# FOUNDATIONS

**The Greenwood Encyclopedia of American Institutions**

Each work in the *Encyclopedia* is designed to provide concise histories of major voluntary groups and nonprofit organizations that have played significant roles in American civic, cultural, political, and economic life from the colonial era to the present.

1. *Labor Unions*
Gary M Fink, Editor-in-Chief

2. *Social Service Organizations*
Peter Romanofsky, Editor-in-Chief

3. *Fraternal Organizations*
Alvin J. Schmidt

4. *Political Parties and Civic Action Groups*
Edward L. Schapsmeier and Frederick H. Schapsmeier

5. *Research Institutions and Learned Societies*
Joseph C. Kiger, Editor-in-Chief

6. *Private Colleges and Institutions*
John F. Ohles and Shirley M. Ohles

7. *Government Agencies*
Donald R. Whitnah, Editor-in-Chief

8. *Foundations*
Harold M. Keele and Joseph C. Kiger, Editors-in-Chief

The Greenwood Encyclopedia of American Institutions

# Foundations

editors-in-chief
HAROLD M. KEELE AND
JOSEPH C. KIGER

GREENWOOD PRESS
Westport, Connecticut • London, England

**Library of Congress Cataloging in Publication Data**

Main entry under title:

Foundations.

(The Greenwood encyclopedia of American institutions, ISSN 0271-9509 ; no. 8)
Includes bibliographical references and index.
1. Charities—United States—Societies, etc.—History.
2. Social service—United States—Societies, etc.—History. 3. Corporations—Charitable contributions—United States—History. 4. Endowments—United States—History. I. Keele, Harold M. II. Kiger, Joseph Charles. III. Series.
HV88.F68   1984        361.7'632'09        83-10750
ISBN 0-313-22556-7 (lib. bdg.)

Copyright © 1984 by Harold M. Keele and Joseph C. Kiger

All rights reserved. No portion of this book may be reproduced, by any process or technique, without the express written consent of the publisher.

Library of Congress Catalog Card Number: 83-10750
ISBN: 0-313-22556-7
ISSN: 0271-9509

First published in 1984

Greenwood Press
A division of Congressional Information Service, Inc.
88 Post Road West
Westport, Connecticut 06881

Printed in the United States of America

10  9  8  7  6  5  4  3  2  1

# CONTENTS

*Contributors*   xix

*Preface*   xxiii

## A

| | |
|---|---|
| Adolph Coors Foundation | 3 |
| Ahmanson Foundation, The | 3 |
| Alcoa Foundation | 5 |
| Alden Trust. See George I. Alden Trust | 6 |
| Alfred P. Sloan Foundation | 6 |
| Alliss Foundation. See Charles and Ellora Alliss Educational Foundation | 10 |
| Ambrose Monell Foundation, The | 10 |
| Amherst H. Wilder Charity. See Amherst H. Wilder Foundation | 11 |
| Amherst H. Wilder Foundation | 11 |
| A. M. McGregor Home, The | 18 |
| Amoco Foundation, Inc. | 18 |
| Amon G. Carter Foundation | 21 |
| Anderson Foundation. See John W. Anderson Foundation; M. D. Anderson Foundation | 22 |
| Andrew W. Mellon Foundation, The | 22 |
| Annenberg Fund, Inc., The | 24 |
| Annie E. Casey Foundation, The | 24 |
| Arie and Ida Crown Memorial | 25 |
| Arie Crown Memorial Fund. See Arie and Ida Crown Memorial | 25 |
| Arthur Vining Davis Foundations, The | 25 |
| Association for the Aid of Crippled Children. See Foundation for Child Development | 27 |
| Astor Foundation. See Vincent Astor Foundation, The | 27 |
| Atlantic Foundation, The | 27 |

Aurora Foundation, The 27
Avalon Foundation. See Andrew W. Mellon Foundation, The 29

## B

Babcock Foundation. See Mary Reynolds Babcock Foundation,
  Incorporated 31
Baker Foundation. See R. C. Baker Foundation, The 31
BankAmerica Foundation 31
Bank of America Foundation. See BankAmerica Foundation 32
Beatrice P. Delany Charitable Trust 32
Benedum Foundation. See Claude Worthington Benedum
  Foundation 32
Benwood Foundation, Inc. 33
Boettcher Foundation 35
Booth Ferris Foundation 36
Boswell Foundation. See James G. Boswell Foundation, The 37
Bremer Foundation. See Otto Bremer Foundation 37
Brown Foundation. See Brown Foundation, Inc., The; James Graham
  Brown Foundation 37
Brown Foundation, Inc., The 37
Bush Foundation. See Bush Foundation, The; Edyth Bush Charitable
  Foundation, Inc. 38
Bush Foundation, The 38
B. W. Foundation. See Weingart Foundation 41

## C

Cafritz Foundation. See Morris and Gwendolyn Cafritz
  Foundation, The 43
Calder Foundation. See Louis Calder Foundation, The 43
California Charities Foundation. See William Randolph Hearst
  Foundation 43
Callaway Community Foundation. See Callaway Foundation, Inc. 43
Callaway Foundation, Inc. 43
Campbell Foundation. See J. Bulow Campbell Foundation 45
Cannon Foundation, Inc., The 45
Carnegie Corporation of New York 46
Carnegie Foundation for the Advancement of Teaching, The 52
Carrie Estelle Doheny Foundation 55
Carter Foundation. See Amon G. Carter Foundation 56
Cary Charitable Trust. See Mary Flagler Cary Charitable Trust 56
Casey Foundation. See Annie E. Casey Foundation, The 56
Castle Foundation. See Harold K. L. Castle Foundation 56

| | |
|---|---|
| Champlin Foundations, The | 56 |
| Charles A. Dana Foundation, Incorporated, The | 56 |
| Charles A. Frueauff Foundation, Inc. | 59 |
| Charles and Ellora Alliss Educational Foundation | 60 |
| Charles E. Culpeper Foundation, Inc. | 61 |
| Charles Engelhard Foundation, The | 63 |
| Charles Hayden Foundation | 63 |
| Charles H. Revson Foundation, Inc. | 65 |
| Charles Stewart Mott Foundation | 68 |
| Chatlos Foundation, Inc., The | 73 |
| Chicago Community Trust, The | 74 |
| China Medical Board of New York, Inc. | 76 |
| Christian A. Johnson Endeavor Foundation, The | 77 |
| Clark Foundation. See Clark Foundation, The; Edna McConnell Clark Foundation, The; Robert Sterling Clark Foundation, Inc. | 78 |
| Clark Foundation, The | 78 |
| Claude Worthington Benedum Foundation | 79 |
| Cleveland Foundation, The | 79 |
| Coleman Foundation, Inc., The | 83 |
| Columbus Foundation, The | 83 |
| Commonwealth Fund, The | 85 |
| Communities Foundation of Texas, Inc. | 89 |
| Connelly Foundation | 92 |
| Conrad N. Hilton Foundation | 93 |
| Coors Foundation. See Adolph Coors Foundation | 93 |
| Cowell Foundation. See S. H. Cowell Foundation | 93 |
| Crown Memorial. See Arie and Ida Crown Memorial | 93 |
| Cullen Foundation, The | 93 |
| Culpeper Foundation. See Charles E. Culpeper Foundation, Inc. | 94 |

## D

| | |
|---|---|
| Dallas Community Chest Trust Fund, Inc. See Communities Foundation of Texas, Inc. | 95 |
| Dana Foundation. See Charles A. Dana Foundation, Incorporated, The | 95 |
| Danforth Foundation, The | 95 |
| Dan Murphy Foundation | 98 |
| David and Lucile Packard Foundation, The | 100 |
| Davis Foundations. See Arthur Vining Davis Foundations, The | 100 |
| DeCamp Foundation. See Ira W. DeCamp Foundation, The | 100 |
| Delany Charitable Trust. See Beatrice P. Delany Charitable Trust | 100 |

| | |
|---|---|
| Del E. Webb Foundation | 100 |
| De Rance, Inc. | 101 |
| DeWitt Wallace Fund, Inc. | 105 |
| Dodge Foundation. See Geraldine R. Dodge Foundation, Incorporated | 105 |
| Doheny Foundation. See Carrie Estelle Doheny Foundation | 105 |
| Don and Sybil Harrington Foundation, The | 106 |
| Donner Foundation. See Independence Foundation; William H. Donner Foundation, Inc., The | 106 |
| Douglas Foundation. See McDonnell Douglas Foundation, Inc. | 106 |
| Dow Foundation. See Herbert H. and Grace A. Dow Foundation, The | 106 |
| Dr. Scholl Foundation | 107 |
| Duke Endowment, The | 107 |
| Du Pont Fund. See Jessie Ball du Pont Religious, Charitable, and Educational Fund | 110 |

## E

| | |
|---|---|
| Eastman Kodak Charitable Trust | 111 |
| Edna McConnell Clark Foundation, The | 111 |
| Edward John Noble Foundation | 113 |
| Edyth Bush Charitable Foundation, Inc. | 116 |
| El Pomar Foundation | 117 |
| Engelhard Foundation. See Charles Engelhard Foundation, The | 118 |
| Esso Education Foundation. See Exxon Education Foundation | 118 |
| Eugene McDermott Foundation, The | 118 |
| Exxon Education Foundation | 120 |

## F

| | |
|---|---|
| Fairchild Foundation. See Sherman Fairchild Foundation, Inc., The | 123 |
| Fannie E. Rippel Foundation | 123 |
| Ferris Foundation. See Booth Ferris Foundation | 124 |
| Fikes Foundation. See Leland Fikes Foundation, Inc. | 125 |
| Fleischmann Foundation. See Max C. Fleischmann Foundation | 125 |
| Florence and John Schumann Foundation, The | 125 |
| F. M. Kirby Foundation, Inc. | 125 |
| Fondren Foundation, The | 126 |
| Ford Foundation, The | 127 |
| Ford Motor Company Fund | 135 |
| Foundation for Child Development | 136 |
| Frank E. Payne and Seba B. Payne Foundation | 140 |

Frueauff Foundation. See Charles A. Frueauff Foundation, Inc. 141
Fuld Health Trust. See Helene Fuld Health Trust 141
Fuller Foundation. See George F. and Sybil H. Fuller Foundation 141

## G

Gannett Foundation, Inc. 143
Gates Foundation 145
General Education Board 146
General Motors Foundation 153
George F. and Sybil H. Fuller Foundation 153
George Foundation, The 154
George Gund Foundation, The 155
George I. Alden Trust 156
Geraldine R. Dodge Foundation, Incorporated 158
Godfrey M. Hyams Trust 159
Grant Foundation. See William T. Grant Foundation 160
Guggenheim Foundation. See John Simon Guggenheim Memorial Foundation 160
Gund Foundation. See George Gund Foundation, The 160

## H

Haas Community Fund. See William Penn Foundation, The 161
Hallmark Educational Foundations 161
Harold K. L. Castle Foundation 162
Harrington Foundation. See Don and Sybil Harrington Foundation, The 163
Harry G. Steele Foundation 163
Hartford Foundation. See Hartford Foundation for Public Giving; John A. Hartford Foundation, Inc., The 164
Hartford Foundation for Public Giving 164
Hayden Foundation. See Charles Hayden Foundation 167
Hearst Foundation. See Hearst Foundation, Inc., The; William Randolph Hearst Foundation 167
Hearst Foundation, Inc., The 167
Heinz Endowment. See Howard Heinz Endowment 168
Helena Rubinstein Foundation, Inc. 168
Helene Fuld Health Foundation. See Helene Fuld Health Trust 168
Helene Fuld Health Trust 168
Helen K. and Arthur E. Johnson Foundation 169
Henry J. Kaiser Family Foundation, The 170
Henry Luce Foundation, Inc., The 173

| | |
|---|---|
| Henry P. Kendall Foundation, The | 174 |
| Herbert and Margaret Turrell Foundation. See Turrell Fund | 175 |
| Herbert H. and Grace A. Dow Foundation, The | 175 |
| Herrick Foundation | 177 |
| Hess Foundation, Inc. | 178 |
| Hewlett Foundation. See William and Flora Hewlett Foundation, The | 179 |
| Hillcrest Foundation | 179 |
| Hilton Foundation. See Conrad N. Hilton Foundation | 179 |
| Hoblitzelle Foundation | 179 |
| Houston Endowment, Inc. | 180 |
| Howard Heinz Endowment | 181 |
| Hunt Foods Charitable Foundation. See Norton Simon, Inc. Museum of Art | 182 |
| Hyams Trust. See Godfrey M. Hyams Trust | 182 |

# I

| | |
|---|---|
| Independence Foundation | 183 |
| International Cancer Research Foundation. See Independence Foundation | 184 |
| Ira W. DeCamp Foundation, The | 184 |
| Irvine Foundation. See James Irvine Foundation, The | 185 |

# J

| | |
|---|---|
| Jackson Hole Preserve, Incorporated | 187 |
| James G. Boswell Foundation, The | 189 |
| James Graham Brown Foundation | 191 |
| James Irvine Foundation, The | 194 |
| J. Bulow Campbell Foundation | 199 |
| J. E. and L. E. Mabee Foundation, Inc., The | 199 |
| Jessie Ball du Pont Religious, Charitable, and Educational Fund | 200 |
| Jessie Smith Noyes Foundation, Inc. | 201 |
| J. Howard Pew Freedom Trust | 202 |
| J. M. Foundation, The | 203 |
| J. M. Kaplan Fund, Inc., The | 205 |
| J. N. Pew, Jr., Charitable Trust | 206 |
| John A. Hartford Foundation, Inc., The | 207 |
| John and Mary R. Markle Foundation, The | 208 |
| John D. and Catherine T. MacArthur Foundation | 212 |
| John McShain Charities, Inc. | 221 |
| John Motley Morehead Foundation, The | 222 |

| | |
|---|---|
| John Simon Guggenheim Memorial Foundation | 222 |
| Johnson Foundation. See Christian A. Johnson Endeavor Foundation, The; Helen K. and Arthur E. Johnson Foundation; Robert Wood Johnson Foundation, The | 226 |
| Johnson New Brunswick Foundation. See Robert Wood Johnson Foundation, The | 227 |
| John W. Anderson Foundation | 227 |
| Jones Foundation. See Jones Foundation, The; W. Alton Jones Foundation, Inc. | 227 |
| Jones Foundation, The | 227 |
| Joseph and Helen Regenstein Foundation. See Regenstein Foundation, The | 228 |
| Joseph B. Whitehead Foundation | 228 |
| Josiah Macy, Jr., Foundation | 231 |
| Joyce Foundation, The | 235 |
| Julius Rosenwald Fund | 238 |

# K

| | |
|---|---|
| Kaiser Foundation. See Henry J. Kaiser Family Foundation, The | 243 |
| Kalamazoo Foundation | 243 |
| Kaplan Fund. See J. M. Kaplan Fund, Inc., The | 244 |
| Kate B. Reynolds Charitable Trust | 244 |
| Keck Foundation. See W. M. Keck Foundation | 246 |
| Kellogg Foundation. See W. K. Kellogg Foundation | 246 |
| Kenan Charitable Trust. See William R. Kenan, Jr., Charitable Trust | 246 |
| Kendall Foundation. See Henry P. Kendall Foundation, The | 246 |
| Kenneth T. and Eileen L. Norris Foundation, The | 246 |
| Kerr Foundation, Inc., The | 247 |
| Kirby Foundation. See F. M. Kirby Foundation, Inc. | 249 |
| Kleberg Foundation. See Robert J. Kleberg, Jr., and Helen C. Kleberg Foundation | 249 |
| Kodak Charitable Trust. See Eastman Kodak Charitable Trust | 249 |
| Krannert Charitable Trust | 249 |
| Kresge Foundation, The | 250 |
| Kress Foundation. See Samuel H. Kress Foundation | 251 |
| Kroc Foundation, The | 251 |

# L

| | |
|---|---|
| Laura Spelman Rockefeller Memorial | 255 |
| L.A.W. Fund, Inc. | 259 |

xii / CONTENTS

| | |
|---|---|
| Leavey Foundation. See Thomas and Dorothy Leavey Foundation | 259 |
| Leland Fikes Foundation, Inc. | 259 |
| Lettie Pate Whitehead Foundation, Inc. | 262 |
| Lexington Foundation. See Northwest Area Foundation | 264 |
| Liberty Fund, Inc. | 264 |
| Lila Acheson Wallace Fund, Inc. See L.A.W. Fund, Inc. | 264 |
| Lilly Endowment, Inc. | 264 |
| Longwood Foundation, Inc. | 270 |
| Louis Calder Foundation, The | 270 |
| Louis W. and Maud Hill Family Foundation. See Northwest Area Foundation | 271 |
| Luce Foundation. See Henry Luce Foundation, Inc., The | 271 |
| Lyndhurst Foundation | 271 |

## M

| | |
|---|---|
| Mabee Foundation. See J. E. and L. E. Mabee Foundation, Inc., The | 273 |
| Mabel Pew Myrin Trust | 273 |
| MacArthur Foundation. See John D. and Catherine T. MacArthur Foundation | 274 |
| McDermott Foundation. See Eugene McDermott Foundation, The | 274 |
| McDonnell Douglas Foundation, Inc. | 274 |
| McDonnell Foundation, Inc. | 276 |
| McGregor Fund | 278 |
| McGregor Home. See A. M. McGregor Home, The | 282 |
| McKnight Foundation, The | 282 |
| Maclellan Foundation, Inc., The | 284 |
| McShain Charities. See John McShain Charities, Inc. | 285 |
| Macy Foundation. See Josiah Macy, Jr., Foundation | 285 |
| Marjorie Merriweather Post Foundation of D.C., The | 285 |
| Markle Foundation. See John and Mary R. Markle Foundation, The | 286 |
| Mary Flagler Cary Charitable Trust | 286 |
| Mary Reynolds Babcock Foundation, Incorporated | 288 |
| Max C. Fleischmann Foundation | 291 |
| M. D. Anderson Foundation | 292 |
| Meadows Foundation, Inc. | 293 |
| Mellon Foundation. See Andrew W. Mellon Foundation, The; Richard King Mellon Foundation | 296 |
| Memorial Welfare Foundation. See Lyndhurst Foundation | 296 |
| Metropolitan Life Foundation | 296 |
| M. J. Murdock Charitable Trust | 297 |
| Monell Foundation. See Ambrose Monell Foundation, The | 298 |

| | |
|---|---|
| Moody Foundation, The | 298 |
| Morehead Foundation. See John Motley Morehead Foundation, The | 302 |
| Morris and Gwendolyn Cafritz Foundation, The | 302 |
| Mott Foundation. See Charles Stewart Mott Foundation | 303 |
| Murdock Charitable Trust. See M. J. Murdock Charitable Trust | 303 |
| Murphy Foundation. See Dan Murphy Foundation | 303 |
| Myrin Trust. See Mabel Pew Myrin Trust | 303 |

## N

| | |
|---|---|
| Nelda C. and H. J. Lutcher Stark Foundation | 305 |
| New Haven Foundation, The | 307 |
| Newhouse Foundation. See Samuel I. Newhouse Foundation, Inc. | 310 |
| New York Community Trust, The | 310 |
| Noble Foundation. See Edward John Noble Foundation; Samuel Roberts Noble Foundation, Inc., The | 316 |
| Norris Foundation. See Kenneth T. and Eileen L. Norris Foundation, The | 316 |
| Northwest Area Foundation | 316 |
| Norton Simon Foundation, The | 319 |
| Norton Simon, Inc. Museum of Art | 321 |
| Noyes Foundation. See Jessie Smith Noyes Foundation, Inc. | 321 |

## O

| | |
|---|---|
| Old Dominion Foundation. See Andrew W. Mellon Foundation, The | 323 |
| Olin Foundation, Inc. | 323 |
| Otto Bremer Foundation | 324 |

## P

| | |
|---|---|
| Packard Foundation. See David and Lucile Packard Foundation, The | 329 |
| Parsons Foundation. See Ralph M. Parsons Foundation, The | 329 |
| Payne Foundation. See Frank E. Payne and Seba B. Payne Foundation | 329 |
| Penn Foundation. See William Penn Foundation, The | 329 |
| Permanent Charity Fund of Boston, Committee of the | 329 |
| Pew Charitable Trust. See J. N. Pew, Jr., Charitable Trust | 330 |
| Pew Freedom Trust. See J. Howard Pew Freedom Trust | 330 |
| Pew Memorial Trust, The | 330 |

| | |
|---|---|
| Philadelphia Foundation, The | 335 |
| Phillips Foundation, The | 338 |
| Phoebe Waterman Foundation. See William Penn Foundation, The | 339 |
| Pittsburgh Foundation, The | 339 |
| Post Foundation. See Marjorie Merriweather Post Foundation of D.C., The | 340 |
| Prudential Foundation, The | 341 |
| Public Welfare Foundation, Inc. | 343 |

## R

| | |
|---|---|
| Ralph M. Parsons Foundation, The | 345 |
| Ramapo Trust | 346 |
| Raskob Foundation for Catholic Activities, Inc. | 346 |
| Ray A. Kroc Foundation. See Kroc Foundation, The | 347 |
| R. C. Baker Foundation, The | 347 |
| Regenstein Foundation, The | 348 |
| Research Corporation | 349 |
| Retirement Research Foundation, The | 352 |
| Revson Foundation. See Charles H. Revson Foundation, Inc. | 354 |
| Reynolds Charitable Trust. See Kate B. Reynolds Charitable Trust | 354 |
| Reynolds Foundation. See Z. Smith Reynolds Foundation, Inc. | 354 |
| Richard King Mellon Foundation | 354 |
| Richardson Foundation. See Sid W. Richardson Foundation; Smith Richardson Foundation, Inc. | 355 |
| Rippel Foundation. See Fannie E. Rippel Foundation | 355 |
| Robert A. Welch Foundation, The | 355 |
| Robert J. Kleberg, Jr., and Helen C. Kleberg Foundation | 356 |
| Robert Sterling Clark Foundation, Inc. | 357 |
| Robert Wood Johnson Foundation, The | 358 |
| Rockefeller Brothers Fund | 361 |
| Rockefeller Foundation, The | 364 |
| Rockefeller Memorial. See Laura Spelman Rockefeller Memorial | 373 |
| Rosenwald Fund. See Julius Rosenwald Fund | 373 |
| Rowland Foundation, Inc. | 373 |
| Rubinstein Foundation. See Helena Rubinstein Foundation, Inc. | 373 |
| Russell Sage Foundation | 373 |

## S

| | |
|---|---|
| Sage Foundation. See Russell Sage Foundation | 381 |
| Saint Paul Foundation, The | 381 |
| Samuel H. Kress Foundation | 382 |

| | |
|---|---|
| Samuel I. Newhouse Foundation, Inc. | 383 |
| Samuel Roberts Noble Foundation, Inc., The | 385 |
| San Francisco Foundation, The | 387 |
| Sarah Scaife Foundation, Inc. | 390 |
| Scaife Foundation. See Sarah Scaife Foundation, Inc. | 392 |
| Scherman Foundation, Inc., The | 392 |
| Scholl Foundation. See Dr. Scholl Foundation | 392 |
| Schumann Foundation. See Florence and John Schumann Foundation, The | 392 |
| S. H. Cowell Foundation | 392 |
| Shell Companies Foundation, Incorporated | 394 |
| Sherman Fairchild Foundation, Inc., The | 395 |
| Shubert Foundation, Inc., The | 396 |
| Sid W. Richardson Foundation | 397 |
| Simon Foundation. See Norton Simon Foundation, The | 398 |
| Simon Museum of Art. See Norton Simon, Inc. Museum of Art | 398 |
| Sloan Foundation. See Alfred P. Sloan Foundation | 398 |
| Smith Charitable Trust. See W. W. Smith Charitable Trust | 398 |
| Smith Richardson Foundation, Inc. | 398 |
| Spencer Foundation, The | 400 |
| Standard Oil (Indiana) Foundation. See Amoco Foundation, Inc. | 403 |
| Stark Foundation. See Nelda C. and H. J. Lutcher Stark Foundation | 403 |
| Starr Foundation, The | 403 |
| Steele Foundation. See Harry G. Steele Foundation | 404 |
| Stoddard Charitable Trust, The | 404 |
| Surdna Foundation | 405 |
| System Development Foundation | 407 |

# T

| | |
|---|---|
| Teagle Foundation, Incorporated, The | 411 |
| Texaco Philanthropic Foundation, Inc. | 412 |
| Thomas and Dorothy Leavey Foundation | 412 |
| Timken Foundation of Canton | 413 |
| Tinker Foundation, Incorporated, The | 414 |
| Tropicana Foundation. See Aurora Foundation, The | 415 |
| Turrell Fund | 415 |
| Twentieth Century Fund, Inc. | 420 |

# U

| | |
|---|---|
| United States Steel Foundation, Inc. | 423 |

xvi / CONTENTS

# V

| | |
|---|---|
| Victoria Foundation, Inc. | 425 |
| Vincent Astor Foundation, The | 426 |

# W

| | |
|---|---|
| Wallace Fund. See DeWitt Wallace Fund, Inc. | 431 |
| W. Alton Jones Foundation, Inc. | 431 |
| Warren Foundation. See William K. Warren Foundation, The | 432 |
| Webb Foundation. See Del E. Webb Foundation | 432 |
| Weingart Foundation | 432 |
| Welch Foundation. See Robert A. Welch Foundation, The | 434 |
| Western Electric Fund | 434 |
| Whitehead Foundation. See Joseph B. Whitehead Foundation; Lettie Pate Whitehead Foundation, Inc. | 435 |
| Wilder Foundation. See Amherst H. Wilder Foundation | 435 |
| William and Flora Hewlett Foundation, The | 435 |
| William H. Donner Foundation, Inc., The | 436 |
| William K. Warren Foundation, The | 438 |
| William M. Scholl Foundation. See Dr. Scholl Foundation | 439 |
| William Penn Foundation, The | 439 |
| William Randolph Hearst Foundation | 440 |
| William R. Kenan, Jr., Charitable Trust | 443 |
| William T. Grant Foundation | 445 |
| W. K. Kellogg Child Welfare Foundation. See W. K. Kellogg Foundation | 446 |
| W. K. Kellogg Foundation | 446 |
| W. M. Keck Foundation | 451 |
| W. R. Hewlett Foundation. See William and Flora Hewlett Foundation, The | 453 |
| W. W. Smith Charitable Trust | 453 |

# Z

| | |
|---|---|
| Z. Smith Reynolds Foundation, Inc. | 455 |

| | |
|---|---|
| *Appendix 1* | |
| Assets | 457 |
| *Appendix 2* | |
| Family-Connected Foundations | 463 |

*Appendix 3*
  Locations                                    465
*Appendix 4*
  Chronology                                   471
*Appendix 5*
  Genealogy                                    477

*Index*                                        489

# CONTRIBUTORS

*W. Stevenson Bacon,* Director of Communications, Research Corporation, New York, New York

*Joy A. Blakslee,* Staff, The Joyce Foundation, Chicago, Illinois

*Norrine M. Bohman,* Assistant to the President, Amherst H. Wilder Foundation, Saint Paul, Minnesota

*Jack Brauntuch,* Executive Director, The J. M. Foundation, New York, New York

*Leslie Caine Campbell,* Professor of History and Journalism, Auburn University, Auburn, Alabama

*Carla Capizzi,* Assistant Editor, Editorial Services, Public Affairs Department, The Prudential Insurance Company of America, Newark, New Jersey

*James P. Carroll,* Public Relations Associate, Lilly Endowment, Inc., Indianapolis, Indiana

*James C. Cobb,* Associate Professor of History, University of Mississippi, University, Mississippi

*Kenneth M. Cuthbertson,* Administrative Vice-President, The James Irvine Foundation, San Francisco, California

*Dorothy D. DeMoss,* Associate Professor of History, Texas Woman's University, Denton, Texas

*Karl F. Drlica,* Professor of Education, Oregon State University, Corvallis, Oregon

*Jane Dustan*, Vice-President, Foundation for Child Development, New York, New York

*Mary Earle,* Program Officer, The Vincent Astor Foundation, New York, New York

*Sara L. Engelhardt,* Secretary, Carnegie Corporation of New York, New York, New York

*Herbert C. Englert,* Executive Vice-President, Fannie E. Rippel Foundation, Morristown, New Jersey

*Marion M. Faldet,* Vice-President and Secretary, The Spencer Foundation, Chicago, Illinois

*Thomas J. Farnham,* Department of History, Southern Connecticut State College, New Haven, Connecticut

*A. G. Fiedler, Jr.,* Manager, Communication Services, Standard Oil Company (Indiana), Chicago, Illinois

*Carl Fjellman,* Executive Director, Turrell Fund, East Orange, New Jersey

*M. Laney Funderburk, Jr.,* Director, Education Division and Public Information, The Duke Endowment, Charlotte, North Carolina

*Barbara J. Getz,* Program Officer, The Kresge Foundation, Troy, Michigan

*Larry D. Givens,* Associate Professor of History, University of Mississippi, University, Mississippi

*David C. Hammack,* Associate Professor of History, University of Houston, Houston, Texas

*Janice Lynn Hartoch,* Administrative and Research Assistant, The Charles A. Dana Foundation, Incorporated, New York, New York

*A. McGehee Harvey,* Professor of Medicine and Physician-in-Chief, School of Medicine, Johns Hopkins University, Baltimore, Maryland

*Robert E. Hencey,* Director of Communications, W. K. Kellogg Foundation, Battle Creek, Michigan

*Marilyn Hennessy,* Executive Director, The Retirement Research Foundation, Park Ridge, Illinois

*J. William Hess,* Associate Director, Rockefeller Archive Center, North Tarrytown, New York

*Milton J. Huber,* Professor of Urban Affairs, University of Wisconsin-Milwaukee, Milwaukee, Wisconsin

*Evans C. Johnson,* Professor of History and Chairman, Department of History, Stetson University, DeLand, Florida

*John F. Joline III,* Executive Director, Edward John Noble Foundation, New York, New York

*Frank Karel,* Vice-President of Communications, The Robert Wood Johnson Foundation, Princeton, New Jersey

*Norton Kay,* Director of Public Information, John D. and Catherine T. MacArthur Foundation, Chicago, Illinois

*John C. Kilkelly,* Associate Professor of Political Science, St. Cloud State University, St. Cloud, Minnesota

*Nancy Klinghoffer*, Communications Manager, The Glenmede Trust Company, Philadelphia, Pennsylvania

*James D. Koerner*, Vice-President, Alfred P. Sloan Foundation, New York, New York

*John Kostishack*, Executive Director, Otto Bremer Foundation, St. Paul, Minnesota

*Robert L. Kroc*, President, The Kroc Foundation, Santa Ynez, California

*David C. Lamb*, Research Assistant, The John and Mary R. Markle Foundation, New York, New York

*Thomas W. Lambeth*, Executive Director, Z. Smith Reynolds Foundation, Inc., Winston-Salem, North Carolina

*Sally R. Lancaster*, Vice-President for Grant Administration, Meadows Foundation, Inc., Dallas, Texas

*S. Whitney Landon*, Chairman, Board of Trustees, Turrell Fund, East Orange, New Jersey

*Leslie Lenkowsky*, Director of Research, Smith Richardson Foundation, Inc., New York, New York

*Susan Little*, Research Associate, The San Francisco Foundation, San Francisco, California

*Amy P. Longworth*, Executive Assistant to the President, Rockefeller Brothers Fund, New York, New York

*Janet Maughan*, Program Officer, The William H. Donner Foundation, Inc., New York, New York

*Calvin Mayne*, Director of Communications, Gannett Foundation, Inc., Rochester, New York

*Robert E. McArthur*, Professor of Political Science and Director of the Bureau of Governmental Research, University of Mississippi, University, Mississippi

*Clyde V. McKee, Jr.*, Trustee, Nelda C. and H. J. Lutcher Stark Foundation, Orange, Texas

*Anne Hodges Morgan*, Vice-President for Programs, The Kerr Foundation, Inc., Oklahoma City, Oklahoma

*Raymond L. Muncy*, Professor of History and Chairman, Department of History and Social Science, Harding University, Searcy, Arkansas

*Jack Murrah*, Associate, Lyndhurst Foundation, Chattanooga, Tennessee

*Michael V. Namorato*, Associate Professor of History, University of Mississippi, University, Mississippi

*Roger M. Olien*, Associate Professor of History and Chairman, Faculties of History and Government, The University of Texas of the Permian Basin, Odessa, Texas

*Harriet Chappell Owsley*, Former Director, Tennessee State Library and Archives, and Editor, The Papers of Andrew Jackson, Nashville, Tennessee

*Don M. Pace*, Staff, Brewton-Parker College, Mount Vernon, Georgia

*Elaine Perachio*, Staff, The Moody Foundation, Galveston, Texas

*Carol Piasente*, Research Associate, The San Francisco Foundation, San Francisco, California

*Elizabeth F. Purcell,* Editor, Josiah Macy, Jr., Foundation, New York, New York

*Renate Rennie,* Program Officer, The Tinker Foundation Incorporated, New York, New York

*Henry Romney,* Director, Information Service, The Rockefeller Foundation, New York, New York

*David L. Rowe,* Assistant Professor of History, Middle Tennessee State University, Murfreesboro, Tennessee

*William Rudman,* Staff Associate for Communications, The Cleveland Foundation, Cleveland, Ohio

*Robert M. Salter,* Assistant Director, Hartford Foundation for Public Giving, West Hartford, Connecticut

*Gene W. Setzer,* Vice-President, Jackson Hole Preserve, Incorporated, New York, New York

*James Howell Smith,* Associate Professor of History, Wake Forest University, Winston-Salem, North Carolina

*John Sobotka,* Law Archivist, University of Mississippi, University, Mississippi

*Joseph F. Steelman*, Professor of History, East Carolina University, Greenville, North Carolina

*Marilyn A. Stein,* Assistant Vice-President of Communications, Charles Stewart Mott Foundation, Flint, Michigan

*Susan D. Steinwall,* Research Fellow, Social Welfare History Archives Center, University Libraries, Minneapolis, Minnesota

*Oona Sullivan*, Office of Reports, The Ford Foundation, New York, New York

*John D. Taylor,* President, Northwest Area Foundation, Saint Paul, Minnesota

*Ralph W. Tyler,* President, System Development Foundation, Palo Alto, California

*James Van Patten,* Professor of Education, University of Arkansas, Fayetteville, Arkansas

*William K. Wallach,* Assistant Director, Bentley Historical Library, University of Michigan, Ann Arbor, Michigan

*Steven K. Weber,* Editor, The Henry J. Kaiser Family Foundation, Menlo Park, California

*Carol Weiland,* Program Officer, Charles H. Revson Foundation, Inc., New York, New York

# PREFACE

The beginnings of our private philanthropic foundations are to be found in the ancient civilizations of the Middle East, particularly the city-states of Greece. Plato's Academy, for example, received an endowment from him for its support, and prior to the birth of Christ the Ptolemaic rulers of Egypt established funds for the operation of the famous Alexandrian Museum and Library. Somewhat later, several of the Roman emperors set aside funds for the relief of the empire's poor, and the medieval church established funds for the operation of hospitals and other charitable institutions for the relief of the sick and the poor. But not until the seventeenth and eighteenth centuries in Europe was there a significant increase in the number of institutions which properly can be considered to be foundations. In the second year of the seventeenth century, the English Parliament passed the memorable Statute of Charitable Uses (1601), which placed the governmental stamp of approval on the establishment of foundations in England.

In the late eighteenth and early nineteenth centuries, the private foundation as we know it today was first created in the United States by forward-looking men such as Benjamin Franklin and Stephen Girard as vehicles for their private benefactions. It is interesting to note that some of these early foundations are still in existence. The first truly modern foundations in this country were not established until after the Civil War, and the motivation for the founding of some of them was concern for the plight of the defeated and stricken South. The Peabody and Slater Funds and the General Education Board* are prominent examples of such postbellum war-related institutions.

In the post-Civil War period it was Andrew Carnegie who first gave prominence to the concept that wealthy men were in fact trustees of their wealth and that they should therefore assure that their wealth was used for the benefit and betterment of all mankind. Having convinced himself that the foundation was the best instrument for carrying out this belief, Carnegie established a number of foundations in the early years of this century, the largest being the Carnegie Corporation of New York.* Soon other men of great wealth adopted Carnegie's

---

*An asterisk (*) after a title indicates that there is a brief history of the foundation in this work.

philosophy, with the result that the United States has experienced the continuing creation of foundations with large assets down to the present. An outstanding example of the continuing emergence of large foundations is the Robert Wood Johnson Foundation,* which embarked with assets of over $1 billion on its sizable program as recently as 1971. (For a chronology and genealogy of foundations established in the twentieth century, see Appendix 4 and Appendix 5, respectively.)

Modern U.S. foundations are private, not-for-profit organizations created to provide aid for socially useful purposes and projects, which, according to section 501 (c) (3) of the Internal Revenue Code, qualify for tax exemption only if they operate exclusively for one or more of the following purposes: charitable, religious, scientific, literary, educational, testing for public safety, and prevention of cruelty to children or animals. The code further provides that no "substantial" part of a foundation's activities may be devoted to efforts to influence legislation and that no foundation may participate in any manner in any candidate's campaign for political office.

Foundations in the United States can be chartered by either a state or the United States. They can be legally established as not-for-profit corporations or as trusts. The latter can be set up in a deed but is more frequently established by a will. Trusts are governed by one or more trustees, corporations by a board of directors. The life-span of a foundation and the manner in which its assets are to be expended may be specified in its trust instrument or charter. For example, a foundation's expenditures may be: (a) limited to income only, or (b) limited to principal and income to be expended within a specified period of time, or (c) left to the discretion of trustees or directors. Outstanding examples of foundations in each of these categories are: (a) Carnegie Corporation of New York, (b) Mary Flagler Cary Charitable Trust,* (c) the Rockefeller Foundation.* It should be added that relatively few foundations fall into category (b).

Foundations are usually categorized by type as community, company or corporation sponsored, operating, or independent.

The community foundations are usually those which have been established and are located in cities and urban areas. Most major cities in the United States have acquired community foundations since the establishment of the first one, the Cleveland Foundation,* in 1911. Civic-minded individuals, many of them well-to-do and often bankers, have led in their establishment. They are usually administered by trustees designated by local political, banking, educational, and other officials and their grants are generally made for local purposes. They were predominantly palliative in their giving in the early decades of their existence. In the past two decades, however, the larger ones have gradually shifted a substantial portion of their grants to the support of more venturesome projects. See Eugene C. Struckhoff, *Handbook for Community Foundations* (1977), for a recent account of the rationale and activities of this type of foundation.

Foundations created by U.S. business corporations have increased dramatically in recent years, both in their numbers and in the size of their individual endowments. Their source of funds may be in endowments or annual contributions, or both, from a business corporation. Since the level of charitable giving by corporations has often declined during periods of economic downturn, a major rationale for the creation of company foundations has been the stabilization which they provide for contributions to charitable institutions in depressed times when such institutions are most in need of financial support. They are usually administered by officials of the sponsoring corporation, and normally the grants have been concentrated in those communities in which the funding corporation has plants or facilities. See Beardsley Ruml and Theodore Geiger, eds., *The Manual of Corporate Giving* (1952), an earlier work which deals in part with this type of foundation. A more recent account is that of James F. Harris and Anne Klepper, *Corporate Philanthropic Public Service Activities* (1976).

The operating foundations are those which use members of their own staff to carry out their projects. In other words, they actually use their assets to pay salaries to a permanent or semipermanent staff for work carried out by the staff or to provide for the maintenance and upkeep of a library, museum, or other such facility. The line between a foundation of this type and research institutions, libraries, or museums is sometimes a fine one and, in the last analysis, rests on how an organization views itself plus, in some cases, the degree to which it makes grants to individuals other than its own staff and whether its income is derived from single or multiple sources. Moreover, the trustees of some foundations in this category have, through their direction, changed the classification of their organizations. Thus, the Carnegie Endowment for International Peace and the Carnegie Institution of Washington, which originally followed a policy of making substantial grants to other organizations and to individuals, now restrict their activities almost wholly to programs and projects carried out by their own staffs and the maintenance of libraries, laboratories, and other research facilities. Brief histories of these two and similar organizations, such as the Charles F. Kettering Foundation, are to be found in a companion volume in the Greenwood Encyclopedia of American Institutions, Joseph C. Kiger, *Research Institutions and Learned Societies* (1982).

Historically, most of the larger U.S. foundations have been of the independent type. This can be seen by reference to Appendix 1 herein, which ranks foundations included in this volume according to the size of their assets and also designates the relatively few community, company, and operating foundations. Those not so designated are independent foundations which usually have been set up by an individual or the members of a family. This is why they are sometimes referred to as "family foundations." See Appendix 2 herein for a listing of those foundations funded by or with close connections to the same family.

A number of reasons have been advanced for the predominance of the independent type: the tax benefits to be derived by individuals and families creating them; the fact that many have been set up as memorials, sometimes designated as such, to departed loved ones; and their ability, when properly set up and organized, to dispense large sums of money to individuals and to any number of organizations, namely, educational and research institutions, hospitals, museums, libraries, and so forth, to enable them to carry out a wide variety of programs and projects enjoying the favor of the donors or their successors. Consequently, many of the independent foundations are also referred to as "general purpose foundations." See David F. Freeman, *The Handbook on Private Foundations* (1981), for a recent work discussing this and other types of foundations and their operation.

Thus, it may be seen that America's largest foundations vary in the manner in which they have been and can be created, their life-span, and their method of operation. Within this diversity, however, have emerged several principles held by the vast majority of the largest and most significant foundations that differentiate them from earlier charitable organizations and also from many present-day smaller foundations. See Joseph C. Kiger, *Operating Principles of the Larger Foundations* (1954), for a full account of the development of these beliefs. See also F. Emerson Andrews, *Philanthropic Foundations* (1956), still a standard comprehensive work on the subject.

The foremost and most striking of such principles is that foundation funds should be used for preventive rather than palliative purposes. It holds that rather than attempt to relieve distress in given situations, the foundations should use their money in efforts to eliminate the cause of the distress, thereby preventing its repetition. This is aptly called the "venture capital" concept. It is based on the following reasoning: since foundations often have large resources with relatively few restrictions upon their expenditures, and since they have no profit motive and no shareholders to which they are financially responsible, they are free to seek out and support the new, the novel, the experimental. There are those who go so far as to hold that the foundation should support the risky where the chance of failure is large but the rewards of success, even though facing highly unlikely odds, are enormous.

If the venture capital principle is to be allowed full play, then it follows that onerous and undue restrictions on foundation operations should be kept to a minimum. Historically, our federal and state governments have afforded our foundations great freedom of action by allowing them considerable latitude in their interpretation of what constitutes socially useful purposes, and governmental auditing of their activities has been relatively minimal. Since 1943, federal law has required foundations to file annual information returns with the Internal Revenue Service (IRS), and since 1969 they have been required to pay to the U.S. government a percentage of their income to enable the IRS to audit their activities. Prior to that year, they were completely tax exempt. None of the states has ever collected money from them for audit purposes, and the reporting provisions of state laws vary from the stringent one of New York to much less rigorous ones in other states. On this subject, see Eleanor K. Taylor, *Public Accountability of Foundations and Charitable Trusts* (1953). On balance, then, our foundations have had great freedom in their establishment, their choice of grantees, and their operation.

Of the approximately twenty-three thousand legal entities in the United States today which may properly be called "foundations," probably one half or more of them have assets of less than $100,000 and give less than $10,000 annually for philanthropic and charitable purposes. Typically, these foundations reflect the particular interest of their donors, have no staff, and are concerned with purely local projects. They are overwhelmingly palliative in purpose rather than innovative or preventive.

There are roughly thirty-four hundred foundations in the United States with assets of $1 million or more which average annual gifts of $100,000 or more. Although comprising only 15 percent of the foundations in the country, this group accounts for about 93 percent of the assets and 89 percent of all grant dollars paid out by all of our foundations. See Marianna O. Lewis and Alexis Teitz Gersumky, eds., *The Foundation Directory*, 8th edition (1981), particularly the introduction, for a more detailed discussion of such fiscal data on foundations. This group of thirty-four hundred foundations forms the seminal core of the foundation world.

In preparing this volume of the Greenwood Encyclopedia of American Institutions, the editors first had to determine the criteria for selecting the most significant foundations from this core group for inclusion in the volume. Investigation demonstrated that those foundations which historically have exerted the greatest impact on society have almost without exception been those which were among the largest of this group. It thus became readily apparent that the single most important factor was that of the magnitude of a foundation's assets. Put another way, the most notable and the most far-reaching achievements of foundations have been concentrated among those with the largest assets. Having established to their satisfaction that magnitude of assets was the single most important criterion for selecting the most significant foundations, the editors were faced with a second critical problem—how far to apply that criterion in arriving at a feasible number of foundations for inclusion in this volume.

Further investigation revealed that a cut off figure of $30 million in assets would yield approximately 200 foundations which the editors believed included an overwhelming proportion of foundations (with exceptions noted hereafter) that had made outstanding societal contributions. Accordingly, included in this volume are brief histories of 230 of the foundations having the largest assets (usually as of 1980-1981), which in each case exceeds $30 million. Three foundations with assets slightly below the $30 million criterion are included because of the uniqueness of their programs. These 230 foundations hold approximately 65 percent of total foundation assets, which aggregate approximately $41 billion and dispense annually about 48 percent of total foundation grants of about $2.7 billion dollars. It should be emphasized that the foregoing figures and percentages are approximations derived from projections based upon *The Foundation Directory* (1981), table 2, p. viii, referred to above.

There are also an additional four foundations, now defunct and so listed in Appendix 1, for whom brief histories are included herein because the magnitude of their assets while in existence would, if they were now in existence, have placed them in the category of the larger foundations.

In the effort to provide, in condensed form, these interpretive historical sketches of the foundations selected for inclusion in this work, letters were sent by the editors to the executive officers of the some two hundred largest foundations, asking that an article on their foundation be prepared by someone familiar with its history and operation. The editors offered to provide guidelines and editorial direction in the preparation of the article, with the assurance that attribution would be accorded the author of the article. Seventy-seven contributors (and they are so designated) have prepared articles on their foundations for inclusion herein. Many foundations, while not providing the author of the respective articles appearing in this volume, did provide historical information, annual reports, informational brochures, and so forth, sufficient to enable the preparation of brief histories by the editors or other contributors. The historical sketches of those foundations failing to supply requested information are primarily based on two legally required and therefore publicly available sources of information, IRS forms 990AR and 990PF, which are primarily statistical in nature, plus other sources discussed below.

For these reasons, the articles appearing herein vary greatly in length, content, amount of interpretation, and major sources cited for additional information. The founders or officials of some foundations apparently prefer not to furnish the public with much more information than that required by the IRS, arguably because they do not have to raise money for their operation from the public or from stockholders concerned with their performance. Other foundations are more cooperative. Some, especially the larger ones such as the Rockefeller Foundation (RF), have voluntarily established archival centers which are open to scholars and other interested persons; and the RF and others, such as the Carnegie Corporation of New York and the Commonwealth Fund,* have consistently published annual and other reports on their activities and have aided in the preparation of histories of their organizations, including those appearing in this work. (Unless otherwise noted, foundations included herein keep their files and archives at their central offices, the home states of which are indicated in Appendix 3.)

A foundation's annual reports, in which the organization's history, programs, and activities are usually discussed, are the best sources of information. Obituaries in newspapers such as the *New York Times* and biographies on some foundation donors and officials appearing in the *Dictionary of American Biography* have provided the editors with important background material for some foundations. Although not cited in the bibliographical material appearing at the end of the sketches herein, the Foundation Center publications, particularly its *Source Book Profile*, have been of inestimable value to the editors and to many of the contributors in their research efforts and the resultant brief histories of foundations presented herein.

It should not go unnoted that since 1956 the Foundation Center (prior to 1968 known as the Foundation Library Center) has become an increasingly valuable depository for historical and other information about foundations. The officials and staff of the center, particularly President Thomas R. Buckman and the late Marianna O. Lewis, while unstinting in their efforts to provide the editors with information and counsel, carefully avoided any attempts to influence our editorial prerogative. In acknowledging our debt to them, we should also like to thank Landrum Bolling, former chairman of the Council on Foundations, who kindly gave us the benefit of his extensive knowledge and experience. We are deeply appreciative to the University of Mississippi for its generous support, which was attendant upon the location on the campus of the editorial offices for this project. Our thanks are due, too, to Vice-President James T. Sabin and Editor Cynthia Harris of Greenwood Press, together with members of the editorial staff of the press for raising and helping us to answer numerous questions anent meaning and style in the preparation of this volume. Any errors, in this and other aspects of the work, however, are the sole responsibility of the editors.

Finally, the editors wish to express their appreciation for the assistance they have received from contributing authors both within and without the foundations herein chronicled. Their names follow their contributed entries and are listed with their foundation position or other affiliation in the contributor's section. All articles for which there is no attribution have been prepared by the editors.

Harold M. Keele
Joseph C. Kiger

# A

**ADOLPH COORS FOUNDATION.** Adolph Coors, Sr., who left Germany because of political and economic oppression, founded the brewery bearing the family name in 1873 in Golden, Colorado. The years following saw the growth of the brewery and the successful launching of porcelain and other business enterprises by the Coors family, particularly by Adolph Coors, Jr., who died in 1971. Through a bequest from the Adolph Coors, Jr., Trust, the Adolph Coors Foundation was established in 1975 with the stipulation that the funds from the trust were to be used only in the state of Colorado. A 1977 bequest to the foundation from the estate of Gertrude Steele Coors specified that income from this later bequest might be used outside Colorado. With total assets which in 1981 were valued at $54 million, grants are still primarily made to organizations located in Colorado.

Since its inception, the foundation has devoted approximately 40 percent of its grants to colleges, universities, and other educational organizations. Approximately 20 percent went to public affairs organizations, including ones concerned with economic and legal issues and domestic and foreign policy. Human service programs, health, and youth organizations each received about 10 percent of total funding, and the remainder was divided among a variety of donees.

Four members of the Coors family serve on its six-member board of directors. Its programs and activities are carried out by an administrative staff headed by an executive manager from offices located at 350–C Clayton Street, Denver, Colorado 80206.

For further information, see *Annual Reports* of the foundation, published continuously since 1980.

**AHMANSON FOUNDATION, THE.** The Ahmanson Foundation was incorporated in California in 1952 as a private charitable organization. Its funding was donated by Howard F. Ahmanson; his wife, Dorothy G. Sullivan; members of the Ahmanson family; and family business affiliations. Howard F. Ahmanson was a graduate of the University of Southern California who became a noted philanthropist and art collector. He was a member of the board of directors of the Kennedy Center for the Performing Arts, the Los Angeles County Museum of Art, and the University of Southern California. The Ahmanson wealth derived primarily from savings and loan associations and insurance companies, which are currently owned and operated by H. F. Ahmanson and Company, a holding company for Home Savings of America, the nation's largest savings and loan association (net worth, April, 1982, approximately $722 million).

Officers and directors of the foundation include members of Ahmanson's family and officers of H. F. Ahmanson and Company. Robert H. Ahmanson, a nephew, is foundation president and trustee; William H. Ahmanson, also a nephew, is foundation vice-president and trustee as well as chairman and chief executive officer of H. F. Ahmanson and Company. Other trustees of the foundation include Howard F. Ahmanson, Jr., Franklin D. Murphy, Robert M. DeKruif, and Daniel M. Belin.

The Ahmanson Foundation is a general charitable institution with a primary interest in and focus on the greater Los Angeles area. In its grant giving, there is an emphasis on education, health and medicine, arts and culture, social and community programs, and some support for various religious organizations. Since its incorporation, education has received the largest share of funding, accounting for approximately 50 percent of all grants. The foundation especially supports universities, colleges, and independent schools in southern California with grants for capital and building funds, equipment and materials, renovations, endowments, scholarships, matching and challenge grants, and public school districts. In a notable exception to its general emphasis on local giving, in 1979 the Kansas University Endowment Association in Lawrence received $550,000, the Ahmanson Foundation's largest grant of that year.

After education the next largest share of funding is made in support of arts and humanities programs and institutions, which include museums, performing arts groups and centers, and historical societies and preservation programs. Approximately 20 percent of all grant dollars are allocated to arts and culture. Reflecting the founder's interest, the Los Angeles County Museum of Art is generally a recipient of the foundation's larger grants.

Grants for health and medicine account for about 15 percent of expenditures. Recipients include hospitals, university-affiliated cancer research programs, clinics for family services and counseling, and some disease–related research institutions, such as the Arthritis Foundation of Southern California and the Leukemia Society of America.

Social welfare and community services continue to be a major area of emphasis for the Ahmanson Foundation and receive approximately 10 to 15 percent of all dollars in grant disbursements. Child welfare agencies, family services, programs for minorities, community civic programs, and public service groups are supported. The foundation's remaining grants are generally distributed for support of religious organizations, including churches and church-sponsored social service agencies. The foundation makes no grants to individuals.

In 1979, the Ahmanson Foundation expended about $7 million on 374 grants. Twenty-five percent of the grantees were first-time recipients. The general range of grants was between $500 and $50,000, while the high was $550,000 and the low $100. In 1981 the foundation had assets of about $120 million, consisting mainly of shares of the H. F. Ahmanson and Company.

The offices of the Ahmanson Foundation are located at 3731 Wilshire Boulevard, Los Angeles, California 90010. It is administered by four full-time staff members headed by Kathleen A. Gilcrest, vice-president and secretary.

For further information, see "Ahmanson Posts $42.4 Million Loss for First Quarter," *Wall Street Journal* (May 18, 1982), p. 56; and Melinda Marble, *Guide to California Foundations* (1982). See also a foundation statement (n.d.) explaining grant application guidelines.

LARRY D. GIVENS

**ALCOA FOUNDATION.** Originally established as a trust on November 17, 1952, by the Aluminum Company of America, and initially funded by a gift of $16.9 million from that company, the Alcoa Foundation was succeeded by a nonprofit Pennsylvania corporation by the same name, established February 7, 1964.

For the period 1953–1980, the Aluminum Company of America made additional gifts, including $5 million in each of the years 1978, 1979, and 1980. Excluding capital gains on sales of its securities, net income of the foundation from its inception in 1952 to 1980 has amounted to approximately $67 million, with grants of almost $80 million made during the same period. In 1980, the foundation had assets of about $151 million.

Funded principally by income from its investments, grants have been made to educational, cultural, health and welfare, civic and community development, and youth organizations. Programs and activities of organizations and educational institutions located in or near communities where Alcoa Company plants or offices are located have received special consideration. Emphasis has also been placed upon educational institutions with strong engineering and professional programs and various local, regional, national, and international organizations. With the exception of a scholarship program for sons and daughters of Alcoa Company employees, Alcoa Foundation does not make grants to individuals, nor does it make grants to elementary and secondary schools except to those secondary schools aided under a recently established Educational Gift Matching Program.

The foundation is governed by a seven-member board of directors, composed principally of directors, officers, and executives of the Aluminum Company of America, which meets approximately every four weeks. Its programs are carried out by a small administrative staff located at 1501 Alcoa Building, Pittsburgh, Pennsylvania 15219.

For further information, see *Annual Reports* of the foundation, published since the 1970s.

**ALDEN TRUST.** See George I. Alden Trust.

**ALFRED P. SLOAN FOUNDATION.** The Sloan Foundation was established in 1934 by Alfred P. Sloan, Jr., and incorporated in the state of Delaware. Sloan, who for many years was the chief executive officer of General Motors Corporation, was active in the affairs of the foundation until his death in 1966. Annual grant expenditures of the Sloan Foundation averaged $14 million between 1975 and 1980, and the foundation's assets at market value at the end of 1980 were about $266 million.

In its early years, the foundation was small and its fields of activity few. Grant expenditures over the first ten years averaged about $300,000 a year, support going to Sloan's *alma mater*, the Massachusetts Institute of Technology; to local charities; and to economics. Research and education in economics was a major interest of Sloan, and his conviction was strong that ignorance of the principles of capitalism and free enterprise was both a danger and an opportunity. Hence in its first period, the foundation supported a variety of projects whose purpose was to assist research in economics and provide schools and the general public with nontechnical, low-cost instructional materials, including materials suitable for radio broadcasting, later for television, and for popular magazines. This approach to mass education in a complex subject was phased out in the early 1950s, and it is fair to say that the foundation learned much but accomplished little with this activity. Today, economics remains a major interest of the foundation, but that interest is expressed mainly in the support of research.

In the 1940s, the foundation's assets increased, and its fields of activity expanded to include research in pure science, medical research, technical research, and industrial management. By 1950, the foundation's assets were $29 million and its annual grant expenditures were about $5 million.

The decade of the forties also marked the beginning of a special chapter in the history of the Sloan Foundation and in American philanthropy—the establishment by Alfred P. Sloan, Jr., of what was to become one of the world's leading centers for cancer research and treatment. As the Second World War drew to a close, Sloan joined the board of New York City's Memorial Hospital for Cancer and Allied Diseases, where he soon became persuaded that the kind of team-based scientific research that had proved so effective during the war, both in industry and university laboratories, could be applied equally well to the conquest of cancer.

In 1945, Sloan founded the Sloan-Kettering Institute for Cancer Research (as the research arm of Memorial Hospital) with grants of $4.2 million from the Sloan Foundation and prevailed upon his close associate over many years at General Motors, Charles F. Kettering, to join his name to the enterprise. For the next thirty-four years, the Sloan Foundation maintained a special relationship with "Sloan-Kettering," as it is popularly known. General support grants were made each year, as well as frequent grants for particular projects. Many, but by no means all, of these grants came from a special fund within the foundation called the General Motors Dealers Appreciation Fund for Cancer and Medical Research. This fund was established in 1949 with gifts to the Sloan Foundation from General Motors dealers who sought to express their appreciation to Sloan for the work he had done over a period of many years to strengthen the relationship between General Motors and its dealer organizations.

Between 1945 and 1980, the foundation's support of Sloan-Kettering came to $34 million. Personal gifts from Alfred P. Sloan, Jr., during his lifetime and at his death came to an additional $33 million, bringing the total benefactions attributable to Mr. Sloan to $67 million. Today, Sloan-Kettering (the official name is now Memorial Sloan-Kettering Cancer Center) is the largest private institution in the world for the treatment of cancer and for cancer-centered research and training. Its operating budget in 1980 was $183 million, of which $44 million was spent on research and training.

The history of growth at Sloan-Kettering is as good an illustration as might be found of the function private foundations can sometimes fill in providing venture capital for the first stages of an attack on a major problem of society—to be followed by government with its far greater funds that are indispensable to the ultimate solution of the problem. Private funds alone could not hope to meet the present budget of Sloan-Kettering or to finance the pace of research and treatment; and for that reason, the foundation brought to an end its special relationship with Sloan-Kettering in 1980 with a grant of $3.5 million, representing the residue of the General Motors Dealers Appreciation Fund.

If there is little public discussion nowadays about the intractability of cancer, much of the credit goes to Sloan-Kettering. Few informed persons now doubt the eventual success of the struggle to control this ancient affliction of mankind. The Sloan Foundation looks back on its relationship with Sloan-Kettering with both pride and humility; both are interwoven in the part the foundation and Alfred P. Sloan, Jr., played in creating and helping grow beyond the foundation's own ken one of the world's preeminent cancer centers.

Also of particular note among the foundation's activities has been its support over the last twenty-six years of basic research in physics, chemistry, pure mathematics, and since 1972 in neuroscience, through its program called Sloan Research Fellowships. Established in 1955, these fellowships give support and recognition to creative young scientists at a time in their careers when funds for personal research may be the hardest to find and scientists may have the most to contribute to their discipline. A well-developed nomination and selection process governs this program, and the support provided, although modest in size, is used for a wide variety of purposes of the fellows' choice.

The Sloan Research Fellowships now have an alumni of 1,641 persons, many of them of great distinction in their fields. That alumni now includes eight Nobel laureates; the winners of two Fields Medals, the highest honor in mathematics; and the recipients of hundreds of other honors. In 1981, the Sloan Research Fellowships were expanded to include six fellowships a year in economics and four in applied mathematics; a total of eighty-eight awards of $20,000 each were made in 1981. A brochure titled "Sloan Research Fellowships" is available from the foundation, on request, giving the details of this program.

Another institution with which the foundation maintained a special relationship for a great many years is the Massachusetts Institute of Technology, from which Sloan graduated in 1895 with a B.S. degree in electrical engineering. For most of the lifetime of the foundation, MIT has been a major recipient of Sloan grants. Support had been given to the Sloan School of Management (which was founded with the help of a Sloan grant), the Executive Development Program, the Center for Advanced Engineering Study, and for many other projects in research and instruction in science, technology, economics, and management. Grants to MIT from the inception of the foundation to June 1981 totalled $48 million, making MIT by far the largest recipient of the foundation's grants to institutions of higher education.

In 1969, the foundation adopted a new mode of operation that distinguished between the "general program," under which the established interests of the foundation were pursued, and a set of "particular programs," which focused on more sharply defined topics for limited periods of time. Four particular programs were developed and carried to completion between 1969 and 1979: one to increase the number of minority students in medicine and management; one to support experimental work in educational technology; one to help establish the new discipline of neuroscience; and one to increase the number of minority students in engineering.

Inflation has reduced the value of the foundation's grant dollar by more than half since the concept of particular programs was adopted; and since the foundation's income has not kept abreast of inflation, the original plan, which called for two or three such programs to operate concurrently, has had to be modified. It now appears likely that the foundation can sustain at most two, and possibly only one, particular program at a time. The fifth particular program, in cognitive science, is now in operation.

The foundation's current principal interest is higher education, with an emphasis on science, engineering, economics, management, and public policy education; and the foundation over the last twenty years has conducted many programs and made many grants in these disciplines (in public policy since 1976). The foundation is reexamining its role, however, in science and engineering, fields in which the cost of research has now reached a level that can be sustained only by federal agencies, possibly in cooperation with industry.

The foundation's principal support of science currently is in its particular program in cognitive science, a pure research program focused on problems of understanding human mental processes. Support under this program goes for highly interdisciplinary research in psychology, linguistics, neuroscience, philosophy, anthropology, and computer science. Beyond that, the foundation's support of science and engineering is likely to diminish in the future. The foundation does provide limited support for work in the history and philosophy of science. On occasion, it also supports curriculum development and instructional experiments in science and technology, and it supports a variety of other low-cost projects related to these fields. It also supports a program that permits senior scientists to spend a year at a nongovernmental institution in Washington to take an active part in public discussion and policy formation in science and in other fields.

In economics, the foundation over the last five years has concentrated on research. Doctoral-student workshops in applied microeconomics research have been supported in a large number of leading institutions. Research projects have also been supported at the Brookings Institution, the American Enterprise Institute for Public Policy Research, the National Bureau of Economic Research, and at other independent research organizations.

In management education, the foundation's principal activity in recent years has been in "public" management, that is, in the analysis of public problems and the management of government. New master's degree programs in public policy have been supported at leading universities, and new courses have been financed at liberal arts colleges. Having helped establish a variety of such programs, the foundation is now turning its attention to two other problems in this field: developing a sound base of research in public policy, and increasing the number of minority students in high-quality public policy programs.

The foundation's funds are spent in two ways: on programs and activities developed by the foundation's staff and for which grants are made, usually on a competitive basis, in support of individuals and institutions; and in response to proposals that come unsolicited to the foundation and that are also judged competitively, often with the help of outside reviewers.

Application for a grant can be made at any time for support of activities that fall within the interests of the foundation, as indicated above. The foundation's activities do not extend to primary or secondary education, or to the humanities, religion, the creative or performing arts, or to medical research or health care. Grants are not made for endowment, buildings, or equipment, and are very rarely made for general support or for activities outside the United States.

Grants of $20,000 or less are made throughout the year by the officers of the foundation; grants over that amount are made by the trustees, who meet five times a year for that purpose. Letters of application are normally sent to the president of the foundation and include, in addition to a discussion of the work the applicant proposes to do; information about the applicant; the cost and the duration of the work; and, in the case of new applicants, the tax status of the organization that would administer the grant unless it is a recognized institution of higher education. The foundation has no deadlines or standard application forms. Often a brief letter of inquiry, rather than a fully developed proposal, is an advisable first step for an applicant, conserving his time and allowing the foundation to give the applicant a preliminary response as to the possibility of support. The program and activities of the foundation are directed from offices located at 630 Fifth Avenue, New York, New York 10020, under the direction of the president.

For further information, see *Annual Reports* of the foundation, published since 1938. See also occasional papers and reports published by the foundation relating to its programs and activities, particularly Warren Weaver, *Alfred P. Sloan, Jr.—Philanthropist* (1975), a biographical sketch of Sloan as a philanthropist.

JAMES D. KOERNER

**ALLISS FOUNDATION.** See Charles and Ellora Alliss Educational Foundation.

**AMBROSE MONELL FOUNDATION, THE.** This foundation was established in 1952 as a memorial to Ambrose Monell by his widow. From unrelated families, Maude Monell and Ambrose Monell married in 1899. In 1917, he resigned the presidency of International Nickel Company to become a colonel in the American aviation forces in France. He died in 1921 without resuming the presidency of the company, though he was serving as director on the boards of several major corporations. In 1932, his widow married Norwegian ship builder and shipping line executive George Unger Vetlesen. The G. Unger Vetlesen Foundation, incorporated in 1955, memorialized Vetlesen, who died that year. Maude Vetlesen died in 1958.

Committed generally to the improvement of the physical, mental, and moral condition of humanity throughout the world, the Monell Foundation has emphasized health and medical care, though it has also supported the fields of art and culture. The market value of its assets in 1979 was about $57 million. Its grant disbursements had risen from $1.63 million in 1976 to about $2 million in 1979. Awards in the fields of health and medical care accounted for approximately 44 percent of the disbursements in 1978, with major recipients being the Massachusetts General Hospital ($170,818) and the Menninger Foundation ($75,000). In addition, there were smaller grants to museums, dance theaters, educational institutions, and social agencies. The market value of its assets in 1980 was listed at $83,828,944, with $2,551,334 in grants. Though the scope of its philanthropy is national, its emphasis has been on the New York area.

In 1968, the foundation awarded a $1 million grant to establish the Monell Chemical Senses Center, Inc., at the University of Pennsylvania. Since its founding, the Chemical Senses Center has been a major recipient of Monell Foundation grants.

For several years, the foundation was guided by four officers. Edmund C. Monell, son of Maude and Ambrose Monell, served as president until his death on March 27, 1980. The vice-president and treasurer, also the recipient of applications, was Harmon Duncombe of the New York law firm of Fulton, Walter, and Duncombe, later to be Fulton, Duncombe, and Rowe. Duncombe was also a director of the International Flavors and Fragrances Corporation, secretary of the G. Unger Vetlesen Foundation, and a director of the van Ameringen Foundation, which was established in honor of the founder of the International Flavors and Fragrances Corporation. Another vice-president was Henry G. Walter, a member of the law firm and chief executive officer of International

Flavors and Fragrances. Walter was also a director of the van Ameringen Foundation and the G. Unger Vetlesen Foundation. The secretary and fourth director of the Monell Foundation was George Rowe, Jr., of the same law firm. When Monell died, Duncombe became president and Rowe vice-president of the foundation. Thus, the present governing board of the foundation consists of these three individuals. Administration of the foundation is carried on from offices located at 30 Rockefeller Plaza, New York, New York 10020.

Almost the only additional information readily available to the public on this foundation are the annual reports and returns filed by it with the Internal Revenue Service, and the various Foundation Center publications. See, however, Maude Monell Vethesen obituary, *New York Times* (May 24, 1958), p. 21.

JAMES HOWELL SMITH

**AMHERST H. WILDER CHARITY.** See Amherst H. Wilder Foundation.

**AMHERST H. WILDER FOUNDATION.** A private operating foundation located in St. Paul, Minnesota, the Wilder Foundation is one of the oldest and largest foundations in the United States devoted exclusively to providing direct health and welfare services.

The Amherst H. Wilder Foundation was incorporated as a nonprofit corporation under the laws of the state of Minnesota on December 1, 1910, as the Amherst H. Wilder Charity. The name was changed to Amherst H. Wilder Foundation in 1953. The events leading up to the incorporation of the foundation began with the establishment of three trusts in 1903, 1904, and 1905 resulting from the wills of Amherst Holcomb Wilder; his wife, Fanny Spencer Wilder; and their daughter, Cornelia Day Wilder Appleby.

Early in the year 1859, Amherst Wilder left his home in Lewis, New York, and came to St. Paul, apparently to explore business adventures in this area. He was thirty-one years old. After developing a successful partnership in a trading and freight business, he became involved in most of the business interests of the day—trading, banking, insurance, real estate, manufacturing. Between 1860 and 1880, Wilder was financially involved in almost all of the business activities of St. Paul and was recognized as one of the millionaires of that city.

Amherst Wilder died on the eleventh day of November, 1894. He had been a resident of the city of St. Paul for thirty-five years. By his last will, a considerable part of his estate was directed to be disposed of in such a way as would "best operate in a permanent manner to relieve, aid and assist the poor, sick, and needy people of the City of Saint Paul." During the late 1800s, housing in St. Paul was inadequate, tuberculosis was rampant, and there was much unemployment. Wilder's will also provided that in the event he survived his wife and his daughter, his entire estate would go to the citizens of St. Paul.

Wilder was survived by both his wife and his daughter. The latter died childless on January 20, 1903. Fanny Wilder, his wife, died on April 5, 1903. Both left wills which, after making minor bequests and devises, were designed to carry out the charitable purposes expressed in Mr. Wilder's will—that the family fortune should be devoted to the relief and assistance of needy people in St. Paul.

From 1903 until 1910, the estates were involved in litigation precipitated by certain heirs who sought to set aside the wills. Various decisions were reached by the court which ultimately established the validity of the philanthropic provisions in the wills. Despite court litigation, the expenditure of funds for charitable purposes, as specified in the three Wilder wills, began within three years of the passing of Fanny and Cornelia Day. The first expenditure on record from any of the Wilder trusts was a cash payment made to a widow with two children on July 7, 1906, the birthdate anniversary of Amherst Wilder.

In its early years, the foundation provided direct cash aid to the "helpless poor" of the city. It also provided direct services through the operation of health and welfare programs. A visiting-nurse program to care for the sick and aged was started by the foundation. The foundation also constructed a "bathhouse" for working men and women, day-care centers for preschool children, and a medical outpatient clinic for the poor. It operated a child guidance clinic for emotionally disturbed children, implemented a school lunch program, and fostered a social work program in hospitals.

Programs initiated by Wilder were innovative and filled a vital and necessary need in the city at the time. The foundation has always been an organization in transition. Programs are deleted, added, or changed as needs in the community dictate.

The Wilder Foundation is classified as a private operating foundation by the Internal Revenue Service. As such, the foundation is required to be "organized and operated exclusively for . . . charitable . . . purposes" and to regularly expend substantially all of its adjusted net income directly for the active conduct of the charitable activities constituting the purpose or function for which it is organized and operated.

The foundation's charitable purposes are specified in its restated (1974) articles of incorporation as follows:

. . . to promote the social welfare of persons resident or located in the greater Saint Paul metropolitan area by all appropriate means, including relief of the poor, care of the sick and aged, care and nurture of children, aid to the disadvantaged and otherwise needy, promotion of physical and mental health, support of rehabilitation and corrections, provision of needed housing and social services, operation of residences and facilities for the aged, the infirm, and those requiring special care, and in general the conservation of human resources by the provision of human services responsive to the welfare needs of the community, all without regard to or discrimination on account of nationality, sex, color, religious scruples, or prejudices. . . .

In carrying out these purposes and as an operating rather than a grant-making charitable entity, the foundation devotes a substantial portion of its resources through capital funding, operating subsidy, and management services to the direct provision of social, health, and welfare services to children, their families, the elderly, and the general community in the greater St. Paul metropolitan area. The restated (1974) articles of incorporation specify a change in the geographical service area of the foundation from the said city of St. Paul to the four-county area comprising the greater St. Paul metropolitan area. To carry out its services, the foundation owns, manages, or maintains twenty-five functional program buildings with a book value of $22,295,000. In the fiscal year ending June 30, 1981, the foundation funded thirty-five human service programs and had total operating expenses of $16,679,000 and capital expenditures of $6,057,055.

The Wilder Foundation has ten members who also constitute the board of directors and as such are the governing body of the corporation. Each director is required to be a resident of the city of St. Paul or maintain a principal place of business or principal interest and activity in the city. Each is elected by the members and holds board membership until he or she resigns, is removed by a court having jurisdiction over such matters, or reaches his or her seventieth birthday. The board of directors is vested with and exercises responsibility for the determination of overall policy of the foundation, including matters pertaining to setting objectives, establishing policy, and appointing the chief executive officer.

The officers of the foundation consist of a chair, first vice-chair, second vice-chair, secretary-treasurer, and president. Each officer must be a member of the board of directors, and each holds office for a term of five years, with the exception of the president, whose term is one year.

The president of the corporation is also the chief executive officer of the foundation. He or she is responsible for directing, administering, and coordinating the operations of the foundation in accordance with goals and strategies. He or she plans and directs the foundation's efforts to provide a constant or expanding level of health and social services to the St. Paul area while increasing endowment financial strength to ensure foundation continuity. The president and chief executive officer is assisted in administering the foundation by a management support team consisting of two division directors, administrator of housing, director of planning and development, controller, personnel director, and two executive assistants.

The original and significant continuing source of the foundation's operating income is interest and dividends from investments of its trust endowment. In December, 1910, when the foundation was incorporated, the market value of the original Wilder family endowment was $2,602,000. In 1981, total assets of the foundation were valued at about $191 million and the market value of the foundation's endowment was $94,927,000. Investment income used to finance operations during the 1980-1981 fiscal year amounted to $4,876,334.

Investment policies are made by the full board of directors. Recommendations made and actions approved by the investment committee of the foundation, composed of four members of the board of directors appointed by the chair, are reviewed, ratified, or modified by the board.

In addition to its investment income, a significant portion of the foundation's operating revenues is derived from outside sources, which include private fees and rents, state of Minnesota funds, county contracts, grants, and gifts.

More specifically, private fees include fees paid for services provided by the foundation to other nonprofit organizations, clients of its various social services, and rent receipts from its housing projects. County contracts include purchase-of-service agreements with various county or city governmental agencies and with schools in the St. Paul metropolitan area. Grants and gifts are received from other public and private organizations to subsidize operating costs of specific programs. These sources include: United States government funds used primarily for senior employment programs and community corrections; state of Minnesota grants directed to services for children with mental health problems or developmental disabilities; private foundations' and organizations' gifts for children with learning and developmental disabilities and program start-up costs; and county government funds for children's mental health services (actually state funds administered by the county) and community corrections. The total outside income from all of these various sources for the fiscal year ending June 30, 1981, was $11,802,378.

With respect to funding and resources, the policy of the foundation has been to use income from its trust endowment and investments of the same primarily to formulate, plan, develop, and operate social welfare programs and projects which will attract outside sources of revenue in order to increase its charitable services to persons living in the greater metropolitan St. Paul area. Interest and dividends from the foundation's trust endowment are also used to subsidize administrative and supportive services and, as needed, all direct service programs which are not self-supporting from such outside funding sources.

The Wilder Foundation is currently organized into four operating divisions:

The *Division of Services to Children* provides direct outpatient and residential mental health services for children and their families, and education, training, and consultation for adults who affect the lives of children.

Programs operated by the division include: child guidance clinics which provide comprehensive outpatient mental health services for children and adolescents with personal, family, and developmental difficulties; a learning center which provides diagnostic, treatment, education, and rehabilitation services for children with special education and mental health needs; an adolescent education program which provides intensive special education and mental health services for severely learning-disabled junior high and senior high youth; a children's placement service which provides placement, either in foster care, group homes, or residential settings, as a treatment approach for emotionally disturbed children; a community care unit which trains and supports community care givers and provides mutual-help support systems for family members in situations of crisis, stress, or developmental change; and a children's day-care center.

Approximately four thousand children were served in the division during the fiscal year ending June 30, 1981. Total expenses to finance operations was $4,577,772.

The *Division of Services to the Elderly* provides comprehensive, integrated health and social services, including a full spectrum of community-based and residential services to chronically impaired elderly persons and leisure, educational, recreational, cultural and employment programs to the relatively well elderly.

The division operates a skilled nursing facility for 147 older persons, a facility which provides a range of long-term care for 108 persons, including board, intermediate nursing care, and skilled nursing care. The division also operates a facility which offers board and room for 133 older persons and intermediate or skilled nursing care for 43 persons.

The division also provides community-based and outreach services for elderly persons: an outpatient health center offering a pharmacy, comprehensive dental care, counseling and personal development, eye care, podiatry services, health education, and primary medical care; an adult day-care program; nursing services, personal care, and homemaker and chore services for older persons living in their own homes; two multiservice centers, one in the downtown area and one in an inner-city neighborhood; a senior citizens sales shop which serves as a retail outlet for articles made by older persons; a senior employment program; a care-giver support program for persons who care for elderly family members; a senior information service which reaches isolated elderly neighborhood residents; and a transportation and escort service for elderly and handicapped persons.

An information and assistance office provides timely and accurate information to prospective clients and their families, community agencies, and the interested public about all the services offered in the foundation's elderly division. The office also conducts preservice assessments and evaluations to assist clients, their families, and participating professionals in securing the required service and in designing a plan for the optimal care of the client.

Over fifteen thousand older persons were served by the division during fiscal year 1980–1981. Total expenses to finance the programs amounted to $8,226,573.

The *Division of Correction Services* provides community-based programs for felons and misdemeanants and an environmental program for treatment of adolescent boys and girls.

The division operates a highly structured residential program—consisting of supervised living, group interaction, and counseling—for twenty male felons as a community alternative to imprisonment in adult correctional institutions. Also for adult offenders, primarily misdemeanants, the division operates a community-based, nonresidential service center, offering various kinds of counseling, driver's training, and development of educational and self-skills.

In addition, the division supervises a three-month wilderness-oriented program in northern Minnesota for seventy delinquent adolescents who are referred from the juvenile courts of the four counties comprising the metropolitan St. Paul area. This program places emphasis on outdoor, year-round activities designed to build confidence and self-reliance in the youth.

During the fiscal year ending June 30, 1981, approximately five hundred persons were served in the foundation's correctional programs. The cost to operate the programs was $1,892,198.

The *Division of Housing Services* provides housing for low-, moderate-, and middle-income adults and families. It manages foundation-owned housing and acts as management agent for other housing developments.

The division provides low-cost rental housing for older persons in two apartment buildings, 41 units each, and also operates a 120-unit facility on the same campus for older residents who are eligible to participate in the U. S. Department of Housing and Urban Development Section 8 rental program which subsidizes rental payments.

The division is responsible for the management of two housing projects which were developed and constructed by the foundation. Wilder Square consists of an 11-story, 136-unit high-rise building, owned and managed by the Wilder Foundation, which provides rental housing to elderly and handicapped persons, and a 163-unit cooperative, which includes five 3-story apartment buildings and 43 townhomes that are sold to individuals and families of all ages. Wilder Park is condominium housing, managed by the foundation, which consists of a 231-unit, 17-story apartment tower and 52 townhomes designed for low-, moderate- and middle-income persons.

All Wilder housing is located in residential neighborhoods in the city of St. Paul. The rental apartments were built in 1963 and 1980; Wilder Square was constructed in 1975; and Wilder Park was completed in 1980.

Over eleven hundred persons were served in Wilder housing during fiscal year 1980–1981. The cost to finance housing operations was $1,621,068.

In addition to programs operated in the four divisions, the foundation operates a 980-acre camp, thirty miles from downtown St. Paul, which provides educational and recreational activities in a natural environment for children and adults. Current projects at the camp include expanding and improving its program as an educational resource, developing a 60-acre operating farm, and constructing year-round energy-self-sufficient facilities for retreats, conferences, and classroom programs. During fiscal year 1980–1981, nine thousand persons participated in outdoor activities and programs at Camp Wilder. Total expenses amounted to $232,637.

Nine hundred employees of the foundation helped to provide services to more than twenty-six thousand persons who participated in Wilder programs during fiscal year 1980–1981.

To assist and complement staff, the foundation internally provides professional administrative, technical, and supportive services. These services include:

- a planning and development office which is responsible for maintaining computer-based record systems of foundation service programs, surveying and studying the needs

of various age and socioeconomic population groups in the metropolitan St. Paul area, and performing demonstration projects and client follow-up studies of foundation programs;
- an accounting and data processing department which prepares monthly and annual financial reports processed on an in-house computer;
- a personnel department which develops and administers personnel policies and practices for the foundation's nine hundred employees;
- a building maintenance/compliance department whose staff—consisting of painters, carpenters, electricians, plumbers, and mechanics—maintains the foundation's buildings and vehicles;
- a purchasing department which is responsible for the operations and control of purchasing within designated areas in the foundation.

The Wilder Foundation, during fiscal year 1980–1981, formed a new, wholly owned subsidiary. Named the AHW Corporation, the subsidiary was established to develop, construct, and market three interrelated projects in the proposed Saint Paul Energy Park. The park is a cooperative venture among the city of St. Paul, the federal government, and private organizations to combat deterioration and underutilization of certain portions of the St. Paul community by providing a compatible, energy-efficient environment for residential housing and commercial and industrial development. The AHW Corporation will be involved in the construction of 950 housing units and community facilities in Energy Park.

Another recent undertaking of the foundation was the establishment of a Management Support Program to provide consultation, training, and technical assistance to other nonprofit agencies in the community as well as to programs in the foundation.

The Amherst H. Wilder Foundation, from its very beginning, has responded to the needs of the St. Paul community. Over the last seventy-five years, the foundation, working in cooperation with other public and private agencies and organizations in the community, has tried to do something about those needs. Since the first expenditure in 1906, the Wilder Foundation has spent more than $68 million of its trust endowment and investment income in carrying out its mission.

Archival material on the Amherst H. Wilder Charity/Foundation consists of some business papers of Amherst H. Wilder, newspaper clippings on the Wilder family and Wilder Charity/Foundation, last wills of the Wilder family, official minutes of the meetings of the board of directors dating to December, 1910, annual reports of Wilder Charity/Foundation, legal documents related to purchase of foundation properties and agreements with other organizations and businesses, and various files and reports on foundation programs and activities. A noteworthy point is that there are practically no personal papers of the Wilder family.

The archival material is deposited in the corporate office of the Amherst H. Wilder Foundation, 355 Washington Street, St. Paul, Minnesota, and at the Minnesota Historical Society, St. Paul.

For further information, see Merrill E. Jarchow, *Amherst H. Wilder and His Enduring Legacy to Saint Paul* (1981). See also the following publications of the foundation: *Wilder Charity: Legal History and Documents* (1948); *Amherst H. Wilder Charity Resumé 1906–1952* (1952); *Diamond Anniversary Report of the Amherst H. Wilder Foundation* (1967); and *Annual Reports* from 1912 to 1920, 1947, 1949, 1959, and from 1971 continuously to the present.

NORRINE M. BOHMAN

**A. M. MCGREGOR HOME, THE.** Founded in Ohio in 1904, the 1981 assets of the A. M. McGregor Home amounted to about $33 million. Annual expenditures are about $3 million, with some $2.5 million of the total being devoted to the care of destitute aged persons living in the home. The remainder is used to provide support for various social agencies for the elderly located in the greater Cleveland, Ohio, area.

The home is governed by a fifteen-member board of trustees. Administration of the home, including its limited grants program, is carried on from its location at 14900 Terrace Road, East Cleveland, Ohio 44112 under the direction of an executive director and with a staff of ninety-two persons.

Almost the only additional information on the home readily available to the public are the annual reports and returns filed by it with the Internal Revenue Service, and the various Foundation Center publications.

**AMOCO FOUNDATION, INC.** The Amoco Foundation traces its roots back to 1952, with the founding of the Standard Oil (Indiana) Foundation, funded by Standard Oil Company (Indiana). The company itself had donated to charitable causes for many years previously. The Amoco Foundation came into existence to provide a more structured and stabilized giving pattern. Yearly giving no longer would be dominated by the vagaries of the business cycle, and both donor and recipients would be better able to institute long-range planning. The foundation continues to derive its funding from Standard Oil Company (Indiana).

The predecessor, Standard Oil (Indiana) Foundation, was incorporated on May 21, 1952, and held its first meeting in Chicago, the corporation's home base. Robert E. Wilson was the foundation's first chairman and was Standard board chairman at the time. In 1973, to form the present Amoco Foundation, that foundation was consolidated with two others. These were the Pan American Petroleum Foundation, founded in 1953; and the American Oil Foundation, established in 1957. The latter two were foundations originated by two Standard Oil subsidiaries: an exploration and production company now known as Amoco Production Company; and a refining, transportation, and marketing company now called Amoco Oil Company. These two foundations had been funded mainly by the Standard Oil Foundation, although the Pan American Foundation also received income from oil and gas royalties.

Foundation officers historically have been executives of their sponsoring companies and have served the foundations without additional pay. At the time of the consolidation in 1973, John E. Swearingen was chairman both of Standard Oil Company (Indiana) and of the Standard Oil (Indiana) Foundation. He continues to retain both positions, in the company and in the renamed Amoco Foundation.

The president of the former American Oil Foundation was Blaine J. Yarrington, then president of American Oil Company (now Amoco Oil Company). F. Randolph Yost was president both of Amoco Production Company and of Amoco Production Foundation. The current president of the foundation is Richard M. Morrow.

Amoco Foundation and its predecessors have contributed only to recognized, tax-exempt organizations. It does not make grants to individuals, special interest groups, endowment funds, or human service groups that are essentially supported by United Way giving; nor to organizations which are religious, fraternal, political, social, or athletic in nature. Instead, support is offered to highly qualified organizations that have established programs and reputations for service and effectiveness in the areas of higher education, health, community services, arts, and civic responsibilities.

Over the years, the company's contributions to the foundation have followed a relatively conservative policy. In the recent past, there has been a shift in philosophy, as well as a major increase in budgets. The foundation has intensified its efforts to finance needed changes in specific areas of education and community services.

In the educational sector, which has historically received at least half of the foundation's annual disbursements, new grants are specifically earmarked to help stem the critical shortage of engineering and geophysics doctoral candidates and engineering faculty members. In the community service field, which now receives about one-third of the foundation's giving, large sums are now being directed to individual neighborhood renewal and rehabilitation projects. The foundation's redirection is sensitive both to critical needs within these areas and to sharply reduced government funding of such programs.

Educational grants are made to accredited colleges, universities, and other organized links to higher education. Assistance ranges from unrestricted grants to help private institutions retain academic freedom, to faculty awards, scholarships and fellowships, employee gift matching (with some portions actually two-for-one), awards to libraries and to science museums, plus aid to other related programs. Unrestricted grants can be used for any purpose except endowment. In some cases, they take the form of leadership grants, generally reviewed annually, in order to encourage sustained giving by others. Since 1965, the foundation has underwritten a series of awards to outstanding faculty members at state universities.

In early 1981, Amoco Foundation established a major program to award three-year fellowships for engineering and geophysics Ph.D. students and to provide faculty with research grants in order to retain or attract doctoral candidates into a university teaching career. The fellowships provide tuition, fees, and $10,000 annual stipends; engineering faculty grants have $20,000 annual stipends. This was the first major industrial program of its type introduced in the United States. In announcing the program, the foundation noted that the number of engineering doctoral candidates had declined by one-quarter in the past decade.

Two other new programs are directed at helping more minority members enter the field of engineering. The first finances the start-up of a chemical engineering curriculum at a minority university; the second underwrites a precollege curriculum for various inner-city Chicago high school students who plan to enter engineering school.

The Amoco Foundation plans significant increases in funding for existing and new community support projects, to reaffirm the foundation's belief that inner-city problems can best be solved at the local level. Rehabilitation projects are being funded in two deteriorating neighborhoods.

Other funds are helping charitable organizations cut their heating bills. Many such organizations are housed in older buildings. Foundation grants help finance energy audits and pay for equipment and services, ranging from more sophisticated temperature-sensing and control devices on heating plants to additional insulation and storm windows throughout the building.

A large share of community service giving has been to United Way organizations, essentially in metropolitan areas where Standard Oil Company and its subsidiaries have operations and employees. Standard itself regularly has provided such organizations with leadership support and ancillary services. In addition to combined appeals, the foundation funded a variety of other community service efforts that emphasize individual development, for example: youth-oriented social service groups (such as Junior Achievement, boys' and girls' clubs, YMCAs, Scouts, and so on) and additional neighborhood self-help efforts (such as job preparation and placement, entrepreneurial business development). In addition, the Amoco Foundation supports medical research and other health-related projects.

Grants are made to finance research and the study of political and economic systems, traffic safety, energy and environmental conservation, community economic issues, and foreign relations. The foundation also makes funds available to libraries and museums and for the performing arts and other cultural activities. To a lesser degree, the foundation supports educational, youth, health, cultural, and social service activities in foreign countries where Standard operates. In 1981 total foundation assets amounted to about $52 million and the foundation made grants of about $9 million.

Candidates for foundation grants should write to Donald G. Schroeter, executive director, at the foundation offices: Amoco Foundation Inc., 200 East Randolph Drive, Chicago, Illinois 60601. Requests should contain the following information: a brief description of the organization (that is, formal name, activities, history, objectives, plus annual report or other comprehensive financial data, as well as a list of contributors; amount of aid sought, its uses, how anticipated results would be objectively audited; and an Internal Revenue Service statement affirming the organization's tax-exempt status under Internal Revenue Code Section 501(c)(3).

For further information, see a *Cumulative Report* of the foundation, 1952–1968; and *Annual Reports* of the foundation and its predecessors, published continuously since 1969.

A. G. FIEDLER, JR.

**AMON G. CARTER FOUNDATION.** Amon G. Carter (1879–1955), the founder of and principal donor to the foundation, was a poor boy with little schooling who became a successful newspaperman and a rich man. He entered the newspaper field in Fort Worth in 1905 and in 1909 launched the *Fort Worth Star-Telegram* with borrowed money. He acquired the controlling interest in the newspaper in 1923 and became publisher and president. Subsequently, he acquired substantial interests in real estate, oil, and ranching. As his wealth grew, he gave money and made gifts to individuals and institutions, with most of his large gifts going to educational institutions in the Fort Worth and West Texas region.

The Amon G. Carter Foundation was established in 1945 with funds provided by Amon G. Carter, N. B. Carter, and the Star-Telegram Employees Fund, with the major portion of its initial assets of about $13 million coming from the proceeds of the sale of some of Amon G. Carter's oil holdings. The foundation was established as a limited-life corporation, but its charter has since been amended to provide for perpetual existence. While appropriations from capital can be made, the foundation's endowment has continued to grow from income on investments and additional gifts of about $7 million following Amon Carter's death plus those from the Carter Foundation Production Company. Its 1980 assets were about $118 million.

The original stated purpose of the foundation was to support benevolent, charitable, educational, and religious undertakings of a missionary nature. From its beginning, the foundation has concentrated its gifts to institutions in the Fort Worth area. This policy reflects the principal donor's intense interest in and concern with Fort Worth. One of the foundation's early grants, for example, provided funds for the purchase of an outstanding collection of manuscripts and first editions of sixteenth- to nineteenth-century English and American authors for presentation to Fort Worth's Texas Christian University. In 1980, this same university received the largest grant in the foundation's history, $3,231,000, for support of the university's communications buildings. Other major grants for that year, out of a total of some $10 million, included one of $1,467,507 to Fort Worth's Amon Carter Museum of Western Art, one of $500,000 to the Museum of Science and Industry of Fort Worth, and two of slightly over $1 million each to Fort Worth's YMCA and St. Joseph Hospital.

The foundation is governed by a three-member board of directors which includes Amon G. Carter's daughter, who is also president of the foundation.

Administration is carried on from offices located at 400 West Seventh Street, Fort Worth, Texas 76101, under the direction of a secretary.

Almost the only additional sources of information readily available to the public concerning Amon G. Carter Foundation are the annual reports and returns filed by it with the Internal Revenue Service, and the various Foundation Center publications. See, however, Amon G. Carter obituary in the *New York Times* (June 24, 1955), p. 21.

**ANDERSON FOUNDATION.** See John W. Anderson Foundation; M. D. Anderson Foundation.

**ANDREW W. MELLON FOUNDATION, THE.** A reflection of the deep and continuing interest in philanthropy by members of the Mellon family, the Andrew W. Mellon Foundation is the latest and largest of a number of charitable organizations established and funded by the Mellon family dating back to the early years of the twentieth century.

Andrew W. Mellon (1855–1937), for whom the foundation is named, and his brother, Richard B. Mellon (1858–1933), built sizable fortunes in the late nineteenth and early twentieth centuries and simultaneously turned to philanthropy. For example, records show that, exclusive of his contributions to the A. W. Mellon Educational and Charitable Trust and to the National Gallery of Art, personal charitable contributions of Andrew W. Mellon for such purposes from 1902 until his death in 1937 were about $10 million. In 1913, the brothers established and funded the Mellon Institute of Industrial Research, one of the predecessor institutions of the present-day Carnegie-Mellon University. In 1930, Andrew W. Mellon set up the A. W. Mellon Educational and Charitable Trust, which became the major beneficiary of his estate. This, together with previous gifts, amounted to over $100 million, making the Mellon Trust one of the larger U.S. foundations at that time. Its most notable accomplishment, which was personally initiated by Andrew Mellon, was the establishment of the National Gallery of Art in Washington, D.C. However, because of continuous and large appropriations over the years from principal, the foundation's size has been greatly reduced, and its program is now largely restricted to the Pittsburgh area.

Ten years after the establishment of the Mellon Trust, Andrew Mellon's daughter, Ailsa Mellon Bruce, founded the Avalon Foundation, which concentrated its grants in the fields of medicine, health, and artistic and cultural projects. It also focused on projects pertaining to the development of youth and the preservation of our natural resources. Its grants were generally made only to organizations operating in its chosen fields and primarily in the New York area.

The Avalon Foundation was founded in 1940. A year later, Ailsa Bruce's brother, Paul Mellon, founded the Old Dominion Foundation. Its chief areas of concern were education, the arts, mental health, the preservation of nature areas, and the conservation of natural resources. It also maintained a special program of grants limited to the state of Virginia from which its name was taken and in which its founder made his home. In 1945, the foundation, which had made few grants to individuals in its early years, established and funded the Bollingen Foundation, which, until its termination in the 1960s, made grants to individuals working in the fields of the arts and humanities.

In 1969, the Andrew W. Mellon Foundation was established under the laws of New York through the merger of the Avalon and Old Dominion Foundations. By that time, the combined assets of these two foundations, which had received from their donors gifts amounting to $167 million, had increased in value through appreciation of assets and income to $273 million, despite having made grants in the neighborhood of $148 million. Upon the death of Ailsa Bruce in 1969, the newly formed foundation received more than $400 million from her estate. This brought the foundation's assets to approximately $700 million. In 1981, these assets amounted to approximately $817 million, making the foundation one of the largest in this country. Annual grants made by the foundation range from $35 million to more than $58 million.

The Mellon Foundation has reflected the interests of the trustees of the predecessor foundations, particularly those of Paul Mellon, who was a continuous member of the board of trustees of both the Avalon and Old Dominion foundations, was active in a number of other Mellon philanthropies, and has served on the board of the Mellon Foundation since its founding. Hence the major programs of the Mellon Foundation from 1969 to the present have been in higher education, the arts, medicine, population, conservation and the environment, and public affairs. In terms of number of grants and total dollars appropriated, the foundation's largest commitment has been to higher education, particularly for the nation's research universities. Aid in this program area has included the funding of professorial chairs, primarily in the humanities at selected colleges and universities; subventions for university presses to aid in scholarly publication; aid for libraries, including the nation's independent research libraries and leading historical societies; and allocations for advanced language instruction, area studies centers, and centers for advanced learning. An unusual feature of the millions of dollars appropriated by the foundation for institutions of higher education in the 1970s was that approximately a quarter of this money was in endowment form. Such support of higher education and the humanities is projected into the future. As the foundation enters the 1980s, it has announced a graduate fellowship program in the humanities with a projected underwriting, over a ten-year period, of $24 million.

The program and activities of the foundation are directed from offices located at 140 East Sixty-second Street, New York, New York 10021, by an administrative staff headed by President John E. Sawyer, formerly president of Williams College.

For further information, see *Reports* which were published periodically by the A. W. Mellon Educational and Charitable Trust, the Avalon, Bollingen, and Old Dominion foundations, particularly those for the Mellon Trust dated 1930–1945, 1946–1950; and *Annual Reports,* 1951 to the present for the Mellon Trust, those for the Bollingen Foundation dated 1945–1953 and 1954–1958, and those for the Old Dominion Foundation dated 1941–1950, 1951–1955, and 1956–1958. For a recent history of the Bollingen Foundation, which includes an account of the lives of Paul Mellon and his wife Mary Conover Mellon together with a description of their roles in the foundation and operation of other Mellon philanthropies, see William McGuire, *Bollingen, An Adventure in Collecting the Past* (1982). The papers of the Bollingen Foundation are deposited in the Library of Congress, Washington, D.C. See also *Annual Reports* of the Andrew W. Mellon Foundation, published continuously since 1969, particularly that for 1979, which presents a review of the decade 1969 through 1979.

**ANNENBERG FUND, INC., THE.** The Annenberg Fund was set up in Delaware in 1951 by funds donated by Walter H. Annenberg. By 1958, its assets amounted to approximately $1.5 million, and it was making annual grants of about $100,000, chiefly for elementary and secondary schools, a community fund, and music. By 1969, the fund's assets had increased to about $44 million, and grants for that year were approximately $1.5 million. Since that time, assets declined to about $32 million in 1980, while annual grants have climbed to between $3 million and $4 million. In recent years, most of this fund's giving has been concentrated upon cultural programs, historic preservation, education, and health and medical research. The majority of the grantees of the fund have been located in the states of Pennsylvania, New York, and California and primarily in the cities of Philadelphia, New York, and Los Angeles.

Three of the four members of the Annenberg Fund's governing board of trustees are members of the Annenberg family, and Walter H. Annenberg, the donor, serves as president, with his wife as vice-president. The administration of the fund is carried on from offices located at 100 Matsonford Road, Radnor, Pennsylvania 19088.

Almost the only additional sources of information readily available to the public on this foundation are the annual reports and returns filed by it with the Internal Revenue Service, and the various Foundation Center publications.

**ANNIE E. CASEY FOUNDATION, THE.** Established in California in 1948, the Annie E. Casey Foundation reported assets of about $135,000 and grants of about $5,000 for that year. The following approximate figures for subsequent years show a steady growth in assets and resultant annual grants: in 1957, assets of $750,000 and grants of $25,000; in 1969, assets of $15 million and grants of $0.5 million; in 1975, assets of $35 million and grants of $1,300,000; and in 1979, assets of $46 million and grants of $3 million.

The corpus of the foundation initially consisted of stock in United Parcel Service of America, Inc. (UPS) donated by members of the Casey family, including Annie E. Casey, for whom the foundation was named, and J. E. Casey. The latter was one of the founders and an official of UPS.

Throughout its history, the foundation has operated almost wholly in the area of child welfare support, particularly in the Seattle, Washington, area. Since the removal of its offices from New York City to Greenwich, Connecticut, in the 1970s, the foundation has concentrated most of its grant support to a child welfare program headquartered in Seattle, called the Casey Family Program, and more recently in Connecticut, called the Casey Family Program East. The foundation also continues to provide some support to the Roman Catholic Archdiocese of Seattle, earmarked for use to prevent juvenile delinquency. It also operates a park in downtown Seattle, named Waterfall Gardens.

The foundation, with 1981 assets of about $56 million, is governed by a five-member board of trustees. Administration is carried on from offices located at 51 Weaver Street, Greenwich Office Park 5, Greenwich, Connecticut 06830, under the direction of the chairman.

Almost the only additional sources of information on this foundation readily available to the public are the annual reports and returns filed by it with the Internal Revenue Service, and the various Foundation Center publications.

**ARIE AND IDA CROWN MEMORIAL.** Established in 1947 in Illinois, this foundation was originally named the Arie Crown Memorial Fund. In 1960 the name was changed to its present one by the Crown sons so as to honor both parents, Arie and Ida. Initially, the foundation was funded with gifts of about $400,000 from members of the Crown family. These assets, through appreciation from income and other gifts from the Crowns, had grown to about $10 million by the time of the name change in the 1960s. In 1980 the foundation had assets of about $33 million.

The foundation has concentrated its giving, presently about $1.75 million annually, on organizations located in the Chicago and New York metropolitan areas. These organizations have traditionally included higher and secondary education, together with social, cultural, welfare, and religious organizations. Many of them have been Jewish organizations. The foundation is governed by a five-member board of directors, each of whom is a member of the Crown family. Administration of the Arie and Ida Crown Foundation is carried on from offices located at 300 West Washington Street, Chicago, Illinois 60606, under the direction of a secretary.

Almost the only additional sources of information readily available to the public on this foundation are the annual reports and returns filed by it with the Internal Revenue Service, and the various Foundation Center publications.

**ARIE CROWN MEMORIAL FUND.** See Arie and Ida Crown Memorial.

**ARTHUR VINING DAVIS FOUNDATIONS, THE.** Named for the industrialist-businessman who made one fortune producing aluminum and another in developing Florida real estate, there are three Arthur Vining Davis Foundations, designated as foundations No. 1, No. 2, and No. 3. Foundation No. 1 was organized in 1952 during the lifetime of Mr. Davis. It is of relatively modest size, its total assets amounting to about $1 million during most of its existence.

Foundations No. 2 and No. 3 are substantially larger, having been created by the will of Arthur Vining Davis following his death in 1962 to receive the major share of his $50-million estate. They commenced operations in 1965. The Mellon Bank N.A. serves as corporate trustee for foundations No. 1 and No. 2; the Southeast First National Bank of Miami serves foundation No. 3 in a similar capacity.

The three foundations are operated and administered as separate legal entities. All funds are handled separately by the appropriate corporate fiduciary and are subject to the various individual reporting requirements. In dealing with grant applications, the situation is different. In an effort to achieve efficiency and economy of operation, the three foundations share the cost of a single office located in the Haskell Building, Oak and Fisk Streets, Jacksonville, Florida 32204.

Since the first year of operations in 1965, the trustees have striven to adapt the particular interests of Arthur Vining Davis during his lifetime to the contemporary needs of society. For example, private education has been a continuing major field of support, whereas public television programming has received sizable grants only recently.

The boards of trustees have chosen to operate nationally in several fields of service to the community. However, under the terms of Davis's will, they may make grants only in the United States. It was initially determined as a matter of policy that funding would be limited to those institutions which exist only through private support, in contrast to those receiving their basic financing from federal or state sources. This continues as foundation policy. Thus, the trustees continue to concentrate their grants in private education, medicine, religion, hospitals, and public television. Depending upon the income available, however, the board hopes to reach a position from which it can consider other areas of need without curtailing its support of traditional fields in which it has operated.

There is one board of trustees for foundations 1 and 2 and another for foundation 3. The nephew of the founder, Nathaniel V. Davis, chairman of Alcan Aluminum, Ltd., serves as chairman of both boards. Several trustees also serve on both boards.

Assets of the Arthur Vining Davis Foundations were worth about $60 million in 1980. Annual grants at that time amounted to about $4 million. The programs and activities of all three foundations are conducted and administered by a single staff headed by an executive director.

The foregoing brief history was primarily based upon a statement furnished to the editors by Max K. Morris, executive director of the foundations. For further information, see *Annual Reports* of the foundation, published continuously since 1970. See also Arthur Vining Davis obituary, *New York Times* (November 18, 1962), p. 86, and (November 27, 1962), p. 43; and "Arthur

Vining Davis," *Dictionary of American Biography,* Supplement Seven (1980), pp. 166–167.

**ASSOCIATION FOR THE AID OF CRIPPLED CHILDREN.** See Foundation for Child Development.

**ASTOR FOUNDATION.** See Vincent Astor Foundation, The.

**ATLANTIC FOUNDATION, THE.** The Atlantic Foundation was established in 1964 in New Jersey by J. Seward Johnson, brother of Robert Wood Johnson who was the founder of the Robert Wood Johnson Foundation.* The Atlantic Foundation was funded with shares of stock in the Johnson and Johnson Company.

In the first decade of its operations, the foundation made grants to a wide range of institutions and organizations. These included secondary schools, hospitals, cultural institutions, conservation, and oceanographic projects, many of which were organizations located in the New Jersey area.

Since the mid-1970s, the foundation has devoted almost all of its grants to the support of marine sciences and ocean engineering projects. In allocating this support, the Atlantic Foundation has allotted nearly 100 percent of it to two operating foundations, the Harbor Branch Foundation, Incorporated, in Dayton, New Jersey, and the Harbor Branch Institution, Incorporated, in Fort Pierce, Florida. For example, in 1978 the Harbor Branch Foundation received a grant of $3.85 million, which was the sole grant made in that year, and in 1979, two grants totalling $3.9 million were made to these two operating foundations.

In 1975, the Atlantic Foundation's assets were about $85 million; by 1980 they were about $69 million.

The foundation is governed by a six-member board of directors which includes J. Seward Johnson, chairman; J. Seward Johnson, Jr., president and treasurer; and Barbara P. Johnson, vice-president. The other directors are: James L. Johnson, Marilyn C. Link, and Reuben F. Richards. Administration of the foundation is carried on from Post Office Box 6337, Lawrenceville, New Jersey 08648.

Almost the only additional sources of information readily available to the public concerning this foundation are the annual reports and returns filed by it with the Internal Revenue Service, and the various Foundation Center publications.

**AURORA FOUNDATION, THE.** Located in Bradenton and with assets in 1981 of about $83 million, the Aurora Foundation is the largest in Florida.

Aurora was founded by Anthony T. Rossi, a Sicilian immigrant to New York City at the age of twenty. After holding a variety of jobs in New York, Rossi became proprietor of a grocery. Rossi moved to Florida and entered the restaurant business. During World War II, he laid much of the basis for his fortune by packaging fruit for shipment to the North as gifts. He pioneered in packing chilled grapefruit and orange sections in glass jars. He organized Fruit Industries,

Incorporated, which revolutionized the juice business. The name was changed in 1955 to Tropicana (based upon a mannequin, "Tropic Ana," depicting the daughter of an employee). Chilled citrus juice was shipped, much as fuel oil is transported, in stainless steel containers by rail or by ship. Rossi's business was a sensational success: stock was offered to the public on the over-the-counter market in 1969 and on the New York Stock Exchange in 1970. In 1978, Rossi sold Tropicana to Beatrice Foods for $488 million. His share of this, plus his net from previous stock sales, would have made him the richest man in citrus. However, he gave most of his assets to the Tropicana Foundation, established in 1969, which was renamed the Aurora Foundation after the sale.

Rossi has no children. After his first wife, Florence, died, he married Sanna, a former worldwide missionary for Gospel Recordings who has written several books. There are no children by either marriage. Rossi had come to America with the hope of earning enough money to produce a film about Africa. His love of America led him to abandon plans to live in Africa, but he did not give up his interest in it.

Reared as a Roman Catholic, Rossi, through study of the Bible, became an energetic convert to evangelical Christianity—first the Methodist Church, then the Southern Baptist, and still later an independent Baptist church in which he now serves as deacon. In about 1970, he conducted revivals in Messina, Sicily, and organized an evangelic Baptist church, which he still supports.

The Aurora Foundation maintains at Bradenton, Florida, a missionary village with 220 homes and a recreation hall on 400 acres of land embodying four lakes. The residences are for missionaries without assets, who occupy them rent-free, paying only for utilities. The foundation maintains two other organizations, Bible Alliance Dissemination and Bible Alliance Missions. They produce Bible translations and religious tracts on cassettes and ship them from the missionary village, many going to Africa and the West Indies.

The foundation occasionally funds scholarships, especially for children of preachers, but disclaims interest in funding chairs for colleges or giving bricks-and-mortar grants to schools and colleges. However, two recent grants have been made—one to Bethune-Cookman College, Daytona Beach, and one to the University of Tampa. More typical are 1976 grants of $300 to the World Radio Missionary Fellowship, Miami, Florida, and $500,000 to the West Indies Mission, Coral Gables, Florida. In the same year, a grant of $2,000 went to the Sarasota Jewish Community Council and a $1,000 grant to the Westminster Presbytery, St. Petersburg, Florida. Many other grants are made for interdenominational evangelical purposes, but no grants have been made for Roman Catholic causes. Although the foundation does not limit its grants geographically, they tend to be concentrated in the South; New England and the Pacific Northwest have received none.

Trustees of the foundation are Anthony T. Rossi, Chairman; Ralph Nicosia, Rossi's nephew; Ed H. Price, Jr., who heads a public relations firm in Bradenton;

and A. Lamar Matthews, an attorney from Sarasota. Price and Matthews are deacons in Southern Baptist churches.

Although Rossi feels that there has been too much attention to his foundation and he discourages publicity, a number of articles about him are available. For further information, see *Florida Investment Letter* (June 15, 1969); "The Faith of Anthony Rossi," *Tampa Sun* (July 20, 1969), pp. 1, 6–7; Wayne King, "Tropicana: Anthony T. Rossi and Little Tropic-Ana Together Have Earned Millions in Citrus," *Tampa Tribune* (June 23, 1974); "Tony Rossi Can't Let Go," *Fortune* (January 16, 1978), pp. 120–124; Jim Powell, "Florida's Unspoiled Orange Barons," *Town and Country* (March, 1981), pp. 72–84; and Otis White, "Giving Money is Not Always an Easy Task," *Florida Trend* (July, 1982), pp. 60–65.

EVANS C. JOHNSON

**AVALON FOUNDATION.** See Andrew W. Mellon Foundation, The.

# B

**BABCOCK FOUNDATION.** See Mary Reynolds Babcock Foundation, Incorporated.

**BAKER FOUNDATION.** See R. C. Baker Foundation, The.

**BANKAMERICA FOUNDATION.** The company-sponsored BankAmerica Foundation was established in California in 1968 as the Bank of America Foundation and was and is supported by donations from BankAmerica Corporation and its subsidiaries. In the 1970s, the foundation's name was changed to BankAmerica Foundation simultaneous with a similar change in name by its sponsoring company. In its first decade of existence, the foundation's assets increased from a few million dollars to approximately $22 million in 1979. During this same period, annual gifts from the BankAmerica Corporation and its subsidiaries to the foundation ranged from several million dollars to $7 million. The foundation's 1981 assets were about $31 million.

The continuing inflow of capital to the BankAmerica Foundation has enabled it to conduct a sizable grant-making program. Since its founding, the foundation has concentrated most of its grants in the fields of community improvement and education. These grants have been primarily limited to California, where BankAmerica Corporation is headquartered, and to communities where the bank has significant operations.

In 1979, for example, of approximately $7 million disbursed by the foundation, 43 percent was provided for the support of community affairs organizations. Two of the largest grants in this area were one of $827,000 to the United Way of San Francisco and one of $779,000 to the United Way of Los Angeles. Education was awarded 31 percent of foundation funds for the year; this included over $1 million for the foundation's Educational Initiatives Program and about $800,000 to various colleges and universities. The former program was set up to make awards to public elementary and secondary schools, devoted to promoting innovation and excellence in California schools. Of the remaining 26 percent of the total monies granted in 1979, 20 percent went to cultural and arts groups and organizations, such as $625,000 to the San Francisco Opera Association, with the remaining grant monies used for the support of national and international affairs organizations.

The BankAmerica Foundation is governed by an eight-member board of trustees. Also, the foundation has a distribution committee of nine members to set foundation goals, operating procedures, and make decisions on grant applications. Many of the members of the board of trustees and some of the members of the distribution committee are senior officers of BankAmerica Corporation. Administration of the foundation is carried on under the direction of an executive director. The mailing address of the foundation is Bank of America Center, Post Office Box 37000, San Francisco, California 94137.

For further information, see *Annual Reports* of the foundation, published since the 1970s.

**BANK OF AMERICA FOUNDATION.** See BankAmerica Foundation.

**BEATRICE P. DELANY CHARITABLE TRUST.** This foundation was established in New York about 1977 by Beatrice P. Delany. In 1978, assets were valued at about $18 million. Since then, as the partial result of ensuing contributions in the millions of dollars, the foundation's assets grew to about $23.5 million in 1980 and to $32.25 million in 1981.

Since its beginnings, the Beatrice P. Delany Charitable Trust has concentrated its giving on hospitals, higher education, and religious organizations. In 1980, for example, with grants totalling about $3.64 million, 51 percent was appropriated for hospitals and medical research, including a grant of $1.47 million to Rush Presbyterian/St. Luke's Medical Center, Chicago; 37 percent was appropriated for higher education, including a grant of $1.07 million to the Illinois Institute of Technology, Chicago; and the remaining 12 percent was appropriated for various religious organizations, secondary education, and social service and cultural programs. Geographically, most of the forty-six recipients of grants in 1980 were located in Chicago.

All powers and duties with respect to the property and assets of the trust are vested in the sole trustee of the foundation, the Chase Manhattan Bank. The distribution of principal and income from the trust for charitable purposes, however, is lodged in a three-member trust committee. The mailing address of the foundation is The Chase Manhattan Bank, 1211 Avenue of the Americas, New York, New York 10036.

Almost the only additional sources of information readily available to the public on this foundation are the annual reports and returns filed by it with the Internal Revenue Service, and the various Foundation Center publications.

**BENEDUM FOUNDATION.** See Claude Worthington Benedum Foundation.

**BENWOOD FOUNDATION, INC.** The Benwood Foundation, of Chattanooga, Tennessee, has been called the most important institutional supporter of cultural activity and philanthropic causes in the Chattanooga region. With 1980 market value of assets over $38 million, it is the largest private foundation in Tennessee and one of the largest in the South. Since 1950, when it received its principal bequest from the estate of its founder, George Thomas Hunter, the Benwood Foundation has annually provided from $1.5 million to $2.5 million to assist educational, health and welfare, artistic, and religious organizations, primarily in Chattanooga and southeast Tennessee.

George Thomas Hunter achieved wealth during a life devoted to service to the Coca-Cola Company. Born in Maysville, Kentucky, in 1877, he moved to Chattanooga in 1904 to attend Baylor School and to work in a new Coca-Cola bottling company there. His maternal uncle, Benjamin F. Thomas, was a principal founder of Coca-Cola, and he had established the company's new branch in Chattanooga. Presumably under his uncle's tutelage, Hunter rose rapidly in the corporate administration, serving as secretary from 1906 to 1915 (while Thomas was president) and then succeeding his uncle as president in 1915. In 1941, the corporation elected him chairman of the board, a post he held until his death in 1950.

Hunter chartered the Benwood Foundation in 1944 in Delaware (state laws there made such incorporation relatively uncomplicated) and in 1945 in Tennessee. The name of the foundation supposedly derives from an incident associated with his uncle. Benjamin F. Thomas purchased some land on Lookout Mountain before it became as heavily developed as it is today. When Thomas's sister visited the overgrown and seedy patch, she was shocked that he had bought it and exclaimed, "Well, Ben would!" Whether truth or legend, this is the best explanation for the name available. The full development of the foundation's organizational structure and charitable philosophy took place after Hunter's death in 1950. Hunter had no children, and his only survivors were five sisters. So the bulk of his Coca-Cola holdings went to the foundation, and he directed in his will that the money be used for "the advancement of mankind."

To interpret and apply his specific wishes, a board of trustees was created that today consists of five individuals appointed from among Chattanooga's financial and corporate leaders. The current trustees are Scott L. Probasco, Jr., vice-chairman of American National Bank and Trust Company; E. Y. Chapin III, president of Rock City Gardens, Inc.; Sebert Brewer, Jr.; Joseph Davenport, who holds executive positions with the Volunteer State Life Insurance Company, American National Bank and Trust, Coca-Cola Bottling Company of Miami, Inc., and other corporations; and W. R. Randolph, Jr., consultant to the Coca-Cola Company. Administrative responsibilities are lodged with the executive director, currently W. A. Walter.

Hunter left instructions that foundation support be given in five broad areas, "religious, charitable, scientific, literary, and educational activities." For each, the trustees have formulated guidelines for assessing requests. By far, education has received the largest share of the foundation's total giving (about 50 percent). According to the written guidelines, unrestricted gifts go to universities, colleges, and secondary and elementary schools to support the institutions' athletic and academic scholarship programs (no scholarships are awarded directly to individuals) and to assist capital construction and research projects. The largest recipient in this category has been the University of Tennessee for the university's foundation, for capital projects, and for athletic and research scholarships. Covenant College has received over $100,000 for capital improvements as well. Schools benefiting from foundation gifts for scholarships include Hunter's *alma mater*, Baylor School, as well as Sewanee Academy, Tennessee Tech University, and other secondary and elementary schools.

Gifts to the arts and humanities provide the second largest area of donation (about 25 percent of total giving). Grants go to organizations which "encourage or engage in artistic and cultural programs, performances or activities." The principal recipient has been the Hunter Museum of Art, in Chattanooga, which is housed in George T. Hunter's home. General support has gone to the Chattanooga Community Foundation; gifts for acquiring artifacts and for general development to museums like the Tennessee State Museum, the Houston Antique Museum, and the Tennessee Valley Railroad Museum; and operating support for the Chattanooga Symphony Orchestra and other performing arts organizations.

Only slightly below this level of giving has been the assistance rendered to health and welfare organizations. The foundation gives principally to charitable hospitals and teaching hospitals, for research in disease prevention and cures (including specialty clinics), and to social service and welfare organizations. The foundation has awarded funds in this category for construction; the Chattanooga-Hamilton County Hospital Authority, for example, received $300,000 for construction. Other funds have been used for medical scholarships.

The foundation's efforts to support religious activities have been for religious instruction and worship. It specifically excludes gifts for operations or building programs, although it did contribute to the construction of a chapel at Covenant College as part of a broad capital improvement program. Principal recipients under this category have been the Christian Business Men's Committee, Reachout, Inc., and the Public School Bible Study Committee—programs designed to increase Bible awareness and to inculcate active religiosity. Total giving in this category has amounted to about 10 percent.

The trustees have developed application procedures quite similar to those of most foundations across the country. They require letters of intent that include a brief description of the program to be funded. A formal application form is used. The board considers requests at each quarterly meeting (January, April, July, and October). Recipients submit audit statements at the end of the grant period.

Each year, the Benwood Foundation contributes to from 90 to 110 projects, with an average donation of about $24,000. Amounts of these grants range from $100 to over $300,000. The great majority of grants goes to organizations in

Chattanooga and the rest of Tennessee, but the foundation has awarded grants for projects as well in Arkansas, Connecticut, Georgia, North Carolina, and Texas.

For further information, see Gilbert Govan and James W. Livingood, *The Chattanooga Country, 1540–1976* (1977). See also George Thomas Hunter obituaries, *New York Times* (October 4 and 8, 1950) and *Chattanooga Times* (October 4, 1950).

DAVID L. ROWE

**BOETTCHER FOUNDATION.** Incorporated December 22, 1937, in Colorado, the incorporators of the Boettcher Foundation were Claude K. Boettcher, the principal donor; Charles Boettcher II, his son; and James Quigg Newton, Jr. The three constituted the first board of trustees. The articles of incorporation stated the purpose for which the foundation was incorporated in the following:

> To receive and maintain a fund or funds and apply the principal and income thereof, and any other property or funds of the Foundation, to such religious, charitable, scientific or educational uses and purposes as will, in the absolute and uncontrolled discretion of the Trustees of Foundation, most effectively assist, encourage and promote the general well-being of mankind, within the territorial limits of the present State of Colorado; and it shall be within the objects of the Foundation to use as means to that end research, publication, the organization, establishment and maintenance of religious, charitable, scientific and public educational activities, agencies and institutions, and to aid any such activities, agencies and institutions already established and any other means and agencies which, from time to time, shall seem expedient to said Trustees, provided, always, that the Foundation shall never have or exercise any objects or purposes, except such as shall in law be deemed charitable, . . .

Thus the people and institutions of Colorado became and remain the Boettcher Foundation's foci of interest. The explanation for this lies in the history of the Boettcher family in the last hundred years. Charles Boettcher, the founder of the family fortune and the father of Claude K. Boettcher, was born in Colleda, Prussia, in 1852. He left Germany at the age of seventeen and made his way to Cheyenne, Wyoming, in 1869, and thence to Colorado in 1873, at which times both Wyoming and Colorado were still territories. After establishing a successful hardware business serving the agricultural and mining interests of Colorado, he expanded his interests into utilities, banking, cement, and the then fledgling sugar beet industry with notable success.

Claude K. Boettcher (1875–1957), the son of Charles Boettcher, was the moving spirit in the founding of the Boettcher Foundation. Born in Boulder, Colorado, in 1875, he graduated from Harvard University in 1897 with a degree in engineering and became associated with his father in the latter's manifold business enterprises. Both he and his wife, born Edna Case, the daughter of a pioneering Colorado physician, early in their married life expressed a desire to contribute to the well-being of the people of Colorado, from which much of the

Boettcher family's wealth derived. The Boettcher Foundation was the instrument by which they planned to accomplish their goal.

Initially, Charles Boettcher and Claude K. Boettcher and their wives provided the major part of the foundation's funds. Subsequent contributions from other family members and associates have increased the fund, which in 1981 amounted to over $80 million. From 1937 through 1982, the foundation, now governed by a board of seven trustees headed by C. Bruce Flick, chairman, and Mrs. Charles Boettcher II, vice-chairman, has made grants aggregating more than $63 million.

Boettcher Foundation grants are usually of a substantial size and are made to well-conceived projects or to established Colorado institutions or organizations, ordinarily where there is participating support. It is foundation policy to avoid initiating projects or making continuing commitments of support or grants to individuals.

From its establishment in 1937 to the present, educational organizations have received about 50 percent of the total amounts granted. Hospitals and health services have received approximately 20 percent, and civic and cultural programs and community and social services approximately 30 percent. Over the years, the University of Colorado and the University of Denver have been major beneficiaries of the foundation's giving. The foundation has also made grants to various Colorado hospitals, the Denver Symphony Orchestra, the Denver Museum of Natural History, and the Denver Art Museum. It also has continuously supported undergraduate scholarship and postgraduate fellowship programs wherein grants are made to Colorado colleges and universities to be distributed to selected individuals.

A small administrative staff headed by John C. Mitchell, president and executive director, conducts the programs of the foundation from offices located at 828 Seventeenth Street, Denver, Colorado, 80202.

For further information, see *Annual Reports* of the foundation, published since the 1960s, particularly the report for 1967, which contains a historical review of the foundation's first thirty years of operation with a record of foundation grants for the years 1937-1967.

**BOOTH FERRIS FOUNDATION.** The Booth Ferris Foundation is the result of a merger in 1964 of two previously established trusts. The first trust was established under the will of Chancie Ferris Booth, who died in 1957, the second under the will of her spouse, Willis H. Booth, who died in 1958. Willis Booth was for many years the vice-president of the Guaranty Trust Company (now Morgan Guaranty Trust Company) and served on the board of trustees for many large corporations.

The foundation, with initial assets of about $17 million and with 1981 assets of around $60 million, has provided support for a wide variety of institutions, schools of art, theological seminaries, educational associations, social service, child welfare agencies, museums, performing arts companies, and schools of health and health services, to name a few. However, the majority of these grants have been for education, the arts, social services, and welfare and have been concentrated in the northeastern United States, particularly New York City.

The Booth Ferris Foundation is governed and administered by two trustees, Robert J. Murtagh, 30 Broad Street, New York, New York, 10004, and Morgan Guaranty Trust Company of New York, 9 West 57th Street, New York, New York, 10019. An original trustee of the foundation, Thomas G. Chamberlain, died in 1978.

About the only additional sources of information readily available to the public on this foundation are the annual reports and returns filed by it with the Internal Revenue Service, and the various Foundation Center publications. See, however, Willis H. Booth obituary, *New York Times* (February 22, 1958), p. 17, and Booth estate (September 12 , 1958), p. 52; and Mrs. Willis H. Booth obituary, *New York Times* (May 12, 1957), p. 86.

**BOSWELL FOUNDATION.** See James G. Boswell Foundation, The.

**BREMER FOUNDATION.** See Otto Bremer Foundation.

**BROWN FOUNDATION.** See Brown Foundation, Inc., The; James Graham Brown Foundation.

**BROWN FOUNDATION, INC., THE.** The Brown Foundation was established in Texas in 1951 by Herman and George R. Brown. Both men were officers of and associated with Brown and Root, Inc., one of the world's largest construction companies, with subsidiaries which included oil and gas companies, hotels, paper mills, mines, real estate companies, and other interests.

In its early years, the foundation was relatively small. In 1957, its assets amounted to slightly over $1 million, and it made grants in that year totalling approximately $125,000. Following the death of Herman Brown in 1962, however, the foundation became the major recipient of his estate; and by 1969, assets were valued at about $110 million, with annual grants amounting to about $2.75 million. The foundation has from its inception focused its grants upon the local area, that is, Texas and Houston, with grants made primarily to institutions concerned with higher education, hospitals, museums, and for population control, the performing arts, and conservation. This pattern of giving has been followed continuously down to the present.

By 1980, the foundation reported assets of about $226 million. This marked an increase of about $40 million from the figure for 1979. In 1980, the foundation made grants totalling almost $14 million and approved grants for future payment totalling almost $40 million. As in previous years, the foundation confined the major part of its giving in 1980 to Texas, particularly the Houston area. By far the largest share of grants (50 percent or $7 million) was made in the field of higher education, with William M. Rice University receiving about $2.5 million,

Southwestern University receiving $1,627,072, and Colorado School of Mines receiving $1,430,000. Museums were granted about $2.5 million or 18 percent of the total giving for the year, with Houston's Museum of Fine Arts receiving $2,449,704. The city of Houston was given almost $1.75 million or 13 percent for various civic purposes. The approximately 19 percent remaining was devoted to aid for churches, hospitals, secondary education, artists and cultural groups, and other purposes.

The Brown Foundation is governed by a nine-member board of trustees, with George R. Brown serving as president until his death on January 22, 1983. Most of the other officers and members of the board are members of the Brown family. The mailing address of the foundation is Post Office Box 13646, Houston, Texas 77019.

Almost the only additional information on this foundation readily available to the public are the annual reports and returns filed by it with the Internal Revenue Service, and the various Foundation Center publications. See, however, Herman Brown obituary, *New York Times* (November 16, 1962), p. 32; and George R. Brown obituary, *The Houston Post* (January 23, 1983), pp. 1, 29.

**BUSH FOUNDATION.** See Bush Foundation, The; Edyth Bush Charitable Foundation, Inc.

**BUSH FOUNDATION, THE.** In its short history, this St. Paul, Minnesota, foundation has grown from a relatively small family organization into one of the region's most solid foundations that provides essential support to professional arts organizations and four-year colleges, as well as to projects in the humanities, human services, and health fields. The foundation usually limits its work to Minnesota and the Dakotas.

Archibald Granville Bush, one of the early figures in Minnesota Mining and Manufacturing Company (3M) history, and his wife, Edyth, established the Bush Foundation on February 24, 1953. Bush, born in 1887 to a western Minnesota farming family, is said to have left home at age twenty-one seeking freedom from hay fever. By 1909, Bush had a bookkeeping degree from Duluth Business University and a job as a bookkeeper for a small sandpaper manufacturer—3M. Bush joined 3M shortly after William L. McKnight, founder of the McKnight Foundation* and another Duluth Business University graduate. Together, Bush and McKnight built the faltering company into a giant organization, and Bush ultimately rose to the post of chairman of 3M's executive committee.

Little is known about the Bush Foundation's early years or the Bushes' motivation for establishing the foundation. The childless couple apparently wished to make provisions for their fortunes after their deaths. The foundation's stated purpose is to "encourage and promote charitable, scientific, literary, and educational efforts."

The foundation's first years were modest ones. Between 1953 and 1962, its gifts totalled $594,126. "In its early years, the foundation had no set pattern of giving, and in its first two years, the larger undertakings were accomplished through direct contributions of capital,'' the 1963 annual report explained. Grants were made to colleges and schools, student aid, alcoholism treatment projects, and "general welfare," the report continued.

During the same period, the Bushes gave through other channels besides the foundation. Bush told the *Orlando Sentinel* (Florida) in October, 1959, that his annual giving totalled about $300,000. His favorite charities were reported to be Hamline University in St. Paul, "3M employees who have hardship," and projects in Granite Falls, Minnesota, a town near his boyhood home.

Among the early projects that received foundation support were the establishment of the A. G. Bush Library of Management, Organization, and Industrial Relations at the University of Chicago; scholarships to teachers of the Granite Falls school district; and various alcoholism treatment programs for women, including major grants to Granville House, a half-way house in St. Paul for recovering female alcoholics.

In 1965, Bush and the foundation approved a fellowship program to support individuals in midcareer who wished to further their educations. The result was the Bush Leadership Fellows Program, which had granted continuing training and internship stipends to 238 individuals as of 1982. The Bush Foundation's fellowship program was expanded in 1973 to include a summer leadership program. In 1976, similar fellowship programs for artists and public school executives were announced, and in 1979, the Bush Foundation created a fellowship program for rural physicians. While the Leadership Fellows are open to individuals living in Minnesota, the Dakotas, and western Wisconsin, the other programs are limited to Minnesotans.

Bush's death on January 16, 1966, marked a turning point in the Bush Foundation's history. He left some $1.7 million to family and friends and stipulated that the remainder of his estate, estimated at $127 million (including approximately 1.6 million shares of 3M stock), was to go to the foundation. Its assets were reported to be $11.4 million in 1964 and approximately $20 million by 1966. By 1979, the year the final payment from the estate to the foundation was made, the Bush Foundation's total assets had jumped to nearly $218 million.

Huge payments from the estate, together with the dictates of the U.S. Tax Reform Act of 1969 and probate court rulings, prompted the board of directors to make changes that appreciably changed the foundation's character. The board was enlarged and reorganized in 1970. The board then wrote specific grant-making guidelines and policies in April, 1971, diversified its stock portfolio by selling most of its 3M holdings, and in August, 1971, enlarged its full-time staff from two to eight, including, for the first time, professional program and business staff.

The years between Bush's death in 1966 and the arrival of the professional staff in 1971 were marked not so much by grant-making activity as by legal difficulties. Little is recorded about any grants distributed during the late 1960s; even the Bush Leadership Fellows Program was suspended until 1969.

The legal difficulties stemmed from disputes regarding Bush's will and the structure and make-up of the Bush Foundation's board of directors. In 1953, when the foundation was established, the board of directors consisted of five members, including Archibald and Edyth Bush. The articles of incorporation were amended in 1959 to create a seven-person board of directors.

However, in August 1966, eight months after Archibald Bush's death, Edyth Bush threatened to renounce her husband's will, citing disagreement over the foundation's management and the composition of the board of directors. She subsequently agreed to stand by her original consent to the will and was given $2.1 million and other considerations. At the same time, the foundation's articles and bylaws were amended in an attempt to resolve the dispute over board composition by creating a bicameral board of directors. The bicameral board included a four-member class, whose original members were individuals with 3M ties, and a three-member class, consisting of Edyth Bush, her nephew, and an attorney. Majority votes were required from each class for any board action.

The bicameral board structure proved to be a failure, and the foundation was unable to function effectively in the face of continuing legal battles. In 1968, the minority board sued the majority and the executors of Bush's will, charging them with breaches of their financial duties. The case went to trial in September, 1969, and ended with the parties agreeing to a settlement that provided for a sixteen-member board that included Edyth Bush as a lifetime member.

The Bush Foundation's legal problems were still far from over, for Edyth Bush and her representatives continued to contest the issue, first in 1971 by filing renunciations of A. G. Bush's will, and in 1972 by seeking to set aside the 1966 and 1969 agreements. Court decisions in both cases went against Edyth Bush, culminating in 1975 when the U.S. Supreme Court refused to review the cases. In the meantime, Edyth Bush had died in her Florida home on November 20, 1972, leaving the bulk of her estate, valued at $132 million at her death, to the Edyth Bush Charitable Foundation, Inc.* of Florida.

With a new board of directors, multiplying assets, and a professional program staff, the Bush Foundation gained stature during the 1970s. The board of directors reaffirmed the foundation's earlier position as a strictly regional foundation, fine tuned grant-making policies and procedures, and through a series of grant-making decisions, directed the foundation's efforts toward the field of education, the arts and humanities, and human services. By 1981, more than half (54.3 percent) of the foundation's grant appropriations were directed toward education, while human service projects claimed nearly 14 percent of the grants and the arts received 12 percent of the appropriations. The fellowship programs, health programs, and miscellaneous projects divided the remainder of the $15.3 million appropriated that year.

The foundation's educational grants have been primarily for the support of undergraduate education. In 1976, the board launched a seven-year matching capital grants program for four-year private colleges in Minnesota and the Dakotas. A similar capital funds program for four-year colleges associated with the

United Negro College Fund was undertaken in 1980 in conjunction with the William and Flora Hewlett Foundation.* The third major component of the Bush Foundation's educational program began in 1979: faculty development grants to foster improvements in undergraduate instruction. Between 1980 and November, 1981, the foundation had distributed more than $4.8 million in faculty development awards to eighteen public and private universities. A scholarship program for junior college students who wished to enroll in four-year institutions began in 1972.

The Bush Foundation's major support of arts organizations began in 1969 with a $250,000 grant to the Minnesota Orchestra and a $300,000 award to the St. Paul Chamber Orchestra. In 1970, the Bush Foundation added the Guthrie Theater and the University of Minnesota's Theater Fellowship Program to its list of beneficiaries. By 1971, when the program staff arrived, the foundation board had already set an established pattern of support of Twin Cities-area professional arts organizations.

"Those early grants quickly did three things," a 1978 foundation staff report noted. "They made the foundation the largest single local contributor to arts organizations in Minnesota; they provided a large proportion of the unearned income for the arts organizations which were funded; and they may have helped save the Guthrie Theater and the St. Paul Chamber Orchestra." Since 1969, the Bush Foundation has directed such grants to major arts and humanities organizations to support operating expenses, special projects, and building renovations or construction, and, as of 1981, approximately $14.2 million had been disbursed throughout Minnesota.

The foundation's 1981 annual report notes that it has no set pattern of giving in the human services fields, although since the mid-1970s, it has favored projects serving the handicapped and youth, together with proposals designed to reduce the incidence of family violence.

The foundation is governed by a fifteen-member board of directors; board membership fell by one when Edyth Bush died in 1972. The administration of the foundation is carried on from offices located at E-900 First National Bank Building, St. Paul, Minnesota 55101. Foundation archival material is presently located at its St. Paul offices, but it plans to eventually transfer such material for deposit with the Minnesota Historical Society.

For further information, see *Annual Reports* of the foundation, published since the 1970s. See also periodic newsletters, concerning its fellowship programs, published by the foundation.

SUSAN D. STEINWALL

**B. W. FOUNDATION.** See Weingart Foundation.

# C

**CAFRITZ FOUNDATION.** See Morris and Gwendolyn Cafritz Foundation, The.

**CALDER FOUNDATION.** See Louis Calder Foundation, The.

**CALIFORNIA CHARITIES FOUNDATION.** See William Randolph Hearst Foundation.

**CALLAWAY COMMUNITY FOUNDATION.** See Callaway Foundation, Inc.

**CALLAWAY FOUNDATION, INC.** The Callaway Foundation was the culmination of the charitable and philanthropic impulses of Fuller E. Callaway, Sr., and his family. Born in LaGrange, Georgia, in 1870, the son of a Baptist minister, by the time he was eighteen years old Fuller Callaway had earned and saved $500. Going into the mercantile business in LaGrange, by the time he was twenty-five years old he had opened "Callaway's Mammoth Department Store." Inaugurating the buying of household, farm, and other items on a carload basis, he ran spectacular and successful sales which attracted shoppers from miles around the town.

Toward the end of the nineteenth century, Callaway and the other business leaders in LaGrange were responsible for the erection of a cotton mill there in the hopes that it would provide jobs and money for the people of the region. Then, when it appeared that the mill was going to go bankrupt, Callaway reorganized its operations and was largely instrumental in rescuing the mill. This had been accomplished, in part, by his making a trip North in order to secure credit and the engagement of a selling agent. During this time, he had made friends with a number of textile men. In 1899, a member of this group traveled to LaGrange and offered to put up some money if Callaway would raise the balance and then build and operate a new cotton mill there. The decision was made to go ahead, and the outcome was the chartering, in 1899, of the Unity

Cotton Mills. The enterprise prospered and eventually became the Callaway Mills, employing thousands of people.

Fuller Callaway, although he read widely, attended school for only one year. What was the secret of his phenomenal business success? Callaway himself attributed much of it to his life-long marriage to the former Ida Cason of Jewell, Georgia, beginning when he was twenty and she was eighteen. Others have pointed out that he loved his work, was constantly aware of the needs of the people who worked for and with him, and had the ability to pick good men and delegate authority to them. Finally, it was clear that he had the ability to sense and seize opportunities as they arose and carry them through to successful conclusions.

Although Fuller Callaway had always been interested in and actively promoted the betterment of the people of the community and region in which he lived and worked, the substantial monies which began to flow to him in the twentieth century spurred him to organized efforts in this regard. In 1907, he provided the impetus and funds for the building, equipping, and support of a hospital in LaGrange. In 1913, the hospital was made part of a corporate entity, entitled the LaGrange Settlement, with activities expanded to include other charitable work in addition to the medical. In 1919, the Textile Benefit Association for charitable, religious, and educational purposes was formed and funded by Callaway and several of his associates. Although Fuller E. Callaway, Sr., died in 1928, by 1943 these pioneering philanthropic organizations had been merged into the Callaway Community Foundation, which, in 1962, became the Callaway Foundation, Inc.

Callaway Foundation, Inc., between the time it was organized in 1943 and the present, has made charitable contributions in excess of $84 million, in large part for the benefit of people and projects in LaGrange and Troup County, Georgia. A few grants have been made for projects elsewhere in Georgia, but they have very seldom been made elsewhere in the United States. Callaway Foundation, Inc., in 1981 had assets with a fair market value in excess of $80 million.

Over the years, led initially by Fuller E. Callaway, Jr., the board of trustees of the foundation has preferred to contribute its funds for capital equipment and construction projects in order to provide benefits to people over a long period of years. Thus, many hospitals, churches, schools, universities, and similar institutions have been provided aid for such purposes. Some of the outstanding benefactions of the foundation have been: a $1 million grant for the construction of a Science Center and a $2 million grant for the construction of the Lamar Dodd Art Center, both at LaGrange College; a $3 million challenge grant toward the construction of a City-County Hospital in LaGrange; a $2 million challenge grant toward the construction of an intercollegiate athletic center at the Georgia Institute of Technology; and a grant of $1 million to the University of Alabama, Birmingham, toward the constructing and equipping of a medical research facility. Also, in celebration of its twenty-fifth anniversary in 1968, the foundation created a trust of $10 million which provides funds to the senior colleges and graduate schools in Georgia for their establishment of Fuller E. Callaway Professorial Chairs.

With offices located at 209 Broome Street, LaGrange, Georgia 30240, the projects and activities of the foundation are carried on by a small administrative staff headed by J. T. Gresham, president and general manager.

For further information, see *Annual Reports* of the foundation, published continuously since 1969. See particularly the *Annual Report* for 1969–1970, which provides biographical information about the Callaway family, together with a detailed history of the background and operation of the foundation.

**CAMPBELL FOUNDATION.** See J. Bulow Campbell Foundation.

**CANNON FOUNDATION, INC., THE.** The Cannon Mills Company was organized in 1887 as a small cotton manufacturing plant in Concord, North Carolina. From its modest beginnings and over a span of nine decades, this company emerged as the world leader in the production of household textiles. Its founder, James W. Cannon, focused attention upon the production of basic textile products for consumers—towels, sheets, pillowcases, bedspreads. Upon James's death in 1921, Charles A. Cannon, the youngest son of the founder, became head of the company and served in that capacity for the next fifty years until his death in 1971.

The Cannon Foundation was incorporated in North Carolina in 1943 under Charles A. Cannon's leadership. By 1951, its assets amounted to slightly over $9 million, and grants for that year totalled about $0.5 million. Assets climbed to approximately $16.5 million in 1957, but grants were still about $0.5 million for that year. In 1975, assets were listed at about $25 million, and grants for that year totalled about $1.5 million. Assets in 1979 were slightly over $30 million, and grants totalled about $1.25 million.

The foundation has focused much of its attention upon local giving, with 55 percent of its grants in 1979 going to hospitals, of which the Cabarrus Memorial Hospital of Concord and the Stanly County Hospital of Albemarle were principal beneficiaries. Altogether, amounts of $596,713 were awarded to Cabarrus Memorial Hospital and $100,000 to the Stanly County Hospital in 1979. Additional support of $7,300 was awarded to other hospitals.

The local character of the Cannon Foundation's giving is also reflected in grants to education that comprised 22 percent of sums designated in 1979. Of $272,051 in funds set aside for educational institutions in that year, $95,000 went to Cabarrus Academy, Incorporated, of Concord; $72,500 was appropriated to Barber-Scotia College, a junior college of Concord; and $68,301 was allocated for the Kannapolis, North Carolina, city schools. Lesser amounts were awarded to public and private universities, junior and senior colleges, an academy, and high schools. About the only institution outside of North Carolina to receive educational support was Springfield College, of Massachusetts, with a $1,000 grant.

In its contributions to educational activities, the Cannon Foundation set up $57,625 in scholarship grants in 1979. North Carolina State University, of Raleigh, was the largest recipient with $25,625; Wingate College was awarded $12,500; and Barber-Scotia College, of Concord, received $12,000. Lesser amounts were provided the University of North Carolina at Chapel Hill, Wake Forest University, and Western Carolina University.

Thirty-four grants totalling $55,000 were made to churches in 1979, representing 4 percent of the Cannon grants for the year. Denominations in the Concord and Kannapolis areas that were awarded funds included the Baptist, Methodist, and Presbyterian churches and the Church of God. Eight community funds were awarded $105,844 that represented 8 percent of the Cannon grants in 1979. These awards were designated for United Fund and United Way drives, of which the principal amount, $93,344, went to Cabarrus County. The other counties received $5,000 or less.

The balance of Cannon Foundation grants in 1979, thirteen in number for $73,650 and representing 6 percent of the grant dollars, was expended for various social services and civic activities, including a workshop for youth, Boy Scouts, the YMCA, a rescue squad, and a residential development center.

The foundation is governed by a seven-member board of trustees. The mailing address of the foundation is Post Office Box 467, Concord, North Carolina 28025.

Almost the only additional information on this foundation readily available to the public are the annual reports and returns filed by it with the Internal Revenue Service, and the various Foundation Center publications.

JOSEPH F. STEELMAN

**CARNEGIE CORPORATION OF NEW YORK.** Andrew Carnegie, the founder of Carnegie Corporation of New York, was born in Dunfermline, Scotland, in 1835. In 1848, his family emigrated to the United States, settling in Allegheny, Pennsylvania, where he began his career as a bobbin boy in a cotton factory. Books provided most of Carnegie's education, as he moved from bobbin boy to Western Union mesenger to telegraph operator and then through a series of positions leading to superintendent of the Western Division of the Pennsylvania Railroad. While still employed by the railroad, Carnegie invested in a new company to manufacture railway sleeping cars. From that beginning, he expanded his business ventures to encompass the building of bridges, locomotives, and rails. In 1873, he organized the first of his steelworks, the beginning of a major steel enterprise which he sold in 1901 to J. P. Morgan for $400 million.

Carnegie's philanthropic career began around 1870. He is best known for his gifts for free public library buildings, which he made to 2,509 communities in the English-speaking world. In 1889, he wrote the "Gospel of Wealth," in which he articulated his view that the rich are merely "trustees" of their wealth and are under a moral obligation to distribute it in ways that promote the welfare and happiness of the common man.

By 1911, Carnegie had endowed five organizations in the United States and three in the United Kingdom and had given away more than $42 million for public library buildings and close to $110 million for other purposes. Nevertheless, ten years after the sale of the Carnegie Company, he still had more than $150 million and, at age seventy-six, was tiring of the burden of philanthropic decision making. He decided to establish a trust to which he could transfer the bulk of his remaining fortune and, ultimately, the responsibility for distributing his wealth, even after his lifetime. Carnegie Corporation of New York was chartered by a special act of the legislature of the state of New York on June 9, 1911.

Using the simplified spelling that he tried to promote, Carnegie's first letter of gift to the corporation's trustees (November 10, 1911) set out the purpose of the new institution: "to promote the advancement and diffusion of knowledge and understanding among the people of the United States by aiding technical schools, institutions of higher lerning, libraries, scientific reserch, hero funds, useful publications, and by other such agencies and means as shall from time to time be found appropriate therefor." He wrote further:

My desire is that the work which I hav been carrying on, or similar beneficial work, shall continue during this and future generations.

Conditions upon the erth invitably change; hence, no wise man will bind Trustees forever to certain paths, causes or institutions. I disclaim any intention of doing so. On the contrary, I giv my Trustees full authority to change policy or causes hitherto aided from time to time, when this, in their opinion, has becom necessary or desirable. They shall best form to my wishes by using their own judgment.

During 1911 and 1912, Carnegie gave the corporation $125 million, making it the largest single philanthropic trust ever established up to that time. As the residual legatee under his will, the corporation received an additional $10,336,868 when the estate was settled. Carnegie earmarked a portion of the endowment, which has since been fixed at 7.4 percent of the total, to be used for philanthropic purposes in Canada and what were then the British colonies.

In the corporation's early years, Carnegie himself was president and a trustee. James Bertram, his private secretary, and Robert A. Franks, his financial agent, were also trustees and secretary and treasurer, respectively, of the corporation. These three constituted the first executive committee and made most of the funding decisions. The other seats on the board were held *ex officio* by the presidents of the five previously established Carnegie organizations in the United States: Carnegie Institute (1896), Carnegie Institution of Washington (1902), Carnegie Hero Fund Commission (1904), Carnegie Foundation for the Advancement of Teaching* (1905), and Carnegie Endowment for International Peace (1910).

Initially, corporation grants followed the pattern of Carnegie's personal philanthropies. Until 1917, gifts for the construction of public libraries and for the purchase of church organs were continued, and the other Carnegie organizations in the United States received substantial grants for their programs. Other grant recipients included universities, colleges, schools, and general educational agencies.

When Carnegie's health began to fail in 1915, the corporation's trustees began to play a more active role in the affairs of the foundation. Following Carnegie's death in 1919, however, the trustees elected a full-time, salaried president as chief executive officer and made him an *ex officio* member of the board. This move ushered in the now-strong tradition of the professionally managed foundation which, while attempting to carry out the founder's general intentions, operates independently of the current interests of the donor's family.

Carnegie clearly left room for such a mode of operation when he wrote his letter of gift. Nonetheless, the transition was gradual. Despite the corporation's broad mandate, Carnegie had made the presidents of the five other Carnegie institutions *ex officio* trustees, and several of these trustees argued strongly that Carnegie's intention was that the corporation should first and foremost take care of their trusts' needs. Indeed, during the first thirty years of its history, approximately 30 percent of the corporation's grant funds did go to the other Carnegie institutions.

Legal interpretations of Carnegie's intentions for the corporation have identified only two formal restrictions—in purpose and in geographic scope. "The advancement and diffusion of knowledge and understanding" has been taken to mean research and education in the broadest sense. Carnegie's intention as to the beneficiaries of the corporation's grants was originally simply "the people of the United States," where over 90 percent of its support currently goes. The relatively small program, now called the International Program, that Carnegie subsequently endowed to see to his philanthropic interests in other parts of the English-speaking world outside of the United Kingdom has been maintained, although the corporation has, at various times, elected to exclude portions of those areas in which it is empowered to operate.

As a professionally staffed foundation, the corporation's programs and emphases have been formulated to a large extent by its presidents. The following men have served as president after Carnegie himself: James R. Angell, 1920–1921; Henry S. Pritchett, 1921–1923; Frederick P. Keppel, 1923–1941; Walter A. Jessup, 1941–1944; Devereux C. Josephs, 1945–1948; Charles Dollard, 1948–1955; John W. Gardner, 1955–1965; Alan Pifer, 1965–1982; and David A. Hamburg, 1982–.

James Angell stayed for less than a year before going on to become the president of Yale University, but during his brief tenure, appropriations of $22.8 million in excess of income were made, leaving a deficit that claimed about half the corporation's income for the next decade. Henry Pritchett, the president of the Carnegie Foundation for the Advancement of Teaching, served as the corporation's acting president for a brief period and was instrumental in hiring Frederick P. Keppel.

Under Keppel's leadership, the corporation's current program orientation began to take shape. Grants reflected Keppel's own concern for the arts, adult education, educational testing, and higher education, as well as the traditions of the foundation. Andrew Carnegie's interest in public libraries was transformed into a major program in library education. Keppel was also responsible for recruiting Gunnar Myrdal, a Swedish social economist, to undertake the landmark study that resulted in *An American Dilemma: The Negro Problem and Modern Democracy*. This project and a number of grants for black colleges had historical precedents in Carnegie's personal support of Tuskegee and Hampton institutes and his provision of a pension for Booker T. Washington. The international program during Keppel's tenure concentrated on Canada, although after 1926, grants were also made in Africa, Australia, and New Zealand.

It was not until 1946 that the foundation's constitution was amended to eliminate *ex officio* trustees (with the exception of the president of the corporation), and a "grandfather clause" exempted those already serving. Nonetheless, Keppel was responsible for phasing out most of the other Carnegie organizations' reliance on the corporation. He gradually substituted the principle of supporting only those projects run by the other organizations that fit within the corporation's interests. The Carnegie Foundation for the Advancement of Teaching, with its focus on higher education, was still a major recipient of grants and, in addition, received a loan of nearly $15 million, most of which was later forgiven. On the whole, however, the corporation's funds were available for support of interests developed through its own staff work.

World War II brought a hiatus in normal operations, and grants, for the most part, supported the emergency programs of various national organizations. During the postwar period, several major shifts in program were made. The international program was restructured so as to concentrate on Africa, particularly African education and its place in national development. International affairs became a dominant theme in the domestic program, entailing the development of American universities as resources in this field through support of research, training, and international exchange. Improving the quality of future American leadership was another important program theme, reflected in grants to provide special opportunities for the academically talented and to develop new high school curricula. During the presidency of John W. Gardner, who was himself a psychologist, the corporation began to support research on cognition and creativity as well.

Two central developments influenced the corporation's development during Alan Pifer's tenure as president. In 1971, the trustees formed a special committee to study the structure and role of the board. The recommendations of the committee resulted in expansion and diversification of the board, substantial changes in the committee structure and meeting schedules, and greater opportunity for interaction between board and program staff. The executive committee was abolished, and the full board, now consisting of sixteen elected members and the president, *ex officio*, meets five times a year to consider policy issues and approve grant recommendations. In addition, an annual two-day retreat was instituted to permit extended discussion among trustees and senior staff. The finance and administration committee meets at least five times a year to consider the corporation's investment policies and consult with its investment advisors, as well as to take up any other financial or administrative matters delegated to it. The nominating committee meets as needed to identify and recommend new board members, who may be elected to four-year terms, renewable once, and to nominate board members for the positions of chairman and vice-chairman and for membership on the finance and administration committee.

The second major development under Pifer's presidency was the interest in social justice as a theme running through all program areas. This theme evolved from a specific concern for individual opportunity (particularly the opportunity to attend college) and was fully consistent with previous programs, such as the interest in black colleges and the Myrdal study. However, a corporationwide commitment to promoting greater equity in American life for minority-group members and for women dates only from the mid-1960s. For the most part, a belief in education as the means to achieve social equity still pervades corporation grant making, although some activities, particularly in the public affairs program, have looked beyond education to other social institutions.

The corporation's current grant making is organized into five broadly defined program areas—higher education, elementary and secondary education, early childhood, public affairs, and the International Program—each with a number of relatively focused subprograms. A program officer is in charge of each of the five areas, although other administrative officers may be responsible for a subprogram. Four program associates assist in the development of programs and the review of proposals. Except for the International Program, there is no program budgeting; grant recommendations developed by individual staff members are considered by the entire program staff at its weekly staff meetings. Grants of $15,000 or less may be made at the staff level; larger grants are made by the board, upon recommendation of the staff.

While most of the corporation's appropriations support proposals presented by outside institutions or organizations, occasionally it initiates a major project of its own, as it did in the 1930s with the Myrdal study. Modern examples of corporation-initiated projects are the development of the children's television program, Sesame Street; the two Carnegie commissions on public broadcasting, one of which reported in 1969 and the other in 1979; and the Carnegie Council on Children, which resulted in several publications on the status of children and families in the United States.

Andrew Carnegie intended that the capital he transferred to the corporation be a permanent fund. The charter specified that only income could be spent; both realized and unrealized capital gains were to remain with the corpus. Carnegie's own preference, and the dominant mode of investment for the corporation until the mid-1950s, was investment in corporate bonds and other fixed-income securities. The emphasis on the safety of principal was to the corporation's advantage during the depression years, but the lack of attention to growth of capital was a serious disadvantage both before and after the 1930s.

The purchase of common stocks for investment purposes was first authorized in 1933. By 1950, equities still represented only a quarter of the total portfolio's market value, but they approached two-thirds by 1969. The fiscal years from 1953 through 1965 represent the high ground of the corporation's investment results. The enlarged commitment to common stocks coincided with a substantial rise in stock market values and very little inflation. Developments since 1965 have been complex because of the behavior of the securities markets, inflation, and substantial changes in the corporation's spending and investment policies in the wake of the Tax Reform Act of 1969. In 1969, Congress specified that private foundations spend either all of their income or a designated proportion of the market value of their assets, whichever was higher. This presented a potential conflict between the new federal law and the corporation's charter, so in 1970, the charter was amended to permit the expenditure of "realized appreciation of principal."

This enlarged discretion in spending policies also increased the range of options for investment policies. The corporation's finance and administration committee has been responsible for developing new investment strategies to produce adequate levels of funds for grant and administrative expenditures while at the same time maximizing the long-range value of the foundation's assets. Outside investment counselors manage the corporation's portfolio.

During fiscal 1981, the corporation made grant commitments of about $12.7 million and had administrative, investment, and tax expenses totalling approximately $3.8 million. The market value of its assets on September 30, 1981, was approximately $335 million. Each year, the board designates the amount to be made available for grants and administrative expenses, usually within a range of 5 percent to 6 percent of the average market value of the endowment over the past three years.

The executive and support staff of the foundation currently numbers about forty. The corporate officers normally include the president, vice-president, secretary, and treasurer and assistant or associate secretary and an assistant or associate treasurer. In addition to the program officers, the executive staff also includes a corporate liaison officer, a director of publications, and a personnel director and office manager. The corporation's offices occupy one floor of a midtown Manhattan office building located at 437 Madison Avenue, New York, New York 10022.

For further information, see *Annual Reports* of the corporation, published continuously since 1921; the *Carnegie Quarterly*, published since 1953, which describes in some detail the results of one or more projects supported by the corporation; and a "Review Series," forty informational pamphlets published intermittently between 1930 and 1968. See also Alan Pifer, "The Management of Carnegie Corporation, 1911–1977," *The Art of Giving: Four Views on American Philanthropy—Proceedings of the Third Rockefeller Archive Center Conference,* October 14, 1977 (1979). Also, the Oral History Research Office at Columbia University maintains an oral history of the corporation that was conducted between 1966 and 1970.

SARA L. ENGELHARDT

**CARNEGIE FOUNDATION FOR THE ADVANCEMENT OF TEACHING, THE (CFAT).** Although Andrew Carnegie, the world-renowned American steel titan, had little formal education, he had a life-long respect and admiration for learning and educators. When he became a trustee of Cornell University in 1890, he was surprised and appalled at the low salaries paid professors and the resultant poverty for most when they retired. He came to realize, too, that many were teaching far too long because universities and colleges did not want to put them out to starve. Carnegie eventually decided to correct this situation, and in 1905 he set up the Carnegie Foundation, with an endowment of $10 million, to provide money for a pension system for college teachers. The foundation's first board of trustees consisted primarily of distinguished college and university presidents, including Charles W. Eliot of Harvard, Woodrow Wilson of Princeton, Nicholas Murray Butler of Columbia, and with Henry S. Pritchett, then president of the Massachusetts Institute of Technology, enlisted as the first president of the new foundation.

Pritchett knew that, although there were more than six hundred institutions of higher education in the United States at that time, the vast majority had very low standards, and most had sectarian ties. He saw in the new organization a means to achieve Carnegie's goals and, at the same time, uplift and rejuvenate the college and university system of the United States. Thereupon, a new congressional charter for the foundation, renamed the Carnegie Foundation for the Advancement of Teaching (CFAT), was obtained in 1906 with the expanded goal of doing "all things necessary to encourage, uphold and dignify the profession of the teacher and the cause of higher education within the United States, the Dominion of Canada, and Newfoundland."

From its beginning, the foundation had considerable influence on the standards and policies of our higher educational institutions. Initially, the foundation trustees decided that only professors located at institutions meeting certain standards could qualify for pensions. In addition to being nonsectarian, the standards specified were that qualifying institutions must have a minimum endowment of $200,000, a faculty of at least six professors, and maintain certain minimal entrance requirements.

As an ever-increasing number of institutions raised their entrance requirements and made other changes necessary to qualify their professors for pensions, Pritchett and the CFAT trustees soon realized that the income from the foundation endowment alone could not support this increase, much less those among the first to be admitted to the plan. They eventually came to believe, for practical as well as equity reasons, in the superiority of a retirement system to which both institutions and professors could contribute. This system would be open to all higher educational institutions and would be one whereby a professor could be assured of carrying his pension rights with him to any institution rather than just among those associated with the foundation.

After much study and negotiation, the Teachers Insurance and Annuity Association (TIAA), designed along these lines, was ultimately set up in 1918. Operating with an initial subsidy of $1 million from the Carnegie Corporation of New York,* with Pritchett acting as president of the foundation and TIAA until 1930, the latter, although nominally independent, actually operated as an agency of the foundation. After 1930, however, it became completely independent of both the Carnegie Corporation and the Carnegie Foundation, although both continued to supply it with needed assets after that date. In 1952, the TIAA organized an affiliated organization, the College Retirement Equities Fund (CREF), which offered the first variable annuities based on the value of equity investments.

The growth of TIAA/CREF has been phenomenal, particularly in recent decades. By 1931, the TIAA had 15,000 policy holders and by 1941, a total of some 36,000. In 1965, there were 200,000 TIAA/CREF policy holders, and currently there are 700,000 located in 3,300 educational institutions and other eligible organizations. Some 85,000 retired persons or survivors are presently receiving benefits from the income from the present TIAA/CREF assets of about $15 billion. Such figures make the combined organization the seventh-largest insurance company in the United States. In detailing this growth of TIAA/CREF, it should also be noted that its creation and administration must have had a significant, although largely undocumented, influence on later private and public insurance systems, including the U.S. Social Security System.

In addition to setting up and then operating a pension system for a time, the CFAT always carried on educational projects and studies. Probably the best-known and most influential early project was Abraham Flexner's 1910 study of medical education in the United States. Visiting every medical school (over 150) in the United States, Flexner found virtually all of them deficient, some deplorably so. His detailed findings were published by the foundation in its famous *Medical Education in the United States and Canada, Bulletin Number Four* (1910). It resulted in the closing of about half of the country's medical schools, higher standards overall for the medical profession, and greatly increased funding for medical education and research.

The 1913 establishment by the foundation of its Division of Educational Enquiry provided the organizational base for later projects and studies of similar scope and significance. These included studies and resultant reports on: engineering education (1926); legal education (1918, 1921, 1928–1935); and a study of college athletics (1929). Other studies dealt with vocational, teacher, and graduate education.

An important project of the Carnegie Foundation in the 1930s and 1940s was its development of the Graduate Record Examination. Administered by the foundation itself until 1947, testing activities of the foundation and other organizations were merged at that time to form the Educational Testing Service (ETS), which now conducts tests in a variety of educational fields.

From 1950 to 1965, the Division of Educational Enquiry made such studies as the academic presidency, the relationship between higher education and the federal government, student activists, and innovations in liberal education. As these titles indicate, research on higher education has become the preeminent activity of the foundation in recent years. In 1967, the Carnegie Commission on Higher Education was organized under the chairmanship of Clark Kerr, formerly president of the University of California. With an eventual membership of nineteen, including educators, businessmen, and a few foundation trustees, this semi-independent commission produced twenty-three general commission reports, twenty-three technical reports, and sixty sponsored research reports during its life span of six years. These reports covered eight aspects of higher education: functions, structure, governance, innovation and change, demand, expenditure, available resources, and effective use of resources.

The commission's reports provided a very comprehensive, analytical, and descriptive body of literature about higher education in the United States, and some of its recommendations were enormously influential. One of the best indications of a belief that its efforts were a success was the fact that it was replaced in 1973 by the Carnegie Council on Policy Studies in Higher Education as an integral part of the foundation. In contrast to the commission, more than half of the council's members were trustees of the Carnegie Foundation. The council, too, issued a number of influential reports and studies, concentrating on federal and state relationships with higher education.

As has been previously touched on, throughout its history the foundation has always had close ties with the Carnegie Corporation of New York. The corporation provided the Carnegie Foundation with needed funds at critical junctures in its history. For many years, the two organizations shared office space and, occasionally, one or more officers. Indeed, between 1954 and 1979, all of the foundation's officers were simultaneously officers of the corporation. During this period, some consideration was given to abolishing the foundation outright or merging it with the corporation. The resounding success of the commission/council efforts, however, convinced corporation officials, particularly Alan Pifer, its president, and others, that there was a decided need for CFAT's continuance. Thus, in 1979, the foundation was reorganized as a completely independent foundation with assets which in 1981 amounted to about $29 million.

The full-time president of the reorganized foundation is Ernest L. Boyer, former chancellor of the State University of New York and former U.S. Commissioner of Education. The twenty-five-member governing board of trustees, as in the past, consists largely of educators. The CFAT's staff includes about eight professionals and some ten supporting staff personnel. They are augmented by Carnegie Fellows, outstanding educational leaders who participate in the work of the foundation on term appointments. A Research Review Board, consisting of scholars distinguished in various educational fields, is advisory to the president and reviews and monitors the technical quality of foundation reports.

The Carnegie Foundation, with offices located at 1785 Massachusetts Avenue, N.W., Washington, D.C. 20036, is currently engaged in two principal types of studies. First, it conducts studies which focus on current major concerns in higher education. Presently, these include a study of high schools and their relationship to colleges and universities, the control and governance of higher education, and the quality of undergraduate education. Second, the foundation monitors and reports on trends in higher education and examines higher education characteristics which can and need to be studied on a recurring basis.

The foregoing brief history is largely based upon the following recent accounts of the foundation by the president and secretary, respectively, of the Carnegie Corporation of New York: Alan Pifer, "A Foundation's Story: The First Seventy-Five Years of The Carnegie Foundation for the Advancement of Teaching," CFAT *Annual Report* (1978–1979), and Sara L. Engelhardt, "The Carnegie Foundation for the Advancement of Teaching," *The Carnegie Trusts and Institutions* (1981).

For further information, see *Annual Reports* of the foundation, published continuously from 1905 to the present. See also a detailed, although now outdated, history of the foundation by Howard J. Savage, *Fruit of an Impulse. Forty-Five Years of The Carnegie Foundation, 1905–1950* (1953); a detailed biography of Andrew Carnegie by Joseph F. Wall, *Andrew Carnegie* (1970); and a 1983 study by Ellen Condliffe Lagemann, *Private Power for the Public Good* (1983), on the foundation's role in shaping public policy.

**CARRIE ESTELLE DOHENY FOUNDATION.** Edward L. Doheny was a highly successful pioneer in the oil industry. His widow established the foundation bearing her name in 1949 in California. Long active in civic and social welfare organizations and an outstanding Roman Catholic communicant, Carrie Estelle Doheny had received numerous decorations from the church; in 1939, for example, she was named a "papal countess" by Pope Paul XII.

The initial assets of the foundation were about $500,000, and its annual grants in 1952 were about $70,000. Following Carrie Doheny's death in 1958, some $15 million flowed to the foundation from her estate, and by 1969, foundation assets were valued at around $36 million. In 1980 they were in the neighborhood of $48 million.

From the 1960s on, the foundation's pattern of giving placed heavy emphasis on Roman Catholic churches, schools, and organizations in the Los Angeles area. In 1979, for example, a grant of $150,000 was made to the Roman Catholic archbishop of Los Angeles for educational purposes, and $100,000 was given to St. Vincent's Hospital in the same city.

The trustee of the foundation is the Carrie Estelle Doheny Corporation. The seven-member board of directors of the corporation are thus governors of the foundation. They consist of two Roman Catholic clergymen, one of whom serves as chairman of the board, and several prominent Catholic laymen. Administration of the foundation is conducted from offices located at 714 West Olympic Boulevard, Los Angeles, California 90015.

Almost the only additional sources of information readily available to the public on this foundation are the annual reports and returns filed by it with the Internal Revenue Service, and the various Foundation Center publications. See, however, Mrs. Edward L. Doheny's obituary, *New York Times* (October 31, 1958), p. 29, and Doheny estate (November 7, 1958), p. 23.

**CARTER FOUNDATION.** See Amon G. Carter Foundation.

**CARY CHARITABLE TRUST.** See Mary Flagler Cary Charitable Trust.

**CASEY FOUNDATION.** See Annie E. Casey Foundation, The.

**CASTLE FOUNDATION.** See Harold K. L. Castle Foundation.

**CHAMPLIN FOUNDATIONS, THE.** The Champlin Foundations consist of two trusts established in 1932 and 1947, by George S. Champlin, Hope C. Neaves, and Florence C. Hamilton, and a third trust established in 1975, by George Champlin. The Bank of Delaware is trustee for all of the trusts, and the charitable purpose of each is identical. Furthermore, the members of the distribution committees of the trusts overlap, and their functions are carried out by the same staff, headed by an executive director. The mailing address of the foundations is Post Office Box 637, Providence, Rhode Island 02901.

The Champlin Foundations make grants for capital needs to tax-exempt organizations, primarily in Rhode Island. Typical capital needs include the purchase of real property and reduction of mortgage indebtedness. Grants have been made to youth and health agencies, libraries, hospitals, secondary and public schools, colleges and universities, social welfare agencies, humane societies, arts, sciences, and historic preservation. In 1982, grants totalled $4.2 million and ranged from a low of $300 to a high of $352,000. In this same year, the assets of the foundations increased by $47 million, including $38 million received from the late George Champlin's estate, to a total of $87 million.

Almost the only additional sources of information readily available to the public on these foundations are the annual reports and returns filed by them with the Internal Revenue Service, and the various Foundation Center publications. See, however, an information sheet for prospective grant applicants (January 11, 1983), which is available from the foundations.

**CHARLES A. DANA FOUNDATION, INCORPORATED, THE.** Charles Anderson Dana was born on April 25, 1881, in Gramercy Park, New York City. His formal education was concentrated in New York, where he attended the Cutler School and then Columbia University for his bachelor and law degrees.

However, Dana's independent and conservative philosophy was, to a certain extent, a reflection of his Vermont heritage.

During his ninety-four years, Charles Dana's pursuits spanned the fields of law, industry, and philanthropy. As a young attorney, Dana served on the legal staffs of the Pennsylvania Railroad and the New York district attorney's office. After more extensive law experience, he became active in politics and represented New York City's Twenty-seventh District for three terms in the New York legislature.

Dana developed a keen understanding of business through his adjudication of bankruptcy cases. While maintaining his practice in law, he assumed the presidency of the New York and New Jersey Water Company. In 1914, recognizing the potential greatness of the Spicer Universal Joint Manufacturing Company, of Plainfield, New Jersey, Dana provided financial support in return for a majority interest in the firm. In 1946, the company's name was officially changed to Dana Corporation, which is now an international automotive parts firm, with headquarters in Toledo, Ohio.

In 1950, Charles and Eleanor Dana founded the Charles A. Dana Foundation, Incorporated, in Connecticut, their state of residence. In its early stages, the foundation served as an effective vehicle for the founders to conduct their personal philanthropy without the pressures of year-end tax considerations. Gradually, while reducing his business responsibilities, Charles Dana began to view his foundation as a flexible and selective instrument by which he would make a return to society, through financing projects to improve the condition of his fellow man, while meeting his own exacting standards of stability and management. As Charles and Eleanor Dana began to appreciate the long-term importance and potential of their charitable interests, their personal concerns in a local hospital, cancer center, youth programs, and certain colleges and universities ultimately became the basis for the foundation's long-term focus on health and higher education. Later, the directors expanded this focus to include various cultural activities.

Early in its history, an identity was acquired which continues to be characteristic of the foundation today. Since Charles Dana insisted on simplicity and even austerity of organization, the foundation existed without any full-time staff for ten years. Dana believed that each grant must be a sound investment and large enough to make a significant impact. As a result, the number of grants per year was destined to be limited. The founders of the Dana Foundation were able to conduct frequent site visits and maintain a close working relationship with the recipients until the completion of the supported facility or program. Dana's extensive and successful use of the challenge grant served as an incentive for recipients to help themselves.

As the foundation's resources increased and as its directors became more experienced, the maturing needs of the foundation were no longer satisfied by its informal and personal approach. Accordingly, a set of guiding principles was drawn up and adopted by the directors in 1963. This new document increased the foundation's objectivity in screening proposals, greatly limited the number of eligible projects, and improved the efficiency of an operation geared to minimal overhead.

These guiding principles, as revised for the third time in 1980, are as follows:

## GENERAL

1. The Directors favor challenge grants on a matching formula whenever appropriate.
2. With a few special exceptions the eastern part of the United States is the region with priority of consideration.
3. Project requests from areas outside the United States are not supported.
4. Grants are not made to individuals.
5. Grant requests for operating expenses for professional organizations and other such associations, and for the cost of conferences and colloquia are normally not approved.
6. Consideration may be given to a limited number of grants supporting significant and unusual efforts of institutions of recognized quality in higher education, health, science, or the arts.

## HIGHER EDUCATION

1. The Foundation limits its support to private, regionally accredited colleges and universities offering a minimum of four years of studies beyond secondary school.
2. The Foundation normally requires a minimum enrollment of 1,000 students.
3. Priority is usually given to requests from institutions which do not have substantial endowment per student.
4. The Foundation makes challenge grants for its Dana programs for scholarships, professorships and alumni annual giving. Participation in these programs is by invitation.
5. Recognizing the changed context of higher education as institutions enter the so-called steady state, the Foundation will consider grants for projects which are designed to respond to the needs of this new condition.

## HEALTH

1. Priority is given to proposals in the field of health from organizations which have demonstrated the national effectiveness of their activities.
2. Requests from local institutions, organizations and associations are seldom given favorable consideration.
3. Consideration is given to a limited number of proposals in medical education which seek to advance medicine's service to society through the disciplines and training which aim at disease prevention.

## ANNUAL GIFTS

The Directors' review of grant proposals for support of an "annual giving" nature is limited to those assisted by the foundation prior to 1979.

At present, the board of the Charles A. Dana Foundation consists of ten directors. David Mahoney, chairman of Norton Simon, Inc., has been the chairman of the board since 1977, when Eleanor N. Dana (deceased May 30, 1982) assumed the responsibility of vice-chairman after having served as chairman. Walter Corcoran (a director since 1970), chairman of the finance committee of Emery Air Freight Corporation, is vice-president of the board, while Clark M. Whittemore, Jr. (1969), a partner in the law firm of Whitman and Ransom in Greenwich, Connecticut, is secretary-treasurer. The other directors are Edward C. Andrews, Jr., M.D. (1976), president of Maine Medical Center; Charles A. Dana, Jr. (1950), the founder's son; James H. French (1972), past vice-president and treasurer of Asiatic Petroleum Corporation and Shell Caribbean Petroleum; Judge William S. Hirschberg (1950), Connecticut attorney and former state senator; Donald B. Marron (1978), president of Paine Webber; and Donald C. Platten (1978), chairman of Chemical Bank.

The administrative staff of the foundation presently consists of four full-time employees. At the April, 1982, meeting of the board, the directors elected Robert N. Kreidler as president of the foundation. David L. Davies has served as administrative vice-president since March, 1980. Patricia J. Hokanson has been with the foundation as executive assistant since 1975. Janice L. Hartoch has been an administrative and research assistant since 1981. In addition, Dr. Henry W. Littlefield, former vice-president of the foundation (1961–1975) and president-emeritus of the University of Bridgeport, has provided continual service as consultant.

During 1980, the foundation moved its offices from Greenwich, Connecticut, to 150 East Forty-third Street, New York, New York 10017. This move reflected a desire to broaden the foundation's perspective by exchanging ideas with other grant-making organizations. Inspired by its new location and new leadership as of 1982, the foundation is currently conducting a careful evaluation of its directions as it begins the formulation of its programs for the future.

The Charles A. Dana Foundation has made grants totalling $88,970,421 over its thirty-one-year history. With assets at $92,904,175 at the end of 1981, the foundation will continue to implement Charles Dana's wish to consider grants as investments in the betterment of health and opportunity for all.

For further information, see *Cumulative Report* (1960), published by the foundation, covering the years 1950–1960. A review was also published in 1967. *Annual Reports* of the foundation have been published since 1970, periodically including a comprehensive review of its history. The *Annual Report* (1980), for example, included a review of the foundation's first thirty years.

JANICE LYNN HARTOCH

**CHARLES A. FRUEAUFF FOUNDATION, INC.** Pursuant to the will of Charles A. Frueauff, who was a lawyer and the general counsel for Cities Service Company, the Charles A. Frueauff Foundation was established in New York in 1950. With initial assets of about $4 million, the foundation's corpus steadily increased to a 1980 value of approximately $31 million.

Over the years of its existence, the Frueauff Foundation has devoted most of its grants to higher education. In 1980, for example, with grants for that year of approximately $1.5 million, 58 percent went to higher educational institutions. The remainder was allocated to hospitals and health programs (21 percent) and to youth, handicapped, and community service organizations (21 percent). Larger grants for that year included the following: Sweet Briar College—$150,000; Westminster College—$75,000; Southern Research Institute—$100,000; and Recording for the Blind—$17,000.

The Frueauff Foundation is governed by a seven-member board of trustees, with a nephew of the founder serving as president and with the nephew's wife on the board. Administration of the foundation is carried on from offices located at 70 Pine Street, New York, New York 10005, under the direction of a secretary.

Almost the only additional sources of information readily available to the public on this foundation are the annual reports and returns filed by it with the Internal Revenue Service, and the various Foundation Center publications.

**CHARLES AND ELLORA ALLISS EDUCATIONAL FOUNDATION.**
Charles Clifford Alliss (1880–1958) was a long-time employee of Minnesota Mining and Manufacturing Company (3M). He began his employment with 3M in Duluth in 1906 and became foreman of the company's first sandpaper plant in 1907. Alliss worked his way up the corporate ladder and upon his retirement in 1945 was a vice-president of the firm.

The Charles and Ellora Alliss Educational Foundation was established in 1958 with one-half of Charles Alliss' estate ($6 million), and upon the death of Ellora Alliss in 1966, an additional $10 million was willed to the foundation. The foundation in 1981 had assets totalling $31,873,111. The wills of Charles and Ellora Alliss, with respect to the foundation, contained identical provisions, namely that First Trust Company of Saint Paul, Minnesota, would act as corporate trustee and would have custody of assets. The distribution of said assets, however, was to be under the exclusive control of two individual trustees. The number of trustees of the foundation was increased from two to five in 1980. With the exception of a secretary, Jeffrey T. Peterson, designated by the trustees, the Alliss Foundation is unstaffed. Foundation trustees meet four times per year for purposes of reviewing accountings and investment performance, as well as reviewing grant proposals.

According to the wills of the Allisses, "the purposes of the trust shall be educational purposes in the broadest sense." Recognizing that changes will occur over time, the Allisses further stated the trustees are to have "broad discretion to determine the means by which such purposes are to be accomplished." The primary purpose of the Alliss Foundation is to further the education of young people up to postgraduate study through a program of loans, gifts, awards, scholarships, and fellowships.

Grant making of the foundation is generally limited to Minnesota colleges and universities. Examination of grants awarded from 1960 to 1981 reveal that most scholarship money was awarded to private colleges, with some also going to various branches of the University of Minnesota. Grants are made in lump sums to designated colleges, with responsibility resting with the grantee institution for administration of the funds. Individual student applications are not entertained. Grantee institutions may provide scholarships ranging from a minimum of $500 to a maximum of $2,400. The grantee college is obligated to fulfill three basic terms in awarding scholarship money: (1) to identify those students requiring aid and who will be benefitted; (2) to assure that scholarships will be identified as those of the Charles and Ellora Alliss Educational Foundation; (3) to make to the foundation reports of fund disbursement and student progress. Reports are to be submitted as soon as possible following the close of the academic year for which the grant was made but no later than September 15. Since 1960, the foundation has awarded grants totalling $23,486,324.

The selection of students and the manner in which grants are to be distributed are at the discretion of the grantee institution. Scholarships may be granted to both graduate and undergraduate students. Without impairing the discretion of the grantee institution, the foundation trustees express the view that scholarships are not to be confined to students with the highest scholastic rank but rather that the upper 40 percent of any class should be regarded as eligible. Those of even lower rank are also entitled to consideration.

The Alliss Foundation is operated by First Trust Company of Saint Paul, Minnesota, subject to the jurisdiction of the District Court of Ramsey County, Minnesota. The five trustees have designated Jeffrey T. Peterson, a trust officer of First Trust Company, as secretary of the foundation, and his offices are located in the First National Bank Building, St. Paul, Minnesota 55101.

Almost the only additional information readily available to the public on this foundation are the annual reports and returns filed by it with the Internal Revenue Service, and the various Foundation Center publications.

JOHN C. KILKELLY

**CHARLES E. CULPEPER FOUNDATION, INC.** On March 20, 1940, the *New York Times* (p.29) reported that "Charity in effect will become the largest stockholder in the Coca-Cola Bottling Company of New York under the will of the late Charles E. Culpeper." A native of Georgia, Culpeper had built his fortune with the growth of the New York bottling company. His will called for the establishment of a foundation to use the income from his wealth—and, if necessary, its principal—for charitable, religious, and/or educational programs. The philanthropist did request that the greater part of the principal be conserved for the benefit of future generations. Under these provisions, the Charles E. Culpeper Foundation was incorporated in Connecticut in 1940 and in New York in 1955.

Under the direction of the will, the funds were placed in a trust that made specific contributions to beneficiaries such as members of the family. The balance of the income was to be distributed to the foundation. Ultimately, the bulk of the fortune would come to the foundation. Newspaper reports estimated the initial stock bequest to be worth $8 million. In mid-1977, the foundation received an additional $37,217,205 as remainderman under the trust. With smaller gifts from other sources, the addition raised the assets of the foundation to about $57 million at the end of 1977. By the end of 1980, the assets grew to about $68 million. A better index of the growth of the Culpeper Foundation was the growth of its grants, which rose from $240,970 in 1965 to $2,101,720 in 1977 to $4,118,152 in 1980.

The Charles E. Culpeper Foundation has engaged in a program of general giving, though approximately 65 percent of its grants goes to the fields of health, education, and the arts. In general, the foundation has been willing to make multiyear commitments. Recent notable grants include substantial gifts to the Carnegie Institution of Washington for genetic research in its Department of Embryology, the teaching hospitals of the Harvard Medical School to establish within its Affiliated Hospitals Center the "Culpeper Laboratory for Transplantation Biology," to the March of Dimes Birth Defect Foundation to establish a Birth Defects Information System, and to the Yale University School of Medicine for the Center for Human Genetics and Inherited Diseases. In what was termed perhaps the most significant development in recent years in its efforts to offer innovative programs, the foundation is establishing twelve annual fellowships for medical students, postgraduate medical students, or medical school faculty members who will spend one or two years in full-time research and teaching. The foundation also established a series of grants that will be rotated among medical schools to create visiting professorships. Its initiative in improving medical education also led to the establishment of eight "History of Medicine" lectureships funded at selected medical schools.

The foundation's support of the arts and humanities has included endowing the position of chairman of the faculty of the Berkshire Musical Festival, funding the concertmaster chair of the New York Philharmonic Society, and helping defray the costs of the opera telecast intermissions of the Metropolitan Opera Association, as well as other aid toward bringing the fine arts to the public.

In the field of general education, the foundation has established the Charles E. Culpeper Fellowships in the social sciences to give annual grants to postdoctoral students whose work emphasizes the influence of the social sciences on public policy choices. For the benefit of private secondary schools, the foundation has instituted, for a three-year period, a program providing scholarship funds and faculty salary support to assure that such schools will remain in existence without becoming centers only for the financial elite. In the realm of public education, the foundation helped fund, in 1981, a public television series of half-hour documentaries, "ENTERPRISE," developed with the Harvard Business School to look "nonideologically" at how U.S. business works.

The foundation has also made grants to programs designed to improve the process of the administering of justice and, to a lesser extent, to youth support programs, such as Covenant House in New York City.

The Culpeper Foundation is governed by a seven-member board of directors that includes Chairman Francis J. McNamara, Jr., President Helen D. Johnson, Vice-President and Treasurer Nicholas J. Nardi, and Secretary Philip M. Drake. The other members are Colin G. Campbell, William W. L. Glenn, and John A. Huston. Administration of the foundation is carried on from offices located at 866 United Nations Plaza, Room 408, New York, New York 10017.

For further information, see *Thirty-Fifth Anniversary Report* (1975) and *Fortieth Anniversary Report* (1981), published by the foundation, and an information brochure published intermittently. See also Charles E. Culpeper obituary, *New York Times* (February 2, 1940), p. 17; and Charles E. Culpeper will, *New York Times* (March 20, 1940), p. 29.

JAMES HOWELL SMITH

**CHARLES ENGELHARD FOUNDATION, THE.** The donor of this foundation, incorporated in New Jersey in 1940, was Charles Engelhard. Engelhard took over an inconspicuous precious-metal business in 1950 from his father and turned it into Engelhard Hanovia, Inc., a minery and smelting colossus. By the time of his death in 1971, Engelhard's fortune was estimated at $300 million.

Assets of the Charles Engelhard Foundation increased from about $450,000 in 1941 to about $760,000 in 1968. Following Engelhard's death, assets surged to about $21 million in 1975 and in 1981 amounted to approximately $35 million.

The foundation's grants program has emphasized giving to educational, cultural, medical, religious, and wildlife and conservation organizations. Grants have generally been restricted to the New Jersey-New York area. Representative larger grants for 1979 included the following: Metropolitan Museum of Art—$400,000; Educational Broadcasting Corporation—$100,000; St. Paul's School—$100,000; Rockefeller University—$200,000; Nature Conservancy—$100,000; and Pierpont Morgan Library—$100,000. Grants totalled about $1.5 million for 1979.

The foundation is governed by a ten-member board of trustees, with the widow of the founder serving as president and with several daughters of the founder on the board. Administration of the foundation is carried on from offices located at 75 Claremont Road, Post Office Box 761, Bernardsville, New Jersey 07924, under the direction of a secretary.

Almost the only additional sources of information readily available to the public on this foundation are the annual reports and returns filed by it with the Internal Revenue Service, and the various Foundation Center publications. See, however, an article appearing in the *Wall Street Journal* (March 3, 1971), p. 8, on the occasion of Charles Engelhard's death.

**CHARLES HAYDEN FOUNDATION.** Charles Hayden (1870–1937) was born into a well-to-do Boston family whose forbears had been prominent in the American Revolution, and he was educated at the Massachusetts Institute of Technology. In 1892, he and Galen Stone formed the brokerage firm of Hayden, Stone, and Company, in Boston, with $40,000 of borrowed money. Through initial specialization in the stock of copper companies, the brokerage firm prospered, and, following a move to New York in 1906, it rapidly became one of the more prominent brokerage firms in the country. The personal wealth of Charles Hayden grew as the success of his company grew. Noted for his business acuity and probity, at the time of his death, he held fifty-eight directorships in a wide variety of companies and was regarded as one of the most powerful figures in the financial world.

Hayden began making gifts to a variety of institutions before his death. One of his best-known philanthropies was the one by which he provided the funds for the apparatus of the planetarium which bears his name at the American Museum of Natural History. It is not known exactly when he became concerned with the welfare of the boys and young men of our country, but in 1926 he contributed $100,000 to the Boys Club of New York. He also made gifts to the Red Cross and the Massachusetts Institute of Technology to help young men to obtain an education.

Charles Hayden was a bachelor, and a brother was his only survivor. Upon his death, he left the major portion of his estate, amounting to approximately $50 million for the establishment, in 1937, of a foundation for the purpose of assisting needy boys and young men. The foundation in its first few decades of existence made grants to assist only organizations concerned with this particular goal. With the experience gained in years of giving, the foundation trustees have broadened their interpretation of the wishes expressed in Hayden's will and are now guided by the following statement of policy:

Grants are restricted to institutions and organizations that are primarily concerned with the mental, moral, and physical development of youth.

Consideration is limited to those institutions and organizations that serve young people of the metropolitan areas of New York and Boston with preference given to those which are well established with recognized reputations and demonstrated capabilities.

Emphasis is on assisting those groups in need of better physical facilities to improve the availability and quality of their services to young people. [*Annual Report* (1980), p. 3]

With 1981 assets amounting to about $73 million, the foundation has distributed over $100 million in grants during its existence. The trustees have consistently aided a broad spectrum of organizations primarily concerned with the youth of the New York and Boston metropolitan areas. Approximately 75 percent of the annual gifts of about $3 million was given to organizations in the New York area, while the remaining 25 percent went to organizations in the Boston area.

The Hayden Foundation is governed by a board of trustees. Its programs and projects are directed by a member of the board of trustees and a small staff. Its offices are located at One Bankers Trust Plaza, 130 Liberty Plaza, New York, New York 10006.

For further information, see *Annual Reports* of the foundation, published continuously since the 1950s, particularly *Story of the Charles Hayden Foundation* (1952) and the fortieth anniversary *Annual Report* (1977). See also Charles Hayden obituary, *New York Times* (January 9, 1937), p. 17, and *New York Herald Tribune* (January 9, 1937), p. 13; and "Charles Hayden," *Dictionary of American Biography*, Supplement Two (1958), p. 292.

**CHARLES H. REVSON FOUNDATION, INC.** Incorporated in 1956 by Charles Revson, the founder of Revlon, Inc., the Charles H. Revson Foundation received half of Revson's estate after his death in 1975. The board of directors determined that the foundation would focus on four broad program areas, derived from the pattern of Revson's giving during his lifetime: urban affairs, with special emphasis on New York City; education; biomedical research policy; and Jewish philanthropy and education. With its first full-time staff and formal grant-making procedures, the foundation began in 1978 to make special project grants in these four program areas.

Over the first two years (1978–1979), the board and staff consulted hundreds of people in many fields to develop grant-making strategies in the foundation's areas of interest. A number of themes emerged from these discussions that, in the opinion of board and staff, warranted particular attention in the foundation's initial agenda: the forces shaping the future of New York City; the changing role of women; the impact of modern communications on education and other areas of life; and the need in a democratic society to keep government accountable to its citizens. These themes have provided a framework for the foundation's program areas. In some cases they help define a program, while in others they cut across program lines.

The Revson Foundation has tried to take a public policy perspective in grant making, aware that such funding must be carefully monitored so that it remains relevant. A part of the urban program has endeavored to address long-range issues; for example, what forces are shaping the New York City of the year 2000, and what can be done to make it more democratic and the conditions of life therein more equitable? Several early grants have attempted to help individuals and institutions to explore fresh approaches to urban issues and to develop realistic options for the future.

One program the foundation has originated, the Charles H. Revson Fellows on the Future of the City of New York, gives talented people involved with urban issues the chance to spend a year at Columbia University. Modeled loosely on the Nieman Fellowships, at Harvard University, the program's premise is leadership development, and it is open to people in midcareer who are already at work in a variety of fields.

Policy-oriented research on urgent New York City issues is the agenda of the new Center for Urban Studies, at New York University, launched with a five-year foundation grant. The plan calls for a large initial commitment of unrestricted private funds to ensure the center's independence, a mix of public research contracts and foundation grants in subsequent years, and a recruiting effort to attract leading scholars from all over the nation to lend their talents to the solution of city problems ranging from land-use planning and housing to tax policy and education.

The foundation has used a portion of its funds to explore migration trends affecting New York City, particularly its links with the Caribbean. To shed more light on the impact of immigration, the Revson Foundation has made grants to the North American Congress on Latin America for case studies of the lives of undocumented aliens in New York City; to the Brookings Institution for a study of the economies of "source countries" and the impact of immigration on selected areas in the United States, including New York City and New Jersey; to the Puerto Rican Legal Defense and Education Fund for a project to address the civil rights problems of first- and second-generation mainland Puerto Ricans; and to the National Opinion Research Center, at the University of Chicago, for an analysis of the history of immigration policy in the United States.

In view of its profound implications for virtually every aspect of American life, the foundation has adopted the changing role of women as a theme to be reflected throughout its programs. At the same time, the staff surveyed foundation and government funding in the women's field over the past ten years to find areas for special emphasis and found that despite the serious underrepresentation of women in public life, very little private or public money was available for programs aimed at leadership development for women.

The foundation has sought in a number of ways to draw larger numbers of women into public life and to develop leadership at all levels. It has made grants to the National Women's Education Fund for nonpartisan campaign techniques workshops for women who wish to run for public office; to the Women's Action Alliance for monitoring of state and federal action in the area of sex discrimination; to organizations headed by women working on the concerns of parents and children, such as the Children's Defense Fund; and to organizations whose programs are designed to include strong participation by women, such as the Law Students Civil Rights Research Council for summer internships in public interest law for law students, half of them women and more than half minority group members, and fellowship programs at Columbia University, City College, and the National Urban League.

A grant to George Washington University in cooperation with the Women's Research and Education Institute of the Congresswomen's Caucus has launched a new kind of congressional fellowship, in which graduate-student fellows concentrate on issues affecting women. The program is designed to enhance the fellows' career options while providing much-needed research on topics of concern to women.

The Revson Foundation supports a variety of private groups dedicated to ensuring government accountability and strengthening the voices of citizens in policy debates. In its urban affairs program, for example, the foundation has made grants to such organizations as the Legal Defense and Educational Fund of the National Association for the Advancement of Colored People, for a Washington office to monitor compliance with federal civil rights laws, and to the New York City Legal Aid Society, for a center to give poor people access to administrative agencies that make crucial decisions regarding their lives. The program in education stresses the mobilization of citizen interest and participation to improve government and community life. One example is support of the Educational Priorities Panel, in New York City, a consortium of parent and citizen groups that monitors the education budget to protect the needs of children.

In the biomedical research field, the foundation has adopted the concerns of policy making as its emphasis, to monitor the more than $3 billion of government money allocated to biomedical research each year. The foundation's strategy is to help decision makers, the scientific community, and the public explore the implications of policy choices in biomedical research. An example of this approach is a grant to the Institute of Medicine of the National Academy of Sciences to support discussions of past practices and future priorities in four aspects of cancer research, including prevention research and its role in the "war" on cancer.

The Revson Foundation has sought to support uses of modern communications technology for the public benefit, particularly in the areas of education and Jewish philanthropy. For example, one of its education grants is supporting the work of New York University's Alternate Media Center, which is establishing an experimental mobile laboratory to help schools, hospitals, and social agencies explore the uses of interactive (two-way) television to improve service delivery.

It has assisted several projects that tap television's power to enhance understanding among people of diverse cultures and histories. One such project, being produced by Children's Television Workshop, is "Simple Justice," based on the book by Richard Kluger, which will tell the story of the 1954 Supreme Court school desegregation decision.

The program in Jewish philanthropy stresses Jewish education, and it involves the modern media as a means to communicate Jewish history, values, and culture to both Jews and non-Jews. A project that will take advantage of the power of television and film to bring the past to life is a ten-part series entitled "Civilization and the Jews," narrated by Abba Eban and initiated by WNET-Channel 13 in New York City with foundation funding. To ensure that the primary programming on the Jewish experience already recorded in the media is not lost and that it is accessible to the widest possible audience, the foundation has made a grant to the Jewish Theological Seminary of America and the Jewish Museum in New York City to create the National Jewish Archive of Broadcasting. To give the archive a broad educational function, the Jewish Museum plans to program the materials for interfaith and school groups.

During 1980 and 1981, the foundation has continued to make grants in the areas discussed above. With a focus on New York City, for example, it has helped establish a research and training program at Columbia University to study immigration as it affects New York. One recent grant for women's leadership development is assisting the Center for the American Woman and Politics, which is part of the Eagleton Institute of Politics, at Rutgers University, in a project to investigate institutional factors that influence women's participation in politics and identify the most effective channels of access to public office. In the area of government accountability, the foundation supported the planning and development of a program at Harvard University that will address national biomedical and health issues in an interdisciplinary way. And, in the education and communications area, it made a grant to Children's Television Workshop for coproduction of an Israeli version of "Sesame Street," which has as an additional experimental objective eventual use of the programs as a supplemental tool for learning foreign languages in the United States.

As of the end of 1981, the Revson Foundation had assets of about $65 million. It made grants totalling $3.2 million in 1978, $3.5 million in 1979, and $4.1 million in 1980.

The foundation is governed by a twelve member board of directors including Charles H. Revson, Jr., and John C. Revson. Administration of the foundation is carried on from offices located at 444 Madison Avenue, New York, New York 10022 under the direction of a president.

For further information, see *Two Year Report,* for 1978 and 1979, published by the foundation in 1980, and *Interim Report,* summarizing grants made between January 1980 and May 1981. The foundation plans to publish another two-year report in 1982 and *Annual Reports* thereafter.

CAROL WEILAND

**CHARLES STEWART MOTT FOUNDATION.** Flint, Michigan, was transformed by the automobile from "a nice little town—all Yankees" into a dynamic melting pot that now boasts the country's largest concentration of General Motors (GM) operations. The community, which became a carriage-manufacturing center when the Saginaw Valley's white pine was all cut, is known as the birthplace of General Motors, founded by William C. Durant in 1908, and also as the birthplace, in 1937, of the United Automobile Workers Union. In addition, Flint is the home of an institution that resembles neither of these but owes its origin to the prosperity that GM brought to the city. This is the Charles Stewart Mott Foundation, which gave Flint the community school/community education program, a product that has been outranked in "distribution" only by Buicks, Chevrolets, AC spark plugs and Bodies by Fisher. The program spread nationally and has become global. After nearly fifty years, community education is still a major concern of the foundation, but growth in other directions, and standing as one of the ten largest private foundations in the United States, have added to its national stature. Its broad commitment is to the well-being of community—the individual, the family, the neighborhood, the systems of government.

Many persons made their names and fortunes in the Flint plants. Two of the most eminent were Walter P. Chrysler and Charles W. Nash, both of whom left to found other major corporations (Nash Motors today is American Motors).

One of those who stayed was Charles Stewart Mott, educated as an engineer, who had moved his Weston-Mott Company from Utica, New York, to Flint in 1906 to build wheels and axles for Buick and other developing automotive firms. Buick, Weston-Mott, and Flint all underwent swift and tremendous growth. Mott, confident of the future of the automobile and General Motors, sold his company to GM on a straight stock-exchange basis. Years later, the bulk of the large fortune thus created went into the Charles Stewart Mott Foundation.

Long before he established the foundation, Mott began expressing his gratitude to the people of Flint for the success he enjoyed in his adopted community, as when he successfully ran for mayor in 1912 and 1913, offering his skills and experience in business and engineering. The city was sorely in need of both to cope with problems of inadequate sewers, streets and fire protection, and questionable water supply.

Incorporation of the foundation, in 1926, formalized Mott's charitable giving and gave him assurance that funds he left for philanthropic, charitable, and educational purposes would be used in accordance with his ideas and ideals after his death.

He already had provided money to start a medical and dental clinic for school children. Many years later, the clinic grew into the Mott Children's Health Center, now independent, endowed by the foundation, housed in its own fine building and dedicated to the care of the "whole child." In the early prefoundation years, he also gave a building for Flint's Hurley Hospital (now Hurley Medical Center), land for a city park, and country acreage to the YMCA, which developed a camp on the site.

Through the foundation, he set up a summer camp for underprivileged boys and helped to support other programs. Then, in 1935, he heard a talk by Frank J. Manley, supervisor of physical education in the Flint Public Schools, who was growing bitter over his inability to interest Flint's "men of influence" in what seemed to him a sound and even obvious idea. That was to open the schools the year around for after-hours recreation to keep children off the streets for their safety and to combat delinquency.

Mott, inviting Manley to his estate, Applewood, asked him if he would like to start a boys' club. Manley said each of Flint's forty schools could become a community center with a boys' club, a girls' club, a mothers' club, a family club. That vision of a program serving both children and adults, and offering adult credit courses as well as fun classes and physical recreation, proved out. Mott contributed $6,000 to start it in five schools. That was the beginning of a never-interrupted flow of foundation dollars into the Flint schools. The figure has since exceeded $100 million.

In a process that continues today, many experimental and innovative K-12 projects were introduced—breakfasts for undernourished children and homemaking instruction for their mothers in a rundown, largely black area; a special curriculum for potential school dropouts; subsidized jobs and special guidance for young offenders; efforts to guard the health of elementary school children by eliminating correctible physical and dental defects. Mott gave the credit for all this to Manley, an intense, charismatic leader who inspired immense dedication in his staff. "The Mott Program is Frank Manley," Mott often said.

Year after year, the foundation increased its budgets for the Flint community school program, but Mott was well aware of a need for additional higher education facilities for young people who could not afford to go away to college. Six days before an election in 1950, at a civic dinner on the eve of his seventy-fifth birthday, Mott announced a challenge: if the voters would authorize a $7 million bond issue for educational projects, he would give $1 million in land or funds, or both, toward establishment of a four-year college in Flint. The proposal was adopted. The subsequent gift of money and a large part of Applewood, Mott's "farm in the city," went for a combined campus of Flint Junior College, now Mott Community College, and a Flint college of the University of Michigan.

In the 1960s, the foundation began developing national outreach. The "Flint model" of community education (there were others) was spreading, and the foundation made its first grants for community education centers. There now are over eighty of them serving most of the country. The 1960s also brought more grants unrelated to education. After Genesee County's residents voted to tax themselves for the development of a system of regional parks, the foundation made the first of a series of contributions that now totals over $10 million.

The 1970s brought two milestone changes. One was the adoption in 1975 of a foundation operating philosophy that established a dynamic system of missions, or program areas, all dedicated to "making community a practical reality." Almost overnight there was a marked increase in national programming as the foundation reached out to support projects demonstrating the principles of the pluralistic philosophy. The change ended private worries that the people of Flint might become too dependent on the foundation if it continued putting most of its grant resources into its home community.

The other major development involved another deep concern: whether the foundation should continue supporting Flint school programs that had been funded for as long as forty years. The decision of the foundation's board of trustees, announced in 1977 in a position paper entitled "A Long, Fruitful Relationship," was to phase out grants for many ongoing programs, over a period of seven years (since changed to ten years), but also to lift a $5 million-a-year ceiling on grants to the schools. They were invited to submit proposals for new and innovative programs. Two of a number of projects developed since then with foundation help, a prevocational center and a program of experience-based career education, were aimed at easing youth unemployment, an area in which the foundation has made a series of grants to agencies in other states as part of a national attack on this serious problem.

In 1976, the Mott Foundation program staff completed development of mission statements covering the many facets of foundation grant making. The mission of community identity and stability, for example, as revised in 1981, has three program areas: family relationships, too-early childbearing, and family education. Within those areas, the foundation is supporting a broad range of programs that include a half-dozen aimed at finding solutions to the problem of teenage pregnancy, several in behalf of the elderly, and others on hunger, nutrition, and health. When another mission, opportunity for the individual, was developed, the foundation was doing nothing in the fields of quality of work life and black higher education, but the mission statement was a framework for subsequent programming in the two areas.

Assistance to historically and predominantly black colleges and universities and their support organizations has become a long-range commitment. This program began in 1978 with a $1 million grant to the capital-development campaign of the United Negro College Fund. In 1979, $1.8 million was granted to eighteen black institutions for a variety of purposes and $550,000 to four support agencies. In a third set of actions, in late 1980 and early 1981, nearly $4 million was divided among thirty-one colleges and universities and six support groups. The foundation expects grants for this program to reach $20 million during the 1980s.

Ascribing high importance to neighborhoods as the building blocks of the cities, the Mott Foundation has been reaching into urban areas throughout the country, 267 of them through its Project SNAP (Stimulating the Neighborhood Action Process). Other hundreds are served through direct grants, seed funds, and technical assistance channeled through agencies with broad outreach and experience, and through a partnership with other major foundations and corporations in the new Local Initiatives Support Corporation (LISC). This helps community groups of proved capability with housing and other projects.

The foundation has turned increasingly to grants and endowments assuring long-range use of large appropriations of program funds by qualified organizations for objectives in keeping with its philosophy. For example, the Institute on Man and Science, Rensselaerville, New York, was enabled to create a revolving fund to continue financing exemplary projects, such as the rural New Village being built in Pennsylvania at this writing by the families that will live there. Through an investment membership in the Cooperative Assistance Fund, Washington, D.C., the Mott Foundation works with other foundations to provide capital for program-related investments going to disadvantaged communities and enterprises. Through a grant to the endowment fund of Resources for the Future, also in Washington, there is ongoing support for public policy research on energy, natural resources, and the environment.

Other broad approaches have been brought about through the Inter-American Center for Community Education, based in Washington, D.C., which is advancing the movement and attacking the endemic social problems in Latin America. Great potential for diversity is built into their programs to improve the quality of life. In 1980, the foundation began support for centers in Canada and the United Kingdom.

The foundation, which has been making over 360 grants annually for the last three years, was relatively small until 1963. In that year, Charles Stewart Mott added the bulk of his estate, $195 million, to the foundation's assets, which were thus increased to $246 million. Income, which had been about $3 million a year, rose to $10 million. By 1970, assets had climbed to $365,630,260 and income to $13,779,079.

Assets and income peaked in the mid-1970s, assets at $462,494,873 in 1976 and income at $32,181,000 in 1977. Only two years earlier, in 1975, income had been $18,178,000 and assets $377,043,000. At the end of 1980, assets stood at $428,147,565. Fluctuations in the stock market and changes in the foundation's portfolio, as managed by three financial analysts in its Detroit investment office, accounted for a $21 million increase in assets during 1980, but income fell from $30,030,001 in 1979 to $26,646,324. The decline was attributed to recessionary conditions, chiefly in the auto industry. Income has averaged $30.4 million during the last five years.

At the end of 1980, the foundation was the ninth largest in the country on the basis of assets and eighth largest in expenditures for grants, according to "Giving USA," the annual report of the American Association of Fund-Raising Counsel. It had been among the largest since the 1960s.

As recently as 1967, almost 80 percent of the foundation's grant resources were going to the Flint Board of Education. In 1980, the board received 9 percent of grants and 15 percent of grant funds. The amount going to the schools declined less in actual total than in percentage of foundation income. All Flint grants, 21 percent of the total, took 40 percent of program funds.

The Flint share of program funds would have been smaller except for a number of capital grants. These went for support of a public/private structure that is changing Flint's downtown area and neighborhoods. There is an $11 million commitment for AutoWorld, a $60 million Disney-style attraction counted on to develop tourism into the area's second major industry. AutoWorld was planned as part of a great semicircle of redevelopment projects for which the foundation has contributed or pledged over $40 million to help restore downtown as the hub of a metropolitan area of about 450,000 people. Among the other projects are a new Hyatt Regency Hotel and Convention Center; the growing new riverfront campus of the University of Michigan-Flint; Riverbank Park, a "people's" park that has quickly become a center of activity; and River Village, a model residential area. Foundation grants for some of the downtown projects were made in the form of investments that will yield many thousands of dollars over the years for neighborhood improvements in Flint. Other grants go directly for major neighborhood rehabilitation.

Governance of the foundation is in the hands of the eleven trustees, two of whom started their service at the beginning of 1981. William S. White, foundation president and chief executive officer, said the newest members were chosen because of their background and expertise in some of the foundation's new program areas, such as black higher education and youth employment. They are Dr. Willa B. Player of Akron, Ohio, former president of Bennett College,

Greensboro, North Carolina; and Dr. John W. Porter, president of Eastern Michigan University.

C. S. Harding Mott, chairman of the board, is a son of Charles Stewart Mott. He, White, and the other seven trustees are all Flint-area or former Flint residents. In retirement, some of these seven divide their time between Sun Belt and Michigan homes. They are Joseph A. Anderson, former general manager of AC Spark Plug Division and a former vice-president of General Motors; William S. Ballenger, Jr., a banker; Charles B. Cumings, an attorney; Maryanne Mott, of Santa Barbara, California, daughter of Charles Stewart Mott; C. S. Harding Mott II, a rancher; Dr. Harold P. Rodes, retired president of General Motors Institute; and George L. Whyel, a retired banker. Mrs. Charles Stewart (Ruth) Mott continues to serve as a trustee emeritus.

The foundation is housed on two floors in the sixteen-story Mott Foundation Building, opened by a bank in 1930 and bought by the foundation in 1944.

Charles Stewart Mott, who ordered the purchase of the Mott Foundation Building, died in 1973 at the age of ninety-seven, less than nine months after the passing of Frank Manley, his long-time partner in community education and leadership of the foundation. If he were alive today, the foundation's patriarch would find the staff of more than fifty persons working innovatively, adapting to new needs and mindful of both the Mott motto, "Let us be known by our deeds," and the words he once added, "and not by our money."

For further information, see Clarence H. Young and William A. Quinn, *Foundation for Living: The Story of Charles Stewart Mott and Flint* (1963) and *In Memoriam* (n.d.), a booklet about the life of Charles Stewart Mott. See also *Annual Reports* of the foundation, published continuously since 1970, together with *Facts on Grants* and *Report to the People,* published since 1977, which elucidate and explain foundation grants and programs. The Mott Foundation has also issued *Foundation for Living*, containing a statement of its operating philosophy, and other materials, such as *A Guide to Community Education Resources* and *Reading Up*, a quarterly listing of publications resulting from foundation grants.

MARILYN A. STEIN

**CHATLOS FOUNDATION, INC., THE.** The Chatlos Foundation was incorporated in New York in 1953. Donors were William F. Chatlos and the Bristol Door and Lumber Company, Incorporated, in which Chatlos was financially interested. Chatlos (1889–1977), upon whose fortune the foundation was built, was born in Bridgeport, Connecticut. He built thousands of homes in Connecticut, New York, New Jersey, and Florida. In 1926, at the age of thirty-seven, he built and retained ownership of 369 Lexington Tower, a twenty-six-story office building at Forty-first Street and Lexington Avenue in New York City. At the time of its completion, Lexington Tower was one of the tallest buildings in the area. Upon his "retirement" to Florida, he built and operated the Golden Gate Hotel in Miami Beach, consisting of forty buildings on twenty acres "from ocean to bay."

Following the death of Chatlos in 1977, the foundation received more than $35.6 million from his estate, increasing the foundation's assets from $4.1 million in 1976 to nearly $37 million in 1977 and to over $41 million in 1981.

The Chatlos Foundation divides its funds, according to a formula, among its interests in higher education, religious education and activities, health/hospitals, and social services. Child welfare is included in social services. Well over 50 percent of the funds awarded by the foundation have been in the first two categories: higher education and religious education and activities. Among its larger awards in 1979 were: Florida Southern College, Lakeland, $500,000; Billy Graham Center, Wheaton College, Illinois, $260,000; and Florida United Methodist Children's Home, $190,000.

The foundation's governing board of trustees consists of William J. Chatlos, grandson of the founder, president; Alice E. Chatlos, daughter of the founder, treasurer; and five other members. Offices are maintained at 2 Penn Plaza, Room 1648, New York, New York 10001, and Sweetwater Plaza, Longwood, Florida 32750.

Almost the only additional sources of information readily available to the public on this foundation are the various Foundation Center publications and the annual reports and returns filed by the foundation with the Internal Revenue Service.

EVANS C. JOHNSON

**CHICAGO COMMUNITY TRUST, THE.** Late in 1914, Albert W. Harris, president of Harris Trust and Savings Bank, of Chicago, heard about the community foundation concept developed and implemented earlier that year by a fellow banker, Frederick Goff, of Cleveland. After securing a copy of the 1914 resolution and declaration of trust creating the Cleveland Foundation,* the first community foundation to be established in the United States, Harris discussed the idea with officers of his bank and conferred with other bankers, lawyers, educators, and numerous other influential citizens interested in charitable affairs. As a result, on May 12, 1915, a resolution and declaration of trust creating the Chicago Community Trust was adopted by the board of directors of the Harris Trust and Savings Bank.

The Chicago Community Trust was created in order to provide for a general fund in Chicago which could be managed so as to provide a conduit for charitable giving in the Chicago area and, in the words of the resolution, "to permit of change in the particular objects or enterprises to be assisted or encouraged." Thus, there would be assurance to donors that their charitable gifts and bequests would not become obsolete with the passage of time.

When, in 1919, Frank D. Loomis became the secretary (later the first executive director) of the trust, reported capital funds consisted of $725,000, most of which had come from members of the Harris family. During its first four years of operation, $67,520 was distributed. In 1924, the first major non-Harris family gift was received: $1 million from James A. Patten for distribution to institutions designated by him. Smaller contributions were prompted by group luncheons for civic leaders arranged by the trust, by advertisements, and by personal solicitation of wealthy individuals by the officers and staff of the trust. In this connection, Frank D. Loomis makes the statement (p. 17) in his history of the trust: "Selling the Community Trust was not like soliciting a gift to a college or some specific charitable service—we really did not *need* the money; we had to learn to wait." These methods paid off in the 1920s. By the end of 1929, the trust reported assets of almost $2.5 million and total distributions for its first fifteen years of operations of more than $500,000. During the Great Depression, the trust participated in the setting up of a community chest for welfare and relief purposes. Despite this necessary diversion of effort and money, the end of 1939 saw a doubling of trust assets to almost $5 million and total distributions of over $1.3 million.

Following the close of World War II, the trust became an established Chicago institution, with assets of about $9 million and grants of about $2.5 million made in its first twenty-nine years of existence. Later, in the 1940s, several other significant changes took place at the trust. A number of other Chicago banks became trustees along with the former sole trustee, Harris Trust and Savings Bank; and James Brown IV, formerly a dean at the University of Chicago, succeeded Frank D. Loomis as executive director.

During Brown's tenure as executive director (1949–1973), the assets of the trust grew to over $80 million and grants of $3 to $4 million annually were being made during the last few years of his administration. Significantly, by this time more than half of the funds contributed for charitable purposes were being left to the discretion of trust officials, with the remainder designated for specific institutions or purposes.

Assets of the trust in 1982 were approximately $130 million, and grants, restricted to the Chicago area, of over $16 million were made in 1982, with some 65 percent of grant money being made from discretionary funds. In recent years, education, health, hospitals, civic affairs, cultural programs, human services, and welfare have been the major recipients of trust grants.

In the governance and operation of the trust, the trustees are responsible for the management and investment of the funds donated to it. As has been pointed out, at its beginnings there was a sole trustee, but today, nine Chicago banks and trust companies serve in this capacity. The trust's first executive committee, which is responsible for all grant allocations and the trust's general operation, originally consisted of five members, three appointed by public officials and two by the then sole trustee. Today, there are nine members, three appointed by the trustees and one designated by each of six Chicago civic and educational leaders, such as the senior judge of the United States district court and the president of

Northwestern University. Offices of the trust are located at 208 South LaSalle Street, Suite 850, Chicago, Illinois 60604, and administration is carried on under the supervision of an executive director.

For further information, see Frank D. Loomis, *The Chicago Community Trust, A History of Its Development 1915–62* (1962). See also *Annual Reports* of the trust, published since the 1950s; and a pamphlet, *The Chicago Community Trust, History and Review* (n.d.).

**CHINA MEDICAL BOARD OF NEW YORK, INC.** Organized in 1914 as a division of the Rockefeller Foundation,* the China Medical Board in 1928 was incorporated as an independent organization. At that time, the Rockefeller Foundation provided it with an initial endowment of $12 million, which was added to by another and final Rockefeller Foundation grant of $10 million in 1947. Despite its expenditures of approximately $75 million from 1928 to the present, the board's assets, as the result of the increase in value of its investments, in 1981 stood at about $55 million.

During the period from 1914 to 1951, almost all of the funds expended by the China Medical Board were devoted to the construction and support of the Peking Union Medical College. During this period, the college revolutionized the teaching and practice of medicine in China and was appropriately labelled "the Johns Hopkins of China."

With the nationalization of the college by the People's Republic of China in 1951, the board launched a more diverse program involving eight countries and territories in East and Southeast Asia. Its program involved support for operations and research in the areas of medicine, nursing, and public health education in those countries. Grants were not made for those activities which the board felt that medical and nursing schools should be doing for themselves. Rather, they were made to support projects wherein it was believed a school could do more to improve the health of the people of the country in which it was situated.

A statistical analysis of expenditures of $66.5 made by the board during 1951–1980 shows the following:

| | |
|---|---|
| Construction or repair of buildings | 17% |
| Supplies and equipment | 23 |
| Library books and journals | 6 |
| Fellowships | 18 |
| Visiting professorships | 4 |
| Research | 8 |
| Teaching programs | 8 |
| Endowment funds | 16 |

With the renewal of relations between the United States and the People's

Republic of China in the late 1970s, some trustees of the board visited China, and, as a result, the decision was made to reestablish programs in China and continue those being carried on in the other eight countries of Asia. Since the major problem in Chinese medical schools is the lack of a sufficient number of trained teachers and research workers, the board has instituted a training program at centers in Asia and in western countries. Under the program, the board is presently furnishing funds enabling Chinese medical schools to provide some fifty fellowships for training in medicine, nursing, and public health.

Reflecting its stated purpose, "to extend financial aid to the Peking Union Medical College and/or like institutions in the Far East or the United States of America," a number of the members of the China Medical Board's governing board of trustees have always been M.D.'s. Likewise, the chief executive officer, formerly a director and now president, has always been an M.D. The board's activities are directed from offices located at 622 Third Avenue, New York, New York 10017.

For further information, see *Annual Reports* of the board, published continuously since 1928, particularly the one for 1977–1978 which reviews the board's programs for the period 1928–1978. See also Raymond B. Fosdick, *The Story of the Rockefeller Foundation* (1952).

## CHRISTIAN A. JOHNSON ENDEAVOR FOUNDATION, THE.

Christian A. Johnson, a financier with a lifelong interest in education, medical research, and youth development, donated the funds for the 1952 establishment of the foundation bearing his name. The value of its assets varied from some $20 millions to $30 millions during the 1960s and 1970s, and annually, grants ranged up to about $1.25 million during these decades. In 1982, assets were valued at about $32.7 million.

Though the foundation's traditional support program emphasized higher education, health care, medical research, the environment and the arts, the board of trustees narrowed the focus of the foundation in 1981 to education and the arts. Since that time grants other than in the areas of education and the performing and visual arts have been made only to complete funding of earlier commitments to health care, medical research and the environment. In 1982, for example, 60.8 percent of that year's grants of almost $1.8 million were devoted to education, 23.4 percent to health care and medical research, 7.9 percent to the arts, 5.2 percent to protection of the environment and historic preservation while the remaining 2.7 percent went to social welfare through a small Venture Fund. Representative larger grants in 1982 included the following: Hamilton College—$300,000; Memorial Sloan-Kettering Cancer Center—$300,000; Johnson O'Connor Research Foundation—$277,000; Cardigan Mountain School—$200,000; Museum of the American Indian—$60,000.

The foundation has established a modest Venture Fund as a means of allowing for occasional response to an area of need not falling within its established guidelines. Whenever practicable the foundation will make its grants on a challenge basis if it will provide a multiplier effect for the grantee.

The foundation is governed by a five-member board of trustees, with the donor's widow serving as chairman of the board and a daughter as president. Administration of the foundation is carried on from offices located at 1060 Park Avenue, New York, New York 10028 under the direction of the president.

Although the foundation does not presently publish an annual report it does publish grant application guidelines and procedures. With the close of its 1982 fiscal year it commenced publication of a short year-end report covering its grants for the year. Other sources of information available to the public are the returns filed by it with the Internal Revenue Service and the various Foundation Center publications.

**CLARK FOUNDATION.** See Clark Foundation, The; Edna McConnell Clark Foundation, The; Robert Sterling Clark Foundation, Inc.

**CLARK FOUNDATION, THE.** The donors who were responsible for the establishment of the Clark Foundation were heirs to a fortune which originated in the 1800s with a Cooperstown, New York, lawyer, Edward Clark, one of the founders of the Singer Sewing Machine Company. Members of the Clark family, including Edward S. Clark, Stephen C. Clark, and F. Ambrose Clark, established this foundation in New York in 1931.

By 1953, assets of the foundation amounted to about $7 million, and annual grants for that year were approximately $250,000. Since then, the following approximate figures show the foundation's growth: 1958, assets—$8.5 million, grants—$250,000; 1970, assets—$37 million, grants—$5 million. Following the foundation's 1973 merger with the Scriven Foundation, another Clark philanthropy, the 1976 figures were as follows: assets—$69 million, grants—$4 million. In 1980 they were: assets—$114 million, grants—$4 million.

Throughout its history, the Clark Foundation's program has been centered on support of a hospital, museums, and a historical association located in Cooperstown, New York. The foundation has also rendered support for other welfare, cultural, and educational purposes in Cooperstown, including scholarships to students residing there and in surrounding rural central school districts. Through the years, other grants for similar purposes to organizations in New York State and a few elsewhere have been made. Sample grants in 1980, illustrative of the foundation's giving, included the following: scholarships for students from the Cooperstown area—$975,062; Hartwick College, Oneonta, New York—$150,000; New York State Historical Association, Cooperstown—$195,000; the Farmers' Museum Inc., Cooperstown—$54,700; and St. Luke's Hospital Center, New York City—$100,000.

The foundation is governed by an eleven-member board of directors, with Stephen C. Clark, Jr., serving as president and two other members of the Clark family on the board. Administration of the foundation is carried on from offices located at 30 Wall Street, New York, New York 10005, under the direction of a secretary.

Almost the only additional information readily available to the public on this foundation are the annual reports and returns filed by it with the Internal Revenue Service, and the various Foundation Center publications.

**CLAUDE WORTHINGTON BENEDUM FOUNDATION.** In Pennsylvania in 1944, the Claude Worthington Benedum Foundation was established by Mr. and Mrs. Michael L. Benedum. Michael Benedum was the founder of the Benedum-Trees Oil Company, which developed major oil fields in the United States and abroad. The foundation was named in memory of their only child, who was killed in World War I at the age of twenty. When Mrs. Benedum died in 1951, the foundation benefitted from her estate, and by 1952 its assets amounted to about $6.5 million. Similarly, when Michael Benedum died in 1959, approximately $50 million from his estate of about $100 million went to the foundation. Its assets in 1980 were approximately $90 million.

Michael Benedum's hometown was Bridgeport, West Virginia, and his company was founded in that state. Later, it was moved to Pittsburgh. Understandably, therefore, the foundation has given priority to projects and programs designed for the uplift and improvement of the well-being of the people of West Virginia, southwestern Pennsylvania, and the Pittsburgh area. Traditionally, grants have been made to institutions of higher education, both public and private, and to health, cultural, civic, and social organizations in the areas. In 1980, for example, some of the larger grants included: $238,690 to Salem College, West Virginia; $200,000 to the Pittsburgh Symphony Society; $375,000 to Shadyside Academy, of Pittsburgh; and $200,000 to the Western Pennsylvania Hospital, of Pittsburgh.

The foundation is governed by a six-member board of trustees which includes the president and vice-president of the Benedum-Trees Oil Company, the last-named official being the grand-nephew of Michael Benedum. Administration of the foundation is carried on from offices located at 223 Fourth Avenue, Pittsburgh, Pennsylvania 15222, under the direction of a secretary.

Almost the only additional information on this foundation readily available to the public are the annual reports and returns filed by it with the Internal Revenue Service, and the various Foundation Center publications. See, however, Michael L. Benedum obituary, *New York Times* (July 31, 1959), p. 23.

**CLEVELAND FOUNDATION, THE.** As the nation's pioneer community trust, the Cleveland Foundation has become the model for most community foundations in the United States. When formed in 1914, it represented an unprecedented approach to philanthropy by and for the people. That the Cleveland Foundation not only survived but prospered as one of the nation's largest community trusts,—its 1981 assets totalled approximately $224 million,—is in part a tribute to its brilliant architect and his single-minded vision.

Frederick Harris Goff (1858–1924) is an often-overlooked giant of Midwest history. A native of Blackbury, Illinois, and a formidable self-made man, Goff as a young attorney exhibited such exacting prowess that he won an invitation from John D. Rockefeller to handle the oil magnate's legal affairs in New York City. Goff elected to stay in Cleveland, however, where he practiced law for twenty-five years and eventually served as bank president of the Cleveland Trust Company (now AmeriTrust).

As a civic-minded lawyer and banker, Goff became increasingly—even compulsively—concerned that turn-of-the-century philanthropy was so often hampered by bequests that had outlived their usefulness. Substantial funds lay unused, helping no one, the victim of binding and inflexible provisions that an English writer, Sir Arthur Hobhouse, labeled "The Dead Hand."

After several years of thoughtful planning led by Goff, the board of directors of the Cleveland Trust Company adopted, on January 2, 1914, a resolution and declaration of trust which brought into existence the Cleveland Foundation. Here was a new kind of philanthropic agency: a living trust designed to meet in perpetuity the changing needs of the community it served. Its specific purpose was stated thus: "[to assist] charitable and educational institutions . . . for promoting education, scientific research, for care of the sick, aged, or helpless, to improve living conditions or to provide recreation for all classes, and for such other charitable purposes as will best make for the mental, moral, and physical improvement of the inhabitants of the City of Cleveland . . . regardless of race, color, or creed."

Goff had conceived a remarkable alternative to philanthropy based only on great personal fortunes. The Cleveland Foundation, in his view, would accept gifts of one dollar as readily as gifts of millions of dollars. As he once remarked: "Our trust, lacking the resources of the Rockefellers, is especially open [to all] people with enough idealism about . . . philanthropy to warrant [this] to be kept always useful as the years go by."

Goff's singular design ensured that the new foundation would provide the most comprehensive response to the public's changing needs—and eliminate, in his words, the "withering, paralyzing blight of the Dead Hand." Members of the distribution committee, charged with the responsibility to select purposes for and distribution of foundation funds, served from the outset without compensation for set terms, and the majority were to be appointed by public officials. Another mechanism by Goff to make certain that the foundation remained accountable to the people was the provision of an annual audit of all foundation transactions and the dissemination of the audit through advertisements in the local newspapers.

During its early years, the foundation—whose then-limited assets severely restricted grant disbursement—embarked on a vigorous prologue to grant making that exerted some influence on national policy and practice while it prepared the community for future foundation work. These were the Cleveland Foundation "surveys" (1914–1922): systematic investigations—and often searching criticisms—of the community's civic, industrial, and social institutions. Instruments of diagnosis and reform, the studies set the stage, as the report on education (1915–1916) articulated it, for "an entire [institution] to pass in complete review before the public's eye."

Goff, who underwrote many of the surveys out of his own pocket, engaged the country's leading specialists to direct the major research efforts. Dean Roscoe Pound and Professor Felix Frankfurter of Harvard University Law School, for example, supervised the landmark work in criminal justice (1921–1922). Colonel Leonard P. Ayres, the noted statistician and director of education research for New York's Russell Sage Foundation,* led the exploration of the schools.

Palpable remedies and results emerged, underlining Frankfurter's credo that the starting point of reform was the education of the public to the necessity of a sustained interest. The criminal justice survey, which attracted attention around the world, helped clear the path for progress in such areas as prosecution and probation procedures. Among the one hundred recommendations of the education survey, ninety were implemented within ten years of the work's completion. Today, this impressive and seminal body of work is still cited for its progressive yet realistic thinking by urban planners and sociologists.

Actual foundation grant making began in 1919 with allocations of $600. Within thirty-eight years—by 1957—annual disbursements had reached in excess of $1 million; and less than twenty-five years later—by 1981—grant making totalled more than $16 million per year. Clearly the foundation had in the process forged a dynamic relationship with the Greater Cleveland community. Also, it had fulfilled Andrew Carnegie's prediction that the Cleveland Foundation plan seemed well calculated to promote the important ends in view.

Among the projects and programs the foundation helped to nurture during its middle years (1923 to 1973) were the nation's first chest X rays using small film equipment, medical training for World War II national defense, vital research in rheumatic heart disease and infantile paralysis, one of America's first neighborhood redevelopment projects (1956), equal housing, the 1936 Great Lakes Exposition, hundreds of scholarships, and a prized woodland arboretum.

More recently, in response to the sobering needs of its community, and particularly an aging industrial center teetering on the brink of financial collapse in the late 1970s, the foundation has placed special emphasis on Cleveland's economic development and infrastructure, housing and neighborhood development, improved police response time through computer technology, the peaceful desegregation of the Cleveland Public Schools, maternal and child health, parks and the Cleveland lakefront, and the financial stability and development of the community's professional performing arts organizations.

Cleveland Foundation grants support both private and public services; they are made primarily to not-for-profit, private agencies and in some cases to governmental agencies. The latter support, rare among community foundations, has involved a number of significant projects. For example, 1979 foundation funding spearheaded the Operations Improvement Task Force, made up of ninety top business executives loaned to the city, whose work in improving efficiency and municipal management played a key role in restoring public confidence—and turning around the city's perilous financial condition.

General program areas addressed by the foundation are health, civic affairs, social services, education, and cultural affairs. Unless specified otherwise by the donor, grants are limited to the Greater Cleveland area and are not made for sectarian or religious activity.

The Cleveland Foundation is governed by an eleven-member distribution committee, composed of community leaders selected in a variety of ways for their knowledge of the charitable needs of the Greater Cleveland area. There are five public appointees; they, in turn, select a member who is a trustee or principal officer of another philanthropic foundation. Five additional members are appointed by the trustees committee, comprised of the chief executive officers of the seven trustee banks, whose major responsibility is the management of foundation assets.

Several internal foundation developments have been replicated by many community trusts. In a design originally conceived by Goff, the Cleveland Foundation was the first community trust to devise plans for deferred giving—for instance, plans which provide for the payment of annuities to specified individuals, with the balance of income to the foundation. The combined funds, established in 1943, pool the smaller gifts of donors for investment purposes.

In addition, the foundation has, since 1973, pioneered the concept of supporting organizations. In that year, the twenty-year-old Sherwick Fund became the first private foundation in the country to seek suppporting organization status with a community trust in accordance with section 509(a)(3) of the Internal Revenue Code. By agreeing to commit the assets of the fund to the benefit and charitable purposes of the Cleveland Foundation, and by complying with certain other regulations, the Sherwick Fund was able to achieve the greatly enlarged benefits a public charity provides.

In all, seven supporting organizations had affiliated with the foundation by 1981, including The Treu-Mart Fund, the nation's first supporting organization affiliated with both a community trust and another public charity (Cleveland's Jewish Community Federation). Combined assets of the foundation's supporting organizations were nearly $8 million at 1981 market value.

The 1980 Cleveland Foundation annual report lists 243 large trust funds and 287 contributors to the combined funds. Moreover, the foundation, through the years, has accepted thousands of nontrust contributions—usually smaller funds paid out soon after they have been received. Its undesignated funds are approximately 80 percent of total assets—underlining the foundation's ability to address the pressing issues of the day with considerable grant-making flexibility.

The director of the Cleveland Foundation is Homer C. Wadsworth, who, prior to his 1974 appointment, had served, among other posts, as the twenty-five-year president of the Kansas City Association of Trusts and Foundations. Foundation staff is recognized nationally for expertise in specific program areas.

For further information, see Nathaniel R. Howard, *Trust for All Time: The*

*Story of the Cleveland Foundation and the Community Trust Movement* (1963); and *Annual Reports* of the foundation, published continuously since 1926. See also *Frederick Harris Goff* (1923), a brief sketch of Goff's life, published by the Cleveland Trust Company; and William Ganson Rose, *Cleveland: The Making of a City* (1950).

WILLIAM RUDMAN

**COLEMAN FOUNDATION, INC., THE.** J. D. Stetson Coleman, former official of the Pennzoil Company, and Dorothy W. Coleman established the Coleman Foundation as a trust in Virginia in 1951 and in Illinois in 1953. Its assets were relatively small in its early years, in 1977 amounting to about $4.25 million. The deaths of Coleman in 1975 and his widow in 1977 saw the incorporation of the foundation in Illinois in 1978 and a dramatic increase in its assets from the estates of the Colemans.

Foundation assets in 1982 were about $50 million and grants are averaging about $2 million to $3 million annually. In recent years, grants have been devoted to the support of higher education, social programs, hospitals, the handicapped, cultural programs, religion, and research.

Giving has generally been restricted to the Chicago metropolitan area and the state of Illinois. Representative larger grants from 1981 through early 1983 included the following: University of Illinois Foundation—$750,000; Illinois Institute of Technology—$500,000; Misericordia Home, Chicago—$165,000; Illinois Masonic Medical Center, Chicago—$100,000; Rehabilitation Institute of Chicago—$500,000; Glenwood School for Boys—$160,000; and Art Institute of Chicago—$75,000.

The Coleman Foundation is governed by a six-member board of directors. Administration of the foundation is carried on from offices located at 1137 West Jackson Boulevard, Chicago, Illinois 60607, under the direction of an executive director.

For further information, see unpublished annual reports filed by the foundation with the Foundation Center and the Donor's Forum, Chicago, together with a *Guidelines to Grant Requests and Application Procedures,* published periodically by the foundation. See also J. D. Stetson Coleman obituary, *New York Times* (September 8, 1975), p. 87.

**COLUMBUS FOUNDATION, THE.** Harrison M. Sayre, Columbus civic leader and president of American Education Press, was the leader in the formation in 1943 of this Ohio community foundation. Sayre had long been interested in the community foundation as a philanthropic medium. He knew Frederick Goff, the man who is given credit for originating the concept of the community foundation and who established the first one, the Cleveland [Ohio] Foundation* in 1914. Sayre also was a trustee of the Alfred L. Willson Charitable Trust, which had been formed in Cleveland in 1922 and which provided some of the initial funds for the newly formed Columbus Foundation.

Modeled after the Cleveland Foundation, the assets of the Columbus Foundation were, from the beginning, and still are held and managed by the trustee banks. A trustees committee, consisting of officers of three Columbus banks, meets as frequently as required to conduct the foundation's financial affairs. The selection of the recipients of the foundation's grants is made by a governing committee. It consisted originally of five members: two were appointed by the trustees committee and one each by the president of the United Community Council, the president of Ohio State University, and the judge of the Franklin County Probate Court. In 1969, the committee was enlarged to include two more members, one to be appointed by the president of the Battelle Memorial Institute and the other by the chairman of the Columbus Area Chamber of Commerce. Governing committee members may serve two five-year terms.

Many of the early assets of the foundation were given by Preston Davis, principal owner of American Education Press, and by Harrison Sayre, along with other donors of lesser amounts. In 1947, the assets of the Columbus War Chest in the amount of $85,000 were transferred to the foundation, which by then had assets of almost $200,000. Ten years later, the $1 million mark was passed with the $350,000 bequest of Robert W. Stevenson. By 1967, the foundation's assets totalled over $5 million. The greatest period of growth for the Columbus Foundation, however, occurred as the result of the 1969 Tax Reform Act of the United States Congress. The more stringent payout and reporting procedures and the 4 percent tax on income led many smaller foundations to terminate their activities and become part of community foundations in their areas. Thus, the community foundations generally benefitted, and the assets of the Columbus Foundation reached approximately $25 million by the end of 1975. A $7 million bequest from James W. "Red" Overstreet added substantially to the foundation's assets. In 1981 assets of about $50 million make the Columbus Foundation one of the largest community foundations in the United States.

Grants by the Columbus Foundation have been made in the fields of arts and humanities, civic affairs, conservation and environmental protection, education, hospitals and health, religious organizations, and social services. As in the case of other community foundations, the bulk of these grants have been made to organizations located in Columbus or the central Ohio region.

In addition to the management of its own programs, the foundation over the years has served as advisor to other foundations and civic groups. For example, the foundation staff assisted the Battelle Memorial Institute Foundation in its establishment and in the formulation and initial implementation of its grants program. In 1981, the Columbus Foundation made grant commitments in excess of $5 million.

For the first twenty-five years of operation, Harrison Sayre served as the unpaid executive head of the foundation. In 1969, the position became salaried and the first Columbus Foundation office was opened. The present executive director and six full-time employees conduct the programs of the foundation from offices located at 17 South High Street, Columbus, Ohio 43215.

For further information, see *Annual Reports* of the foundation, published since the 1970s. See also *Once an Acorn* (1977), a historical leaflet published by the foundation.

**COMMONWEALTH FUND, THE.** The Commonwealth Fund was founded in 1918 with a gift of approximately $10 million from Anna M. Harkness. Her husband, Stephen, had been a founding investor in the Standard Oil Company. After his death in 1888, first his oldest son, Charles, and after 1916, his youngest son, Edward, managed the family's funds. It was Edward who guided his mother in establishing a charitable foundation so that a portion of her benefaction might be accomplished with greater efficiency and purpose.

After three years of supporting European relief work upon the conclusion of World War I, the fund made its first long-range commitment in educational (1920–1927) and legal research (1920–1943).

The fund's next effort was establishment, in the early 1920s, of the Program of Prevention of Juvenile Delinquency. The fund's interest in preventing delinquency quickly led to the treatment of the emotional and behavioral problems of young children—an interest that could be described as "child guidance." A five-year program involving three national committees and the New York School of Social Work resulted in the training of a corps of more than 350 psychiatrists, psychologists, and social workers in childhood mental development, and child guidance demonstration clinics were operating in seven cities across the United States, with new clinics under development.

During the course of the child guidance program, the Commonwealth Fund recognized that the quality of the services rendered was limited by the level of scientific knowledge and professional expertise. The fund therefore established fellowships to further basic training in psychiatry at teaching hospitals. The original program was revised in 1927, creating the Division of Community Clinics, to oversee development of new clinics, and the Institute for Child Guidance.

The fund's interest in the welfare of children led to its second major endeavor, the Child Health Demonstration Program. In 1922, under the leadership of Barry C. Smith, the second general director, two clinics were set up in small cities and two in rural areas. As in the Child Guidance Clinics, a temporary staff was installed to give pediatric service of a preventive and educational sort, nursing service for children and mothers, and health education leadership in the schools. By the end of the program in 1929, the clinics had been incorporated into the existing county health departments. Thus, these demonstrations broadened current concepts of public health; improved the public health records; emphasized the utility of postgraduate education for practicing physicians; and set a pattern for a few good local health departments. When the clinics came to an end, the fund turned to a new program in which the primary objective was to better the full range of local, particularly rural, health service.

The Division of Rural Hospitals was established in 1925–1926 as the second administrative division of the fund, the first being the Division of Education. A grant was made to Rutherford County, Tennessee (the site of the second Child Health Demonstration) for the establishment of a hospital to support the activities of the Child Health Demonstration Project and the county department of health. As the rural hospitals program was worked out, it took into account the capacity and willingness of rural communities to help themselves. In selected districts containing no town of more than twelve thousand people and without a hospital, the fund set out to supply the greater part, but not all, of the building cost. These hospitals were to concern themselves with professional education and public health. Five additional small hospitals were built in as many different states between 1926 and 1930. From 1930 to 1934, attention was concentrated on the strengthening of administration and service. After 1934, awards for new buildings, reconstruction, and reorganization brought the total number of hospitals aided by the fund in these ways to fifteen.

To overcome some of the difficulties and limitations faced by the small hospitals, the fund, in 1943, offered a plan for the formation of closer ties among the hospitals in small cities and towns and those in a metropolitan center in the area. The Rochester Regional Hospital Council offered promise for cooperative regional development: joint planning of hospital building and expansion; joint operation of institutional services that could be performed more efficiently by the group than by the individual institutions; and pooling of administrative and technical skills.

In the rural hospitals, educational programs were easily established with nearby professional schools. This burgeoning interest in medical education was reflected in Edward Harkness's additional bequest, in 1937, of five million dollars, intended specifically for the support of medical research and medical education.

The Medical Fellowship Program, an important outgrowth of Harkness's bequest, reflected the Commonwealth Fund's continuing interest in training of professional personnel. Beginning in the late 1920s, the fund established fellowships for the more general preparation of psychiatrists. In 1938, the fund began to provide a more general kind of assistance: fellowships for advanced study to junior instructors in medical schools. From 1956 to 1966, the fund supported an additional fellowship program: funds were given to qualified individuals in midcareer and to senior scholars and scientists who were near the peak of their accomplishments.

Another outgrowth of Harkness's gift was increased emphasis on grants for medical research. Support of medical research, beginning in 1920, reflected yet another aspect of the Commonwealth Fund's interest in the welfare of children— essentially all the fund-supported research related to diseases affecting children. After 1937, grants were made for projects such as the development of apparatus for the separation of proteins (Dr. Edwin J. Cohn), study of kidney function (Drs. A. N. Richards and Homer W. Smith), and study of cardiorespiratory physiology (Drs. Dickinson W. Richards, Jr., and Andre Cournand).

The fund's intensified interest in medical education began in 1937, but it was not until the considerable augmentation of the fund's endowment from Harkness's estate, in 1950, that larger grants for medical education became possible.

In the 1950s and 1960s, during the presidencies first of Malcolm P. Aldrich and then of Quigg Newton, the Commonwealth Fund gave major support to medical schools to integrate into the curriculum medical knowledge from several disciplines. Special emphasis was given to reconciling medical education and social needs for medical services. (The major curriculum revision at Western Reserve University Medical School was considered one of the most significant developments in American medical education since the famous and influential 1910 Flexner report.) Grants were also provided for the planning of new medical schools and the expansion of others from two- to four-year schools and for the development of training programs for new categories of health practitioners. Support to established medical schools allowed them to reorganize premedical and medical education; integrate behavioral and social sciences into the curriculum; update their programs in response to the explosion in biomedical knowledge; and educate more students from minority groups. In an attempt to strengthen medical education in whatever manner each school viewed its needs, the fund in 1955 and 1956 made a series of unstructured grants totalling $12.6 million to nineteen university medical schools.

During the presidency of Quigg Newton, tertiary-care medical institutions were successfully encouraged to develop medical services in their communities, and university health centers were led to work more closely with community health services. Important social problems were addressed through support to the Population Council for family planning programs and to medical schools for a new curriculum on human sexuality.

In 1975, under the leadership of Carleton B. Chapman, the Commonwealth Fund turned its attention to the interface between the premedical undergraduate college years and the basic medical sciences usually taught in the first two years of medical school. Abraham Flexner's 1910 report stressed that physicians should be competent in the basic sciences. When the universities could not provide the needed knowledge and skills, the medical schools created the appropriate disciplines oriented to the needs of medicine. Issues deriving from the resulting artificial separation of sciences between the schools of medicine and their parent universities were examined in the fund's interface program, including restriction in opportunities for medical students to study human biology; the stylized curriculum with emphasis on mathematics, physics, chemistry and nonhuman biology; the competition for admission to medical school and its impact on students in general and medical students in particular; and, as a corollary of the intense competition and limited breadth of the traditional premedical education, the lack of counseling for alternative options in health careers. The fund declined to indicate a preference for a particular model, intending that a number of institutions would develop designs which might be used by other colleges and medical schools. In 1975, the fund selected seven universities to explore the role of the humanities and social and behavioral sciences in the education of physicians and to examine the use of the entire natural and basic medical science faculties of a university in teaching future physicians at both the college and professional-school levels. The final awards of these programs were made in 1981.

With the retirement of Carleton B. Chapman in 1980, Margaret E. Mahoney became the Commonwealth Fund's fourth president. Under her leadership, the long-term health needs of Americans continue to be the focus of the fund's activities, as health-care institutions seek solutions to the complex problems facing the country. The fund will concentrate its support on two types of institutions: academic health centers, and public and volunteer health-care institutions in New York City. The fund will particularly consider programs that present specific plans for collaborative use of existing staff and facilities; programs that can be modified or replicated by other institutions; and programs that present plans to retain or expand educational and patient-care services crucial to residents of the center's region.

The Commonwealth Fund has chosen for current attention problems in health-care delivery affecting five specific groups: the elderly who are both functionally dependent and poor; low-income families who must find a way to pay for their medical care; people with personal habits (such as alcoholism) that could lead to major disabilities and premature death; working women with difficulty in obtaining care for their young children; and members of minority groups looking toward careers in the health professions. The fund will make a limited number of grants for research and models that address these problems by supporting investigators for two or three years of work in fields such as medicine, economics, law, political science, sociology, and epidemiology. Priority will be given to work plans designed to examine a problem in its larger social, economic, and political context, as well as from the viewpoint of medical care; to test and analyze changes that may intensify or alleviate the problem; to compare the dimensions of the problem historically, cross-culturally, or in relation to similar problems; to expand the range of new approaches to addressing the problem; and to specify ways through which these new approaches could be put into action.

Three additional programs continue to receive Commonwealth Fund support. The fund's publishing program began in the early 1920s as an accompaniment to the Program for Prevention of Juvenile Delinquency. Since then, the fund's Division of Publications has: provided grants to individual scholars writing about health care, medical education, and the biomedical sciences; subsidized publication of journal articles and books; and distributed books to medical school libraries. The Harkness Fellowship Program, originally known as the Commonwealth Fund Fellowship Program, was established by Edward Harkness in 1925. These fellowships enable young citizens of the United Kingdom, Australia, and New Zealand to pursue graduate-level studies in the United States. At present, twenty fellowships are awarded each year in the United Kingdom, four in Australia, and two in New Zealand. In addition to these two programs, the fund will make a small number of grants to assist those seeking important new ways to make more discerning use of medical technology.

The fund's commitment has been both to the social side of medicine (as reflected in preventive work and community programs), as well as to humanistic medical care (best evidenced by the integration of psychiatric concepts with general training and a basic concern for the quality of the physician-patient relationship). Since its founding, the Commonwealth Fund has directed its attention and resources primarily to the development of ideas, talents, institutions, and arrangements promising to strengthen the extent and quality of medical care in American society.

The Commonwealth Fund, with assets in 1980 of about $139 million, is governed by a nine-member board of directors. Administration of the fund is carried on from offices located at One East Seventy-Fifth Street, New York, New York 10021 under the direction of a president.

For further information, see James W. Wooster, *Edward Stephen Harkness, 1874–1940* (1949), and *The Commonwealth Fund. Historical Sketch. 1918–1962* (1963). See also *Annual Reports* of the fund, published continuously since 1919, and *New Program Directions* (1981), an informational pamphlet about the fund and its future.

A. MCGEHEE HARVEY

**COMMUNITIES FOUNDATION OF TEXAS, INC.** Formerly the Dallas Community Chest Trust Fund, Inc., this is an independent, nonprofit, publicly supported, tax-exempt, philanthropic foundation designed primarily to assist in meeting the long-range and capital needs of health, welfare, cultural, and educational institutions in Texas and adjoining states. Encouraged by the suggestion of Dallas attorney Paul Carrington, seven distinguished civic and business leaders—J. B. Adoue, Jr., R. R. Gilbert, J. L. Latimer, B. F. McLain, Henry S. Miller, Sr., John E. Mitchell, Jr., and Harold F. Volk—established in 1953 the Dallas Community Chest Trust Fund. The fund, renamed in 1981 as the Communities Foundation of Texas, Inc., exists in perpetuity to receive gifts, endowments, bequests, annuities, properties, cash donations, and other type of contributions from public-spirited citizens who wish to make lasting gifts for the long-term needs of the community. The essential purpose of the organization in its early years was to assist, through grants and loans, agencies of the Community Chest (now United Way) that had almost no endowment funds or other provisions for the repair, improvement, or expansion of buildings.

The auspicious beginning of the Dallas Community Chest Trust Fund was greatly benefitted by the appointment of Dr. Fred M. Lange as executive vice-president in 1953. Lange, who had come to Dallas in 1932, was internationally known for his work with philanthropic organizations and was recognized as a leader in welfare financing and administration. Lange's guidance during almost thirty years as president and chairman of the executive committee enabled the fund to achieve impressive growth.

In 1955, Pearl C. Anderson gave the first large gift to the fund, with a donation of highly valued downtown property. Contributions steadily increased, and the organization was incorporated in 1960. By 1961, the fund was able to make annual grants of more than a quarter-million dollars to fifty-eight health, welfare, and cultural organizations in Dallas County. Among the diverse recipients were the Baylor Hospital Building Fund, the Dallas Council on World Affairs, Dallas Day Nurseries, the Salvation Army, and the Episcopal Community Services.

The major problem in the fund's early years was one of communication—to inform the Dallas public of the need for the organization and how it would serve. To facilitate the effort, an advisory council of ninety-nine key business, labor, professional, and community leaders was established to communicate information to potential donors concerning opportunities to help their community. In order to assure continuity and vitality, the council members served three-year, rotating terms. To encourage interest in the fund, brochures were distributed to attorneys, bank trustees, and tax counselors, and extensive advertising was carried out in newspapers. Large donations were made to the fund by W. W. Caruth, Jr., Granville C. Morton, and H. Ross Perot.

In 1971, the fund gained its own permanent office headquarters, the Fred M. Lange Center, located at 4605 Live Oak Street, Dallas, Texas 75204. The building and land were made possible by contributions from Lange's friends in tribute to his dedicated humanitarian service. In addition to housing the fund's staff, the center also contained several meeting rooms available to community groups. During almost two decades of operation, the fund granted more than $3 million to some one hundred organizations.

Through the years the fund's greatest strength lay in the wise and continuing governance of its board of trustees. Composed of seven outstanding business and civic leaders, the trustees serve three-year terms, without remuneration, and cannot succeed themselves immediately, in order that new vision and ideas are always provided. Three of the trustees compose the executive committee, which has a chairman, vice-chairman, and treasurer. A subcommittee of the board carries out the important decision making concerning grants distribution. The trustees also appoint members of the advisory council. Voluntary legal and tax counsel is provided by local attorneys.

Fred Lange served as executive vice-president and chief executive officer of the Dallas Community Chest Trust Fund from its founding until 1969, when he was elevated to the position of president. Succeeding him as executive vice-president was J. Lynn Roberts, who had been associated with the fund for sixteen years. In 1978, Lange became chairman of the executive committee; and Roberts, a recognized leader in the administration of philanthropic donations, became president. Edward M. Fjordbak later became executive vice-president, and the size of the full-time staff grew to eleven.

The caliber of leadership enabled the fund to grow at a steady rate from its very inception, but dramatic changes took place in the decade 1971–1981. Assets grew from $10 million in 1971 to over $60 million in fiscal 1981. Grants rose from under $1 million a year to over $6 million a year, and the number of component funds (family, corporate, and support foundation within the general fund) grew from 76 to 221.

In recent years, the largest percentage of the year's funding was awarded for broad educational purposes in grants to schools, colleges, universities, and special groups for instruction and training. Health grants to hospitals, clinics, medical centers, and disease research associations comprised the next most heavily funded category of recipients. Grants to religious organizations are the third-highest percentage of gifts but reflect the intentions or prior designations of various donors, as the general fund does not make grants to religious causes for the propagation of a certain faith. The fourth category in terms of percentage of grant dollars was that of cultural programs, including funding to the Dallas Museum of Fine Arts, Dallas Symphony Association, and various historical projects.

By 1978, the twenty-fifth year of its existence, the fund was well established within the top ten of the nation's two hundred community foundations in terms of assets and value of annual grants given. Traditionally, grants have been made primarily to organizations that promote the well-being of inhabitants in Dallas County and adjoining counties in Texas. Recently, however, substantial grants have been made to organizations and individuals in other areas of the state and nation. Because the fund had grown beyond the limits of Dallas and had become an area-wide organization, in April of 1981 it was deemed wise to change its name. It became the Communities Foundation of Texas, Inc., which reflected its expanded operations and new role of service to donors and recipients throughout the state.

The foundation recently developed an innovative "branching" technique whereby it helped create and administer community philanthropic funds in cities around the state. The first of these branch offices was established in Palacios, near Matagorda Bay. Such local branches maintain their own executive director and grants distribution committee, but they benefit from the cost-effective business procedures of the principal office in Dallas. In order to offer greater flexibility and service in meeting the needs of donors and their community, the foundation in recent years has made extensive use of such procedures as advise and consult funds, pooled income funds, and support foundations.

For further information, see (Dallas) *Morning News* (April 16, 1965), I, 25; (November 14, 1965), n.p.; and (June 30, 1978), A, 21; informational brochures published by the foundation, particularly *Depository of Good Deeds* (May, 1972); and *Newsletter*, published by the foundation, particularly those for 1981. See also "Remarks by William E. Collins Delivered at the Annual Meeting of the Advisory Council," Communities Foundation of Texas, Inc., (1981), and

"Scrapbooks of Clippings," Communities Foundation of Texas Archives (1961–1981).

DOROTHY D. DeMOSS

**CONNELLY FOUNDATION.** The Connelly Foundation was incorporated in Pennsylvania in 1955 with John F. Connelly and Josephine C. Connelly as the sole donors. John Connelly is also chairman and chief executive of the Crown Cork & Seal Company, of Philadelphia, a firm he acquired in the late 1950s and which is now 373rd on the "Fortune 500" list of companies in the United States. In 1981, the assets of the Connelly Foundation were valued at approximately $56 million, a substantial portion of which is composed of Crown Cork & Seal Company stock.

The majority of Connelly Foundation grants are awarded to educational institutions in the Philadelphia area, followed by grants to church and religious organizations. Lesser amounts go to health-related institutions and civic, social welfare, and cultural programs. Most educational grants are given to schools that have a Roman Catholic affiliation, although certain Protestant schools are recipients. The foundation also gives substantial financial assistance to Roman Catholic churches and religious organizations. The foundation's support of Jewish causes was so extensive in 1980, however, that Connelly was given the "Americanism Award" of the Anti-Defamation League of B'nai B'rith. In 1981, for example, $285,000 of the foundation's funds were invested in state of Israel bonds.

The Connelly Foundation generally assists with annual campaigns, building funds, and institutional internships. Grants often take the form of Crown Cork & Seal Company stocks, although some cash awards are given. No grants go to individuals, for the support of endowment funds, or to requests involving "research-related programs."

In 1981, the Connelly Foundation's grants totalled $2,802,813, of which $1,755,312 was awarded for educational purposes, $522,775 was designated for medical use, $451,375 for religious purposes, and $73,351 was for support of civic activities. Of the total figure, $2,600,525 was in the form of stock contributions, and $202,288 was in cash. In 1980, over 220 grants were awarded, with $12,125 as the average donation. The highest grant was $666,625, while the lowest was $84.

The foundation is governed by a ten-member board of trustees which includes John F. Connelly as president and several members of the Connelly family. The foundation is administered from offices located at 9300 Ashton Road, Philadelphia, Pennsylvania 19136, under the direction of the president.

Almost the only additional information readily available to the public on this foundation are the annual reports and returns filed by it with the Internal Revenue Service, and the various Foundation Center publications. See, however, an article concerning John F. Connelly, "Making Cans and Money and Breaking All the

Rules," *Philadelphia Enquirer* (October 25, 1981), pp. 1–2; and *The Directory of Pennsylvania Foundations* (1981).

JOHN SOBOTKA

**CONRAD N. HILTON FOUNDATION.** The son of a Norwegian emigrant, Conrad N. Hilton was born in New Mexico in 1887. From modest beginnings in 1919, he became a millionaire who owned or controlled a string of hotels all over the world by the time of his death in 1979.

The foundation which bears his name was organized in 1944 and incorporated in 1950 in California. Its assets by that time were about $250,000. By 1969, assets of the foundation were valued at about $1 million, which increased to about $3 million in 1975 and $18 million in 1980. Upon Hilton's death, the bulk of his estate went to the foundation, which reported assets totalling about $59 million in 1982. The first *Annual Report* (1982–1983) of the foundation states that it anticipates receipt, by the end of 1983, of an additional $200 million from Hilton's estate.

Traditionally, the Hilton Foundation has concentrated its giving on Roman Catholic educational institutions and religious organizations, higher education, youth agencies, hospitals, and health and social service organizations. In 1981–1982, grants in the amount of about $1 million were made. Representative larger grants by the foundation included the following: University of Houston—$230,000; University of Houston Foundation—$133,215; Little Sisters of the Poor—$35,000; Children's Home Society of California—$25,000; and Desert Hospital Mental Health Center—$25,000.

The foundation is governed by a nine-member board of directors which includes two sons of Conrad N. Hilton. Administration of the foundation is carried on from offices located at 10100 Santa Monica Boulevard, Suite 775, Los Angeles, California 90067, under the direction of a president.

For further information, see the *Annual Report* (1982–1983) of the foundation referred to above. See also Conrad N. Hilton obituary, *New York Times* (January 5, 1979), p. 22.

**COORS FOUNDATION.** See Adolph Coors Foundation.

**COWELL FOUNDATION.** See S. H. Cowell Foundation.

**CROWN MEMORIAL.** See Arie and Ida Crown Memorial.

**CULLEN FOUNDATION, THE.** Hugh Roy Cullen was born in 1881 in Texas. He stopped school and started to work for three dollars a week when he was twelve years old. He went on to make a billion dollars in the petroleum industry in Texas and Oklahoma in the 1920s and 1930s. Beginning in the 1930s, he and his wife donated hundreds of millions of dollars to philanthropic purposes, and primarily to Texas educational institutions, particularly the University of Houston. Their initial gift was one of $260,000 in 1937 to the University of Houston to erect the Roy Gustave Cullen Memorial Building in memory of their only son who had been killed in an oil field accident the preceding year.

In 1947, the Cullens established the Cullen Foundation to aid educational, medical, and charitable institutions in Texas, particularly in the Houston area and especially the University of Houston. It was planned that the foundation should receive the income from some eighteen thousand acres of oil-bearing land which was expected at the time to eventually yield about $160 million.

Until the end of the 1960s, the assets of the foundation were always listed at less than $10 million, and grants up until the end of that decade never exceeded $700,000 annually. By 1980, however, valuation of foundation assets had jumped to about $82 million, and grants also had risen dramatically, all as the result of the dramatic increase in the production and value of the petroleum products forming the major portion of the corpus of the foundation. For example, in 1977 the foundation made grants totalling more than $8 million; in 1978 almost $10 million; in 1979 more than $11 million; in 1980 almost $14 million; and in 1981 almost $18 million.

It is worthy of note that in 1979, of the total amount given in that year, the foundation awarded 67 percent for the establishment of three trusts: the Cullen Trust for Higher Education ($4.5 million); the Cullen Trust for Health Care ($2 million); and the Cullen Trust for the Performing Arts (slightly over $1 million). These trusts are independent of the foundation, have their own board of trustees, and their own income from their own endowments, which will provide support for their own specific areas of philanthropy in Texas. The foundation has made and continues to make a variety of other sizable grants to other Texas and Houston institutions such as the Houston Museum of Natural Science, South Texas College of Law, and YMCA of the Greater Houston area. Since its inception, the foundation has made grants totalling about $87 million.

The Cullen Foundation is governed by a five-member board of trustees, most of whom are related to the donors. They include the two surviving daughters of the Cullens, who act as president and vice-president of the foundation, and two grandsons of the donors. The mailing address of the foundation is Post Office Box 1600, Houston, Texas 77001, and administration of the foundation is carried on under the direction of an executive secretary.

Almost the only additional information readily available to the public on this foundation is to be found in the annual reports and other returns filed by it with the Internal Revenue Service, and the various Foundation Center publications. See, however, Hugh Roy Cullen obituary, *New York Times* (July 5, 1957), pp. 1, 17; Mrs. Hugh Roy Cullen obituary, *New York Times* (November 17, 1959), p. 35; and "Hugh Roy Cullen," *Dictionary of American Biography,* Supplement Six (1980), pp. 135–136.

**CULPEPER FOUNDATION.** See Charles E. Culpeper Foundation, Inc.

# D

**DALLAS COMMUNITY CHEST TRUST FUND, INC.** See Communities Foundation of Texas, Inc.

**DANA FOUNDATION.** See Charles A. Dana Foundation, Incorporated, The.

**DANFORTH FOUNDATION, THE.** Established by Adda and William H. Danforth in May, 1927, this foundation is a national educational philanthropic organization. Eighty-five percent of the annual budget is awarded nationally and fifteen percent is allocated for programs in St. Louis, the home of the Danforth Foundation. According to its charter, it was founded "for charitable and humanitarian purposes and to promote the well-being of mankind." The primary commitment of the foundation has been to education, and throughout the years of its existence, the goals of the Danforth Foundation have been to educate those persons with potential and to improve educational institutions. These endeavors have been considered the best means of improving the human condition.

William H. Danforth (1870–1955) graduated in 1892 from Washington University, in St. Louis, and began his business career as a manufacturer of livestock feed. He was one of the first manufacturers in the nation to offer employees the opportunity to purchase company stock on installments and to encourage productivity by developing sales incentive programs. Danforth's company became the Ralston-Purina Company and very soon grew to million-dollar proportions.

While developing his manufacturing business, William Danforth served as a Sunday school teacher at the Pilgrim Congregational Church, of St. Louis. In this work he enjoyed contacts with capable young people and soon became interested in ways of helping with their careers. He set up a trust fund for financing college educations for a few young people of outstanding ability, prior to the establishment of the Danforth Foundation, which later took over this work.

Adda and William Danforth helped start the American Youth Foundation, a summer program for leadership training, at about the same time that the Danforth Foundation was established. The first formal activity of the foundation was to award a series of scholarships to the American Youth Foundation's summer camps in Michigan and New Hampshire. Underprivileged young people of outstanding ability were the recipients of these scholarships.

The Danforth Foundation, as it has been expanded, serves three areas: higher education, through grants and programs administered by the staff; precollegiate education, through grant-making and program activities; and urban education in metropolitan St. Louis, through grants and program activities.

In 1940, the foundation began an expansion under the guidance of Dr. William J. Hutchins, president emeritus of Berea College who was appointed advisor to the foundation. His belief in the importance of the teacher influenced him to initiate, in 1941, a program to encourage the growth and development of college teachers, with emphasis on women and ethnic-minority faculty members. The Danforth Associate Program, as it was called, is one of the ongoing programs of the foundation. In 1943, the Danforth Graduate Fellowships Program, designed to encourage the leadership and character development of women college graduates, was added. This program emphasized the importance of women in the field of higher education, but it was discontinued in 1955. Hutchins retired in 1951. During his administration, the activities of the Danforth Foundation were greatly increased.

Dr. Kenneth J. Brown, past president of Hiram College and Denison University, succeeded Hutchins as executive director of the foundation. A number of educational activities were added during his administration. Support was given to teachers from India wishing to study in the United States, and internship programs in campus ministry for students of theology were begun. The primary interest of the foundation during the 1950s was higher education. The Danforth Teacher Grants were established in 1955 to provide graduate fellowships for competent young teachers who had not completed a doctoral degree. Also, a workshop on liberal arts education was begun in the late 1950s. Groups of faculty, students, and administrators met for three weeks to consider issues regarding the quality of liberal arts education. The program was successful and was continued for twenty years. The Danforth Graduate Fellowship Program was started in 1952 to provide graduate study for those pursuing a career in college teaching, and judging by the amount expended and the number of persons receiving grants, it is the largest of all the programs.

It was during the 1950s that the Danforth Foundation sponsored a program to assist colleges in their efforts to bring scholars of national reputation to their campuses and to provide for faculty sabbatical programs in colleges where this was not done. In 1957, the foundation initiated a program for improving the quality of education of racial minorities. Financial awards were made to fifty-five black colleges and universities to help them meet accreditation standards, and Negro College Faculty Fellowships were established to help faculty members improve their qualifications. During Brown's tenure, the staff was increased from two to ten persons and funds allocated for grants increased from $100,000 in 1951 to $1 million in 1961. In addition, six new programs were added.

In the 1960s, under the direction of Dr. Merriman Cuninggim, who became president of the Danforth Foundation in 1961, the foundation began an intensified study of the inequities in education. Large grants were made to the Council of Southern Universities to strengthen faculty qualifications at predominantly black schools and to a number of graduate schools to recruit minority Ph.D. candidates. The Postgraduate Black Studies Program, begun in the late sixties, was established to help develop courses in black studies.

Secondary education was designated as an area of foundation activity in 1963. Three fields of interest in precollegiate education were selected for attention and study: citizenship education of youth, emphasizing moral and ethical development; the professional growth and development of administrators; and new ways to deal with high school education. To further these three fields of interest, the foundation supported the development of new curricula in social studies for school-age students. Curricular activities in which lawyers, police officers, and members of the social service systems participated were initiated. The school principal was considered the most important figure in this learning process, and so the foundation encouraged the professional growth of administrators. Grants were made to the American Association of School Administrators and to the National Association of Secondary School Principals.

In 1968, the foundation began its urban activities. Support was given to projects planned to better the quality of life in the city of St. Louis, with particular attention directed toward improving the educational opportunities of those who had been denied equity. Four concerns were chosen for funding. They were the reconciliation of black and white persons; the encouragement of blacks in management; the support and encouragement of programs in fair housing; and the support of education for minorities with emphasis on preparing them for community-leadership roles. Grants were made to the St. Louis Board of Education to enable it to cope with the educational problems related to school desegregation and quality education. These urban development activities had the full support of the new president of the Danforth Foundation, Dr. Gene L. Schwilch, who became president in the early seventies.

The Danforth Foundation currently (1982) administers the following programs:

1. The Danforth Associate Program—for college and university teachers (begun in 1941, the oldest program)
2. Danforth Graduate Fellowship Program—designed to prepare college graduates for careers in college and university teaching
3. Dorothy Danforth Compton Fellowships—awarded for minority college seniors and graduate students to study for doctoral degrees, in preparation for college teaching
4. Danforth College Project Fund—awards for working with administrators, students, and other faculty members for the improvement of learning and teaching
5. Danforth Seminars for Federal Judges and Educators—workshops for examining issues of education and courts

6. Danforth School Administrators Fellowship Program—for senior high school principals in selected districts
7. Danforth St. Louis Leadership Program—a year-long program of activities for St.Louis-area leaders
8. Danforth Community Seminars—workshops on issues for educators and leaders in metropolitan St. Louis

From its inception in the 1920s, the value of the assets held by the foundation increased slowly to about $8 million in 1950, and grants amounting to about $100,000 were made in that year. Following William Danforth's death in 1955 and bequests from him to the foundation, the value of its assets leaped to about $110 million in 1958, and the foundation made grants that year in excess of $2.5 million. Since that date, there have been a number of fluctuations in the value of foundation assets. In 1970, they totalled approximately $162 million; in 1977 about $97 million; and in 1980 about $87 million. Annual grants made by the foundation have varied accordingly, from $2 million to $12 million annually.

The foundation is governed by a nine-member board of trustees, of which the chairman is the grandson of William Danforth. Administration of the foundation is carried on from offices located at 222 South Central Avenue, St. Louis, Missouri 63105, under the direction of a president.

For additional information, see *Annual Reports* published by the foundation since the 1950s, especially the report for 1977, the fiftieth anniversary of the foundation. See also William H. Danforth obituary, *New York Times* (1955), p. 48.

HARRIET C. OWSLEY

**DAN MURPHY FOUNDATION.** The Dan Murphy Foundation was incorporated in California in 1957 as a private charitable trust. Its funding was donated by the late Bernadine Murphy Donohue.

Officers and directors of the foundation include Daniel J. Donohue, president; Joseph D. Peeler, vice-president, assistant secretary, assistant treasurer, and a member of the Los Angeles law firm of Musick, Peeler, and Garrett; Richard A. Grant, Jr., secretary and treasurer of the foundation and a member of the board of directors of California Portland Cement Company. Oscar T. Lawler, Monsignor Benjamin G. Hawkes, and Rosemary E. Donohue are other trustees of the Dan Murphy Foundation. Lawler is a former chairman of the executive committee of the Security Pacific National Bank of Los Angeles, a member of the board of directors of the Union Pacific Corporation, and serves on the board of several Los Angeles area philanthropic organizations. James Francis Cardinal McIntyre, who died in 1979, was a foundation Vice-President and Trustee.

The Dan Murphy Foundation is a general charitable institution with an emphasis on local giving in the Greater Los Angeles area. It provides grants for

Roman Catholic Church support, religious and charitable associations, hospitals, secondary education, and youth and child welfare programs.

While many foundations saw erosion of their assets due to inflation and stock market reverses during the decade of the 1970s, the portfolio of the Dan Murphy Foundation increased to $82,206,415 (year ended 12/31/79) from $48,634,586 (fiscal 1975). By the beginning of the 1980s, it was among the one hundred largest foundations in the nation.

In 1979, the foundation awarded fifty-three grants totalling $12,211,285, five times the amount awarded in 1975 ($2,517,450). This dramatic increase in funding was due exclusively to a $9.8 million grant to the Roman Catholic archbishop of Los Angeles in the form of 212,065 shares of California Portland Cement Company common stock.

Under section 4943 of the Internal Revenue Code, a part of the stock which the foundation held in the California Portland Cement Company constituted "excess business holdings" which would have become subject to an annual 5 percent excess tax if not disposed of by February 4, 1980. The stock the foundation had to dispose of was slightly more than 6 percent of the outstanding stock of California Portland Cement Company. Acting on the advice of counsel, such stock was transferred in 1978 and 1979 to the archbishop of Los Angeles in lieu of cash contributions. By so doing, the foundation was able to rid itself of its excess business holdings without incurring the costs of filing a registration statement and also satisfying Internal Revenue Code distribution requirements. Thus, on December 4, 1978, 50,000 shares were transferred to the archbishop, and on April 19, 1979, 212,065 shares were transferred to the archbishop.

Twenty-one grants and fully 83 percent of all grant dollars were in the form of Roman Catholic giving, primarily to the Los Angeles archbishop, although other church recipients were located in Alaska, New York, West Virginia, and Wisconsin. Youth and child welfare programs—especially for summer camp programs sponsored by the Boy Scouts of America, Los Angeles, and the YMCA, Los Angeles—received support. However, the Youth Education Fund administered by the Roman Catholic archbishop of Los Angeles received over 90 percent of all funding in the youth and child welfare categories.

All hospitals and health-related institutions which received support by grants from the Dan Murphy Foundation were affiliated with the Roman Catholic Church. Education, social welfare, and cultural programs together received less than 4 percent of all grant dollars. In 1979, most grantees had been previous recipients of Dan Murphy Foundation grants.

The offices of the Dan Murphy Foundation are located at 3701 Wilshire Boulevard, Suite 320, Los Angeles, California 90010.

Almost the only additional sources of information readily available to the public on this foundation are the annual reports and returns filed by it with the Internal Revenue Service, and the various Foundation Center publications. See, however, *Guide to California Foundations* (1976) and 4th ed. (1982). See also John Fleischman, "Future of Foundations in Los Angeles," *Los Angeles Times*

(January 26, 1975), section V, p. 5; and "California Portland Stake Draws Offer by Martin Marietta," and "California Portland Cement," *Wall Street Journal* (April 11, 1979, p. 12; April 23, 1979, p. 20).

LARRY D. GIVENS

**DAVID AND LUCILE PACKARD FOUNDATION, THE.** Incorporated in 1964 in California, the Packard Foundation is named for its donors. David Packard is one of the two founders and chairman of the board of Hewlett-Packard Company, a leading manufacturer of electronic measuring instruments.

Assets of the foundation were valued at about $1.4 million in 1968. Since that time, gifts of $580,000 in 1975, over $6 million in 1979, and over $9 million in 1980 have swelled assets to about $33 million in 1981.

Foundation giving has been restricted primarily to the San Francisco and Monterey Bay areas of California, although a few grants may be made in the Pueblo area of Colorado. Also, a few national and international grants in the areas of population studies and the environment may be made. Foundation support is concentrated in the following areas: arts, particularly the performing arts; community programs; conservation; education; and health. The foundation made 242 grants in 1980 in amounts ranging from a few thousand dollars to $50,000.

The Packard Foundation is governed by an eight-member board of trustees, with the donors serving as president and vice-president and with their four children on the board. Administration of the foundation is carried on from offices located at 330 Second Street, Post Office Box 1330, Los Altos, California 94022, under the direction of an executive director.

For further information, see *Annual Reports* of the foundation, published since the 1970s.

**DAVIS FOUNDATIONS.** See Arthur Vining Davis Foundations, The.

**DECAMP FOUNDATION.** See Ira W. DeCamp Foundation, The.

**DELANY CHARITABLE TRUST.** See Beatrice P. Delany Charitable Trust.

**DEL E. WEBB FOUNDATION.** Del E. Webb, former semiprofessional baseball player, a principal owner of the New York Yankees from 1945 to 1964, the founder-owner of the multimillion-dollar Del E. Webb Corporation with large interests in real estate, construction, and hotels, established the foundation bearing his name in Arizona in 1960.

The assets and grants of the Del E. Webb Foundation were modest until the death of Webb in 1974 and the receipt in 1977 of some $37 million from his estate. Since then, the foundation has been making grants of approximately $3 million annually.

The foundation has concentrated its grants in Arizona, Nevada, and southern California, primarily to support medicine and medical research institutions. Two directors administer its assets, which in 1979 amounted to about $41 million, from offices located at 3800 North Central Avenue, Phoenix, Arizona 85012.

Almost the only additional sources of information on this foundation readily available to the public are the annual reports and returns filed by it with the Internal Revenue Service, and the various Foundation Center publications. See, however, Del E. Webb obituary, *New York Times* (July 5, 1974), p. 24.

**DE RANCE, INC.** The largest foundation in Wisconsin, holding one-third of the total foundation money in the state, De Rance, Inc., is also the largest foundation in the country devoted to Roman Catholic interests. The foundation's present principal source of funds was a $97 million package of cash and securities that came to De Rance in 1970 from Philip Morris, Inc., in exchange for Miller Brewing stock.

De Rance, Inc., was founded in 1946 by Harry G. John, a grandson of the founder of the Miller Brewing Company and president of the brewery at the time. As heir to nearly half of the Miller stock, John decided to incorporate a private foundation to steer money primarily to religious sources, particularly those identified with the Roman Catholic Church. Accordingly, John soon stepped down from the Miller presidency to devote his full-time energies and resources to the foundation.

Prior to the Philip Morris take-over, all of the assets of the foundation came from Harry G. John himself, who received his inheritance in 1952 and gave most of it to De Rance, Inc. John named De Rance for an obscure French monk, Abbé Armond-Jeans de Rance, who led the strictly contemplative Trappists in the seventeenth century and encouraged among his monks the practice of austerity even at the cost of ruined health.

During the first twenty years of its operation, a period of more limited assets and more modest grants, De Rance, Inc., emphasized support to the contemplative orders of the church, particularly the Trappists, both at home and abroad. During this same period, growing out of Harry John's personal interests and travels among native Americans in the Dakotas, grants were made to establish Roman Catholic mission schools and community centers in those areas.

Grants along these lines conformed to the fundamental purpose of De Rance to aid religious, charitable, and educational organizations: to promote religion, education, and the care of the sick, aged, or helpless; and to improve the religious, mental, moral, and physical well-being of all persons who may be selected as beneficiaries. The religion to be promoted in carrying out the foregoing purposes is Roman Catholicism, but the assistance and promotion of educational and charitable programs need not be confined entirely to Roman Catholic agencies. Of specific concern are blacks and native Americans and the missions in the developing countries of Latin America, Africa, and Asia.

The 1970 take-over of Miller Brewing Company stock by Philip Morris exploded the foundation's assets some twentyfold. Grants previously amounted to one million dollars a year. Since then, grants have averaged better than $10 million a year. For the year ending December 31, 1980, the market assets of De Rance were $161,641,649; and grants, 371 of them, totalled $11,429,651.

In recent years, grants have also become more systematized. Geographically, grants are categorized into four units: Wisconsin, the United States, Latin America, and foreign (the rest of the world). The categories themselves indicate priority interests in the needs of Wisconsin and Latin America. Areas of current special interest include the needs of a select number of small colleges (scattered from upstate Wisconsin to Nairobi, Kenya), electronic communications, prolife initiatives, and promotion of devotion to the Sacred Heart of Jesus.

The International Institute of the Heart of Jesus (IIHJ) was established early in the seventies after lengthy and detailed correspondence with Vatican officials. Its purpose is to promote donations to the Heart of Jesus, which, in more concrete terms, aims to help institutions, organizations, and movements dedicated to promoting the Roman Catholic Church and her missions in the world. The Sacred Heart symbolizes Christ's love of humanity. According to Harry John, spiritual criteria, including loyalty to the official teaching of the church and signs of love for Christ, are used in determining its grants. The teachings, it should be emphasized, come from bishops and the pope, not from theologians. IIHJ now has main offices in Rome and also at the foundation headquarters in suburban Milwaukee, with others in Colombia, Ireland, Ghana, and Spain. In 1981, IIHJ received six grants, five for religious, educational, and charitable activity ($1,075,000) and another for administrative costs ($206,751). The largest grants of the institute itself go to organizations established to preach and propagate devotion to the Heart of Jesus.

De Rance's grants for propagation go far beyond those awarded through the institute. In 1981, for example, its largest grant was one of $700,000 to aid in the purchase and furnishing of the Pope John Paul II Pilgrims' Center, in Rome. Of its twenty-seven grants of over $100,000 each in 1981, half were awards to propagate the faith in such far away places as Uganda, Kenya, Ecuador, India, Thailand, Egypt, Sudan, Poland, and Japan.

Perhaps the most exciting new area of interest at De Rance since 1980 has been in the field of electronic communications, marked by the purchase of interests in a variety of radio and television stations across the country. In El Paso, Texas, a T.V. station has been purchased from an evangelical group. De Rance credits "evangelicals" as being "way ahead" of other religious institutions in propagating the faith via electronic media. Viewing radio and T.V. stations as "windows" by which to view the Roman Catholic Church, De Rance has interests in other stations in St. Louis and Los Angeles and is exploring the acquisition of others. Much attention is being given to researching formats other than preaching that will prove to be innovative and effective means of propagating the faith. The use of drama is one approach under consideration. Undergirding the foundation's movement into radio and television is its conviction that much commercial programming today is antifamily in orientation. Suggestive of this concern was its 1981 grant of $47,500 to Morality in Media, in New York City, an agency which monitors regulation of the cable industry and conducts a nationwide alert on "cableporn."

Also expressive of De Rance's views concerning the deterioration of family values in modern society is its aggressive and sometimes controversial support of the natural family planning and antiabortion movements in recent years. In 1979, for example, $1,168,424 was awarded to organizations involved in the natural family planning and antiabortion movements. Its largest grant, $439,280 that year, was to the Human Life Center at St. John's University, in Minnesota, which at the time considered itself the largest antiabortion organization in the nation. Other antiabortion agencies receiving grants that year included Americans United for Life, the Friends for Life, the National Family Planning Guild, and the Catholic League for Religious and Civil Rights.

Less money was provided for this purpose in 1981. The Divine Word Missionaries of the Japan Family Life Association, in Tokyo, received $275,000, largely for production of the movie *Mother Teresa on Reverence for Life* and for support of a study of natural family planning. Nationally, the largest grant in this area, $75,000, went to the National Commission on Human Life, Reproduction and Rhythm, based in Oak Park, Illinois, whose initial focus has been broadened to include the right-to-life issue. Other antiabortion organizations receiving lesser grants in 1981 included Catholics United for Life, the Human Life Center at St. John's University, in Minnesota, and the Pro-Life Action League, in Chicago. The Pro-Life League's aggressive techniques of sit-ins and confrontation of clients at clinics which perform abortions have become highly controversial within the antiabortion movement itself.

While these unique and controversial areas of grant activity stir up public controversy, they constitute only a small portion of De Rance's annual giving. In 1981, for example, the foundation approved 375 grants totalling $9,456,546, with gifts ranging from $700,000 to $500 each. De Rance's generosity consistently exceeds by a large margin minimum federal requirements for foundation giving.

More typical of De Rance's giving are its contributions to small parochial educational institutions and missions serving the underprivileged and handicapped at home and abroad. Cardinal Newman College, in Normandy, Missouri, for example, received over $650,000 in gifts in 1981, largely for operational support. Similarly, Mount Senario College, in Ladysmith, Wisconsin, which educates poor native American students living in the area, received in 1981 some $280,000, mainly to discharge its debts. Numerous, more modest grants have been awarded to inner-city private schools, both Catholic and non-Catholic, serving minority students. Abroad, the largest gift in the educational and foreign missions field in 1981 was to an archdiocese in Sudan ($300,000) to construct a center for the rehabilitation of handicapped children. Another large sum ($200,000) was given to the Christ of the Andes Mission, in Ecuador, for its Working Boys' Center. All in all, roughly half of De Rance support has been going abroad in recent years, mostly to the poorer areas of the world and to programs discovered by the foundation's directors while visiting grantee-programs abroad.

Foundation personnel claim that the biggest problem confronting them is the overwhelming number of requests for funding they receive from all around the world. Each year, grant requests total more than the market asset value of the foundation itself, which was $151,413,317 in 1981. As has been suggested, however, the aggressive posture of De Rance on sensitive issues, such as abortion and propagation of the Roman Catholic faith, results in controversy and attracts the press. For example, in 1981 an association of six inner-city Roman Catholic schools refused a grant of $60,000 because the foundation insisted the schools choose certain religion textbooks for their classes. A De Rance representative commented that the texts in use did not reflect "the fullness of [Catholic] doctrine." One of the school's priestly administrators claimed that the foundation was using its money "to force its religious orientation on others."

In 1979, a special grant of $20,000 to the Human Life Center at St. John's University, in Minnesota, "to sponsor a national conference on alternatives to Planned Parenthood" received press attention. The conference was eventually cancelled. A document published by the National Organization for Women (NOW), in Washington, D.C., listed the Human Life Center as "a virulently anti-birth-control group that focuses its venom on the contraception-abortion link and on Planned Parenthood." That year, the Human Life Center received $439,280 from the foundation.

Issues of the above nature underscore both the strict interpretation of Catholic doctrine, reflective of the namesake of the De Rance foundation and the strong hand of Harry G. John in making awards in line with the "spiritual criteria" mentioned earlier. He serves as president and treasurer of the foundation. Assisting him in a major way are three other directors: his wife, Erika; his longtime associate and Catholic philosopher, Donald Gallagher, who serves as executive vice-president; and Gallagher's wife, Adele, who serves as project evaluator. Both wives serve also as vice-presidents. The staff of some twenty-two individuals includes a librarian and a cook to accommodate the steady stream of priests, nuns, missionaries, and theologians that make their way from all over the world to seek support for their projects.

The personality of Harry John figures prominently also in the financial management of De Rance's market assets. As one who has a reputation of liking "to see a lot of action" in the foundation's portfolio, John has engaged portfolio managers with matching reputations in recent years. In the mid-seventies, for example, he engaged one of Wall Street's most storied and controversial figures, Gerald Tsai, the prototype of the aggressive, fast-trading money manager. In recent years, First Wilshire Securities Management, in Los Angeles, has had the De Rance account. Wilshire's Fred Astman and Noble Trenham have increased the foundation's assets by about 50 percent since 1979.

In short, then, De Rance, Inc., represents the institutionalization of the generosity, philosophy, and resolute commitment to a deepening relationship with his church of a very extraordinary man, Harry G. John, and a foundation which gives away $10 million a year.

Administration of the foundation is carried on from offices located at 7700 West Blue Mound Road, Milwaukee, Wisconsin 53213, under the direction of the president.

Almost the only additional information readily available to the public on this foundation are the annual reports and returns filed by it with the Internal Revenue Service, and the various Foundation Center publications. See, however, "Armand Jean Le Bouthillier De Rance," *The New Catholic Encyclopedia,* vol. 12 (1967), p. 78. See also the following articles appearing in the *Milwaukee Journal*: David L. Beale, "Obscure Foundation Gives Away Millions" (October 31, 1976) and "The Quiet Man Who Gives Millions" (November 1, 1976); Anne Curley, "Foundation Here Gets Top Investor Marks" (July 17, 1979); and Barbara Dembski, "Big Money Finances Abortion Battle" (August 6, 1981).

MILTON J. HUBER

**DEWITT WALLACE FUND, INC.** DeWitt Wallace and his wife, Lila Acheson Wallace, were the founders in 1921 of the Reader's Digest Association, Inc. The ensuing profits from the association's publication of the *Reader's Digest* and from other business ventures enabled Wallace to establish the DeWitt Wallace Fund, Inc., in New York in 1965; it had been preceded by the establishment of the L.A.W. Fund, Inc.,* by Lila Wallace in 1956.

With its assets, which grew from about $27 million to approximately $46 million at present, the fund has primarily supported independent schools through a variety of grants. In 1980, 36 percent of the approximately $5 million granted in that year was given to two community foundations, the New York Community Trust* and the Saint Paul Foundation* (Minnesota), which in turn made grants within those funds' traditional areas of giving. Well over 50 percent of the grantees of the DeWitt Wallace Fund have been located in the northeastern United States, particularly New York City.

The fund is governed by a five-member board of directors, all of whom, including Lila Wallace, have past or present connections with the Reader's Digest Association, Inc. Administration of the fund is carried on from offices located at 200 Park Avenue, 34th Floor, New York, New York 10166, under the direction of a secretary who is also secretary of the L.A.W. Fund, Inc. The Wallace Fund also has some of the same directors and occupies the same offices as the L.A.W. Fund, Inc.

Almost the only additional information readily available to the public on this foundation are the annual reports and returns filed by it with the Internal Revenue Service, and the various Foundation Center publications.

**DODGE FOUNDATION.** See Geraldine R. Dodge Foundation, Incorporated.

**DOHENY FOUNDATION.** See Carrie Estelle Doheny Foundation.

**DON AND SYBIL HARRINGTON FOUNDATION, THE.** Established in Texas in 1951, the Harrington Foundation bears the name of its founders, Donald D. Harrington and his wife, Sybil Harrington. Donald D. Harrington was born in Illinois, educated in Missouri, and associated with the Standard Oil Company early in his career in Mexico and South America. He was associated with Shell Oil Company in the early days of the Smackover Field, Arkansas, and Corsicana, Texas. In 1926, he entered the Texas panhandle oil boom. This was the beginning of a success story leading to an international reputation in the oil and gas industry, real estate, and other investments. Initially, the foundation was small, and until 1974 its assets amounted to only about a million dollars. In that year Harrington died, and his property was bequeathed to the foundation. The distribution of the assets proved to be very complicated, and the foundation did not begin to receive funds from Harrington's estate until 1976. From that time until 1980, the foundation received some $32 million in gifts. Foundation assets in 1981 stood at about $55.5 million, and its grants for 1981 amounted to over $4.5 million.

Throughout its entire existence, the Harrington Foundation's areas of interest have remained substantially the same. In 1957, for example, when its assets were about $330,000 and its grants for the year amounted to $41,000, the foundation's stated areas of interest were: hospitals and health services; scholarships and educational associations; support for Protestant churches; and music and the entertainment arts. Today, its interests include hospitals and health-care agencies, cultural programs, higher education, youth agencies, social services, and civic affairs. The primary locality of interest is the city of Amarillo and the panhandle of Texas. Illustrative of the aid provided by this foundation over the years are the following contributions: over $6 million to the Don and Sybil Harrington Cancer Center, Amarillo; $1.2 million in scholarships grants to West Texas State University; $2 million to St. Luke's Hospital, Phoenix, Arizona; $1 million to the Metropolitan Opera Association, New York; and $3.5 million to the Panhandle Plains Historical Society.

The foundation is governed by a six-member board of trustees. Sybil Harrington served as president of the board from April, 1974, to April, 1982. She retired at that time but is still a board member. Administration of the foundation is carried on from offices located at 700 First National Place, 801 South Fillmore, Amarillo, Texas 79101, under the direction of the president.

Almost the only additional information on this foundation readily available to the public are the annual reports and other returns filed by it with the Internal Revenue Service, and the various Foundation Center publications.

**DONNER FOUNDATION.** See Independence Foundation; William H. Donner Foundation, Inc., The.

**DOUGLAS FOUNDATION.** See McDonnell Douglas Foundation, Inc.

**DOW FOUNDATION.** See Herbert H. and Grace A. Dow Foundation, The.

**DR. SCHOLL FOUNDATION.** The Dr. Scholl Foundation was originally incorporated in 1947 in Illinois under the name of the William M. Scholl Foundation. Dr. William M. Scholl, the foundation's principal donor, was a leader in medical care of the lower extremities of the human body, particularly the feet. He founded the Scholl Manufacturing Company, which brought Scholl a considerable amount of wealth. Eventually, this company became a division of the Schering-Plough Corporation and now is an international manufacturer of footwear and foot-care products.

In its early years, the foundation's assets and resultant grants were small. In 1953, for example, assets were valued at about $160,000, and grants totalled about $10,000. By 1968, the year of Scholl's death, assets had risen in value to about $0.5 million, and grants for that year amounted to about $35,000. During these early years, foundation grants were largely for the Roman Catholic Church, higher and secondary education, including medical schools, and were restricted primarily to the Chicago area.

Following Scholl's death in 1968, the name of the foundation was changed to its present one in 1973 and assets swelled to about $12 million by 1975. Grants of about $1.5 million were made in that year. It was in this period, too, that the foundation targeted orthopedics as a special area of interest within its general ones of education and the health sciences.

From the 1970s and on into the 1980s, the value of the assets held by the foundation grew considerably. By 1979, for example, assets were worth about $68.5 million, and in 1980 they increased to about $83 million. During these same years, annual grants increased from about $3.25 million to approximately $5 million. Education, particularly medical education and research, received about 33 percent of annual funding; civic and economic associations, social welfare agencies, and hospitals and ancillary organizations each received about 17 percent of funding; the remainder was disbursed to religious, cultural, and other organizations. Geographically, the foundation continued to make grants primarily in the Chicago area.

The foundation is governed by an eleven-member board of trustees which includes members of the Scholl family acting as president and vice-president of the board. Administration of the foundation is carried on from offices located at 111 West Washington Street, Suite 2137, Chicago, Illinois 60602, under the direction of an executive director.

Almost the only additional sources of information readily available to the public on this foundation are the annual reports and returns filed by it with the Internal Revenue Service, and the various Foundation Center publications. See, however, "Guidelines for Grants" (n.d.) a one-page sheet issued by the foundation which contains some general information about it.

**DUKE ENDOWMENT, THE.** The Duke Endowment was established by the late James B. Duke on December 11, 1924, by trust indenture. Duke's original gift was $40 million. He died on October 10, 1925, and through his will, left additional assets worth $67 million to the Duke Endowment.

The Duke family's tobacco products manufacturing business began modestly in the years immediately following the Civil War. By the early 1890s, however, James B. Duke, through a series of mergers and consolidations, became president of the American Tobacco Company. At that time, the American Tobacco Company was reported to control more than 90 percent of the domestic paper cigarette manufacturing business. This corporation was dissolved in 1911 when the United States Supreme Court upheld the constitutionality of the Sherman Anti-Trust Act. Duke's attention then turned to the development and production of hydroelectric power in the Piedmont of North and South Carolina. The Southern Power Company, later named Duke Power Company, was incorporated by Duke interests in 1905. Duke had other business interests in textiles and in the early 1920s held a major block of shares of stock in the Aluminum Company of America.

Duke, through the trust indenture, established four groups of beneficiaries of his philanthropy: higher education, hospitals, orphanages, and the rural United Methodist Church in North Carolina and retired Methodist preachers. Recipients were limited to organizations and institutions located in North Carolina and South Carolina.

The Duke family had a long-standing interest in Trinity College, a small liberal arts college located in Durham, North Carolina. James B. Duke was a trustee of Trinity College, as were his father, Washington, and his brother, Benjamin. The Duke family had contributed heavily to Trinity College in 1892 when it was attracted to Durham from its more rural setting in Trinity, North Carolina, near Asheboro. Through the indenture which established the Duke Endowment, James B. Duke agreed to give financial support to Trinity College sufficient to transform it into a national university if its governing board would agree to change the name of the college to Duke University, in honor of his father. The Trinity College board of trustees unanimously agreed to the name change on December 29, 1924.

Immediately, trustees made available $6 million to Duke University for purchasing land and construction of a physical plant. Duke suggested that Trinity College be retained as the men's undergraduate college and that new colleges and schools be organized, including "a School of Religious Training, a School for Training Teachers, a School of Chemistry, a Law School, a Co-ordinate College for Women, a School of Business Administration, a Graduate School of Arts and Sciences, a Medical School, and an Engineering School, as and when funds are available."

The following year, through Duke's will, an additional $4 million was bequeathed to Duke University to build "a Medical School, Hospital and Nurses Home," and $7 million more was bequeathed for other capital purposes.

In addition to capital funds described above, totalling $17 million, Duke University has received a major share of income from the Duke Endowment's investments. By the end of 1980, Duke University had received $243,873,645 from the Duke Endowment, 45 percent of the endowment's total grants and distributions.

Three other educational institutions were named as beneficiaries: Davidson College, Furman University, and Johnson C. Smith University. As of December 31, 1980, trustees of the Duke Endowment had directed the following amounts to these institutions:

| | |
|---|---:|
| Davidson College, Davidson, N.C. | $20,546,299 |
| Furman University, Greenville, S.C. | $20,675,175 |
| Johnson C. Smith University, Charlotte, N.C. | $16,933,567 |

Hospitals were selected as another principal object of the Duke Endowment because James Duke believed that hospitals had become indispensable institutions, not only by way of ministering to the sick but by generally increasing human efficiency and prolonging human life. Therefore, hospitals not operated for private gain in North Carolina and South Carolina are eligible for annual Duke Endowment support. In 1980, 186 hospitals in the two states received $15,325,390 for both operating programs and capital purposes. Support of hospitals during the last fifty-six years totals $187,395,712.

The third area of concern selected by James Duke was the care of orphaned children—those, he felt, who are most unable to help themselves. During 1980, forty-three residential child-care agencies and institutions received $1,488,785. Trustees have directed $22,676,289 to the care of orphaned and half-orphaned children since 1924.

Finally, Duke selected the rural United Methodist Church in North Carolina and retired Methodist preachers for assistance. In 1980, trustees directed $1,316,452 toward the building, operation, and maintenance of such churches. An additional $361,873 went to the United Methodist church in North Carolina for distribution to retired ministers and their widows and dependent children. Support over the years for building, operating, and maintaining rural United Methodist Churches in North Carolina totals $20,649,233; $5,683,897 has been directed to retired preachers and their families.

Total appropriations to all beneficiaries since 1924 exceeded $538 million dollars at the close of 1980.

Trustees of the Duke Endowment are concerned that support of the four educational institutions named by James Duke has not kept pace with needs. Trustees are faced with trying to do more for these institutions and at the same time maintain a desired level of assistance for hospitals and child-caring institutions in North and South Carolina, and for rural United Methodist Churches in North Carolina and retired ministers. Many of the recipient institutions have received annual support in each of the intervening years since the 1924 establishment of the endowment. This partnership has led to many creative and imaginative approaches to meeting the long-term needs of these institutions and those served by them.

Trustees of the Duke Endowment employ thirty-four full-time professional and support personnel. The endowment's executive director, other administrative staff, and the programs staff in child care, education, and hospitals are located in Charlotte, North Carolina. The Duke Endowment maintained an administrative office in New York City from its founding until 1979.

A board of fifteen trustees directs the affairs of the Duke Endowment. James Duke suggested in the indenture, but did not require, that a majority of trustees should be natives or residents of North Carolina or South Carolina. Trustees of the Duke Endowment meet ten times a year. Trustees' committees are organized coincidental with the four major areas of interest: educational institutions, rural churches, hospitals, and child care. Other committees include: audit, finance, investments, personnel and retirement plan, and public information. Most trustees serve on at least three committees. Trustees of the Duke Endowment also serve as directors and members of the Angier B. Duke Memorial and the Fund Established by Will of Nanaline H. Duke for Duke University.

Assets of the Duke Endowment were valued at $406,513,218 in 1981. Almost $450 million of the total income earned on the investments of the Duke Endowment since 1924 has come from dividends on the common stock of Duke Power Company. This represents 68.4 percent of total income. Other investments include a broad range of United States government obligations, corporate bonds and notes, and stocks.

Offices of the Duke Endowment are located at the City National Center, Charlotte, North Carolina 28202, and at 3329 Chapel Hill Boulevard, Durham, North Carolina 27707.

For further information, see *Annual Reports* of the endowment, published continuously since 1960. See also the following biographies: John Wilber Jenkins, *James B. Duke—Master Builder* (1927); and Robert F. Durden, *The Dukes of Durham, 1865–1929* (1975). Some archival material of the endowment is housed in its Charlotte office. The major portion, however, is located in the Duke University Archives.

M. LANEY FUNDERBURK, JR.

**DU PONT FUND.** See Jessie Ball du Pont Religious, Charitable, and Educational Fund.

## E

**EASTMAN KODAK CHARITABLE TRUST.** A company-sponsored foundation, the Eastman Kodak Charitable Trust was established in New York in 1952 with an initial gift from the Eastman Kodak Company, of Rochester, New York. As the result of further contributions by the company, the foundation's assets grew to about $41 million in 1981.

The foundation's grants traditionally have been made to Rochester organizations, such as local institutions of higher learning, the local community chest, and a local photographic museum. Applications for grants from other areas are not invited. Typically, eight grants totalling about $3 million were made to local institutions in 1978. The following year there were twenty-four such grants totalling about $5 million, of which the University of Rochester received $1,400,000, the Rochester Institute of Technology was awarded $200,000, the community chest obtained $1,875,000, and almost $1 million went to the International Museum of Photography, which is located in the George Eastman House.

In 1981, grants totalling in excess of $10 million were made by the foundation. Of this total, 47 percent was devoted to education; 30 percent to health and community services; 16 percent to civic and cultural programs; and 7 percent to other purposes.

The sole and governing trustee of the Kodak Charitable Trust is the Lincoln First Bank of Rochester, Post Office Box 1412, Rochester, New York 14603. This bank is also the mailing address of the foundation, whose administration is carried on by trust officers of the bank.

Almost the only additional information on this foundation readily available to the public are the annual report and returns filed by it with the Internal Revenue Service, and the various Foundation Center publications. See, however, *Sharing* (1981), an informational brochure published by the foundation.

**EDNA MCCONNELL CLARK FOUNDATION, THE.** Edna McConnell Clark, for whom this foundation is named, was the daughter of David H.

McConnell, who, in 1886, founded Avon Products, Incorporated. Avon subsequently grew to be a giant in the cosmetics industry.

W. Van Alan Clark, following college and an early association with several other companies, in 1920 joined the California Perfume Company, which was later absorbed by Avon. In the 1920s, Clark married Edna McConnell and also became Avon's vice-president in charge of manufacturing. In 1944, Clark was elected chairman of the board of trustees of Avon Products and remained a director until the year before his death in 1975.

Established by the Clarks in New York in 1950, assets of the Edna McConnell Clark Foundation in 1953 consisted of about $30,000 worth of stock in Avon Products, Incorporated; by 1958, assets amounted to about $350,000. Annual grants during this period ranged from about $8,500 to $16,500. Stated interests of the foundation during this time included higher and secondary education, nursing education, youth agencies, child welfare, care of the aged, and rehabilitation of the handicapped.

The slow growth in assets and grant-making activity of the Clark Foundation continued until 1969. In that year, the Clarks donated $126,750,000 worth of stock in Avon Products, Incorporated, to the foundation which had been separately incorporated in that same year in Delaware. The Delaware foundation listed as its mailing address that of the New York foundation. In 1972, the foundation sold a substantial portion of its stock in Avon Products and acquired diversified stocks in other corporations. In 1974, the Delaware foundation merged into the New York foundation, with the sole address of the foundation since then listed as Room 900, 250 Park Avenue, New York, New York 10017. It appears probable that these developments were due to the passage of the U.S. Tax Reform Act of 1969 as nearly one-third of the provisions of that act affected tax-exempt organizations and charitable contributions.

Up until the 1960s, Edna Clark had run the foundation virtually by herself, her creed and that of the foundation being to help those persons least helped by the established institutions and organizations of society. With the significant increase in foundation assets at that time and consequent broadening of its scope of activities, a professional staff was then added.

By the time W. Van Alan Clark died in 1976, at the age of eighty-eight, (Edna Clark died in 1982, at the age of ninety-six), the foundation had embarked on a program of aid for children, the elderly, the poor, and the developing world. Since that time, the foundation has refined its operations to cover four specifically designated programs: the Program for Children, which seeks to assure that children now in foster and institutional care are provided permanent families; the Program in Jobs for the Disadvantaged, which seeks to improve the school-to-work transition of urban disadvantaged youth; the Program for Justice, which seeks more rational, humane, and effective ways of dealing with those in the criminal justice system; and the Program in Tropical Disease Research, which seeks the reduction of schistosmoiasis (snail fever). In making grants, which now total about $12 million annually, it has become the foundation's policy to allocate about 90 percent of the total grants to these four programs, with the remainder going to out-of-program projects.

Illustrative of its grants program are the following major grants awarded in 1982 in each of the four program areas: $205,000—the Children's Defense Fund, Washington, D.C.; $100,000—Youthwork, Inc., Washington, D.C.; $110,000—Vera Institute of Justice, New York, New York; $215,000—University Hospitals of Cleveland, Cleveland, Ohio.

Three sons of the founders are on the six-member governing board of trustees of the Clark Foundation, which in 1981 had assets of about $200 million. One of the sons serves as chairman of the board. Administration of the foundation is carried on from offices located at 250 Park Avenue, Room 900, New York, New York 10017, under the direction of a president.

For further information, see *Annual Reports* of the foundation, published continuously since 1976; and an information pamphlet, *Current Goals and Programs* (1981). See also W. Van Alan Clark obituary, *New York Times* (October 16, 1976), p. 26; and Edna McConnell Clark obituary, *New York Times*, (April 22, 1982), p. 23.

**EDWARD JOHN NOBLE FOUNDATION.** The founder of the Edward John Noble Foundation was born in northern New York in 1882. He grew up there, gaining a love for the St. Lawrence Valley region that stayed with him all his life. In 1905, he graduated from Yale University, and in 1913, he founded the Life Saver Company. He became interested in aviation, and in 1938, he was appointed as the first head of the Civil Aeronautics Authority. Leaving government service in the 1940s, he entered another field of business activity—broadcasting, acquiring the Blue Radio Network from the National Broadcasting Company and founding the American Broadcasting Company.

In 1940, Noble created the Edward John Noble Foundation and made contributions to it at intervals thereafter. At his death, in 1958, the bulk of his estate also went to the foundation.

The foundation was established as a charitable trust under Connecticut law "for such...charitable, religious, scientific, literary, or educational purposes as the trustees...shall deem likely to promote the welfare of mankind." In its early years, the foundation's activities were initiated mainly by Noble, who combined keen business acumen with a strong sense of service.

For example, in 1947, aware of a serious shortage of hospital facilities in the smaller towns of the St. Lawrence Valley region, Noble conceived a plan by which a group of three new hospitals could be built and run under a central management system. The plan was to stimulate community involvement by sharing the costs between private citizens and the foundation and to realize the advantages of centralized management and services. Three communities were selected for the experiment, and following pledges by the foundation, highly successful local fund-raising drives brought together the remainder of the needed sum. By 1952, the three Edward John Noble Hospitals were complete and in operation. The joint management plan devised by Noble proved to be extremely workable and attracted national attention.

Noble was also convinced of the importance of developing leadership potential in American youth. In 1957, the foundation initiated a large new program to finance the graduate training of students who had demonstrated outstanding leadership potential by the time they had reached their senior year in college. Convinced that such potential could not necessarily be determined by any conventional academic measurement, Mr. Noble instead selected a group of colleges and universities across the country and asked the president of each to nominate one candidate a year for a National Leadership Fellowship, with personal leadership qualities rather than academic distinction as the principal criterion for selection. The number of institutions involved in this successful experiment eventually reached nearly fifty. In all, more than five hundred young students participated in the program, which was later merged with a new International Fellows Program initiated by the foundation in 1960 at Columbia University.

The purpose of this latter program was to develop leaders in a number of different academic and professional fields—economics, law, journalism, business administration, engineering, medicine, and others—who also possessed the interest, ability, and training to act effectively on the international scene. Selected from among the most promising graduate students accepted by the professional schools and graduate faculties of Columbia University, fellows took part in one or two years of seminars, lectures, and discussions with officials of the United States government and the United Nations and conducted independent study of a particular foreign country or region. The ultimate objective of the program was to inspire the fellow with an interest in the international aspects of his chosen profession and to encourage him to spend at least part of his career in government service. From 1960 to 1974, over seven hundred fellows took part.

During its first three decades, the foundation made numerous other grants for medical education and research and for general education, as well as for social services to disadvantaged young people.

After Noble's death, the board of trustees that he had appointed as "a single small group of active and interested individuals familiar with his life, background, thinking and purpose" carried on the direction of the foundation's work and the management of its assets. That board included a member of his family, a university president, and several other business and professional leaders with interests in education and health, a concern for broadening educational opportunity, and a strong belief in the value of the arts and humanities.

During the 1960s and 1970s, massive government financing and soaring costs of medical research and hospital care led the Noble Foundation to focus its health concerns on very specific issues, that is, encouragement of the development of family-practice physicians motivated to serve in rural communities in northern New York, dissemination of effective family planning programs, and education on the effects of population growth.

In these same years, the trustees became increasingly concerned about strengthening the impact of the arts in American culture and education, and they expanded the Noble Foundation's support of programs to assist artists, to develop audiences, and to support education in the performing and visual arts. The diversity and the magnitude of the needs in these fields were so great that the foundation felt compelled to concentrate its support geographically on New York City institutions, and in the last few years on one art form at a time (the current priority is music). During the 1970s, nearly one hundred organizations, museums, schools, and colleges were assisted in efforts to develop improved educational programs in the arts for New York City school children, especially the most disadvantaged, and their teachers.

The central, general aim of the trustees has consistently been to enhance the quality of life in America. In recent years, this has led to a growing concern for conservation, especially of the natural environment, wildlife habitats, and protection of endangered species. Included in Noble's estate was St. Catherine's Island, one of the large barrier islands that shields the coast of Georgia, an especially appropriate site on which to implement programs in conservation. With the cooperation of the New York Zoological Society, the foundation established a survival center and breeding program for threatened species of mammals and birds on St. Catherine's in 1974, and that project has been growing ever since. Biological and archaeological research are also encouraged on the island, through projects jointly sponsored with the American Museum of Natural History. These projects, as well as the survival center, enable senior scientists to train student interns in environmentally sound principles and techniques of field research and curatorial practice.

The necessity for American leadership in helping to resolve worldwide problems of population growth, deterioration of the environment, and loss of natural resources has also led the foundation to a renewed emphasis on university students. In particular, the Noble Foundation seeks to support interdisciplinary programs which may give students the breadth and depth of understanding to wrestle successfully with the complexity and interrelationships of these issues. All in all, the current activity of the foundation may be described as an intensified effort to conserve both environmental and human resources, primarily through programs of an educational nature. This effort is rooted in the belief that helping gifted and talented young people to expand their horizons is of central importance in order to sustain the creativity, vision, and confidence needed by a new generation of leaders if the global problems facing us are to be solved.

The Edward John Noble Foundation is governed by a self-perpetuating board of six trustees. Under the stewardship of these trustees, the foundation's asset value has grown from $18 million in 1958 to its 1980 market value of $57 million. A reorganization is now underway, to create a corporate form for the foundation, with nine or ten directors, and to split off the St. Catherine's Island projects as a separate operating foundation.

The trustees have employed a small staff, currently consisting of an executive director, assistant treasurer, and two administration assistants, along with a St.

Catherine's curatorial and maintenance staff of six. The program office is located at 32 East Fifty-Seventh Street, New York, New York 10022 and the business office is located at Post Office Box 162, Washington Depot, Connecticut 06794. The foundation's assets are managed by two advisers, one a major bank and the other a small firm of investment managers, under the direction of an investment committee of the trustees. The foundation's charitable contributions and grants from 1940 to 1980 have amounted to $31,579,000, several million dollars more than the income earned during that period.

The Noble Foundation issues an annual report describing its activities, grants, application procedures, and financial condition. A certified audit is available for inspection at its business office, and its annual reports to the Internal Revenue Service and to the states of New York, Connecticut, and Georgia are public records. It is a member of the Council on Foundations and contributes to the Foundation Center.

For further information, see *Report of Activities 1940–1971* (1971); and *Annual Reports* of the foundation, published continuously since 1971. See also several monographs and articles related to projects on St. Catherine's Island, together with a number of staff and evaluation reports, filed at the program office in New York City.

JOHN F. JOLINE III

**EDYTH BUSH CHARITABLE FOUNDATION, INC.** Founded in 1966 by Edyth Bush, this foundation received sizable assets after her death in 1972. Edyth Bush was the widow of Archibald G. Bush, an officer and director of the Minnesota Mining and Manufacturing Company (3M), and both were large stockholders in that company. Earlier, Archibald Bush had set up the Bush Foundation* in Minnesota, and for several years Edyth Bush served as chairperson of the board of directors of both foundations. Presently, there is no connection between the two organizations.

In 1973, the Edyth Bush Charitable Foundation received its first distribution from Edyth Bush's estate, and this, plus subsequent accretions of estate principal and income, has increased the foundation's assets to approximately $32 million in 1981. Edyth Bush lived in central Florida during the last years of her life, and much of her charitable giving was centered in that region. In 1977, the foundation's board of trustees decided to continue her pattern of giving. Since that time, the foundation has operated primarily to benefit grantees in central Florida and, to a lesser extent, the state of Florida. In a few exceptional cases, grants have been made in the states of Arizona and California, in which members of the donor's family presently reside.

Foundation granting has focused upon education, social and human welfare services (especially for the elderly and handicapped), hospitals, and arts and humanities (particularly the performing arts). Grants approximate $2 million annually.

The Edyth Bush Charitable Foundation is governed by a nine-member board of directors. Its programs are administered by a staff headed by a president, from offices located at 650 Barnett Bank Building, Winter Park, Florida 32790.

For further information, see an informational sheet, *Grant Policies,* published intermittently by the foundation. The foundation plans to issue biennial reports on its programs and activities in the near future.

**EL POMAR FOUNDATION.** In 1937, El Pomar Foundation was established with an initial gift from Spencer Penrose (1865–1939). Scion of a distinguished Philadelphia family and brother of U.S. Senator Boise Penrose, the Republican "boss" of Pennsylvania for over twenty years, Spencer Penrose left Philadelphia for the West in the early 1890s, following his graduation from Harvard. He settled in Colorado Springs, Colorado, and engaged initially in the real estate business with Charles L. Tutt, also a member of an old Philadelphia family. The two subsequently struck and laid claim to one of the richest gold veins in the Cripple Creek area of Colorado. Penrose then turned to the mining and refining of Colorado copper ore with such spectacular success that he was a multimillionaire by the early 1900s. Later he extended his business interests into agriculture, banking, the promotion of tourism in the Pikes Peak area, and the construction and operation of the famous Broadmoor Hotel.

In 1906, he married a widow, Julie McMillan. They had no children; and upon Penrose's death in 1939, his bequeathment of approximately $11 million went to El Pomar Foundation. Upon Julie Penrose's death, in 1956, the foundation received from her estate an additional fund, and El Pomar's assets presently amount to about $82 million, making it the largest foundation in Colorado.

Named for Penrose's luxurious estate, which he built near Colorado Springs, El Pomar Foundation has restricted its grants to Colorado, nonprofit organizations. Two-thirds of the grants have provided support for education and health care. Among the organizations that the foundation has traditionally favored and supported are Colorado College, Penrose Hospital, Cheyenne Mountain Zoo, and Fountain Valley School. The foundation makes between thirty and forty-five grants per year, amounting in the aggregate to about $3.5 million to $4 million annually.

El Pomar Foundation is governed by a five-member board of trustees, of which two are sons of Charles Tutt, Jr. They also serve as chairman and president of the foundation, respectively. El Pomar's programs and activities are directed by a small administrative staff headed by a vice-president/executive director. The mailing address of the foundation is Post Office Box 158, Colorado Springs, Colorado 80901.

For further information, see *Annual Reports* of the foundation, published since the 1970s. See also Spencer Penrose obituary, *New York Times* (December 7, 1939), p. 27, and (December 19, 1939), p. 21; *Conversations* (n.d.), report of an interview with William J. Hybl, vice-president and executive director of the foundation; and "Spencer Penrose," *Dictionary of American Biography*, Supplement Two (1958), p. 525.

**ENGELHARD FOUNDATION.** See Charles Engelhard Foundation, The.

**ESSO EDUCATION FOUNDATION.** See Exxon Education Foundation.

**EUGENE MCDERMOTT FOUNDATION, THE.** With offices located at 3803 Euclid Street, Dallas, Texas 75205, the Eugene McDermott Foundation is a private, nonprofit, philanthropic corporation whose primary focus of giving is in the areas of culture, health, education, and general interests of the local community. No grants are extended to individuals. The foundation was established and incorporated in 1972 by Eugene McDermott and his wife, Margaret Milam McDermott, outstanding benefactors of the fine arts and education activities in Dallas.

A native of Brooklyn, New York, McDermott earned an M.E. degree from Stevens Institute of Technology, Hoboken, New Jersey, in 1919 and an M.A. degree from Columbia University in 1925. In 1930, he moved to Dallas and, along with Dr. J. Clarence Karcher, founded Geophysical Services, Inc. (GSI), the predecessor of Texas Instruments, Inc. The two scientists pioneered in developing the reflection seismic techniques for locating potential oil deposits.

As a geophysicist, McDermott supervised oil explorations that ranged from Canada to the Middle East to South America. He was keenly interested in geochemical means of exploration and received several patents in the field. During his corporate career at GSI, he served as vice-president, president, and board chairman. With the formation of Texas Instruments in 1951, he became president and first board chairman of the diversified engineering, electronics, and manufacturing enterprise. In 1957, he became executive committee chairman and, after 1964, served as a company director until his death in 1973. In addition to his scientific and business activities, McDermott coauthored several books and scholarly papers dealing with human growth and development. He was the recipient of numerous awards and several honorary doctorate degrees.

Contemporary with his success in science and industry, McDermott developed major philanthropic interests. He and his wife established the McDermott Foundation in 1958 (which is not to be confused with the 1972 Eugene McDermott Foundation), and they were major donors to the fine arts in Dallas. Because they were desirous of good theatre for the city, they helped sponsor the Margo Jones Theater, which led the movement toward theatre-in-the-round in the United States. In 1965, the McDermotts gave $200,000 to Southern Methodist University (SMU) for the establishment of the Margo Jones Experimental Theater and served as directors of SMU's Fine Arts Association. Their interest in drama later aided the creation of the Dallas Theater Center, of which McDermott became a member of the executive committee. The couple also created a $225,000-plus trust fund to acquire art objects for display at the Dallas Museum of Fine Arts, and they were instrumental in obtaining the Stillman and Schindler collections of African art. In addition, they supported the Museum of Modern Art, in New York City.

McDermott was a heavy contributor to education in the Dallas area and elsewhere. Among recipients of his time, interest, and financial support were St. Mark's School of Texas, the Hockaday School, Southern Methodist University, the University of Dallas, Lamplighter School, the Dallas Community College system, and the University of Texas system. He was instrumental in establishing the University of Texas at Dallas (UTD) by making initial guarantees of funding for UTD's predecessor facilities, the Graduate Research Center for the Southwest and its Southwest Center for Advanced Studies. At the University of Texas Southwestern Medical School, in Dallas, he helped fund construction of the new Academic Administration Building, established the Eugene McDermott Center for the Study of Human Growth and Development, and endowed a chair in anesthesiology. McDermott was also a prominent financial backer of Stevens Institute and the Massachusetts Institute of Technology.

In 1972, less than a year before his death, McDermott established a new foundation, the Eugene McDermott Foundation, separate entirely from the earlier McDermott Foundation, which then had assets exceeding $8 million. McDermott served briefly as president of the new organization and after his death was succeeded by his wife as principal officer and president. Eric Jonsson was vice-president and trustee, and C.J. Thomsen and Mary McDermott served as trustees. Over the next several years, major funds were transferred at a steady rate from the McDermott estate to the Eugene McDermott Foundation. The 1975 *IRS Annual Report* (990-PF) showed a dramatic increase in foundation assets of over $24 million, derived primarily from contributions to the foundation of a large amount of Texas Instruments, Inc., common stock. Major grants were made to the University of Texas at Dallas, University of Texas Health Science Center, Dallas Museum of Fine Arts, and Stanford University.

In December, 1977, all assets of the McDermott Foundation were transferred to and merged with the Eugene McDermott Foundation, creating a net worth in excess of $30 million. Grants and contributions continued to be made primarily for educational, medical, and cultural purposes. Among the major recipients in 1977 were the University of Texas system, Bishop College, Methodist Hospital Building Fund, Southwestern Medical Foundation of Dallas, and the National Gallery of Art. One million dollars was approved for future payment to the Friends of the Dallas Public Library for the construction of a new downtown facility. During the following year, over a million dollars in grants was disbursed to such organizations as the Dallas Arboretum, Dallas Symphony Orchestra, Dallas Museum of Fine Arts, and the Massachusetts Institute of Technology (MIT).

As president and chief manager of the foundation, Margaret McDermott played the major role in all decision making concerning grants. A native of Dallas, she attended Sweet Briar College and the University of Texas and, after her marriage in 1954, joined with her husband in making major contributions to educational, philanthropic, and cultural undertakings throughout the United States.

She served as president of the Dallas Art Association, the Dallas Museum of

Fine Arts, and Friends of the Dallas Public Library; was a trustee of the University of Dallas; a vice-chairman of the board of the Dallas County Junior College System; and was active in the Goals for Dallas program. She received numerous awards for her philanthropic activity and was granted an honorary doctorate from SMU in 1976 in which she was cited for her support of artistic freedom. She is a private person who believes that publicity for herself or the foundation is inappropriate. She values highly the individualism of the private foundation in making policy and controlling funds, and she declines most association with other foundations.

In the years 1979–1981, the main emphasis of the Eugene McDermott Foundation continued to be the support of a wide variety of cultural and educational organizations, primarily in the city of Dallas. These included the Children's Medical Center, Dallas Museum of Fine Arts, Hockaday, St. Mark's, Dallas Heritage Society, Dallas Symphony Orchestra, Majestic Theater, and the University of Dallas. There were also substantial contributions made to the University of Texas at Austin, Folger Library, and MIT. In 1980, assets of the foundation were valued at about $37 million. Mary McDermott, daughter of the founders, had become secretary/treasurer, as well as trustee, and Patricia Brown was assistant secretary of the foundation.

For further information, see the (Dallas) *Morning News* (August 26, 1973), A, 1, and (February 28, 1965), n.p. See also *The National Cyclopedia of American Biography,* vol. 58 (1979), pp. 493–494.

DOROTHY D. DeMOSS

**EXXON EDUCATION FOUNDATION.** In 1955 in New Jersey, the Exxon Education Foundation was organized as a company-sponsored foundation by the Standard Oil Company (New Jersey). Originally it was titled the Esso Education Foundation, but in 1972 its name was changed to its present one. Major contributors to the foundation have been Exxon Corporation and affiliated companies.

The growth in assets and the increase in annual giving of the foundation is shown in the following approximate statistics for sample years: 1958—assets $2.5 million, grants $1.6 million; 1970—assets $5.5 million, grants $3 million; 1975—assets $9 million, grants $4 million; 1979—assets $13.75 million, grants $10.5 million; and 1981—assets $36 million, grants $42.5 million. The extraordinarily high rate of annual giving in comparison to the year-end assets of the foundation reflects the continued annual infusion of support, typical of company-sponsored foundations, by its sponsoring company. Such infusion ranged from earlier annual gifts of several million dollars to that for 1981 amounting to about $31.5 million. The impact of this foundation, therefore, in its special field of interest—education—is far in excess of what it would be if the foundation were dependent primarily upon the income from its assets.

Reflecting the word *education* in its title, the Exxon Foundation's major area of interest has always been higher education. In its early years, the foundation provided unrestricted grants to private colleges and universities, particularly for undergraduate education. Gradually, however, the foundation expanded its educational program and at the present time conducts five programs to support improvements in the quality of education. Two of these programs are open to application, two are programs for which the foundation does not invite application, and one is a matching-gift program.

In the first two programs, the Exxon Foundation aids higher education in the United States through numerous programs for research and development. This is the foundation's largest program, with special interest in educational activities that cross disciplinary lines and deal with major social issues. The other application program is designed to provide support for improved management and allocation of resources in our colleges and universities. Grants in both of these programs have been made to our public and private colleges and universities and to higher educational associations. Examples of grants provided by the foundation under these programs have included ones to Harvard University to help it establish a new program in business and public policy and a series of grants to establish and develop the Higher Education Management Institute.

The two programs for which the foundation does not solicit applications consist of the precollege area and sustaining programs. The former includes grants, for example, to promote interest in engineering among minority students, and grants to extend the application of television in the educational process. The latter program includes grants to provide help within particular areas of concerns to the foundation; in 1980 more than 60 percent of funds granted in this program supported research and manpower production in fields related to business and to the chemical and petroleum industries.

The fifth program of the foundation, labelled the Incentive Program for Individual Aid to Education, matches Exxon employee and annuitant dollar contributions to accredited colleges and universities of their choice. As of 1981, an individual could contribute as much as $5,000 in a single year and the foundation would match the sum given on a $3 to $1 basis.

The foundation is governed by a ten-member board of trustees, all of whom are officers and managers of the Exxon Corporation. Administration of the foundation is carried on from offices located at 111 West Forty-ninth Street, New York, New York 10020, under the direction of a president.

For further information, see *Annual Reports* of the foundation, published since the 1970s. See also informational booklets, particularly *An Introduction and Guide to Application* (1982), published periodically by the foundation.

# F

**FAIRCHILD FOUNDATION.** See Sherman Fairchild Foundation, Inc., The.

**FANNIE E. RIPPEL FOUNDATION.** Julius S. Rippel had long considered how his estate might be used for the benefit of large numbers of people over a lengthy period of time. As a result, in his last will and testament, he provided for the incorporation in 1953 of Fannie E. Rippel Foundation in memory of his wife, and he bequeathed his residual estate to it.

Born in Newark, New Jersey, Rippel maintained his residence and business headquarters in that city until his death in December, 1950, at the age of eighty-two. Orphaned as a boy, he started working early, and while still a young man he began to prosper as an investment dealer. He invested mainly in the enterprises of his community, particularly in banks and insurance companies. Widely known in his later years as a banker, he exerted an important influence in the affairs of his city and state, and many honors were conferred upon him. Rippel remained active in business until the very day of his death.

Unlike many other foundations, Fannie E. Rippel Foundation has a limited group of objectives and purposes to which it is legally restricted. These are: (a) to aid, assist, found, equip, and provide for maintenance of corporations, institutions, associations, organizations, or societies which are maintained for the relief and care of aged women; (b) to provide and furnish funds for the erection of or to aid in the erection of hospitals; to provide and furnish funds for the equipment of or to aid in the equipment of hospitals either in whole or in part; to aid or provide for the maintenance of hospitals in whole or in part; (c) to provide and furnish funds for corporations, institutions, and other organizations organized, maintained, and existing for the purpose of treatment of and/or research concerning heart disease; (d) to provide and furnish funds for corporations, institutions, and other organizations organized, maintained, and existing for the purpose of treatment of and/or research concerning cancer.

These fields of permissible operation were specified by the founder. They are quite closely related, and the foundation is restricted to them. The trustees may concentrate upon any one or more of them. Applicants outside these fields should not make requests. No grants may be made to individual persons, and the foundation does not use institutions as a syphon to supply grants to individuals. Although the founder imposed no geographical limitations upon the foundation's operations, the trustees have given major emphasis to institutions located in New Jersey. For special reasons, it has also assisted institutions in New York City, the general Northeast Seaboard, and, occasionally, elsewhere.

The foundation is concerned with supporting projects which will move along promptly to a full completion so that the service to be provided by the project will start as soon as possible. More recently, the trustees have given emphasis to physical facility and equipment needs of qualifying institutions. It has rarely supported operational programs. It does not make so-called challenge grants. The foundation has tended to make grants which are relatively large for its resources, rather than trying to make numerous, scattered, smaller ones. This pattern has followed careful deliberation and analysis. However, the foundation will continue to maintain flexibility and to undertake periodic consideration of its operation within the scope of its restricted purposes. It tries to adhere to the spirit as well as the letter of governing statutes. It considers its overall purpose to help institutions to serve constructively large numbers of individual persons.

All requests received by the foundation are reviewed by the foundation staff. Those which come clearly within the foundation's restricted purposes are referred to the foundation's trustees for consideration and decision as to whether or not the foundation will give the request further consideration. All such applicants are notified of the trustees' decision. The foundation's trustees usually meet at least ten times during the year.

The foundation does not use application forms, and there are no deadlines for submission of a request. Applications should be by a letter to the foundation offices at 299 Madison Avenue, Morristown, New Jersey 07960, which gives details of the project and its costs. Such a letter should be signed by a senior corporate officer of the institution, and it should be made clear that the project for which the request is being made is a project of the institution, one which the institution itself supports and wishes to propose for a grant.

Although it had assets in 1981 of about $32 million, it should be emphasized that the foundation receives a great many more qualified requests than it has the financial resources to support. Consequently, many worthy requests must be declined.

As soon as it is practicable after the end of each fiscal year (ending April 30), the foundation prepares an annual report. Such a report gives a summary of the foundation's financial position and operations for the year and lists the grants appropriated during that year. This report is sent to those who request it.

For further information, see *Reports* issued by the foundation for the periods: May 1, 1953–April 30, 1959; May 1, 1959–April 30, 1965; and May 1, 1965–April 30, 1969. See also *Annual Reports* issued continuously since 1971.

HERBERT C. ENGLERT

**FERRIS FOUNDATION.** See Booth Ferris Foundation.

**FIKES FOUNDATION.** See Leland Fikes Foundation, Inc.

**FLEISCHMANN FOUNDATION.** See Max C. Fleischmann Foundation.

**FLORENCE AND JOHN SCHUMANN FOUNDATION, THE.** Named for its founders, the Florence and John Schumann Foundation was established and funded by them in New Jersey in 1961. Following John Schumann's death in 1964, additional assets from his estate flowed to the foundation; and by 1969, its corpus amounted to about $33 million, with grants for that year of about $0.5 million. Since that time, the market value of the foundation's assets increased to about $41 million in 1980, with grants of up to about $3 million annually.

The Schumann foundation has traditionally concentrated its activities and provided support for programs dealing with the problems and needs of the city of Montclair and Essex County, New Jersey, where the foundation has always been located. Funding has been provided for a wide range of health and welfare programs, secondary and higher education, youth agencies, and urban affairs. In 1980, a total of 118 grants were made in these areas, ranging from one for $150,000 to the Frost Valley YMCA, Montclair, New Jersey, to one for $600 to the New Jersey Historical Society, Newark, New Jersey.

The foundation is governed by a nine-member board of trustees, with Robert F. Schumann, a son of the founders, serving as chairman and including other members of the Schumann family. Administration of the foundation is carried on from offices located at 33 Park Street, Montclair, New Jersey 07042, under the direction of a president.

For further information, see *Annual Reports* of the foundation, published since the 1970s.

**F. M. KIRBY FOUNDATION, INC.** Fred Morgan Kirby (1861–1940) went to work at age fifteen in a store in Watertown, New York. During eight years of employment, he saved $500 from his meager wages, which he invested in establishing a store in Wilkes-Barre, Pennsylvania, in partnership with Charles S. Woolworth, brother of the better-known Frank W. Woolworth. After three years, Kirby bought out Charles Woolworth and commenced the development of a chain of ninety-six five-and-ten-cent stores. At the end of 1911, Kirby merged his chain with four others, including that of Frank W. Woolworth, to form the F. W. Woolworth Company. Kirby continued as an officer and director of the combined company, and he extended his business interests to banking, insurance, railroads, utilities, lumber, and other enterprises.

Among Fred Kirby's early charitable benefactions were gifts to Lafayette College and Wyoming Seminary, both located in Pennsylvania. In 1931, he established the F. M. Kirby Foundation in Delaware. The foundation's initial assets were modest. Yet despite the fact that when he died, in 1940, Fred Kirby bequeathed the major portion of his fortune to his son, Allan Price Kirby, by 1957 the foundation's assets had increased to about $7 million and by 1969 to approximately $18 million.

During his business career, Allan Kirby vastly increased the wealth he had inherited from his father. His business interests were varied and substantial. He was chairman of the board of directors and controlling stockholder of Alleghany Corporation, the holding company which controlled the New York Central, Chesapeake & Ohio, and other railroads, as well as Investors Diversified Services, Inc., a multibillion-dollar mutual fund and insurance concern. He was a director and major owner of banks and other corporations. At the time of his death in 1973 at age eighty, Allan Kirby left approximately $10 million to the F. M. Kirby Foundation. In 1980 the assets of the foundation were in the neighborhood of $67 million.

The foundation's pattern of giving has been focused largely upon education, health, social welfare, and community services, and it has concentrated a major portion of its grants within the states of Pennsylvania, New York, and New Jersey. Notably, the foundation in making grants has favored institutions in which past or present members of its board of directors had or have a personal interest. Lafayette College, for example, from which six members of four generations of the Kirby family have received degrees, was awarded a grant of $246,500 from the foundation in 1980. In the same year, Lawrenceville School, the *alma mater* of four Kirbys in three generations, received a grant of $259,000, which was the largest grant made by the foundation in 1980. Annual grants now total about $3 million.

The F. M. Kirby Foundation exemplifies the cohesiveness of a family foundation. The four members of the governing board of directors consist of the two sons and two daughters of Allan P. Kirby. The sons are also the president and vice-president of the foundation. The offices of the foundation are located at 17 De Hart Street, Morristown, New Jersey 07960, and the program of the foundation is administered under the direction of an executive director.

For further information, see Frederick Morgan Kirby obituary, *New York Times* (October 17, 1940), p. 25, and (October 26, 1940), p. 9; and Allan Price Kirby obituary, *New York Times* (May 3, 1973), p. 46. See also an information sheet (n.d.) issued by the foundation.

**FONDREN FOUNDATION, THE.** Funds from the estate of Walter W. Fondren, a Houston, Texas, oilman and founder of the Humble Oil and Refining Company, provided the assets for the 1948 establishment of this Texas foundation. Mrs. Fondren was the administrator of her husband's estate, and she became the principal donor to the foundation. With an initial capital of several million dollars, the Fondren Foundation made grants in the 1950s ranging from $150,000 to $500,000 annually, primarily for the support of institutions of higher education and hospitals in Houston. By the late 1960s, the assets of the foundation had increased in value to about $20 million. Grants of some $500,000 were being made annually, primarily to specific projects in the Texas area. In the early years of the 1980s, the foundation has been awarding grants of about $1.5 million annually from assets which in 1982 were valued at about $30 million.

Following its traditional pattern, these grants have been primarily for educational, medical, and cultural organizations in the Texas area. In 1981, for example, grants were made in the following categories: health—44.39 percent; education—28.77 percent; humanities and the arts—13.69 percent; welfare—10.46 percent; and civic—2.69 percent.

The foundation is governed by an eight-member board of trustees, each one of whom is a member of the Fondren family. The mailing and administrative address of the foundation is Post Office Box 2558, Houston, Texas 77001.

Almost the only additional information on this foundation readily available to the public are the annual reports and returns filed by it with the Internal Revenue Service, and the various Foundation Center publications.

**FORD FOUNDATION, THE.** The Ford Foundation was established in 1936 in Michigan by Henry Ford and his son Edsel with an initial gift of $25,000. That was supplemented the following year by 250,000 shares of nonvoting stock in the Ford Motor Company. From 1936 until 1950, the foundation's grants went largely to charitable and educational institutions in Michigan. With the death of the founders (Edsel in 1943 and Henry in 1947) and the settlement of their estates, the Ford Foundation was transformed from a relatively small, essentially unstaffed institution with mainly local interests to the country's largest foundation, with assets estimated at $474 million.

To plan for this change, the foundation's board of trustees, in 1948, had appointed an eight-member committee of independent consultants, chaired by San Francisco attorney H. Rowan Gaither, Jr. Their recommendations, presented in 1950, were the basis for a broad program of national and international giving. The trustees designated five major areas of foundation interest: the establishment of peace, the strengthening of democracy, the strengthening of the economy, education in democratic society, and individual behavior and human relations. It is worth noting that in assets the foundation was one-tenth the size it would achieve by the mid-1960s. Yet it already had taken aim against a multiplicity of objectives "so broad and comprehensive that virtually everything the Foundation has done in the ensuing years can be rationalized as following the original blueprint." (Richard Magat, *The Ford Foundation at Work: Philanthropic Choices, Methods, and Styles* [1978], p. 19.)

In 1951, national headquarters were set up in Pasadena, California. Program activities were planned and directed from there; fiscal management remained in Detroit, Michigan, and a skeleton staff in New York received grant applications. Two years later, all these functions were consolidated in rented quarters in New York City. In 1967, the Ford Foundation moved into its own headquarters building on East Forty-third Street, not far from the United Nations. The eleven-story, glass-walled and granite structure with a large interior garden was designed by the architectural firm of Kevin Roche/Dinkeloo and has won numerous design awards.

The period 1950–1966 was marked by enormous growth by almost any measure—in the foundation's assets, in the size of the staff, in the number of program interests, and in the geographical spread of its interests. This period was also characterized by a rapid growth of the U.S. economy; the rebuilding of war-ravaged European and Japanese economies; U.S. domination of world economic and military arenas; the rise of nationalism in many parts of the world; decolonization in Asia and Africa and widespread change in Latin America; and at home, the opening chapters of profound social movements that would call attention to the "forgotten Americans," millions to whom the doors to human fulfillment were closed by virtue of race or endemic poverty. The Ford Foundation's emphasis within its programs reflected these realities.

The external relations and management of the foundation's early years were far from tranquil or stable. Two congressional investigations in the mid-1950s absorbed substantial energies of the board and staff. In the same decade, the foundation had three presidents: Paul G. Hoffman, H. Rowan Gaither, Jr., and Henry T. Heald.

On the financial side, the Ford Foundation owned 88 percent of Ford Motor Company stock—all of it nonvoting. Dividends from this holding provided virtually all of the foundation's income in the early years. But the concentration seemed risky, so in 1956 the foundation took initial steps to diversify its holdings by the first public sale of the company's stock. Some 22 percent of the foundation's holding was converted into voting stock and sold. Parenthetically, the foundation continued to diversify its holdings over the next eighteen years—selling, granting, and exchanging 92.7 million shares of Ford Motor Company stock worth $4.2 billion. The divestiture was completed in 1974, and the foundation now owns no stock in the Ford Motor Company.

Because of the yield from the sale ($641 million), along with the sharply rising value of the stock still held, trustees and staff were concerned that the foundation might be perceived as "too big." Thus most of the proceeds of the sale were distributed in a massive block of grants to colleges and universities, hospitals, and medical schools—nearly $550 million in all. Of this amount, $260 million went to six hundred private liberal arts colleges and universities in the United States to increase faculty salaries. Some $200 million went to approximately thirty-five hundred voluntary, nonprofit hospitals in the United States and territories to improve services to their communities, and $90 million in endowment grants went to forty-four privately supported medical schools to strengthen their academic programs.

The style of large block giving (even as more finely targeted programs were developing) continued into the 1960s—for example, $349 million in challenge grants to develop selected private colleges and universities as national and regional centers of excellence (1960), $80 million for symphony orchestras (1965), and $72 million to develop international studies programs at U.S. universities (1965).

In the 1950s, the foundation spun off some of its major interests by the creation and endowment of separate foundations—principally the Fund for the Advancement of Education ($71.5 million), the Fund for Adult Education ($47.4 million), the Fund for the Republic ($15 million), and Resources for the Future ($55.8 million). Today, only Resources for the Future still exists, but a number of the program interests of these organizations later became the basis of internal foundation programs, for example, education, resources and the environment, civil liberties, and equality of opportunity. In addition, the foundation helped establish many new institutions—for example, the Center for Advanced Study in the Behavioral Sciences, the Center for International Legal Studies (at Harvard), the National Merit Scholarships (established jointly with Carnegie Corporation of New York*), the Council on Library Resources, the Woodrow Wilson National Fellowship Foundation, the Center for Applied Linguistics, and the International Institute for Strategic Studies (in London).

The Ford Foundation's overseas work also began in this era—first in Asia and the Middle East (1951), then in Africa (1958), and finally in Latin America and the Caribbean (1959). In 1957, activities related to Europe were expanded, including an appropriation of some $1.1 million to aid Hungarian refugees. (Five years earlier, the foundation had first declared its interest in refugees with a $2.9 million grant to the U.N. High Commissioner, which went to help mainly those in western Europe who had been displaced byWorld War II). Programs of scholarly and cultural exchanges between the West and eastern Europe were also begun in 1957. Gradually, the foundation's international interests expanded to virtually every region of the globe. At one point, the foundation maintained more than twenty field offices in the developing countries, each with resident staffs and an array of project specialists. Indeed, in many places the foundation was the major, if not exclusive, aid-giving agency. Among the foundation's special interests abroad were agriculture, education, strengthening government institutions, rural development, and language problems.

In the 1950s, too, the foundation began supporting research on world population problems. The initial emphasis was on poor countries abroad where marked increases in population were making it increasingly difficult for those nations to feed themselves. Much of the foundation's assistance was channeled through the Population Council. Support over a decade led to the establishment, in 1963, of a population program within the foundation, which resulted in a long series of grants for basic and applied research in the reproductive sciences, demographic studies, and research on population policy. Foundation grants in the population field totalled some $251 million since 1952.

The foundation also showed an early interest in advancing the arts and enhancing the potential of radio and television. For example, in 1951 the Ford Foundation set up the Radio and Television Workshop to improve cultural fare on commercial networks. The workshop's "Omnibus" series provided a tantalizing glimpse of the kind of program television could offer. In addition, considerable emphasis in the early years was put on instructional television.The foundation provided several million dollars for construction of educational stations and released time of faculty to help design and teach courses on T.V.

Among the best known was "Continental Classroom," an open-circuit experiment launched in 1958 and broadcast over commercial channels that featured courses in subjects such as mathematics, physics, Shakespeare, and history. Between 1953 and 1970, the Ford Foundation also provided $90.1 million for a major production resource, the National Educational Television and Radio Center (NET), which subsequently merged with Educational Broadcasting Corporation, New York's public television station.

After passage of the Public Broadcasting Act of 1967, the foundation's efforts focused on strengthening the capability of the new public system to provide a lively alternative to commercial television. Projects supported included the Public Broadcast Laboratory, production centers across the country, the Children's Television Workshop, the Station Program Cooperative, and the New American Drama Project. When the foundation phased out its major assistance to the field in 1977, support had totalled some $293 million.

The Ford Foundation began a program of support for the creative and performing arts in 1957. The major aims were to develop professionals in music, theater, dance, and the visual and literary arts, and to strengthen professional groups and institutions that serve as outlets for artists' careers. The foundation's assistance has ranged from the development of nonprofit repertory theaters, off-Broadway groups, and ballet and modern dance companies to subsidies for the production of new American plays, for the recording of original musical compositions, and for the publication of poetry. Support has gone for the training of professional musicians in the nation's leading conservatories, of student painters, sculptors, and graphic artists in studio art schools and college and university art departments throughout the country, and of graduate students in art history for careers as museum curators. An integral part of the Ford Foundation's arts program has been support for the training and career advancement of minority and women artists. Among the various arts organizations serving minority communities assisted have been the Dance Theatre of Harlem, the Negro Ensemble Company, the Newark Community School of the Arts, and the Puerto Rican Traveling Theater.

In addition to its ten-year, $80.2 million program of operating and endowment support for symphony orchestras, the foundation since 1971 has granted some $28 million to seventy-two performing arts groups in the theater, opera, and dance to help stabilize their financial position, improve their planning and management, and help them build both working capital reserves and endowment funds.

Apart from the foundation's regular program in the arts, special assistance has been granted to the Detroit Museum of Art ($1.9 million), the Museum of Modern Art ($1 million), the Lincoln Center in New York City ($25 million), and the Kennedy Center in Washington, D.C. ($5 million). Foundation support for the arts over the past quarter of a century totals some $293 million.

Other highlights of foundation activities that began during the fifties and sixties include support for projects to ease the problems of the urban poor, improving the nation's public schools, reforms in American graduate education, advancing science and engineering education, strengthening graduate schools of business administration, help in creating international agricultural research centers, and establishment of National Achievement Scholarships to assist academically promising black students.

With McGeorge Bundy's assumption of the Ford Foundation's presidency in 1966, increasing emphasis was put on assuring the civil rights of blacks and other minorities and promoting their equal access to higher education, job opportunities, and decent housing. In 1972, for example, a special $100 million program was launched to improve opportunities for minorities in higher education. Lasting six years, the program had two components: support for a selected group of private black colleges, and doctoral fellowships for blacks, Puerto Ricans, Mexican-Americans, and native Americans. The program was followed in 1979 by the Minority Postdoctoral Fellowship Program, established by the foundation and administered by the National Academy of Sciences.

In the late 1960s, support began for community development corporations in rural and urban sections with large concentrations of the poor and minorities, for housing rehabilitation in declining neighborhoods, for reforms in prisons and in the administration of justice, and for public interest law firms. Large-scale assistance was also begun for legal defense groups representing blacks, Puerto Ricans, Mexican-Americans, and native Americans.

During the 1970s, the Ford Foundation turned its attention to the special needs of women, assisting projects to secure their legal rights, expand job opportunities and training, and improve child-care services. Special emphasis was also placed on that group of severely distressed people sometimes called the "underclass"—mostly unskilled, untrained, lacking in even the basics of education, and dependent on welfare for survival.

Despite the foundation's growth, an undercurrent of concern over the proliferation of programs periodically ran through the board of trustees. The concern was voiced in the second major review of Ford Foundation activities, completed in 1962. A statement by the trustees in that year acknowledged that "the vast demands on the foundation, even the large portion consisting of meritorious proposals, greatly exceed its financial capacity to act favorably." The market value of the foundation's portfolio at the end of 1962 was $3.3 billion; two years later it was $4.1 billion.

Spending in the first half of the 1960s averaged over $300 million annually. In the expectation of long-term capital gains, spending was substantially higher than income—double in some years. As the capital markets turned sharply downward in the late 1960s, the foundation lowered its annual rate of giving somewhat, but expansion of program scope continued. The situation was aggravated by a large "overhang"—grant commitments approved but not yet paid—of $600 million. By 1971, inflation had so eroded the capital base that a further reduction in annual budgets was made.

By 1974, the market value of the Ford Foundation's portfolio had dropped to

$1.7 billion, from a high of $4.1 billion in 1964. The foundation's trustees faced a fundamental choice. The alternative to budget cuts was a continual erosion of the corpus to the point where eventually the foundation would liquidate. They decided to remain in business and therefore began a drastic reduction in the annual level of giving, to $100 million, one-third the level of the preceding decade in nominal dollars and substantially less in real dollars. The foundation targeted both the program grant budget and the staff roster for 50 percent reductions over the four-year period 1974–1978. Substantial progress was made toward each goal.

In anticipation of the change in administration that would occur after McGeorge Bundy's retirement in 1979, the trustees commissioned a major study to assess the likely problems of the 1980s and their implications for the foundation's program. The study underscored the continuing need to align the foundation's grant-making activity more closely with its resources.

At the outset of the administration of the current president, Franklin A. Thomas, in 1979, the Ford Foundation's assets had rebounded in nominal dollars to $2.3 billion, but in real dollars the foundation was one-fourth its mid-1960s size. Despite staff reductions, management costs continued to rise. The foundation was overextended programmatically and geographically. The retrenchments of the 1970s had reduced expenditures unit by unit, but the foundation retained basically the same priorities, divisions, and program areas.

In mapping the future direction of the foundation, therefore, the new administration focused on three key areas: program content, organization and structure, and the geographical spread of foundation activities. After an intensive review, the staff identified six major areas in which the Ford Foundation would be best qualified to work and in which its efforts were most needed.These areas are: urban poverty; rural poverty and resources; human rights and social justice; governance and public policy; education and culture; international affairs.

At the same time, the president proposed a management reorganization to the board of trustees. The principal feature was the consolidation of existing programs into a single program division. This unified structure was designed to concentrate the foundation's resources selectively for greatest effect through coordinated domestic and international programs. It reflected the natural links between the foundation's work in the United States and abroad. Since many issues confronting American society have counterparts in the Third World, and vice versa, closer cooperation could benefit staff and grantees in both domestic and overseas programs.

The Ford Foundation also decided to continue to spend from 30 percent to 40 percent of its program budget on international activities but in fewer overseas locations and with a more concentrated effort on selected themes. In the nine current overseas offices—Dacca, Bangladesh; New Delhi, India; Jakarta, Indonesia; Lima, Peru; Rio de Janeiro, Brazil; Planco, Mexico; Nairobi, Kenya; Cairo, Egypt; and Lagos, Nigeria—foundation representatives work closely with local institutions and leaders in devising programs to further mutual goals and interests.

The trustees approved both the new program themes and the management reorganization at their quarterly meeting in March, 1981. They also confirmed the staff recommendation to phase out several programmatic interests, such as resources and the environment, school finance reform, energy, population, public interest law, women in politics, and day care. The foundation had worked in most of these areas for more than a decade and had either achieved its objectives (sometimes attracting other funds to provide major support) or had come to believe that other opportunities showed more promise of important results. As the foundation phased out some lines of activity, transitional funds were provided as necessary. Thus, to help insure the stability and vitality of two of the country's principal centers of population work, the foundation made a substantial tie-off grant to the Population Council and a large grant to the Allan Guttmacher Institute. In some cases, the decision to leave a field did not mean a total departure but simply the cessation of major institutional support. For example, although support for population research has declined, the foundation has retained, within the Urban Poverty program, a strong interest in teenage pregnancy and fertility-related health issues.

Besides incorporating the new program and management structures, the 1982–1983 budget approved by the trustees in September, 1981, also increased the level of program expenditures by 17.6 percent over the budget for the previous biennium, to $240 million.

The most dramatic programmatic change was the approximate doubling of funds allocated to the critical problems of urban poverty. Although the bulk of this activity is concentrated in the United States, urban poverty is receiving increased attention in developing-country programs as well.

In the United States, the Ford Foundation's future objectives include new work to build local community development organizations; expanded efforts to improve secondary schools serving low-income populations, with special emphasis on mathematics; new programs to reduce teen pregnancy, youth unemployment, and welfare dependency; experiments designed to reduce health and developmental problems among young children in high-risk families; and projects to aid the adjustment of U.S. immigrants and refugees. In each area, these objectives are pursued through a combination of direct experimentation and research.

In the developing world, increased attention is being devoted to the employment needs of recent migrants to the cities and the opportunities and rights of shanty-town dwellers. As in the United States, innovative efforts to enhance the prospects for child survival and provide children from disadvantaged backgrounds with a fair start in life are being assisted.

In other program areas that show no dramatic changes in level of funding, programmatic shifts have occurred. For example, in the foundation's work in international human rights, increased emphasis is now placed on funding locally based human rights projects, a shift from earlier reliance on internationally oriented organizations. Another example can be seen in the effort, now under way, to understand the effects of various fiscal containment measures in the United States. This includes work to measure funding cuts and their efforts, to ease institutional and individual adjustments to these cutbacks, and to reexamine the economic and behavioral assumptions that underlie governmental programs now being reduced. In international peace, security, and arms control, the foundation is exploring the possibilities for new work in nonspecialist education.

Pervading all the Ford Foundation's themes and strategies is a heightened awareness of the present capacity and unrealized potential of local institutions and individuals to undertake and sustain initiatives toward improvement in the quality of life. The community development movement has proved to be an effective means for bringing new life back to stranded neighborhoods and disadvantaged people. Innumerable local organizations have become skilled in ways of leveraging private and public capital to carry out local tasks more effectively than government agencies usually can. Community development also yields byproducts that cannot be measured by numerical indices—restored confidence on the part of local residents, a new sense of hope, and the easing of ethnic and racial friction. The foundation's previous work in many places in the United States and abroad has helped develop community-based organizations, but the surface has just been scratched.

The Ford Foundation has therefore placed special emphasis on the support of community-managed innovations through on-site tests and model demonstrations. The need for government support in the billion-dollar range is as vital as ever. But just as there is no substitute for that scale of aid, there is no substitute for community-based efforts in effectively producing social and economic change.

A prominent example of this emphasis is the Local Initiatives Support Corporation (LISC), which the foundation helped establish with six major insurance, industrial, and banking firms. In several cities and regions throughout the country, LISC is helping local organizations draw business, community, and government resources into an effective coalition for revitalizing neighborhoods and communities. LISC's success in its first two years of operation prompted several corporations and local foundations to ask LISC to join them in establishing similar community development funds specifically targeted to their localities.

On other issues, too, such as neighborhood crime and arson prevention and teenage pregnancy in the United States, and, in the Third World, income-producing activities for women and projects in social forestry and water management, the foundation is capitalizing on the capacity of local nongovernmental resources, ranging from community foundations to corporations.

Though leaner as a result of programmatic and structural changes, the foundation continues to work toward far-reaching objectives through a rich array of programs. Some have evolved from long-standing interests. For example, the Ford Foundation has been deeply engaged in improving agricultural productivity in the Third World for nearly a quarter of a century, with notable success. Now the aim is to redress imbalances in the distribution of those benefits, which is as important for the well-being of the hungry as overall gains in productivity—and even more difficult to achieve. Other efforts represent new departures—for example, the new program to reduce teenage pregnancy, the developing program to insure a fair start for children, and a new international center in Sri Lanka aimed at resolving ethnic, tribal, and religious conflicts in various societies.

Also essentially new is the foundation's emphasis on collaboration with other institutions—foundations, corporations, public and private agencies—in pursuing its various program activities. The foundation seeks partners across national, organizational, and program boundaries and among individuals with many different skills. Since its inception, the Ford Foundation has made commitments totalling $5.7 billion, including grants to some eight thousand institutions and organizations. Recipients have been located in all fifty states, the District of Columbia, and various foreign countries, especially in less-developed parts of the world.

There is no full-length and up-to-date history of the Ford Foundation. For further information, see the previously cited work by Richard Magat, former director of the Office of Reports of the foundation. See also *Study for the Ford Foundation on Policy and Program* (1949), which chartered the course of the foundation in the 1950s; and Dwight Macdonald, *The Ford Foundation: The Men and the Millions* (1956), for an earlier, jocular, but informative account of foundations and the Ford Foundation in particular.

OONA SULLIVAN

**FORD MOTOR COMPANY FUND.** A company-sponsored foundation, the Ford Motor Company Fund was established by the Ford Motor Company in Michigan in 1949. During the 1950s, its assets were in the neighborhood of $15 million and it made annual grants of about $3 million or $4 million annually. The fund's stated purpose in the 1950s was to provide aid in the fields of health, education, social welfare, the humanities, and scientific research, and its operations were limited to the United States, primarily to the Michigan area.

In the 1960s and early 1970s, the fund's assets fluctuated, reaching as much as $26 million in some years and in others dropping to less than $20 million. Yet during these same years, the fund was making annual grants in excess of $10 million in some years and in others dropping down to $6 million or $7 million. Since the late 1970s, assets have ranged from between $36 million and $60 million, with grants of about $10 million being made annually. This fluctuation in assets and grants has been due primarily to fluctuations in the company's annual profits.

From its inception, the Ford Motor Company Fund has concentrated its support on education, community funds, urban affairs, hospitals and health endeavors, and civic and cultural programs. In recent years, for example, the United Funds of Detroit, Michigan, Cleveland, Ohio, and Camden, New Jersey, have received grants in the millions of dollars. Various universities, such as Michigan State

University and the University of Detroit, have received sizable grants for capital and development. The Detroit Symphony Orchestra has similarly benefitted from the fund. In addition to such direct grants, the fund administers the Ford Fund Educational Aid Program, which gives matching grants to educational institutions for employees of the Ford Motor Company and its subsidiaries. Special consideration has always been given to the state of Michigan, particularly the Detroit area, and to communities where Ford Motor Company plants are located.

The Ford Motor Company Fund, with 1980 assets of about $36 million, is governed by a nine-member board of trustees. Two trustees are members of the Ford family, with Henry Ford II serving as president. The other seven members of the board are Ford Motor Company executives. Administration of the fund is carried on from offices located at the American Road, Dearborn, Michigan 48121, under the supervision of a director.

Almost the only additional sources of information on this foundation readily available to the public are the annual reports and returns filed by it with the Internal Revenue Service, and the various Foundation Center publications. See, however, *Educational Aid Program Report*, published annually by the foundation.

**FOUNDATION FOR CHILD DEVELOPMENT.** Unlike most of its sister organizations, the Foundation for Child Development did not begin life as a foundation but rather as a child-welfare agency. In its more than eighty years of existence, it has undergone several major transformations.

In 1900, Mable Irving Jones, a dedicated woman concerned about crippled children who had no access to educational facilities incorporated an agency under the wing of New York City's Children's Aid Society to provide transportation and a special class for three crippled children. A horse-drawn wagon was the vehicle used to transport them. Jones persevered in her efforts to help these hitherto home-bound youngsters and others. By 1904, the number of children served had grown to 117. In 1906, thanks to her pushing and prodding, the New York City Board of Education incorporated into Public School 104 the first public school class for crippled children.

In 1908, the organization, which now had a staff of about ten and was funded through voluntary contributions in the amount of some $10,000 annually, broke away from the Children's Aid Society and established itself as the Association for the Aid of Crippled Children, the name it kept until 1972, when it was changed to the Foundation for Child Development. Throughout its history, the organization has maintained its early dedication to the welfare of the child at risk, although the definition of risk has changed. What follows is an attempt to show how the organization's program has been both a bellwether and a measure of society's idea of the nature of risk.

From 1900 until 1940, the work of the organization broke new ground in both child-welfare practice and policy. Under the successive leadership of three trained nurses, the association initiated free transportation to schools and clinics, provided braces and other therapeutic devices and procedures, and established facilities for physical rehabilitation of crippled children in a variety of settings in New York City. In all its programs, a conscious effort was made to draw the handicapped child into the "normal" life of other children—in school, in the family, and in the community—a concept that is just now resurfacing under the label of "mainstreaming."

By the middle of the 1940s, close to thirty thousand children had been treated. It was then that the idea of the crippled child was broadened from the original, almost total concern for victims of polio to an involvement with many other diseases with crippling effects on children, including cerebral palsy and other disorders of fetal and neonatal origin.

In 1944, the Association for the Aid of Crippled Children received two bequests, one of $8 million and another of $3 million, from the estate of Milo M. Belding, a silk manufacturer and banker whose wife had served on the association's board for over twenty years. The receipt of these funds, which have subsequently been augmented by smaller bequests from a number of other people, marked a turning point in the organization's history, causing it to change from a direct-service agency to a grant-making foundation. Annual assets in 1980 and 1981 were about $30 million, with annual grant expenditures ranging from approximately $1.5 million to $2 million.

After considerable discussion and analysis, the association decided that while a continuation of the service program of education, nursing care, and therapy would improve the lot of those children and families who came into contact with the organization's services, the effect of the program would be extremely limited. The organization would be doing no more than it did when supported by voluntary, year-to-year contributions. Most important in the minds of the directors was the need to begin to look at the *causes* of crippling conditions that locked out of the world of childhood not only children in New York but also handicapped children throughout the country and in other parts of the world.

From these deliberations came the decision to use the Belding bequests to conduct a grant-making program in support of projects involving research, demonstration, and education for the aid of crippled children. At the same time, the association's direct-service program was not completely curtailed, and for a number of years the nursing service was continued. In the 1950s, the Visiting Nurse Service of New York took over this aspect of the organization's work, and like so many of the earlier service programs of the association, it became part of the community's accepted responsibility for handicapped children.

The thrust of the new use of funds was to support innovative patterns of care and research on the identification and prevention of handicaps. As a joint enterprise with New York University-Bellevue Hospital, the Association for the Aid of Crippled Children helped establish the Children's Division of the Institute of Physical Medicine and Rehabilitation (often referred to today as the Rusk Institute). Here, lessons learned in rehabilitating soldiers during World War II (new prosthetic devices and physical therapy, plus the importance of the patient's own role in understanding and overcoming his handicap) were applied to crippled children to equip them physically and psychologically to take their places in homes, schools, and communities.

In later years, the term "handicap" came to cover a much broader range of disabilities and disorders than those obviously visible and readily identified. The nonvisibly handicapped—the retarded, the emotionally disturbed, or the child with a circulatory or metabolic disorder—often remained untreated because such defects were more easily overlooked.

In the 1950s, the foundation had initiated research that spanned many years, and often several continents. With the handicapped children as their point of departure, researchers supported by the foundation sought to identify the causes of handicaps at various stages in the child's development.

In the early 1970s, the organization, known since 1972 as the Foundation for Child Development, again reviewed its purpose and role. Just as in previous years, when the service initiated by it had been gradually taken over as the continuing responsibility of other institutions in the community, so, too, in the field of biological research, support from public bodies had become government policy, as embodied by the National Institutes of Health and their satellite agencies. It had also become increasingly apparent that although genetic and physical handicaps play an important part in the health and well-being of the child, the definition of the child at risk had again to be examined and redefined. In the cities of America and throughout the world, it was clear that the various systems in which the child lives and grows—the family, the day-care center, the neighborhood, and the school—were major determinants of the child's development.

Reflecting this change in perspective, the Foundation for Child Development, in 1974, appointed Orville G. Brim, Jr., a sociologist, as president. Formerly president of Russell Sage Foundation,* Brim has brought to the foundation a deep concern for child development as well as a keen interest in the entire process of human development throughout the life-span.

At present, the foundation supports projects that affect large numbers of children. The three major areas of its work are:

- child development research—the social-emotional development of the child and child development within environmental contexts such as the family and school, including the interrelationship of the child's sense of self-efficacy and his environment;
- public policy and advocacy—the effects of government and corporate policies on children and families;
- New York City/State Program—improving services for families and children in the communities in which they live and monitoring publicly mandated services for children and families at risk.

An example of a project falling under these three broad programmatic areas is, in the field of child-development research, a foundation-operated program for young scholars conducting research on the social and affective development of children. The purpose of the program, initiated in the summer of 1981, is to promote both the career development of young scholars (holders of doctoral degrees) and knowledge about ways in which such qualities as cooperation, self-esteem, and empathy can develop during childhood.

Another example of an effort to pursue the three programmatic goals listed above is an examination of marital disruption in a life-span perspective under the auspices of the University of Pennsylvania, Child Trends, Inc., and the Institute of Social Research, of Temple University. Since World War II, there has been a dramatic increase in divorce in this country. While conventional wisdom assumes that divorce has negative effects on children, these consequences have never been identified in a large-scale survey. The research is exploring the ways in which children's lives and their social development are altered by a changing family context. The project also is developing an inventory of warning signals that will help identify children who are most in need of preventive services in cases of divorce. The National Institute of Mental Health is a joint funder of the project.

Two examples of projects falling in the public sector are as follows. The first is the Congressional Fellowship Program in Child Development, under which mid-career and younger child-development scholars spend a year acting as aides to members of Congress and to congressional committees. The project is jointly funded by the William T. Grant Foundation.* Another public-sector project involves an examination of public interest litigation on behalf of children. As a funder of advocacy groups that use litigation as one of their tools, the Foundation for Child Development decided several years ago that the time was ripe for an examination of the effectiveness of litigation as a method of improving the lives of children. In a series of case studies that will be the main part of a volume to be published in 1982 or 1983, five legal scholars probe the reasons for the decision to use litigation in these instances, the way in which they were handled, and their intended and unintended consequences for children.

In the New York City/New York State sector of its program, the foundation has carried out two studies of children and families, Trude W. Lash, *State of the Child: New York City I and II*, (1976), each of which examines data on various aspects of children's lives, including their health, their schools, and the family and community environments in which they live. By looking at the subject over a period of years, the studies tell us not only how children are, but also whether or not their lives are getting better or worse.

Other projects in New York City and State are directed at reducing the number of children placed out of their homes in foster care and improving the juvenile justice system.

Change comes slowly to foundations. With occasional exceptions, the programs of most foundations are products of evolution rather than transformation. The abiding concern for the child at risk that has run through the history of the Foundation for Child Development provides further testimony for this phenomenon. While there are no immediate plans for changes, the foundation's program undoubtedly will reshape itself from time to time in anticipation of and in response to the needs of children.

The Foundation for Child Development is governed by a council of forty-seven members and a seventeen-person board of directors. The council meets annually to receive the officers' report and to elect the board. The board meets four times a year to determine foundation policy and to approve projects brought by the staff for consideration. There are ten elected officers of the foundation, two of whom, the president and vice-president, are members of the staff.

Offices of the Foundation for Child Development are located at 345 East Forty-sixth Street, New York, New York 10017.

For further information, see *Annual Reports* of the association and foundation, published, annually or biannually, continuously since 1900. See also *Growth: The Story of Forty-Five Years of Service Performed by the Association for the Aid of Crippled Children, 1900–1945* (1945); and *The Story of the 50th Year* (1949).

JANE DUSTAN

**FRANK E. PAYNE AND SEBA B. PAYNE FOUNDATION.** Established as a trust in 1962 in Illinois, the Frank E. Payne and Seba B. Payne Foundation was initiated with funds provided by the late Seba B. Payne. By 1975, the foundation's assets amounted to about $3 million, and it made grants for that year totalling $16,500. In 1980, its assets were valued at about $10 million, and it made grants for the year amounting to about $300,000. In 1981, as the result of diversification of its holdings, which up to that year consisted primarily of stock in Crane Packing Company, the market value of the foundation's assets increased to about $31 million.

The Payne Foundation has always made grants primarily to educational institutions and hospitals, with emphasis on those located in the Chicago area and the state of Pennsylvania. In 1981, for example, 77 percent of its total grants of about $560,000 were made in these educational and health areas, with the remainder allocated for cultural programs, youth/social welfare programs, and religious organizations. The largest grant for that year was one of $200,000 to Moravian College, Bethlehem, Pennsylvania. Other larger grants included one of $50,000 to the Allentown (Pennsylvania) Art Museum; $20,000 to the Evanston (Illinois) Hospital Association; and $40,000 to the Leaning Tower YMCA of Chicago.

The foundation is governed by a five-member board of trustees, which includes a corporate trustee, the Continental Illinois National Bank and Trust Company of Chicago. The address of the foundation is in care of Continental Illinois National Bank and Trust Company of Chicago, 30 North LaSalle Street, Chicago, Illinois 60693.

Almost the only additional sources of information readily available to the public on this foundation are the annual reports and returns filed by it with the Internal Revenue Service, and the various Foundation Center publications.

**FRUEAUFF FOUNDATION.** See Charles A. Frueauff Foundation, Inc.

**FULD HEALTH TRUST.** See Helene Fuld Health Trust.

**FULLER FOUNDATION.** See George F. and Sybil H. Fuller Foundation.

# G

**GANNETT FOUNDATION, INC.** Frank E. Gannett, in explaining why he established the foundation which bears his name, stated that he was not interested in personal financial reward but sought only the joy that came from contributing to the general welfare.

Gannett did, in fact, gain considerable personal financial reward, rising from the poverty of the western New York farmland where he was born in America's centennial year to multimillionaire wealth when he died in 1957. But his personal philanthropy and that of the Gannett Foundation also have contributed over $65 million to the general welfare of Gannett communities.

At Gannett's death, his group of nineteen daily newspapers was, as now, the nation's largest numerically. Twenty-two years earlier, its founder and sole owner began to worry over how to keep his company from falling into irresponsible hands and how to find an appropriate instrument for benevolence. The Gannett Foundation provided both benefits. Its founder incorporated the foundation in 1935 in Rochester, New York, and gave it fifteen hundred shares of his personally owned Gannett stock, then worth less than $1 million. In his will, Gannett bequeathed to the foundation most of his remaining stock, with the intention that the Gannett Foundation would perpetually control the company. That did not work out since Gannett Co., Inc., "went public" in 1967, and government regulations required the foundation to slash its 34 percent ownership of the new stock. Additional stock issues and stock gifts have reduced the foundation's piece of the company to 11 percent (six million shares) today. But the foundation remains Gannett's single largest shareholder, and the name and charitable spirit of its founder are perpetuated in its grants. Those have averaged about $6.5 million in recent years, including $8.7 million in 1980. The money for them comes primarily from dividends on the foundation's Gannett stock. The foundation's assets in 1981 were about $207 million, making it one of America's largest foundations.

Since Frank Gannett's death, Gannett Co., Inc., has grown explosively under the leadership of chief executives Paul Miller and Allen H. Neuharth, who are also trustees of the Gannett Foundation. The company now includes the nation's largest newspaper group in circulation (3.6 million) as well as in number of papers. Furthermore, it has diversified into a varied communications conglomerate with annual revenues of more than $1 billion and an impressive profit record. Specifically, Gannett Co., Inc., owns eighty-two daily and twenty-two nondaily newspapers. In addition to its newspapers, Gannett operates seven television stations; thirteen radio stations; the largest outdoor advertising group in North America; news, marketing research, and satellite communications; and film production services. These far-flung properties are located in more than one hundred communities in thirty-five states, two U.S. territories, and Canada. They range from St. Thomas, Virgin Islands, to Agana, Guam, and from Saskatoon in Canada to Fort Myers in Florida.

Each of those communities is eligible to receive the civic, charitable, cultural, educational, and health grants of the Gannett Foundation. They are recommended to the foundation's headquarters in Rochester by local newspaper publishers or chief executives of other Gannett subsidiaries, who are familiar with local charitable needs and priorities. Then the grants are reviewed by the foundation's staff and approved by the trustees. This local screening process enables the Gannett Foundation to maintain a relatively small headquarters staff (eight full-time employees) and to channel most of its resources to philanthropy.

In recent years, the Gannett Foundation has made far fewer large grants and many more smaller ones, to enable assistance to a broader variety of human needs and services. The average grant is now about $5,600, with many more contributions below that level than above. These grants are indexed in national directories; and the Gannett Foundation's assets, revenues, and disbursements are detailed in its federal tax returns, which are public documents. The foundation's primary national interest is journalism education and professionalism, and its grants in those fields are made in non-Gannett communities as well as those served by Gannett subsidiaries. Gannett Foundation president is Eugene C. Dorsey, a former publisher of Gannett and other newspapers. Offices are in Lincoln Tower, Rochester, New York 14604.

What manner of man was Frank Gannett, who started all this philanthropy? He went to Cornell University with $80 in his pockets and a $200 annual state scholarship, and he worked his way through college. He built his newspaper group at first on borrowed money, starting in Elmira, then moving to Rochester and on to other points in New York, New Jersey, and Illinois with the help of two able and devoted colleagues, Frank Tripp and Erwin Davenport. A sharp businessman, Gannett also paid and treated his employees well by the standards of the time. A teetotaler, he did not allow liquor advertisements in his newspapers. A newspaper carrier in his youth, he also established scholarships that have helped more than fourteen hundred young Gannett carriers through college. A conservative Republican, he opposed President Franklin Roosevelt and made a futile try for the GOP presidential nomination in 1940—but he also plugged for creation of a U.S. Department of Peace. He called both famous men and apprentice printers by their first names. He also established a pioneering policy of autonomous newspapers to counter criticism of his ownership of (usually) the only papers in the small- to medium-sized cities long predominate in the Gannett group. That policy continues as strong as ever in today's Gannett newspapers. Gannett was a devoted husband and father; and his widow, Carolyn Werner Gannett, emulated both his civic leadership and philanthropy until her death in 1979. She was long a member of the Gannett Foundation's trustees, and the Gannetts's daughter, Sally G. McAdam, continues to serve on the board.

Shakespeare wrote that the good men do lives after them. And as foundation chairman Jack Scott has said, "Millions of people have benefited from the generosity and the wisdom and the foresight of Frank Gannett." Or as Vincent S. Jones, the foundation's first chief executive, once quipped, "Frank Gannett didn't take it with him. He didn't even try."

For further information, see *People/Purposes,* an informational brochure published by the foundation. See also "Frank E. Gannett," *Dictionary of American Biography,* Supplement Six (1980), pp. 226–227.

CALVIN MAYNE

**GATES FOUNDATION.** In 1946 in Denver, Colorado, the Gates Foundation was established by Charles C. Gates, Sr., members of the Gates family, and businesses owned by the Gates family. Gates, who died in 1961, was the founder and chief executive of the Gates Rubber Company, of Denver. The initial assets of the foundation were token in nature, amounting to only $2,500 in 1951. By 1957, however, assets had grown to about $660,000, and grants for that year amounted to about $150,000. The stated purpose of the foundation from its inception to that time was to help mankind, particularly U.S. citizens, by exploring and disseminating "methods and techniques for applying the discoveries and benefits of the science of Humanics so as to promote the well being, the health, and the security of individuals employed or engaged in industry." To further this purpose, Gates Foundation grants in the late 1950s were made to community funds, institutions of higher education, youth organizations, and hospitals and health agencies located principally in Denver.

Following the death of the senior Gates, the application of humanics to better the situation of industrial workers was dropped from the foundation's stated purpose, and the list of donee organizations was broadened to include museums, recreational facilities, and music. The area of primary giving was also broadened to include all of Colorado. By 1968, foundation assets amounted to almost $3 million, and grants for that year totalled more than $400,000.

Following a review of its program in the late 1970s, the Gates Foundation announced its major current interests. With a deep concern for and confidence in the future of Colorado, and with a special concern for Denver and its surrounding communities, the foundation intends to make a steady commitment to the improvement of the quality of life for those who live and work in that community. The foundation believes that a critical characteristic of every nonprofit organization must be the ability to be largely financially self-sufficient from income earned by the performance of services related directly to the purpose of the organization. Committed to finding the ways and means to encourage greater cooperation between the government and public and private sectors, the Gates Foundation will make every effort to help provide elected and appointed public-sector managers and leaders with those skills they need in order to serve the citizenry in the most effective manner possible. In conjunction with its continuing belief that the arts and cultural activities of a community are important, the foundation has an ongoing interest in encouraging the development of those positive life-styles which are most effective in helping individuals to improve and maintain their good health and physical well being. Parallel to its ongoing interest in the growth and development of independent schools and private colleges, the foundation believes that there is much to be learned by young people in nonacademic settings—programs engaged in character and leadership development will continue to be of interest. Likewise, the foundation views conservation and outdoor recreation as supportive of its interest in health, education, leadership training, and youth services and will continue to maintain an active interest in those areas. The Gates Foundation has a continuing interest in the preservation of the free-enterprise system. It maintains an interest in parks and historic preservation. Finally, the foundation will, from time to time, initiate programs of special interest to the trustees. In light of these interests, and with giving generally restricted to Colorado, the Gates Foundation has made most of its recent grants to organizations operating in the following areas: education, humanistic and cultural affairs, youth and human services, health, and conservation/recreation.

In 1981, the Gates Foundation had assets in excess of $48 million, and its annual grants in the preceding few years ranged from about $1.5 million to $3 million. Since its inception, the foundation has made grants totalling more than $25 million.

The foundation is governed by a six-member board of trustees. Charles C. Gates, the son of the founder, is currently the president of the board and also chairman and chief executive officer of Gates Rubber Company, part of the newly formed Gates Corporation. One other board member of the foundation is a retired officer of the company. Administration of the Gates Foundation is carried on from offices located at 155 South Madison Street, Denver, Colorado 80209, under the direction of an executive director.

For further information, see *Annual Reports* of the foundation, published continuously since the 1970s. See also *Information for Grant Applicants* (1982–1983), which contains biographical material about the Gates family, together with a brief account of the foundation's establishment and operation.

**GENERAL EDUCATION BOARD (GEB).** The General Education Board was established by John D. Rockefeller, Sr., for "the promotion of education within the United States of America, without distinction of race, sex, or creed." It was set up and began operations in New York in 1902 and was incorporated by act of the United States Congress in January, 1903.

Judged by the standards of today, public education in the United States at the beginning of the twentieth century, outside of occasional centers in the North and Middle West, was backward and crude. In the rural areas, one-room schoolhouses were common. Teachers' salaries were low, and in many places schooling ended at the elementary level.

This situation was particularly true of the southern states, which still suffered from the economic chaos and poverty of the post-Civil War era. Where schools existed, the South had the added expense of two separate school systems for white and black children. Less than half of the children were regularly enrolled in schools. Eighty-five percent of the people in the southern states lived in the country, where the average annual school term was about eighty school days. The teachers in these schools were often lacking in education beyond the elementary level.

In 1901, Robert C. Ogden, a Philadelphia businessman, invited a group of prominent men and women to visit some of the leading black schools of the South. Among those on the trip was John D. Rockefeller, Jr., who had been assisting his father in philanthropic activities for several years. The younger Rockefeller had been raised in an atmosphere of concern and sympathy for blacks. Having observed southern conditions, he at first considered creating an institution to promote education for blacks, but he was advised that to aid blacks would be impossible unless the southern white was aided also. It was then decided to create the General Education Board, which began with a pledge from Rockefeller, Jr., on behalf of his father, of one million dollars to be spent over a period of ten years. In subsequent years, Rockefeller's gifts to the GEB, figured at the market value on the day of the gift, reached a total of $129,209,167.

The first secretary and chief executive officer of the GEB was Dr. Wallace Buttrick, a former Baptist minister who was secretary of the American Baptist Home Mission Society. Buttrick and Frederick T. Gates, the senior Rockefeller's lieutenant and advisor, who became the GEB's chairman in 1907, dominated its activities for the first two decades.

The first undertaking of the GEB was the improvement of elementary and secondary schools in the South. In cooperation with the Southern Education Board, the John F. Slater Fund, and the Peabody Fund, campaigns were conducted for the establishment of improved elementary schools, for passage of laws calling for the creation of secondary schools, and increased financial support for schools. One of the methods employed was to provide salaries for professors of secondary education at state universities. The task of these professors, southerners, was to inform, cultivate, and guide professional, public, and legislative opinion. Because a high percentage of the South's population lived in rural areas, the GEB also provided salaries for supervisors of rural schools within the state superintendents' offices. These officials aided with planning and organization of schools and attempted to develop a curriculum with special significance for farmers' children. Improvement of rural schools required increased prosperity in those areas. The GEB therefore cooperated with the U.S. Department of Agriculture in a program of farm demonstrations to increase agricultural productivity.

Much remained to be done when these campaigns were ended; but increased interest and support for public education had been aroused, and a permanent organization for the development of rural schools had been created.

In its earliest years, the General Education Board was unable to do much in promoting public education for blacks. The bulk of its donations for black education went for schools that emphasized agricultural and industrial training in the pattern of Hampton and Tuskegee institutes. This emphasis on practical education was in harmony with general schooling trends of the late nineteenth century but also was a form of education that was most harmonious with southern prejudices with regard to blacks. The GEB's view was that whatever education could be provided was better than none.

The Anna T. Jeanes Fund had begun work of this type in 1908 by offering to support a black industrial teacher for any county which wished to employ one. The teachers visited the small rural schools in the county and introduced and supervised simple forms of industrial work. They also organized and encouraged local teachers. There were soon more requests for teachers than the income of the Jeanes Fund could meet. The GEB came to the fund's aid and from 1914 to 1949 made periodic grants toward the teachers' salaries. As the decades passed, the role of the Jeanes teachers became increasingly one of general supervision. In many cases, they acted, in effect, as assistant county superintendents for black schools.

In 1910, with support from the Peabody Fund, the state of Virginia named Jackson Davis as the first state supervisor of rural schools for blacks. Two years later, the General Education Board offered to support such an official for any southern state that might apply. Within two years, the GEB was subsidizing white agents for black schools in several southern states. It supported state agents as the chief medium of its black education program until 1946.

In the absence of public high schools for blacks in rural areas of the South, the GEB in 1915 undertook a cooperative program with the Slater Fund to provide some training for black teachers. By 1937, when these schools became part of the public school systems, the GEB had contributed almost $1.5 million for them. Well into the 1930s, county training schools provided in many localities the only secondary education, and often the only adequate elementary schooling, available to blacks.

Although the problems of the South were a major concern of the General Education Board throughout its existence, that area was only one of its interests. Northern state school systems also suffered from poor organization, lack of trained administrators, and a paucity of clearly defined goals and procedures. Beginning with the Maryland system in 1914–1916, the GEB conducted a series of studies of state school systems, which led to substantial reforms. In 1928, this task was turned over to George Peabody College for Teachers, which created a Division of Surveys and Field Services. This function was first supported by a series of grants and later with an endowment fund of $750,000. Peabody broadened the program to include activities such as curriculum conferences, school building improvement programs, and the publication of bulletins and materials on a wide variety of educational problems.

In the 1920s, the GEB expanded its work in three areas: improvement of higher education, raising the standards of American medical schools, and exploration of other needs in education.

In 1902, the year of the GEB's founding, there were nearly seven hundred private and state colleges and universities. Many of them had inadequate revenues and were hardly more than secondary schools. At first the GEB undertook to assist the schools which showed the most promise in favorable locations—centers of commerce, population, and wealth and near transportation lines. Later, the most important criterion was the promise of the institution itself. Individual promise had to be interpreted generously in the case of institutions in the South and Middle West and liberally when it came to black institutions. The GEB encouraged schools to concentrate fund-raising efforts on endowments. It usually preferred private institutions and cooperated with schools affiliated with all religious denominations.

The GEB's practice was to require that its gifts be matched by a specific sum given by others, usually an equal or larger amount. This practice was criticized, and even resented, by some institutions. The GEB's view, however, was that the assets of all foundations could not meet the needs of higher education alone and that making grants in this manner would win a wider base of support from the institutions' alumni and friends. By 1925, it had made endowment grants totalling about $60 million to 291 colleges and universities, not including medical schools. In matching these gifts, the institutions raised $140 million.

In its many contacts with academic institutions, the General Education Board was very much aware of the problems caused by low academic salaries. The period of inflation that followed World War I exaggerated this situation. Jerome D. Greene, who had been a trustee since 1912, focused the GEB's attention on this problem at a meeting in September, 1919. John D. Rockefeller, a few months later, made a gift of $50 million to be specifically devoted to the increase of teachers' salaries. Distribution of this fund was almost completed by June, 1924, although the final date set for collection of matching subscriptions was June, 1933. As a result, the endowments of 173 colleges, including 8 black institutions, were increased by approximately $116 million.

The problems of higher education for blacks were difficult to address. These institutions had been established mostly by religious denominations. There had been no consideration of regional needs, and the schools competed for the available teachers and students. One major effort of the GEB was to encourage cooperation between the black institutions of Atlanta—Spelman College, Morehouse College, and Atlanta University—through large grants for a joint library and future development. Clark College, Morris Brown College, and Gammon Theological Seminary were later brought into the cooperative arrangements.

The earliest of black colleges to receive support from the General Education Board was Fisk, which received grants of more than $5.2 million between 1905 and 1952. Two institutions in New Orleans were merged to form Dillard University, which was named after a trustee of the GEB. Dillard received more than $2 million for endowment and buildings. Jackson College, in Mississippi, and Howard University each received $500,000 in addition to assistance provided for Howard's medical school. In making these gifts, the GEB again faced questions with regard to the desirability of supporting separate schools for blacks. It acted in the belief that until integration was accomplished, the stronger predominantly black colleges were essential.

The GEB's program in medical education was led by Abraham Flexner, who conducted a study of American medical schools for the Carnegie Foundation for the Advancement of Teaching* which was published in 1910. Flexner reported that most medical schools were hardly deserving of the name. The teaching staffs almost always consisted of local practitioners who gave little attention to their classes. Laboratories and clinical facilities were poor, if they existed at all.

Flexner joined the staff of the General Education Board in 1913. He had already recommended that a large grant be made to Johns Hopkins Medical School, which had placed its laboratory departments on a "university basis" with instructors devoting full time to their teaching. In 1913, the board made an appropriation to Johns Hopkins for the purpose of placing the clinical departments on a full-time basis also. Subsequent grants were made to provide full-time teaching at Washington University, in St. Louis, at Yale, the University of Chicago, and Vanderbilt.

The full-time principle aroused great hostility among many laymen and doctors, who contended that this requirement involved interference with the domestic management of an institution, which the GEB said was against its policy. After receiving additional gifts of more than $45 million from Rockefeller, Sr., which were earmarked for medical education, the officers began to ease the full-time requirement. Compromises were reached with Columbia University and Cornell which provided for token observances of full time. The practice which evolved was called "geographical full time," under which the professor or physician conducted all of his practice at the institution with various arrangements for the office and collection of fees. The GEB appropriated $94 million for medical education through 1960, most of it on the condition that matching funds be raised.

The only medical schools for blacks which the GEB considered worthy of major support were Howard and Meharry. From 1920 until 1936, it contributed almost $600,000 to the Howard medical school to supplement its support from the United States Congress. To Meharry, the GEB appropriated $8,673,706, exclusive of fellowships, between 1916 and 1960.

One of the General Education Board's most controversial projects was the establishment of the Lincoln School of Teachers College, Columbia University, which opened in 1917. Over the next twelve years, it appropriated almost $6 million for the school. The goal of the school was the construction of new curricula and the development of new methods. In the 1920s, methods developed by the Lincoln School were introduced in many public schools. Innovations such as the core curriculum, the merging of history, geography, and civics into "social studies," a fresh and practical approach to science teaching, and a greater vocational emphasis came to be characteristic, in many school systems. Teachers College ultimately merged the Lincoln School with its demonstration school and after a long series of legal battles dissolved it altogether in 1948.

In 1923, Wallace Buttrick became chairman of the GEB, and Wickliffe Rose, who had led the International Health Division of the Rockefeller Foundation,* became president. Rose developed a program to stimulate the sciences by encouraging, in a limited number of institutions, programs designed to establish a high order of training for promising scientists. Between 1925 and 1932, the GEB endowed scientific investigation through expenditures of nearly $19 million. Grants were made to the California Institute of Technology, Princeton, Cornell, the University of Chicago, Stanford, and Harvard, among others.

In 1928, the decision was made to correct overlapping that had developed among the various Rockefeller boards. The General Education Board ended its work in medicine, the natural sciences, and the humanities. These fields were taken over by the Rockefeller Foundation. Trevor Arnett, an expert in college and university finance, became president of the GEB.

During the depression of the 1930s, the high-school population of the country practically tripled in five years. The school curriculum, however, was still geared to pupils who might be prepared for more advanced academic work, and the traditional college preparatory curriculum did not hold the new students in school. Between 1933 and 1940, the GEB carried on a general education program to promote changes that would make the system more responsive to the needs of the new school population.

An important part of the general education program was support of agencies working for reorganization of education at the high-school and junior-college levels. Groups working, with assistance from the GEB, toward more flexible curricula and new instructional materials and methods included the American Council on Education and its subsidiary, the American Youth Commission; the National Education Association; the Progressive Education Association; the Board of Regents of the State of New York; the Michigan State Board of Education; and the Washington State Planning Council.

The coming of World War II, which caused a sharp increase in employment, made the program in general education seem irrelevant, and it was terminated in 1940 after an expenditure of $8.5 million. It had created an element of ferment in the educational system. The projects supported had stimulated widespread interest in ways to improve the care and education of young people, and it built up a new body of knowledge about youth.

Another of the GEB's influential programs of the 1930s involved the study of child growth and development. Aid was given to eight major university research centers for studies of the physical and psychological development of children from infancy through adolescence. This work, for which almost $2.5 million was appropriated, provided support for the nursery-school movement, for the modern practice of pediatrics, and for textbooks on child development and adolescence.

In 1920, Rockefeller, Sr., removed all restrictions on the purposes and use of his gifts to the General Education Board, and the trustees began to use the principal as well as the income. By 1937, the GEB had only about $8.7 million in uncommitted funds. This figure increased as market conditions improved, and the Rockefeller Foundation, beginning in 1946, provided almost $16 million in additional funds; but the GEB's days of numerous large gifts had ended. Many of its officers were now also officers of the Rockefeller Foundation.

The GEB decided, in 1940, to concentrate its remaining funds on the South, where the need was still great. From the beginning, the officers had believed that one of the best ways to improve education in the South was to strengthen its economy. Grants were made to southern institutions for studies of agricultural economics and rural sociology, for work in farm management and markets and community development, and for research in soils, forestry, and fish biology. In 1946, the GEB began a series of grants to selected universities to strengthen graduate education. More than $12 million was appropriated to Vanderbilt, Tulane, Duke, Emory, and Atlanta universities.

The General Education Board was one of the first foundations to use systematically fellowships and scholarships in the conduct of its work. Its first fellow, Bruce R. Payne, who later became president of Peabody College, was appointed in 1903. The formal fellowship program began in 1921–1922. It naturally reflected the GEB's major interests—first in public education in the South, then medical education throughout the country, later in higher education. In its final years, the GEB once again concentrated on strengthening southern institutions by giving fellowships to teachers and able college graduates who intended to teach. Such opportunities were especially important for black educators, and almost all black college presidents, deans, and ranking faculty members held GEB fellowships at some time in their careers. About $8 million of the GEB's funds went for fellowships, and more than two thousand fellows were appointed.

As the GEB's program ended in 1964, its last funds, approximately $150,000, were granted to Berea College, in Kentucky, to establish a Special Student Aid Program. The grant was an appropriate indication of the continuity of the GEB's programs, as Berea, serving an isolated and impoverished area, had been the recipient of one of the first grants in 1902.

Spending principal and income, the General Education Board appropriated more than $324.6 million between 1902 and 1964. Of this amount, more than $208 million was spent for universities and colleges (other than black), mostly for general endowment, buildings, facilities, and current expenses; medical education and sciences; natural sciences; and graduate education. Almost $8.5 million was spent for public education (other than black). More than $62.6 million was appropriated for black education, public and private, including fellowships and scholarships. Almost $25.8 million was spent for the science of education.

General Education Board records, approximately 350 cubic feet of correspondence and reports, may be consulted at the Rockefeller Archive Center, Pocantico Hills, North Tarrytown, New York 10591.

The GEB issued a report on its activities for the years 1902–1914 and an annual report thereafter through 1956. It published *General Education Board, Review and Final Report, 1902–1964* (1964). The foregoing brief history is based largely on that account and on Raymond B. Fosdick, with Henry F. Pringle and Katherine Douglas Pringle, *Adventure in Giving: The Story of the General Education Board* (1962).

J. WILLIAM HESS

**GENERAL MOTORS FOUNDATION.** General Motors Corporation (GM) established this company-sponsored foundation in Michigan in 1976 with the announced purpose of leveling the peaks and valleys of the company's charitable contributions, which had often declined in periods of economic downturn when charitable institutions were most in need of support. The management of the company believed that a foundation would, over the years, enable GM to stabilize its contributions to such institutions. As a founding contribution, GM gave $40 million to the foundation in 1976 and added another $40 million the following year. Its 1980 assets of about $82 million makes the General Motors Foundation one of the largest, company-sponsored foundations in the United States.

Since it began operations in 1977, the foundation has made grants of more than $10 million annually. Grants have been concentrated in the following areas in the following approximate percentages: community funds (such as United Way), 35 percent; higher education, 35 percent; hospitals and urban and civic affairs, 15 percent; cultural, youth, business, and international, 15 percent. The foundation has concentrated its grants in Michigan, Ohio, New York, and Indiana, which are the states in which GM divisions and plants are concentrated.

The trustees of the General Motors Foundation are drawn, for the most part, from the executive ranks of the General Motors Corporation. The administration of the foundation's programs is conducted by a manager from offices located at 3044 West Grand Boulevard, Detroit, Michigan 48202.

For further information, see *General Motors Public Interest Reports*, published annually since 1970 by the General Motors Corporation. Since 1976, a section therein, entitled "Philanthropic Activities," discusses in a summary way the operations of the foundation.

**GEORGE F. AND SYBIL H. FULLER FOUNDATION.** The Fuller Foundation was created by George F. Fuller and his wife, Sybil H. Fuller, by declaration of trust dated May 4, 1955.

George Fuller was born in 1869. His father died at an early age, and the burden of support of the family fell on George. At the age of eighteen, he went to work for what later became the Wyman-Gordon Company, of Worcester, Massachusetts. His mechanical genius and hard work contributed greatly to the success of the company. He became successively president, chairman of the board, and was honorary chairman of the board at the time of his death in 1962, as well as a substantial owner of the company. He was active in Worcester business affairs and a very generous contributor to civic and charitable causes.

George and Sybil Fuller left the great bulk of their property to the foundation, including all of their shares of the stock of Wyman-Gordon Company, which is the foundation's principal asset.

The purposes of the Fuller Foundation are to apply its funds for religious, charitable, scientific, literary, or educational purposes, or for the prevention of cruelty to children, within the United States or its possessions.

Grants have been largely to local projects of a capital nature. Major grants have been to the American Antiquarian Society, Worcester Art Museum, Worcester Natural History Society, Mechanics Hall Restoration Fund, Worcester Polytechnic Institute, Clark University, and Assumption College. In 1981, grants aggregated approximately three million dollars, and since its founding through 1980, its has distributed over sixteen million dollars in grants.

Assets of the Fuller Foundation had a 1982 value of approximately $70 million. The present trustees and officers of the foundation are: Sacket R. Duryee, chairman; Paris Fletcher, vice-chairman; Robert P. Hallock, secretary; Russell E. Fuller, treasurer; and Ernest M. Fuller, trustee. Administration of the foundation is carried on from offices located at 105 Madison Street, Worcester, Massachusetts 01601.

Applications for funding may be made by letter, which should contain relevant information, including proof of tax-exempt status, and should be received prior to December 1. No grants are made to individuals.

The foregoing brief history of the foundation was based on information supplied by Paris Fletcher, vice-chairman of the George F. and Sybil H. Fuller Foundation.

**GEORGE FOUNDATION, THE.** The George Foundation was established in Texas in 1945 by the late Albert P. and Mamie E. George. The trust indenture expressed a very strong preference for the limiting of grants by the foundation to projects within Fort Bend County, Texas, home of the Georges.

Initially, the assets of the George Foundation were relatively small, amounting to about $675,000 by 1956. Since that time, they have swelled to approximately $7 million in 1968; $12 million in 1975; and in 1979, following receipt of the final distribution from the estate of Mamie George, they were valued at about $66 million. In 1980, they amounted to about $80 million.

Throughout its history, the George Foundation has limited its giving to a broad range of projects in Fort Bend County, Texas. In the county, the foundation was responsible for: the establishment and funding of the Polly Ryan Memorial Hospital; provision of the land and substantial improvements for the T. W. Davis Memorial Park; the restoration of a number of historic buildings and homes; the construction and maintenance of a central and branch libraries; the granting of college scholarships to high school students; and aid for a number of junior colleges and all of the churches located in Fort Bend County.

Annual grants in recent years have amounted to about $2.5 million to $4.5 million. In 1979, about 97 percent of the grants made went for civic affairs, parks, and historic preservation. One million dollars, for example, was appropriated for construction of a central library and $1,384,480 for fieldhouse construction in a park.

The George Foundation is governed by a three-member board of trustees. The mailing address of the foundation is 207 South Third Street, Post Office Box 536, Richmond, Texas 77469.

For further information, see an informational statement issued by the foundation, together with annual reports and returns filed by it with the Internal Revenue Service, and the various Foundation Center publications.

**GEORGE GUND FOUNDATION, THE.** The founder and major donor of this philanthropy was George Gund (1888–1966), born in La Crosse, Wisconsin. The Gund family settled in Cleveland, Ohio, in 1897. George Gund graduated from Harvard College in 1909 and attended the first business school class at Harvard. His early career included real estate and banking activities in Seattle; army service during World War I; and ranching in Nevada. In 1936, he married Jessica Roessler and began a career in banking in Cleveland, culminating in his being named president of Cleveland Trust Company (now Ameritrust) in 1941 and ultimately, chairman of its board of trustees. In addition, Gund during his lifetime served as a director of some thirty other large corporations.

George Gund began a program of charitable giving in 1937 which, even in this early period, centered on the educational and other institutions which had influenced him in early life. Although he had little personal interest in the arts, he was devoted to fostering them. For example, he had a life-long association with the Cleveland Institute of Art and served as its president from 1942 until his death.

The George Gund Foundation was created in 1951 because Gund believed that the private philanthropic foundation was the most effective medium for charitable giving if it were organized and operated in an effective manner. Furthermore, its work for good would not be limited to the donor's lifetime.

The history of the Gund Foundation falls into three rather distinct periods. The first is the period from its beginnings down to George Gund's death in 1966. Small at the beginning (in 1956 its grants amounted to about $40,000), the foundation eventually gave away a total of $2 million during this early fifteen-year period. Approximately 65 percent of this sum went to three institutions—the Cleveland Institute of Art, Harvard University, and Kenyon College—and the largest and most significant grants to each occurred in the 1960s. Smaller grants to 171 other institutions ranged from $10 to $10,000. Ninety percent of all of the grants were to educational institutions or programs.

The second period, from George Gund's death in 1966 through 1969, was essentially a transitional period. About $6.5 million of the total of approximately $9 million disbursed during this period went to six institutions in memory of the donor, but the foundation began to enter new areas.

During the period from 1970 to 1981, there was a sizable growth in the Gund Foundation's assets and resultant disbursements. Grants during this period totalled about $45 million. The foundation trustees (four children of George Gund now serve as trustees) and staff made an extensive review of its activities and as a result broadened its range and scope of activities. By 1981, the George Gund Foundation's program areas included education, social and economic progress, the arts, environmental quality, and civic affairs. Within each of these broad areas, the foundation has developed areas of concentration, that is, funds of substantial magnitude are concentrated upon one project. In art, for example, the foundation had made contributions to the George Gund Collection of Western Art, which has been exhibited as a traveling collection throughout the country. Grants in the areas of education and social and economic progress, however, have received highest foundation priority. Approximately 65 percent of available grant funds are now being allocated for projects in these two areas.

To summarize, in about thirty years, the George Gund Foundation changed from a small foundation to a large one, with 1981 assets of about $88 million and with annual disbursements of some $5 million to $6 million. At the same time, it has moved from a foundation with a relatively narrow focus related to the interests of its founder to a broader concern with all of the interests of the community and region in which it is located and, to a degree, the nation.

The foundation's programs and activities are conducted from offices located at One Erieview Plaza, Cleveland, Ohio 44114, by a staff headed by James S. Lipscomb, executive director.

For further information, see Geoffrey Gund, *The George Gund Foundation, 1952–1977* (1977), a brief history prepared by a son of the founder. See also *Annual Reports* of the foundation, published continuously since 1978.

**GEORGE I. ALDEN TRUST.** George Alden was a New Englander, born in 1843 in Templeton, Massachusetts, who earned money for his education in the furniture factories of nearby Gardner. He attended Harvard's Lawrence School of Science and subsequently taught mechanical engineering for twenty-eight years at the newly established Worcester Polytechnic Institute (WPI).

As one of the first faculty members of WPI, George Alden and his colleague, Milton Higgins, received national recognition in the 1880s and 1890s for their successful espousal and implementation of an engineering education which interlarded and combined practice with theory. In addition, both Alden and Higgins were innovators whose skills and energies carried them beyond the campus into the world of industry. In 1885, they joined forces with a number of Worcester businessmen in the founding of the Norton Emery Wheel Company, wherein Alden became treasurer and Higgins became president. By 1896, the Norton Company had developed to the point that both men were devoting full time to its operation. By this time, too, Alden had invented a dynamometer for measuring the power of all kinds of machines, and he established and directed one of the first hydraulic laboratories in the United States and one in which the first hydraulic elevators were invented and produced by him and Higgins.

After 1896, as both Alden and the Norton Company prospered as the result of his concentration on its activities, he maintained his interest in education, particularly those aspects that he believed would help young people become effective and productive members of society. Thus he became a trustee of the WPI, a trustee of the newly formed Worcester Boys Trade School, and a member and moving force on the Worcester School Committee. As the second president and later chairman of the board of the Norton Company, Alden launched one of the first programs in the United States to provide help for company employees desiring further education.

It occasions no surprise, therefore, to read in George Alden's will that he wished to care for members of his family and also,

favored helping where earnest, self-sacrificing workers on small salaries are teaching eager pupils... and promoting education in schools, colleges, or other educational institutions, with a preference for industrial, vocational, or professional education....

The George I. Alden Trust was the outcome of these sentiments and was established by Alden on August 24, 1912. He gave his shares of the Norton Company to the trust. As the provisions therein for the benefit of the Alden family and their descendants have expired, the trust income available for philanthropic purposes has increased to the point that now all of the income is used for these purposes.

With the passage of years, the trustees of the Alden Trust have broadly interpreted George Alden's strong interest in career-oriented and related education for serious youth. Thus, scholarship support of students has been of importance, as well as aid for laboratories and other equipment and buildings, where relevant. The trust has been and is especially supportive of institutions that can show a combination of educational excellence together with efficient and economical administration. Its grants have been largely in the northeastern United States, with a special interest in Worcester institutions. The quality of a proposed program and institution, however, are the major factors in grant decisions. Outstanding grants have been those for the Alden Memorial Auditorium, the Alden Research Laboratories, the renovation of the Salisbury Laboratories, and the Atwater Kent building at the Worcester Polytechnic Institute, and for the construction of the Greendale YMCA and educational annex to the Worcester YMCA building.

The 1981 market value of the assets of the Alden Trust was approximately $54 million. Since its establishment in 1926, gifts to recipients have totalled over $25 million.

George Alden served as chairman of the trust's board of trustees from its founding until his death in 1926. Since that time, its operations have been carried out, from offices located at Room 1250, 370 Main Street, Worcester, Massachusetts 01608, by a four-member board of trustees. The present trustees and officers are: Paris Fletcher, chairman; Robert G. Hess, vice-chairman; Francis H. Dewey III, treasurer; George W. Hazzard, clerk.

The foregoing information was based on a booklet, *The George I. Alden Trust* (1980), supplied by the trustees. The booklet is revised annually by an addendum.

**GERALDINE R. DODGE FOUNDATION, INCORPORATED.** Geraldine Rockefeller Dodge (1882–1973) was the daughter of financier William Rockefeller, brother of John D. Rockefeller. In 1907, she married Marcellus Hartley Dodge, heir to the Remington Arms fortune. This union made them one of the wealthiest couples in the United States. Their only son, M. Hartley Dodge, Jr., was killed in an automobile accident in 1930, and the tragedy profoundly affected his mother's life. Thereafter, Geraldine Dodge, who with her husband had been one of the country's leading horse and dog fanciers, turned her interests increasingly to concern for the welfare of animals. For example, she founded and for years maintained a shelter for homeless animals, St. Hubert's Giralda. And in her will, which bequeathed her entire residual estate to the establishment of the Geraldine R. Dodge Foundation, she directed that the foundation be devoted "to the following general and unrestricted objects and purposes: for charitable, scientific, literary, or other educational purposes, or for the prevention of cruelty to animals, or for the encouragement of art."

Incorporated in New Jersey in 1974, the Dodge Foundation initiated and completed a study in 1976 to determine its program priorities. Aside from several small grants, the foundation did not begin active operation until 1977. The guidelines for the foundation's program that emerged from the study called for support in six program areas: animal welfare, the arts, education, critical issues, public interest, and local projects. Except in the fields of animal welfare and secondary education, the foundation has restricted its grants to programs in New Jersey. The largest share of the foundation's grants has been for secondary education in a number of private schools in the New England and Middle Atlantic states. The foundation has excluded from consideration the fields of higher education, health, religion, and international projects.

Beginning with assets of about $30 million in 1977, further distributions of Geraldine Dodge's estate raised the foundation's assets to a 1981 level of approximately $81 million. Grants totalling about $1.5 million were made in 1977 during the foundation's first year of operation. Since then, grants have risen steadily, and it is anticipated that future grants will approximate $4 million annually.

The ten-member board of trustees, of which the chairman and one other member are nephews of Geraldine Dodge, directs the affairs of the foundation. Its programs and projects are carried out by a small administrative staff, headed by an executive director, from offices located at 95 Madison Avenue, Post Office Box 1239 R, Morristown, New Jersey 07960.

For further information, see *Annual Reports* of the foundation, published continuously since 1977, and an information brochure published by the foundation in 1976. See also Geraldine R. Dodge obituary, *New York Times* (August 14, 1973), p. 36, and (September 25, 1973), p. 47.

**GODFREY M. HYAMS TRUST.** In 1921 in Massachusetts, the Godfrey M. Hyams Trust was established by Godfrey M. Hyams, a director of the Virginia Railway. Upon his death in 1927, the trust received its major endowment from his estate. In its early years, the Hyams Trust was among those foundations in the United States having the largest assets. In 1944, for example, its approximately $10 million in assets placed it among the thirty largest foundations then in existence; and in 1952, with assets of about $11 million, it still ranked among the fifty largest. By the end of that decade, although its assets had approximately doubled, it was no longer among the very large foundations. In 1979, its assets stood at about $30 million.

Under the declaration of trust establishing the foundation, the trustees were authorized to spend net income from the foundation's assets as they saw fit. They decided to make the majority of the grants for social service programs and not to make grants to purely educational programs. That policy has been continued to the present day.

Within the above policy guidelines, the Hyams Trust has, through the years, provided aid to a wide variety of what may be called social service organizations to help children, the handicapped, the sick, and the elderly. In 1944, the trust made grants of about $400,000, in 1954 of about $750,000, in 1958 of about $850,000, in 1969 almost $1.5 million, and in 1979 of about $2.2 million.

The 166 grants which were made by the trust in 1979 are within the pattern of its earlier grants. Grantees were overwhelmingly social service organizations in the Boston area, particularly those which served low-income families. They received over 89 percent of all funds granted in 1979. Major recipients in that year, for example, included the following: Lena Park Community Development Corporation, Dorchester—$100,000; American National Red Cross, Boston chapter—$50,000; Family Service Association of Greater Boston—$52,000; and Massachusetts Council of Human Service Providers—$50,000. A limited number of grants, generally for smaller sums, were made to cultural organizations and mental health programs.

The original governing board of trustees of the trust consisted of Godfrey Hyams and his two sisters, Isabel and Sarah. In 1929, an expanded board established two smaller funds, the Clara C. Hyams Fund (now named Sarah H. Hyams Fund) and the Solomon M. Hyams Fund (now named Isabel F. Hyams

Fund). The former was initially established to support the work of various nonincorporated charitable organizations in the Boston area. Today it supports the activities of the East Boston Social Center, Inc. The Isabel F. Hyams Fund was initially founded and has been used to fill gaps in social service needs in East Boston. In 1981, the trustees decided and have since followed the policy of making grants from this fund primarily for the support of summer programs in the social service area.

The trustees of the Godfrey M. Hyams Trust serve on the boards of trustees of the smaller funds. The three are administered from offices located at One Boston Place, Boston, Massachusetts 02108, under the direction of an executive director.

For further information, see *Annual Reports* of the trust and funds, published continuously since 1971. See also an application pamphlet (1982) published by the trust.

**GRANT FOUNDATION.** See William T. Grant Foundation.

**GUGGENHEIM FOUNDATION.** See John Simon Guggenheim Memorial Foundation.

**GUND FOUNDATION.** See George Gund Foundation, The.

# H

**HAAS COMMUNITY FUND.** See William Penn Foundation, The.

**HALLMARK EDUCATIONAL FOUNDATIONS.** The Hallmark Educational Foundation was established by Mr. Joyce C. Hall and Hall Brothers, Inc., in 1943 in Missouri. Hall parlayed two shoeboxes of imported postcards into Hallmark Cards, Inc., known until 1954 as Hall Brothers, Inc., the world's largest greeting-card concern. Self-educated, Joyce Hall personally chose and approved the messages on thousands of these cards, and he had an unerring sense of what the American people wanted said on these cards. As chief executive officer of Hallmark for fifty-six years, Hall guided its growth until, at the time of his death in 1982 at the age of ninety-one, it had over seventeen thousand employees and some twenty thousand nationwide Hallmark shops. With operations centered in Kansas City, Missouri, the Hallmark Educational Foundation has always focused its programs and provided support primarily for organizations located there together with the adjacent areas of Missouri and Kansas.

Initial assets of the foundation were relatively small. In 1951, for example, they were about $0.75 million, and grants for that year amounted to aproximately $32,000. The following approximate annual figures as to assets and grants attest to the foundation's growth since its early years: 1956—assets, $2.25 million; grants, $47,000; 1969—assets, $7 million; grants, $360,000.

It should be noted that, in 1954, the Hallmark Educational Foundation of Kansas was set up and funded by members of the Hall family. It was specifically organized to make grants in the state of Kansas, and its origins can probably be traced to a desire on the part of Kansans to partake of the Hall and Hallmark Cards, Inc., philanthropy. Dr. Franklin D. Murphy, then president of the University of Kansas, served then and continued until 1983 to serve on the board of directors of both foundations. The initial corpus of the Hallmark Foundation of Kansas was small when compared to the Hallmark Educational Foundation. In 1969, for example, the former had assets of about $275,000 compared to about $7 million for the latter. By 1981, however, their situations were reversed, with the Hallmark Educational Foundation of Kansas having assets of about $46.75 million while the Hallmark Educational Foundation had slightly over $21 million.

The two foundations, however, have always shared the same offices, administrative staff, and board of directors. Furthermore, their grants programs have been essentially the same for both foundations. For all practicable purposes, they have operated as one foundation although existing legally as two separate entities. The description of program and grants which follows, therefore, makes no attempt to distinguish between the two.

In addition to limiting their grants to Kansas City and adjacent areas of Missouri and Kansas, the foundations have been equally consistent in their support areas: education, health, welfare, cultural organizations and activities, and civic purposes. An analysis of their grants, totalling about $3.5 million for 1980, shows that 43 percent of foundation grants were for educational purposes. This included 21 percent for higher educational institutions, 12 percent for secondary and other educational programs; and 10 percent for a scholarship program limited to children of Hallmark Cards employees. Artistic and humanistic organizations were alloted 29 percent of grant monies for 1980. Twenty-six percent was devoted to the support of hospitals and health research and social welfare and youth programs, with the remaining 2 percent given for the support of civic, public policy, and other organizations. The largest dollar grants for 1980, all located in Kansas City, Missouri, unless noted otherwise, included the following: Nelson Gallery of Art—$729,086; Kansas University Endowment Association, Lawrence, Kansas—$533,120; the Menninger Foundation, Topeka, Kansas—$455,000; Salvation Army—$200,000; and the Learning Exchange—$131,374.

The Hallmark foundations, with 1981 assets of about $68 million, are governed by a seven-member board of directors, with Donald J. Hall, son of Joyce C. Hall, serving as chairman of the board. Administration of the foundations is carried on from offices located at Twenty-Fifth and McGee Streets, Kansas City, Missouri 64141, under the direction of a president.

For further information, see the *Annual Report* (1982) of the foundations. See also a pamphlet, *Guidelines for Grant Applicants* (n.d.), published by the Hallmark Educational Foundation; and Joyce C. Hall obituary, *New York Times* (October 30, 1982), p. 35.

**HAROLD K. L. CASTLE FOUNDATION.** The late Harold K. L. Castle, a Hawaiian business executive, and his wife, Alice, established the Harold K. L. Castle Foundation in Hawaii in 1962. The foundation's growth in assets and increase in annual giving is shown in the following approximate statistics for sample years: 1969—assets, $0.75 million; grants, $200,000; 1975—assets, $20 million; grants, $1.75 million; 1979—assets, $24 million; grants, $187,000; and 1981—assets, $30 million; grants, $1 million.

The Castle Foundation has always made grants primarily to organizations located in Hawaii. Its support has been directed primarily to education. In 1981, for example, it made only the following six grants, and all grantees were located in Hawaii: Hawaii Loa School—$500,000; St. Andrew's Priory School—$350,000; Iolani School—$1,124; Punahou School—$1,000; Honolulu Symphony Orchestra—$50,000; and Castle Memorial Hospital—$50,000.

The foundation is governed by a five-member board of directors, with a member of the Castle family serving as president and other family members on the board. The address of the foundation is in care of Kaneohe Ranch, Kaneohe, Oahu, Hawaii 96744.

Almost the only additional sources of information readily available to the public on this foundation are the annual reports and returns filed by it with the Internal Revenue Service, and the various Foundation Center publications.

**HARRINGTON FOUNDATION.** See Don and Sybil Harrington Foundation, The.

**HARRY G. STEELE FOUNDATION.** Grace C. Steele established the Harry G. Steele Foundation in 1953 in memory of her husband. By 1969, its assets amounted to about $21 million. Upon Grace Steele's death, in 1974, further funds were bequeathed to the foundation, whose major assets, then and now, consisted of stock of the Emerson Electric Company.

From its inception, the major objective of the Steele Foundation has been to aid projects and organizations which "foster people's desire for self-improvement by providing the necessary tools to deal effectively with the social environment." Grants for higher and secondary education have always been in the forefront in furthering this objective. The foundation has consistently supported organizations devoted to the fine arts, population control, hospitals, clinics, and youth agencies.

In 1975, the foundation made grants of about $1 million from assets which, by then, had risen to around $37 million. In 1979, the foundation made awards of approximately $8.5 million; the overwhelming proportion of the funds awarded were for education. Two schools, Mills College and Occidental College, received slightly over $1 million each. Other major grants were: California Institute of Technology—$222,337; Planned Parenthood, World Population—$148,225; Laguna Beach Museum of Art—$98,750; Boy Scouts of America—$84,112; the Nature Conservancy—$77,481; and Hoag Memorial Hospital—$50,531. All of the foregoing organizations are located in California, and they illustrate the foundation's policy of largely restricting grants to California and particularly to Orange County.

The foundation, with 1981 assets valued at about $35 million, is governed by a six-member board of trustees, each of whom is a member of the Steele family. Administration of the foundation is carried on from offices located at 441 Old Newport Boulevard, Newport Beach, California 92660, under the direction of a vice-president.

For further information, see *Annual Reports* of the foundation, published continuously since the 1970s.

**HARTFORD FOUNDATION.** See Hartford Foundation for Public Giving; John A. Hartford Foundation, Inc., The.

**HARTFORD FOUNDATION FOR PUBLIC GIVING.** One of the nation's oldest and largest community foundations, the Hartford Foundation for Public Giving was established in 1925.

Two bank officers in Hartford—Maynard T. Hazen, an officer in the trust department of the United States Security Company (now part of Hartford National Bank and Trust Company), and Clark T. Durant, trust officer with the Hartford-Connecticut Trust Company (now the Connecticut Bank and Trust Company)—were the founders of the community foundation in Hartford. Both men were attorneys, and both were familiar with the Cleveland Trust Company and the Cleveland Foundation* established by Frederick H. Goff in 1914. Durant and Hazen introduced enabling legislation, which passed the Connecticut General Assembly in 1925, and they drafted a resolution and declaration of trust, modeled on those of the Cleveland Foundation and the New York Community Trust.* In early December, two banks adopted the charter, and the Hartford Foundation for Public Giving was officially created.

The Hartford charter, like those of Cleveland and New York, established a seven-member distribution committee to be appointed as follows: one member each by the chief justice of the Supreme Court of Connecticut, the president of Trinity College, the president of the United Way, the judge of the probate court for the district of Hartford; and three by the trustees committee, which consists of the chief executive officers of the trustees banks. Presently, there are four banks holding and managing trusts for the foundation. They are the Connecticut Bank and Trust Company, Hartford National Bank and Trust Company, United Bank & Trust Company, and the Simsbury Bank and Trust Company.

The members of the distribution committee serve without pay for five-year terms and may be reappointed to a second term. The committee has broad discretionary powers in carrying out the purpose of the foundation, which "is to provide a perpetual source of income to help meet the medical, educational, social welfare, cultural, and civic needs of the people of Hartford and 28 contiguous communities."

A headline in *The Hartford Courant* announced the establishment of the new community foundation in December, 1925. But it was eleven years before there was enough money accumulated to justify the formation of a distribution committee.

On January 29, 1936, a distribution committee met for the first time. Charles A. Goodwin, a respected attorney, banker, civic leader, and public servant, was elected chairman. Other members of that first committee were Spencer Gross,

John M. K. Davis, Mrs. Herbert Fisher, Mrs. Bernard T. Williams, Henry J. Marks, and Earle Dimon.

Goodwin led the foundation for eighteen years, and some of the policies formulated during those early years still serve the foundation today. When Goodwin died in 1954, he left the foundation on a firm basis, and he knew it would grow. History now shows that he was instrumental in securing several large bequests to benefit the foundation, and one of those, the $5.5 million Howard Hunt Garmany estate, was in probate when Goodwin died.

J.M.K. Davis, who became the foundation's second distribution committee chairman, had watched Goodwin closely and literally had taken notes for these first eighteen years as secretary of the foundation. Under Davis's leadership over the next seventeen years, the foundation became a tower of philanthropic strength to Greater Hartford, and it gained a national reputation as one of the outstanding community foundations in the United States and Canada.

Davis gave countless hours to the Hartford Foundation for Public Giving, despite demands on his time from a printing firm he headed and from his numerous other charitable and civic responsibilities. While he adhered strictly to a policy of not publicly campaigning for funds, he was an advocate of the foundation and privately would sing its praises whenever given the opportunity. The foundation continued to grow during the Davis years. In its first eighteen years, the Hartford Foundation had paid grants totalling $942,000. During the next seventeen years, under Davis, the total distribution exceeded $11 million. When he retired voluntarily in 1971, he was given the title "Mr. Foundation" for Greater Hartford.

Under Davis, the foundation hired its first full-time paid director, Russell T. Foster, took a leadership position in grant making in central Connecticut, and was instrumental in establishing a national association of community foundations, the forerunner to the Council on Foundations. In 1971, Lucian E. Baldwin succeeded Davis as chairman, and William H. Connelly succeeded Foster as executive director. As the son of former Governor and retired Chief Justice Raymond E. Baldwin, the Hartford Foundation's third distribution committee chairman brought an unusual perspective to the foundation, which included a law background, considerable experience as a business executive, and volunteer service. Baldwin worked with the trustee banks to establish common trust funds, a first among the nation's community foundations, in which several component trusts were pooled as one for investment purposes, allowing improved management at lower costs. There was a 43 percent increase in the number of agencies receiving grants, assets reached nearly $40 million at market, and income was up 90 percent.

In 1975, following the foundation's fiftieth anniversary, Baldwin was succeeded as chairman by Michael Suisman, a businessman who had served the distribution comittee for ten years, including seven as treasurer. He was an advocate of aggressive grant making and postgrant evaluations; during his chairmanship the number of grant recipient agencies tripled. He instituted special policy meetings for planning and discussions and was an active participant in national conferences for foundations.

In 1979, Suisman voluntarily stepped down and was succeeded by William E. Glynn, an attorney and former Hartford mayor with ten years' service on the committee, including four as vice-chairman. Under Glynn, the foundation has extended its territory to the entire capital region (Hartford and twenty-eight surrounding towns), and a corporate entity, HFPG, Inc., was created to receive and hold property for the benefit of the foundation. In 1981, the Hartford Foundation took another leap forward when it received $6.5 million, the largest gift in its history and believed one of the largest received by a community foundation from a living donor. Annual income is now expected to exceed $4 million. The newest gift brought the original book value of donations to the foundation to $32 million over its first fifty-six years. During the same period, the foundation has paid out in excess of $30 million in grants. While the distribution committee does not budget by category, over time about 34 percent of the grants voted has gone to social services (families, youth, elderly), 26 percent to hospitals and health care, 20 percent to education, 14 percent to culture, and 6 percent to civic projects, libraries, and all others.

The distribution committee approves grants for a variety of purposes to agencies located in the capital region. Grants outside the region are made only to agencies specified by the donor, and there are not too many of those as 90 percent of the foundation's 112 named trusts are unrestricted. The percentage of unrestricted trusts is one of the highest among community foundations and is a tribute to Goodwin and Davis and others, who stressed the advantages of such gifts to take maximum advantage of the strength of a distribution committee and to allow it maximum flexibility.

The Hartford Foundation for Public Giving has shown this flexibility from one of its earliest grants, which was to assess the needs for social services following the flood which covered much of Hartford in 1936, to the creation of a Tornado Recovery Task Force to help people recover from the twister in 1979 which leveled hundreds of Windsor and Windsor Locks homes and businesses near Bradley International Airport. Between these natural disasters have been thousands of grants to deal with man-made problems and needs. Foundation grants were responsible, in part, for the establishment of public television in Hartford in the 1950s, creating a number of parks and recreation areas in the region, launching a consortium of higher education, and creating a transportation network for the elderly in the city.

Not all grants have been successful, of course, and two were actually controversial. One came following the unrest of the 1960s, in which a foundation-sponsored study of community/police relations was debated in the press. The other was a grant for public sculpture in 1975, with the National Endowment for the Arts, which received mixed reviews.

Generally, the Hartford Foundation for Public Giving makes grants in response to applications, feeling that the agencies are closer to the problems and more capable of finding the solutions. However, where it sees an unmet need, the distribution committee has initiated programs. This was particularly true under Davis following riots in the city in the late sixties, and more recently the committee under Glynn is advocating taking initiatives in addition to the more traditional reacting to applications.

With 1981 assets valued at about $58 million, the Hartford Foundation is among the largest community foundations in the nation, and in terms of assets per capita, it leads all principal cities.

For further information, see Glenn Weaver, *Hartford Foundation for Public Giving: The First Fifty Years* (1975). See also *Annual Reports* of the foundation, published intermittently since 1925.

ROBERT M. SALTER

**HAYDEN FOUNDATION.** See Charles Hayden Foundation.

**HEARST FOUNDATION.** See Hearst Foundation, Inc., The; William Randolph Hearst Foundation.

**HEARST FOUNDATION, INC., THE.** Established in New York in 1945, the Hearst Foundation is three years older than the William Randolph Hearst Foundation.* The Hearst Foundation's 1980 assets in the $60 million range, however, represent only about half as much value as the holdings of its sister philanthropy. Annual expenditures amount to approximately $2.5 million.

The foundation's purposes are to aid health-delivery systems and medical research, education, cultural programs, and poverty-level and minority groups. In a typical year, two-thirds of the Hearst Foundation's grant funds will go to recipients in New York and California. Over 40 percent of funding will ordinarily go to health care and research. Educational programs and cultural programs each receive funding in the 20 percent range. Other approximate shares are: social welfare, 10 percent; public affairs, 5 percent; youth agencies, 3 percent; and religious groups, 1 percent.

Grants above $100,000 are infrequent; the general pattern of the foundation's giving is in amounts less than $50,000. Among larger grant recipients have been the Roosevelt Hospital and the Lincoln Center for the Performing Arts, both in New York City, and Ormond Memorial Hospital, in Florida.

Randolph A. Hearst is president of the foundation. He is one of five sons of William Randolph Hearst (1863–1951), the newspaper baron who established the foundation. Charles L. Gould, former publisher of a Hearst newspaper, the *San Franciso Examiner*, was made executive director of the foundation in 1974. Since 1979 he has served as senior executive. In that year, he was succeeded as executive director by Robert M. Frehse, Jr.

The common genesis of the two Hearst foundations lies in the estate planning of their founder. Likewise, their purposes are identical, and their officers, operations, and officer structures are intertwined. For these reasons, the reader should consult the William Randolph Hearst Foundation entry, herein, for background, additional information, and bibliographical notes on the Hearst Foundation, Inc.

LESLIE CAINE CAMPBELL

**HEINZ ENDOWMENT.** See Howard Heinz Endowment.

**HELENA RUBINSTEIN FOUNDATION, INC.** Established in 1953 in New York, Helena Rubinstein Foundation, Inc., was named for its sole donor, Helena Rubinstein Gourielli, who made a fortune in cosmetics and the ancillary beautification of women. She believed that, since her wealth had come from women, her foundation should concentrate its efforts upon the betterment of women and their children. Consequently, when she died in 1965, the foundation, following her views and with augmented assets from her estate, continued to focus its program on the rights and welfare of women and children by making grants to innovative educational projects, the arts, community services, and health and medical agencies.

With 1980 assets of about $31 million the Rubinstein Foundation's grants are between $2 million and $3 million annually. Although grants have been awarded throughout the United States, in Israel, and in Europe, the majority has gone to the New York City area.

The foundation is governed by a four-member board of trustees, which includes Helena Rubinstein's son as president and her nephew as executive vice-president and treasurer. Administration of the foundation is carried on from offices located at 405 Lexington Avenue, New York, New York 10174, under the direction of an executive director.

For further information, see *Annual Reports* of the foundation, published since the 1970s; and "Helena Rubinstein," *Dictionary of American Biography*, Supplement Seven (1980), pp. 666–667.

**HELENE FULD HEALTH FOUNDATION.** See Helene Fuld Health Trust.

**HELENE FULD HEALTH TRUST.** Leonhard Felix Fuld (1883–1965) and his sister, Florentine M. Fuld, established the Helene Fuld Health Foundation in 1935 in memory of their mother. The trust was established in 1951 and, in 1969, was activated as a successor to the foundation. Born in New York City in humble circumstances, Leonhard Fuld attended its public schools and then entered Columbia University in 1902 where he earned the following degrees: B.A.—1903; M.A.—1904; LL.B.—1905; LL.M.—1906; and Ph.D.—1909. Fuld worked for the city of New York in various capacities until 1918 and then in a number of academic posts where he lectured in economics and acquired a knowledge of the stock market. He subsequently acquired a fortune measured in millions as a result of stock market operations and real estate acquisitions.

Leonhard Fuld was a recluse and a bachelor. He lived alone with his sister in a Harlem tenement until her death in 1956; and he died in 1965, leaving no direct descendants. During the thirty-five years from the time he set up the foundation until his death, it gave away millions to promote Fuld's special interest in the health of student nurses. This had become the stated purpose of the foundation as early as the 1940s, and neither he nor others ever explained the reason or reasons for his interest and concern for student nurses. In any case, for over three decades, many hospitals and nursing schools in the northeastern United States were visited by the shabbily dressed Fuld, who dangled a Phi Beta Kappa key. Oftentimes, he was summarily ejected by hospital officials, but, when he was not, the hospital or school would become the beneficiary of a new nurses' residence, a scholarship program, or other gift. By 1951, such grants were running about $150,000 a year from foundation assets of about $3.5 million. In 1956, foundation assets were about $8 million, and grants exceeded $400,000 in that year. When Fuld died in 1965, he left approximately $25 million in trust to the foundation. Since then, these assets have grown to the 1980 figure of approximately $45 million. Annual grants are in excess of $1.5 million, ranging from several thousand dollars to as much as $150,000. The foundation's grant-making program is now restricted to state-accredited nursing schools affiliated with accredited hospitals all over the United States. This is the primary change from the earlier, more free-wheeling procedures of Fuld, but the purpose of the foundation, of course, remains essentially the same.

Since the Helene Fuld Health Trust was activated in 1969, the Marine Midland Bank, 250 Park Avenue, New York, New York 10017, has been its sole trustee, and the trust's direction is carried on from that address.

For further information, see *Annual Reports* of the trust, published since the 1970s. See also Leonhard Felix Fuld obituary, *New York Times* (September 1, 1965), p. 37.


**HELEN K. AND ARTHUR E. JOHNSON FOUNDATION.** This foundation was established in Colorado in 1948 by donations from Helen K. and Arthur E. Johnson. Arthur Johnson, an oil and banking executive, served as vice-president of the foundation until his death in 1976, and Helen Johnson served as its president until her death in 1978. Following their deaths, the assets of the Helen K. and Arthur E. Johnson Foundation increased by some $20 million from their bequests. In 1981 assets amounted to about $35 million. Annual grants from the foundation never exceeded $500,000 until receipt of the bequests from the Johnson estates. Since then, they have increased to over $1.5 million annually.

Throughout its history, the Johnson Foundation has primarily aided civic and cultural, youth, educational, community and social services, and health organizations. Its grants have been limited almost completely to Colorado. For example, out of ninety-four grants made in 1979, only one recipient was located outside of Colorado. In that year, major foundation grants included: Children's Hospital, Denver—$260,000; University of Colorado Medical Center—$100,000;

University of Denver—$100,000; and Denver Museum of Natural History—$90,000.

The Johnson Foundation is governed by a nine-member board of trustees, which includes members of the Johnson family, with the donors' daughter serving as president. Administration of the foundation is carried on from offices located at 1700 Broadway, Denver, Colorado 80290, under the direction of an executive director.

Almost the only additional information on this foundation readily available to the public are the annual reports and returns filed by it with the Internal Revenue Service, and the various Foundation Center publications. See, however, *Annual Reports* of the foundation, published in the past few years.

**HENRY J. KAISER FAMILY FOUNDATION, THE.** The story of the Henry J. Kaiser Family Foundation is the story of the vision of its founders, the distinguished industrialist Henry J. Kaiser and his wife, Bess. Since its inception, the foundation's emphasis has been on medicine and health care. Kaiser's lifelong interest in medicine reflected his belief that his mother, who died when he was sixteen, might have lived longer had medical care been more readily available and more effective. In large measure, the foundation exists as an expression of Henry Kaiser's determination to make quality health care more accessible to all.

In 1938, Kaiser, his son Edgar, and Dr. Sidney Garfield organized a comprehensive, prepaid health-care program for the large work force constructing the Grand Coulee Dam. A few years later, during World War II, a similar program provided care for some two hundred thousand workers employed in the Kaiser shipyards on the West Coast. After the war, rather than disband the enterprise, the Kaisers opened the program to the public. This early experience with what was to become the Kaiser-Permanente Medical Care Program demonstrated the potential of prepaid health-care programs to bring quality medical care within reach of all Americans.

The Kaiser Family Foundation was established as a charitable trust in 1948. Its original trustees were members of the Kaiser family and others closely associated with Kaiser industrial interests. Its office was located in Kaiser Center in Oakland, California. From 1950 to 1968, Eugene E. Trefethen, Jr., served on a part-time basis as the foundation's first chief executive officer. From the first, the emphasis in its grant making was on health care, and, consistent with the tradition of the pioneer American philanthropic foundations, its giving also supported general higher education. To a lesser extent, the foundation assisted nonprofit community organizations in the Oakland, California, area.

The foundation's original assets consisted of gifts from Henry Kaiser and his family, as well as smaller gifts from Kaiser Industries officers and family friends. Almost all of these assets were in the form of shares of Kaiser Industries Corporation common stock, which, because it returned no dividends, had to be sold in small blocks to finance the foundation's grants. Annual grant authorizations during the first few years were relatively small, ranging from $9,450 in 1949 to

$125,450 in 1954. The foundation's corpus was increased significantly in the 1950s and 1960s with the receipt of the estates of Bess Kaiser and Henry J. Kaiser, Jr.

In 1957, the foundation's trustees authorized the first of several substantial grants to Kaiser Foundation Hospitals (KFH) in support of the expansion of the Kaiser-Permanente Medical Care Program. Additional major grants to KFH in 1968, 1972, 1978, and 1981 reflected the foundation's commitment to the concept of comprehensive, prepaid health-care plans. The Kaiser Family Foundation support also enabled KFH to establish Kaiser-Permanente Advisory Services, which provides technical and managerial assistance to prepaid care programs.

Following Henry Kaiser's death in 1967 and the foundation's receipt of his estate in 1968, George D. Woods, one of the nation's most respected investment bankers, was elected chairman and chief executive officer. The next year, the Kaiser Family Foundation acquired a full-time financial officer. In 1972, with the foundation becoming one of the larger philanthropic institutions in the country, the trustees elected a full-time president and chief executive officer. Robert J. Glaser, M.D., was named to the post, bringing to the foundation his knowledge and experience as dean of the medical school and vice-president for medical affairs of the University of Colorado and Stanford University, respectively, and as vice-president of the Commonwealth Fund* of New York. Woods remained as chairman of the board of trustees, and his wisdom and experience continued to guide the foundation's philosophy. A second senior officer was added to the staff, and the foundation's offices were established in Palo Alto, California.

The same year, the trustees and officers undertook a review of the Kaiser Foundation's programs and policies. Medicine—broadly defined to include health-care delivery, medical and paramedical education, and interdisciplinary efforts—was confirmed as the foundation's principal area of interest. Support of San Francisco Bay Area community organizations and of general higher education were identified as secondary funding priorities. In addition, a President's Revolving Fund (now called the President's Discretionary Fund), from which small grants could be made without trustee approval, was created to allow the officers flexibility in awarding funds for planning and research activities in the foundation's areas of interest. The officers adopted formal procedures for receipt, consideration, and evaluation of grant proposals.

A similar program and policy review was conducted in 1979, with the foundation reiterating its commitment to the Kaiser family's vision of making high-quality health care accessible to all. Specifically, priority was accorded to the encouragement of prepaid health-care programs, the improvement of medical and paramedical education, the advancement of health-services administration and management, and the promotion of health-services research. A formal Community Grants Program was established to continue the foundation's tradition of supporting local nonprofit community agencies, and the funding category of general higher education was eliminated.

The Kaiser Family Foundation's giving is carefully targeted to achieve specific goals in the field of medicine and health. Its support encourages cost-effectiveness in the provision of health-care services through the promotion of health-maintenance organizations (HMOs). Foundation grants underwrite efforts to establish new HMOs and to improve the management skills of HMO administrators. Grants to the business schools of major universities make possible research and training in health-care policy research and analysis, furthering the development of rational health-care policies for the United States. Grants in the area of medical education support the upgrading of medical school curricula, the efforts of many medical schools to find new sources of student scholarship aid, and the encouragement of minority medical student education.

Other foundation efforts promote the resurgence of training in general internal medicine, the application and evaluation of new medical technology, the improvement of education in the allied health professions, and the strengthening of training in geriatrics. Through the Kaiser Family Foundation's support, leading medical schools are examining the balance between the training of generalists and subspecialists, HMO administrators are improving their management skills, the achievements of minority medical students are being recognized, community social welfare organizations are serving their constituents more effectively, and quality health care is being made more cost-effective and more readily accessible to many Americans.

The Kaiser Family Foundation is constituted as a charitable trust, and its policies are set by its board of trustees. In 1981, the trustees included W. L. Hadley Griffin, chairman; and Edgar F. Kaiser and Edgar F. Kaiser, Jr., vice-chairmen. The board meets three times each year to consider grant recommendations from the staff; with the exception of the President's Discretionary Fund and the Community Grants Program, all awards must be approved by the trustees.

A portfolio committee of the trustees is responsible for supervision of the foundation's assets and engages professional investment managers to assist in this responsibility. The foundation's principal consists largely of stock holdings in Kaiser Aluminum and Chemical Corporation, Kaiser Steel Corporation, and Kaiser Cement Corporation, along with investments in other equity and fixed-income securities. As of December 31, 1980, the foundation's assets were valued at approximately $250 million. Grants authorized from the foundation's inception through 1980 totalled almost $64 million. Congressional action in 1981 setting the payout requirement for philanthropic foundations at 5 percent of assets will enable the Kaiser Family Foundation more effectively to guard its corpus against inflation, thereby maintaining its "buying power."

For its financial size, the foundation operates with a relatively small staff consisting of the president, an executive vice-president, a treasurer, a secretary and senior program officer, and two program officers. They are assisted by a librarian, a writer, an accounting clerk, and secretarial personnel. In 1980, the foundation occupied new offices at 525 Middlefield Road, Suite 200, Menlo Park, California 94025.

The foundation has issued an *Annual Report* since 1973 and periodically publishes materials describing specific grant programs as well as proceedings and summaries of foundation-sponsored research or conferences. A general information brochure describing program guidelines and application procedures is also available from the foundation.

STEVEN K. WEBER

**HENRY LUCE FOUNDATION, INC., THE.** Born in China in 1898, Henry Robinson Luce was the eldest son of American missionaries to China, Henry Winters Luce and Elizabeth Middleton Root. Henry R. Luce revered and adored his father, learned Chinese before he learned English, and developed a life-long attachment for things Chinese. Luce attended preparatory school in the United States, graduated from Yale University—his father's *alma mater*—where he formed a close friendship with a fellow student, Briton Hadden. In 1922, after working on various newspapers, he and Hadden left their jobs to found a new magazine, *Time*, on some $86,000 which they had raised by selling stock in their newly formed publishing corporation. The magazine prospered, and by 1927 it began to show a profit. In 1929, Hadden died, and the business and editorial control of the publication shifted to Luce. Publication of *Fortune* magazine began in 1930, and the most popular of all Luce publications, *Life*, was started in 1936. By that time, these publications and a number of others owned by Luce had made him a wealthy man.

Henry Luce's first marriage ended in divorce, in 1935. Shortly after his divorce, he married Clare Boothe Brokaw, who is credited with having been the prime mover in getting Luce to launch *Life*. It is also said that she exerted considerable indirect influence on her husband's publishing and other business activities, including the Luce Foundation. During the 1950s, she served as a director of the foundation while pursuing her own notable career in theatrical, political, and diplomatic fields.

In the same year he first published *Life*, Luce established the Henry Luce Foundation as a tribute to his father. Significantly, its primary interest in its early years was in Protestant churches, schools, seminaries, and welfare programs in the Far East. By 1960, its assets had grown to about $1.5 million.

When Henry R. Luce died in 1967, his obituary in the March 1, 1967, issue of the *New York Times* began on page 1 and continued on to occupy another entire page of that edition. Among the statements made about him were that he was the creator of the Time-Life magazine empire, that he created the news magazine, and that he had played a large part in shaping the reading habits, politics, and cultural tastes of the United States. By the time of his death, Luce had amassed a fortune in excess of $100 million, and the major beneficiary of his estate was the Henry Luce Foundation.

Since his death, the foundation has broadened the scope and increased the magnitude of its activities on both the national and international levels. Its assets have grown from about $38 million in 1971 to around $119 million in 1981 and its annual grants are between $2 million and $3 million. The foundation has recently established a number of educational programs—including the Henry R. Luce Professorship Program (established in 1968), the Luce Scholars Program (1973), and the Luce Fund for Asian Studies (1975)—which now absorb over half of the foundation's annual grants. Most of the remainder of the annual grants have been for theological and religious purposes and special projects dealing with Asian affairs. After the establishment of U.S. diplomatic and commercial relationships with the People's Republic of China in the 1970s, Luce Foundation officials, including Mr. and Mrs. Henry Luce III, were among the first to visit China. The *Annual Reports* of the foundation since that time have expressed the hope that its programs and activities can be extended throughout East and Southeast Asia.

By 1958, Henry Luce III was serving as president and a director of the foundation—posts that he still held in 1981. Other directors on the seven-member board of directors are Roy E. Larson, long-time business associate of Luce, and one of Luce's two sisters. The administration of the foundation's activities are carried on from offices located at 111 West Fiftieth Street, New York, New York 10020, under the direction of an executive director.

For further information, see *Annual Reports* of the foundation, published continuously since the 1970s. See also the Henry E. Luce obituary referred to above; and an autobiography by a former Luce publications editor, T. S. Mathews, *Names and Addresses* (1960).


**HENRY P. KENDALL FOUNDATION, THE.** The Henry P. Kendall Foundation was established in Massachusetts in 1957 by Evelyn L. Kendall, Henry W. Kendall, and John P. Kendall, all members of the family of Henry P. Kendall, deceased. From its inception, the foundation has concentrated most of its grants in Massachusetts, New England, and the Mid-Atlantic states. Environmental and conservation groups, particularly those concerned with the protection of wilderness areas and conservation of our natural resources, have been among the foundation's major beneficiaries. Other grants have been made to educational institutions, hospitals, social welfare and public interest groups, and cultural organizations. Included in this last group has been aid for various historic preservation projects.

The Kendall Foundation's assets in 1980 stood at about $34 million, and annual grants amounted to about $1.5 million. Typical recipients of grants in recent years have included Friends of the Earth, Massachusetts Audubon Society, St. Paul's School, the Kendall Whaling Museum, Boston Hospital for Women, and the Opera Company of Boston.

The foundation is governed by a three-member board of trustees, which includes Henry W. Kendall and John P. Kendall. Administration of the foundation is carried on from offices located at One Boston Place, Boston, Massachusetts 02108, under the direction of a vice-president.

Almost the only additional information on this foundation readily available to the public are the annual reports and returns filed by it with the Internal Revenue Service, and the various Foundation Center publications.

**HERBERT AND MARGARET TURRELL FOUNDATION.** See Turrell Fund.

**HERBERT H. AND GRACE A. DOW FOUNDATION, THE.** This foundation was established in 1936 by Grace A. Dow in memory of her husband, Dr. Herbert H. Dow, founder of the Dow Chemical Company. The trust agreement specifies that the trust is to be used "for religious, charitable, scientific, literary, or educational purposes for the public benefaction of the inhabitants of the City of Midland and of the people of the State of Michigan."

Midland, Michigan, is located in the middle of the lower peninsula of Michigan. In 1980, its population was 37,016. It is the home of the Dow Chemical Company. Far removed from metropolitan Detroit, Midland enjoys a cultural and leisure life-style unique among communities of its size, thanks to the generosity of the Herbert H. and Grace A. Dow Foundation. The largest foundation in Michigan, it gave away $7,172,590 in 1981, over half of which went to Midland organizations.

The Chippewa Nature Center and the Midland Center for the Arts exemplify the distinctive cultural flavor that the Dow Foundation is able to bring this upstate city of modest population. Grants totalling two million dollars make the nature center the focal point for a wide and growing variety of nature-oriented, educational, and recreational activities for the Midland area. It is considered one of the premier facilities of its kind in the Midwest. Equally unique is the Midland Center for the Arts, which consists of six units, including a symphony orchestra, a concert series, a Hall of Ideas, a variety of theater groups, and other expressions of the arts—all rare for a city of 37,016 people. In 1981, for example, the foundation made a pledge of $2.6 million for administration and maintenance of the art center. Similarly, the Midland Community Center received $1.18 million to expand its tennis center and other facilities in 1981. Other local beneficiaries of the foundation's generosity include the Dow Gardens, the Midland Beautification Trust, the Midland County Council of Aging, Midland County Churches, City of Midland, and the Midland-Gladwin Community Mental Health Services.

The interest of the Dow Foundation in the city of Midland includes a concern for its physical attractiveness as well as its quality of life. An initial gift of $150,000 in 1981, plus additional pledges totalling $0.5 million in the near future, financed a flood-plain project that is transforming a problem area into a public golf course. Similarly, the Beautification Trust was established and funded with $81,599 in 1981 to beautify the eastern approaches of the city.

Increasingly, two recurrent themes appear to characterize the foundation's grants in recent years, both within Midland and across the state. The president of the foundation likes to refer to one of the themes as the "symbiotic relationship" between the arts and the sciences. Illustrative of this trend locally was its provision of up-front money to start Midland Matrix, a responsibility of the Midland Center for the Arts, which merges the arts and sciences for a two-week extravaganza in June each year and brings to the small city renowned lecturers on scientific topics on the one hand, and big-name bands on the other. Similarly, the Interlocken Center for the Arts, formerly known as the Interlocken National Music Group, now hosts the Dow Science Buildings and has been able to expand to year-round programming, thanks to three million dollars in grants the last two years.

Interestingly, Midland Matrix also illustrates the other strategy running through recent Dow Foundation grants, namely, the provision of seed money to get innovative projects underway, followed by conditional grants based on matching money provided by other local resources. In 1981, the foundation provided one million dollars to endow a challenge-grant program to continue the annual festival of arts and sciences. Also benefitting from this approach is Michigan Artrain, a traveling art gallery for rural Michigan. An initial $0.5 million grant to begin the program has been followed in 1980 and 1981 by grants of $242,662 and $263,841 respectively as matching grants to stimulate the art train's endowment fund.

In terms of financing, the assets of the foundation come exclusively from the Dow Chemical Company, reported currently to represent 5 percent of its market asset value. Therein lies the chief problem of the foundation. The depressed economy and stock market of recent years have resulted in depressed assets from which to make grants. For example, the market value of its securities dropped from $177 million in 1975 to $94 million by 1978, resulting in a drop of its grants from $8.4 million in 1976 to $5.3 million in 1978. More recently, after increasing again to more than $118 million in assets by 1979, 1981 found its assets lowered again to about $98 million.

This means that the Dow Foundation must spread its giving program to the institutions it assists over a longer period of time. Grants for a particular year become substantially less and must extend farther into the future. It also obviously means, in the long term, fewer dollars available for such funding. This phenomenon of diminishing market asset value impacts on everyone—the receiving institutions, the general public served by these agencies, and even the state government which benefits from Dow Foundation grants. This was exemplified by pledges totalling $5.5 million in 1977 to construct or expand the University of Michigan facilities, including its law, chemical engineering, and Gerald Ford library buildings. By the end of 1981, some $3 million of this pledge was still forthcoming. Undoubtedly, the dependency of the foundation upon the vagaries of the stock market, and one stock in particular, complicates the programming of grants by the foundation.

The governance of the Dow Foundation is a family affair. Herbert H. Dow, grandson of the founder of Dow Chemical Company, serves as president, treasurer, and trustee of the foundation. He also is secretary and a director of Dow

Chemical Company. Other family members serve as the other officers and trustees of the foundation. Dorothy D. Arbury, daughter of the foundation's donor, is vice-president and trustee; Herbert D. Doan is secretary and trustee; and Alden B. Dow, son of the foundation's donor, and Margaret Ann Riecker are the other trustees of the foundation. Administration of the Dow Foundation is carried on from offices located at 414 Townsend Street, Midland, Michigan 48640, under the direction of the president.

For further information, see *Annual Reports* of the foundation, published since the 1970s. See also "Herbert Henry Dow," *Dictionary of National Biography*, Supplement One (1944), pp. 261–262; and Mrs. Herbert H. Dow obituary, *New York Times* (June, 1953), p. 23.

MILTON J. HUBER

**HERRICK FOUNDATION.** The Herrick Foundation was established in Michigan in 1949 with funds provided by Ray W. Herrick and his wife, Hazel M. Herrick. Ray Herrick, who died in 1973 at the age of eighty-two, was an early associate of Henry Ford and, in the embryonic days of the automotive industry, was in charge of production for Ford. With some help from Ford, Herrick founded the predecessor of the Tecumseh Products Company, a manufacturer of refrigeration units. He became a chief shareholder in the company, chairman of its board of directors, and acquired a considerable fortune.

The assets of the foundation which Ray and Hazel Herrick set up has consisted almost totally of shares of common stock in the Tecumseh Products Company. Initially, their value was relatively modest. In 1953, for example, assets of the Herrick Foundation were valued at about $338,000, and grants for that year totalled about $60,000. Since then, as the following approximate figures for sample years attest, the value of the foundation assets and its annual grants have shown a continuing and substantial rise: 1956—assets $5.5 million, grants $300,000; 1968—assets $58.5 million, grants $1 million; 1979—assets $115.5 million, grants $5.75 million; 1981—assets $90 million, grants $9 million.

Support by the Herrick Foundation has always been limited primarily to Michigan, although in recent years a limited number of grants have been made in other states. Too, there has always been an emphasis on giving for educational purposes by the foundation. Thus, in its early years of operation, the foundation helped to build Adrian College (Michigan), and the city of Holland, Michigan received funds for a public library which now bears Ray Herrick's name.

Contributions by the foundation since its first decades continue to reflect its traditional giving pattern. In 1978–1979, for example, 52 percent of the total of about $5.75 million granted for the fiscal year went for educational purposes. Larger grants in this area for the year, all to recipients located in Michigan, included: Michigan State University—$1 million; Adrian College—$200,000; Hillsdale College—$100,000; Olivet College—$100,000; Siena Heights College—$100,000; and Western Michigan University—$100,000. Civic, artistic, and cultural organizations accounted for 25 percent of total grants for the year.

Larger grants in this area were ones of $850,000 to the city of Tecumseh, Michigan, for the construction of a civic center and one of $500,000 to the Toledo (Ohio) Museum of Art. The remaining 23 percent of foundation giving was divided among a variety of religious, medical, social, and child welfare organizations. These included, for example, grants of $50,000 to the First Baptist Church, Tecumseh, Michigan; $55,000 to the Herrick Memorial Hospital, Tecumseh, Michigan; and $50,000 to the Honey Creek Christian Homes, Lowell, Michigan.

The Herrick Foundation is governed by a five-member board of trustees which includes Kenneth G. Herrick, son of the founders, serving as president, and his son, Todd W. Herrick, serving as vice-president. The address of the foundation is 2500 Detroit Bank and Trust Building, Detroit, Michigan 48226.

Almost the only additional sources of information readily available to the public on this foundation are the annual reports and returns filed by it with the Internal Revenue Service, and the various Foundation Center publications. See, however, Ray W. Herrick obituary, *New York Times* (April 15, 1973), p. 61.

**HESS FOUNDATION, INC.** This foundation was established in Delaware in 1954 by Leon Hess. Hess had made a fortune in the oil and gas business as chairman of the board and chief executive officer of the Hess Oil and Chemical Corporation.This corporation merged in 1969 with the Amerada Petroleum Corporation to form the present Amerada Hess Corporation, of which Leon Hess is currently chairman and chief executive officer. Most of the assets of the Hess Foundation are in the stock of the corporation. In 1969, they were valued at about $40 million; in 1980 they stood at about $120 million.

Grants of the foundation have primarily been for higher and secondary education, youth and child welfare agencies, hospitals, cultural programs, and denominational, particularly Jewish, support. Also, they have been concentrated in New York and New Jersey. Annual grants of the foundation totalled less than $500,000 from its inception down to the 1970s. Since then, they have climbed to the approximately $1.3 million disbursed in 1979. Grants for 1980, of about $2.17 million, included the traditional pattern of giving described above, such as $335,000 to New York's Park Avenue Synagogue. However, 1980 grants also included one sizable and a number of smaller grants to organizations active in the Virgin Islands: $757,500—the Hurricane Allan St. Lucia Rebuilding Fund; $50,000—Boys Club of St. Croix; $25,000—Island Center of St. Croix; $10,000—United Way of St. Thomas; $25,000—the Good Hope School, St. Croix; and $10,000—Antilles School, St. Thomas.

The Hess Foundation is governed by a five-member board of directors, most of whom are members of the Hess family, and with Leon Hess acting as president. The foundation's mailing address is 1185 Avenue of the Americas, New York, New York 10036.

Almost the only additional information readily available to the public on this foundation are the annual reports and returns filed by it with the Internal Revenue Service, and the various Foundation Center publications.

**HEWLETT FOUNDATION.** See William and Flora Hewlett Foundation, The.

**HILLCREST FOUNDATION.** Established in 1959 in Texas by Mrs. W. W. Caruth, Sr., in 1968 the Hillcrest Foundation's assets were valued at about $5 million, and grants for the year amounted to about $200,000. By 1975, assets of the foundation had climbed in value to about $21 million, and grants for the year totalled about $0.75 million. In 1980 foundation assets were worth about $30 million, and grants totalled about $1.5 million.

Grants by the Hillcrest Foundation are restricted to Texas organizations, and most have gone to those located in Dallas. Emphasis in granting has always been on hospitals and health (38 percent), education (16 percent), youth and social welfare programs (30 percent), and cultural and civic programs (16 percent). The percentages following the foregoing breakdown shows the percent of grant dollars allocated by the foundation for the year ending May 31, 1981. Major grants for 1981 included the following: American Cancer Society Dallas—$100,000; three hospitals located in Dallas—$100,000 each; Child Care Association of Dallas—$125,000; Southwestern University, Georgetown—$50,000; United Way of Dallas—$50,000; Friends of the Dallas Public Library—$100,000; and Public Communications Foundation for North Texas—$65,000.

The Hillcrest Foundation is governed by a five-member board of trustees, which included a son and grandson of the donor together with a corporate trustee, the First National Bank in Dallas. The address of the foundation is in care of First National Bank in Dallas, Post Office Box 83791, Fifth Floor, First International Building, Dallas, Texas 75283.

Almost the only additional sources of information readily available to the public on this foundation are the annual reports and returns filed by it with the Internal Revenue Service, and the various Foundation Center publications.

**HILTON FOUNDATION.** See Conrad N. Hilton Foundation.

**HOBLITZELLE FOUNDATION.** The founders of the Hoblitzelle Foundation were Karl St. John Hoblitzelle and his wife, Esther Thomas Hoblitzelle. Karl Hoblitzelle was a native of St. Louis, and it was as an employee of the 1904 World's Fair in that city that Hoblitzelle acquired a liking for show business. For ten years he lived in Chicago while building a theatrical circuit which was concentrated in the southwestern United States. In 1915, he moved to Dallas. By the close of the 1930s, the Hoblitzelles had become recognized theater, banking, realty, and civic leaders in Dallas. They set up the Hoblitzelle Foundation in 1942, the year before Esther Hoblitzelle's death, to channel grants to a variety of educational, scientific, literary, and charitable organizations, primarily in the Dallas area.

By 1961, the foundation's assets amounted to about $8 million. At his death in 1967, Karl Hoblitzelle left his fortune to the foundation, thereby increasing its assets to about $40 million. In 1980 they stood at about $48 million.

Over the years, the Hoblitzelle Foundation has focused its support on hospital and medical service, education, and, more recently, cultural institutions such as museums and theater companies. The support has gone primarily to organizations in the state of Texas, and more particularly Dallas, and the present policy of the foundation restricts grants to organizations so situated. It is noteworthy, however, that in the 1960s the Hoblitzelle Foundation was one of the several foundations which, according to information supplied to the Internal Revenue Service, acted as a conduit for Central Intelligence Agency funds sent to organizations based abroad.

The nine-member governing board of trustees of the foundation has included five members with close ties to hospital and medical organizations in the Dallas area, particularly the Southwestern Medical Foundation. The foundation's affairs are conducted from offices located at 2522 Republic Bank Building, Dallas, Texas 75201.

For further information, see *Annual Reports* of the foundation, published continuously since the 1970s. See also Karl St. John Hoblitzelle obituary, *New York Times* (March 10, 1967), p. 39.

**HOUSTON ENDOWMENT, INC.** Mr. and Mrs. Jesse H. Jones established the Houston Endowment, Inc., in Houston, Texas, in 1937. Jesse Jones was a prominent Houston builder and developer with extensive real estate and other holdings in the city. In addition, he was associated with and controlled a number of Texas banking institutions and was the publisher of the *Houston Chronicle*, a leading newspaper in the city and state. He was also a significant force in the Democratic Party, at both the state and national level, from the election of President Woodrow Wilson in 1912 through the years of Franklin D. Roosevelt's administrations.

Although in its early years the endowment was primarily supported by annual gifts from Mr. and Mrs. Jones, by 1951 the assets of the foundation amounted to about $20 million and it made grants for that year amounting to about $400,000. Jones died in 1956, leaving no descendants. Through bequests from his estate, the foundation's assets grew to about $35 million by 1958. Grants for that year were over $2 million. During the 1950s, the Houston Endowment's grants were concentrated on higher education, hospitals, medical and dental institutions, social welfare agencies, and churches. Although not restricted to making grants in Texas and Houston, the foundation gave these areas highest priority.

In the 1960s, the assets of the foundation grew enormously, largely by reason of bequests from the estate of Mrs. Jones, who died in 1962. By the end of the decade, they totalled more than $209 million, and the grants had increased to about $5 million per year. In the 1970s, the foundation assets were pretty well stabilized due to a marked increase in the grants being made. For example, in

1975, assets of the foundation were still listed as about $209 million, but the value of grants for the year were slightly over $9 million.

In 1980, the assets of the Houston Endowment were valued at more than $242 million, making it the largest foundation in Texas and one of the largest in the United States. The grants for that year totalled about $15 million, and they continued to reflect the pattern of giving followed by the foundation from its inception. About 42 percent of the total was given to colleges and universities; some 27 percent went to hospitals and health programs; about 19 percent was devoted to cultural and welfare programs; and approximately 9 percent was used to aid secondary education and youth programs. The remainder was devoted to other educational organizations and denominational giving. Some of the major grant recipients in these categories for that year included the following: Southwestern University, Georgetown, Texas—$1,057,350; Scott and White Memorial Hospital, Temple, Texas—$500,000; Southwest Foundation for Research and Education, San Antonio,Texas—$620,000; Museum of Fine Arts of Houston—$575,000; Family Service Center, Houston—$500,000; Houston Independent School District—$400,000; YMCA, El Paso, Texas—$200,000; and American Bar Association, Chicago—$250,000.

The Houston endowment is governed by a seven-member board of trustees. The address of the endowment is Post Office box 52338, Houston, Texas 70052. An additional address of a grants coordinator of its programs is 1023 Bankers Mortgage Building, Houston, Texas 70052.

For further information, see *Biennial Reports* of the endowment, published since 1960. See also "Jesse Holman Jones," *Dictionary of American Biography*, Supplement Six (1980), pp. 324–326; and Bascom N. Timmons, *Jesse H. Jones* (1956).

**HOWARD HEINZ ENDOWMENT.** The Howard Heinz Endowment was established in Pennsylvania in 1941 under the will of Howard Heinz. He was the son of Henry J. Heinz, who had founded the H. J. Heinz Company, which, by the time Howard assumed its presidency in 1919, had become a very successful, international food concern. The foundation's initial assets of several million dollars grew, through accretion plus additional donations from Mrs. Heinz, who died in 1952, so that by 1954 they amounted to about $10 million. Grants in 1954 of about $600,000 were limited to the state of Pennsylvania but covered a wide variety of religious, scientific, educational, and artistic purposes.

By 1958, the assets of the Heinz Endowment had doubled to about $20 million but grants for that year still were at the same level as in 1954. Its grants were chiefly in the fields of music and the arts, community planning, education, health, religion, and social welfare and were limited to organizations located in Pennsylvania, primarily in Pittsburgh. Finally, the foundation came to follow the policy called for in Howard Heinz's will of giving first consideration to various organizations with which Heinz had been associated during his lifetime. These recipients, which still receive preference from the foundation, include Heinz

Memorial Chapel, at the University of Pittsburgh; Sarah Heinz House Association; the Pittsburgh Symphony; Shadyside Hospital; United Way of Allegheny County; the University of Pittsburgh; and Western Pennsylvania Hospital.

In 1979 the foundation made grants amounting to over $4 million. A listing of some of the major grants in that year illustrates the continuing adherence, over almost forty years, to the pattern of giving discussed above. Among them are: Pittsburgh Symphony Society—$1,384,733; Carnegie-Mellon University—$100,000; United Way of Allegheny County—$275,000; Sarah Heinz House Association—$265,000; and the Western Pennsylvania Hospital—$125,000.

The foundation, with 1981 assets of about $101 million, is governed by five individual trustees and a corporate trustee, the Mellon Bank N.A. Henry J. Heinz II, son of Howard Heinz, serves as chairman of the board of trustees, and two other members of the Heinz family are also on the board. The Howard Heinz Endowment has been administered by an executive director from offices located at 301 Fifth Avenue, Pittsburgh, Pennsylvania 15222, which it shares with the Pittsburgh Foundation.* The executive director of the Heinz Endowment also acts as director and chief executive officer of the Pittsburgh Foundation.

For further information, see *Reports* published in booklet form by the foundation for the years 1941–1950 (1951); 1951–1956 (1957); and 1957–1962 (1963). Since the 1970s, the foundation has published *Annual Reports*. See also "Henry John Heinz," *Dictionary of American Biography*, vol. 4 (1932), pp. 506–507; Howard Heinz obituary, *New York Times* (February 10, 1941), p. 20; Howard Heinz will, *New York Times* (February 18, 1941), p. 18; and Mrs. Howard Heinz obituary, *New York Times* (September 26, 1952), p. 22.

**HUNT FOODS CHARITABLE FOUNDATION.** See Norton Simon, Inc. Museum of Art.

**HYAMS TRUST.** See Godfrey M. Hyams Trust.

# I

**INDEPENDENCE FOUNDATION.** The genesis of the Independence Foundation appears to have been the 1929 death from cancer of a son of William H. Donner (1864–1953). Three years after his son's death, Donner, who had made a fortune in the manufacture of steel, established the International Cancer Research Foundation with an endowment of $2 million to encourage cancer research. As Donner grew older, his philanthropic interests broadened and he began to make gifts in other areas, such as the establishment of a park and swimming pool in Columbus, Indiana, his birthplace, and several grants to Hanover College, in Indiana, where he had been a student in the 1880s.

In 1945, the name of the foundation was changed to the Donner Foundation. At about the same time, Donner and the foundation became increasingly interested in precollegiate education in the United States. They believed that while there were many programs and considerable support for collegiate education, there was little available for what they considered to be the crucial period from ages twelve to eighteen.

Donner died in 1953. The Donner Foundation, during the 1950s, devoted a considerable portion of its grant money to a program supporting secondary education in the United States. By 1961, however, the trustees of the foundation had split over the kinds and amounts of grants to be made from its now some $40 million in assets. As a result of this divergence, the foundation's assets were divided equally between Donner's lineal descendants, who established a new William H. Donner Foundation, Inc.,* and a group which promptly set up the Independence Foundation.

In 1961, the Independence Foundation instituted a study of its secondary education program which convinced the directors that the program had been a success and should be continued.

Since 1951, the Independence Foundation and its predecessor has paid the costs of attendance of some ten thousand students at some of the leading secondary schools in the United States. There are currently ninety such schools participating in the program, and individual grants range up to about $6,000 per grant. Every five years, the foundation has updated its list of participating institutions through questionnaires and other means of evaluation. In 1961, the foundation also began the funding of teaching endowments of $300,000 each at a few selected secondary schools. By 1981, some $11 million had been awarded in support of these programs.

In 1980, the foundation embarked on a pilot program, running from 1981 through 1985, involving nursing education. While continuing its support of earlier programs, the foundation designated 73 percent of its appropriations in 1980 for this program.

In 1982, the Independence Foundation announced that it was discontinuing its earlier scholarship program for independent secondary schools and was inaugurating a new loan program for them. In this program, the foundation appropriated a total of $10.5 million to be granted at $1.5 million annually over a seven-year period beginning in 1982–1983. Grants ranged from $2,000 to $100,000 per year per school to eighty-five independent secondary schools located all over the United States. The intent of the programs, according to the foundation's president, Robert A. Maes, "is to stretch the scholarship dollars of these (85) academically strong schools, in effect permanently endowing part of their financial aid programs, so they can continue to offer places and financial aid packages to able students from lower income brackets."

Under the loan program, parents or guardians of a student attending one of the schools would be required to cosign a student's loan. The loan would be at a flexible but nominal interest rate. Repayment would begin after the student completed college and would be due in full no more than five years after college. The initial reluctance of some schools to introduce the loan program was overcome by inflationary pressures on their available scholarship funds plus the high loan repayment rate on the few schools already having loan programs.

The Independence Foundation, with 1981 assets of approximately $41 million, is governed by a six-member board of trustees. The president of the board also acts as the foundation's chief executive officer in carrying out its programs from offices located at 2500 Philadelphia National Bank Building, Philadelphia, Pennsylvania 19107.

For further information, see *Annual Reports* of the foundation, published continuously since the 1970s. See also William H. Donner obituary, *New York Times* (November 4, 1953), p. 23; "A Fund for Teenaged Go-Getters," Delaware Valley Agenda (n.d.); and "Independent Schools; 85 Receive Grants for Student Loans," *Education Week* (February 17, 1982).

**INTERNATIONAL CANCER RESEARCH FOUNDATION.** See Independence Foundation.

**IRA W. DECAMP FOUNDATION, THE.** Elizabeth DeCamp McInerny established the Ira W. DeCamp Foundation in New York in 1975. In 1976, the foundation received almost $800,000 from her estate and in 1977 an additional

$7.48 million. Subsequent additions to its corpus, plus revenue from income, have brought its 1980 assets to about $33 million.

The DeCamp Foundation's program has been limited to grants for health-care facilities and for medical education and research. Over half of the recipients of aid have been located in New York, but grants have also been made in California, New Jersey, and several New England states. Representative of the program are the following major grants for 1979: Massachusetts General Hospital—$200,000; St. Charles Hospital, Port Jefferson, New York—$200,000; St. Vincent's Hospital, New York—$200,000; and Adelphi University, for nursing research program—$100,000. Also in 1979, the foundation approved grants totalling over $2 million in future payments to be made to such institutions as the Yale Medical School, Massachusetts General Hospital, and St. Barnabas Hospital.

The DeCamp Foundation is governed by two trustees, James H. McInerny and Herbert H. Faber. The mailing address of the foundation is in care of Mudge, Rose, Guthrie, and Alexander, 20 Broad Street, New York, New York 10005.

Almost the only additional information on this foundation readily available to the public are the annual reports and returns filed by it with the Internal Revenue Service, and the various Foundation Center publications.

**IRVINE FOUNDATION.** See James Irvine Foundation, The.

## J

**JACKSON HOLE PRESERVE, INCORPORATED.** A nonprofit charitable and educational foundation established in 1940, the goal of the Jackson Hole Preserve, Incorporated, is to preserve and protect, for the benefit of the public, the primitive grandeur and outstanding natural beauty of some of our nation's most scenic areas. The foundation takes its name from the Jackson Hole country in northwestern Wyoming, a flat, forty-mile-long valley, or "hole," bordered on the west by the majestic Grand Teton Mountains and dotted with crystal-clear lakes and streams, flowing into the winding Snake River.

Mr. and Mrs. John D. Rockefeller, Jr., visited Jackson Hole in 1926 with three of their sons, Laurance, Winthrop, and David. Their guide was Horace M. Albright, superintendent of the nearby Yellowstone National Park and later National Park Service director who was Rockefeller's inspiration in protecting the Jackson Hole area. The Rockefellers were profoundly moved by what they saw—the grandeur of the snow-capped Tetons rising to more than 13,700 feet, with the valley below where the twisting Snake River and clear lakes and streams helped sustain an abundance of wildlife and flora. The area's spectacular scenery and its colorful history, dating back to the Indians, fur trappers, homesteaders, and ranchers, made a lasting impression. Rockefeller, however, was dismayed and shocked at the growing number of roadside stands, abandoned ranchers' cabins, and other structures already marring the valley and the vistas of the Tetons. He believed that the area should be protected, "so that people not only from our land but from all lands might find in the awesome majesty of its snow-clad mountains and the peace of its verdant valleys both refreshment of body and inspiration of spirit'' (Informational Brochure, Jackson Hole Preserve, Incorporated, n.d.).

Consequently, Rockefeller organized the Snake River Land Company to acquire properties from willing sellers and to hold lands in Jackson Hole temporarily until they could be conveyed to the federal government as parklands. However, the project prompted a fierce controversy in the valley, and cattlemen and conservationists formed their ranks. Despite the opposition, for twenty years, Rockefeller held firm in his wish to provide the lands for the public's benefit and enjoyment for all time. In 1945, the lands were transferred to Jackson Hole Preserve, Incorporated, which maintained them until 1949. Then, on December 16, 1949, Laurance S. Rockefeller, president of Jackson Hole Preserve, presented a gift of 33,562 acres in Jackson Hole to the federal government as an addition to the Grand Teton National Park. Laurance Rockefeller handed the deed to then Secretary of the Interior Oscar L. Chapman during ceremonies in Washington. This presentation fulfilled the commitment made almost twenty-five years earlier by Rockefeller's father, John D. Rockefeller, Jr., to preserve the unparalleled natural beauty of Jackson Hole.

In addition to the original gift of lands for the Grand Teton National Park, Jackson Hole Preserve has donated funds to the federal government, which the government matched, to help acquire other privately owned properties within the park as they became available.

Visitors soon began arriving at Jackson Hole in numbers greater than existing facilities could handle. However, federal funds were unavailable for adequate visitor accommodations. To provide these facilities, Rockefeller, Jr., in a long-term experiment in serving the public, gave funds to construct Jackson Lake Lodge and to improve Jenny Lake Lodge. With National Park Service assistance in providing roads and utilities, a complete camping center was developed at Colter Bay, including log cabins, a tent-cabin village, campgrounds, and a trailer park.

Another principal area of concern to Jackson Hole Preserve is the island of St. John in the U.S. Virgin Islands, an unspoiled semitropical area of the Caribbean. President Eisenhower signed a bill on August 2, 1956, which established on St. John the Virgin Islands National Park, with five thousand acres given to the nation through Jackson Hole Preserve. The park was made possible by Jackson Hole Preserve's acquisition of the lands with funds contributed by Laurance S. Rockefeller, other members of the Rockefeller family, and the Rockefeller Brothers Fund.*

St. John, nine miles long and five miles wide, is the smallest of the three major U.S. Virgin Islands. Stretches of gleaming white beaches ring much of the islands, and semitropical trees and shrubs cover its hillsides. Laurance Rockefeller visited St. John in 1952 and stopped at Caneel Bay, site of a former sugar mill. He found the combination of mountains, beaches, and sea at St. John unique in the Caribbean and resolved that the beauty of the island should be preserved and protected for the public's enjoyment.

Two years later, he learned that the National Park Service, in 1939, had recommended St. John highly as a national park. A new study reinforced this conclusion and Rockefeller, through Jackson Hole Preserve, began acquiring the lands. Congress passed a bill authorizing the park, and President Eisenhower's signature on the bill soon followed.

Rockefeller, as president of Jackson Hole Preserve, formally presented the land to Secretary of the Interior Fred A. Seaton in ceremonies on St. John on

December 1, 1956. Subsequent gifts by Jackson Hole Preserve helped acquire other available properties within the park boundaries.

To provide visitor facilities, Rockefeller donated to Jackson Hole Preserve the Caneel Bay property, which he had acquired and for which he contributed funds for necessary improvements. Other accomodations at the national park include a tent campground on Cinnamon Bay and day-use facilities at Trunk Bay.

Jackson Hole Preserve, as a means of helping the public enjoy the U.S. Virgin Islands and Grand Teton national parks, has conducted a carefully planned experiment in public service for more than twenty-five years. Since federal funds up to now have not been forthcoming for public accommodations in the two national parks, Jackson Hole Preserve, through two wholly owned subsidiaries, provides facilities for the public at the two parks. All income is devoted to operating and maintaining the facilities and to furthering Jackson Hole Preserve's conservation work.

Among its conservation programs, Jackson Hole Preserve has helped save the giant redwoods along the northern California coast and in the Sierra Nevada. Contributions to the National Audubon Society also helped to save the greatest stand of virgin bald cypress and its bird rookery, now known as the Corkscrew Swamp Sanctuary, in Collier County, Florida.

Jackson Hole Preserve cooperated with New York State in purchasing land through which the 2,500-acre Hudson Highlands State Park was created on the Hudson River's eastern shore approximately forty miles north of New York City. This park complements the Palisades Interstate Park on the Hudson's western side, thus preserving the beauty of the Hudson River Gorge.

Also, Jackson Hole Preserve has assisted in acquiring privately owned lands within national parks for additions to public parklands and has supported conservation activities by other groups, primarily on national levels.

The scenic and historic preservation work of Jackson Hole Preserve has been made possible largely through the personal contributions of the late John D. Rockefeller, Jr.; his son, Laurance S. Rockefeller; other members of the Rockefeller family; and by grants from the Rockefeller Brothers Fund. The 1982 assets and holdings of the preserve are valued at about $29 million.

Jackson Hole Preserve is governed by a ten-member board of trustees, with Laurance S. Rockefeller serving as president. Administration of the foundation is carried on from offices located at 30 Rockefeller Plaza, Room 5510, New York, New York 10112, under the direction of an executive vice-president.

For further information, see an informational brochure published intermittently by the Jackson Hole Preserve, Incorporated. Because it is an operating foundation, with only minor activity in grant making, the foundation does not issue published annual reports.

GENE W. SETZER

**JAMES G. BOSWELL FOUNDATION, THE.** Incorporated in California in 1947, the James G. Boswell Foundation was established as a private charitable organization. Its funding was donated by the late James G. Boswell, Ruth C. Boswell, and Walter O. Boswell.

Colonel James G. Boswell, the principal donor, was a native of Penfield, Greene County, Georgia, who had become a highly successful cotton merchant in Los Angeles, California. He organized the James G. Boswell Company, an agricultural, processing, and farm supplies company. By 1980, approximately 18 percent of the foundation's assets consisted of stock in the James G. Boswell Company. James G. Boswell II, an officer and trustee of the foundation, is also president of the Boswell Company and a director of the Security Pacific National Bank, Los Angeles, California. Ruth C. Crocker and Rosalind M. Boswell are the other foundation trustees and officers.

Throughout the 1950s and the 1960s, the assets and grant expenditures of the James G. Boswell Foundation remained consistent. By the end of 1951, the foundation's assets were $3,541,019, and grants totalled $438,489. In December, 1960, assets were listed as $3,489,655, and grants equalled $387,287. Nine years later (year ended December 31, 1969), assets remained $3,596,413, and $559,153 were disbursed in nineteen grants. The next three years (years ended December 31, 1972) saw a phenomenal increase in the foundation's portfolio ($21,813,356) and a doubling of its grant expenditures ($1,086,300) to over forty grantees.

By the end of 1978, the market value of the assets had reached $39,351,119, and the James G. Boswell Foundation paid out $2,402,238 in thirty-six grants. The grants reflected the foundation's diversity of concerns and giving patterns, with emphasis on higher education, youth, hospitals and health, cultural programs, and social welfare. The majority of recipients were institutions located in California and Arizona.

Higher education in 1978 received a total of eleven grants, which amounted to $925,858 and accounted for 39 percent of all grant dollars expended. Two recipients accounted for more than four-fifths of grant monies for educational purposes: Stanford University, $500,000; and the Agricultural Education Foundation, San Mateo, California, $270,000. Municipal scholarship programs in Corcoran, California, and Sydney, Australia, were funded, as was a student exchange program in Philadelphia, Pennsylvania. Lesser amounts of educational grants were awarded to a diversity of institutions of higher education, primarily in the Southwest.

Grants to youth recreation and development agencies in 1978 accounted for the second-largest shares of funding (30 percent). While nine grants to youth agencies received a total of $714,400, one institution, the City of Corcoran, California, YMCA, was allocated $704,000, the largest amount disbursed by the James G. Boswell Foundation to any organization. The remaining youth grants ranged from a high of $3,000 to a low of $250.

Hospitals and health were allocated 25 percent of all 1978 grant dollars. While six grants were funded, one grantee, the Walter O. Boswell Memorial Hospital, in Sun City, Arizona, accounted for $600,000 out of a total of $608,000 disbursed for health-related giving.

The foundation funded three cultural programs (4 percent of all grant dollars) in the amount of $102,280. The Up with People program, Tucson, Arizona, received $100,780 of all cultural grants dollars. The remaining 2 percent of 1978 grants were to social welfare agencies and community services. Of seven grantees, the Corcoran Community Foundation, California, received $50,000 out of $54,300 disbursed.

By December of 1979, the assets of the James G. Boswell Foundation had increased to $41,059,031, and $3,929,425 was allocated to forty grantees. The grants again reflected an emphasis on local giving, primarily in California and Arizona, and the grant range was $500,000 to $500. A large number of the agencies and organizations which were awarded grants during 1979 were recipients in previous years.

The offices of the James G. Boswell Foundation are located at 4600 Security Pacific Plaza, 333 South Hope Street, Los Angeles, California, 90071. Administration of the foundation, with 1980 assets of about $44 million, is carried on under the direction of an executive secretary.

Almost the only additional sources of information readily available to the public on this foundation are the annual reports and returns filed by it with the Internal Revenue Service, and the various Foundation Center publications. See, however, "Gin at Porterville Sold to Boswell," *Los Angeles Times* (January 1, 1928), p. 11; Sam Clarke, "News About Georgia," *Atlanta Constitution* (July 20, 1947), p. 14; and J. K. Lasser, "Why Do So Many Businessmen Start Foundations?" *Dun's Review* (February, 1949), pp. 15-17, 35-44.

LARRY D. GIVENS

**JAMES GRAHAM BROWN FOUNDATION.** The James Graham Brown Foundation, of Louisville, Kentucky, more than most private giving institutions, memorializes the personal philosophy of its creator. There are two reasons for this. The first is that J. Graham Brown (he preferred to use his middle name) began making sizable charitable contributions long before his death in 1969. He established a trust in 1943 and incorporated the James Graham Brown Foundation in 1954; so, long before his final bequest of about $70 million, the foundation's donation policies were well established. Second, Brown's personality—colorful, energetic, and determined—shaped the foundation during twenty-six years of personal direction.

J. Graham Brown was born in Madison, Indiana, in 1881, one of two sons of W. P. Brown, who owned timber lands and a lumber mill in eastern Kentucky. It was probably to help manage these holdings that, after completing a degree at Hanover College, near Madison, Graham moved to Louisville in 1903. He and his brother, Martin, inherited the business and an estate of about $500,000 upon the death of their father, and Graham began immediately to expand it.

Changing the company's name to W. P. Brown and Sons, he purchased huge timber tracts in Alabama, Mississippi, and Florida, and by 1925 the corporation owned over two billion board feet of standing timber. Despite financial setbacks during the Great Depression, Brown refused to sell any of his holdings; so when the military necessities of World War II raised the price of timber, Brown was able to realize a fortune from his patient investment. Lumber provided the core of a personal fortune that, upon his death, was estimated to be $100 million, making him one of the richest people in Kentucky.

Brown diversified his holdings by investing in hotels and commercial real estate, principally in Louisville. In 1925, he built the Brown Hotel and personally welcomed as its first guest, David Lloyd George. Five years later, he built a new office tower and named it the Martin Brown Building, in memory of his brother. In 1949, he purchased the Kentucky Hotel and three years later built a $2 million addition to it. His most active investment year appears to have been 1955, when he built a towering office addition to the Martin Brown Building (today it is called the Commonwealth Building), bought the Campbell House hotel in Lexington, and built the Brown Suburban Motel outside Louisville. This latter must not have been profitable, for in five years he tore it down and built a twelve-story apartment house on its site. At various times, Brown also invested heavily in commercial properties in Kansas City. Naturally, therefore, concern for civic development would become a principal consideration in Brown's charitable giving.

And so did a love of sports, especially horse racing and breeding. Brown kept stables of thoroughbreds which won over seven hundred races and amassed more than $3 million in purses. He was the largest stockholder in Churchill Downs and served as one of its directors for thirty-two years. He long served as president of the Kentucky Thoroughbred Breeder's Association.

Finally, Brown's personality helped to shape the philosophy of the foundation he created. Somewhat along the lines of a latter-day Horatio Alger character, Brown believed in individual responsibility for success. Though far from reclusive, he was something of a loner. He once commented on his bachelorhood, "I never married—I got out of that trouble." He also never formed partnerships, preferring to control investments personally and directly. This probably proved an advantage when, in the 1930s, creditors tried to foreclose on his Brown Hotel. Brown simply, and adamantly, refused to allow foreclosure, and he arranged a settlement that was acceptable to everyone. He applied this same individualism to his employees—he never allowed unions in his companies. But, on the other hand, he showed personal interest in the welfare of his workers. Brown was decidedly practical, also. He lived in a suite in the Brown Hotel, from where he observed the hotel's services and maintained its high quality. Whenever possible, he paid in cash for everything.

So it is not surprising that the James Graham Brown Foundation gives to self-help programs, particularly in the area of education; to health services that provide help to the needy; to community improvements—both municipal and through private business—that beautify the environment, inculcate civic-mindedness, promote a healthy business life, and encourage individual improvement; and to programs and facilities, particularly athletic, that teach youth self-reliance and competitiveness. Brown formalized this policy in his will by directing that his money be used "to promote the well being of Kentucky residents in matters of business, education, health, and the advancement of general welfare," but this only systematized the philosophy toward contributions that he had personally developed from 1943 to 1969. Brown also specifically ordered that money *not* go to performing arts groups—the theater, opera, ballet, and so forth. He had built the Brown Theater in Louisville in 1925, and had found the experience decidedly unprofitable!

Until Brown's death in 1969, the foundation made large grants to communities and organizations directly related to the donor's personal growth and development. Hanover College, his *alma mater*, received over the years a total of $2.5 million to build a faculty residence, a student center, and a chapel. Brown also donated money to the city of Madison, Indiana, for a new park, a wing for the municipal hospital, and the renovation of the high school gymnasium that the city then named after him. The city of Louisville received $1.5 million for the zoo, and Brown contributed $750,000 to the University of Louisville, most of which went toward the construction of a new gymnasium. Just before his death, he gave $1.5 million for the construction of a Red Cross Regional Blood Center, in Louisville.

When J. Graham Brown died in March, 1969, the trustees inherited the responsibility for continuing his charitable program. Currently ten in number, the trustees lodge administrative responsibilities in a president, vice-president, and treasurer (presently Ray E. Loper, H. Curtis Craig, and Charles F. Wood, respectively). A special committee of the trustees makes recommendations on awarding grants, and the trustees meet monthly to award donations. Application procedures require a letter of intent and brief program description; a formal application is sent to organizations whose programs are of interest to the foundation. Offices of the Brown Foundation are located at 132 East Gray Street, Louisville, Kentucky 40202.

The largest gifts to the foundation were the bequests of J. Graham Brown and his sister, Agnes Brown Duggan. In 1980, the foundation's assets were about $106 million. It awards from sixty to ninety grants a year and prefers to make large dollar contributions. Its highest grant during each fiscal year has often exceeded $1 million, and its average grant ranges from $50,000 to $80,000. Its annual giving has varied from slightly over $2 million to over $5 million. The foundation has continued the policy of giving primarily in Louisville and Kentucky, but it has also donated often to projects in Alabama and occasionally in other states in the Mid-South.

Education and other youth programs continue to be the largest area of the Brown Foundation's donations, amounting to about 30 percent of total giving. It has provided additional support to Hanover College and the University of

Louisville, as well as to many other institutions of higher education in Kentucky and Alabama. It has also funded educational research organizations and youth-oriented organizations like the Boy Scouts, YMCA, YWCA, and others. Community development and civic projects account for nearly 30 percent of the foundation's total giving, too. Money has gone directly to communities and to development organizations, like the Louisville Development Foundation. Historic preservation and museum development have benefitted from Brown Foundation grants. Support has gone to the Mobile Museum Board and the Historic Mobile Preservation Society, the Historic Homes Foundation of Louisville, the Danville and Boyle County Foundation for Historic Preservation, and other groups. Millions of dollars have gone to hospitals, specialty clinics, and medical education programs. In 1979, the Brown Foundation donated over $1 million to the Regional Cancer Center Corporation, in Louisville, and it has contributed heavily to the Jefferson County Medical Society, Inc. Finally, the foundation broadly supports social welfare programs, mainly by donating to community funds, like the Red Cross, the United Jewish Campaign of Louisville, Metro United Way, and others. But it also has given directly to such organizations as the Home of the Innocents, in Louisville; the Diocesan Catholic Children's Home; Little Sisters of the Poor, in Mobile; and the Louisville School for Autistic Children.

Almost the only additional sources of information readily available to the public on this foundation are the annual reports and returns filed by it with the Internal Revenue Service, and the various Foundation Center publications. See, however, James Graham Brown obituary, *Louisville Courier-Journal* (March 31, 1969); p. 1.

DAVID L. ROWE

**JAMES IRVINE FOUNDATION, THE.** This California, nonprofit corporation was organized in 1937 by James Irvine, son of an early California pioneer, to promote the general health, education, and welfare of the "People of California." The James Irvine Foundation administers a charitable trust established by an indenture of trust, dated February 24, 1937, between James Irvine, as trustor, and the foundation, as trustee. The original trust property was a majority of the stock of the Irvine Company, whose principal asset was about one hundred thousand acres of land in Orange County, California, known as the Irvine Ranch.

Under the terms of the indenture of trust, James Irvine directed the foundation to hold and administer the Irvine Company stock "as a unit without division or segregation thereof," and with respect to management of the Company's property:

that inasmuch as the development and operation of said property has constituted the life work of the Trustor, it is the purpose of said Trustor, by the creation of this trust and by vesting in the Trustee through its holding of said stock of The Irvine Company, the exercise of a controlling voice in the operation of its properties, to perpetuate the operation thereof and thus insure an adequate foundation for the charitable purposes herein provided.

In 1947, when Irvine died, his charitable gift of Irvine Company stock in trust to the foundation was valued for estate-tax purposes at $5.6 million. In 1977, when the foundation sold its Irvine Company stock in compliance with the requirements of the excess business holdings provisions of the Tax Reform Act of 1969, the value of Irvine's gift had increased to $184 million. By 1981, the foundation's assets had grown to about $272 million, and its charitable distributions for that year totalled over $14 million.

The trust establishing the James Irvine Foundation gave broad powers to the foundation's board of directors to apply income "to or for the advancement of any charitable use or purpose in the state of California," subject only to two limitations beyond the geographic restriction. One limitation was that "all of such income shall not be devoted to any one or two charities to the exclusion of others." The other, stated "that charities receiving the substantial part of their support from taxation should not be beneficiaries, but that all such property, available from time to time for the benefit of charities, shall be used for such charities as do not enjoy any substantial support through taxation."

Myford Irvine, son of the founder, served as president of the foundation from its inception until his death in 1959. Katherine Irvine, wife of the founder, was the only other family member on the original seven-member board of directors. The other five members were business and professional associates of James Irvine. One of these, the late N. Loyall McLaren, a San Francisco partner in an accounting firm (now Deloitte, Haskins & Sells), served forty years on the board and was president of the foundation from 1959 to 1976. Another director providing continuity from the early years was Robert H. Gerdes, a lawyer and subsequently chairman of the Pacific Gas and Electric Company, whose service as a board member began in 1944 and ended with his retirement in 1982.

It was the policy of the James Irvine Foundation to distribute substantially all income in the year in which it was received. Grants amounted to $160,000 in 1949 and grew to $421,000 in 1957; they totalled $2 million for the ten-year period following Irvine's death. By the late 1950s, grants were made to about forty charities each year. About two-thirds of them were annual sustaining grants in amounts ranging from $100 to $5,000 to charities in Orange County and the San Francisco Bay Area. These included, for example, several hospitals, community chests, Crippled Children's Relief, the Children's Home Society, the T.B. Association, the Boy Scouts (a $10,000 grant in 1953 assisted the International Scout Jamboree held on the Irvine Ranch), Boys' Clubs, YMCAs and YWCAs. In addition, the Irvine Foundation responded to less frequent but substantial capital needs of organizations such as Santa Ana Community Hospital ($150,000 in 1949-1950) and Stanford University Medical Center ($100,000 in 1957); this type of grant, developed in the early years of the foundation, became dominant in the foundation's later years. In the early 1950s, the Irvine Foundation began to make occasional grants to various independent colleges and universities and to major cultural institutions throughout California.

In 1950, Kathryn L. (Mrs. Charles) Wheeler, a granddaughter of James Irvine, succeeded Katherine Irvine as a director of the foundation. Kathryn Wheeler, a resident of Orange County, has continued to serve on the board since that time.

During these early years, the foundation initiated the practice of having a northern and a southern distribution committee, each of which recommended grants in its respective area of the state for some portion of the total grants program.

Over the ten-year period ending in 1967, the foundation made grants totalling slightly over $5 million. The numbers of grants grew to seventy-five to one hundred per year, many of which were annual sustaining grants; but most of the foundation's income was distributed in capital grants to selected institutions such as colleges and universities, symphony associations, hospitals, and various youth and community service agencies. By 1965, the foundation had made grants to 225 charitable organizations: 25 hospitals and medical centers, 51 youth organizations, 21 community funds, 88 community service and cultural agencies, and 40 educational institutions.

During the 1960s, activities of the Irvine Company expanded substantially with the rapid population growth in Orange County. The foundation was involved as the majority stockholder in overseeing the master planning and orderly development of the Irvine Ranch properties. The plans provided for residential, commercial, professional, and industrial development, a site for the University of California-Irvine (which opened in 1965), as well as for continuation of a major agricultural enterprise.

Edward W. Carter, a Los Angeles business executive, was elected a director in 1959 to succeed Myford Irvine, who died that year, and membership of the board was expanded to nine in 1963 and to eleven in 1965.

In 1978, the foundation directors, following extensive review of the grants program, reaffirmed the Irvine Foundation's commitment to the fields of higher education, medical and health care, youth programs, services to the community, and cultural projects. Higher education has continued at approximately 50 percent of the total, and applications in this field are considered once a year at a meeting of the full board, dedicated to this part of the program. Grants in other fields are generally recommended by the respective southern and northern distribution committees for approval by the board at meetings twice a year. For occasional small grants calling for earlier response, actions may be taken by each of the committees or by the president to make grants from a discretionary fund.

Most grants are in support of capital needs or major projects, although the foundation has been increasing the number of "seed money" grants to agencies attempting to meet new needs or to meet old needs in new ways. Normally, grantees are not considered for grants more often than once every three or four years. In recent years, the foundation has extended its activities throughout the state, without as great a concentration in Orange County and the San Francisco Bay Area as in earlier years.

Consistent with its particular focus on higher education, the James Irvine

Foundation in 1981-1982 initiated a program of alumni annual-giving incentive grants for nineteen independent colleges and universities in California. Up to $8 million was authorized to match increases in annual alumni giving at these schools over a three-year period.

In the fiscal year ending March 31, 1981, the Irvine Foundation authorized 128 grants ranging in size from $1,500 (to the San Francisco Study Center to provide management counseling services for small, nonprofit agencies) to $2 million (to the University of Southern California toward construction of a new science building). The total grants authorized were over $13 million, and grant payments (including some authorized in prior years) exceeded $14 million.

In 1966, one of James Irvine's granddaughters, Athalie ("Joan") Irvine Smith, filed a suit in the United States District Court to invalidate James Irvine's charitable trust and to recover the trust principal and income for herself and his other heirs. In 1968, a final judgment was entered in the case, denying her claims and upholding the validity of the trust. While the case was successfully concluded, it was a substantial impediment to the operations of the foundation over a two-year period.

The major problem encountered to date by the James Irvine Foundation, however, was created by the "excess business holdings" provision (Section 4943) of the Tax Reform Act of 1969, which prohibits the ownership of a controlling interest in a business enterprise by private foundations. This required the Irvine Foundation, within ten years, to dispose of all but 2 percent of its stock in the Irvine Company. Since this statute appeared to countermand one of the objectives of James Irvine's trust, the foundation brought an action in the California superior court to conform the trust to the new law and to eliminate any legal obstacles to the establishment of a program for marketing the foundation's excess holdings of Irvine Company stock. This action was favorably concluded in 1973. Meanwhile, the directors began the process of assessing the value and marketing opportunities for disposition of the stock. Because the company stock had never been traded and had no established market, Morgan Stanley & Co., of New York, was commissioned by the foundation to assist in valuation and in determining the appropriate means to achieve a favorable sale.

Those efforts were complicated by a law suit filed in the Orange County superior court, challenging the foundation's marketing plan and, in particular, a tentative agreement for merger of the Irvine Company into a wholly owned subsidiary of Mobile Corporation. The court interrupted trial proceedings to allow what became a widely publicized auction for the Irvine Company stock, with bidding by Mobile Corporation, Cadillac Fairview Corporation, Ltd., and Taubman-Allan-Irvine, Inc. In April, 1977, Taubmann-Allan-Irvine, Inc., topped the bidding with a cash offer approved by all shareholders, which realized $184 million for the foundation's shares. The court not only approved the sale but also found that the foundation had acted properly throughout the marketing of its Irvine Company stock.

Although the "excess business holdings" problem was resolved with a satisfactory sale, it required extraordinary time and attention of the foundation's directors over a period of several years.

A primary accomplishment, which in turn has made possible other achievements, is the growth in the value of the foundation's capital and income. Prior to sale of the Irvine Company stock, the foundation's directors exercised sensitivity and far-sighted judgment in encouraging the company's planning and development of one of the largest single parcels of land in California. Not only did this produce an attractive community of varied land uses, it resulted in an increase in the value of the foundation's stock from $5.6 million in 1947 to $184 million in 1977. Following sale of the company stock, a carefully developed and diversified investment program has produced continued growth in the foundation's total assets, from $192 million in 1978 to $272 million in 1981. During the past twenty years, the growth in income made possible increases in annual grant payments from $0.5 million in 1960 to $2.7 million in 1971 to $5.6 million in 1976 and to $14.1 million in 1981. Over the forty-four-year life of the foundation, grants for charitable purposes in California have totalled more than $84 million.

The foundation's capital has derived entirely from gifts of James Irvine prior to his death in 1947. No additional gifts to the foundation have been received or are contemplated. The founding documents clearly direct operation of the foundation in perpetuity, and its investment policies have sought to preserve that objective. Specifically, in keeping with requirements of the Tax Acts of 1969 and 1981, the foundation attempts to invest and manage its funds so that at least 5 percent of average market value is expended for grants each year and that the principal (and future income) will increase over time at a rate equivalent to or better than the inflation rate.

Following receipt of the proceeds from sale of its Irvine Company stock in 1977, the foundation's capital was invested in marketable securities, with 75 to 85 percent in equities. Under guidelines from the foundation, six investment management firms (four for equities and two for debt securities) manage portions of the foundation's investment capital.

Retaining a focus on significant institutional grants, the James Irvine Foundation has contributed to the overall strength of the "independent sector" in California and has done so at relatively modest administrative cost—typically less than 4 percent. With almost 50 percent of grant dollars going to selected independent colleges and universities, the foundation has participated, for example, in the achievement of a uniquely successful pluralism of outstanding private and public higher education in California. In other fields, as well, the foundation has similarly assisted many institutions, large and small, to continue or enhance their services for the benefit of the people of California.

The board of directors of the foundation presently consists of eleven members and meets quarterly. Those directors resident in southern California form the Southern Distribution Committee, and those resident in northern California form the Northern Distribution Committee. President Morris M. Doyle serves in a part-time capacity as chief executive officer as well as chairman of the board. Administrative Vice-President Kenneth M. Cuthbertson is the senior full-time staff officer responsible for the staff activities of fifteen persons.

The Irvine Foundation's principal (corporate) office has remained since its beginning in San Francisco, and its current address is 2305 Steuart Street Tower, One Market Plaza, San Francisco, California 94105. A southern California office was added in 1968 to enhance administration of the grants program in the most populous area of the state. Currently its address is 450 Newport Center Drive, Newport Beach, California 92660. Archival material about the foundation is located in its San Francisco offices.

For further information, see Robert Glass Cleland, *The Irvine Ranch of Orange County* (1952), and "The Irvines, A Family Portrait," in James P. Felton, ed., *Newport Beach 75, 1906-1981* (1981). See also *For the People of California—The James Irvine Foundation* (1965), an informational pamphlet published by the foundation; and foundation *Annual Reports* published in 1966 and then continuously since 1970.

KENNETH M. CUTHBERTSON

**J. BULOW CAMPBELL FOUNDATION.** J. Bulow Campbell, an Atlanta businessman, civic leader, and a Presbyterian layman, established the J. Bulow Campbell Foundation in Georgia, by his will, in 1940. The Trust Company of Georgia was named trustee of the foundation, and provision was also made for a self-perpetuating, seven-member board of trustees to supervise its operation.

The Campbell Foundation has focused its grants on Protestant churches, particularly the (Southern) Presbyterian Church, and the state of Georgia. Geographically, grants are limited to Georgia, Alabama, Florida, North Carolina, South Carolina, and Tennessee. In 1978, foundation grants totalled about $2 million and all grant recipients were located in Georgia.

Cultural programs and education have received the largest share (approximately 60 percent) of this foundation's largess, with the remainder allocated to Protestant churches, health, and welfare. The foundation's 1981 assets were about $52 million.

Administration of the foundation is carried on from offices located at 1401 Trust Company Tower, 25 Park Place, N.E., Atlanta, Georgia 30303, under the direction of an executive director.

Almost the only additional sources of information readily available to the public concerning this foundation are the annual reports and returns filed by it with the Internal Revenue Service, and the various Foundation Center publications.

**J. E. AND L. E. MABEE FOUNDATION, INC., THE.** A Delaware, nonprofit corporation, the J. E. and L. E. Mabee Foundation, Inc., was formed in 1948 by John E. Mabee and his wife, Lottie E. Mabee. As stated in its charter, the purposes of the foundation are to aid Christian religious organizations, charitable organizations, institutions of higher learning, hospitals, and other organizations of a general charitable nature.

Mr. and Mrs. Mabee were natives of Missouri. They had no children. John Mabee died in 1961, and Lottie Mabee died in 1965, leaving a substantial portion of their personal estates to the foundation.

The activities and affairs of the Mabee Foundation, with 1981 assets of about $302 million, are managed by a board of trustees consisting of John H. Conway, Jr., John W. Cox, Guy Mabee, Joe Mabee, and Donald P. Moyers.

The geographical area of interest to the foundation includes the states of Arkansas, Kansas, Missouri, New Mexico, Oklahoma, and Texas.

The Mabee Foundation's giving is divided approximately as follows: 55 percent to private, independent, non-tax-supported educational institutions; 20 percent to general activities, including Boy Scouts, Salvation Army, Girl Scouts, YMCA, YWCA, and organizations which care for retarded and neglected children; 2 percent for church support; and 23 percent for scientific, health, research, and medical activities, principally grants to hospitals and related activities.

With a fiscal year which ends August 31st, the board of the J. E. and L. E. Mabee Foundation meets quarterly—January, April, July, and October—to consider applications for grants. Offices of the foundation are located at Suite 2535, First National Tower, Tulsa, Oklahoma 74103.

The foregoing brief history of the J. E. and L. E. Mabee Foundation, Inc., was based on information supplied by Donald P. Moyers, vice-chairman of the foundation.

**JESSIE BALL DU PONT RELIGIOUS, CHARITABLE, AND EDUCATIONAL FUND.** Jessie Ball du Pont (1884-1970) was born in Hopeside (now Hardings), Virginia, and taught in the rural schools there. In 1908, she moved with her family to California, where she taught in the public schools of San Diego. This experience gave her a life-long interest in education. She firmly believed that our educational institutions—especially the private, independent ones—must be encouraged and strengthened.

Jessie du Pont worked side by side with her husband, Alfred I. du Pont, in their offices in Jacksonville and Wilmington. Following his death in 1935, she not only took an active part in the management and development of the large and varied du Pont holdings in Florida, but assiduously carried out and broadened the philanthropies he provided for in his will. During her lifetime, she provided financial aid for the education of hundreds of boys and girls, aided large numbers of older people, and gave funds for many educational institutions, churches, and hospitals.

Her will provided for the establishment of a trust with four trustees, one of whom was her brother, and requested that the income go to twelve designated institutions and/or those to which she had made contributions during the five calendar years ending December 31, 1964.

The Jessie Ball du Pont Religious, Charitable, and Educational Fund, established in 1976 to carry out the terms of her will, has scrupulously adhered to this request since it first received assets from Jessie du Pont's estate. To be eligible for aid, applicants must show that they personally received support from Jessie du Pont during the period 1960-1964 or that they are one of the twelve institutions named in her will. The religious, health, cultural, charitable, and educational institutions which have received grants under the foregoing stipulations are, for the most part, located in Virginia, Delaware, and Florida, three states in which Jessie du Pont had special interest, and the University of the South, Sewanee, Tennessee. With 1981 assets of about $75 million, the fund disburses about $5 million annually from offices located at 872 Edward Ball Building, Jacksonville, Florida 32202. Since the fund began operation, higher and secondary educational institutions have received about 40 percent of funds granted; welfare 25 percent; historical and cultural projects approximately 20 percent; hospitals, churches, and religious institutions the remaining 15 percent.

For further information, see the *Report of the Trustees* (1976-1979), *A Five-Year Report* (1976-1981), and an informational brochure published by the fund.

**JESSIE SMITH NOYES FOUNDATION, INC.** The Jessie Smith Noyes Foundation, Inc., was established in 1947 by Charles F. Noyes as a memorial to his second wife.

Charles Floyd Noyes was born in 1878 in Norwich, Connecticut, where his father, Charles Dennison Noyes, was copublisher of the sixth-oldest newspaper in the nation, the *Norwich Daily Bulletin*. At age twelve, with earnings from a paper route, Charles bought a profitable newsstand concession on a summer coastal steamer which he operated during his high school years. After graduation from the Norwich Free Academy, he moved to New York City, where he established a partnership in a small real estate firm. Seven years later, in 1905, he founded his own firm, Charles F. Noyes Company, which soon dominated the real estate market of lower Manhattan.

Jessie Smith Noyes, whom Charles Noyes married in 1926, following the death of his first wife in 1920, was a native of Brooklyn, New York, who devoted much of her adult life to community needs. She was a zealous worker for religious tolerance and racial equality and was a strong supporter of education as the key to social progress. Following her death in 1936 and the foundation's subsequent establishment, the Jessie Smith Noyes Foundation has continued her work in these areas. During its first twelve years, by the end of which time its assets had reached some $4 million, the foundation had provided almost $2 million for individual grants to some twenty-five hundred white, black, and other minority students to assist them in attending accredited colleges, universities, and professional schools.

By 1960, in a move to control the administrative costs of the program, the Noyes Foundation decided that instead of making grants to individuals, it would make grants to institutions, which would then select student recipients. Insofar as possible, an equal distribution between white and minority students was maintained, with all foundation aid for black students being channelled through predominantly black colleges.

Since 1974, the Noyes Foundation has restricted its student-aid grants to institutions that have specific programs in selected areas of health care, education, and the environment. In addition, since 1964, the foundation contributes about $300,000 out of annual grants of between $1.5 million and $2 million, to thirteen charities designated by Charles F. Noyes. The 1980 assets of the foundation were in the neighborhood of $35 million.

The foundation is governed by an eight-member board of directors. Its program is administered from offices located at 16 East Thirty-fourth Street, New York, New York 10016, under the direction of a president.

For further information, see *A Brief History* (n.d.), published by the foundation, on which the foregoing account was primarily based. See also a *Ten Year Report* (1957) and *Annual Report* (1981), published by the foundation.

**J. HOWARD PEW FREEDOM TRUST.** In the years following the 1948 establishment of the Pew Memorial Trust,* the sons and daughters of Joseph Newton Pew and Mary Anderson Pew concluded that strong personal interests could be expressed through smaller trusts which would reflect individual concerns. Therefore, over a period of years, each of them established a trust focused somewhat more sharply on selected philanthropic programs.

The J. Howard Pew Freedom Trust was set up by J. Howard Pew in 1957, with the Glenmede Trust Company as sole trustee. The second of the children of Joseph and Mary Pew, John Howard Pew was born in 1882. He lived for eighty-nine years in Pennsylvania, having grown up in Pittsburgh and later moving to the Philadelphia area. In 1907, he married Helen Thompson. The couple had three children. J. Howard Pew was president and chief executive of the Sun Oil Company for thirty-five years. When he reached his sixty-fifth birthday, he requested that he be relieved of his position. He remained on the board of directors, and in 1963 he assumed the chairmanship upon the death of his brother, Joseph N. Pew, Jr. He held that position until the end of his life, November 27, 1971.

Through the J. Howard Pew Freedom Trust, the founder expressed his commitment to the free-enterprise system, limited governmental regulation, and the rights of individual American citizens. Because of his belief in the interdependence of Christian principles and freedom, the trust was designed to give extensive support to Christian educational programs and institutions, in addition to institutional support for private enterprise in theory and in practice.

In the early years of the J. Howard Pew Freedom Trust, grants were made from a relatively small corpus to a variety of religious and economic education organizations that served the basic purposes described in the deed of trust, and developed research and teaching on the freedoms of economic and religious expression. In the years following the founder's death in 1971, the holdings of the J. Howard Pew Freedom Trust grew appreciably; assets in 1980 were about

$249 million, and the grants made accommodated that growth and the changing times. The grants were, as much as possible, within the framework of J. Howard Pew's life-long philosophy and interests as expressed in the trust charter. Grants of $8 million to $9 million annually are currently made, primarily to religious organizations and theological seminaries, youth development and educational organizations, and for programs addressing economic, defense, and public policy issues.

Prominent among the recipients of grants from the beginning was Grove City College, which had, since its founding, received generous contributions from members of the Pew family. J. Howard Pew graduated from Grove City College in 1900. In 1931, he was elected chairman of the board, as his father had been before him, and he held that position until his death. Other continuing major recipients of grant awards from the J. Howard Pew Freedom Trust include the Hoover Institution, at Stanford University, and the American Enterprise Institute for Public Policy Research. Many smaller grants are concerned with Philadelphia-area organizations and projects, but the J. Howard Pew Freedom Trust continues to support a variety of programs nationally which reflect the founder's philosophy in regard to religious activity and private enterprise. The first *Annual Report* for the J. Howard Pew Freedom Trust was published for the year 1981. Such public reports now provide an annual summary of all current projects and an overview of the trust's directions during each year.

Since the Pew charitable trusts were all set up by members of the same family, they share the same offices at 229 South Eighteenth Street, Philadelphia, Pennsylvania 19103. All are administered by the Glenmede Trust Company as trustee, and the reader should consult the brief history of the Pew Memorial Trust herein for background and additional information on this trust.

NANCY KLINGHOFFER

**J. M. FOUNDATION, THE.** Born to one of America's leading philanthropic families, Jeremiah Milbank (1887-1972) dedicated his life in service to others. As a young businessman, Milbank was sensitive to, and concerned about, the needs of disabled individuals. With the outbreak of World War I, his belief that handicapped persons could lead an independent and meaningful life led to his founding, in 1917, of the Red Cross Institute for Crippled Soldiers and Sailors, the first such American organization to address the needs of physically handicapped veterans.

In 1919, the Institute for the Crippled and Disabled (ICD) was founded as a separate, private, voluntary agency. This institute launched the issue of rehabilitation into a national concern, pioneering techniques and standards which would prove unique in the world. For example, it was at the institute that vocational education, medical service, and psychosocial support were integrated to form a new, comprehensive, rehabilitation approach for the physically handicapped. The majority of rehabilitative resources in this country can trace their origins back to those pioneered by the institute. In 1981, the ICD Rehabilitation and Research Center became known as the International Center for the Disabled. Today, the ICD continues its leadership role in providing comprehensive rehabilitation services for the physically handicapped.

Other notable examples of Milbank's personal voluntary leadership include his founding and financing of the International Committee for the Study of Infantile Paralysis, active support of diptheria and other disease-related medical research, and involvement with President Herbert Hoover and others to mold the Boys Club of America into a vibrant national organization serving over one million boys and girls.

The J. M. Foundation, one of the nation's oldest, was established by Jeremiah Milbank in May, 1924, to support three major fields of interest: medical research, rehabilitation of the physically handicapped (primarily through comprehensive rehabilitation centers), and selected projects that focus on strengthening those values essential to the preservation of a free society. Guided by Milbank, his family, and an exemplary board of directors, who are themselves currently trustees of some forty-four major charitable organizations, the J. M. Foundation has made over $25 million in grants during the period from 1924 to 1982. From a modest first-year payout of $61,500, annual disbursements steadily increased, exceeding the $2 million mark for the first time in 1982. Approximately 60 percent of all support has been directed toward health, rehabilitation, and related fields, while 40 percent has enhanced educational, public service, and related organizations and institutions.

Although a wide variety of organizations and institutions have received J. M. Foundation grants, major support has especially furthered the work of the International Center for the Disabled; Columbia University; Boys Club of America; United Hospital Fund; Memorial Sloan-Kettering Cancer Center; and educational organizations such as the American Enterprise Institute; Heritage Foundation; Hoover Institution on War, Revolution and Peace; the Institute for Educational Affairs; and the Robert A. Taft Institute of Government. In addition to strengthening the nation's rehabilitation movement, various J. M. Foundation activities have been directed toward cost-effective alternatives to medical services which incorporate the timeless ideals of home health care and family involvement. Foundation-sponsored forums with internationally renowned Nobel laureates have focused on the systematic evaluation of biochemical pathways leading to malignant (cancerous) changes in cells. Other related J. M. Foundation initiatives involve employment opportunities and meaningful life experiences for disadvantaged youth, handicapped individuals, and senior citizens; promotion of prevention and individual responsibility for health; and educational fellowships in rehabilitation, immunobiology, oncology, and pharmacology.

Through grants to educational projects and public policy research, the J. M. Foundation fosters those philosophical values that are the hallmark of a just society: free enterprise, individual liberty, personal responsibility, and limited government. Foundation activities, such as support for the definitive biography of President Herbert Hoover, Taft Institute Seminars for Teachers, Hoover Institution Domestic Fellowships, and guidance of the Institute for Educational Affairs, reflect an appreciation for the American system of two-party representative government. Education provides the means for making independent judgments in freedom and autonomy, a vital process in our participatory democracy.

In response to prevailing economic conditions and as a symbol of their deep faith in America's future, the J. M. Foundation's directors authorized a substantial increase in grant expenditures during 1983. As in the past, the foundation will concentrate on health-care delivery and human services. Rehabilitation of disabling conditions will be addressed in new projects directed toward prevention, l \g-term care, and alcohol dependency. In addition, the directors are contemplating expanded participation in the following areas: basic research, specific to the cause and treatment of cancer; fellowships and educational programs in physical medicine; excellence in rehabilitation services; and extramural care which is sensitive to the diversity of human life. To foster America's renaissance, the foundation will also promote individual liberty, free enterprise, and limited government.

The challenge of private philanthropy is to meet the essential needs of individuals while enabling them to control their own lives. New programs planned by the J. M. Foundation during the present decade reflect an appreciation of current needs and opportunities, and a recognition that there exists no better system than that of free individuals, institution, and ideas. With an understanding of the past, a balanced view of the present, and a clear vision of the future, the J. M. Foundation pledges itself to the mission of its founder: meeting human needs through an unyielding commitment to freedom of opportunity and individual initiative.

With 1980 assets of about $34 million, the J. M. Foundation is governed by six directors, elected annually, who meet four times each year in January, May, September, and December. Current directors include: Jeremiah Milbank, Jr., president; Mrs. H. Lawrence Bogert, vice-president; Allan Hoover, treasurer; Daniel G. Tenney, Jr., secretary; William Lee Hanley, Jr.; and Frank Shakespeare. Administration of the foundation is carried on from offices located at 60 East Forty-second Street, New York, New York 10165, under the direction of an executive director.

For further information, see *Annual Reports* of the foundation, published since the 1970s, particularly the one for 1982.

JACK BRAUNTUCH

**J. M. KAPLAN FUND, INC., THE.** The J. M. Kaplan Fund was originally incorporated in Delaware in 1944. In 1975, it merged with the Faigel Leah Foundation, Inc. (incorporated in New York in 1948) to form the New York organization named the J. M. Kaplan Fund, Inc. By 1981, the Kaplan Fund had assets of about $47 million. The principal donors of the Kaplan Fund and its predecessors have been Jacob M. Kaplan and members of the Kaplan family.

Jacob M. Kaplan, a successful industrialist, was the owner of the Welch Grape Juice Company and principal architect of a plan whereby that company was transferred to a cooperative of grape owners without the co-op investing any money of its own in the acquisition.

The J. M. Kaplan Fund is primarily concerned with the interests of the city, state, and region of New York. In the words of its 1980 information brochure, "most of our grants stay near home." Within this parameter, the fund's programs have fallen into three major categories: preserving and enhancing the natural and man-made environment of New York City and state; protecting human rights and civil liberties; and encouraging the arts and humanities. Despite these restrictions to local benefactions, it was revealed in the 1960s that the fund had been used as a conduit for some $1 million of Central Intelligence Agency (CIA) funds, much of which presumably was disbursed abroad.

In 1977, the eighty-six-year-old Jacob M. Kaplan, who until then had acted as president and chief executive officer of the fund, yielded his office to his daughter, Joan K. Davidson, while retaining his membership on the board of trustees. Five other members of Jacob Kaplan's family, including his wife, one son, two daughters, and a brother, are also on the fund's nine-member board of trustees. In the past several years, they have annually authorized grants of about $1.5 million for some 125 to 135 projects. The offices of the fund are located at 2 East Thirty-fourth Street, New York, New York 10016.

For further information, see *Annual Reports* of the fund, published continuously since 1978.

**J. N. PEW, JR., CHARITABLE TRUST.** In the years following the establishment of the Pew Memorial Trust,* the sons and daughters of Joseph Newton Pew and Mary Anderson Pew concluded that strong personal interests could be expressed through smaller trusts which would reflect individual concerns. Therefore, over a period of years, each of them established a trust focused somewhat more sharply on selected philanthropic programs.

The J. N. Pew, Jr., Charitable Trust was set up in 1963 under the terms of the will of Joseph N. Pew, Jr. Its donor was the youngest son of Joseph N.Pew and Mary Anderson Pew. Born in 1886, Joseph Pew, Jr., married Alberta Hensel, with whom he had five children. He served as vice-president of the Sun Oil Company and as chairman of the board from 1947 until his death in 1963.

The J. N. Pew, Jr., Charitable Trust operates under the trusteeship of the Glenmede Trust Company and awards grants primarily in the areas of higher education, health care, conservation, and human services. The Salvation Army, the American Red Cross, Church Memorial Park in Nova Scotia, Canada, and the Nature Conservancy have all received support. Cornell University, J. N. Pew, Jr.'s *alma mater*, has been a major recipient of grants from the trust. The trust's assets in 1969 were about $43 million, and it made grants of over $1.5 million for that year. The trust's assets in 1980 were valued at about $122 million, and grants for that year were over $4 million.

Since the Pew charitable trusts were all established by members of the same family, they share the same offices at 229 South Eighteenth Street, Philadelphia, Pennsylvania 19103, and all are administered by the Glenmede Trust Company as trustee. The reader should consult the brief history of the Pew Memorial Trust herein for background and additional information on this trust.

NANCY KLINGHOFFER

**JOHN A. HARTFORD FOUNDATION, INC., THE.** The business that produced the money with which the John A. Hartford Foundation was initially funded was the Great Atlantic and Pacific Tea Company (A&P). The fascinating story of the company's rise from a small New York store, selling only tea, to one of the earliest successful chain stores in the United States is interwoven with the lives of two Hartford brothers, John A. (1872-1951) and George L. (1864-1957). This foundation is named for one of them.

The two brothers quit school when they were sixteen and went to work for A&P, with which their father, George H. Hartford, had become associated in the late 1860s. By 1900, the company had annual sales of approximately $5 million and was merchandising tea and a variety of grocery products from some two hundred company-owned stores. Despite this growth, and against the initial opposition of his father and brother, John A. Hartford by 1912 had convinced them of the advisability of operating the company's stores on a low-cost, limited-service basis involving the principle of cash-and-carry. In the years that followed, A&P's sales volume became one of the largest of any U.S. company, and at its peak it had some fifteen thousand stores and ninety thousand employees. Although it has suffered from increasing competition from other companies in the post-World War II period, particularly from the so-called supermarket chain stores, the Hartford brothers amassed large fortunes from A&P's operation.

John Hartford and his wife had no children. George L. Hartford had only one daughter who predeceased him. Thus, while the two brothers had surviving nephews and nieces when they died in the 1950s, they left no descendants. Understandably, the major portion of their estates went to the John A. Hartford Foundation, Inc., which John Hartford had established in 1929.

From the foundation's inception until the death of John Hartford in 1951, the assets of the foundation never amounted to more than $4 million, from which were made grants amounting to several hundred thousand dollars annually. However, with the accretion from the estates of the brothers, the assets of the foundation had skyrocketed to over $400 million in the late 1950s. Since that time, the foundation's policy of making large donations annually, from principal, has resulted in reducing its worth to about $131 million by 1980.

From the late 1950s to 1979, the Hartford Foundation concentrated its activities on biomedical research. Its contributions of more than $220 million in this area made it a major factor in developing much of the medical technology in common use today in coronary care units, laser eye surgery, and kidney transplants.

The trustees initiated a major review of the foundation's programs and activities in 1979 which resulted in a number of internal and policy changes. In order to increase income, the foundation diversified its portfolio, which entailed the sale of much of its A&P stock. It also broadened its programs, and presently it supports work in three areas: improving the organization and financing of health care, promoting energy efficiency, and the John A. and George L. Hartford Fellowship Program.

The program for improving the organization and financing of health care, which was motivated by the general concern over the rising costs of health care, supports experiments and research to test new systems of payment that encourage physicians and hospitals to make more efficient use of money for health-care purposes.

A second program sponsors experiments and research in improving the energy market and the corollary regulatory environment in which decisions concerning energy production and use are made. This program also supports attempts to get responses from individual communities and regions as to their particular demands in the context of their particular energy situations.

Continuing its long-time interest in medical research, the foundation provides about $1 million annually towards fellowship support for physicians who are interested in and preparing to begin medical research careers. Twelve John A. and George L. Hartford Fellows are chosen annually in this program, and salary support is provided for the fellows for a period of three years.

The programs and activities of the John A. Hartford Foundation are directed from offices located at 405 Lexington Avenue, New York, New York 10174, by a thirteen-member board of trustees and a staff of fourteen headed by Executive Director John Billings.

For further information, see *Annual Reports* of the foundation, published continuously since 1960; and a *Bulletin,* published periodically in the past. See also "George Huntington Hartford," "George Ludlum Hartford," and "John Augustine Hartford," *Dictionary of American Biography*, Supplement Five (1977), pp. 276-278.

**JOHN AND MARY R. MARKLE FOUNDATION, THE.** John Markle, the son of an anthracite miner, was born in 1858 and grew up in Hazleton, Pennsylvania. He was graduated from Lafayette College in 1880 with a degree in mining engineering, which he had opportunity to put to use the following fall, when he assumed charge of the firm his father had founded, George B. Markle and Company. He had a long and successful career heading one of the largest independent anthracite mining operations in the country and became nationally known as the builder of the five-mile Jeddo drainage tunnel which reclaimed Pennsylvania mines inundated by the 1886 floods.

In 1902, Markle and his wife, the former Mary E. Robinson, moved to New York City, where he devoted himself to his financial interests and to philanthropy. On the suggestion of J. P. Morgan, a friend and financial advisor, Markle established the John and Mary R. Markle Foundation in 1927 with an initial endowment of $3 million. The Markles were wealthy and had no children: a foundation presented itself as the reasonable way of consolidating their charitable contributions. Upon John Markle's death in 1933, an additional $8 million came to the foundation; subsequent sums from his estate brought the total endowment to approximately $15 million.

John Markle's charter for the foundation specified—or rather left the door open to—a broad range of activity. The substantive section of the charter sets forth these goals:

> To promote the advancement and diffusion of knowledge among the people of the United States and to promote the general good of mankind; to aid preparatory, vocational and technical schools, institutions of higher learning, libraries, scientific and medical research; to provide shelter, the necessaries of life and financial and medical assistance to such persons as the directors shall select among those in want, poverty and destitute circumstances; to establish and maintain charitable, benevolent, educational, vocational, industrial, recreational, and welfare activities, agencies and institutions engaged in the discovery, treatment, and cure of diseases and in medical research work, and to aid and cooperate with any activities, agencies, and institutions established for similar purposes,... The operations of the corporation may be carried on within the state of NewYork and elsewhere throughout the United States and in foreign countries.

Under these precepts, John Markle presided over the foundation until his death. (His wife also sat on the board for the first year of the foundation's existence.) The charter was broad enough to permit support of virtually any cause and also allowed the directors to spend principal as well as income. With Markle in the lead, the board did spend more than the foundation income in some early years, with the founder rectifying the deficit. Annual disbursements averaged $400,000 and, in the early years, went primarily to the charities which the Markles had previously supported, with funds also being distributed to needy relatives and pensioners.

Shortly after Markle's death, two foundation board members sought advice on how to run the foundation, turning to Frederick P. Keppel, then president of the Carnegie Corporation of New York.* There is no exact record of what Keppel told the trustees at their meeting, but one can safely assume from the account of John Russell, Carnegie Corporation administrator and future executive director of the Markle Foundation, that Keppel advised them to view themselves as representatives of a privately administered public trust. The *Annual Report of 1937*, one of the first published, indicates that this was the direction taken as the Markle Foundation changed from a private philanthropy, characterized by a diversity of aims, to a focused public foundation. These excerpts from the 1937 *Report* define the area of Markle activity and give the tenor of foundation policy even as it stands today:

> In the spring of 1934 the directors decided to authorize no further grants to individuals not then included on the list of the foundation's beneficiaries and in December, 1934,

appointed a special committee to investigate the general policy and plan of operation of the foundation. The committee submitted a preliminary report in January, 1935. At that time it seemed desirable to the directors that the foundation should become something more than a mere clearing house of gifts either to individuals or to organizations for charitable purposes; that its chief aim should be to take an interest in activities that by reason of their magnitude and their experimental nature or their lack of public appeal must turn for support either to individual givers of large wealth or to foundations organized for charitable or semi-public purposes....

On December 27, 1935, the board of directors formally adopted the foundation's present operating policy when it passed a resolution in general limiting new activities to research in the medical and physical sciences. A number of grants were made in support of specific medical research projects and a program was approved under which the foundation would gradually dissociate itself from the social welfare field.

From 1936 through 1945, the Markle Foundation adhered to the principle of supporting medical research, awarding 627 grants in support of 336 projects. One result of this direction, as reported by the foundation's medical director, John A. Ferrell, was the publication of over fourteen hundred scientific papers regarding work directly sponsored by the foundation, plus almost four hundred published works stemming from the Markle-funded National Research Council project on endocrinology.

Just as John Markle's death in 1933 signalled a change in the foundation's program direction, so the death of Archie Woods, who as vice-president and treasurer had superintended the foundation's support of medical research, brought on another, albeit less radical, change in the foundation's emphasis. In 1946, John Russell, who had served in the administration of the Carnegie Corporation and of Harvard University, was made executive director of the John and Mary R. Markle Foundation. The trustees asked him to define a program generally within the area of previous concentration, namely the medical sciences. Subsequently, Russell directed his attention and the program of the foundation to assistance for physicians in academic medicine by initiating the Markle Scholar Program. This program, the principal program of the foundation from 1947 to 1969, was designed to enable physicians to work in academic medicine and research rather than in private practice. At the time that the Markle Scholar Program was begun, Russell was told by at least one person that the program would be so fascinating that the trustees would never permit him to change it. Indeed, the Scholar Program remained in force for twenty-two years, in that time awarding over 506 fellowships. A little over a third came from specialities considered to represent the basic sciences. Internists were the dominant group, with 162 Markle Scholars coming from internal medicine; many of them had subspecialties. Surgeons claimed 110 of the awards, and pediatricians were third-most numerous, with 61. The overall institutional distribution was impressive— ninety medical schools in the United States and Canada successfully nominated candidates during the program's life.

Acting in the foundation's tradition of private stewardship of a public trust, and stressing the freedom of the foundation to address new problem areas, John Russell officially terminated the Markle Scholar Program at the time of his retirement in 1969. Evaluation of the programmatic and fiscal position of the foundation led it to a novel field of endeavor: mass communications. The enthusiasm of the staff and trustees determined the final decision to embark in this area, unique since mass communications lies outside traditional philanthropic interests in several respects. First, the mass media are unusually dependent on technology, in ways that education, for instance, or social welfare are not. Second, private enterprise is overwhelmingly dominant in the field, despite such public entities as the Public Broadcasting Service (PBS) and National Public Radio. Third, the legislation designed to control the media partakes of a paradoxical legal tradition instituted both to protect the media's freedom and to regulate their utility as a public service. Finally, there is the fact that the media in the United States deliver primarily entertainment. These factors dictate that the foundation's work in mass communications will continue to be challenging, innovative, and perhaps frustrating.

The current purpose of the John and Mary R. Markle Foundation, then, is to strengthen the performance of the media and to understand the potential of communications technology. It is clear that the media are playing an important role in today's society by providing information, shaping attitudes and opinions, and influencing our views of ourselves and the world. It is also apparent that many people feel the media could and should render better service. The Markle Foundation supports projects that expand research on the role of mass communications in society; analyze issues on public policy and the public interest insofar as the public is, or should be, served by the media; improve the performance of professionals involved in the mass communications field; explore the relation between the media and politics; and enrich the quality of print and electronic journalism. The foundation has a general interest in all aspects of the media and plans to support a wide range of efforts to improve mass communications, remaining flexible enough to appropriate for its program the new electronic media now emerging. Current disbursements average $2 million annually from a 1981 endowment of approximately $56 million. Administration of the foundation is carried on from offices located at 50 Rockefeller Plaza, New York, New York 10020.

Specifically, over the years that the program in mass communications has been in place, the foundation has sponsored projects including: the establishment of a magazine, *CHANNELS of Communication*, which critiques and explores the television industry, its programing, and its new technologies; a variety of projects, aimed at both production and analysis, to revitalize American radio; research to determine what effect television has on child development, and advocacy for better children's television; a range of studies exploring the effect of media on politics, and vice versa, which have focused on the format of presidential press conferences, election-night reporting of voting results, and the role of debates in elections; the establishment of a National News Council, which investigates and adjudicates complaints against the press; and a set of studies intended to devise a feasible system of qualitative ratings for television.

Lloyd N. Morrisett, who as president of the Markle Foundation has guided the program in mass communications since its inception in 1969, and who had previously served as vice-president of the Carnegie Corporation of New York and as one of the originators of the children's television show "Sesame Street," summed up the position of the foundation in a 1977 address:

> The most difficult task for the Markle Foundation to accomplish, and one in which it has been only partially successful, is building bridges between people in the mass communications field and those in the nonprofit or academic sector. People in mass communications are suspicious of and sensitive to criticism. They tend to mix among themselves, and do not talk much to outsiders. The regulatory interest of government in the communications field has created an area of tension and uncertainty between government and private industry. A foundation, representing the public interest, has the opportunity to act as a neutral party rather than an antagonist. Although Markle is not necessarily yet seen as a friend, it is not automatically regarded as the enemy. The constituency of policy importance that Markle tries to deal with is the nexus between Washington, on the one hand, and private enterprise on the other. It is with this focus in mind that the Markle Foundation has chosen the area of mass communications, the public medium for [as the Markle charter states] "diffusion of knowledge to the people of the United States."

For further information, see John M. Russell, *Giving and Taking: Across the Foundation Desk* (1976); Tamara G. and Stephen P. Strickland, *The Markle Scholars: A Brief History* (1976); and Lloyd N. Morrisett, "The John and Mary R. Markle Foundation," in *The Art of Giving: Four Views on American Philanthropy—Proceedings of the Third Rockefeller Archive Center Conference, October 14, 1977* (1979). See also *Annual Reports* of the foundation, published continuously since 1936.

DAVID C. LAMB

**JOHN D. AND CATHERINE T. MACARTHUR FOUNDATION.** John D. MacArthur, an insurance and real estate tycoon, established the John D. and Catherine T. MacArthur Foundation. He amassed one of this nation's great fortunes through bold financial investments and innovative programs and techniques aimed at making insurance more readily available to a middle-class clientele.

MacArthur started his empire with $2,500 borrowed in 1935 and built it to a point where, in 1976, *Fortune* magazine could comfortably list him as one of the nation's five living billionaires—and perhaps the least well known. At the time of his death, January 6, 1978, his firm, Bankers Life and Casualty Company, was the largest privately held insurance company under single ownership in the nation. The assets of the insurance company, including all of its real estate holdings, exceeded $2 billion.

At one time or another, MacArthur's empire included vast land holdings of one hundred thousand acres in Florida, primarily in the Palm Beach and Sarasota,

Florida, areas; several development companies and shopping centers; paper and pulp companies; a myriad of commercial, office, and apartment buildings in New York City; publishing enterprises; hotels; radio and T.V. stations; public utilities; banks; and eleven insurance companies.

From a table in the coffee shop in a hotel he owned, the Colonnades Beach Hotel, in Palm Beach Shores, Florida, MacArthur held court—listening to businessmen, real estate promoters, developers, and bankers outline their proposed deals. As the sole owner of Bankers, he had the power and wherewithall to close the deal.

Despite his wealth, MacArthur's lifestyle never changed. He occupied a small apartment with his wife, Catherine, in the Colonnades overlooking the hotel parking lot; he dressed casually so that he was occasionally mistaken for the hotel handyman or bellhop; and he was not averse to wrapping his unfinished sandwich in paper and stuffing it in his pocket for eating later in the day.

MacArthur established the John D. and Catherine T. MacArthur Foundation in October, 1970, and two months later created a trust which provided that the foundation would receive all of the stock (of which he was the sole owner) of the insurance company upon his death. Thus the foundation was activated on December 1, 1978, with the award of two grants of $50,000 each to the League of California Cities and to Amnesty International. In 1979, the foundation authorized thirty-six grants which totalled $5,013,928.

The MacArthur Foundation is a private, independent, philanthropic organization created for charitable and public service purposes. Although MacArthur undoubtedly had his own thoughts on philanthropy and what constituted worthy awards, he was determined that the foundation's board of directors should have the flexibility to respond to need and changing times, plus the ability to charter an independent course.

A few months before his death, in a March, 1977 letter to a friend who was urging him to support a major undertaking, MacArthur wrote: "I have established a Foundation and one thing I had in mind was to give the trustees autonomy. I know of a number of foundations where the donors tried to run them from their graves. I have guaranteed to the trustees that when I am gone they can run the show." And to a trustee, he said: "I figured out how to make the money. You fellows will have to figure out how to spend it." (John D. and Catherine T. MacArthur Foundation-*Report on Activities 1980 and 1981*, p. 2).

At the outset of its grant-making activities, the MacArthur Foundation had six directors, including Paul D. Doolen, president and chairman of the board, J. Roderick MacArthur, son of the founder and chairman of the board of trustees of the Bradford Exchange; and Catherine MacArthur, widow of the founder. In May, 1979, the board was expanded to thirteen members with the addition of several distinguished individuals, such as Edward H. Levi, president emeritus and Glenn A. Lloyd distinguished service professor of law, University of Chicago, and former United States Attorney General; Dr. Jonas Salk, founding director of the Salk Institute for Biological Studies; and William E. Simon, chairman, Crescent Diversified Limited and former U.S. Secretary of the Treasury. On December 15, 1981, Catherine MacArthur died. On December 31, 1981, William Simon resigned, leaving the board with eleven directors.

Almost from the outset, when the board still consisted of six directors, there was agreement on a program that would provide awards to individuals of outstanding talent, a program involving health, and a program that would provide funding in the Chicago area where MacArthur had lived and developed his business empire. The program for individuals gradually evolved into what is today known as the MacArthur Prize Fellows Program. The health program developed from what initially was to be a program dealing with hospital cost containment and rehabilitation of physically handicapped into a mental health research program. The program involving Chicago, named the Special Grants Program, initially supported major cultural activities and organizations in the Chicago area but has since been expanded to include numerous other cultural organizations (such as ten off-Loop theaters) and awards to neighborhood development organizations. Finally, the board created the General Grants Program to evaluate all proposals outside the areas covered by Prize Fellows, Health, and the Special Grants programs.

In its early days, the foundation was deluged with mail and grant applications believed to be the result of publicity about the size of the fortune left by MacArthur and to reports about a "genius program" (the MacArthur Prize Fellows Program).

In a sense, the MacArthur Foundation was a foundation in name only. It had no office, no staff, and no clearly defined programs. It did have ideas, money, *and* a requirement by federal regulations to make awards that in a few years would require the distribution of awards totalling in excess of $40 million annually.

The directors set out, with the aid of outside consultants, to develop broad program plans. And, with a staff of four, they sifted through the thousands of pieces of mail that had arrived and was continuing to arrive; ultimately, they filtered out thirty-six grant requests and met the $5 million payout requirements for 1979.

In May of 1979, with the advent of the new directors and the selection of John Corbally as president on Doolen's recommendation, the staff sorted requests into broad subject categories attaching commentary and background information.

While evaluating grant requests, the directors also had to begin shaping plans to meet still other federal regulations which required foundations to divest themselves of at least 80 percent of the ownership of any operating companies they may own.

In the case of the MacArthur Foundation, the law required the foundation to divest itself of at least 80 percent of Bankers Life and Casualty. In order to proceed with divestiture and to determine its payout requirements, the foundation retained the services of an actuarial firm, a land appraisal firm, and two financial consulting firms to prepare the financial evaluations and reports needed for divestiture. The foundation had until December 1, 1983, to meet the divestiture requirements.

The foundation is among the very largest private philanthropic organizations in the nation, given its assets of $927,967,952 as of December 31, 1981. (Fair market value of assets vary from year to year depending on payouts and investments.) Value of assets for 1982 will not be available until well into 1983. On the basis of current federal regulations, the foundation will have to distribute 5 percent of its assets in 1982—approximately $46.5 million.

The foundation is currently governed by an eleven-person board of directors which meets monthly or a minimum of ten times per year, making it a highly active and involved board. (In contrast to the MacArthur board, most foundation boards meet bimonthly or quarterly.) Each of the four major foundation programs is headed by a program director; each program also has a board director as chairman of a board committee of four or more board directors. The committee makes recommendations to the full board, either approving or disapproving proposals. The board committees work very closely with the program staffs.

Two of the foundation's four major programs—Prize Fellows and Health—are self-initiated and do not consider outside applications or grant requests. Health, from time to time, may seek proposals on certain specified projects or undertakings it initiates.

The other two major programs—Special Grants and General Grants—do consider grant applications under a carefully circumscribed procedure. Applicants for grants should begin their procedure with a two-page or less letter of inquiry stating the purpose of the proposal, the solution proposed, and background on the institution or organization by way of illustrating its qualifications to carry out the program proposed. The foundation will acknowledge receipt of such letters. Fully developed proposals will not be considered and will be returned.

After evaluation of the letter of inquiry, the foundation may send a letter of turndown or seek a fully developed proposal. Appointments will be made on the initiative of the foundation. No grant will be awarded without a fully developed proposal.

All recommendations related to inquiries, including inquiries that lie clearly outside the foundations declared interests and those screened out by the staff, are reported to and approved (or rejected) by the board, board committees, or board officers. The foundation has published a brochure which outlines its general policies, its programs, and its procedures. The brochure is available on request. All letters of inquiry should be addressed to: James Furman, Executive Vice-President, John D. and Catherine T. MacArthur Foundation, 140 South Dearborn Street, Suite 700, Chicago, Illinois 60603.

In 1978, the foundation authorized $100,000 in grants; $5,013,928 in 1979; $40,221,613 in 1980; and $41,072,356 in 1981. Including grants authorized in 1982, the foundation has authorized more than $100 million in grants in its brief, four-year history. The total number of grants authorized exceeds 425—2 in 1978, 36 in 1979, 130 in 1980, 226 in 1981, and the balance in the first half of 1982. The awards range in size from a $1,000 award in 1979 to a $22,103,800 award in 1980.

Since its inception, the MacArthur Foundation has made a number of major awards. In July, 1980, the foundation successfully intervened to save *Harper's* magazine from closing. The foundation published the magazine from September, 1980, through January, 1982. Effective February 1, 1982, the foundation ended its role as publisher and awarded the magazine to the Harper's Magazine Foundation, satisfied that the magazine was on sound financial footing. In the course of its stewardship, the MacArthur Foundation expended more than $5.4 million—eliminating the magazine's debt and providing *Harper's* with sufficient funding to continue publishing for several years. The Atlantic-Richfield Corporation also participated in the rescue effort with an award of $1.5 million.

In December, 1980, the foundation made a gift of 82 acres of prime oceanfront property to Palm Beach County and the state of Florida for use in the creation of a 345-acre park which has been named the John D. MacArthur Beach State Park. The award of $22,103,800 in land value is the largest given by the foundation thus far.

In October, 1981, the foundation awarded special, one-time-only endowments to seventeen distinguished liberal arts colleges and nine major graduate research universities for the establishment of John D. MacArthur chairs and professorships. Each of the liberal arts colleges received $300,000 in endowments, and each of the major graduate research universities received $1.2 million in endowments. The total amount awarded through the endowments was $16.9 million—the second-largest award in the foundation's history.

In July, 1982, the foundation helped create an institute to study environment and natural resources through an interdisciplinary approach and on a global scale. The organization was named the Institute for World Environment and Resources, Inc., and is located in Washington, D.C. The institute's commitment is to a global perspective; to the development of a better understanding of large-scale resource, environment, and population problems; and to the development of innovative policy answers to these problems. The foundation will fund the institute for five years with annual awards. The award is expected to total $15 million, making it the third-largest award made by the foundation. The endowment awards and the grant to create the Institute for World Environment and Resources, Inc., however, end the foundation's grant-making role in higher education and environment for the foreseeable future.

The four ongoing major programs of the foundation are described below.

The *Health Program* is initiating its own mental health research projects, with a particular emphasis on the establishment of networks of institutions to study various areas of mental health research. Thus far, three of eight projected networks have been established. The first is a network to study depression. Mental health research focuses on five major areas:

1. Research on developmental processes—normal and deviant—across the life-span but emphasizing development during infancy, childhood, and adolescence
2. The scientific study of states of consciousness and of unconsciousness processes;

scientific testing of psychodynamic concepts; and a reexamination of the relation of these subjects to mental health

3. Development and scientific evaluation of strategies of prevention and early intervention aimed at reducing the incidence of mental disorders and promoting mental health, competence, and coping skills
4. Research in the causes and treatment of major mental disorders, including research on brain function and behavior, and interactions between biological (genetic and biochemical) and experiential (psychological and social) factors
5. Research on the relationships between physical health and mental health, including exploration of the complex interplay between biological factors and psychological and behavioral factors in the promotion of physical and mental health

The *Prize Fellows Program* does not accept self-nominations or informal nominations or recommendations. Instead, the program relies on one hundred or more foundation-selected nominators who submit the names of persons they believe meet the foundation standards for qualification as Prize Fellows. The names of the nominators are not made public. Information on each nominee is assembled by the program staff along with evaluations of each nominee by experts in the field of the nominee. Primary material, such as the nominee's published writings, also are assembled by the staff. The files are then submitted to a selection committee, which then makes recommendations to the board. Thus far, sixty individuals have been selected as MacArthur Prize Fellows. The Prize Fellows receive between $24,000 and $60,000 annually for five years. The amount of the award varies by age. Persons twenty-one years old or younger receive $24,000 annually. The award increases by $800 for each additional year of age. Persons of sixty-six years and older receive $60,000 annually.

The *General Grants Program* is concerned with the effectiveness and improvement of education; governance and public policy formation; justice; and mass communications. Illustrative of the program's interests are:

1. The future of the educational system in promoting educational excellence and equity
2. The use of new information technologies in formal educational settings
3. Defining and improving governmental productivity
4. Improving citizen's participation in governance
5. Critical issues and areas of need in providing criminal and civil justice
6. The improvement of the practice of journalism
7. The impact of media on public opinion and public policy formation

The *Special Grants Program* is concerned primarily with the Chicago metropolitan area. The program provides support for established cultural institutions, emerging arts organizations, technical assistance providers, and a variety of performing and visual arts groups. In addition, the program supports neighborhood organizations that will:

1. Strengthen and restore the viability of neighborhood organizations by providing for community self-help
2. Address the educational and skill development needs of disadvantaged youth
3. Develop more effective and efficient models for delivery of social services and facilitate local planning
4. Demonstrate innovative approaches to emerging problems through small-scale projects and the establishment of coalitions to coordinate community revitalization efforts
5. Support parents and enhance the role of families in their efforts to improve the quality of community life

The actual grants made in the four major program areas since 1978 have been numerous and varied. Here follows an analysis of them with citation to representative grants in each area.

*Health Program*: The board of directors authorized one hundred grants totalling $15.2 million between December 1, 1978, and December 31, 1981, ranging from $24,500 to the Rehabilitation Institute of Chicago (to complete a study of rehabilitation facilities in the Chicago area in the foundation's very early days before the shift in focus to mental health research) to $1 million over five years to the Center for Advanced Studies in the Behavioral Sciences for a fellowship program in Mental Health.

The overwhelming number of awards have been made in mental health research, including $300,000 to Columbia University College of Physicians and Surgeons for a study of neural development, synaptic plasticity, and learning; $650,000 to the Harvard University Division of Health Policy Research for work on mental health policy; $322,000 to Harvard University for a study of the significance of behavioral inhibition during pre-school years; $294,720 to McLean Hospital for the study of molecular biological investigation of the senile brain in Alzheimer's disease; $375,000 to Northwestern University for the study of depression, meaning, and inference; $300,954 to Pennsylvania State University to enhance the archival and future contributions of the New York longitudinal study; $284,095 to the Research Foundation for Mental Health for the study of psychosocial adaptation from adolescence to young adulthood; $316,346 to Stanford University for the study of chronic stress in children and youth; $379,640 to the University of California-Berkeley for the study of stress, coping, and mental health; $715,024 to the University of California-Berkeley, Institute of Human Development, for an interdisciplinary study of the life course; $300,000 to the University of California for the study of facial signals of emotion; $341,735 to the Research Foundation, University of Louisville, for a study of assessment of temperament of infant twins; $395,265 to the University of Virginia for a longitudinal study of adaptation to remarriage in stepfamilies; and $446,438 to the Wright Institute, Oregon Social Learning Center, for a research project on microanalysis of resistance.

*Prize Fellows Program*: The board has selected sixty MacArthur Prize Fellows whose work covers more than forty-five fields of endeavor, including anthropology, history, physics, poetry, and theater. The sixty Prize Fellows represent a commitment of approximately $14 million over the five-year span of the awards. Names of the individual fellows, the years of their awards, and their fields of endeavor are available on request from the foundation.

*General Grants Program*: The board of directors, through the General Grants Program, authorized fifty-five grants totalling $16,150,990 between December 1, 1978, and December 31, 1981. These included a diversity of research areas.

For example, in the field of *civil justice*, two awards totalling $635,000 were made to the American Bar Association to develop programs and procedures to reduce court costs and delays; and two grants amounting to $700,000 were made to the Rand Corporation to create an Institute for Civil Justice to develop programs to make the system more efficient, responsive, and equitable. In *criminal justice*, two awards totalling $600,000 were made to the Safer Foundation of Chicago for a Basic Skills Program for young ex-offenders. In October, 1981, the board voted to retain a half-dozen outside consultants to develop scholarly papers identifying problems and opportunities for future studies in the criminal justice system.

Also under the General Grants Program, through its *energy* grants, the MacArthur Foundation has generally sought projects that would better inform the electorate and public policy makers about the current state of scientific and technological knowledge in the area of energy. The major grants were $250,000 to the Alliance to Save Energy to develop energy-saving techniques for industry; and $100,000 to the American Council for an Energy-Efficient Economy to develop information to aid local government units among others.

In *education*, the MacArthur Foundation awarded more than $200,000 to the American Council on Education to develop ideas and make recommendations on the major issues facing higher education in the next twenty years; a $2.5 million award went to the United Negro College Fund for a Distinguished Scholars Program; $395,000 to the Committee on Institutional Cooperation, at Northwestern University, for the funding of fellowships for two-year Ph.D. programs in the physical sciences and engineering; $250,000 to the National Association for the Advancement of Colored People (NAACP) Legal Defense and Educational Fund to support black law students attending state-supported law schools in the southern states; and $200,000 to the Washington Center for Learning Alternatives to fund a program of internships and seminars for college students to study and work in governmental agencies and public service groups in the fields of the arts, humanities, and labor relations. Other areas of education have benefitted through major awards totalling almost $2 million for programs of the Aspen Institute for Humanistic Studies; the Institute for Philosophical Research; Reading is Fundamental (for the development of reading materials to aid parents seeking to instill reading interest and skills in their children); and to the Exploratorium Museum, in San Francisco (for the development of its educational programs and exhibits.)

In *governance and public affairs*, the MacArthur Foundation's interest is reflected in a variety of grants ranging from almost a half-million dollars to the Aspen Institute, for funding programs aimed at strengthening citizen participation in the democratic process, to a grant to the World Food Corporation, to provide technical help on experimental agricultural projects in developing countries. In between were awards to the Better Government Association of Chicago ($2.5 million); two grants to the Chicago Crime Commission for programs to increase citizen awareness and responsiveness to crime ($200,000 in two annual awards); to the Civic Action Institute to support a technical assistance program to neighborhood organizations ($158,000); to the Committee for Economic Development to study savings incentives for retirement years ($100,000); to the Cosmopolitan Chamber of Commerce to help improve management skills of minority contractors ($43,400); two major grants to Helsinki Watch for its work in monitoring activities in other countries for violations of the human rights provisions of the Helsinki Accords ($400,000); to the International Management Development Institute for its programs designed to accelerate American industrial growth ($250,000); to the Opportunities Industrialization Center of America for training a management corps to operate its minority manpower training programs ($100,000); and $1 million to the National Academy of Sciences to give the academy greater flexibility in undertaking the independent studies it deems necessary, studies that have not received a congressional mandate or funding.

In *mass communications*, reflecting the MacArthur Foundation's interest, were awards to the National News Council ($50,000), to fund new studies on the role of the media in society, and to the Scientists Institute for Public Information ($125,000), which provides the media with the names of scientists who can be called on by reporters to respond to questions about specific events and developments in the fields of science and technology.

*Special Grants Program*: The MacArthur Foundation board, acting through this program, authorized 112 grants totalling $5,865,483 between December 1, 1978, and December 31, 1981. These included, for example, in the Chicago area, cultural grants of $75,000 each to: the Chicago Symphony, Lyric Opera, Art Institute, Field Museum of Natural History, Goodman Theater, and Channel 11/WTTW. In neighborhood development for the Chicago area, a grant of $1 million was awarded in 1981 to help establish the Local Initiatives Support Corp., to help neighborhood organizations; $175,000 went to Chicago United to support a Career Development Center to help high school students find career paths; and a $300,000 grant was made to avert the closing of Providence-St. Mel High school, which primarily serves a black neighborhood.

For further information, see the foundation's first published report, *Report on Activities 1980 and 1981* (1982). See also numerous journal and newspaper articles in recent years about the foundation, for example, Frederick C. Klein, "MacArthur's Millions,"*Wall Street Journal* (April 26, 1979), pp. 8, 9; Bob

Tamarkin, "Bitter Charity,"*Forbes* (June 11, 1979), pp. 113, 114; "Thousands of Dollars to Do With as They Wish," *Trenton Times* (May 19, 1981), pp. 2, 7; Kathleen Teltsch, "Foundation to Support 21 as 'Geniuses' for 5 Years," *New York Times* (May 19, 1981), pp. A1, B13; Greg Braxton, "Prize," *Los Angeles Herald-Examiner* (May 20, 1981), pp. A3, A8; Calvin Trillin, "Variations," *The Nation* (June 13, 1981), p. 718; Harlan S. Byrne, "After the Windfall," *Wall Street Journal* (November 19, 1981), pp. 1, 22; and Kevin Wolfe, "The MacArthur Fellows," *Dallas Morning News* (June 16, 1982), pp. 1C, 2C.

NORTON KAY

**JOHN MCSHAIN CHARITIES, INC.** The John McShain Charities, Inc., was established in Pennsylvania in 1949 by John McShain; John McShain, Incorporated, of Philadelphia; and others. As a builder, John McShain has been responsible for a number of major construction projects. During the administration of President Truman, when it was apparent that the structural condition of the White House had deteriorated critically, McShain's company was selected to perform the renovation. This project involved extensive, detailed work, which required a complete gutting and restoration of the building.

The major portion of John McShain Charities' grants are distributed in the Philadelphia, Pennsylvania, area and are directed to Roman Catholic churches, religious orders, and denominational organizations and agencies. Following such recipients are institutions of higher learning and secondary schools, generally those with a Roman Catholic affiliation.

During the fiscal year ending March 31, 1980, 293 grants were awarded by the foundation for a total of $982,698. Of these, 149 grants, or 51 percent of the total, were given to Roman Catholic churches, religious orders, and missions. Included was a grant of $100,000 to Pope John Paul II.

Colleges, universities, and secondary educational institutions received forty-eight grants, or 33 percent of the total. The remaining 16 percent went to social welfare, cultural programs, and health and public interest recipients. Among these latter categories were the United Way, Federation of Jewish Agencies Capital Fund, Van Cliburn International Piano Competition, the Historical Society of Pennsylvania, and the Scheie Eye Institute.

Prior to 1971, the foundation's assets were approximately $8 million, but in the 1971-1972 fiscal year, John McShain donated about $34 million worth of shares of corporate stock. The market value of the foundation's assets as of March 31, 1981, was about $33 million, which is a slight rise over the corresponding figure from the previous fiscal year.

John McShain Charities, Inc., is governed by a four-member board of directors, with John McShain serving as president and Mary H. McShain as vice-president. The foundation is administered from offices located at 540 North Seventeenth Street, Philadelphia, Pennsylvania 19130, under the direction of the president.

Almost the only additional information readily available to the public on this foundation are the annual reports and returns filed by it with the Internal Revenue Service, and the various Foundation Center publications. See, however, *The Directory of Pennsylvania Foundations* (1981).

JOHN SOBOTKA

**JOHN MOTLEY MOREHEAD FOUNDATION, THE.** The founder of the John Motley Morehead Foundation was born in North Carolina in 1870. Morehead graduated from the University of North Carolina at Chapel Hill in 1891 with a degree in chemical engineering. Subsequently, in the course of holding various industrial positions, he discovered calcium carbide, and by 1900 he had joined the newly formed Union Carbide Company. His continuing research on industrial applications of calcium carbide resulted in many breakthroughs, including the development of acetylene gas and polyethylene. By the time of his death, in 1965, he had become one of the largest stockholders in Union Carbide and had acquired a fortune of several million dollars.

Morehead married in 1915. However, the couple had no children, and, following his wife's death in April, 1945, he created in that same year the John Motley Morehead Foundation, whose primary beneficiary has been the University of North Carolina at Chapel Hill. Major gifts have included a planetarium, bell tower and chimes, and collections of art works. The Morehead Foundation's chief program, however, was the establishment, in 1951, of a scholarship program at the undergraduate and graduate level, designed to attract outstanding students to Chapel Hill. With 1980 assets of about $37 million, the foundation's income is used to provide aid in excess of $1.25 million to almost three hundred Morehead Scholars, plus almost $1 million in grants for other foundation purposes.

The foundation is governed by a five-member board of trustees. Administration of the foundation is carried on from offices located in Chapel Hill and Charlotte, North Carolina, under the direction of an executive director. The mailing address of the foundation is Post Office Box 348, Chapel Hill, North Carolina 27514.

For further information, see *Report* (1945-1959), published by the foundation, and *Annual Reports* published since that time. See also John Motley Morehead obituary, *New York Times* (January 8, 1965), p. 29; and "John Motley Morehead," *Dictionary of American Biography*, Supplement Seven (1981), pp. 553-555.

**JOHN SIMON GUGGENHEIM MEMORIAL FOUNDATION.** Founded in 1925 by Senator and Mrs. Simon Guggenheim, the John Simon Guggenheim Memorial Foundation, as the name indicates, is a memorial to their son, John Simon Guggenheim, who died April 26, 1922. The senator and his wife, according to their statement, wished to establish a foundation which would continue the influence of their son by aiding scholars, scientists, and artists and thus increase the knowledge, appreciation, and understanding in educational, literary, artistic, and scientific disciplines and promote better international understanding.

In making the gift, Senator Guggenheim proposed that fellowships be issued "under the freest possible conditions," and throughout the foundation's existence, since 1925, this wish has been followed. During the early years, the recipients of grants were asked to make reports to the trustees at the end of their fellowships; but little attention was paid to the reports, and they were soon dropped. All that is now asked of the fellows is that they report their successes, and if books are published as a result of the fellowship, the foundation would like to have copies.

The success of Guggenheim Memorial Foundation has been largely due to the hard work and careful guidance of the first secretary, Henry Allen Moe, a scholar, highly qualified in several fields of specialization, including mathematics, journalism, naval science, and law. Senator Guggenheim asked Moe to assist him in formulating plans for setting up the foundation. Moe spent several months of intensive study, working out the details, studying the amounts and sources of scholarship and fellowship funds available at that time, interviewing scholars, creative artists, college presidents, business and professional men, in an effort to find the most useful area in which this foundation should operate. When this study had been completed, Senator Guggenheim asked Henry Moe to run the foundation for him, and for thirty-nine years he ran it, serving in various official capacities. He served first as secretary, 1925-1938; as secretary-general 1938-1954; and still later as secretary-general and vice-president. In 1945, he became a member of the board of trustees, and from 1961 to 1963, he served as its president, resigning in 1964 to conduct a study for the National Science Foundation. In 1970, Moe was made president emeritus of the board and continued in that capacity until his death in 1975. More than any other person, Moe has exerted the greatest influence on the foundation. His scholarship, his love of freedom, and in the words of one observer, "his passion for excellence" (Milton Lomask, *Seed Money, The Guggenheim Story* [1964], p. 264, the quotations below are from this same work) have dominated its operations. On the subject of freedom of the foundation, he wrote, "it is our intent to remain the stronghold of free enterprise in things of the mind and spirit"(p. 251). Moe sincerely believed that "free man produces most and best"(p. 240).

It was, perhaps, this devotion to freedom which brought the charge by Representative E. Eugene Cox, who led in the founding of the (U.S. House of Representatives) Cox Committee, that the funds of the John Simon Guggenheim Memorial Foundation were being used "to spread radicalism throughout the country to an extent not excelled by any other foundation"(p. 266). The Cox Committee was appointed by the U.S. Congress to investigate tax-exempt foundations to determine especially which were "using their resources for un-American and subversive activities"(p. 265). Moe spent months doing the research necessary to answer the questionnaire sent out by the committee. His report was a lengthy and able refutation of the charges, ending with the admission that the investigation had revealed that two of the 2,190 fellowships that had been granted by the foundation were subsequently discovered to have been awarded to communists, which was deeply regretted. In making this statement, Moe wrote "a Guggenheim fellow should be a good citizen," and if the fellows are "members of any movement, organization, group which does their thinking for them or indicates what their conclusions must or ought to be, they are not free to follow their evidence and their own thinking; and they get no money from us"(p. 268).

In setting up the criteria for making grants, Moe considered it most important that the fellowships should be reserved for persons sufficiently advanced in their fields of specialization to justify the belief that, given help, they would be capable of greater achievement. He thought the foundation should be helpful and understanding of men and women endowed with the creative spark. "What they need," he wrote, "is room for the exercise of their imaginations. *We aim quite simply to provide that room*" (p. 252). With these ideas concerning the types of applicants wanted, Moe actively sought them. The successes of the Guggenheim fellows are ample justification for the ideas upon which the foundation was established. Through 1982, 50 fellows have received Nobel Prizes and 127 have won the Pulitzer Prize.

Originally, the grants were made available only to United States citizens and permanent residents and included its territories and some of its possessions. In the 1930s, the foundation extended its grants to several South American countries. This was made possible by an additional gift of one million dollars from Senator and Mrs. Guggenheim in 1929. In 1940, Canada and Newfoundland were added, and by 1950, all of the South American countries and the British Caribbean were included, making the fellowships available to all of the western hemisphere and the Philippines. These islands, as a possession of the United States, were part of the original awards and were retained for awards consideration after their independence was declared.

The organization of the John Simon Guggenheim Memorial Foundation consists of three units in addition to the office staff. First, is the board of trustees, originally composed of seven members but enlarged to eleven with the extension of grants to the entire western hemisphere. The trustees have the final vote on the applicants chosen. The second unit is the educational advisory board, consisting of thirty-six members, appointed so that approximately one-fourth of them retire each year. They assist the trustees and pass on the qualifications of the applicants. The committees of selection are the third unit. There was only one committee at first, but with the expanded program it was necessary to have two, one for the United States and Canada of seven members and the other for the western hemisphere and the Philippines of four members. All members of these two committees are chosen from the educational advisory board. These committees, together with the office staff, do the bulk of the work. Compiling the dossiers for all the applicants, obtaining judgments of the juries and referees, and obtaining the votes requires a tremendous amount of work of these two groups. The foundation operated with a very small staff in the beginning, which included the secretary and three or four assistants. During the first years, Henry Moe personally visited every applicant and made his recommendations to the board of trustees. It was necessary to increase the staff with the extension of grants.

As first set up, the fellowships were confined to individuals ranging between the ages of twenty-five and thirty-five. However, since 1949, no age limitations have been considered—grants have been made to fellows ranging from twenty-two to seventy-seven years of age, and the average age has risen from thirty-four in 1925-1928 to forty-three in 1977-1980. All along the way, flexibility has been the keynote of the Guggenheim Foundation's procedures. Ordinarily, each grant was for one year, but from the first, fellows have been permitted to seek one or more renewals. During the early years, a Guggenheim fellow was expected to spend most of his fellowship period abroad, but that policy no longer prevails. Today, many grants are made to Americans whose work can best be done at home.

During the first four years of its existence, the foundation awarded 197 fellowships, including renewals. Each succeeding four years, from 1937, the number of fellowships has increased, reaching 1,270 for the four-year period 1957-1960. Since that time, they have not dropped below 1,000 for any four-year period, making the total of 10,546 for the years 1925-1980. This number was chosen from 84,629 applicants. The foundation has awarded more fellowships in the humanities than in any other area of knowledge, with science running a close second.

The dollar value of the fellowships has varied. In the early years, the grant was $3,000, although it could be adjusted upward depending on the needs of each fellow. Due to the decreasing value of the dollar, the average award reached $16,634 in 1980. The amount of money granted from 1961 to 1980 was $67,010,900, which is three times the amount that had been granted prior to 1961. Inflation has forced the foundation to reduce the number of fellowships granted since 1972 in order to make some adjustment for the rising cost of living.

Assets of the foundation have increased over the years. In the 1940s, they were about $20 million; in the 1950s, $40 million; in the 1960s, $55 million; and in 1980 they were about $100 million.

The Guggenheim family has had a remarkable record for philanthropy. In addition to the John Simon Guggenheim Memorial Foundation, four other foundations with large endowments have been established by the senator's brothers, Daniel, Murry, and Solomon, in the fields of aviation, aerodynamics, dentistry, and art. The grandparents of Senator Guggenheim, Simon and Rachel Guggenheim, immigrated to the United States with their thirteen children in 1847. They were Jewish people who had lived in a ghetto in a small town near Zurich, Switzerland, the German area of that country. By reason of an inheritance from her first husband, Rachel Guggenheim had enough money to pay the passage of this large family, with none to spare. They arrived in the New World without money or knowledge of the language, clinging only to a dream of freedom. Simon and his twenty-year-old son, Meyer, began their life in Philadelphia as peddlers, with bulging packs of pins, needles, stove and furniture polish, shoe strings, spices, and some bits of lace. Gradually, they improved their earnings by becoming manufacturers of some of the products and importers of others.

By 1869, when the immigrant grandfather, Simon Guggenheim, died, the family was well established in America. Largely due to Meyer Guggenheim, the senator's father, the family was able to purchase interests in the more lucrative business of silver mining and later the tremendous smelting operations which, by good business practices, they soon dominated. Meyer had married his stepsister, Barbara, and the couple had eleven children, eight sons and three daughters, all of whom lived to adulthood, except one son, Robert, the twin brother of Senator Simon. The Guggenheim brothers were closely associated in their business relationships. The four older brothers—Isaac, Daniel, Murry, and Solomon—operated the New York office of the company, and the younger brothers—Benjamin, Simon, and William—worked in the West, in Colorado and New Mexico and in the adjoining countries of Canada, Mexico, and Alaska, maintaining their western headquarters in Colorado. Together, these Guggenheim brothers, east and west, built one of the great American fortunes.

After some years, Simon became interested in politics, and in 1907, Colorado elected him to the U.S. Senate. This senate election brought Simon back to the East, and from this time he became more closely associated with his older brothers, the eastern branch of the family. With the establishment of the John Simon Guggenheim Memorial Foundation, the senator, whose term of office had expired, spent much time working with Henry Moe at the foundation office. Moe described him as constructive, liberal, kind, and generous, always interested, always helpful, and never obtrusive. Simon Guggenheim was the first president of the foundation, from 1925, the time of its incorporation, until his death on November 2, 1941. He was succeeded by his wife, who served as president from 1941 until Henry Moe took over in 1961. After Moe's two years, Gordon N. Ray became president and has held that position until the present. The foundation began its operations at 120 Broadway, in New York City, and moved during its first year to 100 East Forty-second Street; in 1927, the office was moved to 551 Fifth Avenue North, where it continued to operate until 1965, when it moved to 90 Park Avenue, New York, New York 10016, its present address.

For further information, see *Biannual Reports* of the foundation, published from the 1950s until 1972; *Annual Reports* have been published continuously since that date. See, particularly, the *Annual Report* (1978), which contains an excellent account of the foundation by its current president. See also Bernard Peach and Paschal Reeves, "John Simon Guggenheim Memorial Foundation: Investment in Free Individuals," *South Atlantic Quarterly*, vol. 60 (Spring, 1961) pp. 125-204; and Milton Lomask, *Seed Money: The Guggenheim Story* (1964).

HARRIET C. OWSLEY

**JOHNSON FOUNDATION.** See Christian A. Johnson Endeavor Foundation, The; Helen K. and Arthur E. Johnson Foundation; Robert Wood Johnson Foundation, The.

**JOHNSON NEW BRUNSWICK FOUNDATION.** See Robert Wood Johnson Foundation, The.

**JOHN W. ANDERSON FOUNDATION.** John W. Anderson was the founder and president of the Anderson Company, a leading manufacturer of windshield wipers and other automotive equipment. He was a prolific inventor who held well over one hundred patents at the time of his death in 1967. A brother and a sister survived him, but a major portion of the fortune he had acquired was donated to the John W. Anderson Foundation, named for him, which was established in the year of his death.

During his lifetime, Anderson devoted considerable sums of money for the support of Boys' Clubs and other youth organizations located in northwest Indiana. The foundation which he established has continued to support such activities, particularly in Indiana. By 1975, however, with assets which had grown to about $11 million, the foundation broadened the scope of its grant making to include higher education, community funds, aid to the handicapped, and hospitals. Grants in that year totalled about $600,000.

During the three-year period of 1977 through 1979, Anderson Foundation assets rose in value from about $12 million to approximately $42 million. The value of grants disbursed during this period increased proportionately to about $1.5 million in 1979. Grants continued, however, to reflect the traditional giving pattern of the foundation, with more than two-thirds devoted to education and youth programs. The largest grant made in 1979 was one of $155,914 to the Boys' Club of Northwest Indiana, Inc. Other major grants for the year were ones of $140,000 to the Indiana University Foundation and $100,000 to the Associated Colleges of Indiana.

With 1981 assets of about $51 million, the foundation is governed by a five-member board of trustees. Administration of the foundation is carried on from offices located at 2402 Cumberland Drive, Valparaiso, Indiana 46383, under the direction of a secretary.

Almost the only additional information on this foundation readily available to the public are the annual reports and returns filed by it with the Internal Revenue Service, and the various Foundation Center publications. See, however, John W. Anderson obituary, *New York Times* (September 30, 1967), p. 33.

**JONES FOUNDATION.** See Jones Foundation, The; W. Alton Jones Foundation, Inc.

**JONES FOUNDATION, THE.** Fletcher Jones, cofounder of Computer Sciences Corporation, one of the United States' largest computer services corporations, set up the Jones Foundation in California in 1969. The foundation was practically moribund until 1977 when, following the 1972 death of Jones in an aircraft accident, it received some three million shares of stock in the corporation from his estate, thus making possible an increase in the annual giving of the foundation from about $20,000 in 1976 to around $2 million annually.

Grants have been made primarily to institutions in California and particularly those in the Los Angeles area. In 1979, for example, the California Institute of Technology, the University of Southern California, and Stanford University each received $500,000 for the endowment of a Fletcher Jones Chair in Computer Science at each institution. The only other grant for that year was one of about $420,000 to the Los Angeles Art Museum. During the period 1974-1982, almost 50 percent of the total grant money of $11.25 million made during the period went to the foregoing three universities.

The Jones Foundation is governed by a seven-member board of trustees. With 1981 assets valued at about $40 million, administration of the foundation is carried on from offices located at One Wilshire Building, 624 South Grand Avenue, Los Angeles, California 90017, under the direction of an executive director.

Almost the only additional information on this foundation readily available to the public are the annual reports and returns filed by it with the Internal Revenue Service, and the various Foundation Center publications. See, however, an *Annual Report* published by the foundation in 1981, and a leaflet, *Summary of Grants by Institutions 1974-1982*, issued by it in 1982.

**JOSEPH AND HELEN REGENSTEIN FOUNDATION.** See Regenstein Foundation, The.

**JOSEPH B. WHITEHEAD FOUNDATION.** Housed in offices at 1400 Peachtree Center Tower, in Atlanta, Georgia 30303, are four foundations with total assets, as of November 30, 1982, of $263,176,000. The four foundations are the Trebor Foundation, the Lettie Pate Whitehead Foundation, Inc.,* the Lettie Pate Evans Foundation, and, the focus of this article, the Joseph B. Whitehead Foundation. Each foundation is independent, with its separate board of trustees. They, however, employ the same officers and staff, and they derive the bulk of their endowments from an association with the Coca-Cola industry. In the case of the Joseph B. Whitehead Foundation, the assets flow from the Coca-Cola bottling empire started by Benjamin Franklin Thomas and Joseph Brown Whitehead at the end of the nineteenth century.

Benjamin Thomas and Joseph B. Whitehead, young attorneys from Chattanooga, Tennessee, became early devotees of the new soda-fountain drink, Coca-Cola. The young men, from some unknown inspiration, developed an interest in bottling Coca-Cola throughout the nation. Their first task was to persuade Asa G. Candler, owner of the Coca-Cola Company, that bottling could be profitable. This might have proved difficult since Candler had openly stated that he had "very little confidence in this bottling business" (Pat Watters, *Coca-Cola: An illustrated History* [1978], p. 57).

At the request of Thomas and Whitehead, Sam Erwin, also of Chattanooga and a cousin of Asa Candler, arranged a meeting between the two lawyers and the head of the Coca-Cola Company for July 21, 1899. Thomas and Whitehead must have been extremely persuasive because when they walked out of Candler's office, they took with them one of the most important agreements in business history.

In a six-hundred-word contract, Candler agreed that Thomas and Whitehead would have exclusive rights to bottle Coca-Cola, at no expense or liability to the Coca-Cola Company, throughout the United States, with the exceptions of New England, most of Mississippi, and Texas. (In 1902, Whitehead obtained bottling rights in Texas.) The Coca-Cola Company agreed to sell syrup to them and no one else for bottling purposes. The company also agreed to furnish labels and advertising matter. The contract provided for no exchange of money by the parties to the agreement.

Whitehead realized, as they began to make their plans to provide bottled Coca-Cola for most of the country, that he did not have the capital for such a vast enterprise. To secure the needed capital, Whitehead sold one-half of his one-half interest in the bottling contract to John T. Lupton, an affluent Chattanooga lawyer and businessman.

Early in 1900, Thomas and Whitehead decided to split their territory between them. Thomas received the Mid-Atlantic and Eastern states, plus California, Oregon, and Washington. The Southeast, Southwest, and the Midwest went to Whitehead-Lupton.

In April, 1900, Whitehead moved to Atlanta where he opened his first bottling company. From this base of operation, independent bottlers were franchised in towns and cities throughout his territory. Whitehead and Lupton held the sole right to sell syrup to these franchised bottlers, and they, in turn, were guaranteed an exclusive territory in which to sell the bottled drink.

Joseph B. Whitehead died in 1906 at the age of forty-two, only seven years after embarking on his business venture with Coca-Cola. He had, nevertheless, in that time, through the franchise system and holdings in several bottling companies, provided the foundation for the Whitehead family fortune.

Whitehead was survived by his wife, Lettie Pate Whitehead, and two young sons, Joseph B. Whitehead, Jr., and Conkey Pate Whitehead. It was Joseph B. Whitehead, Jr., who established, in his will, the Joseph B. Whitehead Foundation in memory of his father. The junior Whitehead provided that his residuary estate would be used to start the foundation.

In 1935, Joseph B. Whitehead, Jr., like his father before him, died while still in the early forties. Two years later, the Joseph B. Whitehead Foundation was chartered with assets from the junior Whitehead's residuary estate of $5,321,000. Whitehead stipulated that the foundation's giving must be restricted to the Atlanta area.

The Joseph B. Whitehead Foundation is governed by a three-member, self-perpetuating board of trustees, who are currently J. W. Jones, James M. Sibley, and Robert W. Woodruff. Administration of the foundation is carried on by a staff under the direction of a president.

Most grants from the Joseph B. Whitehead Foundation are given for one-time capital projects. Rarely is a grant made for the basic operations of an organization. No grants are made to individuals. Generally, grants are given to support youth programs and child welfare, health, care for the aged, education, the arts, and civic affairs.

Over the years the Whitehead family, the Joseph B. Whitehead Foundation, as well as the other Coca-Cola-connected foundations, have been especially generous with Emory University in general and with the university's college of medicine and hospital in particular. The chairman of Emory's Department of Surgery holds the Joseph B. Whitehead Chair of Surgery, funded by the Whitehead family.

Joseph B. Whitehead, Jr., had an expressed interest in programs for orphans. The foundation has continued to reflect that interest in its giving, while also extending support to various groups working with other dependent or emotionally disturbed children. Boys' and girls' clubs are of special interest to the foundation. One Atlanta organization is named the Joseph B. Whitehead Boys Club.

The Joseph B. Whitehead Foundation in 1981 distributed $3,358,000 in grants. Children-related groups received $395,000; health care for the indigent, $50,000; scholarships, $30,000; and the arts, $2,575,000. Grants to the arts were exceptionally high in 1981 because of a single grant of $2,250,000 to the Atlanta Arts Alliance toward construction of a new High Museum of Art. Other grants included those to the Robert W. Woodruff Library of Emory University to pay the cost of indexing the daily columns of Ralph McGill, former editor of the *Atlanta Constitution*; the Atlanta Botanical Garden for capital development; and the Atlanta Medical Heritage, Inc., toward restoration of the Academy of Medicine Building for community use.

The Joseph B. Whitehead Foundation, as of December 31, 1981, held corporate stock with a market value of $45,990,072 (book value, $5,572,373). These holdings included stock in eight Coca-Cola bottling companies valued at $8,172,734 (book value, $167,473), stock in the Coca-Cola Company valued at $36,484,720 (book value, $4,223,340), and miscellaneous stock valued at $1,332,618 (book value, $1,181,560). Cash, temporary cash investments, accounts receivable, and investments such as land, buildings, and equipment provide the foundation with additional assets valued at $7,047,169.

Income for the Joseph B. Whitehead Foundation in 1981 included $1,049,792 from interest on savings and temporary investments; $2,847,393 from dividends and interest on securities; and $39,750 in rents. The foundation had expenses, primarily for salaries and rents, of $43,082, giving it an adjusted net income of $3,893,853 for the year and with grants amounting to about $3.25 million.

The Joseph B. Whitehead Foundation, since its beginning in 1937, has not altered its purpose or its methods of operation. The trustees and officers, even though the foundation has played a major role in many notable achievements in the Atlanta community, have consistently and tenaciously worked to avoid publicity. The officers and trustees are also modestly reluctant to focus attention on any special achievements.

In addition to the work cited above, the author is indebted to Charles H. McTier, secretary of the foundation, for an interview in which he provided information about its history and operations. Almost the only additional sources of information readily available to the public on this foundation are the annual reports and returns filed by it with the Internal Revenue Service, and the various Foundation Center publications.

DON M. PACE

**JOSIAH MACY, JR., FOUNDATION.** The Macy family traces its American beginnings to the arrival in Massachusetts of Thomas and Sarah Macy, who emigrated from England in the early seventeenth century. In 1659, conflict with the Puritans over religious freedom led the Macys and nine other Baptist and Quaker families to purchase Nantucket Island. Succeeding generations of Macys prospered as merchants, and in 1828, Captain Josiah Macy established a shipping and commission business in New York.

In the 1860s, the company entered the oil industry. Their refinery was purchased by the Standard Oil Company in 1872, and Josiah Macy, Jr., grandson of Captain Josiah, became a close associate of John D. Rockefeller in that company.

Josiah Macy, Jr., died of typhoid fever in 1875 at the age of thirty-seven, but he was already known for his philanthropic activities. Thus his daughter, Kate, the wife of Walter Graeme Ladd, continued the tradition and in 1930 established the Josiah Macy, Jr., Foundation as a memorial to her father with an initial gift of $5 million. When this gift was substantially reduced by the depression in 1931, Kate Ladd made additional contributions to supplement the foundation's resources, and at her death in 1945 at the age of eighty-two, she bequeathed additional monies, bringing her total gifts to some $19 million. The 1981 value of the endowment is about $54 million.

Kate Ladd's letter of gift is remarkable for the clarity of its mandate and the freedom it provides for adapting the foundation's programs to meet changing needs. It reads, in part:

It is my desire that the Foundation...should primarily devote its interest to the fundamental aspects of health, of sickness, and of methods for the relief of suffering...to such special problems in medical sciences, medical arts, and medical education as require for their solution studies and efforts in correlated fields...such as biology and the social sciences....I hope, therefore, that the Foundation will take more interest in the architecture of ideas than in the architecture of buildings and laboratories.

In its early years, in the 1930s, through its support of pioneering studies of the relationship of the mind and body in the functioning of the total human being, the foundation contributed significantly to a wider acceptance of the psychosomatic approach to medicine. In addition, scientific interest in the early stages of human growth and development was not matched in the 1930s by interest in the degenerative processes of later life. During that decade, the Macy Foundation made grants to support a broad spectrum of studies related to the aging process in animals and in humans. A grant made in 1940 facilitated the establishment of a unit on gerontology within the National Institutes of Health. Moreover, in the field to which it has made its most notable contributions, medical education, the foundation's first grant supported a comprehensive survey, published in 1932, of educational principles and practices followed by medical schools in this country and abroad.

In the 1940s, foreseeing the nation's eventual involvement in the war in Europe, the Macy Foundation began to support projects with specific bearing on health problems related to national defense, including investigations on the causes of traumatic shock and psychiatric disorders among the armed forces.

During the 1950s, many factors were working against stable, well-rounded medical faculties. Research grants were causing competition between investigation and education, and some schools were becoming more like research centers than teaching institutions. As a consequence, the Macy Foundation made grants to support teaching-research staffs in selected schools to help them maintain and improve their instructional programs. In 1955, in an effort to establish a scientific base for obstetrics and the study of human reproduction, the foundation launched a broad program, awarding eight-year grants for graduate research and teaching; setting up a medical student summer scholarship research program; and creating three-year fellowships in obstetrics for the purpose of establishing new positions at the level of instructor or assistant professor.

In the 1960s, world health statistics revealed many areas of desperate need, and the Macy Foundation saw in two of them, minority groups for medicine and pediatrics in developing countries, the possibility of attacking what were, at the same time, medical and social problems. Since then, the Josiah Macy, Jr., Foundation has played a leading role in the movement to increase the representation of blacks and other minority group members in medicine. In the early 1970s, it began to fund programs to strengthen the health advisory services and premedical curricula at selected traditionally black colleges. Summer training institutes for premedical advisors were held, as were seminars in modern quantitative biology for faculty from minority colleges. In addition, a collaborative program was initiated with the Marine Biology Laboratory, in Woods Hole, to provide intensive training and research experiences in biomedical sciences for minority faculty members and graduate students. However, as a prerequisite to advanced study, academic deficiency in undergraduate preparation remains the greatest single obstacle to increasing the proportion of minority medical students. Therefore, the foundation continues to support programs to improve basic science training in selected black colleges.

To address its second area of major concern during the 1960s, in 1965 the foundation decided to spend up to 20 percent of its annual income on programs for education and research in pediatrics in developing countries, with special emphasis on Latin America, the Caribbean, and the Philippines. Three basic approaches were followed. One was to enable strategically located medical schools to establish training programs in pediatrics or preventive medicine; a second was to support regional centers where physicians and graduate-level health workers were trained in the principle of social and preventive pediatrics; a third was to provide support to new rural pediatric centers headed by graduates of these training programs. A majority of the participants are now working in hospitals, clinics, or rural health centers. Several hold positions in academic medicine or public health agencies and are thus able to influence government policy in matters concerning maternal and child health.

The traditional isolation of American medical schools from other university units has tended to minimize the role of the humanities in medical education. In 1965, the Macy Foundation established a major program to heighten the awareness of future physicians about the history of their profession and to reinforce the relationship of medical schools and university departments of history and philosophy. Fellowships were awarded to young scholars preparing for academic careers in the field, and grants were made to medical schools and to universities to establish or strengthen undergraduate and graduate programs in the history of medicine and biology.

Up until recently, the percentage of women in the medical profession in the United States was one of the lowest in the Western world. By 1980, however, the percentages had reached 26.5 of all medical students and 28.9 of first-year students; these figures promise to rise still higher. Since 1965, when it underwrote a study of the careers of women medical graduates, the foundation has sought answers to the questions of how to attract qualified women to careers in medicine and what can be done to reduce the number who drop out, either during their residencies or after they enter practice. Pilot grants were awarded to several universities to study these issues and to make recommendations for their resolution. As part of its current program, Preparation for Medical Education, in 1980 the foundation awarded grants to the Seven College Conference to support cooperative research on the careers of women who plan to become physicians.

The Macy Foundation began in 1965 to explore opportunities for the training and utilization of new categories of health-care personnel—practitioners other than physicians who could provide direct primary preventive care. Grants supported the development and implementation of such programs, including one to prepare clinical nurse specialists in maternal and child health care, and another to train physicians' assistants.

The Faculty Scholar Award Program was created by the Macy Foundation to enable outstanding full-time faculty members in schools of medicine and public health to spend up to a year of concentrated scholarship away from their parent institutions. Freed from pressing responsibilities at home, the recipients were able to devote uninterrupted time to projects of their own choosing in a new intellectual environment.

The preparation and selection of medical students has been a subject of long-term interest to the foundation. In a report for 1956-1960, it was noted that the then educational plan was to select self-starting, self-directing, and self-propelling students who had a broad cultural background rather than a concentration in the sciences. The trend, however, has been away from the plan of broad-based preparation in the humanities and sciences toward an overconcentration on science and that in an atmosphere of intense competition. Consequently, in 1979, the foundation launched a major program under which pilot grants have been made to seventeen medical schools and to several groups of liberal arts colleges to enable them to improve the quality of their premedical counseling; encourage diversity of preparation; and reduce the number of competitive pressures on premedical candidates. Other grants have been made to demonstrate that familiarity with the concepts, perspectives, methods, and materials of the humanities is an essential element in a well-rounded medical education.

To develop a multidisciplinary academic program in health policy and to prepare new types of professionals trained to become managers and decision makers in the field, Harvard University has recently established a graduate-level Division of Health Policy Research and Education to which the foundation has made a grant to support senior fellowships in health policy.

The Minority Groups for Medicine programs described above are still receiving foundation support. In addition, the foundation is presently conducting a nationwide review to determine what new initiatives can be defined to prepare minority physicians and other health professionals for careers in medicine.

The foundation's Conference Program has always played an important part in the exploration of potential fields for support and in the review of existing commitments. Since 1965, the emphasis has been on education and current trends affecting medicine and health care at both the national and international levels. Ninety-five conferences were convened between 1965 and 1980. Since 1965, the foundation has published some fifty reports of its conferences and of Macy-sponsored commissions and studies.

In addition to the foregoing programs, the foundation is also currently awarding grants in the following areas: support of special teaching programs, usually involving cooperation between medical schools and university departments or research institutes, with the aim of providing meaningful exposure to human physiology and pathology for Ph.D. candidates who plan careers of basic research in biomedical sciences; and support of experimental programs designed to improve the content, quality, and effectiveness of the academic experience in medical schools.

The Macy Foundation's board of directors, which currently consists of sixteen members, establishes the policies and controls the funds of the foundation; the board meets at least three times a year. The foundation's programs are administered by the principal executive officer, the president. A report of the foundation's activities is published annually.

Grants are made to colleges, universities, and other professional and educational associations. No grants are made directly to individuals. The foundation does not consider requests for support of medical research, endowment funds, general support, or construction or renovation projects.

The Macy Foundation's professional personnel, as of September, 1981, consists of the president, James G. Hirsch, M.D., two program officers, an assistant secretary, an assistant treasurer, and the conference director and editor. Its offices are located at 44 East Sixty-Fourth Street, New York, New York 10021.

For further information, see the following reports which have been prepared by the foundation since its inception: *Annual Report* (1931); *Six Year Review, 1930-1936; Report, 1937-1940; Review of Activities, 1930-1955; Twentieth Anniversary Review, 1950; Five Year Review, 1956-1960; President's Review, 1961-1962; President's Report, 1963; Annual Report, 1964-1965; Annual Reports* published continuously since 1966; and *A Fifty Year Review, 1980*.

ELIZABETH F. PURCELL

**JOYCE FOUNDATION, THE.** The Joyce Foundation was incorporated in 1948 in Chicago, Illinois, by its sole donor, Beatrice Joyce Kean. Organized exclusively for charitable, religious (removed in 1976), scientific, literary, and educational purposes, the foundation's founding directors were Beatrice Joyce Kean, Cushman B. Bissell, and John P. Gregg.

Until the early 1970s, assets of the foundation remained small, and grants were given to the particular philanthropic interests of the donor. Upon Beatrice Kean's death in December of 1972, the Joyce Foundation was bequeathed 90 percent of her estate, an amount in excess of $100 million. A professional staff was retained, and the assets were delivered to the foundation in 1974. The Joyce family wealth was amassed in the lumber industry, and the foundation's first president, Kent F. Peterson, had been an executive of the Tremont Lumber Company.

At the time of Beatrice Kean's death, the annual contributions of the Joyce Foundation totalled less than $100,000. By 1974, annual giving reached $500,000 and by 1976 was $10 million. A college scholarship program was in operation from 1965 to 1977 for children of employees of several family-owned lumber companies. During that time, scholarship support totalled $314,353. During the first twenty-five years, traditional health organizations and hospitals received the majority of the foundation's contributions. After 1973, higher education and cultural institutions were added as major beneficiaries.

In 1978, the Joyce Foundation published its first public annual report under the direction of its new president, Charles U. Daly. Included in that report was a description of the foundation's programmatic interests in culture, education, environment and conservation, government, health, and social service. In December of 1980, the foundation evaluated its performance under those guidelines and refined its goals, particularly in retitling the Social Service category as jobs and housing and in narrowing the focus of environment and conservation to specific midwestern conservation issues.

Currently, the Joyce Foundation makes grants primarily in the fields of conservation, education, health, culture, jobs and housing, and government. Preference is given to nonprofit organizations having a base or program in the Midwest; on rare occasions, the foundation moves beyond the region for projects of special interest or merit. In addition to funding established institutions, the foundation wants to assist new institutions dealing with problems not now being addressed. Applicants will have a better chance for acceptance if they give evidence of sound management practices, including active participation of board of directors and development of constituent support. Grantees are encouraged to challenge constituents to match foundation money in appropriate instances; where management or fund-raising needs are to be further developed or improved, the foundation will consider proposals with that objective. Applicants requesting grants for projects or programs of extended duration are urged to provide plans for financial support from others that would permit phasing out the foundation's assistance since funding of a given organization is unlikely to exceed three consecutive years. Applicants should include provisions for internal and external fiscal and functional auditing. The foundation does not make grants to individuals.

Conservation—the wise use of natural resources and the custodial care of these resources for future generations—is a basic concern of the Joyce Foundation. Realizing that the problems in conservation are complex and difficult to define, the foundation would like to help projects that address the fundamental aim of protecting the ecological system while demonstrating an understanding of the need for a balance between that vital objective and reasonable economic considerations. One of America's great resources—quite possibly its greatest resource—is the combination of the soil of the Midwest and the substantial but deteriorating water supply that lies underground and in the Great Lakes. The foundation is most interested in projects related to the careful use of this soil and water.

The foundation is interested in supporting those very few universities and colleges having the highest academic quality if those institutions demonstrate needs, good management, and continuing, long-term achievement. The foundation is primarily interested in private institutions because these are the most hard-pressed financially and they are essential to maintaining independence and diversity in all of higher education. At universities and colleges, the foundation will fund projects related to its other areas of interest, such as conservation. The foundation is also interested in institutions providing education at all levels for culturally, socially, or financially deprived students, particularly those of high potential. The foundation would like to receive more grant applications from those working in practical ways to improve secondary education in urban centers.

Strongly preferring preventive rather than curative projects, the Joyce Foundation would rather assist those keeping persons out of hospitals than those improving institutional care. Programs addressing cultural and social habits, nutrition, the environment, health education—including consumer education for youths and adults—are of interest. Self-help and other voluntary projects stressing prevention will receive priority attention. In view of the tremendous burden health costs are placing on the nation, imaginative cost-containment concepts are sought.

Cultural institutions will be supported by the Joyce Foundation if they demonstrate need, superior and continuing achievement, and good or at least improving management. In addition to maintaining existing quality, the foundation would like to strengthen newer or less-established institutions of exceptional promise, especially in cases where there is a possibility of reaching a position in the first rank. Making cultural resources available to wider audiences is an objective of the foundation.

The Joyce Foundation's general goal is to lessen the poverty culture instead of contributing to it. The foundation's position is that too few resources are directed toward preventing dependence and assisting people to become more self-reliant. Applicants are sought for grants helping youths, particularly urban youths, move into productive roles instead of into society's courts and custodial or dependency agencies. Specifically, the foundation seeks development of better programs to train and place in meaningful, private-sector jobs the hard-to-employ youths who now work in dead-end jobs in the public sector or are unable to work at all. Also, grants will be made for the planning and implementation of programs aimed at improving housing in cities, including those programs leading to home ownership. Neighborhood economic development groups and other community organizations working on jobs, housing, and related matters will be given priority. In all cases, grant applications with provision for community input and leadership are preferred.

Within the limits imposed upon charitable organizations, the foundation will consider funding projects that examine the effectiveness and efficiency of federal, state, and local government activities in the foundation's geographic and programmatic areas. This position reflects the view that unquestioned government is likely to be poor government and that what is required is not more spending but more thoughtful spending. The foundation wants to promote increased interest and participation in government by all citizens and other permanent residents, particularly those who have recently come to the United States and those who are just reaching voting age.

The Joyce Foundation is governed by an eight-member board of directors that meets four times per year to set policy and review grant proposals. Staff includes seven professional and three clerical personnel. Interns and consultants are retained to assist permanent staff. Assets of the foundation in 1980 were valued at about $164 million, and annual grants totalled approximately $10.5 million. No substantial changes in the foundation's program activities are anticipated for the foreseeable future. Offices of the Joyce Foundation are located at 135 South LaSalle Street, Chicago, Illinois 60603.

For further information, see *Annual Reports* of the foundation, published continuously since 1978. See also *Program, Policy and Grant Proposal Guidelines* (March, 1983), published by the foundation.

JOY A. BLAKSLEE

**JULIUS ROSENWALD FUND.** Founded in 1917 by Julius Rosenwald, the Julius Rosenwald Fund expended more than $22 million on a variety of projects dedicated to human uplift. The fund's major influence was felt in the area of race relations because of its contributions to black education and health services and a highly successful fellowship program that provided a number of black Americans with the opportunity to develop talents that might otherwise have been stifled by prejudice and discrimination. Julius Rosenwald's stipulation that the fund's assets be liquidated within twenty-five years of his death encouraged others to depart from the tradition of establishing philanthropic organizations in perpetuity.

Julius Rosenwald was born on August 12, 1862, in Springfield, Illinois. His father, Samuel Rosenwald, had left Germany hoping to find greater economic opportunity in the United States. Starting as a peddler, the elder Rosenwald was already a partner in a successful clothing firm when his son was born.

Julius demonstrated similar qualities of industry and thrift, working at several odd jobs and helping at his father's store. At seventeen he left high school, two years short of graduation, to become a $5-per-week apprentice in his uncle's clothing firm. Five years later he was an independent merchant in partnership with his brother. A successful young businessman, Rosenwald confided to a friend that his ambition was to have an annual income of $15,000, $5,000 for expenses, $5,000 to be "laid aside," and $5,000 to go to charity.

This secret ambition would soon seem ludicrous in light of Rosenwald's phenomenally successful business career. The turning point in this career came when he borrowed $37,500 to buy into the mail-order firm of Richard Sears, assuming the vice-presidency of what would become the Sears and Roebuck Company, whose profits returned his original investment many times over.

Rosenwald displayed his philanthropic inclinations long before he became one of the wealthiest men in the United States. He gave $2,500 to the Jewish charities in Chicago when he was still only a moderately successful clothing merchant. Over the course of his life, Rosenwald gave away between $60 million and $70 million. In addition to $20 million he gave to his foundation and other miscellaneous donations, he also contributed to various Jewish charity and relief projects. Another $5 million went to war relief programs; $6 million to hospitals, health agencies, education, and research; and $2 million went to various museums.

Rosenwald's interest in projects to aid blacks derived from several sources. Two books were particularly significant in influencing him. One was a biography of William H. Baldwin, Jr., a railroad magnate who had devoted himself to improving educational opportunities for southern blacks, and the other was *Up from Slavery*, Booker T. Washington's autobiography. Rosenwald's meeting with Washington, his election as a trustee of Tuskegee Institute, and his subsequent visits to the South cemented his resolve to devote much of his philanthropic effort to black causes.

The best-known manifestation of Rosenwald's philanthropy was the Julius Rosenwald Fund. Incorporated in Chicago in 1917 with the goal of increasing "the well-being of mankind," the fund remained under Rosenwald's personal control for the first decade of its existence, and its board of trustees consisted of himself and members of his immediate family. During this period, the fund's activities were tied closely to Rosenwald's personal philanthropic interests and activities. Of the more than $4 million spent during this period, most of the money went to the construction of schools for southern blacks.

By 1927, Rosenwald had decided that successful management of his philanthropic activities required more businesslike supervision. As a trustee of the Rockefeller Foundation* he came to appreciate the value of a central policy-making body and a full-time staff in operating a philanthropic foundation at maximum effectiveness. Thus, he announced a dramatic reorganization of the Julius Rosenwald Fund, effective January 1, 1928. As president of the fund, he selected Edwin R. Embree, a former director and vice president of the Rockefeller Foundation. Policy-making authority rested with a board of ten trustees (later expanded to fifteen). At this time, Rosenwald donated an additional twenty thousand shares of Sears stock to the fund, bringing the total market value of his contributions to approximately $20 million.

As Rosenwald presented this gift to the fund, he expressed his desire that "the entire fund...both income and principal, be expended within twenty-five years of the time of my death." Rosenwald's unprecedented action came as a result of his belief "that trustees controlling large funds are not only desirous of conserving principal but often favor adding to it from surplus income." Rosenwald felt that by providing for speedy expenditure of the fund he would forestall the crippling bureaucracy and perfunctoriness that seemed to develop in foundations established in perpetuity. Rosenwald assured his trustees: "Coming generations can be relied upon to provide for their own needs as they arise" (Edwin R. Embree and Julia Waxman, *Investment in People: The Story of the Julius Rosenwald Fund* [1949], p. 31). His bold move cleared the way for other philanthropic organizations to take similar steps in the dispensation of their funds.

The reorganized Julius Rosenwald Fund benefitted greatly from the stock market boom at the end of the 1920s. Between April, 1928, and September, 1929, the value of its holdings rose from $20 million to more than $35 million. A sharp reversal in its fortunes came with the October, 1929, crash that brought the value of Sears stock down from nearly $200 to less than $10 a share. The fund was saved from premature liquidation by the General Education Board* and the Carnegie Corporation of New York* which absorbed some of its projects. It also shifted its emphasis from grants to less-expensive research projects.

Georgia Governor Eugene Talmadge once scornfully described it as "Jew money for niggers," but historian George B. Tindall (*The Emergence of the New South, 1913-1945* [1967], p. 271) praised the Rosenwald Fund's school building program as "one of the most effective stratagems to outflank the prejudice and apathy that hobbled Negro education" in the South. Beginning with the first contribution to build black schools in Alabama in 1912, Rosenwald money supported the construction of 5,357 schools in fifteen states. In twelve of these states, Rosenwald-supported schools represented approximately 20 percent of all black schools. Tindall also noted that the chief importance of the Rosenwald Fund may have been "the stimulus it gave to public support while neutralizing the opposition of white taxpayers." Nearly two-thirds of the money for construction and most of the operating expenses came from public revenue. The Rosenwald Fund supplied 17 percent of the financial support, blacks about 15 percent, and white contributors another 4 percent.

The school building program quickly focused attention on the need for more, better-trained teachers. In 1932, the fund terminated its building grants program in order to focus its resources on high schools, normal schools, and colleges. Like the building grants, however, most of the grants to black colleges were used to secure increased public support. In 1942, for example, when the Rosenwald Fund and the General Education Board each gave $30,000 to a building program, Mississippi's legislature agreed to elevate Jackson State College from a two- to a four-year institution. In Georgia, Fort Valley State College grew with Rosenwald Fund support from a junior college to a four-year college with primary responsibility in teacher education.

Inequities and deficiencies in health care for blacks led to a program of grants to train blacks as physicians, nurses, and health-care administrators and to subsidize their employment in state and municipal health-care departments. A concern for more effective black leadership fostered a fellowship program that was eventually expanded to include southern whites as well. Between 1928 and 1948, more than $1.5 million went into Rosenwald Fellowships for promising young Americans. Of over 1,500 recipients, 999 were black and 538 were southern whites. Among the more famous black Rosenwald Fellows were singer Marian Anderson and Ralph Bunche, the latter who used this support to complete his doctoral studies at Harvard and finance his travel and the work on his books. Among southern whites, Rosenwald Fellowships went to Pulitzer Prize-winning journalist Ralph McGill of the *Atlanta Constitution* and novelist Lillian Smith. Of the Rosenwald Fund, Smith concluded: "I believe—of all the funds that reached down into the South—that it did the most grassroots work" (Wilma Dykeman and James Stokeley, *Seeds of Southern Change: The Life of Will Alexander* [1962], p. 271). The moving force behind the fellowship program was Will Alexander, cofounder of the Commission on Interracial Cooperation and a long-time champion of racial equality, who served as a trustee of the fund from 1930 until 1948 and as a vice-president from 1940 to 1948. The Rosenwald Fund was also a vigorous supporter of organizations committed to improved race relations and provided considerable financial support for groups like the Commission on Interracial Cooperation, the Southern Regional Council, and the Southern Conference for Human Welfare.

Legal ownership and control of the Julius Rosenwald Fund was vested in a membership corporation and its trustees. The corporation was self-perpetuating as members elected their successors as members and trustees. The term of each trustee was three years, and no trustee except the president of the fund and the chairman of the board could serve more than two consecutive terms. Unless they occupied specific salaried posts with the fund, trustees received no stipends. The entire board regularly met twice each year unless called into special session. These meetings centered on program reviews, development, and allocation of funds. The fund's offices were located in Chicago; but because so much of its impact was felt in the South, a number of trustees were leading progressive southerners, like former North Carolina Governor O. Max Gardner, University of North Carolina sociologist Howard W. Odum, and Louisville *Courier-Journal* publisher Mark Ethridge.

The fund's executive committee, which consisted of five members of the board, normally met once a month to serve as a steering group for the fund's ongoing projects and as a planning group for future programs.

Three members of the board served on the finance committee, which was charged with liquidating enough stock to finance the programs approved by the board. Elected annually by his fellow trustees, the president served as the fund's chief executive officer and was responsible for policy development. The three most influential officers of the fund were Edwin R. Emree, the fund's only president between 1928 and 1948; Will Alexander, vice-president from 1940 to 1948 and a director for race relations from 1942 to 1948; and Charles S. Johnson, director for race relations from 1943 to 1947.

When the Rosenwald Fund closed its books in 1948, over $22 million dollars had been spent. More than half went to educational projects, including the school building fund, library services, and teacher education programs. Three million dollars each went to health and medical services projects and race relations programs. Fellowships accounted for $1.6 million; $1.8 million went into miscellaneous projects, including general education, mental sciences, and public administration. The remaining $1.4 million had gone into the cost of administering the fund.

When Julius Rosenwald died in 1932, the *New York Times* obituary (January 7, 1932, p. 1) praised his generosity, noting that "his hand so generously open in its giving, closed upon none of his wealth in his death." The same might have been said of the Rosenwald Fund, which not only achieved its general goal of "the betterment of mankind" but made a monumental contribution to improved race relations and in the process helped to spur the nation to meet an almost forgotten commitment to human equality.

For further information, in addition to the works cited above, see Alfred Gilbert Belles, "The Julius Rosenwald Fund: Efforts in Race Relations, 1928-1948," Ph.D. dissertation, Vanderbilt University (1972).

The archival records of Julius Rosenwald and the fund are located at the University of Chicago (Julius Rosenwald Papers) and Fisk University (Rosenwald Fund Papers).

JAMES C. COBB

# K

**KAISER FOUNDATION.** See Henry J. Kaiser Family Foundation, The.

**KALAMAZOO FOUNDATION.** The Kalamazoo Foundation, with 1981 assets of about $34 million, is among the leaders in per capita assets among community foundations in the nation. The foundation was established in 1925 to hold in trust gifts and bequests made for the benefit of the residents of the city of Kalamazoo and Kalamazoo County, Michigan. More than fifteen hundred major donors and hundreds of memorial gifts have assisted the foundation in carrying out its purposes which are stated as:

Assisting charitable and educational institutions; for promoting education; for scientific research; for care of the sick, aged, or helpless; for the care of children; for the betterment of living and working conditions; for recreation of all classes; and for such other public, educational, charitable, or benevolent purposes as will best make for the mental, moral, and physical improvements of the inhabitants of the County of Kalamazoo.

Established with an initial gift of $1,000, the Kalamazoo Foundation's early grants were very modest. Its first grant of $250 was made in 1930 to help the public-school milk program. In fact, during its first ten years of operation, the trustees authorized total grants of only $3,750. With new gifts and appreciating investments, the foundation awarded thirty-four grants totalling $92,741 during the World War II years. After the war, the trustees were awarding three times as much money each year as they had in the first fifteen years of the foundation's existence. By 1975, annual grants reached nearly $2 million and by 1981 were approximating $3 million.

Traditionally, the Kalamazoo Foundation has supported innovative programs in the local schools. It has given repeatedly to the Bronson Methodist and Borgess hospitals and to health-care programs ranging from the Constance Brown Society for Better Hearing to those designed to alleviate alcohol abuse. In the 1950s and 1960s, the foundation assisted a number of fine-arts projects and continued to support the community's needs with grants for ball parks, tennis facilities, and swimming pools. Social welfare and human services programs, such as aid for agencies and organizations concerned with the family, physically handicapped, mentally retarded, youth, and so forth, have grown increasingly important and presently account for slightly over half of the foundation's outlays.

Federal programs now provide matching grants for many projects, and the foundation has been able to help local organizations in providing the needed locally provided matching funds. Also, the trustees have been willing to provide seed money for new or experimental programs that appear to need only a successful beginning to secure subsequent funding from other sources.

Community groups, such as the Kalamazoo Chamber of Commerce, several area banks, and the probate and circuit courts, appoint the trustees, who bring a variety of backgrounds and interests to their service for the foundation.

One of the early leaders of the Kalamazoo Foundation was Donald Gilmore, who became a trustee in 1928, president of the board in 1934, and thereafter continued to serve in that capacity until 1974. Following his retirement, William J. Lawrence, Jr., was elected president and continues to serve in that capacity. The incumbent executive secretary, Howard Kalleward, who was appointed in 1966, furnished the editors of this volume with the material on which the foregoing brief history was primarily based.

The program of the foundation is directed from offices located at 151 South Race Street, Kalamazoo, Michigan 49007.

For further information, see *Annual Reports* of the foundation, published continuously since the late 1970s.

**KAPLAN FUND.** See J. M. Kaplan Fund, Inc., The.

**KATE B. REYNOLDS CHARITABLE TRUST.** Kate Bitting Reynolds (1867-1946) was a member of the R. J. Reynolds Tobacco Company family of Winston-Salem, North Carolina. For many years prior to her death, she aided hospitals, educational institutions, orphanages, and the poor. Her interests in these areas were reflected in her will, which made provision for the establishment of the Kate B. Reynolds Charitable Trust upon her death in 1946.

In her will she made provision for family and friends and bequeathed substantial sums to various North Carolina institutions. The residuary portion of her estate, consisting of R. J. Reynolds Tobacco Company stock then valued at $5 million, was left in trust, one-fourth of the income from which was to be used to aid the poor of Winston-Salem and Forsyth County, North Carolina, and three-fourths of which was to be used to aid the charity patients in North Carolina hospitals. The grants and other activities of the trust are administered by two separate divisions: the Kate B. Reynolds Poor and Needy Trust and the Kate B. Reynolds Health Care Trust.

From 1946 until 1968, the Reynolds Charitable Trust gave millions of dollars from the Health Care Trust to hospitals in North Carolina which provided health care for the poor. Grants were made from the Poor and Needy Trust to individuals and to nonprofit organizations in Forsyth County.

By 1968, it was found that in a time of rapidly increasing health-care costs, the Health Care Trust was providing only about $3 a day for each charity patient in a hospital. This was only a small fraction of the average daily cost of a hospital room. Health Care Trust officials therefore concluded that the terms of the trust could and should be reinterpreted to better serve the intent of Reynold's will, and they sought and obtained relief in the North Carolina courts. In 1971, the supreme court of North Carolina held that the trustees could use more discretion and flexibility in awarding grants. Thereupon, the trustees created a broadly diversified advisory board of eleven members to advise it on the funding of health-care programs in North Carolina.

In 1973, the trustees and the advisory board consulted with Dr. John Knowles, then president of the Rockefeller Foundation,* and other knowledgable persons in an effort to find a particular area of need to which the major portion of the Health Care Trust's income could be directed for a ten-year period. The conclusion was reached that making health care more accessible, especially in rural areas, was the area upon which the trust should center its attenton. Subsequently the trust joined with the Z. Smith Reynolds Foundation, Inc.,* and the Duke Endowment* in forming a consortium for the improvement of health care in North Carolina. Since 1972, the Health Care Trust has expended over $16 million through the consortium and through direct grants for other projects for the provision of health care for the people of North Carolina.

In 1969, at approximately the same time the Health Care Trust first considered changing its course, the Poor and Needy Trust terminated its program of direct grants to individuals. Since that time, it has awarded grants only to North Carolina charitable organizations who have used the money for operating expenses or to provide direct aid to individuals.

In 1978, the Poor and Needy Trust also set up a broadly diversified, six-member advisory committee to assist it in awarding its grants. Since that time, approximately $350,000 per year in grants have been awarded primarily to organizations active in social welfare and mental health fields.

Kate Reynolds's will provided that her husband, William N. Reynolds, her nephew, John C. Whitaker, and her secretary, L. D. Long, serve as cotrustees with the corporate trustee, Wachovia Bank and Trust Company, in administering the Kate B. Reynolds Charitable Trust. Since all of the individual trustees are now dead, the Wachovia Bank has been left as the sole trustee of the trust whose 1981 assets were about $51 million.

Since 1971, the trust has been administered by the executive secretary of the Health Care Trust and a trust officer from the Wachovia Bank for the Poor and Needy Trust. The Health Care Trust operates from an office located at 910 First Union National Bank Building, Winston-Salem, North Carolina 27101, and the

Poor and Needy Trust is operated by the Charitable Funds Department, Trust Division, Wachovia Bank and Trust Company, Post Office Box 3099, Winston-Salem, North Carolinaa 27102.

For further information, see *Annual Reports* of the Kate B. Reynolds Health Care Trust, published continuously since 1972. See also "SYNOPSIS" of the Kate B. Reynolds Health Care Trust (August, 1979), and "SYNOPSIS" of the Kate B. Reynolds Poor and Needy Trust (June, 1981), which are mimeographed informational accounts issued by the trust.

**KECK FOUNDATION.** See W. M. Keck Foundation.

**KELLOGG FOUNDATION.** See W. K. Kellogg Foundation.

**KENAN CHARITABLE TRUST.** See William R. Kenan, Jr., Charitable Trust.

**KENDALL FOUNDATION.** See Henry P. Kendall Foundation, The.

**KENNETH T. AND EILEEN L. NORRIS FOUNDATION, THE.** The husband and wife for whom the Kenneth T. and Eileen L. Norris Foundation is named established it in California in 1963. Kenneth Norris, who started working while in his teens, formed the Norris Stamping and Manufacturing Company in 1930 with $23,025 in capital—money which he and his wife had saved for a house. Norris and the company prospered in the midst of the depression by producing and selling building and industrial products. During World War II, the company became a leading contractor for military products, particularly artillery and other cases made from steel rather than brass, and its sales and profits soared. By the time of Norris's death in 1972, the company, now known as Norris Industries, Incorporated, had more than nine thousand employees and sales ranging from $225 million to $275 million yearly.

From its initiation, the Norris Foundation limited its giving to southern California, with emphasis on grants to higher education, hospitals, and community funds, and lesser amounts to cultural and youth organizations and for aid to the handicapped. By the end of the 1960s, foundation assets were almost $6 million, and annual grants amounted to over $200,000. Assets of the foundation in 1981 were about $51 million, and annual grants by that year were about $1.5 million.

The grants program through the years has followed about the same course. In 1979, for example, higher education, hospitals and health programs, and cultural programs received about 90 percent of the total gifts, with social services and youth programs absorbing the remainder; all grants were limited to southern California. Major awards for 1979 were: $928,000—University of Southern California; $35,100—Huntington Memorial Hospital, Pasadena; $50,000—Long Beach Civic Light Opera; and $25,000—YMCA of Metropolitan Los Angeles.

The Norris Foundation is governed by a three-member board of trustees, including the wife and son of Kenneth T. Norris. Administration of the foundation is carried on from offices located at 1900 East Ocean Boulevard, Long Beach, California 90802, under the direction of an executive director who is also the third member of the board of trustees.

Almost the only additional information on this foundation readily available to the public are the annual reports and returns filed by it with the Internal Revenue Service, and the various Foundation Center publications. See, however, Kenneth T. Norris obituary, *New York Times* (March 28, 1972), p. 46.

**KERR FOUNDATION, INC., THE.** In December, 1963, Grayce B. Kerr established the Kerr Foundation in Oklahoma. Grayce Kerr was the widow of the late Robert Samuel Kerr, the founder and chairman of the board of Kerr-McGee Corporation. In addition to his business ventures, Kerr was the first native son elected governor of Oklahoma, serving from 1943 to 1946. From 1949 until his death on January 1, 1963, he served as a United States Senator.

Since its founding, the Kerr Foundation has sought to use its resources to improve the quality of life in Oklahoma and the surrounding region. In 1965, the Agricultural Division was organized and located on four thousand acres of foundation-owned land near Poteau in eastern Oklahoma. The agricultural program assists farm and ranch families to become more proficient in agriculture management and production. The division offers programs of consultation, demonstration, and education to provide farmers and stockmen with current agricultural knowledge and technology.

The Agricultural Division's consultation program provides the services of a broad-based team of agricultural specialists who assist individual farmers and ranchers in planning in the areas of animal science, agronomy, agricultural economics, and horticulture. The demonstration program utilizes Kerr Foundation property to develop and demonstrate better techniques, new technology, and potential new revenue-producing enterprises to farmers and ranchers. The education program concentrates on disseminating practical information through a monthly newsletter, frequent articles in newspapers and agricultural publications, special leaflets on a variety of farm management practices, and through special meetings and small seminars. Within the past year, the Agricultural Division has conducted an intensive educational effort through the media and special meetings to help eradicate brucellosis among Oklahoma livestock.

In recognition of the need for objective information on the complete subject of Oklahoma's economic development, the Kerr Foundation established an Economic Studies Division in 1973. The goal was to assist in the design, finance, and implementation of research and educational activities to provide better information upon which future decisions affecting Oklahoma's social and economic development could be based.

Prior to the discontinuation of the Economic Studies Division in 1979, researchers analyzed total Oklahoma state government revenues and expenditures and published an annual report showing in simple terms how the state allocates its revenues. Through a series of project grants, principally to Oklahoma institutions of higher education, the foundation has supported economically related research on demography, regional economic problems, world food and population issues, and the development of a computer simulation model to analyze population and economic trends in Oklahoma through the year 2000. Although the Economic Studies Division was discontinued, the Kerr Foundation continues to fund the annual analysis of state expenditures and other projects designed to provide information about the state's economy needed by decision makers in both the public and private sectors. A list of the major publications of economic research which the foundation has conducted or supported appears at the conclusion of this history.

Since 1965, the Kerr Foundation also has made grants to nonprofit organizations for charitable and educational purposes. Historically, the largest share of grants has been allocated, with the remaining funds broadly distributed among social service and health agencies, cultural organizations, civil and local government projects, and youth programs.

Although the trustees' principal concern has been with the development of Oklahoma's economic, social, and cultural potential, they have frequently joined with other foundations among the membership of the Conference of Southwest Foundations to promote the development of better information about problems of regional, national, and international scope.

After thoughtful review of its goals and programs in 1979, the trustees initiated the Kerr Challenge Grant Program to assist organizations and institutions that aid young people through service, social, education, or medical programs. The Challenge Grant Program is open to institutions and organizations in Oklahoma, Arkansas, Colorado, Kansas, Missouri, New Mexico, and Texas. Successful applicants are required to match, within a year, the amount awarded, with a minimum of a dollar for dollar from private sources. The program was designed primarily to utilize the foundation's resources to stimulate additional private philanthropy in the region.

In keeping with this latter commitment, the Kerr Foundation Fellowship Program was started in 1981. The program assists nonprofit organizations to become more proficient in securing private gift support by providing fellowships which enable a staff member or volunteer to attend a comprehensive fund-raising training institute.

The Kerr Foundation is supported by contributions from the estate of Grayce B. Kerr Flynn and from her children. The foundation is administered by members of the Kerr family, term trustees, and a professional staff. Robert S. Kerr, Jr., chairman of the Kerr Foundation board of trustees, is a senior partner and an attorney with Kerr, Irvine, and Rhodes, of Oklahoma City. The other trustees are Kay Kerr Adair, of Coyle, and Breene M. Kerr, William G. Kerr, and Joffa Kerr, of Oklahoma City. The term trustees are James E. Webb and Elmer B. Staats of Washington, D.C., Walter Woolley, Jr., of Ada, and Gerald R. Marshall and Thomas E. Broce of Oklahoma City. Broce, formerly president and chairman of the board of Phillips University, of Enid, Oklahoma, serves as the foundation's president.

The board of trustees meets twice a year, in June and December. During the remainder of the year, business may be handled through the trustees' executive committee and the trustees' Challenge Grant Committee. The foundation also uses the services of an Agricultural Advisory Committee and Investment Advisory Committee composed of trustees and specialists from the area of agriculture and finance.

With 1981 assets valued at over $50 million, the Kerr Foundation is the fourth largest in the State of Oklahoma. The principal administrative offices are located at 1208 Fidelity Plaza, Oklahoma City, Oklahoma 73102.

For further information, see *Annual Reports* of the foundation, published continuously since 1973, and the following foundation reports: *Oklahoma State Expenditures in Brief*, published each year 1973 through 1980; *A Profile of Oklahoma Economic Development 1950-1975* (1977); *Alcohol Abuse: Report and Recommendations of the Task Force on Alcohol Abuse* (1979); and *Oklahoma's Second Century* (1980). See also Phil Frey, "Museum on a Mountaintop," *Orbit* (November 1, 1960), pp. 4, 6; Clarice Jackson, "The Kerr Foundation,"*Oklahoma Today* (Autumn, 1973), pp. 2, 5; and "Robert Samuel Kerr," *Dictionary of American Biography*, Supplement Seven (1980), pp. 428-429.

ANNE HODGES MORGAN

**KIRBY FOUNDATION.** See F. M. Kirby Foundation, Inc.

**KLEBERG FOUNDATION.** See Robert J. Kleberg, Jr., and Helen C. Kleberg Foundation.

**KODAK CHARITABLE TRUST.** See Eastman Kodak Charitable Trust.

**KRANNERT CHARITABLE TRUST.** Herman C. Krannert and his wife, Ellnora, established the Krannert Charitable Trust in Indiana in 1960. Herman Krannert was the founder and chairman of the board of Inland Container Corporation, one of the world's largest manufacturers of corrugated shipping containers. During their lifetimes, the Krannerts made substantial gifts to numerous universities and cultural institutions, particularly to those located in Indiana, through the Krannert Charitable Trust and a smaller Herman Charles and Ellnora Decker Krannert Foundation which they had set up.

Herman and Ellnora Krannert died in 1972 and 1974, respectively, leaving no descendants. They bequeathed large sums to the trust so that from 1974 through 1981, its assets increased from about $15 million to about $48 million. Although its grants program remained about the same, the value of its annual grants soared from about $750,000 to more than $11 million in 1979. In 1979,

58 percent of its grants went to higher education; 19 percent to cultural programs; 14 percent to medical research; and 9 percent for social welfare and other projects. The following grants are the major ones for that year in these four categories: Indianapolis Center for Advanced Research—$1 million; Indiana State Symphony, Indianapolis—$760,000; Krannert Institute of Cardiology, Indianapolis—$1.6 million; and United Way of Greater Indianapolis—$390,000. With two exceptions, each of the total of thirty-five grants made in 1979 were to Indiana recipients, with particular emphasis upon Indianapolis.

The trust is governed by a five-member board of trustees which includes the Indiana National Bank. The mailing address of the trust is Post Office Box 1021, Indianapolis, Indiana 46206.

Almost the only additional information on this foundation readily available to the public are the annual reports and returns filed by it with the Internal Revenue Service, and the various Foundation Center publications. See, however, Herman C. Krannert obituary, *New York Times* (February 26, 1972), p. 32; and Ellnora D. Krannert obituary, *New York Times* (July 8, 1974), p. 32.

**KRESGE FOUNDATION, THE.** Sebastian Spering Kresge (1867-1966) was best known for the chain of dime stores which bore his name. In this retailing business, as owner of the S. S. Kresge Company which he founded in 1899, he had amassed a fortune of over $100 million by 1924. Desiring to devote a large part of his wealth to charitable purposes, Sebastian S. Kresge established the Kresge Foundation as an independent, private foundation in 1924 with an initial, personal gift of almost $2 million.

On May 19, 1926, the first public announcement was made of the Kresge Foundation's birth. Then, the *New York Times* carried the news of Kresge's second gift to the foundation, which would bring its assets to nearly $25 million and which would make it the fourth largest of then-existing American foundations. By 1953, gifts totalling $60,577,188 had been transferred by Kresge to the Kresge Foundation.

The incorporating trustees of the Kresge Foundation were: Paul W. Voorhies, president until his death in 1952; Amos F.Gregory, secretary until his retirement in 1966; and Sebastian S. Kresge, treasurer until his death in 1966 at the age of ninety-nine.

In 1930, Stanley S. Kresge, the founder's son, was elected a trustee. He became president in 1952, chairman in 1966, and honorary chairman in 1978. In 1981, in addition to Stanley Kresge and his son Bruce A. Kresge, there were five other members of the board of trustees of the foundation.

The first grants made by the foundation totalled $12,500 to ten organizations. In 1926, the first $100,000 grant was made, and in 1929, the first challenge grant was authorized, requiring the grantee to complete additional fund raising. By 1955, the foundation held assets valued at $85,931,560 and had appropriated $33,565,010 in grants during the preceding thirty years.

The number of qualified applications submitted to the foundation more than doubled in the 1971-1981 period. In 1971, 584 applications were reviewed and resulted in 155 grant commitments totalling $8,994,363. In 1981, 1,551 proposals were accepted and 176 grants were announced, totalling $33,354,000.

Beginning in 1974, grant decisions have been made once each year after review of all applications. Announcement of new grant commitments is made in mid-July each year, after a seven-month review period. Qualified applications are accepted only during the period January 1 through February 15.

The Kresge Foundation, unlike most others, has limited its giving primarily to projects involving the construction or renovation of facilities. Today, grants are made almost without exception toward such bricks-and-mortar projects for charitable organizations. Apart from this policy of limitation, the foundation will review and act upon all qualified proposals submitted to it.

Grants continue to be made on a challenge basis and require the raising of the balance of project costs by the grantee. Generally, the foundation will not provide the first project dollars nor the last, desiring to make its commitments in the midst of private fund-raising efforts and to evoke the completion of such efforts.

The Kresge Foundation has, since 1924, authorized grants totalling more than $416 million to organizations operating in the fields of higher education, health care, arts and humanities, social services, science and conservation, and religion. With 1980 assets of about $655 million, the foundation is administered from offices located at 2401 West Big Beaver Road, Post Office Box 3151, Troy, Michigan 48084.

For further information, see public reports of the Kresge Foundation's activities which have been made since 1953, including published *Biennial Reports* until 1966. Since 1966, the foundation has published *Annual Reports* which document all foundation activities. Specific foundation policies and application guidelines are published each year.

BARBARA J. GETZ

**KRESS FOUNDATION.** See Samuel H. Kress Foundation.

**KROC FOUNDATION, THE.** The Kroc Foundation was originally chartered in Illinois in April of 1965 as the Ray A. Kroc Foundation, with Ray A. Kroc as the founder and sole benefactor. Until 1969, when its name was changed to the Kroc Foundation, the foundation made limited charitable contributions in the Chicago area to hospitals, the Salvation Army, and youth organizations.

In mid-1969, Ray Kroc's brother, Robert L. Kroc, with a doctorate in biology and physiology and a background in teaching and pharmaceutical research, became president and a member of the board of directors of the foundation. The programs were then defined more specifically: (1) medical research conferences concerned with any human disease or associated health problems; (2) grants-in-aid for specific basic and clinical research projects on arthritis (and related connective tissue and bone diseases), diabetes mellitus and its complications, and multiple sclerosis.

Ray A. Kroc, the founder and chairman of the board of the foundation, is the founder and senior chairman of McDonald's Corporation, Oak Brook, Illinois. Directly or indirectly, he has made contributions to the foundation totalling approximately $65 million in asset value. The major part of those contributions, starting in 1965, was made in 1979.

In the fall of 1976, Operation Cork was incorporated into the foundation's programs. Its founder, Joan B. Kroc, has been a member of the board of directors of the foundation since 1969 and is the wife of Ray A. Kroc. Operation Cork is a national alcohol education and communication program. It is headquartered in La Jolla, California, whereas the medical research programs offices are in the Santa Ynez Valley, California.

Since 1980, the expenditures for all programs have ranged between $6 million and $7 million annually. The medical research grants *per se* for 1980 and 1981 approximated $4.5 million annually and may be anticipated to rise gradually in the coming years. While most of the projects supported are in the United States, a number of grants have been made to institutions in other countries, such as Canada, Australia, England, Israel, and Sweden. Operation Cork neither invites, receives, or makes grants *per se* but does initiate a small number of special projects.

The staff of the medical research programs is minimal, being limited to a director of conferences and a director of research grants working with the president of the foundation at the Santa Ynez headquarters on the J & R Double Arch Ranch of the founder. The proceedings of most conferences are published either as supplements to standard journals known to be highly selective in refereeing publications, or as monographs.

The research grants program responds to brief "letters of inquiry" by senior investigators. Such responses may invite an application and in such cases guidelines are supplied for the preparation of applications. These are then refereed by an *ad hoc* group of specialists in the area of the research project. Applications may be received and reviewed at any time of the year. Grants are usually limited to a one- or two-year period and are primarily for new and novel start-up projects. The foundation should not be considered a source of primary or long-time support.

The Kroc Foundation makes no general institutional, "bricks and mortar," or endowment grants. Any support of technical assistants and pre- or postdoctoral research associates is limited primarily to those budgeted in approved, specific research projects. The foundation's policies aim for flexibility in programs, excellence in quality, and efficient speed in reviewing conference and grants proposals.

The foundation, with 1981 assets of about $54 million, is governed by a six member board of directors which includes Ray Kroc, his wife, and his brother. The mailing address of the foundation is P.O. Box 547, Santa Ynez, California 93460.

For further information, see informational brochures published by the foundation in 1976 and 1980. See also *Annual Reports* of the foundation, published since 1978.

ROBERT L. KROC

# L

**LAURA SPELMAN ROCKEFELLER MEMORIAL.** The Laura Spelman Rockefeller Memorial was founded by John D. Rockefeller in October, 1918, in memory of his wife. It was incorporated by the state of New York for general charitable and philanthropic purposes and was not limited geographically in its field of operations. Its endowment, which reached almost seventy-four million dollars in a few years, as well as its income, was available for appropriation by a board of trustees.

During the early years of the memorial, its affairs were managed directly by the trustees. It was operated essentially from the office of John D. Rockefeller, Jr., who was its president throughout its existence. Initially, grants were made for activities closely associated with the late Laura Rockefeller's interests. Consideration was given to the idea that the memorial might promote the welfare of women and children, but this course was not fully developed during the early years. Large appropriations were made to the Young Men's Christian Association (YMCA) and the Young Women's Christian Association (YWCA). Boy Scouts and Girl Scouts received appropriations for their regular work and special activities. During the years 1919-1922, Laura Rockefeller's interest in missionary activities encouraged appropriations of $1 million to the Women's Union Christian Colleges, in the Orient, and $366,666 to three missionary colleges in the Near East—Robert College, of Constantinople; American University, in Beirut; and the Constantinople Women's College.

Organized emergency relief in Europe and China received a considerable proportion of the memorial's income as contributions were made to or through the China Famine Fund, the American Relief Administration, the League of Nations, and the American Red Cross.

In 1919, the Laura Spelman Rockefeller Memorial granted $529,426 to the Palisades Interstate Park Commission for the purchase of two steamboats to facilitate access to the park by residents of New York City. The memorial maintained an interest in recreation and use of leisure time throughout its existence.

After this period of general giving, the trustees began to consider a more systematic program. In May, 1922, Beardsley Ruml, a young man in his late twenties trained in psychology, was appointed director of the Rockefeller Memorial. A small staff of program officers was later employed. Ruml sought to discriminate between responsibility to contemporary society, on the one hand, and projects which might contribute substantially to long-range progress in human welfare. He favored appropriations to special projects which would give organizations the opportunity for demonstrations, investigations, and research which their ordinary resources would not permit. Activities previously supported were not abandoned, but under Ruml's leadership the work of the memorial was centered around three major programs—social science and social technology; child study and parent education; and interracial relations.

Shortly after his appointment, Ruml proposed to the trustees that the memorial move boldly into the field of the social sciences. He believed that a practical attack on social problems required more scientific knowledge of social conditions and human behavior. To attempt to become an operating research body seemed impractical and limiting. It was therefore decided that the Rockefeller Memorial would provide funds for others to enable them to carry on freely their own investigations. Emphasis was placed on universities and research institutions rather than on independent individuals and committees.

Because it was believed that the social sciences had been too speculative, bibliographical, or literary in character, an effort was made to encourage a more realistic approach by increasing social scientists' opportunity for immediate personal observation of social phenomena. Funds were made available for traveling expenses, leaves of absence, statistical and clerical assistance, and other means of placing the investigator in more intimate contact with his subject. Funds were given to the University of Chicago for a study of its own urban community; to Harvard and Radcliffe for economic and legal research in international relations; to the University of North Carolina for social, economic, and governmental research in the South; and to the University of Wisconsin for studies in rural tenancy and land ownership.

In addition to furnishing opportunities for realistic studies, the Laura Spelman Rockefeller Memorial attempted to bring about a collaboration between the various academic departments within the university. Ruml was impatient with the traditional departmental divisions and sought to encourage a synthesis of the various disciplines. Perhaps the memorial's most ambitious undertaking in this direction was its participation, along with the General Education Board* (another John D. Rockefeller philanthropy) and the Rockefeller Foundation,* in financing the Institute of Human Relations, at Yale. This involved an attempt to coordinate and invest with a certain physical unity a number of scattered programs—the university's Institute of Psychology, its Psycho-Clinic for child study, work in the Graduate School, the School of Medicine, and the School of Law. Toward this project the three Rockefeller boards ultimately appropriated more than six million dollars.

The development of major research centers at universities became the most important part of the Laura Spelman Rockefeller Memorial's social science program. Chicago, Harvard, Columbia, Yale, Virginia, Texas, North Carolina, Stanford, Vanderbilt, the London School of Economics, the Deutsche Hochschule für Politik (in Berlin), the University of Stockholm, and many others received grants for the development of research centers. This assistance often involved fluid research funds which the university could use at its own discretion; aid to university presses; special funds for publication; grants to enable some of the centers to experiment with various types of training; aid to libraries in Europe whose books and periodicals had been damaged by the war; and other ways of encouraging the development of techniques of teaching in the social studies. Approximately $20 million was appropriated for these several purposes. Notable progress was made in securing recognition that research facilities and opportunities are essential for the social sciences.

Convinced that research without application was pointless, Ruml sought means to encourage practical application of the results of research. In a part of the program that was termed social technology, efforts were made to involve schools of business, law, public administration, and social work. Five such schools were aided: the Atlanta School of Social Work, the NewYork School of Social Work, the schools at Tulane University and the University of Chicago, and the National Catholic School of Social Work.

The Rockefeller Memorial also took a strong interest in special research agencies which were coming into existence. Probably the most significant of these, with which Ruml and the memorial were particularly identified, was the Social Science Research Council (SSRC). Extensive grants were made to the SSRC, which became the most important agency in the United States for promoting communication between students of social problems and for sponsoring cooperative research among the different disciplines. The Brookings Institution, the Institute of Pacific Relations, and the National Bureau of Economic Research were also substantially aided by the memorial.

To increase the number of qualified persons working in the social sciences and to encourage scholars to study in countries other than their own, the memorial relied heavily on fellowships. The memorial had representatives in England, France, Germany, Austria, Czechoslovakia, Italy, the Netherlands, Norway, Sweden, Denmark, and Australia to assist in carrying out its fellowship program. In the United States, fellowships were administered by the Social Science Research Council. Under these plans, 239 fellows were appointed.

The memorial's early concern for the interests of women, children, and youth led eventually to concentration on child study and parent education. In 1924, this activity was only one among many with which the memorial was concerned in the child welfare field. By 1926, it had become clearly a dominant interest and was soon the memorial's only program for the welfare of children. The program was national in scope and exerted an appreciable influence on the development of American education.

The emphasis on the need to study child growth through all relevant sciences gradually gave rise to the concept of child development. The memorial's program included support for research on the growth and development of children, to provide more dependable knowledge of the child and his nature; the preparation of books, pamphlets, study outlines, and other printed aids to help parents of diverse educational backgrounds in solving their problems and gaining an understanding of their children; training men and women for work in this field, as teachers, child-study leaders, administrators, and investigators; and experimentation in the education of parents under different auspices and conditions.

The program of research focused on support for major centers for the study of young children with provision for interchange of experience and findings. Institutions receiving substantial support included the Child Study Association of America, Teachers College of Columbia University, State University of Iowa, University of California, and the University of Minnesota. To prepare personnel for the further development of this field, 160 fellows were appointed. Almost $4.5 million was appropriated for this program.

The interracial work of the Rockefeller Memorial involved enterprises affecting the position of the blacks in American life. Support was given to organizations working for the improvement of relations between the races, such as the Commission on Interracial Cooperation, the National Urban League, the New York Urban League, and the Phelps-Stokes Fund. The Rockefeller Memorial also hoped to increase the number of blacks able to give social, economic, and political leadership to their race. Fellowships were therefore provided for promising black students. A major concern was the absence of scientific knowledge about the black's position in American life and the various social, economic, and political forces which surrounded him. To fill this void would also require existence of competent black professionals. The memorial attempted to build up universities for blacks in three principal centers that would be strongly equipped in the social sciences, law, business, social work, and public administration. A substantial beginning on this program was made at Fisk University. Preliminary steps had been taken at Howard University and in Atlanta when the decision to dissolve the memorial was made. Funds were also provided for the training of black nurses at Lincoln Hospital and for special projects of the Association for the Study of Negro Life and History.

By the mid-1920s, the several Rockefeller philanthropic organizations had developed programs that were overlapping or intimately related. In a reorganization which was completed on January 3, 1929, the Laura Spelman Rockefeller Memorial was consolidated with the Rockefeller Foundation and a new corporation, continuing under the name of the Rockefeller Foundation, was created. The foundation continued the memorial's interest in the social sciences and administered its unpaid grants until their termination.

At the time of the consolidation, the memorial had appropriated more than $55 million. This total did not include $17.5 million which was appropriated in 1928 for memorials in the name of Laura Spelman Rockefeller and $10 million which was granted to establish the Spelman Fund of New York.

The memorial issued reports on its work for the years 1918-1922, 1923, 1924, 1925, 1926, and 1927-1928. Its office files are deposited and may be consulted at the Rockefeller Archive Center, Pocantico Hills, North Tarrytown, New York 10591.

J. WILLIAM HESS

**L.A.W. FUND, INC.** Lila Acheson Wallace and her husband, DeWitt Wallace, were the founders in 1921 of the Reader's Digest Association, Inc. The profits from the *Reader's Digest* and other business ventures enabled Lila Wallace to establish this foundation in New York in 1956 under the name Lila Acheson Wallace Fund, Inc., which was changed in 1969 to the present L.A.W. Fund, Inc. The L.A.W. Fund, Inc. was followed by the establishment of the DeWitt Wallace Fund, Inc.,* by Mr. Wallace in 1965.

The assets of the L.A.W. Fund, Inc., grew from about $5 million in the late 1960s to approximately $37 million in 1980. The fund has primarily provided support for the preservation, restoration, and maintenance of museums, sanctuaries, and places of scenic beauty. It has also provided support for conservation activities, the arts, and, occasionally, educational and medical projects of an unusual nature. 1980 awards have included a grant of almost $1.5 million to the Metropolitan Museum of Art, New York City, and one of $100,000 to the Metropolitan Opera Association. In 1980, however, about 50 percent of the approximately $6 million granted in that year was made to a community foundation, the New York Community Trust,* which in turn is to make grants on behalf of the fund for projects and organizations which fall within the fund's pattern of interest. Well over 50 percent of the grantees of the fund have been located in the state of New York, with most of the remaining beneficiaries located in the northeastern United States.

The L.A.W. Fund is governed by a six-member board of directors which includes Lila Wallace, who is also president and treasurer. Most of the directors have past or present connections with the Reader's Digest Association, Inc. Administration of the fund is carried on from offices located on the thirty-fourth floor of 200 Park Avenue, New York, New York 10116, under the direction of a secretary. The fund has some of the same directors, occupies the same offices and operates under the direction of the same secretary as the DeWitt Wallace Fund, Inc.

Almost the only additional information readily available to the public concerning this foundation are the annual reports and returns filed by it with the Internal Revenue Service, and the various Foundation Center publications.

**LEAVEY FOUNDATION.** See Thomas and Dorothy Leavey Foundation.

**LELAND FIKES FOUNDATION, INC.** With offices located at 3200 Republic National Bank Tower, Dallas, Texas 75201, the Leland Fikes Foundation, Inc., is a private, nonprofit, philanthropic corporation whose primary focus of giving is in the areas of education, medical and social research, cultural programs, population control, and community welfare of the local Dallas region. No grants are made to individuals. The foundation was established in 1952 in Delaware by Leland Fikes, a Texas oil producer and philanthropist.

Born in Chickasha, Oklahoma, in 1903, Fikes graduated from high school by the age of fourteen and attended the University of Texas and New York University where he studied law and petroleum engineering. During and immediately following his college schooling, he became a wildcatter in the oil boom then taking place in eastern Texas. He worked in the fields, bought and sold oil leases as quickly as possible, and was a millionaire before his thirtieth birthday. His life in many ways coincided with the spectacular growth of the petroleum industry. He drilled over two hundred wells in western Texas acreage and later expanded operations to Kansas, Mississippi, New Mexico, and the Rio Grande Valley in Texas.

An oil man first, Fikes was also involved in many other business interests, including real estate, manufacturing, and construction. In the 1940s, he entered the rental housing business in a large way by purchasing the six-thousand-unit Fairlington Apartments in Washington, D.C. Over the years he headed more than thirty corporations involved in such diverse operations as hotels, garages, motels, office buildings, apartments, and industrial parks. A keen student of petroleum exploration and production problems, he was proud of the appellation given him of being an "independent" in the oil business and in his thinking in general. He took pride in never having worked for a corporation except those which he built or owned in whole or part.

Fikes was a hard worker, possessed a retentive memory and was a voracious reader. He especially enjoyed stimulating discussions in which he exchanged ideas and information with people on diverse topics. In 1965, Fikes was awarded an honorary doctor of laws degree from American University, Washington, D.C. He was active in many civic and social organizations in Dallas, where he made his home after 1938. Previously, he lived for a number of years in Corsicana, Texas, where he met and married the former Catherine Whitten in 1932.

Fikes was a benefactor and member of the board of trustees of the Wadley Research Institute and Blood Bank, Dallas, and long had been interested in the work of the institute's director, Dr. Joseph M. Hill, in the study of blood diseases. Shortly before his death in 1966, Fikes donated a large tract of land to the institute, on which a new research, treatment, and teaching complex would be built. Several years later, the foundation authorized a $500,000 grant to establish the Leland Fikes Research Institute for the study of cancer and blood diseases. During the ensuing years, the Wadley Institute of Molecular Medicine, Dallas, has been a major recipient of grants by the foundation.

There has been a family continuity in the governance of the foundation since 1966. Mrs. Leland Fikes became chairman of the board of trustees; Lee Fikes, son of the founder, became president, treasurer, and trustee; John N. Jackson served as vice-president, secretary, and trustee; and Charlyne D. Henslee became assistant secretary. The trustees emphasized a policy of local giving to a wide variety of cultural, medical, and educational organizations in the Dallas area.

In 1972, when airline skyjacking was a national problem, the foundation granted $96,000 to the Aberrant Behavior Center, in Dallas, for a clinical study of skyjackers and the preparation of seminar material to assist airline crews and employees. The next year, when foundation assets exceeded $15 million, grants were made to Southern Methodist University (SMU) to endow a library fund for the purchase of volumes dealing with African studies; to the Dallas Creative Learning Center for the education of disadvantaged children; and to the Planned Parenthood Association to expand its family planning program.

In 1974, educational and medical research recipients once again received the preponderance of the more than $1.5 million disbursed in grants. Institutions such as Bishop College, Howard Payne College, Montessori Academy, Wadley Institute of Molecular Medicine, and the Public Communication Foundation for North Texas (Channel 13-educational T.V.) received large contributions. SMU accepted major funds for the renovation and construction of a rare books center in the library to be known as Fikes Hall of Special Collections.

In 1976, there was a dramatic increase in foundation assets, from $17 million to $28 million, and disbursements exceeded $2.5 million. The largest grants went to the University of Texas at Dallas to fund research concerning the human vestibular system. The Wadley Institute, again, received significant funds to assist in the construction of a blood bank building and for a research project. Southwestern Medical School, of the University of Texas, accepted a grant to develop a new approach to population control, and Planned Parenthood received major funding to finance conferences dealing with the world population problem.

In the years 1976-1980, there were, likewise, significant grants to organizations devoted to improving the arts, culture, historic preservation, and civic enlightenment of the city of Dallas. Among recipients were the Dallas Civic Opera, the Dallas Symphony, Dallas Museum of Fine Arts, Dallas Civic Ballet, and the Dallas County Heritage Society. The largest grant awarded by the foundation during this period was the almost $1 million pledged to the Friends of the Dallas Public Library toward the construction of a new central facility.

In May, 1981, the total market value of the Leland Fikes Foundation's assets exceeded $32 million and more than $3 million had been disbursed in grants payments. In 1982, Mrs. Leland Fikes was given the James K. Wilson Silver Cup Award for her long and significant financial contributions to the Dallas arts.

The Leland Fikes Foundation has no full-time personnel, as offices and staff are shared with the petroleum company owned by Lee Fikes. Like his father, Lee Fikes believes that publicity for the foundation is inappropriate and values highly the large degree of individualism of a private foundation in making policy and controlling funds. As foundation president, he is the major factor in decisions concerning grant awards. He believes, however, that there should be greater sharing of information among private and public foundations to avoid duplication of effort.

For further information, see Leland Fikes obituaries, (Dallas) *Morning News* (September 4, 1966), A, 18; and (Dallas) *Times Herald* (September 4, 1966), A, 14. See also Evelyn Miller Crowell, ed., *Texas Edition of Men of Achievement* (1948).

DOROTHY D. DeMOSS

**LETTIE PATE WHITEHEAD FOUNDATION, INC.** The Lettie Pate Whitehead Foundation shares offices with three other foundations at Suite 1400, Peachtree Center Tower in Atlanta, Georgia 30303. The other foundations are the Trebor Foundation, the Joseph B. Whitehead Foundation,* and the Lettie Pate Evans Foundation. Each foundation is independent, with its separate board of trustees. They all, however, employ the same officers and support staff and derive the bulk of their endowments from an association with the Coca-Cola business.

The assets of the Lettie Pate Whitehead Foundation come from the Coca-Cola bottling business started by Joseph B. Whitehead in 1899. Joseph Whitehead managed to provide, in the short time he had before his death in 1906, the underpinning for a fortune that would subsequently fund three foundations—all but the Trebor Foundation mentioned in the above paragraph.

Lettie Pate, for whom two of the foundations are named, was born in 1872 into a distinguished Virginia family. She was a direct descendant of George Washington's brother, Lawrence. Lettie Pate, in 1894, married Joseph B. Whitehead and moved to Chattanooga, Tennessee, where her husband opened a law office. The marriage produced two sons, Joseph B. Whitehead, Jr., in 1894, and Conkey Pate Whitehead, in 1898. Seven years after the death of her husband, she married, in 1913, Colonel Arthur Kelly Evans, a retired Canadian army officer.

Lettie Pate (Whitehead) Evans was an august woman. Following the death of her first husband, she was active in the management of family holdings, which were grouped in the Whitehead Holding Company and the Whitehead Realty Company. She served as chairman of the former and president of the latter. Lettie Evans was a director of the Coca-Cola Company, one of the first women to serve on the board of directors of a major corporation. She was also a trustee of several institutions: the American hospital in Paris; the Museum of Fine Arts, in Richmond; Emory University; and Agnes Scott College, in Atlanta. She established her own foundation, the Lettie Pate Evans Foundation, in 1945, with assets of $2,116,000. After her death in 1953, her residuary estate went in trust to this foundation, adding another $7,921,000 in assets.

Conkey Pate Whitehead, as his older brother had done for their father, provided in his will for the establishment of the Lettie Pate Whitehead Foundation as a memorial to the mother. He designated that the foundation use the Whitehead name, even though his mother was then known as Lettie Pate Evans.

Conkey Pate Whitehead died in 1940 at the age of forty-two. All three of the Whitehead men died before reaching their forty-third year. The Lettie Pate

Whitehead Foundation was chartered in 1946 with assets from one-half of the residuary estate of Conkey Whitehead. The other half of the residuary estate went into a trust, as a life estate, for the widow of Conkey Whitehead. Upon her death, the assets from the trust came into the Lettie Pate Whitehead Foundation in 1970, bringing the total gifts received to $18,299,000.

The Lettie Pate Whitehead Foundation is governed by a three-member, self-perpetuating board of trustees who are currently Hughes Spalding, Jr., Herbert A. Claiborne, Jr., and Lyons Gray. Administration of the foundation is carried on by a staff under the direction of a president.

The giving of the foundation, specified by the will of Conkey Pate Whitehead, is primarily limited to providing funds for needy Christian girls in nine southeastern states—Virginia, North Carolina, South Carolina, Tennessee, Alabama, Mississippi, Louisiana, Florida, and Georgia. The grants are made to institutions only, never to individuals. The receiving institutions must not reveal to the individual scholarship recipients that the money came from the Lettie Pate Whitehead Foundation. They are told only that it is an anonymous gift. The receiving institutions provide the foundation a list of scholarship recipients for purposes of verification. The scholarships are based solely on financial need.

Whitehead also provided for the foundation to give funds for the support of needy elderly Christian women. Only about 7 percent of the annual grants goes to homes for the aged, while approximately 93 percent is designated for the scholarship program. The officers and trustees of the Lettie Pate Whitehead Foundation select the schools and homes to receive grants. Only a few institutions that have gone to the foundation with requests have been included in the program. A few institutions, in the 1970s, declined to accept money from the foundation, fearing the sex-restricted scholarship would cause the loss of federal funds. This is no longer a problem for the foundation due to later interpretations of federal regulations that allow individual grants on a sex-restricted basis, so long as the school's overall program is not discriminatory.

The Lettie Pate Whitehead Foundation in 1981 distributed $2,039,500 in grants for scholarships and $165,750 to homes for the aged, for a total distribution of $2,205,250. For scholarships the foundation distributed $95,000 in Alabama, $75,000 in Florida, $544,500 in Georgia, $106,000 in Louisiana, $62,500 in Mississippi, $399,000 in North Carolina, $98,000 in South Carolina, $107,000 in Tennessee, and $552,000 in Virginia. Grants to homes for the aged were $104,250 to three homes in Georgia, $33,500 to three homes in North Carolina, and $28,000 to three homes in Virginia.

The Lettie Pate Whitehead Foundation, as of December 31, 1981, held corporate stocks and bonds with a market value of $38,231,223 (book value, $20,332,337). These holdings included stock in eight Coca-Cola bottling companies valued at $6,102,556 (book value, $610,423), and stock in the Coca-Cola Company valued at $27,480,300 (book value, $15,445,575). Cash, temporary cash investments, and real estate provided the foundation with additional assets valued at $1,276,275 at market value.

Income for the Lettie Pate Whitehead Foundation in 1981 included $483,009 from interest on savings and temporary investments, $2,042,511 from dividends and interest from securities, and $39,750 from rents. The foundation's expenses, primarily for salaries and rents, were $113,789, giving it an adjusted net income of $2,451,481 for the year.

The author is indebted to Charles H. McTier, secretary of the foundation, for an interview in which he provided information about its history and operations. Almost the only additional sources of information readily available to the public on this foundation are the annual reports and returns filed by it with the Internal Revenue Service, and the various Foundation Center publications.

DON M. PACE

**LEXINGTON FOUNDATION.** See Northwest Area Foundation.

**LIBERTY FUND, INC.** Since its founding in 1960, in Indiana, the stated purpose of the Liberty Fund, Inc., has been to promote education concerned with human liberty through making grants and conducting seminars. Funded by gifts from Pierre F., Enid, and John B. Goodrich, members of a wealthy Indiana family, the assets of the foundation grew from about $1.75 million in 1969, with grants of about $50,000 for that year, to approximately $56 million in 1981 and with grants in excess of $2 million annually. In recent years, grants have been made by the foundation to higher educational institutions, such as Hillsdale College, Hillsdale, Michigan, and to research institutions, such as the Foundation for Economic Education, Inc., Irvington, New York.

The Liberty Fund, Inc., is governed by an eight-member board of directors, with Enid Goodrich serving as vice-chairman. Administration of the foundation is carried on from offices located at 7440 North Shadeland Avenue, Suite 100, Indianapolis, Indiana 46250, under the direction of an executive director.

Almost the only additional information on this foundation readily available to the public are the annual reports and returns filed by it with the Internal Revenue Service, and the various Foundation Center publications.

**LILA ACHESON WALLACE FUND, INC.** See L.A.W. Fund, Inc.

**LILLY ENDOWMENT, INC.** The Lilly Endowment, Inc., is a philanthropic foundation created in 1937 with gifts from the Lilly family of Indianapolis, a family whose members founded and directed the development of Eli Lilly and Company, an internationally recognized pharmaceutical firm.

The endowment is chartered under Indiana law as a nonprofit corporation empowered to make grants for the promotion and support of religious, educational, and charitable purposes. Its funds are managed by a self-perpetuating board of directors.

The first officers of the foundation were Josiah K. Lilly, Sr., president; Josiah

K. Lilly, Jr., vice-president; and Eli Lilly, secretary-treasurer. Ruth Allison Lilly and Nicholas H. Noyes were the other original members of the board of directors.

In December, 1947, the size of the board of directors was increased from five to seven, and John S. Wright and Walton M. Wheeler, Jr., were elected to membership. The original officers served until the death of Josiah K. Lilly, Sr., in 1948. Then Josiah K. Lilly, Jr., became president, and Carl F. Eveleigh was elected a director.

When the Lilly Endowment was incorporated, the directors decided that it would be a nonoperating foundation, that it would not conduct research or carry out programs. So the endowment always has functioned as a purely grant-making institution, with appropriate facilities and staff.

The endowment's first gift, $10,500 to the Indianapolis Community Chest, was made at a meeting held on December 9, 1937. A total of $14,250 was allocated in four grants at that meeting, including a $1,500 grant to the Library of Congress for "bibliographical research."

As is typical of family foundations, grants made during the first few years of operation were a reflection of the charitable interests of Lilly family members. Grants were made to Christ Church Cathedral, of Indianapolis; the Indiana Historical Society; Christamore Aid Society; and the Indianapolis Symphony Orchestra. Independent and church-related colleges were also favored. Although the endowment's area of interest has broadened over the years, overall grants still reflect the philosophy of the Lilly family.

These grants also continue to reflect the family's commitment to its home community, Indianapolis, and to the state of Indiana. Of course, as the endowment has grown in size, it has attracted applications from all over the United States and from distant parts of the world. Still, the endowment has continued to emphasize projects that will improve the quality of life in Indianapolis and Indiana, although the number of grants with regional, national, or even international implications increased slightly as the years passed.

In April, 1949, Josiah K. Lilly III was employed as the endowment's first full-time staff member. Up until that time, Eli Lilly had accepted responsibility for the foundation's business. Josiah K. Lilly III opened an office in the Merchant's Bank Building, in Indianapolis, where he spent part of his time establishing office procedures and staff responsibilities. In June of the same year, he hired a secretary/bookkeeper, Rubie Myers, who had held a position with Eli Lilly and Company for fifteen years. At the outset, some of the directors were doubtful that there would be enough business to keep one person occupied. But by 1959, this situation had changed, and there were three full-time professional positions on the endowment's staff.

For the first ten or fifteen years of its existence, the endowment operated quietly. Few people knew of its activities beyond the Indianapolis community and outside of the organizations that had received grants. All of this changed by 1948, when an increase in assets made the Lilly Endowment one of the major foundations in the country. In response to this growth, the board decided to publish an annual report, which appeared in March, 1951. Since that time, the endowment has issued an annual report every year.

By the mid-1940s, the officers of the foundation developed an active program involving projects in the social sciences and the humanities, which includes religion, education, cultural projects including art and music, and community services, public health, and natural science. By November of 1956, these chartered fields of interest had been reduced to three: education, religion, and community services.

The general policies of the Lilly Endowment were first formulated in 1950 and, with minor revisions, are the same today. Under the policies established by the board of directors, the endowment regularly declines projects in health care. There have been few exceptions to this rule, and most of them have involved community projects in Indianapolis.

Also declined with regularity are most projects related to biological and physical science research, housing, transportation, environment, population, the establishment of endowment funds, and the funding of scholarships. With the exception of a few projects in Indianapolis, the Lilly Endowment rarely provides funds for the construction of buildings or other facilities.

Requests for grants covering a period of more than two years usually are rejected, and so are most requests involving the production of films and other mass media. The endowment does not make grants to individuals.

In the art and culture field, the endowment makes a very limited number of grants, and all of these are restricted to Indianapolis and Indiana. The grants made by the endowment to international programs are restricted to a handful of developmental and informational programs.

Throughout the years, the Lilly Endowment has been served by distinguished board members. Josiah K. Lilly, Jr., who succeeded his father as president, served in that capacity until his death in 1966. Eli Lilly was then elected to the presidency, and in October, 1972, he was named chairman of the board. He was elected honorary chairman of the endowment's board of directors in 1975.

Eli Lilly was not only one of the principal founders of the endowment, but he gave it leadership as president and chairman and was a board member from its initial meeting in 1937 until his death on January 24, 1977. He was considered largely responsible for the endowment's commitment to programs to support a broad range of activities in the field of religion and to encourage education directed toward ethical, moral, and social values. He was profoundly concerned with the strengthening of human character, and he persisted in his conviction that this was a major direction in which the endowment should move. He also had a passion for history, especially Indiana history, which led him to recommend assistance to a number of projects, and he personally authored several books on historical subjects in Indiana.

Eugene N. Beesley, who succeeded Eli Lilly as chairman of the board in 1975, had been a board member since 1951. He was then president of Eli Lilly and Company, the first to be named to that office from outside the Lilly family.

He served successively as the endowment's vice-president, president, and chairman of the board during a time when his leadership and business experience proved most useful.

In 1975, Landrum R. Bolling was elected president of the endowment. Before joining the institution in 1973 as executive vice-president, he served for fifteen years as president of Earlham College, in Richmond, Indiana. Bolling left the endowment in 1977 to accept a position as chairman of the board of the Council on Foundations.

Thomas H. Lake, a former president of Eli Lilly and Company, was elected chairman of the board in 1977, succeeding Beesley. Later that same year he was named president, to fill the position vacated by Bolling.

The Lilly Endowment board has always been a cohesive, stable body, and this is reflected in the unity of purpose and historical continuity of the institution's grants. The endowment has sought to concentrate its resources in selected fields of interest rather than scattering them among a wide range of programs and projects. From the beginning, it has been the endowment's practice to expend practically all of the income from invested funds in the year in which the funds are received and in keeping with commitments for future years. This policy, along with the publication of annual reports, indicates the endowment's commitment to its charter and its recognition of responsibilities.

In 1969, however, Congress saw fit to legislate additional requirements for private foundations. These were included in the Tax Reform Act of 1969, a law which requires a private foundation to disburse to qualified recipients all of its annual income or a percentage of the average market value of assets, whichever is greater. Although the law settled many issues, it also had a profound effect on thousands of foundations, including the Lilly Endowment. It soon became apparent that during periods of economic distress, when the stock market declines, the new payout formula can seriously erode capital assets. In addition, the Lilly Endowment and many other foundations had to increase greatly their administrative budgets.

In 1973, Landrum R. Bolling, then the endowment's executive vice-president, played a leadership role in the foundation world by testifying before a congressional committee and recommending a reduction in the size of the annual payouts and the excise tax. He pointed out private philanthropy's history of accomplishment in this country and the need for a public policy that prevents abuses and provides support.

The Lilly Endowment's history of grant making is an example of the flexibility and creativity that private-sector financing can provide to a variety of projects. Over the years, the priority interests of the endowment have been synthesized into four basic categories: human development, strengthening independent institutions, encouraging responsive government at all levels, and improving the quality of life in Indianapolis and Indiana.

One of the projects that serves a combination of these interests has been a series of seminars for trustees of Indiana colleges and universities. These training programs were designed to help trustees increase their understanding of institutional problems and their skill to cope with these problems. The seminar presentations brought participants up to date on educational trends, giving them a chance to hear what authorities in the field have to say and allowing them an opportunity to exchange experiences, concerns, and ideas. By assisting college and university trustees to understand their role and responsibilities, it is hoped that the entire hierarchy, including administrators and faculty, would benefit. The ultimate goal, of course, is to improve the quality of education at these institutions.

In that same vein, the Lilly Endowment has long sought to provide national leadership in the area of faculty development. It has made available financial assistance for regional programs that give special attention to the needs of faculty members from small liberal arts colleges. And the Lilly Post-Doctoral Teaching Awards have been described as a significant effort to help junior faculty exercise their stewardship through improved teaching.

For historically black institutions, the endowment has given major emphasis to programs whose goal is strengthening the teaching of the social sciences, in order to help these colleges and universities continue to play a major role in providing quality education to black Americans.

The education of ministers long has been a priority interest of the endowment, and an important thrust has been the strengthening of theological schools. Through their graduates, these institutions exert a powerful influence on churches of all denominations and, through the churches, on millions of people. So there is a need for the seminary to determine its own identity, to decide its mission, and to settle on the programs and policies which will enable it to carry out that mission. Making such decisions is the responsibility of the seminary's board of trustees. To help these trustees, their schools, and all theological education, the Lilly Endowment has initiated a series of competitive grant programs centering on trustee education and development. The competition has resulted in grants of modest size. Yet, the potential impact has been promising as an awakening interest in the seminary and its potential for service becomes apparent.

In the youth services field, the endowment has been involved in a number of programs that have local, state, and national implications. For instance, the endowment has assisted efforts designed to explain free-market economics to young people, a subject not always covered in their standard education.

Through the Legal Services Organization of Indiana, Inc., the Lilly Endowment has helped in the development of a children's rights program. The objective is to protect young people from abuse, to keep the young truant from being thrown into a county jail with hardened criminals, and to educate public officials and the public about the problems faced by young people in our society.

In Indianapolis, in a program called Youth Works, the endowment has been involved in an effort to provide job opportunities for young people in the private sector. In a number of cases, this action has helped young minority men and women break the unemployment pattern and become productive citizens.

Because of a traditional emphasis on programs benefitting Indianapolis and Indiana, the Lilly Endowment has provided financial assistance to some major revitalization projects. A major emphasis has been the establishment of Indianapolis as the nation's capital of amateur athletics, an effort that has involved a broad-based community campaign to attract events that involve top-ranked competitors in amateur sports. The endowment has joined in funding facilities that have expanded public recreational opportunities available within the city while also attracting amateur sporting events.

The endowment has also helped with the financing of the White River State Park, a cooperative effort of state and local government and the private sector that will eventually create a major urban attraction and activity center on the western edge of downtown Indianapolis.

In its grant-making activities, officers and program staff are organized into three divisions—Education, Religion, and Community Development. Through this structure the staff identifies, monitors, and evaluates specific projects. The endowment, with 1980 assets of about $866 million, receives approximately 3,500 grant requests each year, and staff members respond to each inquiry and proposal. They also work closely with potential grantees whose projects seem promising and fall within endowment guidelines. The endowment's board of directors has the final decision on whether or not a project will be funded. Because resources are limited, only about 10 percent of the requests result in grant awards.

The purpose in all areas of Lilly Endowment interest is to produce change, to utilize the resources of the foundation to solve problems, and to make a situation or an institution or a procedure better than it has ever been. That positive transformation is what the endowment's grant-making mechanisms attempt to achieve. During its history, the endowment has striven to commit its resources to efforts that can produce positive changes in human society. As Eli Lilly once wrote, "Ours is the responsibility for preserving the customs and ideals upon which this organization was built, so that we may pass on to those who follow us an even finer inspirational record than that which we inherited" (*SuperVISION*, December, 1947).

Offices of the Lilly Endowment are located at 2801 North Meridian Street, Post Office Box 88068, Indianapolis, Indiana 46208.

For further information, see *Annual Reports* of the endowment, published continuously since 1950, and the following endowment booklets: Robert K. Greenleaf, *The Seminary as an Institution: The Work of the Trustee* (1980), and Alice L. Beeman, *Toward Better Teaching: A Report on the Post-Doctoral Teaching Awards Program of the Lilly Endowment, Inc.* (1981). See also Fred D. Cavinder, "The Problem of Giving Away Money," (Indianapolis) *Star* (December 8, 1974), p. 8; "Josiah K. Lilly, Sr.," *Dictionary of American Biog-*

*raphy*, Supplement Four (1974), pp. 499-500; and Gordon Englehardt, "Precarious Purse Strings," [Louisville] *Courier-Journal* Sunday Magazine (October 23, 1977).

JAMES P. CARROLL

**LONGWOOD FOUNDATION, INC.** The Longwood Foundation, Inc., was established in 1937 in Delaware by Pierre S. du Pont (1870-1954) for the primary purpose of maintaining and improving Longwood Gardens, his estate in Pennsylvania. In addition, the foundation was designed to support nearby educational institutions, libraries, hospitals, and social welfare agencies. Du Pont had been the primary figure in the rise of two of the giants in American industry: the Du Pont Company and General Motors Corporation. While amassing millions from these enterprises during his lifetime, du Pont devoted considerable amounts of money and time to the establishment and maintenance of his Longwood Gardens estate—some one thousand acres of formal gardens, fountains, statuary, and greenhouses.

By 1951, assets of the foundation totalled about $7.5 million, and grants were about $200,000 for the year. Following du Pont's death in 1954, the foundation received a substantial bequest from his estate, and by 1968, despite expenditures from principal in the millions of dollars, the foundation's assets stood at about $226 million. Since then, transfer of capital assets to Longwood Gardens has reduced the assets by 1981 to slightly over $112 million.

From its inception to the present, the foundation's giving program has been relatively constant. In 1979, for example, with grants totalling about $4.7 million, 35 percent of this sum ($1,615,700) was devoted to the support of Longwood Gardens. Other major representative grants included the following ones in Wilmington, Delaware: Tower Hill School—$250,000; Mary Campbell Center—$200,000; United Way of Delaware—$150,000; and Historical Society of Delaware—$100,000. Still others, outside Delaware, were: American Horticultural Society, Mount Vernon, Virginia—$201,570; Chester County Hospital, West Chester, Pennsylvania—$254,660; and Brandywine Conservancy, Chadds Ford, Pennsylvania—$85,000.

The Longwood Foundation is governed by a seven-member board of trustees, several of whom are members of or are connected with the du Pont family. The foundation is administered from offices located in 2024 Du Pont Building, Wilmington, Delaware 19898, under the direction of an executive secretary.

Almost the only additional information on this foundation readily available to the public are the annual reports and returns filed by it with the Internal Revenue Service, and the various Foundation Center publications. See, however, "Pierre Samuel du Pont," *Dictionary of American Biography*, Supplement Five (1977); pp. 192-194.

**LOUIS CALDER FOUNDATION, THE.** Louis Calder (1879-1963) joined the Perkins-Goodwin Company in 1897 as a $4 a week office boy. In 66 years of service to the company, he was named president (1922), chairman of the board and a director, and was largely instrumental in its becoming a leading international pulp and paper marketing and management organization. He founded the Louis Calder Foundation in 1951, and, through his successive gifts, by 1958 its assets were about $27 million and its grants for that year exceeded $600,000. Grants during the first decade of its existence were made primarily to organizations in the New York City area in which Calder was interested and included hospitals, educational institutions and libraries, churches, and youth agencies.

Following Calder's death in 1963, additional funds were bequeathed to the foundation in his will; and by 1969 its assets had risen to over $50 million, and grants for the year exceeded $2.25 million. The earlier pattern of giving established by Calder continued. Grants from principal as well as income have often been made by the foundation. Thus, since its inception, the foundation has paid over $45 million from income and over $6 million from principal.

In 1981, the Louis Calder Foundation, with assets of about $54 million, awarded almost $4 million, with about 70 percent divided between educational and youth programs and the remaining 30 percent divided between hospitals/health organizations and cultural programs. Representative major grants for the year in these major areas of giving were: New York Medical College—$100,000; United Neighborhood Houses of New York—$370,000; Metropolitan Opera Association—$200,000; United Negro College Fund, Inc.—$100,000; and A Better Chance, Inc., Boston—$50,000.

The foundation is governed by a three-member board of trustees which includes one corporate trustee, Manufacturers Hanover Trust Company. Administration of the foundation is carried on from offices located at 10 Rockefeller Plaza, New York, New York 10020, under the direction of one of the noncorporate trustees.

For further information, see *Annual Reports*, published by the foundation since the 1970s. See also Louis Calder obituary, *New York Times* (June 20, 1963), p. 33.

**LOUIS W. AND MAUD HILL FAMILY FOUNDATION.** See Northwest Area Foundation.

**LUCE FOUNDATION.** See Henry Luce Foundation, Inc., The.

**LYNDHURST FOUNDATION.** Though operating under its present name and general guidelines since 1978, the Lyndhurst Foundation was first incorporated and funded by Thomas Cartter Lupton forty years before that as the Memorial Welfare Foundation. Upon Lupton's death in 1977, the foundation received a substantial bequest from his estate, and the board of trustees reevaluated the policies and priorities of their philanthropy, deciding to change the name and the operation of the foundation.

A full-time professional staff was added to explore new areas, evaluate proposals, make recommendations to the board of trustees, and monitor all grants approved. Whereas it had been the practice of the Memorial Welfare Foundation to award grants almost exclusively to programs in the Chattanooga, Tennessee, area, the board announced that the new Lyndhurst Foundation would consider grant requests from throughout the southeastern region of the United States. They further declared that their gifts would be primarily directed to meet specific needs in health, education, and the arts.

The foundation's health-related grants are focused upon primary care, particularly in areas that are poorly served in terms of basic needs. Grants in education are increasingly directed toward secondary schooling, although some support has provided opportunities for older students to gain professional experience and broaden their exposure while performing needed services for communities. Arts organizations generally receive grants to help increase or diversify their audiences, improve management, or strengthen their potential for earnings.

A few of the Lyndhurst Foundation's grants are made to assist various economic development activities or to improve organizations' effectiveness. In addition, the trustees have a keen interest in activities which offer the potential for enhancing the vitality and "livability" of the Chattanooga community, especially its downtown area.

The board of trustees has also, as a matter of policy, decided to restrict or eliminate gifts in the following categories: (1) endowments; (2) capital projects, including buildings and equipment; (3) deficit operations; (4) general support for hospitals, colleges, universities, religious organizations, and traditional arts and social service organizations in metropolitan areas; (5) research; (6) organizations whose purpose is general advocacy on behalf of a particular group or a particular perspective on current public issues; (7) individuals who request assistance.

Grant requests are generally initiated by a letter describing the organization and the specific project for which support is sought. Project budgets and a copy of the organization's tax-exempt ruling from the Internal Revenue Service must also be included. Staff members review all requests and sometimes seek further information, an interview, or a visit with the organization.

The Lyndhurst Foundation is governed by a four-member board of trustees which includes John T. Lupton as president. Administration of the foundation is carried on from offices located at 700 Krystal Building, Chattanooga, Tennessee 37402.

The Lyndhurst Foundation's assets were valued in 1981 at approximately $70 million, and grants totalling $3.5 million to $4 million were being awarded annually by that year. The board of trustees establishes all investment policies and oversees the administration of investments, which is performed by three investment and banking firms.

For further information, see *Annual Reports* of the foundation, published since 1979.

JACK MURRAH

## M

**MABEE FOUNDATION.** See J. E. and L. E. Mabee Foundation, Inc., The.

**MABEL PEW MYRIN TRUST.** In the years following the establishment of the Pew Memorial Trust,* the sons and daughters of Joseph Newton Pew and Mary Anderson Pew concluded that strong personal interests could be expressed through smaller trusts which would reflect individual concerns. Therefore, over a period of years, each of them established a trust focused somewhat more sharply on selected philanthropic programs.

The Mabel Pew Myrin Trust was established in 1957 by the youngest child of Joseph and Mary Pew, under the trusteeship of the Glenmede Trust Company. After Mabel Pew Myrin's death in January, 1972, the trust became the beneficiary of the residue of her estate. Grants were first awarded from the Mabel Pew Myrin Trust in 1974, which by then had assets of about $41 million.

Through the 1970s, grants were made predominantly in the Philadelphia area to social service organizations and health-care and medical research programs. Since 1979, however, the trust has undergone a comprehensive reorientation of funding priorities. In recent years, grants from the Mabel Pew Myrin Trust have been directed toward the arts and the humanities, social welfare, and health care. Funding in the health-care field has focused on mental health and home health care. Arts support and grants for health care and social services are generally restricted to institutions and programs serving the Philadelphia area. Educational grants are awarded occasionally to private secondary schools in the Philadelphia metropolitan area.

Grants now totalling about $6.5 million annually are made to a variety of organizations that represent specific interests of the founder. Myrin was a supporter of the Kimberton Farms School in Kimberton, Pennsylvania, a day school which follows the Waldorf pedagogy based on the teachings of Dr. Rudolf Steiner. She was a trustee of the Presbyterian-University of Pennsylvania Medical Center, in Philadelphia, and a supporter of the University of Pennsylvania School of Veterinary Medicine. She was on the board of directors of Ursinus College and had a strong interest in the Opera Company, of Philadelphia. All of the above groups have been funded by the Mabel Pew Myrin Trust from its assets which, in 1981, were valued at about $145 million.

Since the Pew charitable trusts were all established by members of the same family, they share the same offices at 229 South Eighteenth Street, Philadelphia, Pennsylvania 19103 and all are administered by the Glenmede Trust Company as trustee. The reader should consult the brief history of the Pew Memorial Trust herein for background and additional information on this trust.

NANCY KLINGHOFFER

**MACARTHUR FOUNDATION.** See John D. and Catherine T. MacArthur Foundation.

**MCDERMOTT FOUNDATION.** See Eugene McDermott Foundation, The.

**MCDONNELL DOUGLAS FOUNDATION, INC.** The McDonnell Douglas Corporation is a world leader in aerospace research, development and production. As the McDonnell Douglas Corporation grew over the years, there have been several modifications in its company foundation title to reflect these changes. The McDonnell Aircraft Corporation Foundation was established in 1947 and the McDonnell Aerospace Foundation in 1963 in St. Louis, Missouri. The two were merged in 1975 and with a transfer of assets became McDonnell Aerospace Foundation, Inc., in 1977. The foundation name was changed to its present one in 1980.

The purpose of the foundation has remained fairly constant over the years. Funding is dedicated to general giving, with an emphasis on higher education and community nonprofit organizations. There have been slight shifts from time to time in activities and organizations supported. These have included support for hospitals, community development, the arts, population control, international affairs, international relief, local historical sites, and family service. Although there are no geographical restrictions, primary focus for fund distribution has been Missouri and the St. Louis area in particular. A prime recipient of the funds from early days through the present has been Washington University, in St. Louis.

Major accomplishments of the foundation, therefore, have been the support of programs and activities of higher education and various civic organizations throughout Missouri, particularly in St. Louis. However, some funds are distributed in other states and abroad. The sciences, health, and the arts programs in St. Louis have been particularly benefitted by large and continuing grants from the foundation.

An analysis of foundation grants shows that in 1972 expenditures of $454,300 included $380,325 for sixteen grants, from a single high grant of $150,000 to a low of $100. There were forty-five grants for the fiscal year ending June 30, 1977, in the amount of about $1.8 million, with a high of $904,050 to Washington

University, in St. Louis, and a low of $100. In that year, grants for education comprised 61 percent of the total funding, with primary support to private colleges and universities. The grant to Washington University represented 50 percent of the total funding for the year. Other grants to education included funds for Georgetown University, Washington, D.C.; St. Louis University; Lindenwood College, St. Charles, Missouri; American University, Washington, D.C.; as well as the McDonnell Scholarship Foundation. Sixty-one percent of the grants were for higher education with fourteen grants; 23 percent of the funds went to seventeen United Funds; 7 percent of the funds went to four health organizations or hospitals; 4 percent was distributed to government and/or international relations foundations, with an additional 2 percent for aviation purposes. The remaining 3 percent was distributed to the Missouri Mansion Preservation Association, the National Society of Automotive Engineers, the Missouri Historical Society, and the Michael Lynam Fund.

For the year ending June 30, 1980, there were $2,608,428 in grants given. Percentage distribution varied only slightly from prior years. The largest single grant, for $1,626,225, went to Washington University, St. Louis, accounting for 62 percent of the year's total funding and over 90 percent of the educational support. Other recipients of education funds were the McDonnell Scholarship Foundation; Georgetown University, Center for Strategic and International Studies; United Negro College Fund; Northwestern University; and the David Rankin, Jr., Technical Institute. The percentage breakdown of donations was 66 percent to higher education with thirteen separate grants; 20 percent to nineteen various community funds; 4 percent to aviation and space science organizations; 3 percent for public and international affairs; 3 percent for various cultural programs; 2 percent for social welfare; and 2 percent for health and hospitals. Typical of the larger grants made in the year ending June 30, 1980, in addition to those mentioned, were $300,000 to the United Fund of Greater St. Louis, Missouri, and $143,750 to the United Way, Inc., of Los Angeles, California.

For the year ending June 30, 1981, approximately $3.5 million was distributed, with the largest single grant, of $873,786, going to Washington University. This grant was followed by $600,000 to the City of St. Louis – McDonnell Planetarium; $345,000 to the United Fund of Greater St. Louis; $201,000 to the Missouri Historical Society of St. Louis; $175,000 to the St. Louis Symphony; $120,000 to the United Way of Los Angeles, California; and over $100,000 to the Alabama Space Science Exhibit Commission, in Huntsville, Alabama.

Officers of the McDonnell Douglas Foundation are also officers in the McDonnell Douglas Corporation and have remained fairly constant over the years. Sanford N. McDonnell is chairman and a director of the foundation, as well as chairman and chief executive officer of the McDonnell Douglas Corporation. James S. McDonnell III is vice-president of the foundation as well as vice-president of marketing for the corporation; Michael Witunski is secretary of the foundation and a vice-president of the corporation; Stanley J. Sheinbein is treasurer of the foundation. These officers form the governance organization for making grants and for receiving and preserving funds through investment policy designed to maintain and increase funds. For the year ending June 30, 1977, foundation assets were $29,850,838; and in 1980, $42,661,244.

The mailing address of the foundation is Post Office Box 516, St. Louis, Missouri 63166, shared with that of the McDonnell Foundation, Inc.*

About the only additional sources of information available to the public on this foundation are the annual reports and returns filed by it with the Internal Revenue Service, and the various Foundation Center publications.

JAMES VAN PATTEN

**MCDONNELL FOUNDATION, INC.** McDonnell Aircraft Corporation was incorporated in 1939 and in 1966 became McDonnell Corporation. Douglas Aircraft Company was incorporated in 1928. After their merger on April 28, 1969, both companies continued to operate under their individual names as divisions of the McDonnell Douglas Corporation. The McDonnell Foundation, incorporated in Missouri in 1950, was originated by the early founders of the corporation to contribute to worthy educational and civic organizations in the community and nation. In contrast to the McDonnell Douglas Foundation, Inc.,* which is supported by the corporation, the McDonnell Foundation is supported and maintained by members of the McDonnell family who are or have been officers of the giant aerospace corporation, one of the world's largest.

Founders of the McDonnell Foundation have fulfilled the purposes of a foundation demonstrating a keen sense of the needs of the organizations they support. For example, contrary to problems of recipients of governmental grants caused by the government's lack of long-term commitment to their projects, the McDonnell Foundation has often supported a particular institution or activity for many years. Funds have been distributed for broad purposes, including higher education, secondary education, and the space sciences, with recent focus on community funds, hospitals, community development, and, particularly, the field of research in parapsychology. Through the years, particular attention has been paid to supporting private higher education institutions, especially Washington University, of St. Louis. In 1950, Henry Ford II noted when the Ford Motor Company Fund* was established that traditional sources of financial support of private institutions were tending to disappear. He foresaw negative consequences inherent in having private institutions turn to the government for much-needed financial aid and stated that this situation placed increasing responsibility upon American businesses in their role of industrial citizens. Thus, the McDonnell Foundation is fulfilling this responsibility to support private institutions. As with other foundations, a main problem for this one has been the challenge of careful investment in a cyclical economy in order to protect and preserve fund assets for maximum distribution to worthy institutions and agencies.

As has been pointed out, a major accomplishment of the McDonnell Foundation has been its support of private education and higher educational institutions. For example, grants for the year ending December 31, 1978, were $2,098,484. Some $605,923 ($61,317 cash and 7,900 shares of Mobil Corp. common stock worth $544,606) was given to Washington University, St. Louis; $106,000 to Princeton University, New Jersey; $58,333 to the Mary Institute, Country Day School Endowment Fund, St. Louis; and $5,000 to Stanford University, Department of Computer and Information Science. Smaller grants were given to other public and private higher education institutions.

The largest grant for that year, however, was one of $1.1 million given to the Psychophysical Research Laboratories, of St. Louis, reflecting the foundation directors' increasing interest in parapsychology. Grants ranging from $1,000 to $40,000 were given in the same field to fifteen other individuals or organizations, including Dr. Lawrence L. LeShan, New York, for research on a theoretical model for paranormal phenomena; Psychical Research Foundation, Inc., Durham, North Carolina; ESP Research Associates Foundation, Little Rock, Arkansas; and the Mind Science Foundation of San Antonio, Texas.

For the year ending June 30, 1981, about $3.5 million was donated. The largest grant was $3,005,000 to Washington University, St. Louis. The second-largest grant was $249,984.25 for the St. Louis Children's Hospital, followed by $92,400 to Princeton University, Princeton, New Jersey. Largest of the smaller grants was $24,000 to Dr. Lawrence L. LeShan, New York, for continued research on a theoretical model for paranormal phenomena.

Financial assets and grants awarded have increased substantially over the years. A ledger amount of almost $1 million in assets for the year ending December 31, 1956, witnessed expenditures in grants of $9,512. Ledger assets were over $3.5 million and the foundation expended $209,900 in grants for the fiscal year ending June 30, 1961. Market-value assets of about $60 million for the year ending December 31, 1978, funded fifty-three grants totalling about $2 million. More recently, market-value assets of approximately $68 million as of April, 1981, funded total grants of some $3.5 million. Each year there have been increases in market value assets, gifts to the foundation from the McDonnell family, and in the amount of grants given.

Personnel of the foundation include John F. McDonnell, director; James S. McDonnell III, vice-president and director; Stanley J. Sheinbein, director and secretary-treasurer. These officers also serve in the McDonnell Douglas Foundation, Inc.,* funded by the McDonnell Douglas Corporation. John F. McDonnell and James S. McDonnell III contributed more than 2 percent of total funds to the McDonnell Foundation for the year 1981. When James S. McDonnell, a long-time director of the McDonnell Foundation as well as of McDonnell Douglas Foundation, died, his position was taken by John F. McDonnell. Some officers of the two foundations also serve as directors of the McDonnell Douglas Corporation. The mailing address of the McDonnell Foundation is Post Office Box 516, St. Louis, Missouri 63166.

About the only additional information readily available to the public on this foundation are the annual reports and returns filed by it with the Internal Revenue Service, and the various Foundation Center publications.

JAMES VAN PATTEN

**MCGREGOR FUND.** After more than thirty years of activity in the work and study of spiritual and social welfare, Tracy W. McGregor (1869-1936) established the McGregor Fund in 1925 with a modest gift of $5000 "to relieve the misfortunes and promote the well-being of mankind." McGregor began his work in Detroit in 1891 when he assumed control, upon the death of his father, of the Helping Hand Mission (later renamed McGregor Institute) for homeless and destitute men. Following marriage in 1901 to Katherine Whitney, daughter of a wealthy Michigan lumber baron, McGregor combined his mission work with business and civic activities. Work with homeless men, needy children, underprivileged mothers, epileptics, and feebleminded children acquainted the McGregors with human suffering and the need for well-directed and well-managed financial assistance to alleviate the misfortunes of their fellow citizens.

Concurrently, McGregor formed in 1910 an informal group of wealthy and influential Detroit men, known as the "Thursday Group," who gathered with the announced purpose of working together to do good. Within this group, McGregor encountered and grappled with many of the problems of late nineteenth- and early twentieth-century industrialization and urbanization. The nation of yeoman farmers envisioned by Thomas Jefferson was rapidly being transformed, and although America remained primarily rural and small-town through this era, the significance of the city loomed large in the national consciousness. City governments proved slow in meeting the needs of its dependent classes and the increasing numbers of new arrivals. Immigrants, with languages and customs understood by few, and rural Americans, who had moved to the city seeking work, were crowded together in dirty tenements and neighborhoods marked by inhumane sanitation and health conditions. Educated, middle-class men and women, such as the McGregors, sensitive to the needs of poor, urban dwellers, devised pragmatic strategies to confront the second nation, urban and industrial, growing up around them. The McGregor Fund was one strategy adopted to address the consequences of a rapidly urbanizing society.

Following its modest beginnings in 1925, the McGregor Fund grew substantially through subsequent gifts from the McGregors until the total principal in December, 1932, amounted to over $3 million. By the time McGregor died in 1936, the fund had accumulated more than $8 million. Through additional gifts from Katherine McGregor, who died in 1954, and income from investments, the McGregor Fund's balance in 1981 was in excess of $37 million.

Governed by a board of trustees, of which Tracy McGregor was a member until his death, the early years of the McGregor Fund were devoted to a careful study of needs not adequately met by city or state government or by other local organizations. Before 1933, the fund made only modest contributions to promote the philanthropic and social interests of its founders, while the trustees discussed and developed the scope and purpose of the McGregor Fund. McGregor believed that most of the foundation's money should be viewed as risk capital to be spent for social experiments, for those groups adopting novel approaches to social problems but whose financial base had not yet been firmly established in the community.

Eight years after the creation of the McGregor Fund and following its dramatic growth in financial resources, the board was ready to commence a larger program of giving as Detroit entered the depths of the Great Depression. Annual grants made between 1931 and 1939 increased from $2,000 to over $275,000. This period also saw the tax-exempt status of the charitable foundation challenged by the Internal Revenue Service (IRS). Although originally affirmed by the IRS as a charitable foundation, the IRS altered the McGregor Fund's status in 1934 after a large gift by Katherine McGregor. Threatened with substantial federal taxes the fund appealed, and, in 1939, the IRS reversed its ruling and reaffirmed the fund's tax-exempt status.

Through the thirties the McGregor Fund developed as a general-purpose foundation with major commitments (totalling 92 percent of all grants) in four fields: local philanthropic and charitable organizations (39 percent), health (12 percent), education and research (25 percent), and history of early America (16 percent).

Tracy McGregor had been aware of the problems of poor transients since his early work at the Helping Hand Mission/McGregor Institute in the 1890s. As the economic depression of the 1930s worsened, the McGregor Fund increased gifts to the McGregor Institute to support the feeding and housing of Detroit's destitute men. Welfare agencies across the country noted large increases in the number of transient and homeless people. Guided by McGregor's interests, the McGregor Fund provided seed money for a national Committee on Care of Transient and Homeless. Representatives of fifteen national welfare agencies, along with interested individuals such as McGregor, formed the initial committee. Through local census surveys of transients, sponsored by the McGregor Fund, the committee was successful in influencing legislation, in 1933, establishing the Federal Emergency Relief Administration (FERA). Through the efforts of FERA administrator Harry Hopkins, federal programs and resources were used to address the plight of the homeless.

McGregor was a dominant figure in Detroit in establishing federated community giving in the city. He was instrumental in forming the Detroit Community Fund as an outgrowth of the coordinated Patriotic Fund which he headed during World War I. Following the war, the Thursday Group worked to organize the Detroit Community Fund as a central body to raise money for the city's charitable groups. The McGregor Fund was an early and heavy supporter of this body (over $260,000 in the 1930s) and continues today to support its successor, the United Foundation of Detroit. Coincident with McGregor's push for a central fundraising body was his desire for a centralized administrative organization that would form the city's charitable groups into a more closely knit unit to eliminate overlapping programs and lead to a more efficient use of scarce resources. He was successful in establishing the Community Union, now known as United Community Services, to which the McGregor Fund has contributed steadily.

In the 1930s, the McGregor Fund commenced support of work in the field of health. McGregor was interested in convalescent care and rest as a method of saving persons in danger of serious mental and physical health breakdowns who risked permanent or long-term loss of ability to work. In 1932, the McGregor Fund founded the Committee on Health Activities to provide relief for persons in imminent danger of health breakdowns. In 1939, the McGregor Fund organized the McGregor Health Foundation, with a separate board of trustees, as a vehicle to fund programs and research projects in the emerging fields relating to mental health. The new health foundation, supported primarily but not exclusively by the McGregor Fund, existed until 1967, and it left a legacy of financial aid to pioneering efforts in preventive psychiatry.

The McGregor Fund supported many research projects in the field of health apart from those initiated by the McGregor Health Foundation. In 1934, the fund dispersed grants to investigate costs of medical care, individual and cooperative health insurance plans, medical care for the near-indigent sick, and health security for a variety of industrial workers. The McGregor Fund also supplied funds to create the Michigan Society for Mental Hygiene (1936), an outgrowth of McGregor's support for the National Committee for Mental Hygiene.

Support for educational institutions and students has always been a high priority for the McGregor Fund. Early efforts, reflecting the founder's interests, focused on higher education, particularly research in astronomy, early American history, social work, the improvement of secondary education in Michigan, and programs of the Merrill-Palmer School, a center for family life education, of which McGregor was president from 1920 to 1936. Among the most significant projects sponsored by the McGregor Fund in education were the development of powerful instruments to study solar phenomena at McMath-Hulbert Observatory, University of Michigan; establishment of a School of Social Work at the University of Michigan; assistance to the American Historical Association to initiate the "McGregor Plan," which enabled colleges to purchase primary source books in early American history; and the establishment, upon McGregor's death, and continued support of the founder's valuable special collection of early Americana at the University of Virginia.

The McGregor Fund also provided scholarship money for the education of needy students who showed promise of outstanding achievement. To support this effort, the McGregor Fund established in 1939 another separate foundation, the Student Aid Foundation of Michigan, which was governed by a separate board of trustees. From 1931 through 1970, the McGregor Fund made available almost one million dollars in financial aid for worthy students.

With the advent of World War II, the McGregor Fund confined itself to supporting activities initiated wholly or in part by the fund or its founders and to assist war-relief agencies. The McGregor Fund continued to support heavily its separately incorporated health foundation and Student Aid Foundation. The

Detroit Community Fund remained a prime receiver of aid from the McGregor Fund. Mental health was a high priority, and the McGregor Fund was instrumental in creating several mental health programs at Wayne University College of Medicine, in Detroit. The war years marked a beginning of a trend toward the heavy support of health and education projects. By 1950, over 47 percent of the McGregor Fund's annual giving was in the area of health.

The board of trustees established three new areas of support in the 1950s. The trustees turned their attention to problems of aging and financed a study by the National Committee on Aging (which it helped found) on enforced retirement on the basis of age. In 1951, when the continued existence of the Detroit Symphony Orchestra was at stake, the McGregor Fund and several other foundations agreed to contribute to the orchestra until it established firm financial footing. The last new area of support centered on the trustees' sense of need to explore problems confronting blacks and to select particular areas in the field to which the McGregor Fund might make valuable contributions. A special conference in 1955 outlined potential areas of support.

At the end of the next decade, the market value of the McGregor Fund rose above $30 million for the first time. Support for education succeeded health as the highest funding area for the McGregor Fund. Strong support for the Merrill-Palmer Institute and Wayne State University continued, and in 1961 the fund developed a "Plan for Aid to Private, Liberal Arts Colleges" in the midwest. This ambitious plan recognized the contributions made by these schools and the financial difficulties they were encountering in the 1960s. The aid for these colleges and universities continues today, and the level of annual giving has increased from $25,000 to $50,000.

During the sixties, the McGregor Fund participated in a united campaign, the Metropolitan Detroit Building Fund, to raise money for the rehabilitation of buildings occupied by social and health agencies in Detroit. McGregor Fund contributions to this capital campaign continued for several years, and the fund still supports such ventures.

Following the 1967 riot in Detroit, a committee of citizens, incorporated as New Detroit, organized to mobilize the city's resources to rebuild the city and to combat the problems that precipitated the riot. The McGregor Fund helped establish New Detroit and contributed to its many programs.

The 1970s and early 1980s saw the McGregor Fund continue its long-established pattern of support for education at the secondary and university levels and for local welfare agencies. This period of financial distress for many nonprofit organizations also marked for the McGregor Fund a dramatic rise in the number of requests for support of operations and an increase in the average grant request. As this type of demand has increased, the possibility of McGregor Fund support with risk capital for new social experiments has declined, thus blunting the fund's initial objectives. Elliott H. Phillips, current president of the McGregor Fund, has raised the possibility that general-purpose foundations like the McGregor Fund will become more insular and concentrate increasingly on funding projects within the local community. Noting that the McGregor Fund at that time disbursed 74 percent of its grants in southeastern Michigan, Phillips observed that, in other words, charity will begin at home and stay pretty close to home. This prospect, of course, does not alter the beneficial work that the McGregor Fund has sponsored and continues to support. Through its history, the McGregor Fund has dispersed more than $35 million primarily in the fields of education, welfare, and health.

The fund is governed by an eight-member board of trustees. Administration of the fund is carried on from offices located in Suite 1380, 333 West Fort Building, Detroit, Michigan 48226, under the direction of an executive director.

For further information, see the fund's *Annual* and *Multi-Year Reports*, beginning with a seven-year report for 1931-1937. See also Henry S. Hulbert, an unpublished biographical sketch of Tracy McGregor (1939); Tracy McGregor, *Toward a Philosophy of the Inner Life* (1933); and the records of various organizations funded by the McGregor Fund. Examples of the latter include: records of the Merrill-Palmer Institute located at the Reuther Library, Wayne State University; and the records of the Committee on Care of Transient and Homeless found in the National Social Welfare Assembly Collection, Social Welfare History Archives, University of Minnesota.

WILLIAM K. WALLACH

**MCGREGOR HOME.** See A. M. McGregor Home, The.

**MCKNIGHT FOUNDATION, THE.** Since the McKnight Foundation was incorporated in August, 1953, the Minneapolis-St. Paul metropolitan area has been its primary beneficiary. The McKnight Foundation appropriated $29.6 million in grants in 1981, the bulk of which went to various human services agencies and projects in the Twin Cities area.

The foundation's namesakes, William L. and Maude L. McKnight, accumulated their fortunes through the Minnesota Mining and Manufacturing Company (3M). William McKnight, a White, South Dakota, native, was graduated from Duluth Business University in 1907, the same year he began his sixty-six-year career with 3M. Minnesota Mining and Manufacturing was a tiny sandpaper manufacturing firm at the time the twenty-year-old McKnight joined it as assistant bookkeeper. He was later promoted to president in 1929 and then chairman of the board in 1949. McKnight retired in 1973 as honorary board chairman. One of McKnight's close colleagues at 3M was another Duluth Business University graduate, Archibald Granville Bush. Bush, who ultimately rose to the post of executive committee chairman, also established a foundation bearing his name in 1953 (see the Bush Foundation*).

The McKnight Foundation's early years were relatively modest ones. The foundation's 1974 annual report summarizes the organization's work between 1953 and 1973 by noting that nearly $1.9 million was distributed to 123 organizations, most of them Minnesota concerns. The major beneficiaries of early

McKnight grants include the St. Paul United Way ($492,500); the University of Minnesota ($193,800); the Minnesota Society of Crippled Children ($92,100); Carleton College, in Northfield, Minnesota; Breck School, in Minneapolis; and Hamline University, of St. Paul.

The McKnight Foundation's complexion began to change in 1972, when five charitable funds were incorporated into the foundation. These funds—the McKnight Family Endowment, the McKnight Family Charitable Fund, the McKnight Family Educational Fund, the McKnight Family Literary Fund, and the McKnight Family Scientific Fund—had distributed $389,926 between 1964, when they were organized, and the 1972 merger.

Following the consolidation, Maude McKnight died in 1973, naming the foundation as residual beneficiary of her estate. Maude McKnight's death set the foundation down a course of rapidly increasing assets and also marked a turning point in the foundation's history. Not only would the McKnight Foundation soon be able to award single grants that far exceeded its total assets as of 1974, but it would also hire its first professional staff and reorganize the foundation's governing structure.

By 1977, the McKnight Foundation had received more than $115 million from Maude McKnight's estate. The foundation's financial picture escalated again in 1978, when William McKnight died, also naming the foundation as residual beneficiary. In 1981, the foundation had received more than $176 million from William McKnight's estate and expected to receive additional disbursements. The deaths of the foundation's benefactors multiplied the foundation's assets significantly: from nearly $8 million in 1974 to $338.1 million in 1981.

In November, 1974, the McKnights' daughter, Virginia M. Binger, assumed the presidency of the board of directors. Other new directors included Binger's husband and three children and the foundation's newly appointed executive director. In addition to hiring its first full-time employees in 1974, the foundation also wrote new articles of incorporation, amended the bylaws, adopted guidelines and procedures for grant making, and identified a number of long-term beneficiaries of the foundation.

Since 1974, the foundation's work has been primarily directed toward the Minneapolis-St. Paul metropolitan area and secondarily to outstate Minnesota. The fields of human services, education, and the arts and humanities have received the greatest attention, together with several major multimillion-dollar special projects. In 1975, the McKnight Foundation made its first two grants of at least $1 million each. These grants went to the University of Minnesota to help improve graduate and professional programs and to a consortium of three Minnesota colleges to help develop scholarship programs for disadvantaged minorities.

The 1975 million-dollar mark had been overtaken by 1978, when the board of directors appropriated $10 million toward a massive redevelopment of the "Lowertown" area of downtown St. Paul. This grant was designed to stimulate both private and public investment in the total redevelopment of the inner-city area. The $10 million grant, which was one of the largest foundation grants for inner city development up to that time, was surpassed in 1980 and 1981, when the McKnight Foundation set aside a total of $17 million for the Minneapolis-St. Paul Housing Fund. This fund's aims have been to increase the availability of affordable housing for low- and moderate-income families living in the metropolitan area through new construction and other means. The foundation's 1980 annual report expressed the housing fund's purpose in this way: "to offset the tendency of many young families to leave the city—or not to consider it."

The multimillion-dollar projects and other special projects, such as the William L. McKnight-3M Omnitheater at the Science Museum of Minnesota in St. Paul, attracted public attention but certainly did not supplant the more bread-and-butter work of the McKnight Foundation. In 1981, the foundation awarded $11.6 million, or 47 percent of its total yearly appropriations, to human services projects. The arts and humanities claimed 29 percent of the grants, while education received 8 percent; the health field, 7 percent; environmental projects, 4 percent; with neuroscience research, international projects, and miscellaneous projects receiving the remaining 5 percent.

The foundation has been particularly interested in human service programs and has made grants to programs dealing with such concerns as the aged, handicapped, jobs training, housing, and neighborhood services. In 1981, for example, the foundation appropriated $5 million to the Minneapolis Foundation, enabling it to administer a neighborhood self-help initiatives program. This neighborhood program is designed to bring together the enthusiasm that often accompanies neighborhood self-help schemes with the expertise and resources of the community's institutions. In 1982, the McKnight Foundation announced it had set aside a total of $6.2 million to increase services to the mentally retarded, developmentally disabled, and mentally ill.

Grants to the arts and humanities have provided operational support in addition to matching grants designed to help build the endowments of selected arts organizations. Fellowships to individual artists have also been awarded. The foundation's work in education has been directed toward scholarships, major capital projects, and special education programs in elementary and secondary schools. Health-care grants have been directed toward neighborhood programs. Additionally, since 1977, the foundation has supported neurological research, with particular attention to understanding how memory functions. Experimental energy programs have also received foundation support.

In 1983, the foundation was governed by a six-member board of directors, with Virginia [McKnight] Binger as president. The foundation's full-time staff also numbered six and was headed by Russell V. Ewald, executive vice-president. The McKnight Foundation maintains its offices at 410 Peavey Building, Minneapolis, Minnesota 55402.

For further information, see *Annual Reports* of the foundation, published since the 1970s, and an informational leaflet, *Grant Making Policy and Procedures*.

SUSAN D. STEINWALL

**MACLELLAN FOUNDATION, INC., THE.** The Maclellan Foundation was established in Delaware in 1945 by the late Robert J. Maclellan, who had been chairman of Provident Life and Accident Insurance Company of Chattanooga, Tennessee, and a director of the American Trust and Banking Company. The foundation has been supported by gifts from other members of the Maclellan family, and its assets, worth approximately $66 million in 1981, consist mainly of shares of stock in the Provident Life and Accident Insurance Company.

The support of the Protestant Church, including missionary activities and theological education, and education constitutes the major area of concern for the foundation. A majority of the grants and most of the activities of the foundation have been limited geographically to Tennessee, particularly the Chattanooga area. The annual level of giving of the foundation has increased from around $2.5 million in 1977 to a 1981 magnitude of about $4 million.

The Maclellan Foundation is governed by a five-member board of trustees, which includes three members of the Maclellan family. Administration of the foundation's programs are carried out under the direction of a president who also serves as president of the board of trustees. The foundation's offices are located in the Provident Building, Chattanooga, Tennessee 37402.

Almost the only additional information readily available to the public on this foundation are the annual reports and returns filed by it with the Internal Revenue Service, and the various Foundation Center publications.

**MCSHAIN CHARITIES.** See John McShain Charities, Inc.

**MACY FOUNDATION.** See Josiah Macy, Jr., Foundation.

**MARJORIE MERRIWEATHER POST FOUNDATION OF D.C., THE.** Marjorie Merriweather Post (1887-1973) was the only child of C. W. Post, the man who developed and marketed the cereal foods Post Toasties, Postum, and Grape Nuts. Through her own business acumen, such as her successful advocacy of the production and sale of frozen foods, she eventually led in the formation, in the 1930s, of the General Foods Corporation, the largest food company in the United States. In the process, Marjorie Merriweather Post multiplied many times over the millions she inherited from her father.

A strikingly beautiful woman, Marjorie Post was married four times—to Edward B. Close (1905-1919), E. F. Hutton (1920-1935), Joseph E. Davies (1935-1955), and Herbert A. May (1958-1964)—each marriage ending in divorce. Following her divorce from May, she resumed her name of Marjorie Merriweather Post.

Davies was the U.S. ambassador to Russia for a number of years in the 1930s. Marjorie Post accompanied him there, and she greatly enlarged the art collection she had been gathering over the years by the purchase of czarist treasures from the Russian government. Also, it was during these years that she began to give the lavish parties for which she became famous and which were to be continued to shortly before her death. For her entertaining in the United States, Marjorie Post built a number of palatial estates in Florida, New York, and, particularly, Hillwood—located in the northwest part of the District of Columbia.

Throughout her life, Marjorie Post prided herself on her philanthropic support of social welfare programs and the assistance she provided to various educational and artistic institutions. She, for example, made large contributions to Mount Vernon College, the National Symphony Orchestra, and the John F. Kennedy Center for the Performing Arts, all located in Washington, D.C. When she died in 1973, her New York estate was left to New York State, the Florida one to the U.S. government, and Hillwood, the D.C. estate, to the Smithsonian Institution. The Smithsonian deemed it impossible to operate Hillwood on the income of the $10 million grant given for this purpose, and Hillwood was turned over to the Marjorie Merriweather Post Foundation of D.C., which had been set up by Marjorie Post in the District of Columbia in 1967 with assets at that time of a few million dollars.

In 1980 the assets of the foundation were about $41 million. The Post Foundation now provides support only for what has become the Hillwood Museum, with grants to it amounting to over $1 million annually. The museum, with an administrative staff of twenty-five and some fifty part-time guides, is now open to the public. On display are what has been called the most comprehensive collection of nineteenth-century Russian decorative art outside the Soviet Union. The Russian collection, for example, includes dining plates, chandeliers, portraits, tea services, and crowns formerly belonging to the Russian imperial family, together with icons, jeweled articles, textiles, and furniture.

The Post Foundation is governed by a thirteen-member board of directors, a number of whom are descendants of or related to Marjorie Merriweather Post. Administration of the foundation is carried on under the direction of a secretary from 4155 Linnean Avenue, N.W., Washington, D.C. 20008, which is the address of the Hillwood Museum.

Almost the only additional information readily available to the public on this foundation are the annual reports and returns filed by it with the Internal Revenue Service, and the various Foundation Center publications. See, however, Marjorie Post's obituary, *New York Times* (September 13, 1973), p. 50; an article about her will, "Mrs. Post's Will Filed in Capital," *New York Times* (September 26, 1973), p. 42; Nancy Bourgerie Meo, "Marjorie Merriweather Post," *Notable American Women—The Modern Period* (1980), pp. 556-557; and an article about her, the museum, and the foundation, Barbara Gamarekian, "Little-Known Museum Fit for a Czar," *New York Times* (January 4, 1983), p. A16.

**MARKLE FOUNDATION.** See John and Mary R. Markle Foundation, The.

**MARY FLAGLER CARY CHARITABLE TRUST.** From her childhood until her death, Mary Harkness Flagler Cary (1901-1967) was a part of New York's intellectual and cultural life. She was the daughter of Anne Lamont Flagler and Harry Harkness Flagler, whose father and maternal grandfather were among the founders of the Standard Oil Company. Harry Harkness Flagler had a great interest in music and for years was president of the New York Symphony and its successor, the Philharmonic Symphony Society of New York. Mary Cary was an accomplished musician in her own right and was a leader in the founding of the National Orchestral Association to help young musicians further their careers. From 1930 until her death in 1967, she served as its president in addition to being its principal financial sponsor.

In 1923, Mary married Melbert B. Cary, Jr., whose principal interest lay in printing and typography. Melbert Cary served for a number of years as president of the American Institute of Graphic Arts and the Continental Typefounders Association. Over the years, Mary and Melbert Cary assembled important collections of type and printing materials, along with valuable collections of books, music manuscripts, and playing cards.

During her childhood, Mary Cary had spent her summers in the countryside, sixty miles north of New York City in the area around Millbrook, New York. During the years of their marriage, Mary and her husband acquired a tract of about eighteen hundred acres of hills, woods, and fields in the Millbrook area which they planned to convert into their country estate. They called it Cannoo Hills. Their plan was abandoned upon Melbert Cary's untimely death in 1941, but Mary Cary spent time there after his death and determined that after her own death the land should remain intact and not be subject to real estate development.

Having no descendants, Mary Cary, after making bequests to members of her family, friends, and certain charities, provided in her will that the bulk of her estate be used to establish and fund the Mary Flagler Cary Charitable Trust. Accordingly, following her death on December 27, 1967, the trust bearing her name was established in New York in 1968. Mary Cary also provided that while the income from the trust could be distributed currently, the principal must also be distributed within fifty years from the founding of the trust. Her will directed that the Cary collections, along with funds necessary to preserve them, be given to institutions to be used for educational purposes and that Cannoo Hills be kept intact and conveyed to a donee, selected by her trustees, to be maintained and administered as a natural resource.

During the early years of the trust's existence, the trustees placed the Cary collections in the Pierpont Morgan Library, the Beinecke Rare Book and Manuscript Library at Yale University, and the School of Printing at the Rochester Institute of Technology. They also appropriated the funds necessary to care for and augment these collections. Cannoo Hills was conveyed in 1973 to the New York Botanical Gardens. Now designated as the Cary Arboretum, it has been developed and administered for research and education in the plant sciences, with particular emphasis upon their ecological aspects.

The Cary Arboretum has been the largest single beneficiary of the Cary Charitable Trust. Out of the total of approximately $45 million distributed to grantees from 1968 to the present, about 50 percent went to the arboretum. Some 25 percent has gone for support of the trust's music program, which has included continued support for the National Orchestral Association and the Philharmonic Society of New York and substantial grants to institutions such as the Juilliard

School and the Metropolitan Opera Association, Inc. From the remaining appropriations of the trust, the Cary family collections have received important although decreasing support.

In recent years, the trust has achieved a far more focused program, emphasizing both music and conservation while dropping miscellaneous categories. The decreasing support for the family collections is due to the fact that they have now all been placed in research libraries, and the heavy initial expenses of their installations and conservation have been paid. The Cary Arboretum continues to take, by far, the largest share of the trust's grant budget, while other conservation grants have remained fairly constant at a much smaller (about 10 percent) percentage of the budget. The trust has been particularly active in assisting efforts to conserve those portions of our eastern coast that have remained in a natural state. Through grants to agencies such as the Nature Conservancy, the trust has funded land acquisitions, planning, and legal action where needed.

With 1981 assets of about $70 million, the three-member board of trustees, plus a small advisory group and office staff, conduct the trust's programs from offices located at 16 East Thirty-fourth Street, New York, New York 10016.

For further information, see the following reports published by the trust: *Five-Year Report* (1973), covering the years 1968 through 1973; *Three-Year Report* (1976), covering the years 1973 through 1976; and *Biennial Report* (1978), covering the years 1977 and 1978. See also *Annual Reports* of the trust, published continuously since 1979.

## MARY REYNOLDS BABCOCK FOUNDATION, INCORPORATED.

Chartered in North Carolina on September 11, 1953, the Mary Reynolds Babcock Foundation, Incorporated, was created under a provision in the will of Mary Reynolds Babcock, of Winston-Salem, North Carolina. Daughter of the famed tobacco manufacturer, Richard Joshua Reynolds, Mary Babcock stipulated that twelve million dollars be set aside to establish a foundation whose purpose would be:

the promotion of the well-being and betterment of mankind throughout the world through assistance and support to such charitable, educational, recreational, literary, religious, scientific, or public purposes as shall be in furtherance of the public welfare.

During its early years, the Babcock Foundation spent approximately 74 percent of all grants on institutions of higher learning and other organizations located in North Carolina. Generally, this pattern of distribution has been continued to the present. A substantial number of these early grants were made for "brick and mortar" projects that involved construction of classrooms, libraries, laboratories, dormitories, and other facilities on college and university campuses. In the first thirteen years of its existence, the foundation paid out $17,608,934.54 in grants, while the market value of its assets increased to $22,139,764.40. When the directors evaluated the foundation's program in 1966, however, a decision was made to emphasize grants for specific, well-defined programs and to forego support for the erection of buildings.

It has been a continuing policy of the foundation not to make grants to individuals. The stated goals of the Babcock philanthropy also excluded the funding of programs that benefitted only one city or county, although ideas that transcend a community's geographic boundaries and produce a ripple effect are taken into account. In recent years, grants for construction or restoration projects, or for international programs, have been curtailed. While sizable grants have been made to the medical schools of Wake Forest and Duke universities, the foundation has also tended to forego support of medical research, thus leaving this field to other foundations and to governmental agencies.

The Babcock Foundation has achieved recognition for the diversity and originality of its philanthropies as its program has evolved and expanded since 1966 to meet changing social needs. An outstanding example of such giving involved programs at Wake Forest University, ranging from support to Bowman Gray Medical School and the affiliated Baptist Hospital, to the award of substantial funds for a fine arts center and the Reynolda Village properties, toward establishment of the Charles H. Babcock School of Business Administration, support of a program for Asian studies, and funding for faculty development and excellence. Benefactions to city and county programs in the Winston-Salem area have included the development of Reynolda House and the Piedmont collection of art, the Piedmont University Center, the restoration of Old Salem as a historical site, support of the North Carolina School for the Arts, Salem College's gallery of contemporary art, the North Carolina Advancement School, the Moravian Music Foundation, the Winston-Salem Symphony, and the Piedmont Repertory Company. The enrichment of such a wide variety of educational and cultural programs has made Winston-Salem one of the more attractive of the emerging urban centers in the nation.

At the Johnson C. Smith University, a predominantly black institution in Charlotte, the foundation, in cooperation with the Duke Endowment,* has undertaken to improve the stature of the faculty, curriculum offerings, facilities, and administrative staff of the university. This support was based on the premise that the institution enjoyed dynamic leadership and a faculty capable of growth and improvement.

Throughout its history, the Babcock Foundation has focused attention upon the problems of disadvantaged youth, early childhood, and adolescence. The foundation, for example, provided support for the North Carolina Fund, whose specific purpose was to serve disadvantaged youth; the Learning Institute of North Carolina, whose objective was to study and serve the needs of early adolescence; and the Center for Early Adolescence, at the University of North Carolina. This last program, in which the Babcock Foundation worked with the Ford Foundation,* is currently administered by the university's School of Education. Serving as a national center for the analysis of early adolescence, the program focuses upon the problems of integrating youth between the ages of ten to fifteen into society. Corollary programs of the foundation have involved support for drug rehabilitation, youth centers, summer camps, job-training facilities, art and craft schools, studies of child abuse and neglect, and activities addressed to the special needs of the young in urban areas.

In cooperation with the Carnegie Corporation of New York,* the Babcock Foundation has centered its attention and support since 1976 on the Institute for Public Policy Research based in Raleigh, North Carolina. The stated purpose of the institute is to foster accountability in government at the state level, specifically in North Carolina, and to analyze through published reports and studies the effectiveness of executive, legislative, and judicial functions. The overall purpose of this work has been to encourage state government to become more efficient, responsible, and attentive to the needs of the people. The institute has generally met with cooperation from the various state agencies and departments, and its findings have provided considerable insight into public policies and problems.

In cooperation with the National Endowment for the Humanities, the Babcock Foundation has sponsored training programs in the humanities for college and university teachers, with these programs offered jointly by Duke University and the University of North Carolina, and also at Davidson College. In 1970, the foundation took a leading role in founding the Southeastern Council of Federations. In 1976, in association with the American Academy of Arts and Sciences, the foundation was instrumental in securing the establishment of the National Humanities Center, at North Carolina's Research Triangle Park. This center has achieved national and international acclaim as a preeminent institution for humanistic scholarship.

The responsiveness of the foundation to contemporary issues and problems is reflected in its support for conservation projects, environmental protection, and organizations that are involved with defending the rights of women. Voter registration, economic opportunities, job training, and urban problems of blacks have long warranted foundation support. Recent grants have also dealt with the plight of Mexican Americans and Indians as well as the disadvantaged of particular areas, especially the southern Appalachians.

From the date of its establishment in 1953 through August, 1978, the Babcock Foundation paid out $37,315,455 in grants, of which amount educational institutions received 62.4 percent; health, welfare, and human relations services were paid 22.3 percent; the arts and humanities programs were awarded 12 percent; and international programs were granted 3.3 percent. In the geographic distribution of these philanthropies over a twenty-five-year period, North Carolina received 73.7 percent of the total awarded. For the 1980-1981 fiscal year, the foundation awarded grants of $2,653,200; it processed 1,387 applications during this year and awarded 100 grants. In 1981, the market value of its assets amounted to about $34 million.

In the early years of its development, the governing board of directors of the foundation consisted almost entirely of members of the Babcock family. The present-day seventeen-member board of directors includes a number who are not related directly to the Babcock and Reynolds families. Administration of the foundation is carried on from offices located at 102 Reynolda Village, Winston-Salem, North Carolina 27106, under the direction of an executive director.

For further information, see *Annual Reports* of the foundation, published since the 1960s.

JOSEPH F. STEELMAN

**MAX C. FLEISCHMANN FOUNDATION.** The Max C. Fleischmann Foundation was established in Nevada in 1952. As outlined in Fleischmann's will, the foundation was dedicated to the support of religious, educational, scientific, and charitable projects. Between 1952 and 1980, the foundation spent approximately $190 million on projects like educational buildings and equipment, scholarships, and research in the medical and biological sciences. It gave special consideration to causes to which Fleischmann had contributed in his lifetime and to regional areas in which he had lived or had some special interest.

Max C. Fleischmann was born in Riverside, Ohio. At the age of eighteen, after attending the public schools and Ohio Military Institute, he went to work in his father's yeast factories. He became superintendent of manufacturing in 1920, moved up to vice-president in 1923, and became chairman of the board upon the death of his brother Julius in 1925. He sold the Fleischmann Yeast and Gin Factories in 1929 to the J. P. Morgan banking syndicate for approximately $20 million worth of stock in Standard Brands, of which he became a director and eventually chairman of the board of directors.

Moving to Santa Barbara, California, Fleischmann quickly made a name for himself as a philanthropist, contributing to beach improvements, a Boy Scout camp, polo fields, a museum, and a number of scholarship funds. In 1935, Fleischmann built an impressive estate on the shores of Lake Tahoe. He continued his philanthropy in Nevada, spending over $200,000 to convert the old United States Mint at Carson City into a state museum. He also helped to build a hospital at Carson City, established 178 scholarships at the University of Nevada, and gave the university a large dairy farm for which he provided a special endowment in Standard Brands stock.

For several years, Fleischmann was part owner of the Cincinnati Reds baseball team and was instrumental in securing an agreement between the National and American leagues preventing the raiding of players and avoiding the scheduling of conflicting games. During World War I, Fleischmann commanded the American Expeditionary Forces Balloon Corps and acquired the rank of major, a title by which he liked to be addressed in civilian life. A flamboyant eccentric, he seemed to take pride in attire that seldom matched and often clashed. He sometimes wore a .38-caliber pistol or two strapped to his waist and did not hesitate to use his honorary position as a state policeman to apprehend speeders and generally keep the peace in his part of Nevada.

Fleischmann fell ill in 1951, and an operation disclosed that he was suffering from "an incurable malignancy." Recuperating at his wife's California home, he grew increasingly despondent and finally committed suicide at the age of seventy-four.

His will reflected both his commitment to philanthropy and his unpredictability. He had no children, and his wife, Sara, whom he had married in 1905, received an annual after-tax income of $84,000. His total bequests to friends, relatives, and employees amounted to less than $1 million. The remainder of his fortune, an amount in excess of $50 million, went into the foundation that bore his name. Six trustees each received an annual payment for their services and were given considerable discretion in spending the foundation's money. Fleischmann's only stipulation was that all of the money be spent within twenty years of his wife's death (which came in 1960).

The trustees complied with his wishes, spending more than $90 million in 1980, the last $1.1 million of which went to support wetlands conservation projects in Nevada. Though not widely publicized, the Fleischmann Foundation during its period of existence (1952-1980), was among the nation's largest foundations. In 1976, for example, it had assets of approximately $115 million.

For further information, see *Annual Reports* of the foundation, published from the 1970s to 1980. See also the following articles appearing in the *New York Times*: "Max C. Fleischmann in Hospital" (September 19, 1951), p. 43; "Max Fleischmann a Suicide on Coast" (October 17, 1951), p. 28; "Estate Tops $50,000,000" (October 31, 1951), p. 34; and "Foundation Meets Deadline for Going Out of Business" (July 5, 1980), p. 6.

JAMES C. COBB

**M. D. ANDERSON FOUNDATION.** The M. D. Anderson Foundation was established by Monroe D. Anderson in 1936. He had been one of the founders of Anderson, Clayton and Company, a worldwide cotton merchandising firm with home offices in Houston, Texas. Originally a partnership, it was incorporated in 1929. Anderson continued as an officer and director of the corporation until his death in 1939.

It was in the early 1930s that Anderson, a bachelor, decided to devote the greater part of the fortune he had amassed to philanthropy. He created the M. D. Anderson Foundation as a vehicle to carry out his plans, but he developed a serious illness and died before they could be put into operation. By his will, he provided nearly all of the assets of the foundation, which by 1979 amounted to approximately $56 million.

Since its inception, the Anderson Foundation has adopted the "venture capital" or "seed money" method of operation, that is, it makes grants to other agencies to launch new and untried programs or helps worthwhile projects that are encountering temporary difficulties.

Anderson Foundation support over the years has been given primarily to institutions operating in the area of medicine and to educational and other organizations ancillary to medicine and health. The Texas Medical Center, Houston, Texas, for example, which the foundation helped to establish in the 1950s, has continued to be a major recipient of foundation aid. Similarly, the Baylor University College of Medicine and the M. D. Anderson Hospital and Tumor Institute have benefitted from the foundation's largess. A variety of other institutions working in the field of improving living conditions generally have also received support. Except for aid to medically oriented projects in Houston, however, the foundation has avoided grants to church-related institutions. Also, because of the provisions in Anderson's will and consequent legal limitations, foundation funds are expended only in the state of Texas.

A board of trustees of three members and a small staff headed by a secretary conduct the program and activities of the foundation from offices located at Suite 750, Two Houston Center, Houston, Texas 77001.

For further information, see an *Annual Report* of the foundation, published in 1977.

## MEADOWS FOUNDATION, INC.

To support and maintain hospitals, homes, and institutions for the care of the sick, the young, the aged, the incompetent, and the helpless....

To support the promotion of health, science, education, and the advancement and diffusion of knowledge and understanding among the people of Texas.

With these words of high purpose and resolve, Algur H. Meadows created the Meadows Foundation in 1948 to benefit the people of Texas living at that time and for generations yet unborn. It was his dream and plan that the wealth he was accumulating would be returned, through a private trust for the public good, to enrich the quality of life for the people who inhabited the land where that wealth had primarily been acquired. Since 1960, as a result of his generosity and compassion for others, almost fifty million dollars in grants have been made to hundreds of different organizations and institutions by the foundation which bears his name.

One of seven children born to Dr. John M. Meadows and his wife, Sally, in the small south Georgia town of Vidalia, Algur Meadows's life became yet another chapter in the American story of opportunity successfully united with talent, education, and determination, as well as good luck and good timing. It was the East Texas oil boom that drew and propelled him into a lifetime of involvement in the oil and gas industry. As founder of General American Oil Company of Texas, in 1936, he guided its growth into one of the nation's major independent oil and gas production companies. As the free-enterprise system enabled him to accumulate great wealth, it also enabled him to engage in a lifetime of sharing that wealth with others. He committed not only his material possessions to public charity but also his time and energies.

Feeling that his own life had been immeasurably enriched from participation in charitable activities, he created the Meadows Foundation so that his giving could continue long after his life ended; and he challenged his family and trusted advisors to carry forward his dedication to involvement in philanthropy.

He directed that members of his family should participate in guiding the foundation because they were conversant with his objectives for its efforts. In so charging his family, he wrote that he wanted their involvement because he was "sure they will pass along those objectives to their descendants" and because he wanted "the Meadows name and family not only identified with, but engaged in the accomplishment of the public charitable purposes of the foundation."

Until his death in June, 1978, Meadows was president and a director of the foundation. The securities of the foundation largely represent common stock in General American Oil Company. His interest in art led Meadows to donate $35 million to Southern Methodist University to organize the Meadows Museum of Spanish Art as a memorial to his first wife, who died in 1961, and to endow the School of the Arts. Over the years, Meadows donated many paintings to the museum through the foundation.

His death in mid-1978 ended an era of thirty years of leadership for the foundation and created a need for internal reorganization. Already managing the assets derived from the estate of his first wife, the board of directors now prepared to receive additional major new assets from his estate.

Acknowledging the great potential of the foundation to benefit the people of Texas, the directors began the transition by electing new officers, providing for new offices, and engaging a full-time staff. A review of the past giving of the foundation pointed the way to developing goals and grant directions for the future.

Their first major gift was a $1 million endowment grant to the Meadows School of the Arts, Southern Methodist University, Dallas, Texas, in November of 1978, to establish the Algur H. Meadows Award for Excellence in the Arts, a prize to recognize and reward high levels of international achievement in the creative and performing arts. Because A. H. Meadows was a man of extraordinary foresight who valued the gifts of great artists as one of the ultimate contributions that can be made to society, the Meadows Award for Excellence in the Arts is a living reminder of the legacy of Al Meadows and a continuing expression of the vital role of the arts in human life. The winner of the award, named annually, received a $25,000 cash prize, a gold and bronze miniature of the sculpture "Spirit's Flight" by Isamu Noguchi, which was commissioned to symbolize the award, and professional engagement for corollary events to be scheduled during the year following the artist's selection. The first recipient of the Meadows Award was Ingmar Bergman, internationally acclaimed film director.

In 1980, the foundation disbursed a record $5,172,307 in payments on grant pledges. During the year, 110 new grants, amounting to $1,403,004, were approved, selected from over 600 requests. About one-half of these 1980 grants were to first-time recipients, demonstrating commitment of the officers and directors to build a giving program based on both new and past relationships.

Increasingly concerned about impending difficulties for the charitable sector, the Meadows Foundation, with the encouragement of other Dallas foundations, donee organizations, and business and volunteer groups, has underwritten a program to provide management and technical assistance to charitable organizations—the Center for Non-Profit Management. Through trained volunteers directed by a professional staff, the center will counsel and assist nonprofit groups to establish priorities and set attainable goals, formulate plans to pursue those ends, and utilize management techniques designed to promote increased efficiency and savings in operational expenses. The ultimate purpose of such efforts is not only to try to maintain the critical services and programs of an organization but to enhance their effective delivery to the public.

The five areas of interest and the types of grants currently being made by the Meadows Foundation are the arts, social services, health, education, and civic and cultural programs. The category of religion, *per se*, was deleted in 1981 because of the foundation's policy of giving special consideration to any type of program which is based on religious commitment and ethical concerns, thus testifying to the belief that religion is appropriately a part of all human pursuits and not something apart from other experience.

The foundation is committed to giving preference to funding projects which include innovative ways to promote organizational efficiency, to share resources, and to cooperate with other agencies and thus to increase the efficient use of present funding in order that future needs may continue to be met.

Under the terms of its charter, the Meadows Foundation can distribute grants only in the state of Texas and only to qualified charitable organizations; money is neither lent nor given to individuals.

The foundation is governed by a thirteen member board of directors which includes Algur Meadows' son and second wife. Administration of the foundation, with 1981 assets of approximately $124 million, is carried on from offices located at 310 Meadows Building, Dallas, Texas 75206.

The foundation's full board meets in April and November. A grants review committee, authorized to act on requests not characterized as "major," meets in the remaining ten months.

There is no application form, and proposals may be submitted at any time. Interviews may be granted after the receipt of proposals. Applicants can expect acknowledgment of the receipt of their proposal and notification of final action by the board within three months. The foundation issues guidelines for submitting a proposal; a statement of program policy is included in the foundation's *Annual Report*.

His concern covered Catholic, Jewish, Protestant; it covered Black, White, Chicano, Indian; it went from grade schools to universities, hospitals, blood banks, symphonies, museums, ballets. He was concerned with the whole spectrum of human life....

Generations coming on will profit from being able to see art masterpieces at first hand, from using the scholarships, from the hospital equipment, the schools, the endless lists of good things which poured out of the heart of one of the most genial and likeable human beings one could ever know. [Meadows Foundation, Inc., *Annual Report* (1980), p. 5]

With these words, written at the time of the death of Algur H. Meadows in 1978, an articulate friend captured the spirit of the man and his meaning in the lives of others.

For further information, see *Annual Reports* of the foundation, published since 1980.

SALLY R. LANCASTER

**MELLON FOUNDATION.** See Andrew W. Mellon Foundation, The; Richard King Mellon Foundation.

**MEMORIAL WELFARE FOUNDATION.** See Lyndhurst Foundation.

**METROPOLITAN LIFE FOUNDATION.** The Metropolitan Life Foundation was established in 1976 by the Metropolitan Life Insurance Company, which is its sole supporter. With 1981 assets of about $47 million, annual giving by the foundation has risen from about $275,000 in 1977 to around $4 million in 1981.

Since its inception, the foundation has sponsored a program to assist tax-exempt organizations, particularly in communities in which the Metropolitan Life Insurance Company has a major presence. In carrying out this program, the foundation limits its support to stated goals in defined areas as follows:

*Health*: the foundation's goal is to assist in the development and implementation of educational programs to promote health awareness and to encourage the delivery of adequate health care at reasonable cost.
*Education*: the foundation's goal is to assist higher education and strengthen programs and opportunities for minorities in disciplines directly related to the insurance industry.
*Civic Affairs and Public Policy*: the foundation's goal is to help strengthen the social and economic fabric, to provide education and training opportunities for specific groups that are presently at a disadvantage, and to improve the quality of the environment in which Metropolitan employees live and work.
*Culture*: the foundation's grants recognize the importance of cultural resources on the national and local level to the vitality and quality of life in any community. Contributions are made to both established and pioneering organizations in order to provide opportunities for the development of artists and to bring cultural experiences to wider audiences.
[Metropolitan Life Foundation, *Policy and Guidelines for Grant Consideration* (1981), pp. 4, 5]

Within the above areas, approximately 50 percent of grant money has been divided about equally between donations to various community funds and health agencies. Education and civic affairs have each received about 20 percent of the total appropriations of the foundation, and the remaining 10 percent has been allocated to the cultural area.

The six members of the foundation's board of directors are senior officers of the Metropolitan Life Insurance Company. The program of the foundation is administered from offices located at One Madison Avenue, New York, New York 10010, under the direction of a president.

For further information, see *Annual Reports* of the foundation, published continuously since 1979. See also a foundation brochure, *Policy and Guidelines for Grant Consideration* (1981).

**M. J. MURDOCK CHARITABLE TRUST.** After graduating from Franklin High School in Portland, Oregon, in 1935, Melvin J. (Jack) Murdock had the option of going to college or opening up his own business with the money his father had set aside for his college education. He chose to open a radio sales and appliance store. In the process, Howard Vollum joined him as a radio repairman. After World War II, during which Murdock served in the U.S. Coast Guard, he and Howard Vollum organized and founded Tektronix, Inc., a firm later based in Beaverton, Oregon. Jack Murdock became the chairman of the board of trustees and major stockholder in this firm, which, in 1981, was reported to be the world's largest manufacturer of oscilloscopes and graphic computer terminals and employed some twenty-four thousand workers. Sales were reported to be over one billion dollars annually. Thus, prior to his unexpected death in 1971 from a seaplane accident, Murdock had become a very wealthy man.

The terms of Murdock's will provided for the establishment of the M. J. Murdock Charitable Trust, which was funded by the transfer of assets to it from his estate on June 30, 1975. At the end of the first full year of operation, on December 31, 1976, the fair market value of the trust assets were reported to be slightly over $117 million. A total of about $4.5 million was granted during that period, of which $3.62 million was allocated in Oregon. Forty-nine grants were awarded, ranging from $355 to $1.1 million. Eighteen of forty-eight grants ranged in size from $2,000 to $10,000, while sixteen other grants ranged in size from $10,000 to $50,000.

By 1981, foundation assets were about $127 million, and 106 grants were paid out for a total of slightly over $7 million. The smallest grant was $1,500, while the largest was $1.5 million. The general range was $5,000 to $150,000.

In 1981, 38 percent of the total grant dollars in nineteen grants was allocated to education. Twenty-eight percent in twenty-three grants went for medical and scientific purposes. Fourteen cultural programs were awarded 16 percent of the funds, while social welfare received thirty-six grants for 14 percent of the grant dollars. Four percent of the dollars was awarded to fourteen civic and public interest programs.

The Murdock Charitable Trust is among the fifty largest in the United States and the largest in the state of Washington.

Influenced by Murdock's insatiable appetite for innovation and creativeness, the foundation's board of trustees favors research or the application of existing knowledge to solve or prevent important problems; they do not merely react to "needs." Priority in giving is afforded private institutions in the states of Oregon, Washington, Idaho, Montana, and Alaska.

The trust is governed by a three-member board of trustees, each of whom has served on the board since the inception of the trust. Administration of the trust is carried on from offices located at 915 Broadway, Vancouver, Washington 98660, under the direction of an executive director. The mailing address of the trust is Post Office Box 1596, Vancouver, Washington 98668.

For further information, see *A Report* (1976), covering the years 1975 and 1976, published by the trust; and *Annual Reports* published continuously since that time. See also *A Tribute to Jack Murdock, 1917-1971* (1971), published by Tektronix, Inc.; "Tektronix Executive Feared Drowned," *Oregonian*, (May 18, 1971), p. 1; "75 Million Estate Filed," *Oregonian*, (October 6, 1971), p. 12; "Melvin J. Murdock," *The National Cyclopedia of American Biography*, vol. 57 (1977), p. 38; and *The Guide to Oregon Foundations* (October, 1977), p. 218.

KARL F. DRLICA

**MONELL FOUNDATION.** See Ambrose Monell Foundation, The.

**MOODY FOUNDATION, THE.** Established by William Lewis Moody, Jr., and his wife, Libbie Shearn Moody, of Galveston, Texas, under a trust indenture dated August 22, 1942, the purposes of the Moody Foundation set forth at that time were:

(a)...support and maintenance of churches and other religious institutions or organizations in the State of Texas;

(b)...establishment, support and maintenance of hospitals, homes, and institutions for the care of the sick, the young, the aged, the incompetent, and the helpless among the people of Texas; and

(c)...promotion of health, science, education, and advancement and diffusion of knowledge and understanding among the people of Texas.

The first of the Moody family to arrive in Texas was William Lewis Moody, Sr., who came from Virginia to Texas by boat in 1852, landing in Galveston. He went from there on horseback to Fairfield, Texas, where he set up a law practice. He served with distinction during the American Civil War, where he attained the rank of colonel. He was one of the leaders in the growth of the cotton, railroad, and banking businesses in Texas. Colonel Moody moved his family to Galveston in 1866 and started the cotton firm of W. L. Moody & Co.

Moody's son, William Lewis Moody, Jr., became junior partner in his father's firm in 1886 at the age of twenty-one. The younger Moody was instrumental in succeeding years in adding a private bank and a branch of the expanding cotton business to the activities of W. L. Moody & Co. In 1905, he organized the American National Insurance Co., which grew to be the largest life insurance company west of the Mississippi. In 1907, he organized another bank. He owned several newspapers and started a hotel company which at one time owned thirty-two hotels and motels. His interest in ranching led him to acquire eleven ranches (encompassing over two hundred thousand acres), all of which were fully operational. He married Libbie Rice Shearn, of Houston, in 1890. They had four children: Mary Elizabeth, William Lewis III, Shearn, and Libbie. Moody died in 1954, leaving a substantial financial empire.

The successor to this empire was Mary Moody Northen, his oldest child. She had been a member of the Moody Foundation board of trustees since its establishment in 1942. Upon the death of her father, she assumed the chairmanship and also took on the leadership of some fifty corporations that comprised the Moody enterprises. She was then sixty-six years old, retirement age for many, but for her a career was just beginning. It was one for which she had been well prepared by her father. Moody had made it a daily practice for many years to discuss with his daughter the business transactions in which he was involved. She shared his interest in and acumen for business matters and justified her father's confidence in her abilities as she took charge of his vast financial empire. She soon became known as the "First Lady of Finance."

Now in her nineties, Mary Moody Northen is still active on the board of directors of many Moody enterprises. In addition to her philanthropic work through the foundation, she continues to make personal contributions to many worthwhile projects within the state of Texas and across the nation. She has been an active member of numerous historical and hereditary patriotic organizations, as well as a dedicated member of various state boards that reflect her interest in historical and cultural opportunities. Her commitment to educational excellence has been recognized by the conferring of honorary degrees by five universities. In 1976, she was awarded the Santa Rita Award, the highest honor awarded by the University of Texas system. The tribute paid to her at the time of the award sums up well her character and worth:

Within Mrs. Northen is combined an unusual business genius with a deep sense of obligation to her community and her nation, a feeling of responsibility to the welfare of the individual as well as a strong inclination to provide for the future through improvements, research, and historical preservation. [*Santa Rita Award Program*, September 30, 1976]

The provisions of the Moody Foundation trust indenture specified that the original gift of $815,834 must remain forever intact as a permanent investment or endowment fund from which the income would be used within the state of Texas for religious, charitable, scientific, and educational purposes. From the year of its founding through 1959, the income of the foundation was small, and the total grants made during this seventeen-year period amounted to only $350,000. These grants were primarily to local churches, orphanages, a school for children with cerebral palsy, and other civic and charitable organizations.

William Moody, Jr., provided additional endowment for the foundation under the provisions of his will, which was probated in 1959. The bulk of the assets became available to the foundation in 1960. During the period from 1960 to 1964, the total grants amounted to $20,771,586. By 1965, the value of the assets of the foundation was approximately $240 million. As the assets and income of the Moody Foundation increased over the years, so did the size and number of grants. Through 1981, the Moody Foundation has funded 1,460 grants for a total of over $123 million, with more than $46 million aiding educational institutions throughout Texas, $31 million supporting expansion of health-care services and scientific research advances; $29 million assisting with cultural and historical projects; and $16 million helping the economically disadvantaged through community and social services programs.

A shift in the nature of requests began occurring in 1965 from requests for capital improvement funds to requests for project and program activity funds. In many ways, the growth and evolution of the foundation's grant program has been related to the development of the Southwest. In the late fifties and early sixties, Texas was a rapidly developing state, with tremendous economic growth and influx of people. Almost every major institution was faced with the need for expanding facilities and equipment. The Moody Foundation attempted to respond to these needs with funds for construction and equipment acquisition. By the mid-sixties, the public and private sectors were called upon to collaborate to solve complex social, medical, and human problems, with an emphasis on quality of life. The nature of requests received and the foundation's response to them reflected these new needs.

The shift over the past twenty years in types of grants awarded is significant. Grants to health and science have remained relatively stable at from 20 to 25 percent during these years. Similarly, the percentage of grants in the area of community and social services has remained fairly consistent at around 12 percent. There has been a decrease in the funds allocated to education—in the early years as much as 78 percent of the funds went to education; in recent years this percentage has dropped to a range of 20 to 25 percent. In the field of humanities (including art, history, language, museums, music, performing arts), the percentage of grants has increased from about 16 percent in 1969 to a range of 30 to 40 percent in recent years.

In addition to awarding grants in response to applications, the foundation has initiated several of its own programs, which it administers. A scholarship program was begun in 1969 for Galveston County High School students. The foundation's current commitment is $600,000 to its two local scholarship programs. The feasibility of setting up a Graduate Education Scholarship Program is now under consideration.

In 1977, the foundation began acquiring rare medical books, medical instruments, and other items of historical significance. This ongoing collection is presently on loan to the Moody Medical Library at the University of Texas Medical Branch at Galveston.

Another program undertaken by the foundation was the renovation and restoration of the Santa Fe Building in downtown Galveston. Built in 1913, this ten-story building served as the depot for the Atchison, Topeka, and Santa Fe Railroad until 1946. It had various tenants after that date and then became vacant. Mary Moody Northen was anxious to see it become a part of the historic Strand area restoration and be an attractive and useful addition to the extensive restoration/rejuvenation of the area already underway. The building was purchased in 1976 by the foundation. Restoration has recently been completed, and the building has been named Shearn Moody Plaza for one of the sons of the foundation's founders. Floor space has been leased to various governmental, charitable, research, and educational organizations.

There are other projects planned for the Shearn Moody Plaza area. Antique railroad cars and railroad memorabilia are being purchased by the foundation for a Galveston Center for Transportation and Commerce. Plans are presently being formalized for construction of a facility near the Plaza to house a center for disease prevention, health promotion, and physical fitness.

Initiation of programs by the foundation is a trend that will continue to grow. The more passive mode of giving, which waits for applications to be submitted in order to respond to needs, will be supplemented increasingly by active searching out of needs and determining of what can be initiated by the foundation to meet them.

The Moody Foundation is governed by a board of three trustees who are charged with the responsibility of determining operating policies, acting on all business matters, reviewing investment portfolios, and taking action on all grant requests. Since 1978, the board has been comprised of Mary Moody Northen and two grandsons of the founders, Robert L. Moody and Shearn Moody, Jr. The administrative aspects of the foundation are carried out by a professional staff which includes an executive administrator, and administrator of grants and programs, a comptroller, three program officers, and a scholarship administrator.

The Moody Foundation's assets were valued at $200 million at the end of 1981. Investments include money market instruments, certificates of deposit, common stocks, industrial bonds, and real estate.

Applications for funds are submitted in writing according to guidelines available to the applicant. Interviews and site visits are scheduled when appropriate. The staff reviews all applications and presents them to the trustees at the four or more annual meetings of the board of trustees. Applicants are notified in writing of action taken relating to their requests.

The Moody Foundation is restricted by its trust indenture from granting funds for activities or organizations outside the state of Texas. In general, it does not make grants for deficit financing of buildings and programs, regular operational expenses of established programs, or grants to individuals except through approved scholarship programs. As stated in its 1977 *Annual Report*, the foundation distributes its funds in the following areas:

1. Advancing educational capabilities by the construction of buildings, purchase of equipment for instruction, books for libraries, support of innovative programming, curriculum change and educational reform, endowment of professorships and chairs;

2. Enhancing health care programs through grants for the construction of facilities, purchase of equipment for treatment, development of new treatment modalities, expansion of health care delivery, and development of public education programs about health problems;

3. Sustaining scientific activities through support of established and recognized programs and projects aimed at acquiring and disseminating greater knowledge in the physical, life, and social sciences, the purchase of equipment and construction of facilities for scientific purposes and increasing the public's understanding of technical matters;

4. Encouraging interest in the arts and humanities by assisting in the extension of programs in the visual and performing arts, development of arts and education activities, improvement of audience participation, development of literary works, increasing the public's knowledge of our cultural heritage, construction of facilities, and restoration of historic structures; and

5. Improving community and social services through grants for rehabilitation programs, community development and human relief, development of residential care for dependent youth and support of programs that address special population groups such as the aging, the mentally ill, and the disadvantaged.

The philosophy of giving of the Moody Foundation is moving in the directions of developing community services, encouraging private enterprise, and enhancing economic development, with the foundation itself initiating more and more of the projects and programs. Among submitted grant applications, the foundation will be looking for innovative and forward-looking approaches to the programs and projects being proposed. Cultural and performing arts—first to suffer in times of inflation and cutbacks in federal support—will receive special foundation consideration. Small towns and rural areas will continue to benefit from the commitment the trustees feel to have these locales share the advantages and enrichment opportunities that usually accrue only to larger cities. In the area of health and science, one of the major thrusts will be in the field of rehabilitative medicine and the related areas of disease prevention and health promotion. The foundation will continue its interest in the historical heritage of Texas.

The impact of the Moody Foundation's grant program has affected the quality of life of Texans in all areas; the commitment to help and enrich continues.

For further information, see S. C. Griffin, *History of Galveston* (1931); Earl W. Fornell, "The Moody Era in Galveston" (1966, unpublished); D. Bearden and J. Frucht, *The Texas Sampler: A Stitch in Time* (1976); and R. E. Baker, unpublished speech to the Southwest Council of Foundations (1981). See also *Annual Reports* of the foundation, published continuously since 1965.

ELAINE PERACHIO

**MOREHEAD FOUNDATION.** See John Motley Morehead Foundation, The.

**MORRIS AND GWENDOLYN CAFRITZ FOUNDATION, THE.** Established in 1948 in the District of Columbia, the Morris and Gwendolyn Cafritz

Foundation was founded for the primary purpose of benefitting the district and adjoining areas. The foundation's assets, initially valued at about $100,000, were provided by Morris Cafritz, a spectacularly successful Washington real estate developer and financier. The foundation's size and scope of activities were not significant until the late 1960s, when, upon the death of Morris Cafritz in 1964, a substantial portion of his estate went to the foundation. His gifts and those from other members of the Cafritz family, plus income from its invested assets, raised the foundation's corpus to a 1981 value of approximately $60 million.

The Cafritz Foundation has limited its support to organizations located in the Washington, D.C., area and makes grants of approximately $2 million per year. A major portion of the grants has been for the arts and humanities, with the remainder devoted to community services, education, and health. In the area of the arts and humanities, recent grants have been made for underwriting the costs of a symposia on the American Revolution held at the Library of Congress and support for institutions such as the John F. Kennedy Center for the Performing Arts, the National Symphony Association of Washington, D.C., the Corcoran Gallery and School of Art, and the Opera Society of Washington. A large variety of grants has also been made to community associations, schools, colleges, universities, hospitals, and allied organizations, with emphasis on the needs of the inner-Washington, D.C., city area.

Gwendolyn D. Cafritz, Morris Cafritz's widow, is active in the affairs of the foundation and presently serves as president and a director of the three-member governing board of directors. A son, Calvin Cafritz, is a member of a nine-member advisory board which makes recommendations as to grants to the directors.

The affairs of the foundation are conducted from offices located at 1825 K Street, N.W., Washington, D.C. 20006.

For further information, see an undated summary of information issued by the foundation, together with *Annual Reports* published continuously by it since the 1970s. See also Morris Cafritz obituary, *New York Times* (June 13, 1964), p. 23.

**MOTT FOUNDATION.** See Charles Stewart Mott Foundation.

**MURDOCK CHARITABLE TRUST.** See M. J. Murdock Charitable Trust.

**MURPHY FOUNDATION.** See Dan Murphy Foundation.

**MYRIN TRUST.** See Mabel Pew Myrin Trust.

# N

**NELDA C. AND H. J. LUTCHER STARK FOUNDATION.** In February, 1961, H. J. Lutcher Stark and his wife, Nelda Childers Stark, organized a foundation which would provide funds from their contributions and eventually their estates for charitable purposes. The Nelda C. and H. J. Lutcher Stark Foundation was incorporated under the laws of Texas as a nonprofit corporation to be operated exclusively for public, charitable, religious, and educational purposes. The objectives of the foundation were, with one exception, intentionally stated in all-inclusive terms to leave foundation administrators free to respond to specific areas of interest that were expected to develop with experience in the foundation field. Both Nelda and H. J. Stark had been actively collecting works of art for a number of years, and, with this in mind, draftsmen of the corporate charter specifically authorized the Foundation to build, construct, and maintain a museum to exhibit paintings, porcelains, bronzes, and other works of art.

During the early years of the Stark Foundation, its activities were limited in scope and reflected previously developed charitable interests of the organizers. After the death of H. J. Lutcher Stark in 1965, funds and other assets from his estate became available to the foundation in the next few years. The foundation received substantially all of the very extensive and important art collection which had been accumulated by the Starks. The Stark collection included Roman and Egyptian antiquities, European paintings, porcelain, glass, and American art. Within this diversity, however, the Starks focused on art of the American West. Reflecting the Starks' interest in the land, people, and wildlife of America, the collection provided an excellent survey of the interpretations of the development of the West by nineteenth- and twentieth-century artists. The foundation also received Stark's boyhood home, a Victorian mansion built for his parents, William Henry and Miriam Lutcher Stark.

Because of the excellence and importance of the art collection, as well as the wishes of H. J. Stark, foundation trustees, under the direction of Nelda Stark, began plans for a museum. The selection of a site in the downtown area of Orange, Texas, near the boyhood home of H. J. Stark, contributed to the direction of the foundation's major accomplishments from the 1970s on. This site was in an area being abandoned by businesses moving away from the central commercial district. The Orange city government became interested in foundation plans and the possibility of reversing the deterioration of the area. Through joint efforts of the city and the foundation, architects were employed to develop a master plan for renovation of the downtown area and development of a cultural and civic center. From this master plan, the foundation assumed full responsibility for the construction and operation of the Stark Museum of Art, restoration and operation of the W. H. Stark House, and the design and landscaping of a park, all of which would remain under the ownership of the foundation.The master plan included the construction of a theater for the performing arts, which would be built by the foundation, then donated to and operated by the city, and a new city library. The foundation contributed part of the land and all of the architect's fees for the library. The remainder of the plan, including the renovation of the city hall and a municipal office building, was accomplished by the city.

On November 29, 1978, the Stark Museum of Art opened to the public. Faced with white Vermont marble, the building provides approximately fifty-eight thousand square feet for exhibition space, visitors' services, storage, and work space. On display in the museum are selections from the collection, including rare prints and manuscript material by John James Audubon, sketches by Paul Kane, sculpture by Frederic Remington and Charles Russell, paintings by members of the Taos Society of Artists, American Indian art, porcelain, and Steuben glass. Prior to the opening of the museum, the foundation made several acquisitions to strengthen the holdings, including oil paintings by Thomas Moran, Albert Bierstadt, and other Western artists. Acquisitions since the opening of the museum include an Audubon copper plate and Western prints, and further acquisitions are planned to develop the collection. Conservation of the permanent collection is a priority of the foundation, with a regular program of attention to the works of art. Future exhibitions are planned for portions of the collection, and the museum staff provides tours and gallery talks for the public. The foundation has published four catalogues of the museum's collections. Admission to the museum is free.

Restoration of the W. H. Stark House, designated as a Recorded Texas Historic Landmark–1976 and entered in the National Register of Historic Places–1976, was completed in 1980. The fifteen-room, three-story, wood-frame structure was built circa 1894 and shows the influence of several architectural styles. Mrs. W. H. Stark had traveled extensively and brought home fine china, glass, silver, and other decorative arts from around the world to display in the house. The W. H. Stark House is thought to be unique among such restorations in that, when W. H. Stark died on October 8, 1936, and Miriam Lutcher Stark died on November 27 in the same year, the house was closed, and all furniture, decorations, and accessories remained stored there until restoration was begun in 1973. An inventory of all furniture and accessories in the house had been taken in 1921. This inventory, together with photographs of various rooms of the house and interviews with servants employed by W. H. and Miriam Stark, made it possible to restore the house with all furniture, decorations, and accessories just as it was when the Starks lived there in 1921. Docents were trained to give tours concerning the history of the structure, and the W. H. Stark House opened for guided tours on February 10, 1981.

The Frances Ann Lutcher Theater for the Performing Arts was built by the foundation between 1976 and 1980. Consultants hired by the foundation provided specifications to guide the architects in designing a structure appropriate for a broad range of performing arts. The building has 70,880 square feet of space and seats approximately 1,500. After donating the theater to the city, the foundation has provided additional grant money to support programming and performances. The foundation completed its construction activities in the cultural-civic center area with the development of Stark Park, a block park landscaped with walks and trees, which serves as the focal point for the center.

The Stark Foundation is a nonprofit corporation administered by a board of trustees from which the officers are selected. Officers and trustees are Nelda C. Stark, chairman; Eunice R. Benckenstein, vice-chairman; Clyde V. McKee, Jr., secretary-treasurer; William J. Butler; S. H. Phillips; and Homer B. H. Stark. The foundation is presently classified as a private foundation by the Internal Revenue Service.

Financing of the foundation is by income from investments, except for a relatively small amount collected for guided tours of the W. H. Stark House. The foundation's total assets in 1981 were about $45 million.

The foundation has a total of fifty-five permanent and part-time employees engaged in the operation of the Stark Museum of Art and the W. H. Stark House and in the administrative offices. The foundation's mailing address is Post Office Box 909, Orange, Texas 77630.

For further information, see Julie Schimmel, "A New Museum of the American West," *The American West* (January, 1979); and Sarah Boehme, "The Stark Collection," *Southwest Art* (December, 1980). See also various informational brochures about the Stark Museum of Art, published by the foundation.

CLYDE V. McKEE, JR.

**NEW HAVEN FOUNDATION, THE.** The year 1928 was a good year for New Haven, Connecticut. The year was one of prosperity and growing civic pride; it was also the year that the New Haven Foundation came into existence. The foundation is what is legally known as a community foundation, and its role is to create an endowment from gifts and bequests and then to distribute the income to community causes. Experience had demonstrated that bequests for specific charitable purposes frequently became anachronistic; an eighteenth-century bequest to defray the expense of pasturing the cattle of Yale University's president offered a humorous example to New Haveners of a gift that had lost its usefulness with the passage of time. On the other hand, the New Haven Foundation provided a safe and permanent method of distributing the income from charitable gifts in ways that would always meet the contemporary needs of the community. What was created in 1928 was a flexible and highly responsive resource that was available to the entire community, the foundation itself not being the object of charitable gifts but rather a transmitter of gifts. The community is the beneficiary.

The concept of the foundation had been born three years before, in 1925, when Henry L. Galpin suggested to a group of fellow bankers that they examine the idea of a community trust fund. The death of Nettie J. Dayton on September 13, 1928, led to the first gift to be received by the new organization. She left $135,000, the bulk of her estate, in trust for the foundation, the funds being received in September, 1930. The endowment grew slowly during the years of the Great Depression; not until 1932 did another substantial gift go to the foundation. But during the 1940s, other large gifts began arriving. By 1948, the foundation's twentieth anniversary, the funds which it administered totalled $1,640,000. The largest gift ever received was that of Hayes Quincy Trowbridge, who in 1969 provided through his will a general purpose gift of $5,121,310 to the foundation. During the year 1952, the New Haven Foundation received $2,235,961 from a trust established by Ross Fletcher Gates, of Derby, Connecticut. On July 25, 1954, his brother, Frank Gates, died, leaving a similar trust valued in excess of $2 million to the foundation. In 1958, the estate of Frank Gates was completely settled and a final distribution of $118,000 was made to the Gates Fund, thus creating a total book value of $4,536,000 as of December, 1958.

Smaller gifts have also played an important part in making the foundation's work possible. In 1948, in recognition of the growing general interest in the foundation, a general fund was established to receive gifts as small as $5; since that time, the general fund has grown to well over $1 million. Because of the willingness of persons of various means to support the foundation, it has developed into the seventh largest of 250 community foundations in the United States. Only those in New York, Cleveland, Chicago, Boston, San Francisco, and Hartford have larger endowments. With assets in 1980 of a market value of about $40 million, the New Haven Foundation ranks first in the country on an assets-per-capita basis.

The New Haven endowments are maintained in five trustee banks, and a trustee committee, composed of the presidents of these banks, has as its duty the insurance of unity of purpose and concert of action among the trustees. The committee reports the income produced on a quarterly basis, and a distribution committee assigns the income to various organizations that, in its judgment, best serve the diverse needs of the community. The distribution committee is made up of nine members chosen in rotation by the mayor of New Haven, the judge of probate for New Haven, the president of Yale University, the president of the New Haven County Bar Association, the Greater New Haven Chamber of Commerce, the trustees committee, and the distribution committee. The foundation distributes income from both restricted funds, for which donors have specified particular organizations or fields of interest for receipt of the income, and unrestricted funds, for which the distribution committee has been given the sole responsibility to designate recipients. Grants are made to not-for-profit organizations in the greater New Haven and lower NaugatuckValley regions of Connecticut, within five areas of interest: arts and culture, education, health, religion, and social services. In 1980, the foundation distributed $3 million to deserving programs.

In its early days, most of the foundation's income went almost automatically to established agencies. The former Community Chest (now the United Way) regularly received a large contribution, as did other well-known charities and health organizations (the foundation was especially involved in funding cancer research and treatment). Those funds which might still be available at the end of the year would be divided among New Haven's hospitals. Since then, contributions to established charities such as the United Way have been slowly phased out, the foundation contending that United Way funding should come from current donations rather than endowment income. The foundation has lately provided grants to groups that could hardly be described as "establishment." In 1970, for example, the foundation provided $10,000 to "Number Nine," a group of young nonprofessionals working with teenagers who were reluctant to bring their problems to more formal social service agencies.The group was quartered in a storefront in the heart of the city, where it operated a telephone "crisis line" and provided emergency living quarters. The first secretary of the foundation, Osborne Day, contended that foundation funds should be used for pioneering purposes and that progress was to be made by the advancement of new ideas which may not fit into the existing scheme of things. This attitude is still basic to the foundation's philosophy.

The New Haven Foundation is a resource available to the entire community. Among the important New Haven programs that might never have succeeded without the foundation's assistance are the Center for Advocacy, Research and Planning; Connecticut Women's Education and Legal Fund; the Arts Council; the Children's Museum; the Arts Education Program of the New Haven Board of Education; and the Fair Haven Community Health Clinic. Through projects like these the New Haven Foundation continues to serve its community.

The New Haven Foundation's offices are located at One State Street, New Haven, Connecticut 06510. Norman Harrower, Jr., director, is the present executive head of the foundation.

For further information, see the following series of articles that appeared in the *New Haven Register*: "New Haven Foundation—Origins"; "New Haven Foundation—Early Gifts"; "New Haven Foundation—How It Distributes Its Funds"; "New Haven Foundation—A Lasting Memorial" (February 6, 7, 8, 9, 1978). See also Floyd Shumway and Richard Hegel, eds., *New Haven, An Illustrated History* (1981); and *Annual Reports* of the foundation, published continuously since 1928.

THOMAS J. FARNHAM

**NEWHOUSE FOUNDATION.** See Samuel I. Newhouse Foundation, Inc.

**NEW YORK COMMUNITY TRUST, THE.** One February morning in 1920, readers of the *New York Times* saw a headline, "Community Trust to Guide Charity." The story that followed defined an idea new to New York at the time, the formation of a trust:

...which is to foster educational, charitable, and benevolent gifts, to be administered under a plan which will permit flexibility of distribution to meet changing needs and enable persons of wealth as well as of moderate means to make their gifts more effective. [*New York Times* (February 28, 1920), p. 7]

Prime initiator of the New York Community Trust, which was established by declaration of trust in New York in 1923, was Frank J. Parsons, a vice-president of the United States Mortgage and Trust Company. Parsons's experience in handling trust funds had taught him that, while dead men tell no tales, they have a lot to say about how their money is to be spent—and not infrequently what they say in a last will and testament becomes, with the passage of time, difficult, foolish, or impossible to carry out.

When Parsons broached the idea of the New York Community Trust, he found willing listeners among his friends in banking. So, determined to get the best possible advice, he went to Cleveland to see "Judge" Goff, originator of the community trust idea. Frederick Harris Goff was not a judge but a lawyer turned banker, and prime founder of the Cleveland Foundation.\*

It was important, Goff said, to obtain a broad base of interest in the project. Accordingly, Frank Parsons set out to obtain one. First, he invited twenty banks to serve as a trustees committee. Then, an eleven-member distribution committee was formed. Five members were appointed by the trustees committee, one by the mayor of the city of New York, one by the senior judge of the U.S. Circuit Court of Appeals, one by the president of the New York Chamber of Commerce, one by the president of the Association of the Bar of the City of New York, one by the president of the New York Academy of Medicine, and one by the president of the Brooklyn Institute of Arts and Sciences.

When Frank Parsons went to Cleveland to talk to Judge Goff, he met a bright young man named Ralph Hayes. A graduate of Western Reserve University and a member of Phi Beta Kappa, Hayes had been assistant to Newton D. Baker, secretary of war, before becoming Goff's special assistant coordinating the affairs of the Cleveland Foundation.

Three years later, Ralph Hayes was appointed director of the New York Community Trust. Hayes was twenty-nine years old, and he had a million dollars to spend. At that time, he stated that vast sums of money were being wasted by people who tied up millions in foolish and ill-advised wills and bequests. He urged that philanthropy should be made fool-proof by inquiry into how monies should best be spent for future generations.

Ralph Hayes lived and breathed his new job. He told the story of the New York Community Trust dramatically and well and worked to expedite good appointments to the distribution committee and to get the trust functioning.

In 1924, the first New York Community Trust fund was established and the first grant was made. Rosebel G. Schiff gave $1,000 to create the Teresa E. Bernholz Fund in memory of her beloved principal of Public School No. 9 in New York. She asked that a prize go each year to the girl student of that school who had earned the highest respect of her teachers. In June, at the graduation exercises, the first award—$20—was made.

Meantime, the financial position of the trust grew precarious, and, in March, Ralph Hayes found himself writing to the chairman of the distribution committee, Thomas Williams, that available funds were less than sufficient for thirty days' operation.

Thomas Williams went to work to shore up the organization, personally calling on bank presidents and trust officers. At the same time, Hayes concentrated on enlisting the interest of a number of people who were eventually to be important contributors to the growth of the trust.

In November, 1924, New York newspapers announced that a fund of $500,000 had been created by Mrs. Felix M. Warburg in the U.S. Mortgage and Trust Co. in commemoration of her father, Jacob H. Schiff. In 1925, the Moritz and Charlotte Warburg Memorial Fund of $500,000 was set up in the same bank by Mr. Warburg, in memory of his parents.

With these announcements, the New York Community Trust became not only a living but a thriving entity. Soon it began to attract other donors and became concerned with the entire Greater New York area.

Until this time, the law of the state of New York required that each will utilizing the community trust contain a complete transcript of the detailed "Resolution and Declaration of Trust Creating 'The New York Community Trust' " as originally drawn up. This was a good idea but a cumbersome procedure because the transcript was twenty pages long! Happily, in 1926, bills amending the personal property law and the real property law were steered through the New York state legislature. The result was that attorneys no longer needed to reproduce the entire contents of the twenty-page transcript in a will or trust agreement. Instead, its provisions could be incorporated by a simple reference to a publicly recorded copy.

As the nation sank into the depression, the New York Community Trust found itself weathering the storm. In the year 1930, the capital depreciation of securities comprising the trust was less than 1 percent. The amount of income disbursed that year was nearly 5.35 pecent of the year-end market value of those securities. At the same time, the distribution committee disbursed what amounts it could to such beneficiaries as the Women's Division of the Emergency Unemployment Relief Committee.

In 1932, Herbert L. Griggs told the New York Community Trust officials that, because his wife suffered from arthritis, he and she wanted to do something to help other arthritis victims. They felt that, because so much money and effort were already being spent on medical research, they would like to try to bring comfort directly to the sufferers. Letters asking for ideas were written to more than sixty leading physicians and medical institutions. From the replies, plans for the Emily Griggs Fund were laid. The plan called for small sums to be given through several hospitals to help make arthritics more comfortable. The plan even recognized that an arthritic can sometimes hold a part-time job if he or she can get to and from work, and it provided taxi fares for such cases.

Most donors, being New Yorkers, asked the New York Community Trust to help them do something for New York. But New Yorker Lucy Wortham James added other ideas. Revising her will in the mid-1930s, her thoughts returned to her ancestral home in the Ozark foothills of Missouri. Here her great-grandfather had helped found the Maramec Iron Works; here Lucy had spent her childhood; and here, after the turn of the century, she had acquired much of the rolling acreage of her forebears and envisioned sharing it with generations to come.

Before her death in 1938, Lucy James arranged to make her residuary estate a part of the New York Community Trust, which created the James Foundation to carry out certain purposes she suggested. A small library, supported by the municipality of St. James, Missouri, was put in a handsome new home of Georgian design.Today it houses twenty-one thousand books and spreads its services to thirty-five communities in eight counties. Its story hour brings children to "Lucy's Playhouse," a little, rebuilt structure which was once a childhood haven for Lucy James herself. The picturesque ruins of the old iron works and the great Maramec Spring, with a daily flow of nearly one hundred million gallons, became the hub of a 1,756-acre wooded tract, a quarter of which is developed for recreational use.

Indian lore as well as the area's iron-working history is kept alive in the Maramec museum. The branch from the great spring is stocked daily with creel-sized rainbow trout and has become an angler's paradise. In addition, in the city of St. James, a park has been created with a man-made lake to fish in, three swimming pools, ballfields, and playground equipment.

As the country emerged from the depression, many individuals, like Lucy Wortham James, turned to the New York Community Trust as a means of responding to society's changing needs. New funds, large and small, came in. At the end of World War II, there were seventy-seven different funds, with assets of $17.6 million. Year after year, new funds were set up—two by actor David Warfield, who earned $25 a week in his first theatre role and died at age eighty-four, leaving an estate ultimately valued at more than $2 million, and one by Isabel C. McKenzie, who during her lifetime played fairy godmother to dozens of children but had none of her own. Appropriately, since Andrew McKenzie was an architect, money from the McKenzie Fund has helped mark historic and architecturally important New York buildings.

By the mid-1950s, it had become clear that there was a need for a way to handle smaller charitable trusts. So in 1955, Community Funds, Inc., was established as a nonprofit corporation to meet the need for administration of small or special project funds, whose assets it manages directly. When a fund grows to the point where its assets exceed $200,000, the fund may be transferred to the New York Community Trust.

The board of directors of Community Funds, Inc., is made up of the same persons who serve as members of the distribution committee of the New York Community Trust.

By 1964, the New York Community Trust was managing 173 funds, 27 of them in Community Funds, Inc. In all of these funds, observed a director's report written at the time, two themes persist: administrative similarity and philanthropic variety. While managerial procedures are standardized, the purposes served are endlessly different.

In 1967, Ralph Hayes retired, and the distribution committee sought and found a new director, Herbert B. West. Like Ralph Hayes, Herbert West was a writer. He joined Batten, Barton, Durstine & Osborn, a leading New York advertising agency, as a copywriter in 1936 and ultimately became a vice-president and account supervisor. After thirty years at the advertising firm, Herbert West left the business world to devote his full time to what had become more and more his real life interest: community service.

In this area, he had served as chairman of the board, International Social Service, American Branch; vice-president and board member, Travelers Aid/International Social Service of America; trustee, United Community Funds and Councils of America. He had been appointed by the presiding bishop to the executive council of the Protestant Episcopal Church of the United States, and he had conducted seminars and conferences, lectured, and written articles on philanthropy. A practical idealist, Herbert West came to the New York Community Trust at a time when America was beginning to realize there were few simple solutions to social problems because the problems themselves were increasingly complex.

Responding to the times, under Herbert West's direction, the New York Community Trust began to take an increasingly professional approach. Field representatives were added to the staff to investigate proposals, to evaluate ongoing projects, to make follow-up reports, and to go out into the community in an effort to identify needs and effective means of meeting them. The trust's range of advisors and counselors was enlarged. And greater interaction and exchange of ideas among charities, city and state officials, and other foundations was encouraged.

The year 1969 saw the New York Community Trust grow more rapidly than it had in any single previous year. Twenty-four new funds brought the combined size of the New York Community Trust and Community Funds, Inc., to a year-end total of 239 active funds. The year began with assets of $78.8 million, and, despite the decline in the securities markets during the year, the foundation ended 1969 with assets of $99.2 million, a gain of 25 percent.

Another record was set in 1969. The largest gift that year came from DeWitt

Wallace and Lila Acheson Wallace, who set up funds in the New York Community Trust and in Community Funds, Inc. Interestingly, the money for these funds was derived largely from an idea that had been born back in the twenties, almost at the same time as the New York Community Trust, and which had grown into a worldwide editorial phenomenon, *The Reader's Digest*. The Wallace funds were established as founder-advisory funds to reflect the special concerns of De Witt and Lila Wallace and exist under New York Community Trust auspices separate from the De Witt Wallace Fund, Inc.,* and the L.A.W. Fund, Inc.,* founded by De Witt and Lila Wallace, respectively.

As the sixties ended and the seventies began, the Tax Reform Act of 1969 eliminated some of the principal benefits of private foundations and made community foundations more attractive vehicles for charitable giving. Multiple new requirements and limitations were imposed on private foundations. Community foundations, as "publicly supported charities," were exempt. In effect, the act encouraged private foundations to transfer assets to public foundations. Many did and are continuing to do so.

Herbert West, in his 1969 director's report, pointed out:

We take pains to make sure that each Fund is administered as a suitable individual memorial. Grants from each Fund are made individually. Even the checks in payment of grants carry the name of the individual Fund as the central element. In addition, we prepare an individual biographical sketch of each principal founder. These are printed in check-size leaflets which accompany the grant checks. These life stories are fascinating.

Under West's direction, pre-grant research was strengthened, and efforts were made to integrate the work of the organization with others interested in New York. For example, a series of interfoundation meetings was begun, drawing the attention of New York's major foundations to the needs of the community. Special guests at these meetings were civic leaders and specialists in city problems. In addition, a series of luncheons with attorneys and bankers was inaugurated, and letters were sent to legislators apprising them of grants made in their districts.

In 1974, the New York Community Trust celebrated its fiftieth anniversary. Its assets had crossed the $200 million mark. It had become, at that time, the country's largest community foundation—and perhaps the most challenged. As the fund's director observed, more people seem to have chosen to live in New York City and its vicinity than in any other place on earth. When urban problems develop, they often begin and develop faster in New York than anywhere else. New York City has them all—population, drugs, decay, racial and ethnic tensions, fear, loneliness, disease, traffic. But, he countered, New York has some of the greatest blessings—leadership, beauty, talent, dedication, neighborliness, creativity, medical skill.

In 1975, the Westchester Community Foundation was established, and, two years later, the Long Island Community Foundation was established to concentrate on the special problems and opportunities in Nassau and Suffolk counties. Both foundations were created as divisions of the New York Community Trust, thereby having at their disposal the trust's resources: seasoned administrators, a professional grant staff, very low costs, familiarity with charity-related tax laws, and the financial expertise of sixteen major city and county banks. In addition, the Westchester Community Foundation is served by an advisory committee and the Long Island Community Foundation by a board of advisors composed of residents who know their communities well. They serve without compensation.

In the summer of 1976, when the city of New York was in the throes of a major fiscal crisis, the groundwork was laid to create the Corporate Special Projects Fund. It was established with contributions of $25,000 from each of several participating corporations. Collaboratively, executives from each corporation—along with administrative staff from the New York Community Trust—identify, review, and recommend grants that can have a sizable, long-term effect on the city's institutions and spirit. In its first year, the Corporate Special Projects Fund supported ten projects in the areas of family services, community affairs and economic development, health, and parks improvement. In that same year, the trust published the first in a series of reports that ascertained the depth of need for technical assistance in the areas of art and culture, housing, health care, youth services, and programs for girls and women. The reports examined the extent and types of agency assistance serving those areas and suggested roles that the trust should play in providing further support.

At the heart of the work of the New York Community Trust has always been its dedicated distribution committee, a small group of distinguished citizens serving without compensation to fulfill their responsibilities to the community and to the donors of funds. This committee is still appointed by civic authorities representing the public and by the trustee's committee. The leadership of this committee has been furnished by five unusually talented chairmen over this half-century plus: Thomas Williams, Thomas M. Debevoise, Ralph Hayes, Francis T. Christy, and the current chairman, William Parsons (no relation to Frank Parsons, who led in the founding of the trust).

In 1981, the New York Community Trust had a professional staff of thirty-six operating out of its offices located at 415 Madison Avenue, New York, New York 10017. Its total assets were about $291 million and, combined with community funds, comprised 447 individual funds.

The editors are grateful to Elise Maclay, information officer, the New York Community Trust, for supplying us with most of the information used in the preparation of the foregoing brief history of the trust. For further information, see *Annual Reports* and *Yearbooks*, published by the trust since its inception and, particularly, *The Story of The New York Community Trust: The First Fifty Years* (1974). See also the following trust informational brochures: *James Foundation; The Westchester and Long Island Community Foundations; Heiser Program for Research in Leprosy;* and various ones providing guidance for donors and grantees.

**NOBLE FOUNDATION.** See Edward John Noble Foundation; Samuel Roberts Noble Foundation, Inc., The.

**NORRIS FOUNDATION.** See Kenneth T. and Eileen L. Norris Foundation, The.

**NORTHWEST AREA FOUNDATION.** First-time visitors to the Northwest Area Foundation offices usually are surprised to learn that all of the oil paintings gracing the walls are the work of Louis W. Hill, Sr. Even more surprising is that this man, who inherited the virile personality, constructive mind, and business sagacity of his father, James Jerome Hill, could have found the time to paint, for his days were filled with railroading, banking, mining, and expeditions to the West.

Louis W. Hill, Sr., had a lifetime interest in education, research, health, welfare, and the arts. His intellectual curiosity, his concern for his fellow man, and his belief in and support of thoughtfully conceived pioneering in all fields were evident throughout his life. He had that rare ability to perceive the many potentials inherent in this nation's human and natural resources, and he used his talents as a catalyst for progress and the advancement of economic and social well-being of his community and country.

Louis Warren Hill was born in Saint Paul, Minnesota, on May 19, 1872, the son of James Jerome and Mary Theresa (Mehegan) Hill. He was educated at Phillips Exeter Academy and graduated from Sheffield Scientific School, Yale University, with a Ph.B. degree, in 1893.

James J. Hill once told a friend, "Shares of stock are nothing more than the man behind them—for of what avail are all the equipment and assets of a railroad or any other institution unless there are men in control who know how to run it?" (Louis W. and Maud Hill Family Foundation, *Annual Report* [1973], p. 9). In line with this philosophy, Louis W. Hill went to work for his father after graduation from Yale. His apprenticeship included service in the Great Northern Railway accounting department, then a winter as a mechanic in the Great Northern shops, later as a clerk to a section foreman and master carpenter, finally ending up in the general offices learning how to administer the ever-growing business.

In 1895, Louis Hill became a billing clerk in Duluth, Minnesota. His engineering and geological training at Yale enabled him to see northeastern Minnesota's great iron ore potential, not only as railroad freight, but to the total economy. His initial purchase of twenty-five thousand acres of land from Michigan timber interests on June 22, 1898, was followed by additional purchases and leases, culminating in the creating of the Great Northern Iron Ore Properties Trust in 1906. He was its founding president and board chairman until 1945, remaining as a trustee until his death in 1948.

By 1898, Hill was an executive in the railroad, and he became president of the Great Northern system in 1907 upon his father's retirement, succeeding him as chairman of the board in 1912. He served as both president and board chairman from 1914 to 1919 and continued as board chairman until his retirement on October 10, 1929.

Hill was married on June 5, 1901, to Maud Van Cortlandt Taylor, daughter of Cortlandt M. Taylor, in New York City. They had four children: Louis Warren, Jr., Maud Van Cortlandt, James Jerome II, and Cortlandt Taylor.

Like her husband, Maud Hill had a deep interest in the welfare of mankind. It was expressed throughout her life, especially in the fields of health and music, to which she gave generously of her time, talents, and money.

Hill had a great love for the West and concern for its people. During his frequent business trips, he explored it on horseback, by wagon and automobile, sleeping on the prairies, in ranch houses and primitive communities, studying the land, talking and listening to people. It was said that he knew more people of more kinds west of the Mississippi than any other man. He believed that the basic wealth and prosperity of the nation came from the soil, and his business sense was keen enough not only to encourage the development of mining and agriculture but, once developed, to carry it as freight on the railroad.

Hill was especially interested in Montana's farming potential, and at first people laughed at his dream of turning 93 million acres of semiarid land into wheat-producing country. But in seven years, under his discerning leadership in irrigation and reclamation, Montana was shipping 25 million bushels of wheat instead of 2.5 million, and it was being shipped via the Great Northern.

He knew the lands through which the tracks were laid. He studied its history, the flora and fauna, and especially the Indian lore. He appreciated the natural splendor of Glacier National Park, working to create and preserve it, designing and constructing hotels and chalets so that visitors from other parts of the nation could enjoy its beauty. These were organized into the Glacier Park Hotel Company in 1914. To give visitors a better chance to appreciate the beauties of the Montana Rockies, Hill outfitted two open-air flat cars so that rail passengers could get a full view of the scenery as they crossed the Continental Divide.

Railroads, banking, and mining were Hill's prime interests, but this energetic man also found time for many other activities. He realized that railroads needed good access roads for shipping freight, and this led to his interest in automobiles and road building. He served as chairman of the Minnesota State Highway Commission from 1917 to 1920. In addition to being an accomplished painter and art collector, he also had a great love for music, and for a number of years he was president of the Saint Paul Orchestral Association.

His love of the outdoors was not confined to the West. Determined to make Saint Paul the most popular winter resort in America, he promoted the Saint Paul Winter Carnival in 1916 and 1917. The colorful costumes, ice palace, sporting events, and parades were a time for great festivities, and the event is continued to the present time. He was interested in developing the 4-H program and helped to organize it on a statewide basis. As a part of this effort, he arranged for special Great Northern Railway cars to transport children and their animals through many counties of rural Minnesota several years during the late 1920s.

When the depression-engendered unemployment crisis sent thousands in search of help in 1932, his interest in and commitment to others' welfare deepened. Concerned with the grave unemployment situation not only as it affected individual lives that came to his attention, but also as it was the outgrowth of an unhealthy system, Hill turned to A. A. Heckman—who then headed United Charities of Saint Paul—for advice on how he might provide short-term relief and for discussion on how fundamental changes in the system might be wrought. Because there was little public welfare money available then, the primary responsibility for relief was falling to the private sector. With Heckman's aid, Hill set up a short-term private relief effort, bringing food staples from the West aboard the Great Northern Railway.

In 1934, after studying the structure and performance of a number of foundations, trusts, and endowments, Hill established the Lexington Foundation. In keeping with his broad interests and philosophy, he created the foundation "for charitable, educational, and scientific purposes which contribute to the public welfare in such manner as shall, to its board of directors, seem best."

The fact that the foundation continues to have both trustees and directors is no accident or expression of whim. Both structure and stated objectives reflect Hill's recognition that a foundation must be a viable, flexible organization with safeguards against sterility. Foundation trustees are appointed for specific terms by the Second Judicial District Court of Minnesota. Trustees annually elect the directors who are responsible for determining policy and program, engaging staff to carry out the foundation's program and annually appointing the fiscal agent.

The foundation was renamed the Louis W. and Maud Hill Family Foundation, following Hill's death in 1948. Heckman became its first executive director in 1952 and later was named president. In 1975, the name was changed again, to Northwest Area Foundation, reflecting its growth beyond the scope of the traditional family foundation and a commitment to the region that provided its original resources. Thus, grants generally are made in the states of Minnesota, Iowa, North Dakota, South Dakota, Montana, Idaho, Oregon, and Washington.

In 1973, Heckman resigned from the foundation staff, although he remained on the board until 1979. Taking over as executive director, John D. Taylor became president in 1981. He had joined the staff in 1966.

The policy of the foundation always has been to support programs which give promise of having significant effects within their fields and for which there is no general support from other sources. Objectives are: to aid in the development of new bodies of knowledge; to assist pioneer organizations in health, science, welfare, education, and the arts and humanities; and to support projects directed toward development of a closer relationship between research and practice in the broad field of human welfare.

In translating these objectives into program, the foundation considers such factors as the critical areas in the several fields needing attention and the extent to which funds for the support of research and experimentation are available from other sources. As a result, one field or segment of it and its emerging new problems may receive greater emphasis than others in any given year or period of years.

In recent years, directors have believed that Northwest Area Foundation funds can be used most effectively in support of programs that are more narrowly focused than in the past. Therefore, requests for proposals have been developed giving guidelines and directions as to the kinds of projects the foundation will fund in certain fields. In developing these requests for proposals and in analyzing the proposals that come to the foundation in response to them, foundation staff members are aided by advisory committees made up of academic and practicing experts in the various fields.

The Northwest Area Foundation, with 1981 assets of about $132 million, makes grants in eight fields, plus a smaller number of miscellaneous awards. From its inception in 1934 through November of 1981, the foundation has awarded $10,526,075 in arts and humanities; $35,716,062 in education; $11,453,693 in environmental and physical sciences; $9,194,319 in human services; $21,223,627 in medical sciences and health; $6,850,843 in social sciences; and $932,164 in miscellaneous areas for a total of $95,896,783.

The foundation's offices are located at W-975 First National Bank Building, Saint Paul, Minnesota 55101.

For further information, see the first published report on activities, covering the period 1935 to 1953, which was published by the foundation in 1953. See also *Annual Reports* of the foundation, published continuously since 1953.

JOHN D. TAYLOR

**NORTON SIMON FOUNDATION, THE.** Norton Simon, the founder of this foundation and the Norton Simon, Inc. Museum of Art,* had a meteoric and much publicized rise in the business world. He attended college briefly in the 1920s but left for a stint of buying and selling in the stock market. Taking $35,000 he made there, he acquired control of a bankrupt California food company in 1931 which became the base and/or organization for acquisition by Simon of companies such as Hunt Foods and Industries, Inc., Canada Dry Corporation, and McCall Corporation and their eventual merger into Norton Simon, Inc., a multibillion-dollar conglomerate corporation. In addition, Simon acquired substantial or controlling interests in a significant number of other corporations. Reportedly a millionaire by his late twenties, Simon subsequently became a much wealthier man as the result of these business activities spanning a half century.

Simon began the collection of art works, which have brought him both praise and criticism in the art world, at about the same time, 1952, that he established the Norton Simon Foundation and the Norton Simon, Inc. Museum of Art, 1954, in California. Initially, the foundation was a relatively small one. Its assets in

1958 amounted to about $417,000, and it made grants for that year of about $14,000. Since then, as the following approximate sample figures attest, the foundation has had sizable increases in assets: 1969—$39 million; 1975—$90 million; 1980—$219 million.

During the 1960s and early 1970s, the Simon Foundation program consisted almost entirely of the purchase of works of art. In 1964, for example, some $15 million was spent by the foundation for the purchase, "lock, stock, and barrel, including the building," of New York's Duveen Brothers, one of the world's leading art galleries. Occasionally such acquisitions involved Norton Simon and the foundation in controversy. In 1974, for example, the "Shivapuram Nataraja," a tenth-century Indian bronze, was the subject of a celebrated dispute between the Indian government and Norton Simon and his two foundations. The Indian government brought a $2.5 million suit against Norton Simon, the foundations, and the art dealer who sold the bronze to him, alleging that it had been stolen from an Indian temple. An agreement was finally reached whereby, after ten years on display at the Norton Simon Museum of Art, the "Natajara" would be returned to India.

Simon's move, in 1974, from the collection of art to its exhibition engendered considerably more controversy. This involved the taking of control, through funding provided it by the Norton Simon Foundation and the Norton Simon, Inc. Museum of Art, of the then debt-ridden Pasadena (California) Museum of Modern Art. Several members of the old board of trustees of the Pasadena museum resigned, alleging Simon was engaged in the same ruthless take-over procedures he followed in business. They also expressed displeasure at his announced intention of downplaying the modern art works held by the museum. By the fifth anniversary (1980) of the opening of the now-named Norton Simon Museum of Art, however, one well-known curator of art stated that the museum was "the finest museum established in America since World War II, thanks to the consistently high quality of the works he's [Simon] collected"(*New York Times,* [February 24, 1980], p. 27).

The museum's holdings today are in excess of five thousand works and are conservatively worth in the hundreds of millions of dollars. They include such treasures as Raphael's "Madonna" and a still life by Zurbarán, as well as those by Matisse, Picasso, and dozens of other renowned names. Drawings by Claude Lorrain, Rembrandt etchings, 350 prints by Goya, together with sculptures represented by Rodin, Moore, and David Smith are also included in its holdings.

The Norton Simon Foundation is governed by an eight-member board of trustees. The foundation and the Norton Simon, Inc. Museum of Art are only nominally distinct. Their boards and directors are interlocking and have substantially the same slates of directors and officers, with Norton Simon serving as president of each. They have common headquarters and make use of joint offices at 411 West Colorado Boulevard, Pasadena, California 91105. Close by is the Norton Simon Museum of Art at Colorado and Orange Grove, Pasadena, California 91105. The nineteen-member board of directors includes Norton Simon and several friends and associates from the Hollywood world, with Jennifer Jones Simon, Norton Simon's wife, serving as chairman.

Almost the only additional information readily available to the public on this foundation and the Norton Simon, Inc. Museum of Art are the annual reports and returns filed by it with the Internal Revenue Service, and the various Foundation Center publications. See, however, the following articles about Norton Simon which, while journalistic, are informative about him and his foundations. In the *New York Times*: Milton Esterow, "Norton Simon Foundation to Buy Mansion and $15 Million Art Collection of Duveen Gallery" (April 21, 1964), p. 27; Grace Glueck, "Million in Norton Simon Funds to Aid Pasadena Art Museum"(October 22, 1974), p. 20; Grace Glueck, "Simon Control of Museum Stirs Controversy" (December 30, 1974), p. 8; and Grace Glueck, "The Simon Museum—'The Fief of a Private Acquisitor' " (February 24, 1980), pp. 20, 27. See also "Collectors, the Abstract Businessmen," *Time* (June 5, 1964); David C. Smith, "Not-So-Simple Simon," *Wall Street Journal* (March 4, 1965), p. 1; and Walter McQuade, "Norton Simon's Great Museum Caper," *Fortune* (August 25, 1980), pp. 78, 79, 81, 82, 84.

**NORTON SIMON, INC. MUSEUM OF ART.** Set up in Pasadena, California, in 1954, as the Hunt Foods Charitable Foundation, the foundation's name was changed in 1958 to Hunt Foods and Industries Foundation and then to Norton Simon, Inc. Museum of Art in 1969. It was funded initially by predecessors of Norton Simon, Inc., a for-profit corporation controlled by Norton Simon, and subsequently by it and its subsidiaries. The initial assets of this philanthropy were larger than those of the Norton Simon Foundation,* a sister organization. In 1958, for example, its assets of $1 million were more than twice as large as those of the Norton Simon Foundation. In 1980, the museum's assets were about $147 million, compared to the foundation's approximate $219 million.

One of if not the principal purposes of the museum has been the same as that of the Norton Simon Foundation—purchases of works of art and their loan to major public museums for exhibition.

In 1974, the Pasadena Museum of Modern Art was transformed into the Norton Simon Museum of Art. This is a true museum and not to be confused with the Norton Simon, Inc. Museum of Art, which since that time, along with the Norton Simon Foundation, has provided major support for the museum. In addition, the Norton Simon, Inc. Museum of Art has consistently carried on an auxiliary general grants program which has provided support for health and welfare organizations, educational institutions, and other arts and cultural groups.

The genesis of the two Simon foundations lies with Norton Simon. Although their funding may have been different, their offices, operations, officers, and governing-board structures are intertwined. For these reasons, the reader should consult the Norton Simon Foundation entry, herein, for background and additional information on the Norton Simon, Inc. Museum of Art.

**NOYES FOUNDATION.** See Jessie Smith Noyes Foundation, Inc.

# O

**OLD DOMINION FOUNDATION.** See Andrew W. Mellon Foundation, The.

**OLIN FOUNDATION, INC.** The Olin Foundation was incorporated in New York in 1938 by industrialist Franklin Walter Olin, who was described as one of the wealthiest men in the Mississippi Valley. Born in Vermont, Olin, under his father's tutelage, had worked as a millwright. He eventually graduated from Cornell University and by the 1890s was constructing black-powder plants in New Jersey, Pennsylvania, and West Virginia. In 1892, he established the Equitable Powder Manufacturing Co., and in 1896 he founded the Western Cartridge Company, of East Alton, Illinois. From these beginnings he developed a group of munitions manufacturing companies that served as a major wartime supplier to the United States and its allies. At his retirement in 1944, the group was merged into Olin Industries, which later became part of the Olin Mathieson Chemical Corporation.

From the time of its creation until the death of Franklin W. Olin in 1951, the Olin Foundation's grants generally reflected his personal charitable interests. Over the next twenty-six years, the foundation was guided by Charles L. Horn, of the Federal Cartridge Corporation, Minneapolis, Minnesota; James O. Wynn, a New York lawyer; and Ralph Clark, a former associate of Olin. The three developed for the Olin Foundation a policy of making grants to private colleges and universities for the total cost of new library and academic buildings, exclusive of administrative, physical education, and student service facilities.

The current six-member board of directors includes President Carlton T. Helming; Treasurer Robert D. Moss; William B. Horn, of Minneapolis, Minnesota; and Vice-President Lawrence W. Milas, of New York City. They have followed the directions of their predecessors in what they consider a policy that has had substantial positive impact on higher education.

All funds available for grants are derived from the investment of the original gifts made to the foundation by Franklin W. Olin and his wife, Mary. In December, 1980, the market value of the foundation's assets was $116,324,023.

During that year, the foundation paid $3,736,500 in grants but had approved $10,995,500 for future payment. Its policy of making grants for the total costs of buildings, but paying as the buildings are constructed, distributes the allocations over several years.

The Olin Foundation's primary interest is in making grants to promising private colleges and universities in the United States that offer four-year baccalaureate programs. The foundation attempts to disperse its gifts geographically. Altogether, the foundation has placed twelve buildings on campuses from Johns Hopkins University, in Baltimore, Maryland, to Whitman College, in Walla Walla, Washington, in the last ten years.

In recent years, some misunderstanding has attended the activities of the Olin Foundation because of newspaper reports that have confused the "free enterprise" program of the John M. Olin Foundation, founded in 1953 by a son of Franklin W. Olin, with the long-established educational support program of the Olin Foundation. Neither of the donor's sons, John M.Olin or Spencer T. Olin, nor the foundations that they have formed are involved in the work of the Olin Foundation, Inc.

The Olin Foundation maintains two offices that administer a united program. President Carlton T. Helming is at the Olin Foundation, Inc., 415 Foshay Tower, Minneapolis, Minnesota 55402. Vice-President Lawrence W. Milas is at the Olin Foundation, Inc., 299 Park Avenue, New York, New York 10171.

Almost the only additional information readily available to the public on this foundation are the annual reports and returns filed by it with the Internal Revenue Service, and the various Foundation Center publications. See, however, *Statement of Grant Policies and Procedures and a Report of Recent Foundation Grants* (1982), published by the foundation.

JAMES HOWELL SMITH

**OTTO BREMER FOUNDATION.** Otto Bremer (1867–1951) was born in the village of Seesen near the Hartz Mountains of Germany. The fourth of eight children born to Eduard and Mathilde Maeder Bremer, Otto completed an apprenticeship in banking and, at the age of nineteen, emigrated with his brother Adolf to the United States. They settled in Saint Paul, Minnesota, where there was a large German immigrant community. He began his banking career as a bookkeeper with the National German American Bank, became its chief clerk in 1900, and, in 1921, was elected chairman of what then became the American National Bank, then the largest independent bank in the Ninth Federal Reserve District. As stockholder, director, and chairman of the board, Otto Bremer became known as a successful banker throughout the upper Midwest, where he developed correspondent relations with many rural banks. He remained in this position for thirty years, combining with it a wide range of political, financial, and corporate activities, including the presidency of the Jacob Schmidt Brewing Company, which he assumed at the death of his brother, Adolf, in 1939. Active in community affairs, Bremer served as treasurer of the city of St. Paul for ten years, played a key role in the creation of the Minnesota Democratic Farmer-Labor Party, and was an advisor to presidents Woodrow Wilson and Franklin D. Roosevelt, the latter of whom in 1933 appointed him to direct the Minnesota division of the Home Owners Loan Corporation.

It was his participation in banking, however, that was most important to Otto Bremer. While his holdings were extensive and made him at one point the largest investor in bank stocks in the Midwest, it was his association with what he called his "countryside banks" that proved more enduring and rewarding than other partnerships. He was always invited to become a stockholder in these institutions because of his reputation as a banker, and his relationship with the country banks, which by 1933 numbered fifty-five, was characterized by support and sacrifice rather than control. One of his creeds was that banks should be home banks, independently operated by people of their communities.

His commitment to these countryside banks and their communities was unwavering. Although his holdings in these banks represented a relatively small share of his total assets, they were most important to him. During the Great Depression, Bremer liquidated many of his other assets to strengthen these community institutions, and none of them had to close. His money, he said, was to serve the community in which it was invested—first, last, and always.

Otto Bremer never married but enjoyed a very close family relationship with his brother Adolf and with his sister Frieda who lived with him throughout his life. To a great extent, the countryside banks also constituted his family, and it was his deep concern for these institutions in Minnesota, North Dakota, and Wisconsin that prompted the formation of the Otto Bremer Foundation. Realizing that his death might initiate procedures that could disrupt these banks in which he believed so strongly, he sought to insure their perpetuation and the ultimate return of his wealth to the communities they served.

The Otto Bremer Company was formed in 1943 with the transfer of Bremer's stock in the countryside banks. The Otto Bremer Foundation was created the next year and eventually received ownership of the assets of the Otto Bremer Company. As a charitable trust and a registered bank holding company, the foundation could channel back into the communities philanthropic dollars earned from the deposits made by citizens in their local Bremer bank. In this manner, Bremer's family of countryside banks could be kept together and his wealth used in service of their communities.

Currently, over 95 percent of the foundation's total assets are invested in the ownership of the Otto Bremer Company, which in turn owns majority interests in twenty-nine bank affiliates and associated insurance, building, and agricultural credit companies in Minnesota, North Dakota, and Wisconsin.

Three trustees are charged with the governance of the foundation and its wholly owned subsidiary, the Otto Bremer Company. Appointed for life and empowered to appoint their successors, the current trustees are William H. Lipschultz, Robert J. Reardon, and Gordon Shepard.

The foundation's grant-making activities are determined by the board of trustees and administered by an executive director within the framework of a trust instrument. As written in 1944, the purposes of the foundation are:

- To relieve poverty in the City of St. Paul, Minnesota.
- To establish scholarships and assist poor and deserving students in securing education in any University or College situated in the State of Minnesota and to aid such Universities to increase their efficiency.
- To provide or assist in providing physical training in schools and public grounds.
- To promote citizenship by aiding such movements as the Boy Scouts, Girl Scouts, and Camp Fire Girls.
- To advance religion by aiding in the construction or maintenance of churches, aiding in the up-building of church choirs and music, and the supply of music.
- To aid orphan and baby's homes conducted as charitable institutions.
- To promote the public health by aiding in the construction, enlargement, and maintenance of hospitals and by aiding them to purchase new surgical and other appliances used in treatment and study of human diseases.
- To aid or provide for the study of causes or cure or treatment of diseases and other human ailments.
- To aid persons suffering from catastrophy that affects a section of a community and by reason of which a call for aid to the Red Cross or the public is made.
- The beneficiaries under the foregoing Sections shall be limited to those persons, institutions, corporations, and municipalities, states, or subdivisions who are residents of or who have their situs in the State of Minnesota, or Wisconsin, or North Dakota, or Montana.

Using this instrument as a guide, the trustees update their interpretation of this trust in order to respond to the ever-changing needs of society. Currently, these purposes are organized into five broad areas of interest: community affairs, education, health, human services, and religion. While not exclusive, these comprise the principal areas of foundation funding.

Given Otto Bremer's commitment to the countryside, geography also plays an important role in determining the foundation's funding activity, with most awards going to nonprofit organizations that specifically serve those predominantly rural communities where there are Bremer bank affiliates. A smaller portion is also dedicated to programs designed to relieve poverty in the city of St. Paul, which was Otto Bremer's home and the headquarters of the foundation and company. But just as a concern for the countryside characterized Otto Bremer's career and his banking relationships, giving in rural areas continues to be the principal focus of the foundation.

In 1982, the foundation had assets of $42,409,740 and had distributed $2,361,403 in 386 grants for that year. Administration of the foundation is carried on from offices located at 700 Northwestern National Bank Building, St. Paul, Minnesota 55101.

For further information, see *Annual Reports* of the foundation, published since 1980. See also a biography of Otto Bremer being prepared by the foundation and due to be completed in 1984.

JOHN KOSTISHACK

# P

**PACKARD FOUNDATION.** See David and Lucile Packard Foundation, The.

**PARSONS FOUNDATION.** See Ralph M. Parsons Foundation, The.

**PAYNE FOUNDATION.** See Frank E. Payne and Seba B. Payne Foundation.

**PENN FOUNDATION.** See William Penn Foundation, The.

**PERMANENT CHARITY FUND OF BOSTON, COMMITTEE OF THE.** One of the oldest community foundations in the nation, the Permanent Charity Fund of Boston was established by a declaration of trust in 1915 by officers of the Boston Safe Deposit and Trust Company and incorporated in 1917. Charles E. Rogerson, president of the bank, was the first president of the fund, and his son, Charles M. Rogerson, served as its secretary and part-time director for nearly three decades. The Boston Safe Deposit and Trust Company was the foundation's sole trustee for sixty-seven years; then, in 1983, a new declaration and agreement of trust was drawn up, effecting the conversion of Permanent Charity Fund to a multiple trusteeship. The foundation's new trustees are: the Bank of New England, the Bank of Boston, the Shawmut Bank, and the State Street Bank and Trust Company. They have joined Boston Safe in the management and investment of the fund's assets.

The Committee of the Permanent Charity Fund distributes the fund's income for charitable purposes. A separate corporation, the Committee of the Permanent Charity Fund of Boston, Inc., is comprised of eleven members selected as follows: one by the attorney-general of Massachusetts, four by judicial officials of the commonwealth and the city of Boston, five by the trustees' committee, and one by the chief volunteer officer of the United Way of Massachusetts Bay. Committee members are unpaid and serve for five-year terms.

In its early years, Permanent Charity Fund grew slowly but steadily. It was the committee's practice generally to make a large number of modest grants to health and welfare agencies, family and children's societies, settlement houses, hospitals, and dispensaries. By 1945, the fund's endowment had reached about $6 million, and it was distributing approximately $250,000 annually.

The committee's grant-making policies began to change in the 1960s, as a strengthened United Way responded to the immediate needs of many health and welfare organizations and newly established government programs sought to address the problems of minorities, the poor, and the helpless.The committee decided to reduce its support of agencies' regular operating expenses in favor of an increase in allocations for innovative demonstration projects, planning and research, and building campaigns. The committee also embraced a broader view of charity, thus enabling it to include community development, inner-city housing, education, and the arts among its concerns.The substantial growth of the fund's resources during this period made it possible for the foundation to change direction in this way.

In the 1970s, the Permanent Charity Fund reduced further the number of grants it made for operating budgets and clearly enunciated its policy of being "particularly disposed to supporting" the following kinds of activities within the Greater Boston area: (1) demonstration projects that provide practical approaches to dealing with specific community problems; (2) projects that will help coordinate community services; (3) projects that provide leverage for generating other funds and community resources; (4) capital campaigns for building and renovations. In 1982, with assets of $100 million, the fund distributed $8 million to the following fields of service: social services—33 percent; education—11.9 percent; health—11.3 percent; cultural and performing arts—14.9 percent; community services planning—7.6 percent; community development and housing—6.5 percent; civic affairs and other—13.4 percent. Major representative grants included: Corporation for Boston, a citizens' advocacy organization, $20,000; Federated Dorchester Neighborhood Houses, $66,000; Project STRIVE, Scholarships for Vocational Education, $45,000; New England Medical Center Hospitals, $24,659; Local Initiatives Support Corporation, for community development projects, $250,000; and the Permanent Charity Fund Cultural Arts Fund, to preserve and encourage cultural programs with broad public appeal, $310,000.

The fund is administered from offices located at One Boston Place, Boston, Massachusetts 02106, under the direction of a director.

For further information, see *Annual Reports* of the fund, published since the 1960s; and *The Report*, published quarterly since 1980. See also an informational booklet (undated) published by the fund.

**PEW CHARITABLE TRUST.** See J. N. Pew, Jr., Charitable Trust.

**PEW FREEDOM TRUST.** See J. Howard Pew Freedom Trust.

**PEW MEMORIAL TRUST, THE.** Originally established in 1948 as the Pew Memorial Foundation, the Pew Memorial Trust is both the oldest and largest of the Pew charitable trusts. It was created in memory of Joseph Newton Pew, Sr., founder of the Sun Oil Company (now Sun Company, Inc.), and his wife, Mary Anderson Pew, by their four children, J. Howard Pew, Mary Ethel Pew, Joseph N. Pew, Jr., and Mabel Pew Myrin. Eight hundred eighty thousand shares of Sun Oil Company stock, carrying an estimated value of $50 million, were contributed in equal parts by the four children. Additional gifts were made from time to time by the same donors until June of 1956, when it was agreed that no further additions would be permitted from any source.

Joseph Newton Pew, Sr., had founded the Sun Oil Company in 1886. He was a former teacher and real estate agent whose entrepreneurial skills soon carried him to the forefront of the nation's booming oil and natural gas industries. Even before launching his own natural gas business, he had developed techniques for capping the natural gas that blew off the top of oil wells and for transporting it through pipelines. His initial ventures were confined largely to western Pennsylvania, but after an immense oil field was discovered at Spindletop, in Texas, in 1901, Pew built a refinery at Marcus Hook, on the Delaware River just south of Philadelphia, to accommodate the crude oil shipped in by tanker. Given this impetus, the Sun Oil Company grew dramatically. Joseph N. Pew, Sr., died in 1912, and his sons, Joseph N. Pew, Jr., and J. Howard, were named vice-president and president, respectively, of the Sun Oil Company. J. Howard served as president for thirty-five years, until 1947. During his tenure, Sun Oil began to make its first substantial inroads into the American market.

The Sun Oil Company, now known as Sun Company, was the family's primary financial interest. Although Sun Company common stock comprised a large portion of the Pew Memorial Trust's assets, a percentage of the assets were in the General Crude Oil Company of Houston and other holdings. By 1975, these other assets were sold and the proceeds used to diversify the investment portfolio. Despite the wide diversity of investments, the majority of the assets remain in Sun stock.

The board of directors of the Pew Memorial Foundation met for the first time on April 3, 1948, and made the first grant, of $30,000 to the Southeastern Pennsylvania Chapter of the American National Red Cross, to assist flood victims in Pennsylvania. In 1957, the foundation was restructured and its assets transferred to the Pew Memorial Trust. The purpose of the trust was stated in the originating documents, namely the provision of financial support for "purely religious, charitable, scientific, literary, or educational purposes...all in the promotion of the public welfare."

At the same time, the Glenmede Trust Company was named sole trustee for the trust. The company itself had been created only one year earlier, in 1956, and had been chartered under the banking statutes of the commonwealth of Pennsylvania. This new company was named after "Glenmede," the Bryn Mawr, Pennsylvania, estate of Mr. and Mrs. Joseph N. Pew, Sr. The name was derived from the family name of Glenn (Joseph N. Pew, Sr.'s, mother was Nancy Lee Glenn) and the meadow that was part of the estate.

The structure of the Glenmede Trust Company is unusual. Although it conducts a broad range of fiduciary business for the general public, it has no commercial banking powers. It administers and acts as trustee for numerous accounts, including personal trusts, pension funds, and investment advisory accounts. When the four brothers and sisters who established the Pew Memorial Trust later set up their own charitable trusts, the Glenmede Trust Company became administrator and trustee for these trusts as well. The major discretionary trusts include the Mary Anderson Trust, the Mabel Pew Myrin Trust,* and the J. Howard Pew Freedom Trust,* all established in 1957. The J. N. Pew, Jr., Charitable Trust* was set up in 1963, the Knollbrook Trust in 1965, and the Mary Ethel Pew Medical Trust in 1982. June, 1979, marked the death of Mary Ethel Pew, the last survivor of the four founders of the Pew Memorial Trust.

The Glenmede Trust Company, with offices located at 229 South Eighteenth Street, Philadelphia, Pennsylvania 19103, acts as trustee for all of the trusts. Administration of the trusts is carried on under the direction of an officer of the company. Thus, all applications for grants to any one of the trusts come to the company, which, in turn, directs these proposals to the appropriate trusts for action.

Initially, grants from the Pew Memorial Trust were made predominantly in the Philadelphia area to a wide variety of organizations that represented specific interests of the four founders. While the size and scope of the grants were small in comparison to those today, the diversity was considerable. The assets of the Pew Memorial Trust, the range of its grant-making activities, and the size of the charitable trust staff grew steadily over the years. A total of $12.5 million was awarded in the first ten years of the foundation's existence. In 1973 alone, $13.5 million was distributed, and in 1977, this figure more than doubled as payouts from the trust totalled $28.8 million. Fifty-one million dollars was distributed in 1981. The increase in funding capabilities in the 1970s and 1980s was due primarily to the increased value of assets in the portfolio of the Pew Memorial Trust which were valued at slightly over $1 billion in 1980. As a result of the appreciable growth of the trust and the opportunities it attracted, a deliberate and methodical shift in procedures and methods has evolved for funding organizations in the Philadelphia area as well as across the country.

The trust's first grant, to the American Red Cross, had been given anonymously, and for many years all grants from the Pew Memorial Trust were given in this way. This procedure was rooted in the founders' deep religious convictions that true charity should be a private matter between God and the human conscience, and thus, the Glenmede Trust Company then published no annual reports (other than those required by the Internal Revenue Service) on its stewardship of the Pew Memorial Trust.

By 1972, however, the changing climate for private philanthropy, as well as the legal requirements of accountability, led the Glenmede Trust Company board of directors to change this procedure. The first news release relating to a Pew Memorial Trust grant was approved in November, 1972, with a $200,000 grant from the Pew Memorial Trust for a gymnasium in the Zion Baptist Church's Community Building, in Philadelphia. The first annual report for the Pew Memorial Trust was published for the year 1979. These public reports now provide an annual summary of all current projects and an overview of the trust's directions during each year.

In recent years, grants from the Pew Memorial Trust have been directed toward four primary areas: health care, education, human services, and the arts and the humanities. As with most foundations, the grant requests received by the trust far exceed those which it can support. For every grant approved many worthy requests must be declined. In order to respond adequately to changing conditions and increased demand, there is a need for frequent reevaluation and development of specific guidelines for funding consideration.

In 1980 and 1981, symposia on both the needs of medicine and health care, and on the problems of independent higher education, respectively, were conducted to evaluate past activity as well as new approaches to funding in these areas. The meeting of a Health Advisory Group, in January, 1980, resulted in a dramatic change in focus for health-care support. The majority of the trust's health and medical grants, prior to 1980, had been awarded primarily in the Philadelphia area for hospital construction, patient equipment, or for a variety of programs in specific disease research. These categories of grants were virtually eliminated as funding priorities. In light of national patterns of health-care delivery and financing, it was decided that the trust's traditional support of hospitals was no longer the most appropriate use of private funds. Funding priorities shifted in 1980 to the health sciences, policy research, and the training of health-care professionals, as well as to innovative programs leading either to the containment of health-care costs or to significant improvements in the delivery of and access to health care. As an example of this change in direction, in December of 1980, the trust funded a program to investigate and disseminate strategies leading to a competitive health-care system. Conducted by a health-care research organization, this program resulted in a series of seminars and investigations to help accelerate the progress of health-system change in communities around the country. Such programs had not been considered by the trustee prior to the reevaluation of health-care support.

Funding in the education field has also taken new direction in the 1980s, due in part to the establishment of an Education Advisory Group, which held its initial meeting in February of 1981. In the early years, the grant making to colleges and universities was of a general nature, and funds were appropriated for either "operations" or "capital projects." In more recent years, funding has become increasingly project and program oriented, and, as a result of the 1981 meeting, the guidelines are increasingly more issue oriented. Renovations and occasionally construction of academic facilities are funded, but no support is given for scholarships, two-year community colleges, or for nonacademic facilities. Special emphasis is directed toward programs that aim to strengthen existing academic systems, such as programs that encourage the realignment of existing curricula to address better the value of liberal arts study at a time when an increasing number of students are demanding specific career-based courses. For example, in 1980, the trust funded studies to redefine the meaning of baccalaureate degrees and to consider major changes in undergraduate study programs and policies.

Human-service grants are directed toward programmatic, operational, and capital needs. Emphasis is placed on programs that offer productivity and independence for needy people. Within the cultural field, support is given in many categories of the arts and the humanities to promote the development and maintenance of artistic excellence, particularly in Philadelphia but also, selectively, on a national basis. Segments that receive funding include dance, music, museums, drama, literature, and historical preservation. Grants are made for new programs, operational support, and for capital improvements.

The Glenmede Trust Company would like to retain the trust's historic patterns of support while at the same time be able to leverage its dollars in areas that realistically address today's priority needs, as expounded in the above examples. To this end, the underlying philosophical intent of the founders has remained strongly emphasized. Careful stewardship of the trust's resources has made possible the continuation and expansion of the founders' vision to promote public welfare and to help meet human needs. Within broadly stated aims, the Glenmede Trust Company, as trustee, must weigh hard choices in its decisions about grant making. To be effective, foundation dollars should be carefully directed, and the trustee must regularly assess the resources, interests, and priorities for the trust. Growing resources, along with the pressure of society's ever-increasing needs, have led the trust to expand its operations. A grants-management system was developed to process all incoming proposals in order to handle efficiently the increasing number of grant requests received each year. Each proposal is logged in and reviewed to determine if the request falls within current funding guidelines. Applications are then reviewed by a trust officer and assigned to a program analyst or associate for in-depth analysis. Site visits are made, when appropriate, and outside consultants are sometimes asked to provide a technical evaluation. Each grant application, therefore, passes through a number of reviews before a recommendation is made to the board of directors. The board renders the final decision on each proposal at grant-making meetings held six times during the year.

The company maintains a relatively small staff composed of individuals with broad backgrounds and strong analytical skills, rather than a large staff or experts on numerous narrowly defined disciplines. When particular knowledge or expertise is required in an area of funding consideration, specific analysis of ideas and proposals is developed with the assistance of outside consultants. This system provides great flexibility in allowing funding directions to change with future conditions.

The Pew Memorial Trust regularly revises its outlook in response to the changing needs of society. The focus and direction of grant making is flexible, depending on current needs, but the trustee's aim to provide both leverage and impact from funds does not change. Philanthropic giving by the Pew Memorial Trust is designed to aim to improve the quality of life. The Glenmede Trust Company, as trustee, seeks to support organizations and programs that not only demonstrate the promise of solving real needs in health care, education, human services, and the arts and the humanities, but attempts to do so in a way that is cognizant and respectful of the necessity to produce self-respect, pride, and freedom.

Because of its earlier anonymity policy, biographical and bibliographical material about the early history and activities of the Pew Memorial Trust is limited. Beginning in the 1970s, however, the foundation has publicized its programs and operations and has published *Annual Reports* continuously since 1979. See, too, "Joseph Newton Pew, Jr.," *Dictionary of American Biography*, Supplement Seven (1980), pp. 615–616.

NANCY KLINGHOFFER

**PHILADELPHIA FOUNDATION, THE.** The Philadelphia Foundation was created in 1918 by a resolution of the directors of the Fidelity Trust Company "for the promotion of charitable, educational and civic purposes in the City of Philadelphia and the Commonwealth of Pennsylvania." The foundation was the idea of William Purves Gest, then president of the Fidelity Trust Company. Gest modeled the Philadelphia Foundation after the Cleveland Foundation,* the first community foundation, which had been established four years before in Cleveland, Ohio, by Frederick Goff. Gest had been associated with Fidelity Trust since 1889, serving as an assistant to his father, John B. Gest, who was then vice-president of the bank. William Gest became Fidelity's president in 1915 and later, in 1926, became chairman of the board of its consolidated successor, the Fidelity-Philadelphia Trust Company. He served in this position until his death in 1939.

The Philadelphia Foundation is primarily designed to serve the needs of the five Greater Philadelphia counties of Bucks, Chester, Delaware, Montgomery, and Philadelphia. While a few donors specify that the income derived from their gifts be used elsewhere, the majority of the grants are awarded in the Philadelphia area.

The trustee structure of banks supporting the Philadelphia Foundation has expanded from William P. Gest's single Fidelity Trust Company to eight major Philadelphia banks. A person wishing to establish a trust fund with the Philadelphia Foundation simply contacts one of the participating banks or a foundation staff member, indicating an intent to make a gift. A bequest format is used, and the donor then decides in which category of funds he would like his gift to be placed.

The Philadelphia Foundation has four types of funds. "Class I" funds designate the recipient to whom the donor intends the proceeds from his gift to be awarded, for example, a particular community service or educational institution. The foundation honors the donor's specific intentions, but should the designated recipient of the donor's bequest cease to exist, the foundation can employ the doctrine of *cy-pres* whereby the original intent of the donor is carried out in a closely related area. This can be done without costly court procedures. One of the foundation's annual reports related the sad tale of an orphan's home in Texas that, some years ago, was handsomely supported by the wishes of a generous donor. However, the orphanage was later forced to consider closing its doors as the donor's provisions stipulated that for the institution to continue receiving support, the candidates for the orphanage had to be minus *both* parents–the absence of one simply would not do. As "complete" orphans were increasingly hard to come by, the institution was having difficulty taking advantage of the gift. In this instance, the doctrine of *cy-pres* would have ameliorated the problem. The Philadelphia Foundation desires that the intent of the donor's wishes be honored to the letter; however, it makes little sense not to be able to make adaptations as future circumstances dictate. Indeed, a hallmark of this and other community foundations is permanence tempered with flexibility.

"Class II" funds give the foundation somewhat greater latitude in the disbursement of the proceeds of the donor's gift. The donor selects "one or more specific types of human service or geographic areas as beneficiaries," and the foundation chooses recipients from the specified areas for the awarding of grants. With "Class III" funds, the donor selects types of recipients for consideration, and the foundation awards grants to these agencies when possible.

Finally, "Class IV" is a completely undesignated category. The donor permits the foundation to employ the funds where they are needed the most.

For the year 1980–1981, the Philadelphia Foundation distributed a total of $2,646,313. Of this sum, 23 percent was drawn from Class I funds, 31 percent was from Class II, 37 percent was from Class III, and from Class IV, the unrestricted category, the amount disbursed was 9 percent of the total.

The foundation currently funds projects that deal with the Philadelphia community, including the culture, education, and health of its people. The foundation usually does not make grants to individuals, national organizations, private schools, research projects, or government agencies. Also, normally it will not support capital expenditures or fund-deficit financing. In addition, the foundation does not make grants that will be used for sectarian religious purposes. However, exceptions to these restrictions can occur when stipulated in the donor's trust instrument.

The initial years of the Philadelphia Foundation's existence were marked by rather modest growth. The first donor, Rachel L. Coles, gave, in 1920, the sum of $628.02. This amount was divided among six Philadelphia hospitals. A second fund was established in 1924 with a value of $4510.25, but by 1946, the funds held in trust had a market value in excess of $1,250,000, with an annual net income exceeding $48,000 available for charitable uses. Still, for the forty years following its founding, the Philadelphia Foundation was a relatively small community foundation, with no staff other than a Fidelity-Philadelphia Trust Company trust officer handling its paperwork when the need arose. It was not until the fall of 1958 that a professional executive director for the foundation, Richard K. Bennett, was appointed. His arrival coincided with five other banks joining the Fidelity-Philadelphia Trust Company (in 1968, the Fidelity Bank) as trustee institutions for the Philadelphia Foundation. From this point, the foundation underwent two substantial changes—a marked increase in the amount of trust funds at its disposal, with an allied rise in the level of distributable resources, and a shift in the type of recipient of the foundation's funds, toward those social service institutions and activities that dealt closely with the everyday life of the underprivileged citizen who lived in the inner-city sections of Philadelphia.

Certainly, such changes can be attributed to a national evolution in social thinking that took place in the 1960s, but the change in direction of the foundation and improvement in finances can also be traced to the arrival of Richard K. Bennett and his successor in 1961, Sidney N. Repplier, and an augmented professional staff who guided the foundation. Bennett and Repplier, for example, made concerted efforts to acquaint potential donors in the Philadelphia area with the advantages of establishing trust funds with the Philadelphia Foundation.

Thus, by 1964, the traditional emphasis on grants to "Hospitals and Nursing" had dropped from the 1959–1960 level of 25.6 percent to 10.8 percent, while 17.1 percent of the funds now went to "Youth Group Work"—up from 6.6 percent in 1959–1960. In addition, 8.58 percent was devoted to the category, "Aesthetics," which was adopted in 1959–1960 and involved support of art, theatre, and music for the Philadelphian of modest means.

In 1956, income available for distribution from the funds comprising the Philadelphia Foundation was $162,813. Five years later, in 1961, the figure had risen to $401,135. And in 1968, distributable income had increased to $2,177,919.

Disbursements kept pace with the increase in assets. In 1956, $162,465 was granted, while in 1961, this amount rose to $407,604 and in 1968 approached $2,046,000.

During the decade of the seventies, the foundation continued to serve the more traditional recipients of its funds, such as family service organizations, educational institutions, and child-care facilities, but it also continued its expansion of support to nontraditional groups. In 1971–1972, for example, the foundation disbursed $200,000 to twenty organizations which were active in the field of justice for people of limited means. Foundation grants enabled the Pennsylvania Prison Society to establish an ombudsman to the city's Holmesburg Prison. Also, during that same period, the foundation supported the Lawyer's Committee for Civil Rights Under Law, an organization specializing in discrimination cases in housing, justice, and education. The foundation made grants to the National Caucus on Black Aged, the Presbyterian-University of Pennsylvania Medical Center's clinic for sickle-cell anemia, the Philadelphia Orchestra for a program of visits by groups of its musicians to inner-city schools, and the children's television show, "Sesame Street."

In 1973–1974, the Philadelphia Foundation added a new funding category entitled "Human Rights and Justice," which, according to the annual report for that year, "represents an effort to bring hope, dignity and betterment of the human condition to those who have been powerless far too long—the aged, poor, women, prisoners, mental patients and the like." And throughout the remainder of the 1970s, up until the present time, the foundation has continued to support programs such as "Options for Women, Inc.," which sponsored upward career mobility workshops and affirmative action programs, and neighborhood arts and recreation centers offering inner-city children a chance to develop special skills and broaden their horizons.

Another unique, nontraditional program was begun in 1976 which made fuel funds available for needy Philadelphia residents. The fuel program has been expanded, so at the present time, more than five thousand children and elderly persons receive its benefits during the winter months.

The administrative structure of the Philadelphia Foundation is formed by the director, his administrative staff, the trustees committee, the distribution committee, and the advisory committee. The trustees committee, which consists of the presidents of the eight trustee banks, appoints three of the seven members of the distribution committee. This latter body meets twice a year to disburse the foundation's distributable funds to the appropriate recipients. The remaining four members of the committee are appointed by the officers of the Chamber of Commerce of Greater Philadelphia; the officers of the Philadelphia Bar Association; the presidents of Drexel University, Temple University, and the University of Pennsylvania; and the officers of the Community Services Planning Council of Southeastern Pennsylvania.

The advisory committee is appointed by the distribution committee and consists of persons with an interest and background in philanthropy who also possess special competence in fields such as education, health, welfare, arts, and humanities.

With 1981 assets of about $34 million, administration of the Philadelphia Foundation is carried on from offices located diagonally across from the Philadelphia City Hall, at 1502 Two Girard Plaza, Philadelphia, Pennsylvania 19102, under the direction of the incumbent director, John R. Ruthrauff.

For further information, see *Annual Reports* of the foundation, published 1960 through 1962; *Biennial Reports*, 1964 through 1972; and *Annual Reports*, 1973 to the present. See also an informational booklet, published by the foundation in 1956; Lillian Gest (daughter of the founder of the foundation), *The Philadelphia Foundation: Brief Biographies of the Donors of Memorial Funds* (1974); and *The Directory of Pennsylvania Foundations* (1981).

JOHN SOBOTKA

**PHILLIPS FOUNDATION, THE.** The Phillips Foundation was incorporated in 1944 in Minnesota and funded by Jay Phillips and his immediate family. The foundation by 1982 had assets of $35 million.

The broad purposes of the Phillips Foundation are to provide funding for higher education including medical and theological education, for health, Jewish welfare and temple support, cultural programs, community funds, hospitals, and for youth agencies. Foundation contributions in 1982 were approximately three million dollars, with nearly one-third of this funding being allocated to educational institutions. Approximately 20 percent of 1982 funding was for hospitals and medical research, with particular emphasis in the field of ophthalmology. Another 20 percent of grant funds went toward the support of Jewish welfare agencies, such as the Minneapolis Federation for Jewish Service, and for synagogues. Other recipients of foundation support included public radio and television, the United Way, YMCA, YWCA, and the Boy Scouts.

While the Phillips Foundation has no geographic restrictions on its giving, the majority of grants is awarded to organizations located in Minnesota. Organizations in Colorado, California, and New York have, however, also received support, as have a significant number of Israeli institutions.

The Phillips Foundation, in 1968, established the Phillips Chair in Jewish Studies, at St. John's University, Collegeville, Minnesota. This was the first time such a chair had been installed in a Roman Catholic university in the United States. The foundation has also funded an outreach program at the University of Denver designed for Jewish people residing in sparsely populated areas of Colorado. Major support is also provided for the Jewish Theological Seminary of America, in New York. The Phillips-Wangensteen Building on the campus of the University of Minnesota was funded in part by the Phillips Foundation in honor of the renowned surgeon,Owen Wangensteen. This building houses the university's health sciences and auxiliary departments.

The Phillips Foundation is governed by a ten-member board of directors, a number of whom are members of the Phillips family and with Jay Phillips acting as president. The foundation is administered from offices located at Midwest Plaza, West Building, Minneapolis, Minnesota 55402, under the direction of an executive director.

Almost the only additional information readily available to the public on this foundation are the annual reports and returns filed by it with the Internal Revenue Service, and the various Foundation Center publications.

JOHN C. KILKELLY

**PHOEBE WATERMAN FOUNDATION.** See William Penn Foundation, The.

**PITTSBURGH FOUNDATION, THE.** This community foundation, the Pittsburgh Foundation, was established in 1945 by a declaration of trust and bank resolution. The assets of the foundation, originally consisting of three small grants, were relatively modest during its first few years of existence. By the early 1950s, however, its assets had increased to several million dollars, and it was making grants of approximately $100,000 annually. Grants were generally limited to the Pittsburgh area and were awarded primarily to other organizations for fellowships and scholarships, and for palliative giving through case-work services of established agencies.

By 1958, the foundation's assets, which were tied up in sixty-seven different funds, had grown to almost $7 million and its grants for the year amounted to over $400,000. By that time, the foundation's grants were used largely for programs of research, demonstration, and experiments in new fields, and to support special projects of regularly established agencies, almost all of which were located within the Pittsburgh area. Child care, education, youth agencies, hospitals, community planning, social welfare, and the arts were areas that received foundation support.

In the 1960s and 1970s, the Pittsburgh Foundation's assets continued to grow. In 1969, they amounted to over $17 million; in 1975, assets reached almost $23 million; and, in 1981, they stood at about $43 million. Grants have increased proportionately–they amounted in 1981 to over $4 million.

Major areas of foundation giving in 1981 were education, the arts, health, children and youth, and social services. Representative major grants for that year in these areas were made to: University of Pittsburgh—$45,000; the Pittsburgh Symphony Society—$1,859,648; The Presbyterian Association on Aging—$40,000; Boys' Club of Western Pennsylvania—$24,000; Housing Opportunities, Incorporated—$50,000; and Allegheny General Hospital—$50,000.

At the present time, about 60 percent of the foundation's income is derived from restricted funds and 40 percent from discretionary funds. The former are funds the donor of which has specified the general purpose for which his or her gift is to be expended. In such case, the donor leaves the selection of the particular expenditure to the decision of the foundation's distribution committee. In recent years, the foundation has used its discretionary funds almost wholly to support programs which provide direct human services. All grants on behalf of individuals for scholarships and grants to churches and hospitals are made only from restricted funds. As in the past, grants are primarily limited to the Pittsburgh area.

Four Pittsburgh banks have served and continue to serve as trustees and managers of the gifts which have been made to the foundation. The foundation's distribution committee is responsible for grant-making policy and distribution of the funds turned over to it by the trustees. This committee consists of nine citizens of the Pittsburgh area appointed by the committee and by various public officials of the area.

Administration of the foundation is carried on from offices located at 301 Fifth Avenue, Pittsburgh, Pennsylvania 15222, which it shares with the Howard Heinz Endowment.* Also, the executive director of the Heinz Endowment acts as director and chief executive officer of the Pittsburgh Foundation.

For further information, See *Annual Reports* of the foundation, published since the 1950s.

**POST FOUNDATION.** See Marjorie Merriweather Post Foundation of D.C., The.

**PRUDENTIAL FOUNDATION, THE.** Community involvement and social responsibility have been Prudential's way of doing business throughout its history, spanning more than a century. John Dryden, founder of the Prudential Insurance Company of America, set the stage for the company's future efforts by expecting agents and supervisors in branch offices to become active members of the communities in which they worked.

That attitude of involvement sometimes was manifested in dramatic situations. For instance, in 1917, when a munitions ship exploded in Halifax, Nova Scotia, Prudential insurance agents dashed to the scene to handle claims from victims. But first they spent long hours helping to rescue the injured, digging through debris, carrying stretchers, and handing out food, blankets, and clothing at aid stations.

In more recent years, Prudential has "loaned" the services of professional and executive employees to private organizations, federal agencies, and city and state governments who seek the company's help in revamping their operations. It has been a solid supporter of the United Way and has long provided cash contributions to educational institutions and other nonprofit organizations.

It wasn't until the 1960s, however, that the Prudential Insurance Company began to formulate a structured, targeted approach to corporate giving and social involvement. In response to turmoil in American cities—including a 1967 disturbance in Newark, New Jersey, Prudential's home-office city—the company began an ongoing program of pumping badly needed investment dollars into America's cities. In the program's first five years, Prudential committed $333 million in high-risk, low-interest social investments. Currently, social investments are budgeted at $50 million annually.

Prudential Insurance Company's cash contributions to nonprofit organizations grew from about a half-million dollars in the early 1960s to more than $6 million in 1981. To coordinate and administer these increased contributions, the company established the Prudential Foundation in December, 1977, with a $50 million appropriation.

The Prudential Foundation is a not-for-profit organization governed by an eight-member trustee board and six officers. In its short existence, the foundation has awarded some $15 million in grants to organizations and in gifts to match employee contributions to educational institutions.

When granting funds, the foundation gives highest priority to projects in areas of education, health, urban affairs, and minority assistance. Other grant categories include business and economic research and education, culture, conservation and ecology, public afffairs, and United Way. The foundation's aim is to help improve the quality of life in our country by supporting organizations which are working to solve social problems. Where needed, the foundation will help develop new or more effective solutions to these problems.

As one of Newark's corporate leaders, Prudential is strongly committed to projects that can help to better that city. A substantial portion of foundation dollars goes to programs in the Newark area. Grant priority also is given to U.S.

cities where Prudential home offices are located: Bellaire (Houston), Texas; Boston, Massachusetts; Chicago, Illinois; Fort Washington, Pennsylvania; Jacksonville, Florida; Los Angeles, California; Minneapolis, Minnesota; and South Plainfield, New Jersey.

But grants are only one way that the foundation achieves its goal of helping to change society for the better. The foundation may also request use of company personnel and facilities, in combination with the resources of other institutions, in order to get the results it is seeking.

This has resulted in some innovative and successful joint programs. For instance, in 1980 the foundation worked with the national council of the Girl Scouts of the U.S.A. and Prudential's own printing office to produce the first Spanish-language edition of the Girl Scout Handbook and Leaders Guide.

In another situation, the foundation awarded a grant to the Support Center, a nonprofit management consulting firm that helps nonprofit organizations. The Support Center, in turn, is providing planning and fund-raising assistance to other foundation grant recipients.

For another project, the foundation is teaming up with Prudential's social investment area, the Prudential Property and Casualty Insurance Company, and with the Neighborhood Housing Services of America to rehabilitate urban housing. A $120,000 foundation grant and a $5 million social investment loan are providing financial resources for Neighborhood Housing Services. But going a step further, Prudential is introducing experimental homeowners insurance for the homes undergoing rehabilitation. Moreover, Prudential personnel are helping Neighborhood Housing Services to operate existing programs and develop new ones.

The foundation plans to continue this program of imaginative grant making, using many of Prudential's resources to help assure a healthy society. However, changing social needs and trends will affect the thrust of future foundation efforts.

For example, as the number of older Americans increases, the foundation is getting more involved in funding projects affecting the elderly. It is increasing its support of health-screening fairs, educational programs, and public policy research. The foundation also plans to place more emphasis on the areas of urban affairs, especially economic development and job creation; minority affairs; and family-oriented and neighborhood self-help projects.

As all levels of government reduce support for nonprofit organizations, then business, the private sector, and individual citizens will have to shoulder additional financial responsibility to ensure the continuation of many beneficial services. Consequently, the Prudential Foundation will become increasingly involved in funding projects with other corporations and in joint public-private initiatives.

Whatever direction the foundation moves in, Prudential will aim to be more than a financial arm doling out dollars. Through the foundation, with 1981 assets of about $34 million, and the effective use of company resources and personnel, Prudential plans to be a positive force in the world in which it operates.

The foundation is governed by an eight-member board of trustees who are officers or directors of the Prudential Insurance Company of America. Administration of the foundation is carried on from offices located at 15 Prudential Plaza, Newark, New Jersey 07101.

For further information, see *Annual Reports* of the foundation, published since 1979. See also the following articles: Leah Berton, "It's the Giving That Counts," *Prudential Magazine* (Winter, 1979), pp. 3, 6; Alex Plinio, "Corporate Gift Matching: Seek and You Will Find," *Fund Raising Management* (March, 1981), pp. 24, 31; Alex Plinio, "How Corporate Giving Works," *The Philanthropy Monthly* (April, 1981), pp. 8, 11.

CARLA CAPIZZI

**PUBLIC WELFARE FOUNDATION, INC.** Established in Texas in 1947, the Public Welfare Foundation was reincorporated in Delaware in 1951. It was founded by Charles Edward Marsh, a native of Ohio, who spent his entire adult life in the newspaper business. His major premise was that one should use one's talents and energy for the good of the community and humanity. In carrying out this belief, Marsh performed many public services during his lifetime but always sought to avoid publicity concerning his philanthropic activities. It is for this reason that the foundation which he set up does not bear his name. Rather, it verbalizes his beliefs.

In addition to owning a number of newspapers, Marsh was active in other businesses, such as oil, gas, banking, and real estate, He donated three of his newspapers—*The Spartanburg [South Carolina] Herald and Journal, The Tuscaloosa [Alabama] News,* and the *Gadsden [Alabama] Times*—to the foundation, and their operation provides the income for its charitable giving.

Marsh died in 1964. By the end of the 1960s, the assets of the Public Welfare Foundation had grown to approximately $12 million and annual grants amounted to $500,000. In 1980, the foundation's assets were around $46 million and its grants amounted to about $2 million annually. The foundation's program is worldwide, with some 150 grants per year in the areas of emergency relief, medical services, education, aged and child welfare, and community development. Support is generally for start-up and self-help projects and emergency needs and, in some cases, continuing programs. Grants for 1979–1980 ranged from a high of $100,000, for continued support of the operation of a hospital boat on the Amazon River, to a low of $1,000 to Grace Episcopal Church, Washington, D.C., for a needy Nigerian student.

An eleven-member board of directors, which includes the founder's widow, Claudia Haines Marsh, and her son, Davis Haines, governs the foundation's operations. Administration of the foundation is carried on from offices located at 2600 Virginia Avenue, N.W., Room 505, Washington, D.C. 20037, under the direction of a chief executive officer.

For further information, see *Annual Reports* of the foundation, published continuously since the 1970s.

# R

**RALPH M. PARSONS FOUNDATION, THE.** Ralph M. Parsons (1896–1974) was the founder in 1944 of the California company bearing his name. At that time, it was a partnership consisting of Parsons, Stephen D. Bechtel, and John A. McCone. Bechtel later left and became a chief rival of Parsons in the engineering and construction field, while McCone later became head of the Central Intelligence Agency (CIA). By the 1970s, Parsons's company was involved in projects amounting to more than $1 billion, and Parsons had become a millionaire.

The Ralph M. Parsons Foundation was established in 1961 in California with miniscule assets, and its grants during the first decade of its existence averaged about $13,000 annually. This pattern of relative inactivity by the foundation continued down to 1976, when it received from Parsons's estate shares in the Ralph M. Parsons Company worth about $9 million. The value of the foundation's assets has increased tremendously since that year. By 1977, they were worth over $21 million and, in 1981, about $74 million.

Grants by the foundation were about $850,000 in 1978, $230,000 in 1979, and $1.6 million in 1980. Its primary areas of interest during these years were higher education, social welfare, and cultural and civic projects. Major representative grants in 1980 in these areas included the following: Stanford University—$500,000; the Huntington Library—$450,000; the Salvation Army, Los Angeles—$30,000; and the Girls Club of Pasadena—$30,000. These and most of the other grants made by the foundation have been for the support of organizations located in southern California.

The Parsons Foundation is governed by an eight-member board of trustees. It is administered from offices located at 1545 Wilshire Boulevard, Los Angeles, California 90017, under the direction of an executive director.

Almost the only additional information on this foundation readily available to the public are the annual reports and returns filed by it with the Internal Revenue Service, and the various Foundation Center publications. See, however, Ralph M. Parsons obituary, *New York Times* (December 21, 1974), p. 30.

**RAMAPO TRUST.** A predecessor organization to this foundation, the Montebello Trust, was established in New York in 1968. It was funded with assets of about $8 million by Henry L. Schwartz, and he and three other members of the Schwartz family served on the trust's four-member board of trustees. Grants from the trust were used to support a local hospital.

The Ramapo Trust was established by Henry Schwartz in New York in 1973, and in 1974 the Montebello Trust was liquidated and its assets turned over to the Ramapo Trust. By this time, the trust had assets in excess of $25 million and was making annual grants of about $1.5 million. The 1981 assets of the trust were about $31 million, and its grants amount to about $2 million annually.

Its grants program has always been weighted heavily in favor of Jewish organizations, both in the United States, particularly in the New York-New Jersey area, and in Israel. In recent years, the major share (75 percent) of gifts has gone to religious and higher educational institutions and to Jewish welfare and religious activities, with a minor share (25 percent) to hospitals and Jewish youth and child welfare organizations. The largest grants in the foregoing categories for 1979–1980 have been the following: Hebrew Union College Jewish Institute of Religion, New York—$225,000; Federation of Jewish Philanthropies of New York—$200,000; Mount Sinai Hospital, New York—$119,000; and the American Friends of the Children's Day Nurseries and Children's Town in Israel, Incorporated, New York—$112,000.

The Ramapo Trust is governed by a three-member board of trustees, including Henry L. Schwartz and another member of the Schwartz family. The foundation's mailing address is 100 East Forty-second Street, New York, New York 10017.

Almost the only additional information on this foundation readily available to the public are the annual reports and returns filed by it with the Internal Revenue Service, and the various Foundation Center publications.

**RASKOB FOUNDATION FOR CATHOLIC ACTIVITIES, INC.** The career of John Raskob (1879–1950) followed the pattern of the American success story. Born to poor parents, he rose from a $5 a week position to become a wealthy and influential figure in the business and political world. It was an early association (he was then in his twenties) with members of the du Pont family that proved to be the catapult for his rise to prominence in the du Pont industrial empire. Then, about the time of World War I, it was primarily Raskob who engineered the agreements whereby the Du Pont Company acquired control of the General Motors Corporation. In the process, Raskob had become a very wealthy man by the 1920s.

In 1928, Raskob became the chairman of the national committee of the Democratic Party in the party's unsuccessful drive for the presidency in that year. Following Democrat Franklin D. Roosevelt's election to the presidency four years later, Raskob soon split with F.D.R. and became a leader in the Liberty League and other groups opposed to the New Deal program. Raskob began to curtail his business and political activities in the 1940s and thereafter devoted an increasing amount of time to philanthropic activities, particularly those benefitting the Roman Catholic Church. A major outcome of this interest was the establishment of the Raskob Foundation for Catholic Activities, Inc., in Delaware in 1945.

In its first few years of existence, the foundation's assets amounted to several million dollars. At his death, Raskob left the bulk of his estate to the foundation. By 1956, its reported assets were about $18 million, and grants for that year totalled about $750,000. The assets of the foundation grew to about $40 million by 1968 but since that time have remained relatively stationery and, in 1980, stood at about $43 million. Grants, similarly, have averaged from $1.25 million to $1.50 million annually since the 1960s.

The purpose of the Raskob Foundation since its inception can be simply stated: to support Roman Catholic Church institutions and activities. Grants for this purpose have been made in the United States and abroad to a truly wide variety of institutions. Grantees included: parochial schools, secondary schools, and higher educational institutions; social welfare agencies; hospitals, clinics, and health agencies; and Roman Catholic dioceses, churches and religious orders. Only institutions and organizations formally or informally connected with the church are provided support by the foundation.

The foundation is governed by a thirteen-member board of trustees, with Anthony W. Raskob serving as chairman, Patsy Raskob Bremer as president, and including several other members of the Raskob family. Administration of the foundation is carried on, under the direction of an executive vice-president, from offices located at Kennett Pike and Montchanin Road, Post Office Box 4019, Wilmington, Delaware 19807.

For further information, see the *Annual Report* (1981) of the foundation. See also John J. Raskob obituary, *New York Times* (October 16, 1950), p. 27; an article concerning his will, "Raskob Foundation Gets Bulk of Estate," *New York Times* (October 26, 1950), p. 21; and "John J. Raskob," *Dictionary of American Biography*, Supplement Four (1974), pp. 681–683.

**RAY A. KROC FOUNDATION.** See Kroc Foundation, The.

**R. C. BAKER FOUNDATION, THE.** Reuben Carlton Baker, Sr., was the founder and long-time chairman of the board of Baker International Corporation, makers of equipment for drilling, mining, and oil and gas exploration. He set up the R. C. Baker Foundation in California in 1952. By 1968, its assets amounted to approximately $9 million and by 1975 they had doubled. In 1981, they stood at about $48 million. This increase was primarily due to the appreciation in the value of the original endowment.

Except for restrictions prohibiting grants to individuals or endowment funds, the R. C. Baker Foundation's program has been broad and diverse. It has supported numerous institutions, including colleges and universities, youth agencies, hospitals, social service agencies, museums, churches, institutes, and so forth.

In 1980, for example, its 375 grants totalling about $2 million ranged from a high of $100,000 to the Los Angeles, California, YMCA to a low of $500 to the Los Angeles, California, National Safety Council.

The foundation is governed by a six-member board of trustees, with the Security Pacific National Bank of California acting as corporate trustee. Administration of the foundation is carried on from Post Office Box 6150, Orange, California 92677, under the direction of a trustee.

Almost the only additional information readily available to the public on this foundation are the annual reports and returns filed by it with the Internal Revenue Service, and the various Foundation Center publications.

**REGENSTEIN FOUNDATION, THE.** This foundation was established in Illinois in 1950 as the Joseph and Helen Regenstein Foundation by Joseph Regenstein, the founder of a paper envelope and business supplies company. In February, 1982, the foundation's name was changed to its present one. In its first three years of existence, the assets of the Regenstein Foundation barely exceeded $500,000, and its annual grants ranged from about $8,000 to $12,000. By 1958, however, its assets had climbed to about $2.5 million, and annual grants for the year were about $80,000. During the 1950s, foundation aid was largely restricted to local (Chicago) giving. By 1969, assets had increased to about $40 million, and annual grants for the year amounted to approximately $1.5 million. Since that year, the assets of the foundation have been relatively stable, but the amount of annual giving has more than doubled. The approximate figures for assets and grants for the years 1975 and 1980 illustrate these developments: 1975, assets—$40 million, grants—$1.1 million; 1980, assets—$46 million, grants—$4.1 million.

Throughout its existence, the foundation has limited its gifts primarily to the Chicago area. Emphasis has always been placed on grants for educational purposes, medical research, health care, and artistic and cultural purposes. In 1980, for example, representative major grants in these various areas included the following: University of Chicago (various purposes)—$1,538,000; Menninger Foundation, Topeka, Kansas—$652,210; Art Institute of Chicago—$256,449; Rush Presbyterian, Saint Luke's Medical Center, Chicago—$400,000; and United Charities of Chicago—$91,000.

The foundation is governed by a three-member board of trustees which includes the son of Joseph Regenstein, who serves as president of the foundation. Administration of the foundation is carried on from offices located at 3450 North Kimball Avenue, Chicago, Illinois 60618, under the direction of the president.

Almost the only additional information on this foundation readily available to the public is a *General Guidelines* leaflet, available from the foundation; the annual reports and returns filed by it with the Internal Revenue Service; and the various Foundation Center publications.

**RESEARCH CORPORATION.** Founded in 1912 by a young chemist with the help of the secretary of the Smithsonian Institution and—according to some sources—President William Howard Taft, the Research Corporation has, with reason, been called a unique American institution. It is one of the nation's first foundations and the only one wholly devoted to the advancement of science and technology. It had its genesis in an immensely valuable invention for controlling industrial air pollution, the electrostatic precipitator. The precipitator was perfected by Frederick Gardner Cottrell while a professor of chemistry at the University of California, Berkeley.

Then in his early thirties, Cottrell decided to use his discovery not only to clean up the air, but to create an organization which would promote the practical use of other inventions as well as his own. Any resources generated by this activity were to be plowed back to help support scholarly research in the sciences. It was a highly original philanthropic concept: the fruits of research would be applied in the public interest, and income—in the form of patent royalties—would be used to foster further advancement in science and technology.

In 1911, Cottrell was introduced to Charles D. Walcott, secretary of the Smithsonian, and he persuaded Walcott to help him launch this unusual endeavor, a foundation to make money to give away. Together they recruited a board of directors that included, in addition to several distinguished academicians, such men as General T. Coleman du Pont; Elihu Thompson, founder of the company which later became General Electric; Arthur D. Little, consulting chemist and president of the American Chemical Society; and Elon Huntington Hooker, president of the Hooker Electrochemical Company.

Cottrell, a man of modest means, believed that Research Corporation was so badly needed that it would "prosper from hunger." Thus the foundation came into being in February, 1912, its sole assets Cottrell's patent rights and a small—at Cottrell's insistence—operating fund of $10,100, subscribed by the members of the board.

Although it had been anticipated that Research Corporation would simply license Cottrell's electrostatic precipitator to potential users, the device—which removed soot, dust, and other pollutants from stack gases at smelters, power, and other industrial plants—proved to be too temperamental for inexperienced engineers to construct and operate. To meet demand, Research Corporation established a precipitation division to design, manufacture, and install the units. This was later reorganized as an independent company (Research-Cottrell, Inc.), and the sale of the company to the public in the early 1960s provided the foundation with a more conventional endowment.

Resources to feed back into scholarly research were some time in coming, but by 1917 the infant foundation was able to offer a fellowship in applied science. The first gifts to educational institutions began shortly thereafter, and, as there were very few sources of research support, the opportunities were spectacular. Funds were provided beginning in the early 1920s to assist the early experiments of "father of rocketry" Robert H. Goddard; to help Ernest O. Lawrence acquire the magnet that became the heart of the first large cyclotron, and to build the first high-voltage generators named in honor of their inventor, Robert J. Van de Graaff.

As a result of the prescience of Cottrell, the foundation has been able to help support the early work of some seventeen promising scientists who later won Nobel Prizes. Among them were Max Delbrück, discoverer of the genetic structure of viruses; Edward C. Kendall, who played a crucial role in discovering cortisone; Isidor I. Rabi, who uncovered the resonance method of recording the properties of atomic nuclei; and Robert B. Woodward, who developed the fundamental techniques for synthesis of complicated organic compounds. A total of well over $70 million has been granted since the inception of the foundation to advance basic academic research, largely in support of the best ideas of younger college and university scientists. Many of these grantees have left an indelible mark on science and society.

It had been Cottrell's hope that other inventors would follow his example and donate their inventions to Research Corporation, both to spur industrial innovation and to strengthen the organization's ability to contribute to academic science and technology. Some did indeed contribute, and the royalties their inventions produced made possible a variety of grants programs in areas such as applied nutrition, the cytogenetics of major agricultural crops, advanced physics, and biomedical research. The inventors who made possible these programs were Robert R. Williams and Robert E. Waterman, who first synthesized vitamin $B_1$; Donald F. Jones and Paul C. Mangelsdorf, responsible for a practical method of producing hybrid seed corn; Charles H. Townes, who originated the maser-laser concept; and Elizabeth Hazen and Rachel Brown, who invented the first antifungal antibiotic.

Although the patents on these discoveries have expired, and with them the grants programs made possible by the patent royalties, Research Corporation continues its long-standing support of basic academic science. The foundation's Cottrell Research Program and Cottrell College Science Program make awards to assist basic research in the natural and physical sciences at colleges and universities across the country, currently at a level of over $3 million annually.

These grants programs are essentially open and ongoing competitions for research funding. Grants are made on the basis of scientific significance and originality of the proposed research. The judging process makes use of outside referees, authorities in their respective fields, and reviews by the foundation's grants advisory committee. The committee is drawn from the academic research community, and its recommendations form the basis for approval by the foundation's board of directors.

In keeping with Cottrell's vision, Research Corporation works in the public interest to transmute academic technology into useful products and processes. This task, one of transferring technology from university laboratories to industry, is undertaken by the foundation's major operating program, Invention Administration Program (IAP). A professional staff, trained in the major scientific disciplines, marketing, and patent law, evaluates inventions made at scientific and educational institutions and arranges to patent and license those that appear promising.

Most inventions received by the foundation, about 400 annually, come from among the 280 institutions which maintain cooperative agreements for IAP services. Under these agreements, Research Corporation retains a share of invention royalties for its programs and returns the major portion to the institution and inventor. Evaluation, patenting, and licensing services are donated by the foundation, regardless of the success of licensing efforts.

First placed on a formal basis in 1935, the foundation's Invention Administration Program has played a unique role in bringing to the public products and processes of crucial importance to medicine and nutrition, to industry and agriculture, and to science itself. In addition to the discoveries previously mentioned, Research Corporation has helped make available, through patent licensing, anticancer drugs, cortisone, and antibiotics; vitamins A and $B_{12}$; yield-enhancing hybrid plant varieties; labor-saving agricultural machinery; chemicals and chemical processes; and a host of other inventions. The computer memory core was licensed by the foundation, as have been many other important electronic and mechanical devices.

Over the years, the foundation has evaluated in excess of 12,000 inventions, patenting perhaps 10 percent of them in the United States and other industrial countries. Of these, 150 to 200 have been successfully licensed to industry and developed and marketed to benefit the public and to produce royalties to aid further research.

Research Corporation was chartered in New York as a singular organization: a stock corporation that would own all of its own stock and never pay dividends. This highly unusual arrangement was subsequently ratified by a special act of the New York state legislature in 1932. The foundation is today incorporated as a not-for-profit corporation and is exempt from federal income tax under section 501(c)(3) of the Internal Revenue Code. The foundation is governed by a self-perpetuating board of directors numbering fifteen; by tradition, it includes among its members the secretary of the Smithsonian Institution. The remaining directors include prominent academicians, industry executives, lawyers, and financiers.

Cottrell's gift of patent rights is now embodied in a diversified investment portfolio that, together with other assets, was valued at $46.3 million in 1981. This portfolio was created through the sale by the foundation of a major portion of the electrostatic precipitator business that was built up over the years following 1912. Annual royalties on inventions administered by the foundation recently totalled $6.5 million, of which $4.5 million was returned to the scientific institutions and inventors that originated the discoveries. The balance of $2 million and investment income of $3 million helped sustain foundation programs for advancing academic science and technology.

Resources available through Research Corporation for assisting basic academic research have been supplemented in recent years by other foundations, major industrial companies, and individuals. Over $500,000 is received annually from such sources to help fund scientifically significant research proposed to the foundation by college and university faculty members.

The foundation maintains an expanded Invention Administration Program staff to handle inventions of growing complexity and in a variety of fields. The program employs twenty-two professionals. In addition, a scientifically trained grants staff numbers four members, and four executives are concerned with general foundation administration.

Headquarter offices of the Research Corporation are located at 405 Lexington Avenue, New York, New York 10174, with regional grants offices in Minneapolis, Atlanta, and Burlingame, California. The chief executive officer of the foundation, Dr. John P. Schaefer, formerly president of the University of Arizona, became president of the Research Corporation on June 1, 1982, succeeding Dr. James Stacy Coles, following his retirement.

Records concerning the founding of Research Corporation are located in the Smithsonian Institution's Secretarial Records for 1907–1949; other early and remaining papers of the foundation pertaining to grants, patents, and the development of the precipitation industry are located at Research Corporation's main offices in New York City.

For further information, see Frank Cameron, *Cottrell: Samaritan of Science* (1952); and Harry J. White, "Centenary of Frederick Gardner Cottrell," *Journal of Electrostatics* (1977–1978). See also *Science, Invention and Society: The Story of a Unique American Institution* (1972), an information booklet about the Research Corporation; quarterly and irregular newsletters issued by the foundation; and *Annual Reports* of the foundation, published continuously since 1954.

W. STEVENSON BACON

**RETIREMENT RESEARCH FOUNDATION, THE.** The Retirement Research Foundation was established by John D. MacArthur, a Chicago resident and businessman, in 1950. The foundation was incorporated that year in the state of Michigan "to receive and administer funds for scientific, educational, and charitable purposes, specifically to conduct and provide for research concerning problems of industry and of individuals arising from regular gainful employment, all for the public welfare, and for no other purposes". Upon the death of the founder in 1978, the foundation was the recipient of major assets.

A seven-member board of trustees appointed by the founder over a twenty-year period then assumed responsibility for operation of the foundation. Initial monthly meetings were devoted to the financial aspects of the foundation. By March, 1979, the task of determining the program directions of the Retirement Research Foundation began. The world had changed since the foundation's purpose had been articulated, and the task of the trustees was to determine a program focus for the 1980s. With assistance from consultants, the trustees examined the status of older citizens, the issues of a society growing older, the programs of government and private philanthropy. A five-month study process resulted in a mission and policy statement which would guide the foundation's grant-making activity in the early years.

To improve the quality of life of older persons in the United States, the foundation was to target its resources on projects which would: (1) increase the availability and effectiveness of community programs designed to maintain older persons in independent living environments and to enable the disabled aged to function independently; (2) improve the quality of nursing-home care; (3) provide new opportunities for older persons to engage in employment and volunteer roles; and (4) research the causes and solutions to significant problems of the aging population. Within these priority areas, the foundation would support a variety of strategies but was particularly interested in innovations which have the potential for national or regional impact. Where appropriate, the foundation would give priority to requests from the Chicago metropolitan area.

In December, 1979, the foundation's first grant awards were made. In the period December, 1979, through December, 1981, the foundation awarded $6,575,051 to seventy-nine different projects. A major portion of the foundation's funding has been directed to keeping older persons in their homes and communities. Through support of research, advocacy, education, and service, the foundation has addressed housing, income, access to benefits and services, and the availability of a wide range of community services which offer alternatives to and prevent institutionalization.

To improve the quality of nursing-home care, the Retirement Research Foundation has focused on creating community and citizen presence in nursing homes and the regulatory and policy arenas, on developing legal sanctions, and in improving components of care. Major problems addressed through basic and clinical research include depression, Alzheimer's disease, atherosclerosis, and macular degeneration.

The 1981 White House Conference on Aging presented opportunities for foundation involvement and support. A special project to monitor long-term results was subsequently launched.

As the foundation's program develops, evaluation is a greater focus. Examination of past operations and accomplishments and continued monitoring of the status of the aging population and the environment will enable the Retirement Research Foundation to undertake new initiatives and to respond to new opportunities. As a recently activated foundation, the major accomplishments are yet to be documented.

The original seven-member board of trustees was increased to nine members in April, 1979. This nine-member board of trustees has full legal responsibility for operation of the foundation. The board is actively involved in the operations of the foundation through regularly scheduled quarterly meetings and special meetings as needed. Offices are located at 325 Touhy Avenue, Park Ridge, Illinois 60068.

A consultant retained in May, 1979, was appointed executive director in May,

1980. The director and an additional staff person conduct the day-to-day operations of the foundation. Consultants augment staff in the grant-making process.

The foundation's program is financed by its assets, about $43 million in 1981. Its annual grant distribution is 5 percent of the asset value.

Since the foundation has a short history, information about it is limited and includes only articles of incorporation, minutes, and statements as to grant program activity.

MARILYN HENNESSY

**REVSON FOUNDATION.** See Charles H. Revson Foundation, Inc.

**REYNOLDS CHARITABLE TRUST.** See Kate B. Reynolds Charitable Trust.

**REYNOLDS FOUNDATION.** See Z. Smith Reynolds Foundation, Inc.

**RICHARD KING MELLON FOUNDATION.** Richard King Mellon (1899–1970) was the son of Richard B. Mellon (1858–1933) and the nephew of the more famous Andrew W. Mellon (1855–1937). Destined to become the inheritor of one of the largest private fortunes in the world, Richard King Mellon was trained by his father and uncle to assume direction of the business interests upon which it was based. He did not, however, confine his activities to his family's large business interests. He served with distinction in the armed forces of the United States, ultimately becoming a lieutenant general of the army. He developed a keen and abiding interest in nature and the outdoors, and, as a lifelong resident of Pittsburgh, he had an unflagging concern for its betterment and was a prime mover in the Golden Triangle Project which helped to revitalize that city. Also, he was active in the educational and philanthropic fields, particularly those involving Pittsburgh. His founding of the Richard King Mellon Foundation in 1947 was the natural outgrowth of these interests.

His wife, Constance Prosser Mellon, was closely associated with Richard Mellon in his many and varied activities. She was particularly active in the affairs of the foundation, serving as chairwoman of its board of trustees from the time of its inception until her death in 1980. Their two adopted sons, Richard P. Mellon and Seward Prosser Mellon, became and remain members of the foundation's six-member board of directors. They also serve as chairman of the board and president of the foundation, respectively.

For the first three decades of the foundation's existence, by the end of which time its assets had reached approximately $130 million, its major grants were in the fields of education, health, and civic and cultural affairs, with special emphasis on projects relating to or connected with the Pittsburgh area. Out of a total of $150 million it devoted to charitable and educational organizations during that period, over 50 percent went to institutions located in Pittsburgh and western Pennsylvania.

By 1980, the assets of the Richard King Mellon Foundation had increased substantially from funds received from the estate of Richard King Mellon and from appreciation in investments so that the foundation had assets of approximately $311 million.

The foundation's priorities have shifted dramatically from its earlier interests to the conservation of the natural resources of the United States. For example, out of appropriations of approximately $24 million made in 1980, the foundation allocated $15 million to the Nature Conservancy of Arlington, Virginia, a national conservation agency. This grant, which was the largest in the foundation's history and the largest ever made to a conservation organization, was for the support of a ten-year project to protect the bottomland hardwood forests of six important rivers of the deep South: the Choctawhatchee, Suwanee, Apalachicola, Mobile-Tensaw, Pascagoula, and Pearl. Appropriately entitled "Rivers of the Deep South," the project concentrates upon funding the acquisition of significant national wilderness areas along these rivers, both to protect lands from injurious development and to assist in wildlife preservation.

Despite the shift in the emphasis on its areas of activity, the foundation continues to make sizable grants in its early areas of interest: education, medicine and health, and social and cultural affairs. Also, it continues to maintain special interest in Pittsburgh and western Pennsylvania. In 1980, about $5.5 million was devoted to projects in Pittsburgh and western Pennsylvania communities. Typically, the University of Pittsburgh was the recipient of a grant of over $1.5 million in that year.

A small administrative staff, headed by George H. Taber, vice-president and director, along with an active executive committee, conducts the business and programs of the foundation from offices located at 525 William Penn Place, Pittsburgh, Pennsylvania 15219.

For further information, see *Reports* of the foundation, published trienially until the 1970s, and *Annual Reports*, published continuously since that time. See also periodic information brochures published by the foundation.

**RICHARDSON FOUNDATION.** See Sid W. Richardson Foundation; Smith Richardson Foundation, Inc.

**RIPPEL FOUNDATION.** See Fannie E. Rippel Foundation.

**ROBERT A. WELCH FOUNDATION, THE.** Like many of the large foundations in Texas, the Robert A. Welch Foundation was created with assets that were amassed in mineral industries. Welch's investment in oil began in 1901 and continued in Texas and Louisiana for nearly fifty years. In 1905, he purchased the Mound Company and developed rich sulphur works. Thereafter, he pursued investments in minerals, real estate, and securities.

In Houston, Welch was known for his personal frugality. He rode the public busses to and from his office. It is said that his customary tip was one thin dime. Welch did give large sums away during his lifetime, however, particularly to

Hermann Hospital and to the Community Chest in Houston. He died a bachelor in 1952 at age eighty-two.

From its inception two years later, the Robert A. Welch Foundation committed its resources to aid research in chemistry at colleges and universities in Texas. It has also endowed chairs in chemistry at thirteen universities and supports scholarship programs for undergraduate and graduate students. Additional activities include an international achievement award in chemistry. Each recipient is given a gold medallion and $150,000 for outstanding research achievement. The Welch Foundation also sponsors an annual conference on chemical research. In total, it has presented grants, scholarships, and awards to more than 1,500 recipients since the foundation was established.

The foundation's assets, as of 1982, were about $144 million. During the 1981–1982 year, grants totalling $13, 197,797 were awarded. Income for the year was $15,923,235, of which about 11 percent was paid in taxes, principally the Windfall Profits Tax.

The foundation is governed by a five-member board of directors. Administration of the foundation is carried on from offices located at 2010 Bank of the Southwest Building, Houston, Texas 77002. A separate seven-member advisory board of prominent scientists recommends awards to the directors.

For further information, see *Annual Reports* of the foundation, published since the 1950s. See also Robert A. Welch obituary, *The Odessa American* (January 1, 1953); and *A Biography of Robert Alonzo Welch* (n.d.), published by the foundation.

ROGER M. OLIEN

**ROBERT J. KLEBERG, JR., AND HELEN C. KLEBERG FOUNDATION.** A Texas rancher, Robert J. Kleberg and his wife were the original donors who established the Robert J. Kleberg, Jr., and Helen C. Kleberg Foundation in Texas in 1950. Kleberg was the president and chief executive officer of King Ranch, Inc., one of the largest ranches in Texas, and is famous for his development and introduction of the Santa Gertrudis breed of cattle, new strains of grass, and other ranching and cattle-raising innovations.

The initial assets of the Kleberg Foundation in 1951 consisted of $571, and it made grants out of principal for that year of $450. Its stated purpose at its inception was to use both income and principal for charitable and educational purposes, with special emphasis on agriculture and animal husbandry. By 1974, the assets of the foundation had grown in value to about $4.50 million, and grants for the year amounted to about $0.25 million. By this time, the foundation was primarily providing grants for the purposes of higher and secondary education, medical education, and cultural programs.

By 1980, assets were valued at about $31 million, and grants for that year totalled about $4 million. Following a pattern of giving which it has followed since 1969, the Kleberg Foundation allocated the largest share of its funding, or 75 percent, to medical research and health services, followed by 10 percent to cultural and historical programs, and the remaining 15 percent to wildlife, veterinary, and animal care, education, and various civic and social welfare agencies. By far the largest grant for the year was one of $1,266,930 to the Salk Institute, located in La Jolla, California. This reflects the present foundation policy of giving on a national basis for biomedical research, veterinary sciences, and related areas, although all of the other categories of giving focus mainly on South Texas.

The foundation is governed by a six-member board of directors, with a daughter of the donors serving as president. Administration of the foundation is carried on from offices located at Suite 535, 711 Navarro Street, San Antonio, Texas 78205.

Almost the only additional sources of information readily available to the public on this foundation are the annual reports and returns filed by it with the Internal Revenue Service, and the various Foundation Center publications. See, however, *Annual Reports* of the foundation, published since 1979.

**ROBERT STERLING CLARK FOUNDATION, INC.** Established in 1952 by Robert Sterling Clark, a descendant of one of the founders of the Singer Sewing Machine Company, the Robert Sterling Clark Foundation operated on a miniscule scale in its early years. In 1957, for example, its assets were $144,328, and it made grants of $14,985 for various projects in New York City. With the death of Clark in 1956, approximately one-quarter of his estate was left to the foundation; one-quarter went to the Sterling and Francine Clark Art Institute, Williamstown, Massachusetts, which he had built earlier and which housed his art collection; and one-half was placed in trust for his wife, Francine. Upon her death in 1960, her estate was divided between the foundation and the art institution. The assets of the foundation thereupon rose to more than $25 million and in 1982 stood at about $33 million.

From 1960 to 1972, the Clark Foundation was operated by its five-member board of directors without the benefit of a full-time administrator. During this period, the foundation grants were miscellaneous in nature; however, two clearly discernible characteristics were a marked preference for what may be called cultural endeavors and a preponderance of grants to organizations within the Greater New York City area.

The hiring, in 1972, of a full-time administrator by the foundation was followed by a review of its past giving and the formulation of new guidelines for its future. By 1976, this had resulted in a decision to concentrate the Clark Foundation's grants in three broad program areas: (a) examining the role of the family in a changing society; (b) strengthening private institutions; and (c) ensuring the effectiveness and accountability of public institutions. In making grants to each of these areas, however, the foundation continued its policy of concentrating its grants in the Greater New York City area.

In recent years, the Clark Foundation has refined and developed its grants program. The foundation's current fields of interest are: encouraging permanence and stability for children in, or at risk of, foster care; strengthening the management of cultural institutions in New York City and the greater metropolitan area; and ensuring the effectiveness and accountability of public agencies in New York City and State. No grants to individuals or for building or endowment funds are given.

The Robert Sterling Clark Foundation is presently governed by a five-member board of directors. Its programs are carried out by a small administrative staff, headed by an executive director, from offices located at 112 East Sixty-Fourth Street, New York, New York 10021.

For further information, see *Annual Reports* of the foundation, published continuously since 1971. See also "Art Repository Heir to Millions," *New York Times* (January 18, 1957), p. 23.

**ROBERT WOOD JOHNSON FOUNDATION, THE.** A private philanthropy interested in improving health care in the United States, this foundation's founder was the late General Robert Wood Johnson. General Johnson had a deep concern for human welfare, particularly the improvement of health, and during his lifetime devoted much of his energy to public service. He was the chief executive officer of Johnson and Johnson, which he built from a relatively small family business into a publicly held corporation operating internationally.

In 1936, he established the Johnson New Brunswick Foundation to distribute funds for philanthropic causes, principally in the New Brunswick, New Jersey, area. In 1952, this foundation became the Robert Wood Johnson Foundation. Following Johnson's death in 1968, the foundation received the bulk of his estate and, in 1972, began its work on the national scene.

The foundation is governed by a board of trustees that meets six times annually. Its operations are conducted by a full-time, professional staff of approximately seventy-six persons. In addition, fourteen individuals with academic appointments in medical, nursing, and other professional schools across the country serve as senior program consultants directing multisite programs funded by the foundation. The foundation's offices are at the Princeton Forrestal Center, Post Office Box 2316, Princeton, New Jersey 08540.

When the Robert Wood Johnson Foundation began its work as a national philanthropy in 1972, there were too few health resources in many areas of the country, and many people were unable to get medical and dental services. After careful study of available information, and with the advice of many national leaders in health, the trustees and officers agreed that they would concentrate the foundation's initial efforts on improving access to general medical and dental care, with a goal of helping people regardless of their economic status, race, or place of residence to obtain personal health-care services when and where needed. Improvements in the quality of care and the public policy aspects of health care were also selected as additional areas for activity.

Between 1972 and 1980, the Johnson Foundation made grants totalling $407.4 million, principally to improve people's access to general medical care. During this same period, the problems the foundation selected also received increasing attention from many other private and public funding sources. Available evidence now suggests that access to medical care significantly improved during this period, although difficult problems persist for many.

The foundation therefore continues to be active in aiding those who seek further to improve health services for people who remain inadequately served. However, in late 1980, its focus was broadened and the foundation began phasing in grants for those working in two other areas of health care. Thus, three principal interests now comprise the foundation's agenda for grants: (1) programs to improve access to personal health care for the most underserved population groups; (2) programs to make health-care arrangements more effective and care more affordable; and (3) programs to help people maintain or regain maximum attainable function in their everyday lives.

In 1980, the Robert Wood Johnson Foundation had assets of over $1 billion. By the end of 1981, the foundation's first decade as a national philanthropy, it had made 1,592 grants with appropriations totalling $447.6 million.

To increase the potential impact of the foundation's grant funds within its three areas of program interest, the institution's role has been further defined to assist: (1) developing and testing new and previously untried approaches to health-care problems; (2) demonstrations to assess objectively the operational effectiveness and value of selected new health-care arrangements and approaches which have been shown to be effective in more limited settings; and (3) projects designed to promote the broader diffusion of programs that have been objectively shown to improve health status or to make health care more affordable.

The Johnson Foundation gives priority to proposed programs and projects addressing regional or national problems. The one exception to this and the other guidelines is support for a small number of activities in New Brunswick, New Jersey, where the foundation originated. Policy guidelines established by the foundation's board of trustees normally preclude support for ongoing general operating expenses; endowment, construction, or equipment; basic biomedical research; international activities or programs in institutions in other countries; and direct support to individuals. Also, the foundation does not support programs concerned solely with a specific disease or with certain broad public health problems, except as they might relate to the foundation's three program interests.

The Robert Wood Johnson Foundation uses two general methods in its grant making. One consists of grants made in response to direct, unsolicited requests from organizations or institutions whose work falls within the foundation's principal areas of interest. The other approach consists of invitational programs whereby a number of institutions or agencies compete for funds to conduct similar projects simultaneously addressing a specific national problem, within the guidelines of a well-defined protocol. Appropriations totaling $245.3 million have been made in support of such programs, which have included:

- establishing fifty-one primary-care group medical practices in thirty-seven states and the District of Columbia, sponsored by community hospitals and their medical staffs, to provide care to underserved population groups;

- integrating and coordinating, in areas of eight states, community services needed by elderly citizens with health problems so that these individuals can maintain reasonably independent life-styles;

- expanding of outpatient dental care in twenty-five hospitals with general dentistry residency programs;

- combining resources of local health departments and municipal hospitals in five of the country's fifty largest cities to offer primary medical care through twenty-two urban neighborhood sites;

- strengthening medical-school training and research relevant to the problems encountered by physicians in general pediatrics practice;

- deploying pediatric nurse practitioners, backed up by physicians in nearby practices, in seventy schools serving thirty-seven thousand children in four states;

- developing clinical programs in eleven dental schools to train dental students to care for handicapped patients.

The foundation has expended more than $18.2 million to fund objective, third-party evaluations to measure the outcomes of the major programs it has supported, and additional resources are devoted to helping its grantees communicate the experience and the knowledge they have gained to others who can use this information.

The range of activities assisted by the Robert Wood Johnson Foundation's grants reflects the trustee and staff commitment to the idea that a variety of approaches to bettering health-care services should be encouraged. Moreover, while grants are awarded to many kinds of organizations and institutions, the foundation views this funding as an investment in individuals or groups of individuals who have shown an interest, commitment, and capability in working toward the solution of problems in the health field.

For further information, see the following articles about the foundation: John Walsh, "Robert Wood Johnson Foundation: Planning for a Metamorphosis," *Science Magazine* (March 10, 1972), pp. 1093, 1094, 1095; "Wealthy Foundation Seeks to Affect Care," *American Medical News* (September 10, 1973), pp. 1, 11, 12; Peter Michelmore, "The Johnson Millions: Transfusion for Front-line Medicine," *Modern Medicine* (March 18, 1974), pp. 17, 18, 19, 20, 21; Jack Harrison Pollack, "The Million-dollar Prescriptions of Dr. Rogers," *Signature* (September, 1974), pp. 41, 42, 43; S.G.K., "Catalysts for Model Building," *Hospitals, J.A.H.A.* (March 1, 1975), pp. 44, 45, 46, 47; Frank Jones, "Important Organizations," *Journal of Dental Education* (March, 1977), pp. 135, 136, 137, 138; Betty Holcomb, "Seeking New Directions in Health Care," *Health Care Week* (January 23, 1978), pp. 9, 10; Patrick Young, "Robert Wood Johnson: Assessing Success," *Foundation News* (July–August 1979), pp. 13, 14, 15, 16, 17, 18; "HCMR Interview: David E. Rogers," *HCM Review* (Spring,

1980), pp. 41, 42, 43, 44, 45, 46, 47, 48. See also *Annual Reports* of the foundation, published continuously since 1971.

FRANK KAREL

**ROCKEFELLER BROTHERS FUND (RBF).** The Rockefeller Brothers Fund (RBF), a private, grant-making, philanthropic foundation based in New York City, was established in 1940 by the five sons of John D. Rockefeller, Jr. The brothers, later joined by their sister, Abby Rockefeller Mauzé, provided funds through annual contributions to the RBF and served as its original trustees. Their purpose was to create a system of joint giving, whereby they could share interests and responsibilities while carrying on the philanthropic tradition of their father and grandfather. The central concerns of the trustees have consistently been expressed in the fields of conservation, population, cultural development, economic development, and international relations.

At the outset, the RBF concentrated its activities solely in New York City, but the scope broadened over the next decade to include national and international relief and rehabilitation efforts in response to World War II and its aftermath. By 1950, the fund had developed the philanthropic concept of responsible citizenship in three contexts: New York City, the United States, and the international community. Guided by this idea, much of the fund's early grant making consisted of across-the-board general budgetary support to a wide spectrum of social service, cultural, and civic organizations.

The fund's interests have remained broad and flexible over the past four decades, owing largely to the sensibilities, concerns, and personalities of John D. (III), Nelson, Laurance, Winthrop, and David Rockefeller, and Abby Rockefeller Mauzé. While the brothers established the RBF as a way of sharing their concerns, each brought to bear his own personal and professional interests. John D. Rockefeller III, who devoted much of his life to philanthropy, was especially concerned with population issues, strengthening Asian-American relations, and developing cultural institutions in the United States. Nelson made important contributions to the public life of the country; his offices included governor of New York and vice-president of the United States. He also served as president of the Museum of Modern Art and was deeply interested in Latin America. Laurance, a pioneer venture capitalist, has a fascination for science and technology, as well as a strong conservationist bent. Winthrop, who served the state of Arkansas in numerous ways, including as governor, had lifelong interests in the fields of health, education, and racial equality. David, an art collector and Ph.D. in economics who retired as chairman of the Chase Manhattan Bank in 1981, remains active in urban development and international relations. Abby Rockefeller Mauzé brought to the fund her interests in population, the advancement of education and opportunities for women, and the delivery of social services. The history of RBF grant making reflects both the cooperative nature of the trustee's effort and the full variety of their lives.

The Rockefeller Brothers Fund remained a relatively small foundation during its first decade of operation, when total grants for any given year never exceeded $300,000. However, during those years, the fund consistently gave general support to community service organizations, private hospitals, and other nonprofit groups. The RBF also established relationships and interests which remained vital for years, including contributions to the Museum of Modern Art, the Legal Aid Society, the Conservation Foundation, Planned Parenthood, the United Negro College Fund, the New York Zoological Society, and the Colonial Williamsburg Foundation.

A $58 million gift from John D. Rockefeller, Jr., in 1951–1952 established an endowment and considerably increased the fund's level of activity. While expenditures for the years 1941 through 1950 totalled $2 million, combined grants in 1953 alone exceeded $1 million, and the figure increased thereafter. The fund received additional large gifts in 1960 and in 1971, through bequests from John D. Rockefeller, Jr., and his wife, Martha Baird Rockefeller. Under the direction of Dana S. Creel, the RBF staff expanded to keep pace with its philanthropic activity over the next twenty-five years, from 1951 to 1975. During this period, the board of trustees was also expanded to include members from outside the Rockefeller family.

With the expansion in 1951–1952, the fund began to identify special interest areas and take more initiative in grant making. A special program was established to make grants intended for "experimental or new undertakings" in the fields of international relations and understanding; strengthened national life; and conservation, population, and resources. The general program grants continued to support nonprofit organizations with local (New York City), national, or international impact and in many cases were awarded on a regular annual basis. It is largely through the special program, with its explicitly experimental purpose, that the RBF earned its reputation as a flexible and responsive foundation. However, it is the combination of the two programs that has encouraged both consistency and creativity in grant making.

Special program grants realized many of the RBF's more visible achievements, especially in the national and international fields. The following examples illustrate the wide range of special grants the RBF has made.

In 1953, the theological school fellowship program was created for students interested in exploring the possibility of a theological education, as a contribution to the religious strength of the country.

In 1956, the RBF launched a Special Studies Project to explore "the problems and opportunities facing this country during the coming 10 to 15 years." The seven panels focused on issues such as national defense and economic growth, and included a distinguished membership of leaders in business, labor, science, and education. The resulting publications series, *America at Mid-Century*, influenced national public policy goals over the subsequent two decades.

In 1974, the fund's longstanding concern for population problems, demonstrated most notably through regular grants to the Population Council and to

Planned Parenthood, was merged with a related interest in natural resource conservation. The resulting Environmental Program articulated "a new general awareness of relationships among parts of the natural system." The program approached environmental protection through continued support of population and conservation institutions but also attempted to increase understanding of an emerging new environmental ethic through grants to organizations such as the Lindisfarne Association, Worldwatch Institute, the Zen Center, and the New Alchemy Institute.

RBF activities at the international level, during these years, included grants for South American and Asian agricultural development, education in the Near and Middle East, improved Asian-American relations, and the economic development of West African nations.

In New York City, the fund made steady contributions toward the development of the city's neighborhoods, as well as to those organizations concerned with culture, public education, and improving government and transportation. The fund assisted significantly in the early development of several of the city's most important institutions, including Memorial Sloan-Kettering Cancer Center, Lincoln Center for the Performing Arts, and the Museum of Modern Art.

In 1975, after careful consideration, the trustees decided that the time had come for the fund to discharge certain long-held "special responsibilities." A total of approximately $100 million was appropriated as contributions to eighteen organizations, including the Japan society, Rockefeller University, the Jackson Hole Preserve Incorporated,* the Metropolitan Museum of Art, and Spelman College. In addition to relieving the fund of further major responsibility to these organizations, the resulting endowment reduction led to a reduced level of grant making in subsequent years.

The RBF used this opportunity to redefine its programs. Currently, the national program concentrates on agricultural lands preservation, water conservation, domestic development finance, employment policy and job development, and strengthening the private, nonprofit sector. The New York City program aims to improve the quality of life in the fund's home community by encouraging more comprehensive, efficient, and publicly accountable approaches to problems in the fields of economic development, housing and community development, public education, government efficiency, economic growth and stabilization, human services, employment and skill development, and the creative living environment. The international program encourages international cooperation, with special emphasis on China and Japan, ecodevelopment in the Caribbean, and legal protection of civil and political liberties in areas such as South Africa.

The RBF is governed by a board of fifteen trustees, the majority of whom are members of the Rockefeller family. The board meets twice annually, in the spring and in the fall. The executive committee, composed of seven board members, meets three times a year. All RBF appropriations must be approved by one of these bodies. David Rockefeller is currently chairman of the fund.

William M. Dietel succeeded Dana S. Creel as president in 1975. The RBF, with 1980 assets of about $177 million, employs a program and support staff of approximately twenty-five members, plus consultants on occasion.

No detailed, independent history of the Rockefeller Brothers Fund has been written, although Waldemar A. Neilsen includes a short summary in his book, *The Big Foundations* (1972).The most comprehensive source of information about the RBF is its *Annual Reports*, which have been published with reference to every year the fund has operated. The current report is available from the RBF office, 1290 Avenue of the Americas, Room 3450, New York, New York 10104.

RBF records for the years 1941–1976, including all grant-related documents, are located in the Rockefeller Brothers Fund archive at the Rockefeller Archive Center, Pocantico Hills, North Tarrytown, New York 10591. Research inquiries may be made of Joseph W. Ernst, Director. Recent documents remain on file in the RBF office library. Records covering the most recent ten years are not publicly available.

AMY P. LONGSWORTH

**ROCKEFELLER FOUNDATION, THE (RF).** The idea of establishing a foundation independent of the donor and his family, professionally managed, and with the mandate "to attempt to cure evils at their source" without regard to national boundaries probably came from Frederick T. Gates, a former Baptist minister and a long-time associate of John D. Rockefeller, Sr., who exerted considerable personal influence on all the Rockefeller philanthropies.

Originally it was hoped that such a Rockefeller trust would be chartered by the Congress of the United States, with its organization and program subject to continuing congressional review. Legislation was introduced to this end in 1910, 1911, and 1912, but the Congress, strongly influenced by hostility toward large corporations and their founders, was not receptive to such a proposal.

The result was that the Rockefeller Foundation was finally incorporated by the New York state legislature in 1913 with an initial endowment of $35 million "to promote the well-being of mankind throughout the world."

At their first meeting, on May 14, 1913, under the leadership of John D. Rockefeller, Jr., the trustees of the foundation began to address themselves to the then-vast problem of how to spend the foundation's funds wisely. They decided to concentrate the RF's energies in the fields of public health and medicine, agreeing with Frederick Gates's eloquent arguments that disease is the supreme ill in human life.

The decision grew from two interrelated factors. First, at the turn of the century, disease was the implacable barrier to human welfare everywhere. Even in the United States, life expectancy in 1913 was only fifty-two years, compared with seventy-three years today. One out of every ten American children died in the first year of life, compared with one in seventy-two today. Second, considerable knowledge of many of the great endemic diseases—malaria, hookworm, yellow fever, and typhus, for example—was in hand but was not being applied. A job of organizing, financing, and educating needed to be done.

The trustees voted to continue the programs of the Rockefeller Sanitary Commission (which became the International Health Board of the Rockefeller Foundation) in the field of hookworm control. The Sanitary Commission had, in the years 1910 through 1914, done extensive work in eleven southern states where—with the cooperation of governmental agencies, charities, women's clubs, ministers, teachers, and practicing physicians—massive campaigns of public education and medication were carried out. Over 25,000 public meetings were held, attended by more than 2 million people who were given the facts of the disease and its prevention. Sanitary inspectors examined 250,000 rural homes to check sources of infection; traveling dispensaries provided free examination and free treatment.

Wickliffe Rose, who had directed the work of the Sanitary Commission and now led the foundation's International Health Board, had earlier conceived the idea of carrying this hookworm control work abroad, where the disease prevailed in a wide belt around the equator. Although a relatively effective therapy for the disease—capsules of thymol and salts—was known, the essential job was to demonstrate to hundreds of millions of people that improved sanitation was the only means of preventing hookworm infection. Therefore, in the years immediately following 1913, the hookworm control activity of the Rockefeller Foundation was carried to fifty-two countries on six continents as well as twenty-nine islands. In a typical year, seventy-three foundation staff members were on assignments in thirty-six foreign countries and territories. Everywhere, the foundation's International Health Board worked cooperatively with the governments of the countries involved.

Wickliffe Rose had not gone very far in his work before he began to realize that to extend the great benefits of preventive medicine it would be necessary to create new institutions for the training of specialists to staff the local health agencies on which depends continuing protection against endemic diseases. The Rockefeller Foundation, therefore, appropriated more than $6 million to build and endow the School of Hygiene and Public Health, at the Johns Hopkins University, the first such institution in the world. The RF then spent over $25 million in developing public health schools and institutions in Ankara, Athens, Belgrade, Bucharest, Budapest, Calcutta, Cluj, Copenhagen, London, Madrid, Manila, Olso, Prague, Rome, São Paulo, Sofia, Stockholm, Tokyo, Toronto, Warsaw, and Zagreb, as well as at Harvard University and the University of Michigan. At the same time, the foundation developed a system of fellowships that brought promising students from all over the world to these schools of public health.

Medical and public health fellowships were the beginning of what eventually was to become a global study program, embracing every field of foundation activity. Through the years, over thirteen thousand scientists and scholars from most of the world's nations have been given the opportunity for advanced study; twenty-eight have later in their careers been recipients of a Nobel Prize.

Even more extensive control programs were mounted against malaria and yellow fever, and to a lesser extent against diseases such as typhus, influenza, rabies, yaws, bilharziasis, syphilis, tuberculosis, and amoebic dysentery. For example, in 1915, the Rockefeller Foundation established pilot malaria-control projects in Arkansas and Mississippi to find answers to basic questions such as how to break the chain of transmission from man-to-mosquito-to-man and how to protect populations effectively and economically from infection. The success of these projects led, in 1919, to the beginning of a coordinated attack in ten southern states by the U.S. Public Health Service, state boards of health, and the foundation. The campaign was gradually expanded and intensified, until the final push in the years 1942–1944 virtually eradicated malaria from this country.

In 1938, there exploded in Brazil the most severe malaria epidemic ever recorded in this hemisphere. Over one hundred thousand cases, with at least fourteen thousand deaths, occurred in the first six months. So widespread was this epidemic that crops went unharvested, and starvation added to the ravages of malaria. At the invitation of the Brazilian government, the Rockefeller Foundation brought together a large antimalarial organization to bring the epidemic under control. Operating in the manner of a military campaign, over two thousand people set themselves the almost unbelievably painstaking task of eliminating every single malaria-transmitting mosquito from a twelve-thousand-square-mile area. By the end of 1940, *Anopheles gambiae* could no longer be found in the region: the western hemisphere was free from danger.

The RF's greatest single public-health effort, however, was in the field of yellow fever. For centuries, this disease had periodically ravaged many parts of the world with cataclysmic outbreaks against which no protection was possible. As late as 1905, a yellow fever epidemic, which began in New Orleans, caused one thousand deaths in the southern states. For over thirty years, starting in 1915, the RF fought this terrible disease, whose complexities proved a challenge to laboratory and field-workers alike, with a large staff of scientists in New York, Africa, and Latin America. Many of them contracted yellow fever; six died of it.

The vaccine now used to protect people from yellow fever was eventually developed in 1935 at the Rockefeller Foundation's New York laboratories, from a blood specimen taken in 1927 from a West African native named Asibi. In 1951, Dr. Max Theiler, a member of the New York laboratories, was awarded a Nobel Prize for this achievement.

An extraordinary chapter in the foundation's history is its work in China. In 1913, the RF offered to introduce Western medicine to China. Eight years later, the Peking Union Medical College (PUMC)—"the most beautiful medical school in the world"—was dedicated. Distinguished medical scientists from the United States and Europe complemented largely Western-trained Chinese faculties deployed in fifty-nine buildings over twenty-five acres. For twenty years, PUMC graduates furnished the leadership for China's medical schools and public health programs—fewer than ten entered private practice. Research was focused almost exclusively on disease problems relevant to China.

Of even more far-reaching importance were the pioneering efforts of Dr. John B. Grant to establish community-based health care in China's cities and countryside. This was a successful undertaking that, when joined to the mass literacy and social welfare efforts led by Dr. James Yen, evolved into some of the first large-scale, integrated, rural development models.

The war with Japan and the subsequent autocracy of Mao brought to an end, seemingly forever, an enormously promising collaboration, one which represented the single largest investment the RF has ever made. But with the normalization of relationships between the United States and China in 1972, the RF was asked to return to China. Today, once again, considerable collaborative work is being done, particularly in the fields of the agricultural sciences and reproductive physiology.

It became increasingly clear to those who guided the Rockefeller Foundation that there was little promise for lasting progress in public health unless medical education as a whole could be improved. On receipt of an additional $50 million from John D. Rockefeller, Sr., in 1919, the RF devoted millions of dollars to improving the quality of medical teaching in Belgium, France, Germany, Great Britain, Canada, Brazil, Lebanon, the Pacific Islands, and Southeast Asia. Meanwhile, the General Education Board,* another Rockefeller family philanthropy, gave extensive support to the improvement of medical education in the United States, where low standards of teaching had been revealed by the famous Abraham Flexner report.

By the middle of the 1920s, with the quality of medical education increasingly a national and international concern, the Rockefeller Foundation turned away from the support of teaching and toward the development of new knowledge. A new division of medical sciences, under Dr. Alan Gregg, gave direct support for research into unsolved or unexplored problems in fields such as infectious diseases, human genetics, the behavioral sciences, endocrinology, and, importantly, psychiatry in the medical school context.

The year 1928 marked the consolidation of several Rockefeller philanthropies. The Rockefeller Foundation assumed responsibility for programs leading to the advancement of knowledge in the natural sciences, social sciences, humanities and arts, as well as the medical sciences. These had been previously administered by three other Rockefeller philanthropies: the Laura Spelman Rockefeller Memorial,* the General Education Board, and the International Education Board. The RF thus entered vast new fields of research and scholarship, ending its almost exclusive concentration on medicine and public health.

In the mid-1930s, the Rockefeller Foundation turned to support investigations in relatively new and unexplored fields concerned with "the constitution, structure, and function of living organisms and their component parts." Under the guidance of Warren Weaver, almost $100 million was spent over the next twenty years to support a great variety of projects in the basic life sciences, with the principal focus on the increasingly productive discipline of molecular biology. The work of men such as Linus Pauling, George W. Beadle, George Hevesy, Ernest O. Lawrence, and George E. Hale was encouraged by grants to their institutions.

Support for the physical sciences, while lesser in scope, is typified by a $6 million grant from three Rockefeller philanthropies for the construction of the two-hundred-inch Hale telescope on Mount Palomar.

During the 1930s and 1940s, research funds for experimental biology became increasingly available elsewhere. The RF, therefore, began to place increased emphasis on the application of scientific knowledge then available, especially in the agricultural sciences.

In 1942, the Mexican government invited the foundation to send staff members to work in a cooperative venture for the improvement of Mexico's basic food crops. Under the leadership of J. George Harrar, an accomplished plant pathologist who twenty years later was to become president of the Rockefeller Foundation, the work began with those crops basic in the Mexican diet: maize and wheat. As one project appeared to be on the way to success, additional sections were established—first on potatoes, then on vegetables, sorghum, barley, and forage and pasture legumes and grasses. The last step was to extend the work into the animal sciences.

The pattern of crop improvement began with the collection and study of indigenous varieties and with experimentation on introduced types to select superior strains for prompt release to farmers. It continued with a parallel, longer-term program of plant breeding to create higher-yielding, disease-resistant strains superior to indigenous varieties. Supporting the breeding work, studies in soil fertility and disease and pest control led to knowledge of how farmers could most advantageously manage the improved varieties to secure maximum yields.

As important as the scientific work was the advanced training of many hundreds of young Mexican scientists, and the intensive development of strong agricultural training institutes.

The impact of this cooperative program produced dramatic results. Within twenty years, food production doubled as a result of research, advances in seed production, proper use of fertilizers, irrigation of new lands, and improved communications systems. In 1961, the minister of agriculture could announce the creation of the National Institute of Agricultural Research, staffed and administered by Mexican scientists, to absorb the cooperative program and the entire experiment station system.

In 1950, two members of the RF staff in Mexico City boarded an airplane bound for Bogotá, Colombia, taking with them hundreds of packets of wheat lines developed in Mexico. With their experience in the Mexican program, and with the advantage of possessing seeds representing previous research, the two scientists, later joined by others, started a cooperative program in Colombia which, in a shorter time, has achieved just as outstanding results as the one in Mexico.

Similarly, in 1955, a staff member in Colombia went to Chile to begin another cooperative food crop improvement project. In 1956, the Rockefeller Foundation extended the agricultural program to Asia in response to an invitation from the government of India. These "country programs," as they were called within the RF, laid the bases for the so-called Green Revolution, greatly increased productivity-per-acre due to improved seeds and their proper cultivation. By 1977, an estimated 30 percent of land given to the cultivation of rice in all of Asia was sown to improved varieties, as was 72 percent of the wheat acreage.

Unable to meet the number of requests from individual countries, the RF and the Ford Foundation* developed the concept of international agricultural research agencies devoted to specific food crops and serving whole regions. The first such center, the International Rice Research Institute, was started in the Philippines in 1960, operated with funds from the Ford and Rockefeller foundations. Today, a global network of thirteen such centers is supported by an international consortium of national and international agencies that in 1981 raised more than $130 million for the network's research activities.

The Green Revolution—agriculture-led development in the Third World—is probably, together with the work of the RF's former International Health Division, the foundation's most substantial achievement, one that was recognized in 1970 with a Nobel Peace Prize to Dr. Norman E. Borlaug, a staff member still active in Mexico today.

During its first fifteen years, the Rockefeller Foundation concerned itself almost exclusively with medicine and the exact sciences as a means toward a better life. But many of humanity's predicaments—such as war, poverty, and prejudice—do not lend themselves to clear-cut scientific solutions; they are likely to yield only to an evolutionary process of analysis, systematization, education, and testing. It is the goal of the social sciences to illuminate and help direct this complex evolutionary process.

In 1928, with the absorption of the Laura Spelman Rockefeller Memorial, the RF acquired a working interest in scholarly investigations—principally in economics, political science, and sociology—aimed at the clarification of man's relationship to his social environment. At that time, the social sciences were largely governed by tradition and chance, university social science departments were as often as not poorly developed, and competent men in the social sciences were few. A bold beginning had been made by Beardsley Ruml, the Laura Spelman Rockefeller Memorial's young and imaginative director, to put the social sciences on a sounder scientific footing. His work left the Rockefeller Foundation in a position to carry forward a well-articulated program based on the promotion of systematic research and aimed at achieving concrete improvements in areas such as international relations, economics, and public administration.

On an increasingly expansive front, the Rockefeller Foundation helped develop strong university research centers, here and abroad, to create fundamental knowledge upon which good teaching could rest. Universities given such encouragement include Harvard, Yale, Columbia, Stanford, Vanderbilt, Texas, Geneva, Paris, and Stockholm, among many others. Through various research institutes, the RF supported systematic inquiries into economic, political, and social problems where little empirical knowledge was available. Through the award of fellowships, the foundation increased the number of trained social scientists. Where the will existed, it sought to bring together scholars from several disciplines for joint studies on some of the concrete problems of the times. For example, the Great Depression brought emphasis to studies of economic stabilization. International relations became an important interest in the 1930s as the world scene became increasingly complex and threatening.

After World War II, as scores of countries gained independence, the foundation supported considerable work in the social sciences at universities in such nations to underpin their hopes for rapid growth grounded on economic, educational, and administrative techniques that have grown out of the social sciences over the past fifty years.

For more than fifty years, the Rockefeller Foundation has supported scholarly and creative work in the humanities and the arts. At first, the work of the foundation followed lines established by the General Education Board—support for archaeology, bibliography, biography, and language study. But, in 1934, a trustee committee urged a shift away from supporting the preservation of the past in favor of interpreting the present.

In literature, the foundation began by encouraging talented young writers, to provide a measure of time and freedom for further creative work. Awards were made to gifted writers in the United States, the United Kingdom, Canada, India, Nigeria, Japan, and the Philippines. Latin American literature, too, rarely available in translation, received support through the translation and publication of seventy-five major works.

In history, the foundation gave considerable impetus and assistance to definitive collections of the papers of great American statesmen, among them Lincoln, Madison, Hamilton, Jay, and Wilson. Other approaches that received a great deal of attention were the historical illumination of our own century and historical studies of the non-Western world.

Beginning in the 1930s, the RF intensively supported the effective teaching of major modern languages in America. To extend knowledge and education of other contemporary cultures, the foundation helped develop centers at leading American and foreign academic institutions for the study, in depth, of foreign history, culture, and institutions.

Among the arts, drama is the field in which the foundation has been active over the longest period. In the 1930s and 1940s, the foundation helped advance community and university drama in the United States through new plays, experimental productions, and the training of playwrights, directors, and actors. Foundation grants helped support or establish a variety of lively theatre groups, including the Stratford Shakespearean Festival, in Ontario; the American Shakespeare Festival, in Stratford, Connecticut; the Arena Stage, in Washington, D.C.; and the Lincoln Center for the Performing Arts, in New York City. In the 1950s, the foundation's interest in the performing arts was expanded to include music and the dance.

In the early 1960s, considerable discussion took place among the RF's trustees on how best to draw upon the lessons of the past in a world where pioneer effort by the foundation has been absorbed, on a vastly increasing scale, by programs of government and international organizations. Therefore, in 1963, on the occasion of its fiftieth anniversary, the Rockefeller foundation's trustees focused the RF's financial and professional resources, still substantial by the standards of the day, on five programs or areas in which several disciplines were associated for maximum effectiveness. The five areas defined by the trustees were the conquest of hunger, the populations problem, strengthening emerging centers of learning in the less-developed world, moving toward equal opportunity for all in the United States, and aiding our cultural development.

Under the leadership of Dr. J. George Harrar, who had directed the dramatically successful agricultural programs and had recently been elected president of the RF, considerable work of lasting significance was done over the next two decades in the areas defined by the trustees. Harrar's interest in improving world agriculture naturally remained unabated, but equally decisive was his unflagging insistence on improving educational and economic opportunities for black Americans.

Following its long interest in non-Western cultures, the RF brought its expertise in agriculture, the medical and natural sciences, and the social sciences (particularly economics) to bear on strengthening universities in Africa, Asia, and Latin America, with the objective of enabling these institutions to furnish well-trained men and women to participate in the development of their countries and regions. The methodology of this program, successively called University Development and then Education for Development, consisted of assigning key foundation staff to a university, substantially augmented by visiting professors mostly from U.S. universities, who together fleshed out academic departments while promising younger faculty members received additional training as RF fellows in highly regarded universities before returning to their teaching positions. Grants from the RF, meanwhile, provided improved teaching and research facilities. The objective was for RF and other expatriate faculty to work themselves out of a job. This was accomplished to a highly satisfactory degree, so much so that the trustees were able to phase out this program, the final step taken in 1983. In terms of money spent and staff deployed, it remains the largest program ever undertaken by the RF.

During those same years, the population program played an active role in supporting private and official efforts to create awareness of the consequences of extremely rapid rates of increase, and to stimulate research and availability of culturally acceptable means of family planning.

At home, the Rockefeller Foundation became one of the most consistent advocates and supporters of equality of opportunity for blacks, at first in the field of higher education, later in training black administrators for selected public school systems with largely black student populations. In addition, its arts program expanded vigorously into the support of creative individuals—particularly playwrights, choreographers, and video artists—at a time when the performing arts captured the interest and imagination of the American public as never before.

Realism dictates that the Rockefeller Foundation today must take a more modest view of its potential for influencing progress. The soaring costs of inflation and relatively static capital funds can only diminish the foundation's grant-making ability. As for its well-known operational programs, it is unthinkable today to maintain, as the foundation did in 1970, a field staff of 143 highly experienced professionals, distributed over 15 nations. It is painful that at a time when the private initiative is stressed emphatically that the RF's responses, as those of other private organizations, must necessarily be circumscribed.

But despite adverse circumstances common to all private, nonprofit organizations, the RF is determined, in the words of its president, to "sustain its global vision."

The foundation, with 1981 assets of about $883 million, is organized into six programs staffed by specialists in fields relevant to program interests. Richard W. Lyman, formerly president of Stanford University, is the foundation's chief executive officer; he is assisted by three vice-presidents. A board of twenty-three trustees of widely varying experiences passes on the grant proposals made to them by program officers at regular meetings. The six programs and their 1981 expenditures are: Arts, Humanities, and Contemporary Values—$6.4 million; Conquest of Hunger—$7.9 million; Education for Development—$5.2 million (program being phased out); Equal Opportunity—$4.9 million; International Relations—$3.7 million; Population and Health—$11 million. Each program's specific interests are detailed in the annual report, which is available on request.

An overview of the program areas makes clear the RF's continuing commitment to assist in the economic and social development of the world's poorer countries, with a renewed interest in long-neglected tropical diseases that afflict hundreds of millions of people. At home, its long-standing interest in helping to advance the educational and economic opportunities of blacks has not flagged and now extends to Hispanics and other minority-group members. And a new program in international relations seeks to enhance the global capacity to prevent conflict between nations that would render immaterial all other human effort.

The headquarters offices of the Rockefeller Foundation are located at 1133 Avenue of the Americas, New York, New York 10036. Rockefeller Foundation archival material is located and may be consulted, upon inquiry, at the Rockefeller Archive Center, Hillcrest, Pocantico Hills, North Tarrytown, New York 10591.

For further information, see the RF's standard history, now outdated, by Raymond B. Fosdick, *The Story of the Rockefeller Foundation* (1952); E. C. Stakman, Richard Bradfield, and Paul C. Mangelsdorf, *Campaigns Against Hun-*

*ger* (1967); William Greer, *The Plague Killers* (1969); and Mary Brown Bullock, *An American Transplant: The Rockefeller Foundation and Peking Union Medical College* (1980). See also *Annual Reports* of the foundation, published continuously since 1914.

HENRY ROMNEY

**ROCKEFELLER MEMORIAL.** See Laura Spelman Rockefeller Memorial.

**ROSENWALD FUND.** See Julius Rosenwald Fund.

**ROWLAND FOUNDATION, INC.** Incorporated in Delaware in 1960 by Edwin H. Land and Helen M. Land, as Edwin H. Land-Helen M. Land, Inc., the Rowland Foundation took its present name in 1972. Edwin Land made a fortune through his invention of the Polaroid-Land camera and other scientific discoveries. The foundation has been financed through grants of cash or stock in Land's Polaroid Corporation.

Initially, the foundation was relatively small, but, in the 1970s, its assets grew to about $34 million, which is approximately what its corpus was in 1980. The foundation, with annual grants in recent years ranging from $0.75 million to $1.5 million, has devoted well over 50 percent of its annual giving for the support of higher and secondary education, hospitals, and medical research, with the remainder devoted to the support of arts, culture, and social welfare programs.

In 1979, the Rowland Foundation established a scientific laboratory or research institute in Cambridge, Massachusetts. A 1981 press account stated that the foundation would transfer millions of dollars in its assets to this new institute. Thus, it appears that the institute will become the major beneficiary of future foundation support.

The Rowland Foundation is governed by a five-member board of trustees, with Edwin H. Land serving as president, Helen M. Land as vice-president, and two other members of the Land family on the board. The mailing address of the foundation is Post Office Box 13, Cambridge, Massachusetts 02138.

Almost the only additional information on this foundation readily available to the public are the annual reports and returns filed by it with the Internal Revenue Service, and the various Foundation Center publications. See, however, *Annual Reports*, published since 1979, and an article "Polaroid's Land To Cut Holdings from 11% to 7.7%," *Wall Street Journal* (July 22, 1981), p. 11.

**RUBINSTEIN FOUNDATION.** See Helena Rubinstein Foundation, Inc.

**RUSSELL SAGE FOUNDATION.** Established by Margaret Olivia Sage in 1907, the Russell Sage Foundation is probably the oldest general-purpose foundation in the United States. The foundation's first leaders developed its initial social research and social welfare policy programs out of the private charity organization movement. They pursued those programs with remarkable consistency for forty years, until the increasingly distinct professional development of social research and social work made it impossible for one foundation to contribute to both fields at once. In 1947, the Russell Sage Foundation broke sharply with its past, strengthened its ties to the academic social science disciplines, and shifted its emphasis to the application of those disciplines to social problems and the professions.

Margaret Sage named the foundation after her husband, who left her the entire $65 million fortune he had made in railroad, telegraph, lumber, and other investments. Russell Sage had disliked all forms of philanthropy. Margaret Olivia Sage, alone, decided to put the fortune to charitable purposes, and she made large gifts to many colleges and universities, churches, and charities.

In addition, Margaret Sage wished to create a memorial that would both endure and promote social change. Robert W. de Forest, president of the New York Charity Organization society and her chief advisor, persuaded her that a permanent institution could promote change only if it was empowered to change itself. Accordingly, Mrs. Sage set up the Russell Sage Foundation under a charter that defined its purpose very broadly: "The improvement of social and living conditions in the United States of America" by "any means" that seems appropriate to its trustees from time to time, "including research, publication, education, the establishment and maintenance of charitable or benevolent activities, agencies and institutions, and the aid of any such activities, agencies, or institutions already in existence." Margaret Sage laid down a more precise set of objectives in a letter accompanying her initial gift of $10 million (her will added a $5 million bequest in 1917): the foundation was to promote "social betterment—improvement of the hard conditions of our working classes, making their homes and surroundings more healthful and comfortable and their lives happier; giving more opportunity to them and to their children." It was to take the entire nation for its field but was to be located in New York City and to pay some special attention to the city and its region.

The foundation's initial program reflected the emphasis on the professionalization of social work and the elimination of deleterious environmental conditions that characterized the organized charity movement at the turn of the century. Margaret Sage, Directors Robert W. de Forest and John Glenn (former leaders of the Charity Organization Societies of New York City and Baltimore), Shelby M. Harrison, and a board of trustees that at first included five men and four women active in New York charities defined this program and provided extraordinary continuity of leadership. Operating from an imposing building near New York's United Charities Building, just above Gramercy Park, the foundation became the pioneer American research institute, grant maker, and coordinator of research, experiment, and reform legislation in the fields of social work, urban planning, and industrial relations. These programs were more sharply focused, better financed, more consistently pursued, and more firmly connected to the social policy community than were most competing research initiatives, and they had a considerable impact.

The Sage Foundation soon decided to use its own staff and facilities to carry out most of its activities. Early research grants to social-work schools in Boston, Chicago, Saint Louis, and New York yielded disappointing results; university departments of sociology were doing little research. So the foundation itself set up research departments in fields such as child hygiene, recreation, consumer credit, industrial studies, social surveys, and social statistics, staffing them with highly trained researchers drawn from both universities and organized charities. And it assumed responsibility for housing the library that had been put together by organized charity in New York City and for making it, as de Forest hoped, the best place in the country where practical problems could be studied.

From the beginning, de Forest, Glenn, and Margaret Sage determined to use the foundation to develop the basic and the practical knowledge that was essential if social work was to become a profession. It published books that became standards in several fields of social work—most notably Robert A. Woods and Albert J. Kennedy, *Handbook of Settlements* (1911); Mary E. Richmond, *Social Diagnosis* (1917) and *What is Social Case Work* (1922); and Joanna C. Colcord, *Cash Relief* (1936) and *Your Community* (1939). Under Richmond between 1909 and 1929, and then under Colcord until 1945, the Department of Charity Administration and several related departments published social-work texts, trained social workers, and provided expert advice. These activities, together with the provision of classroom and office space in its West Wing Building (1931), kept the foundation in close touch with the New York School of Social Work. Within the social work movement the foundation persistently emphasized the physical, economic, and social environment, rather than the psychological or cultural characteristics of individuals, as the source of poverty. It did not support the introduction of psychiatry into social work. It did support research and the formulation of reform legislation on social and institutional problems such as child abuse, child labor, women's working conditions, marriage, unemployment, workmen's compensation, and consumer credit. During the first twenty years, the trustees also granted several million dollars to charity organization societies, located chiefly in New York City and New York State, to strengthen their management and support their campaigns against tuberculosis and other environmental and public health problems.

Belief that the physical environment exerted a profound influence on social life also shaped the Russell Sage Foundation's second-largest effort between 1907 and 1947, its sponsorship of the survey and city planning movements. One of the foundation's first research and publishing ventures was the *Pittsburgh Survey* by Paul U. Kellogg et al. (1909–1914), on the economic, health, and social problems and the social agencies of that city. Bringing together ideas about the study of housing, public health, working conditions, and the social, moral, and religious lives of the poor that had been gathering force in Britain and the United States since the last third of the nineteenth century, the *Pittsburgh Survey* and the movement it sparked were widely influential. In 1909, the leading social work journal, *Charities and the Commons,* now edited by Kellogg and supported in large part by the foundation, changed its name to *The Survey*. In 1912, the foundation created a Department of Surveys and Exhibits under the direction of Shelby M. Harrison, who had worked on the *Pittsburgh Survey*; over the next twenty years, Harrison played a central role in the development of social research methods and in the promotion, design, and staffing of hundreds of surveys. Harrison continued to promote innovations in research; he served as chairman of the Social Science Research Council executive committee between 1933 and 1945. But by the mid-1920s many of the surveys served a social-work planning and advocacy more than a social research function.

The foundation's interest in city planning grew both out of the survey movement and also out of its longstanding interest in housing. In 1909, de Forest and Glenn joined Lawrence Veiller in setting up the National Housing Association, which was, in effect, a department of the foundation. Through a series of books and pamphlets, the quarterly *Housing*, and a consulting and reference service, Veiller continued until 1936 to urge that housing be improved through stricter regulation, private investment, and mortage policies designed to make home ownership more widely accessible—not through public or limited-dividend housing. Between 1909 and 1922, the Sage Foundation supported these goals by investing a considerable portion of its capital in the development of Forest Hills Gardens, in the New York City borough of Queens. This experiment succeeded in producing high-quality design but failed to yield the modest profits the foundation had expected (ultimately it cost the foundation several hundred thousand dollars). It also failed to supply low-cost housing for the poor. In 1922, Charles Dyer Norton and Alfred T. White persuaded de Forest and Glenn to turn the foundation resources to city planning. The result was a ten-year, million-dollar investment in the comprehensive, twelve-volume *Regional Survey and Plan of New York and Environs* (Thomas Adams et al., 1928–1931) and considerable subsequent support for the independent Regional Plan Association of New York, which sought to promote the survey's recommendations over the next fifteen years and which still continues to urge comprehensive planning in the New York region. Distinguished from its predecessors by its prescient attention to demographic and economic factors and by its emphasis on the diffusion of population throughout an entire twenty-two-county metropolitan region, the New York regional plan set the standard in its field until the middle 1960s. Between 1922 and 1946, the Sage Foundation also published some of the leading textbooks in city planning and supported several national city planning organizations.

The foundation's original leaders were persuaded that "social and living conditions" could be improved not only indirectly, through professional social work and city planning, but also directly, through bargaining by workers. The foundation supported a third major effort between 1907 and 1947: the study of working conditions and labor relations. Mary A. van Kleeck, who had been publishing papers on women and children at work in New York City for the College Settlements Association since 1905, joined the foundation as head of its Committee on Women's Work in 1910, then served as director of the Department of Industrial Studies from 1916 until 1947. She and her associates produced a steady stream of books and pamphlets, first on women's occupations and, after 1916, on health insurance, unemployment, and collective bargaining in mines, steel mills, and retail stores. Between 1929 and 1946, van Kleeck turned her department's attention to two major projects: a comprehensive study of labor relations during depression and war, with emphasis on industrial unions (never published), and Mary L. Fleddérus and Mary van Kleeck, *Technology and Livelihood* (1944). Van Kleeck's own emphasis shifted from a cautious encouragement of collective bargaining in the early 1920s to forthright advocacy of the socialization of all industry in *Miners and Management* (1934) and of national five-year plans. The foundation's trustees rejected these policy recommendations and began, in 1934, to place a disclaimer at the beginning of all books the foundation issued, stating that the foundation approved the methods but not necessarily the conclusions of the work.

The charter devised by de Forest and Margaret Sage in 1907 did not limit the Russell Sage Foundation to a narrow set of social-work purposes but made it a general-purpose foundation whose trustees were empowered to respond to "other and greater needs for philanthropic action than any which are now apparent." In 1947, the foundation's trustees decided to exercise that power and to make radical changes in both focus and operating procedures. They brought the foundation's direct involvement in the organized charity movement to an abrupt end and abolished their three-pronged program in the fields of social work, city planning, and industrial relations. Henceforth, the foundation would seek to improve "social and living conditions" through the support of social science research.

The decision to shift focus in 1947 was made easier by the fact that many foundation programs had lapsed into routine. Several departments and individuals had made important contributions to the study and relief of unemployment and to the formulation of relief legislation during the Great Depression; but apart from van Kleeck's studies of industrial relations, the foundation had devoted most of its effort to the management of social work and to the support of organizations that it had launched before 1929. Few of its researchers had contributed to the social sciences during the 1930s; much of the staff had left for military service during the war; the federal and state governments had taken over most of the social service activities formerly provided by organized private charity. Harrison's retirement in 1947 brought an opportunity for a new start.

By 1947, lawyers and social scientists dominated the board of trustees, replacing the men and women who managed organized charity. Their emphasis on social science research reflected their own priorities as well as the recommendations of Social Science Research Council's executive director, Donald R. Young, and the other social scientists who had evaluated the Sage Foundation's programs. In 1948, the Sage trustees appointed Young as president of the foundation. They ended support for social work and urban planning agencies and for the New York School of Social Work (which then affiliated with Columbia

University). They distributed the foundation library to Columbia, City College, and the New York Public Library. They curtailed the foundation's research institute activities, retired most of the staff, and sold the foundation's buildings. These actions freed the foundation from long-standing commitments; it added to the resources it could devote to research with the discovery of oil on the March Island (Louisiana) bird refuge, to which it held mineral rights.

Since 1947, the Russell Sage Foundation has used its resources (its endowment was valued at about $49 million in 1981) to support and publish studies in basic and applied social research. These studies are conducted primarily by social scientists who are based in universities and who are selected by peer review of proposals submitted in foundation-specified program areas. In its publication program, the foundation emphasizes book-length works designed for general readers as well as for scholars. The foundation itself also provides facilities for researchers and encourages members of its own small staff to carry on research in their own fields. An operating as well as a grant-making foundation, it has launched several programs that have attracted external resources. In 1982, it moved into newly renovated quarters at 112 East Sixty-fourth Street, New York, New York 10021, enabling it to expand the research activities conducted on its own premises.

The body of work supported and published by the foundation since 1947 is much more diverse and difficult to characterize than the work it produced before that date. This was the almost inevitable result of the foundation's institutional change: it now operated much less like an institute with a permanent research staff, experienced a good deal of staff turnover, especially during the turbulent 1970s, and elected to stay closely in step with the changing and increasingly divergent concerns of academic social science.

Under the leadership of Young and Orville G. Brim, who succeeded Young as president in 1964 and served until 1972, the Russell Sage Foundation continued to publish sociological and practical studies of philanthropy, social-work administration, and related topics. It reduced its activity in these fields when it transferred its twenty-year-old *Social Work Year Book* to the American Association of Social Workers in 1948 and, with Carnegie Corporation of New York* assistance, turned its longstanding program of data collection and studies on foundations and charities into the independent Foundation Library Center (later Foundation Center) in 1956. But it continued to publish works, such as the pioneering *Aging and Society* (three volumes, 1968–1972), by Matilda White Riley and associates, that were of interest to both social workers and sociologists. And it continued its early focus on the social environment and launched a new series of works designed to summarize and interpret specialized social research for a wider audience by underwriting Roland Warren's work on communities, Milton M. Gordon's work on assimilation, and Harold Wilensky and Elliot Lebeaux's *Industrial Society and Social Welfare* (1965).

Young and Brim also moved the foundation in new directions. During their tenure, it supported several studies of educational testing and of the factors that encourage high achievement in school, including Brim et al., *American Beliefs and Attitudes about Intelligence* (1969), and Urie Bronfenbrenner's widely read *Two Worlds of Childhood* (1970). And it launched an effort to promote the use of social science in the medical, military, journalistic, public administration, and especially the legal professions. Anthropologist Esther Lucille Brown had begun work of this sort in 1932; Young, Brim, and sociologists Leonard S. Cottrell, Jr., and Edgar S. Borgatta greatly expanded it after 1947. The foundation supported research on professionalization in general, on the relation between social science and the professions, and on social problems relevant to particular professions by Brown and her associates and, after 1949, by Robert K. Merton, William J. Goode, Morris Janowitz, Philip Selznik, and other leading sociologists. With over $1 million from the Ford Foundation* as well as with its own funds, the foundation also supported exchanges of graduate students and researchers between professional schools and social science departments and underwrote the introduction of sociological perspectives into the curricula of professional schools.

Between 1948 and 1975, the Russell Sage Foundation maintained a special relationship to the discipline of sociology. During the 1950s and 1960s, it supported research on the methods and the personnel of the discipline and provided both pre- and post-doctoral fellowships for sociologists. In earlier years, it had assisted in the creation of the Social Science Research Council (1923), the publication of *Recent Social Trends* (1933) and the *Encyclopedia of the Social Sciences* (1934), and in the publication of U.S. census data for small tracts in New York City (1924–1932); it now helped organize a series of demographic and sociological monographs based on the censuses of 1950 and 1960 and financed by several sources in addition to its own budget. Under the leadership of Eleanor B. Sheldon and Wilbert E. Moore, it also took the lead, from 1966 on, in the movement to define and to demonstrate the effectiveness of social indicators—statistical measures of social phenomena, gathered over time in consistent series. The foundation and the Social Science Research Council supported programs of research designed to persuade the federal government to collect and publish social indicators, just as it publishes indicators of economic trends. This movement had some success but had not, by the early 1980s, secured federal adoption.

Under the relatively brief administrations of Hugh F. Cline, Aaron Wildavsky, and Trustee David B. Truman in the mid-1970s, the foundation revived its early interest in political institutions, public administration, and public policy. Wallace S. Sayre and Herbert Kaufman's *Governing New York City* (1960) was a distinguished early work in this field; now the foundation underwrote several studies of national politics and sponsored research on policy options in specific areas such as criminal justice, privacy, civil liberties, the negative income tax, early childhood education, the management of public bureaucracies, and the history and current problems of New York City.

In 1979, Marshall A. Robinson, an economist and Ford Foundation executive, became president of the Russell Sage Foundation. Two years later the foundation's trustees, now led by Herma Hill Kay, a professor of law at the University of California, decided to continue their emphasis on social science and social policy research. The first programs approved under this decision—the organization of a new series of monographs based on the 1980 census and the sponsorship of a postdoctoral fellowship program—reaffirmed the foundation's postwar role within the social science community.

For further information, in addition to the Sage Foundation's archives, see several relevant manuscript collections located at Columbia University: the Lawrence Veiller Papers in the Community Service Society of New York Papers, the Mary E. Richmond Papers, and Shelby M. Harrison's manuscript biography of John M. Glenn. The archives of the Regional Plan Association of New York are at Cornell University; the papers of George McAneny, president of the Regional Plan Association from 1932 to 1951, are at Princeton University; the Mary van Kleeck Papers are in the Sophia Smith Collection at Smith College. The Paul U. Kellogg Papers and the Survey Associates Papers in the Social Welfare History Archives, University of Minnesota, are also relevant. See also the *Annual Reports* of the foundation, published continuously since 1947.

The fullest account of the foundation for its period is John M. Glenn, Lilian Brandt, F. Emerson Andrews, *Russell Sage Foundation 1907–1946* (1946); other accounts of the foundation itself are F. Emerson Andrews, *Foundation Watcher* (1973); and Orville G. Brim, "Do We Know What We Are Doing," in Fritz F. Heimann, ed., *The Future of Foundations* (1973).

Of the many works that discuss the Sage Foundation's programs, see F. Emerson Andrews, *Philanthropic Foundations* (1956); Robert Bremner, *From the Depths: The Discovery of Poverty in the United States* (1956) and *American Philanthropy* (1960); Roy Lubove, *The Progressives and the Slums: Tenement House Reform in New York City, 1890–1917* (1962); and *The Professional Altruist: The Emergence of Social Work as a Career* (1965); Clarke Chambers, *Seedtime of Reform: American Social Service and Social Action* (1963) and *Paul U. Kellogg and The Survey: Voices for Social Welfare and Social Change* (1971); John F. McClymer, *War and Welfare: Social Engineering in America, 1890–1925* (1980). A brief history of the foundation as a social service organization is provided in Peter Romanofsky, *Social Service Organizations* vol. 2 (1978); and biographical accounts of Margaret Olivia Sage, Mary E. Richmond, Mary van Kleeck, and Joanna Colcord appear in Edward T. James, ed., *Notable American Women* (1971).

DAVID C. HAMMACK

# S

**SAGE FOUNDATION.** See Russell Sage Foundation.

**SAINT PAUL FOUNDATION, THE.** This community foundation, the Saint Paul Foundation, was established in 1940 in St. Paul, Minnesota, by a group of citizens from the city's chamber of commerce. Under their plan of organization, funds coming to the foundation were placed under the management of trust institutions selected by persons making the gifts to the foundation; officers of three trustee banks of St. Paul served as a committee which selected five members of a distribution committee. In 1952, a reorganization resulted in an enlarging of the distribution committee, wherein various political, professional, and educational officials selected six members, and five were designated by the foundation's distribution committee and three by the bank trustees. Despite this reorganization, the foundation had a slow growth. In 1954, its capital amounted to only $5,000, and it made grants for that year of $300. By 1969, assets of the foundation had climbed to about $3 million, and grants for that year amounted to about $64,000. In 1975, assets had grown to about $40 million, and grants for that year amounted to $2.5 million. Since then, primarily as the result of several large bequests, the foundation's assets soared to approximately $58 million in 1982, and grants for that year were about $4 million.

The purpose of the St. Paul Foundation has remained the same throughout its history, which is to benefit the citizens of the St. Paul area. Over time, however, there have been changes. The distribution committee has broadened its area of operations from St. Paul proper to adjacent counties and, under certain circumstances, even beyond this geographic area. Also, the foundation has recently created several new funds to better serve its constituency and has embarked on a number of special projects in the educational area. Thus, while the foundation has continued to engage in the palliative giving which was a characteristic in its earlier years, it is now funding more venturesome projects. In 1980, for example, social welfare organizations in the St. Paul area received 32 percent of total foundation funding, but 57 percent of the total was devoted to humanistic and educational funding, 6 percent for special projects, with the remaining 6 percent devoted to other organizations. Larger grants for 1980 included the following: Twin Cities Public Television—$300,000; Saint Paul Chamber Orchestra—$50,000; United Way of the Saint Paul Area—$153,042; College of Saint Catherine—$60,000; and Citizens Task Force for the Library—$40,862.

The foundation is governed by three corporate trustees: American National Bank and Trust Company of Saint Paul; First Trust Company of Saint Paul; and Northwestern National Bank of Saint Paul. Distribution of foundation grants is administered by a fourteen-member distribution committee under the direction of a president. Offices of the foundation are located at 1120 Northwestern National Bank Building, St. Paul, Minnesota 55101.

For further information, see *Annual Reports* of the foundation, issued since the 1970s, and periodic topical reports which it has published. See also *A History of The Saint Paul Foundation 1940–1980* (1980), a fourteen-page pamphlet published by the foundation.

**SAMUEL H. KRESS FOUNDATION.** Born on July 23, 1863, in Cherryville, Pennsylvania, Samuel H. Kress became one of the better-known American businessmen of the twentieth century. Although starting his career in teaching in 1880, he went on to become the founder of S. H. Kress and Company, operating what was popularly known as a five-and-ten-cent store. Beginning in Memphis, Tennessee, in 1896, Kress quickly built up his chain of stores, and, by 1900, he moved to his avid avocation—art collecting. Over a period of years, he acquired a notable collection of paintings and sculpture, particularly of the Italian school, which he later gave to the National Gallery of Art, Washington, D.C., and to twenty-five other museums and galleries across the United States.

It was in 1929 that Kress incorporated the Samuel H. Kress Foundation, in New York, for the purpose of promoting the "moral, physical, and mental welfare of the human race." Funded initially with relatively small grants from him and from his brothers, Claude W. and Rush H. Kress, assets of the foundation had swelled to several million dollars by the time of Samuel Kress's death in 1955. Until his death, he devoted his energies to the foundation and art collecting, serving as a trustee of the Metropolitan Museum of Art and as president and a trustee of the National Gallery of Art.

The Kress Foundation had always had grant programs predominantly for art history research and art conservation, though, for a time, the foundation did award grants for medical research and facilities. In 1963, however, a decision was reached to return to its former concentration in the art area. In 1981, with assets of approximately $30 million, the foundation operates six major programs: fellowships for predoctoral research in art history; training and research in conservation of works of art; development of scholarly resources in the fields of art history and conservation; conservation and restoration of monuments and works of art; archaeological field work emphasizing art history; and occasional related projects. In recent years, total annual grants have ranged from $1.5 million to

$2 million. Grants have been made to a wide variety of art institutions in all sections of the United States as well as to institutions abroad.

The Kress Foundation is governed by a seven-member board of trustees. Administration of the foundation is carried on from offices located at 221 West Fifty-seventh Street, New York, New York 10019, under the direction of an executive vice-president.

For further information, see *Annual Reports* of the foundation, published since 1962. See also Samuel H. Kress obituary, *New York Times* (September 22, 1955), p. 25.

MICHAEL V. NAMORATO

**SAMUEL I. NEWHOUSE FOUNDATION, INC.** He said he was "not trying to save the world." His abiding concern, he told people, was to provide for his family. Giving his local editors control of newspaper content and letting them try to save the world, S. I. Newhouse attended to the business side of his "properties," as he called them, and made his heirs the wealthiest media family in the country. With holdings that may be worth $2 billion, the Newhouses are even richer than the fabled Hearsts and Coxes. Samuel I. Newhouse's sons, Samuel and Donald, reign over thirty-one big-city, daily papers, six television stations, three radio stations (now up for sale), numerous cable and microwave businesses, and five magazines, including *Vogue, Mademoiselle,* and *Glamour.*

Newhouse established Advance Publications, Inc., as his chief corporate entity. He was sole owner, holding 1,000 shares of common stock. As his will provided, 990 shares became nonvoting stock and the property of the Newhouse Foundation. His two sons each received five shares, all of the voting stock that remained. He also arranged that 10 percent of his estate would go to his wife.

Newhouse and his wife, Mitzi, established the foundation in 1945, when Newhouse was fifty. Among its major projects are support of a communications center at Syracuse University and a law center at Rutgers University. Its general giving is concentrated in New York and is directed toward community funds, music and the arts, education, Jewish welfare funds, hospitals, and youth agencies. When gifts are made outside of New York, they tend to be in areas where Newhouse media properties are located. They are all over, in Mississippi, Louisiana, and Alabama, in Ohio, Michigan, and Missouri, in Oregon, Pennsylvania, and Massachusetts, as well as in New Jersey and New York.

In 1980, the foundation was cited by the National Committee for Responsive Philanthropy (NCRP) as one among 30 percent of 208 foundations queried who declined to provide information for a study conducted by the committee. Also, as part of its policy of discouraging new applicants, the foundation issues no specific application guidelines. It is therefore not surprising that beneficiaries tend to be largely the same year after year; but there is nothing to keep a supplicant from writing a letter of inquiry to the foundation's address, 950 Fingerboard Road, Staten Island, New York 10305.

The Samuel I. Newhouse Foundation fairly fits one of the characterizations that emerged from the 1980 NCRP study, that many foundations "operate in secrecy and refuse to make public the details of their operations, investments, and beneficiaries." On the other hand, Newhouse performs a little better than the foundations accused by the NCRP of giving "startling small" grants to charities devoted to "minorities, women, consumers, the poor, the elderly, the disabled and the environment." The NCRP would urge greater giving by the foundation to newer charities, but Newhouse is involved significantly in minority and poverty-group projects. See Spencer Rich, "Charity Groups' Secrecy Criticised," *Washington Post* (June 5, 1980), p. 4.

Education is the principle activity supported by the foundation, accounting for about 40 percent of disbursements annually. Social welfare and civic and youth affairs receive about one-third, including 7 percent earmarked for Jewish welfare. Cultural programs amount to approximately 15 percent and health programs close to half that share. A major cultural grantee is the Mitzi E. Newhouse Theatre in New York City's Lincoln Center.

S. I. Newhouse made contributions of $25 million through the foundation before his death in 1979 at the age of eighty-four. Indeed, he wanted to see results of his philanthropy during his lifetime, and particularly did he want to see the Communications Center at Syracuse University completed in his span. Gifts to the center accounted for much of the $25 million. Asked how he came to choose the university as his major beneficiary, the publisher explained that his two sons attended Syracuse, he was owner of two newspapers and radio and television stations there, and he was on the board of trustees and had received an honorary degree from the university.

An initial gift of $2 million was made in 1960. It was used for construction of a new School of Journalism building, provisions for mid-career study by active journalists, and support for graduate students and media research. In 1962, the Newhouse foundation made an additional grant of $13 million to Syracuse to implement an I. M. Pei design for a four-building center on an eight-acre site adjacent to the main campus. In addition to the journalism building, finished in 1964, space was provided for radio and television, educational television, audiovisual education, speech, and collateral activities. Until 1977, over half the foundation's disbursements went to the center and to the S. I. Newhouse School of Public Communications housed there. The level of annual support dropped year by year and recently was at the quarter-million-dollar level, about one-eighth of the foundation total.

It was natural that Newhouse would take an interest in making a major grant in New Jersey. He was reared in Bayonne and had begun his publishing career when he was seventeen by managing the *Bayonne Times*. The first paper in which he owned a controlling interest was the *Staten Island Advance*. Newhouse, who had been drawn to support Syracuse University because it was his sons' *alma mater*, ended his own formal schooling when he was thirteen. He later resumed studies at the New Jersey Law School, where he was graduated in 1916, then twenty-one years of age. This institution was later incorporated into Rutgers

University's law school. In 1978, the foundation made a $1.5 million grant to fund the establishment of the S. I. Newhouse Law Center on Rutgers' Newark campus. The grant was used for renovations on a seventeen-story building to house the center, to establish an endowment that would benefit research programs, and for the acquisition of specialized books and journals. In appreciation for the grant and for the publisher's other deeds in the public interest, the Newhouse Law Center name was made to embrace Rutgers' Newark School of Law, School of Criminal Justice, and Institute of Continuing Legal Education. Annual grants to Rutgers have been made subsequently, as high as $300,000.

The publisher's companies were run by the family, and so is the foundation. His widow, Mitzi, is president. His brothers, Norman and Theodore, and his sons, Samuel, Jr., and Donald, are the other directors and officers.

The market value of the foundation's assets hovers around $40 million. In 1979, it stood at about $36 million, and annual grants were around $2 million. In addition to its own income, it receives funding from Newhouse companies and makes grants through them. The accumulation of wealth on which the foundation is based was a result primarily of Newhouse's great profits. It was swelled, however, by the low costs and incredibly simple management system he used for his chain of properties. He ran his properties "out of a battered briefcase." With no central office, he shared desks and secretaries at the various publishing outlets as he made his frequent rounds. Wealth piled up, too, as a result of his living in a manner which, while extravagant by common standards, with a Park Avenue apartment and a large country estate in Jersey, would have to be judged positively frugal in contrast to that of some of his mass-media peers. Born to immigrant parents, he had to leave school as a youngster in order to help support his family on a two-dollar-a-week salary as a judge's clerk. The foundation he established could annually employ a thousand clerks at such wages, even allowing for inflation.

Newhouse termed himself a liberal democrat but left his local editors free to follow their own political philosophies. His papers and broadcast stations were strong in community service, and his foundation is an extension of that inclination, of the fact that he was oriented very much toward the future, of his favorite diversions, the theatre and opera, and, with the foundation's emphasis on the Syracuse center, of his life's work in mass communications.

Deriving its assets from a publishing fortune has not influenced the Newhouse Foundation to issue reports and publications concerning its own activities. Almost the only additional information readily available to the public on this foundation are the annual reports and returns filed by it with the Internal Revenue Service, and the various Foundation Center publications. There is, however, a book, out of print and held by relatively few libraries, which may be consulted. It is John A. Lent, *Newhouse, Newspapers, Nuisances* (1966).

LESLIE CAINE CAMPBELL

**SAMUEL ROBERTS NOBLE FOUNDATION, INC., THE.** The Noble Foundation was created as an irrevocable trust by the late Lloyd Noble, of

Ardmore, Oklahoma, in 1945 as a memorial to his father, Samuel Roberts Noble. Lloyd worked in his father's hardware store as a boy, and after attending the University of Oklahoma, he entered business for himself and formed the Samedan Oil Corporation in 1932 and the Noble Drilling Corporation in 1939.

Lloyd Noble had a particular love for farming, and while directing his oil enterprises in Oklahoma, he observed from his aircraft the erosion of the land and the abandoned farms during the late 1930s. Consequently, the first objective of the newly organized Noble Foundation was to encourage more farmers to conserve and improve their cultivated land, increase the grazing value of their pastures, and produce more and better foods in their vegetable gardens.

The foundation employed a technical staff, and a series of contests were begun in 1946 to stimulate interest in procedures which would improve the agricultural economy of south-central Oklahoma. A laboratory was built and equipped to analyze soils and to experiment with appropriate crops. From these efforts have come Elbon (Noble spelled backwards) and Bonel (rearrangement of the word Noble) ryegrasses, winter pasture grasses that have proved superior in growth and nutrition and have gained worldwide acceptance. Today, under the direction of Gary D. Simmons, three teams comprised of three to five scientists with skills in agronomy, agricultural economics, animal science, horticulture, and wildlife management provide a free farm planning and consultation service to state and area agriculturists as a part of several ongoing programs within the foundation's Agricultural Division. This service is designed to help farmers and ranchers within a 100-mile radius of Ardmore, Oklahoma, attain a balanced economical program in accord with their goals, finances, and land capability. The scientists and staff are involved in ongoing research on three research and demonstration farms which comprise approximately 4,000 acres. Also, demonstration projects are conducted on cooperator farms and ranches where specific problems exist. No limitation is placed on the cooperator as to size of the farm or type of enterprises. There are 450 farms and ranch cooperators actively involved in the foundation's Agricultural Division's research and demonstration. In addition, many other daily, "one-time" contacts by telephone, letter, office, or on farm visit were made with individuals needing technical training assistance. Throughout 1981, 2,885 forage and 3,032 soil samples requiring 35,725 determinations were processed at the foundation's laboratory. An additional 616 determinations were made in digestible dry matter, prussic acid, nitrates, and irrigation water samples. During the year ending October 31, 1981, $1,741,905 in foundation funds were expended by the Agricultural Division.

The Biomedical Division of the Noble Foundation was established in 1951 to provide basic knowledge toward the understanding and control of malignant and degenerative diseases. Using animal and tissue culture models, the scientific staff, under the direction of Dr. M. K. Patterson, Jr., studies the fundamental cause underlying carcinogenesis, tumor-host relations, immunological responses, aging, and nutritional variations of cells. The Biomedical Division operates five research sections: Cell Biology, Nutrition, Biomedical Pharmacology, Tumor-

Host and Immunology. The staff has published more than three hundred papers, including numerous reviews and chapters in books, and has participated in hundreds of seminars. The laboratory receives no federal grants or contracts and has no affiliation with hospitals or universities. The foundation maintains an extensive scientific library utilizing computerized retrieval, on-line terminals to other data bases, microfilm filing, and interlibrary loan.

The Noble Foundation has approximately eighty-five employees engaged in basic biomedical and agricultural research and consultation. It is completely self-supporting, and no outside contributions are sought, although $515 in grants were received in 1981 and $265 in 1980. If funds are available after in-house commitments are met, the foundation makes grants in other areas, principally for health research and for health-delivery systems. During 1981, the amount of funds expended by the foundation's Biomedical Division totalled $1,973,649.75.

There is also an interest manifested by the Noble Foundation in higher education, with grants awarded primarily for capital improvements. The sum of $10,600,075.34 was given to ninety-five organizations or institutions in 1981, an all-time annual high. The foundation also provided scholarship support for forty-two students at twenty-three different schools of higher learning. The students are children of employees of the various Noble-related companies. Both the Biomedical Division and the Agricultural Division employ high school and college students during the summer months.

The Noble Foundation's assets in 1981 were valued at about $336 million, most of which was in governmental and nongovernmental obligations and corporate stocks. The excess of expenditures over receipts in 1981 amounted to $2,289,267.

The Samuel Roberts Noble Foundation is governed in all of its operations by the ten-member board of trustees, three of whom are the children of the founder, Lloyd Noble: Sam, Ed, and Ann Noble Brown. The mailing address of the foundation is Route 1, Ardmore, Oklahoma 73401.

For further information, see *Annual Reports* of the foundation, published since the 1950s. See also "Memorial Living Tribute to Son," *Duncan Oklahoma Banner* (September 2, 1960), p. 4.

RAYMOND L. MUNCY

**SAN FRANCISCO FOUNDATION, THE.** A community trust for the Bay Area, the San Francisco Foundation was established in 1947 by declaration of trust to serve the counties of Alameda, Contra Costa, Marin, San Francisco, and San Mateo.

The foundation had its start in 1946 when Marjorie Elkus, director of the Columbia Foundation, and Leslie Ganyard, director of the Rosenberg Foundation, two private San Francisco foundations, convinced Daniel E. Koshland, a leading philanthropist, civic leader, and businessman, to head an exploratory committee of twenty-five people to study the potential for a local community trust. Elkus was responding to numerous requests from attorneys, trust officers, and others concerned with charitable trusts who were looking for ways to meet community charitable needs. The exploratory committee approved the idea, and with a $20 gift from Elkus as the sum total of assets, the declaration of trust was filed in January, 1948, and Daniel Koshland was named the chairman of the foundation's distribution committee.

Community foundations, as the term implies, are designed to serve a particular locale and to be concerned with that community as a whole. Community foundations, as distinguished from private foundations, are made up of contributions or bequests from a number of donors. The San Francisco Foundation currently embodies 105 separate trusts. Some of these trusts are restricted as to their use, by purpose or geographic location; most are unrestricted trusts.

The responsibility for management of assets is vested in eleven trustee banks; the responsibility for using funds in the public interest is vested in the distribution committee. The seven members of the distribution committee are appointed by outside agencies or institutions, as provided in the declaration of trust. Members are chosen for their experience and knowledge of the community's needs. The distribution committee has the responsibility of modifying the conditions of a trust, if compliance with the donor's instructions becomes "impossible, impracticable, unnecessary, or undesirable," so that the donor's charitable purpose can still be effectively carried out. This power is rarely used. Because community foundations are independent of individual donor control, they enjoy some special privileges under the tax laws. Donors also receive greater tax advantages. The community foundation also has a responsibility for public disclosure of assets and disbursements.

In 1948, the San Francisco Foundation's distribution committee, consisting mostly of members of the exploratory committee, including Daniel Koshland, who was to serve for twenty-six years, hired its first executive director, John R. May, who stayed with the foundation until his retirement in 1974.

The first years of the San Francisco Foundation were devoted to establishing its reputation as an asset to the community. Confidence in the foundation as a stable and worthwhile organization grew, in great measure due to the prominence of the members of the distribution committee. The earliest grants were in social welfare. As the foundation grew, grants were made in the areas of equal opportunity in housing, jobs, and legal assistance; support was given to neighborhood organizations and other civic issues. In its effort to address the whole of the Bay Area community, the foundation quickly moved into granting funds to projects in the arts, education, and the environment. The San Francisco Foundation has frequently joined with other foundations to pioneer a study of a community problem and to promote activity to create solutions. In the mid-seventies, the foundation began to investigate various community needs, decide on funding guidelines in specified areas, and disseminate those findings and guidelines to the community. Martin A. Paley, the foundation's second and current director, commissioned a series of reports on the arts, health, and public interest law that shaped the foundation's granting practices. The foundation has continued to develop studies and concept papers to shape policy and grant making.

The guiding principle of the foundation's granting practices is analogous to a concept of venture capital: the foundation seeks out ideas and projects that will work to make a difference in community life. The general operating credo is to use funds creatively in response to new ideas in the community, rather than to provide general support for existing programs. It can be a risky undertaking, but that is one of the foremost purposes of foundation grants—to put money where more standard sources of funding will hold back until the program has proven its worth. When the idea is successful, the program can look elsewhere for continued support.

Over the years, the foundation has been instrumental in helping to establish the Bay Area's public T.V. station, starting newcomers' centers for immigrants and refugees, enabling public school students to receive instruction from professional artists, among other things. Currently, one major effort of the foundation is stimulating an increase in the supply of low- and moderate-income housing through direct aid to projects, as well as the formation of a task force aimed at addressing the problem in a variety of ways.

In 1975, Mrs. Beryl Buck, who in her will created a trust to be administered by the San Francisco Foundation for the benefit of the people and institutions of Marin County, died. When the foundation received the assets of the Buck bequest in 1980, they totalled $264 million, catapulting the assets of the foundation to $348 million, making it the largest community foundation in the country. The foundation set out to learn more about Marin County and began the process by inviting more than eighty community leaders to discuss the needs of the county with foundation staff. This process proved so useful that the foundation later repeated it in another county. After listening to the community, the foundation set objectives to guide its assessment of proposals. These proved to be not very different from the criteria that guided the foundation before; the foundation's current policies are described below.

From 1978 to 1981, the growth of the foundation increased dramatically—the number of grants awarded jumped from 170 to over 500, awards increased from $7.4 million to $29.4 million, and the number of staff tripled. The foundation's assets in 1981 were valued at about $379 million.

From its main offices located at 500 Washington Street, San Francisco, California 94111, the foundation presently supports programs in a variety of areas, including the arts and humanities, the environment, physical and mental health, education, social services, and urban affairs. Seven major themes guide the foundation: strengthening the family, reducing dependency, sustaining diversity, improving the quality of education, promoting and strengthening the appreciation of arts and culture, promoting the compatibility of environmental preservation with social needs, and promoting problem solving. In addition, the foundation encourages projects that are directed toward the development of public policy, that test new methods of addressing problems, are directed toward changing institutional behavior, or coordinate the activities of two or more established agencies. The foundation also provides technical assistance to projects—a short-term infusion of aid to assist in solving a management problem or to provide a long-range plan for an agency. The foundation also has an awards program which is an integral part of the foundation's efforts to perpetuate important work on the behalf of the community. The awards are designed to identify and reward extraordinary accomplishments in community public service and the arts. Publicly citing the work of individuals or groups who have demonstrated leadership in their fields is one way the foundation encourages and rewards exceptional efforts in making the Bay Area a better place to live.

For further information, see the following interviews published by the Regional Oral History Office, the Bancroft Library, University of California, Berkeley: *Emma Moffatt McLaughlin: A Life In Community Service* (1970); *Daniel E. Koshland, Sr.: The Principle of Sharing* (1971); and scattered portions of *Bay Area Foundation History*, vols. 1–4 (1976). See also *Annual Reports* of the foundation, published continuously since 1948, and various newsletters published intermittently since 1974.

SUSAN LITTLE<br>CAROL PIASENTE

**SARAH SCAIFE FOUNDATION, INC.** The Sarah Scaife Foundation was established in December, 1941, under a deed of trust of Sarah Mellon Scaife, of Pittsburgh. Sarah Scaife was the wife of Alan M. Scaife and the sister of Richard King Mellon.

The Scaife Foundation has sought to achieve its purposes through the awarding of grants to other agencies in the fields of education and culture, health and medicine, scientific research, public affairs, and recreation. It does not make grants to individuals or to national organizations for general fund-raising campaigns. In recent years, it has accelerated its assistance to programs in public policy analysis and public affairs at the national level. As in the case of other philanthropies associated with the Mellon family (see Appendix 2), the Scaife Foundation concentrated in its early years on assistance to local education and charitable organizations in the Pittsburgh area, especially those bearing the Mellon name. Founded in 1941, the foundation was virtually inactive during the Second World War and did not publish an annual report until 1947.

By the time of Sarah Scaife's death in 1965, the organization's grant programs could be classified into three major areas. (1) A portion of its awards were an expression of the founder's personal civic and cultural interest in Pittsburgh, with major support for historic preservation, the city museum, the performing arts, municipal parks, and extensive tree planting. (2) Larger amounts were devoted, in concert with other Mellon foundations, to educational, medical, and research institutions in the Pittsburgh area. (3) There was also assistance to conservation and urban redevelopment, two enterprises in which Sarah Scaife's husband and brother played leading roles. At Sarah Scaife's death, more resources passed to the foundation, and there was a major increase in grants. Net income increased from $928,494 in 1965 to $2,866,439 in 1966; and grant approvals increased from thirty-one, valued at $1,413,950, to fifty, valued at $4,090,980. By 1981, the number of approved grants had increased to sixty-seven, valued at $7,252,900.

The foundation has continued to support local projects in western Pennsylvania, particularly in Allegheny County and Pittsburgh. Of major importance, however, has been the increase in its assistance to organizations in other parts of the country which address major domestic and international questions. This change coincided, to a large degree, with the assumption, in 1973, of Sarah Scaife's son, Richard Mellon Scaife, as chairman of the foundation's board of trustees. Both the number and size of these grants have increased. In 1979, for example, the foundation awarded fourteen such grants of $100,000 or more; in 1980, there were nineteen; and in 1981, there were twenty-six. The largest such grant during this period was to the Hoover Institution on War, Revolution, and Peace, located at Stanford University, which received $1 million. As for consistent support, four organizations were awarded grants of $100,000 or more in each of these three years. The Institute for Contemporary Studies, San Francisco, received $875,000 for research in public policy. The Foundation for American Communications, Los Angeles, was awarded $550,000 to conduct educational conferences for journalists concerning the American economic system. Vanderbilt University, Nashville, received $450,000 for its Television News Archive. Americans for Effective Law Enforcement, Inc., South San Francisco, was granted $375,000 for its program of defending and counseling law enforcement officers faced with lawsuits.

The field of public affairs has received greater emphasis in the foundation's grant program. While public affairs accounted for just over 35 percent of total grants in the entire 1942–1981 period, the field received over 79 percent of the grant funds approved in 1979, over 80 percent in 1980, and over 81 percent in 1981.

In its forty years of operation, the Sarah Scaife Foundation has approved 1,335 grants amounting to $102,329,503. In 1980, foundation assets totalled about $123 million, and grants amounted to about $6 million. The foundation has done much to improve the quality of life in Pittsburgh and western Pennsylvania. Perhaps of even greater significance for the future has been the increasing focus upon grants concerning public affairs at the national level. If this emphasis continues, its relatively large grants are likely to make the Scaife Foundation even more visible as a supporter of research and education in public policy and public affairs. Some critics may decry the policy orientations of some of the grant recipients, but whatever the policy preferences of the grantee organizations, the foundation seems destined in the years ahead to exert far greater national influence than possibly contemplated by its founder.

The foundation is governed by a ten-member board of trustees, with Richard Mellon Scaife serving as chairman. Administration of the foundation is carried on from offices located at 3900 Mellon Bank Building, Pittsburgh—mailing address of Post Office Box 268, Pittsburgh, Pennsylvania 15230—under the direction of a president.

For further information, see *Annual Reports* of the foundation, published since 1979.

ROBERT E. McARTHUR

**SCAIFE FOUNDATION.** See Sarah Scaife Foundation, Inc.

**SCHERMAN FOUNDATION, INC., THE.** With funds supplied by members of the Scherman family, the Scherman Foundation was established in New York in 1941. Harry Scherman, its first president, had founded the Book-of-the-Month Club, which achieved phenomenal success under his leadership. In its first decade, the foundation was a modest one; its assets in the late 1950s had not reached $1 million. However, following Harry Scherman's death in 1969, additional funds flowed to the foundation, and by the end of that year, assets were valued at slightly over $10 million. By 1975, assets were approximately $13 million and they were valued at about $33 million in 1980.

Until the 1960s, the foundation's grants were primarily made to organizations active in the areas of international affairs, economics, and music, and they never exceeded more than a total of $200,000 annually. Since then, the foundation has broadened its areas of interest, with concentration upon social welfare, the arts and culture, located in the New York area, conservation, and family planning. In 1980, for example, out of total grants of approximately $1.75 million, the largest grants made in each of the above areas were as follows: United Jewish Appeal—$100,000; Metropolitan Opera Association—$20,000; Natural Resources Defense Council—$20,000; Association for Voluntary Sterilization—$25,000; New York Public Library—$85,000; and Educational Priorities Panel—$15,000.

The Scherman Foundation is governed by a nine-member board of trustees, which includes Harry Scherman's son-in-law, who is president, and his daughter, who is secretary. Administration of the foundation is carried on from offices located at 250 West Fifty-seventh Street, New York, New York 10019, under the direction of an executive director.

For further information, see *Annual Reports* of the foundation, published since the 1970s.

**SCHOLL FOUNDATION.** See Dr. Scholl Foundation.

**SCHUMANN FOUNDATION.** See Florence and John Schumann Foundation, The.

**S. H. COWELL FOUNDATION.** Samuel H. Cowell was a businessman, rancher, stockman, landholder, and philanthropist. He was born in San Rafael,

California, in 1861 or 1862, and was one of five children in the family of Henry Cowell.The family moved to Santa Cruz in 1865, remaining there until 1879, at which time the family moved to San Francisco.

Samuel Cowell preferred to participate in business and ranching rather than pursue a formal education. Eventually he owned, operated, and was president of the Henry Cowell Lime and Cement Co., a company founded by his father. In 1906, Samuel Cowell built the Cowell Cement Plant in Cowell, California, which remained in operation until 1946. In addition, Cowell opened several other plants in the area and owned property in sixteen counties.

At six feet in height and over two hundred pounds, Cowell was athletically inclined. He participated in rodeos and harness racing. He was also a member of the "Alert Hose Team," a group of volunteer fire fighters.

Samuel Cowell died in 1955 at the age of ninety-three, without heirs, for he had not married and had outlived the other members of his family. At the time of his death, Samuel Cowell's estate was valued at $15 million. His will established the foundation in 1955 as a testamentary trust: "To return to the people of California the fruits of the Cowell enterprise for the advancement of education, religion, and philanthropic enterprises."

In carrying out the obligations of the trust, the trustees encouraged freedom and independence from governmental support. Grants were made for unusual capital needs on special projects, or as seed money to stimulate matching or other grants, as contrasted to support for general operations, expenses, or indebtedness. The trustees indicated it was important for the main funding to come from other sources and for the grantee to have the ability to continue the project without additional funds from Cowell. The trustees preferred to make grants to new applicants and generally did not make more than one grant to an applicant within a three- to five-year period.The trustees desired to increase the magnitude of the Cowell grants by using them to stimulate matching and challenge monies.

The foundation report of 1981 emphasized that grants made in the past should not be used as a "self-limiting" criterion for future requests. Grants made in 1981 were classified in six general categories: aid to the disabled, community services, education, family planning, cultural activities, and youth programs.

During 1955 to 1976, the Cowell Foundation assets increased from $15 million to over $32 million. By 1979, the assets grew to $49.5 million and to about $76 million in 1981. In 1978, California ranked fourth in the nation in terms of total foundation assets, and the S. H. Cowell Foundation ranked eighth on the list of the ten largest foundations in California in terms of money awarded.

Between 1979 and 1981, the total number of grants awarded increased from 70 to 113, but the proportion of money awarded to the six classifications remained approximately the same. Aid to the health and handicapped programs increased from 16 to 19 grants but decreased the proportion of dollars awarded from 23 to 21 percent. The proportion of monies allocated to community service programs increased 5 percent from 17 to 22, while the number of grants almost tripled from 11 in 1979 to 31 in 1981. The grants to primary and secondary education increased from 14 to 17, but the percentage of money decreased from 18 to 14 percent.

In 1979, eight family-planning projects received 16 percent of the funds, but in 1981, eleven programs received only 6 percent of the grant money. Cultural activities received 6 percent of the funds granted in 1979 and 5 percent in 1981. Youth projects were granted 9 percent of the funds in 1979 and 7 percent in 1981.

The total amount granted in 1979, for 70 requests was $2,108,263 as compared to the total awards granted in 1981 of $4,595,247 to 113 grantees.

The trustees supported programs for training, for youth, for minorities, and for disadvantaged in such a way as to provide needed skills and services to the community during the training program. Programs which were operated by and for the disabled to make them self-sufficient were supported. However, the foundation's 1981 *Annual Report* stated that it does not make grants to individuals or for routine program administration, for operating expenses, for annual campaigns, for sectarian religious programs, or for hospitals or hospital programs. Furthermore, the foundation does not make grants for conferences, seminars, workshops, symposiums, to publication projects, or to media programs. Funds from the S. H. Cowell Foundation have been limited to grantees in northern California.

The foundation is governed by a three-member board of trustees, including the Wells Fargo Bank. Administration of the foundation is carried on from offices located at 350 Sansome Street, Suite 620, San Francisco, California 94104, under the direction of an administrator.

For further information, see *Annual Reports* of the foundation, published since the 1970s. See also *The Guide to California Foundations* (1981), pp. *xii* and 71.

KARL F. DRLICA

**SHELL COMPANIES FOUNDATION, INCORPORATED.** This company-sponsored foundation was established in New York in 1953. By 1958, the assets of the Shell Companies Foundation, Incorporated, were valued at about $2.25 million, and grants for that year amounted to approximately $1 million. This pattern of granting, typical of company-sponsored foundations, wherein continual annual infusion of company funds permits annual grants in excess of income from assets, has continued to the present. The following approximate assets and grants figures for representative years illustrate this pattern: 1969—assets $4.66 million, grants $2.66 million; 1975—assets $15.3 million, grants $3 million; 1979—assets $34 million, grants $5 million. During its history, most of the foundation's funds were donated by the Shell Oil Company, with lesser amounts from the Shell Pipe Line Corporation and similar participating companies. From 1953 through 1982, the foundation made grants totalling about $95 million.

Throughout its history, this foundation's preferred areas of giving included education and community funds. In 1980, about 60 percent of the moneys granted went for a number of planned programs which provided scholarships, fellowships, basic research grants, and direct grants to some 600 colleges and universities, 170 independent secondary schools, and a few national educational organizations. Approximately 12 percent of the funds expended for the year went to United Way and similar organizations in cities and towns where significant numbers of Shell company employees resided. The remaining funds were allocated to a number of national organizations concerned with a variety of purposes and to local organizations in places where substantial numbers of Shell company employees resided.

The Shell Companies Foundation, with 1981 assets of about $56 million, is governed by a nine-member board of directors who are executives of the Shell Oil Company and/or the Shell Pipe Line Corporation. Administration of the foundation is carried on from offices located at Two Shell Plaza, Post Office Box 2099, Houston,Texas 77001, under the direction of a senior vice-president.

For further information, see *Annual Reports* of the foundation, published since the 1960s, latterly under the title *Pattern for Giving*. See also *How One Typical Corporation Views Philanthropy* (1981), a booklet published by the Council for Financial Aid to Education.

**SHERMAN FAIRCHILD FOUNDATION, INC., THE.** Originally established in New York in 1955 as the Fairchild Foundation, Incorporated, this foundation's principal donors were Sherman Mills Fairchild and his aunt, May Fairchild. Sherman Fairchild inherited considerable wealth from his father, a founder and the first president of International Business Machines Corporation (IBM). The father's fortune was considerably augmented through his son's invention and development of numerous devices—cameras, aircraft, sound systems, among others—in a wide variety of fields. He pioneered, for example, in the field of aerial photography. Sherman Fairchild dropped out of Harvard College because of illness without obtaining a degree, was a lifelong bachelor, and left no descendants.

The initial assets and activities of the Fairchild Foundation were modest. In 1958, for example, its assets were listed as less than $200,000, and its grants for the year amounted to less than $10,000. Ten years later, however, Fairchild's additional gifts had increased the foundation's assets to approximately $29 million, and the foundation's grants for the year totalled over $350,000. Grants at that time were primarily concentrated in the New York area and were made to a variety of organizations: hospitals, higher educational institutions, youth and social agencies, a botanical garden, and to programs in the areas of business research, urban problems, international affairs, and flight safety.

At the time of Fairchild's death in 1971, it was reported that he left an estate valued in excess of $200 million, with the bulk of it going to the foundation. Thus, in 1975, the then newly named Sherman Fairchild Foundation, Inc., reported assets of almost $102 million and grants totalling almost $6 million.The foundation's areas of giving, however, remained about as they were in 1968.

Since 1975, the foundation has concentrated most of its giving in the area of higher education, with far less emphasis on hospitals, cultural programs, social welfare, and other purposes. In 1978, for example, out of grants totalling about $5.5 million, a large percentage went to the four following universities in the following amounts: $1.3 million—Stanford University; $1.06 million—Lehigh University; $1 million—Columbia University; $750,000—California Institute of Technology. Relatively smaller grants for the year in other areas of interest included: $400,000—Memorial Sloan Kettering Cancer Center; $150,000—Metropolitan Museum of Art; and $100,000—Legal Aid Society of New York.

The Fairchild Foundation is governed by a five-member board of directors, including Walter Burke, a close friend and business associate of Sherman Fairchild who was bequeathed $2 million by Fairchild and is president of the board of directors, and another member of the Burke family. Administration of the foundation, with 1980 assets of approximately $131 million, is carried on from offices located at 2 Greenwich Plaza, Greenwich, Connecticut 06830.

Almost the only additional information on this foundation readily available to the public are the annual reports and returns filed by it with the Internal Revenue Service, and the various Foundation Center publications. See, however, Sherman Fairchild obituary, *New York Times* (March 29, 1971), p. 36; and Sherman Fairchild will, *New York Times* (April 3, 1971), p. 33.

**SHUBERT FOUNDATION, INC., THE.** Lee and J. J. Shubert established the Sam S. Shubert Foundation in 1945 in memory of their deceased brother. Lee and J. J. made substantial contributions to the foundation over the next two decades, and, in 1970, its assets were doubled by assets received from the estate of Lee Shubert following his death in 1953. In 1971, after the death of J. J. Shubert in 1963, the foundation's name was changed to its present one, and, in 1972, as the principal beneficiary of the estate of J. J. Shubert, the foundation received the shares of the various theatrical companies controlled by the Shuberts.

The Shubert Foundation is the sole shareholder of the Shubert Organization, which owns and operates the Shubert theatres. At its peak—prior to the growth of motion pictures and television—the Shubert holdings consisted of over one hundred theatres located throughout the United States. Today, there are twenty-two Shubert houses, of which seventeen are in New York City and one each in Boston, Chicago, Los Angeles, New York, and Philadelphia. These theatres and associated real estate, in 1981 valued at about $30 million, are the principal assets of the Shubert Foundation. While earlier grants were made from a securities portfolio, the foundation's granting program today depends almost wholly on the operations of the Shubert theatres.

Although the foundation has made some grants to organizations not related to the arts, its program focuses primarily on professional theatre and dance groups and their related supporting organizations. In 1980, for example, out of grants totalling about $1 million, 92 percent went to performing art, theatre, dance, and related organizations. The foundation, since 1978, has funded the James N.

Vaughan Award, which carries a $10,000 grant, to an art organization for exceptional accomplishments. In that same year, the foundation began funding the Shubert Archive project, designed to collect and preserve the early materials (back to 1903) of the Shubert theatres.

The foundation is governed by a seven-member board of directors, including the daughter-in-law of J. J. Shubert. Its administration is carried on from offices located at 234 West Forty-fourth Street, New York, New York 10036, under the direction of an executive director.

For further information, see an *Annual Report* (1980), published by the foundation. See also J. J. Shubert obituary, *New York Times* (December 27, 1963), pp. 1, 23; and "Lee Shubert", *Dictionary of American Biography*, Supplement Five (1977), pp. 627–628.

**SID W. RICHARDSON FOUNDATION.** The Sid W. Richardson Foundation was created by Sid W. Richardson, one of Texas' most colorful and successful oilmen. Richardson made and lost several large fortunes as a wildcatter during the 1920s and 1930s. By using his own drilling rigs, Richardson cut corners or "poor-boyed" scores of wells; he borrowed equipment and obtained drilling supplies on credit. Oilfield workers referred to Richardson's wells as "bean jobs" because he occasionally paid them with groceries, which he obtained on credit from local merchants. Richardson began to enjoy greater success during the mid-1930s and developed substantial petroleum properties by the end of World War II in the Slaughter, Keystone, and other fields of the Permian Basin of Texas.

Like many other oilmen, Richardson was often a "soft touch" for children's projects and other charitable causes. He organized his foundation in 1947, in part to regularize his substantial charitable donations. From the beginning, it was limited to the support of institutions and programs within Texas. After his death in 1959, the foundation was greatly expanded with assets from his estate, which became available in 1965.

During the next decade, the Richardson Foundation placed major emphasis on community programs in the Fort Worth area and on the support of construction at educational and health-services institutions. Decisions on funding were made directly by the board of directors until 1973, when Valleau Wilkie, Jr., was hired as the foundation's first professional administrator. Thereafter, Wilkie and his staff have both screened requests for funds and supported a gradual but significant shift in aid of educational and health programs, with less emphasis on providing funds for construction of facilities and greater provision of operating funds for programs. Projects in the arts and humanities and in human services are still largely limited to the Fort Worth area.

The Sid W. Richardson Foundation is now administered by a four-person board of directors, who are aided by a five-person professional staff under the direction of an executive vice-president. Offices of the foundation are located at 309 Main Street, Fort Worth, Texas 76102.

In 1981, the assets of the foundation were about $105 million, largely in marketable securities, cash, and short-term cash investments. Since 1965, grants totalling $60,518,516 have been approved.

For further information, see *Annual Reports* of the foundation, published since 1979. See also "Men in the Industry's News," *The Oil Weekly*, vol. 78, no. 11 (August 26, 1935), p. 14; "West Texas," *The Oil Weekly*, vol. 100, no. 11 (February 17, 1941), p. 54; "West Texas," *The Oil Weekly*, vol. 101, no. 7 (April 21, 1941), p. 56; and "Sid W. Richardson, His Clan Dwindling," *Oil and Gas Journal*, vol. 57, no. 41 (October 5, 1959), p. 101.

ROGER M. OLIEN

**SIMON FOUNDATION.** See Norton Simon Foundation, The.

**SIMON MUSEUM OF ART.** See Norton Simon, Inc. Museum of Art.

**SLOAN FOUNDATION.** See Alfred P. Sloan Foundation.

**SMITH CHARITABLE TRUST.** See W. W. Smith Charitable Trust.

**SMITH RICHARDSON FOUNDATION, INC.** Chartered in North Carolina in 1935, this general-purpose foundation's capital was donated over a period of years by the brothers H. Smith Richardson and Lunsford Richardson, with the former having contributed the larger share. (In the 1960s, an amount equal to the present value of Lunsford's contributions was reorganized as a separate foundation, to be administered by his descendants.) The aim of the brothers was to create an instrument through which they might give back to American society some of the many blessings it had given them. In particular, they hoped that the Smith Richardson Foundation might help preserve or create the conditions that would enable others to enjoy the kind of success they had.

In its early years, by agreement with the Internal Revenue Service, the foundation was allowed to accumulate its income and had neither staff nor programs. Starting in the 1950s, however, the foundation's major preoccupation was with the international problems besetting the United States. Important projects in that period were the creation of the Foreign Policy Research Institute at the University of Pennsylvania, the organization of a summer seminar series for reserve officers at the National War College in Washington, D.C., and a series of grants to a then-unknown junior faculty member at Harvard University, Dr. Henry Kissinger, which enabled him to conduct a program for foreign leaders and publish a journal, *Confluence*. In addition to advancing the careers of foreign affairs specialists like Kissinger, the foundation's efforts produced a number of seminal studies, such as *Protracted Conflict*, a study of Soviet conflict management in the military, economic, and political arenas, which greatly improved public understanding of an increasingly dangerous international environment.

In the next decade, the foundation's focus moved closer to home. Working with the then-governor of North Carolina, Luther Hodges, the Smith Richardson Foundation underwrote the research that led to the creation of one of the nation's first small business credit-development agencies at the state level. A number of other grants went to historic restoration in North and South Carolina, and some were general support grants for schools and colleges in the state.

However, the foundation's major interest in the 1960s reflected the lifelong concern of the founders, particularly Smith Richardson, with the art and science of identifying and developing creative and managerial talent in all kinds of organized endeavors. A large number and variety of projects were undertaken, and the foundation acquired a considerable staff with expertise in this area, including a number with advanced degrees in psychology and management science. Aware that an operation of this scope required greater expertise than the foundation's trustees could provide, it was reorganized, in 1970, as a separate educational corporation with its own governing board. Today, as the Center for Creative Leadership, it is nationally known for its work in personnel identification and development, and numerous businesses, nonprofit groups, and government agencies utilize its programs. Located in Greensboro, North Carolina, the center receives annual funding from the foundation but is otherwise independent, with a board of governors chaired by William Friday, head of the University of North Carolina, and under the direction of its president, Dr. Kenneth Clark, former dean of the University of Rochester.

Following an intensive assessment of past activities and an examination and study of current needs, the Smith Richardson Foundation, in 1973, embarked upon its present program, which is heavily oriented toward scholarship on problems of public policy. Among the topics addressed have been the effects of federal and state government regulation upon economic activity, the impact of taxation on productivity, and various alternatives for reducing inflation. In addition, in 1978, the trustees of the foundation concluded it was necessary to return to supporting work on foreign and national security policies. This decision has led to projects dealing with topics such as new concepts in strategic thinking, the reassessment of American intelligence capabilities, and human rights in totalitarian countries. As a result of these efforts, the foundation has been credited with playing a central role in developing important new ideas in public policy (such as "supply-side economics") and with again enhancing public awareness of America's major international problems.

The foundation's principal office remains at the Smith Richardson Foundation building, 5000 Laurinda Drive, Greensboro, North Carolina, although its main program office is now located at 210 East Eighty-sixth Street, New York, New York 10028. R. Randolph Richardson, a son of one of the founders, currently serves as president, while John W. Red is vice-president and in charge of the Greensboro office. The trustees of the foundation meet quarterly and approve all grants. In 1980, the foundation expended approximately $3.5 million for grants and operations. Its assets, in 1980, were approximately $101 million. No further additions to this fund are anticipated.

For further information, see *Annual Reports* of the foundation, published continuously since 1962. All files and archival material pertaining to the foundation are located at its Greensboro offices.

LESLIE LENKOWSKY

**SPENCER FOUNDATION, THE.** The Spencer Foundation was organized in 1962 as an Illinois not-for-profit corporation, with offices in the John Hancock Center, 875 North Michigan Avenue, Chicago, Illinois 60611. It possessed an endowment valued in 1982 at about $90 million. The foundation is governed by a board of directors consisting of ten members, and it employs a staff of eleven professional and clerical people. The foundation program, broadly stated, is to enhance understanding of the learning process through support of research in the behavioral sciences.

The Spencer Foundation was the creation of Lyle M. Spencer, a long-time resident of Chicago, founder of Science Research Associates, Inc. (SRA), and president of that company until his death. Born in Atlanta, Georgia, in 1911, he grew up in Wisconsin and South Carolina, his father a professor and university president. Spencer graduated from the University of Washington in 1933 and spent the following year touring the world as a member of a championship college debating team. He returned to the University of Washington, receiving the M.A. degree in 1935 with a major in sociology. Moving then to the University of Chicago, he pursued advanced graduate study in sociology as a University Fellow and as a Marshall Field Fellow.

With characteristic entrepreneurial zeal, he and a colleague responded to the need they observed during the depression of the thirties for a scientific approach to the problems of unemployment by founding Science Research Associates in 1938. The new company began its work by underwriting a series of research studies on occupations that were overcrowded and occupations with an insufficient supply of new workers, analyzing the typical patterns of preparation for each occupation. This research, extremely helpful to young people seeking jobs and to those responsible for their training, was published by SRA the same year, in a series of studies entitled *Occupational Information System for High Schools*. The company went on to develop further career-guidance and testing materials and later became a publisher of school texts and curriculum guides. SRA, now a subsidiary of IBM Corporation, continues as a leading publisher of educational materials.

Lyle Spencer, while pursuing a highly successful career in business, maintained an abiding interest in educational research. His writings often reflected his interest in social science research in particular. Describing the early years of the company he founded, he stated that willingness to take a chance on new research ideas kept it out on the frontier of the social sciences. When he came to establish the Spencer Foundation in 1962, it was natural for him to direct that it be dedicated to furthering the understanding of education. He made clear his feeling that since the Spencer fortune had been earned through educational publishing, "much of this money should be returned eventually to investigating ways in which education can be improved around the world" (The Spencer Foundation, *Annual Report* [1981], p 3). Spencer gave further evidence of his belief in the value of education by serving on the boards of many institutions involved with the social sciences and with education, and by making generous gifts to those institutions, both directly and through the foundation he established. One of his major efforts was connected with Roosevelt University in Chicago, where he served as chairman of the board of directors. Roosevelt was, at that time, a brand-new institution seeking to establish itself as a purveyor of high-quality education for young people of all ethnic backgrounds in an urban setting. He successfully involved the Chicago business community in the enterprise, convincing them of the need for a first-class institution dedicated to these goals. He held that it was important for society's mobility systems to remain open.

Spencer died after a short illness in August, 1968, and his will revealed that the Spencer Foundation would come into a substantial portion of his estate, valued at the time of distribution at more than $80 million. The following month, the board of directors established an office for the foundation and hired its first employee, the corporate secretary. Search for a chief executive began immediately and culminated with the appointment of H. Thomas James, a scholar and administrator with degrees from Wisconsin State University, the University of Wisconsin, and the University of Chicago, and who was, at the time, dean of education at Stanford University. James began his work as president of the foundation in September, 1970.

During the early years of the foundation, the board of directors was expanded to its current size of ten members, in an effort to bring a broader perspective to its consideration of program. In 1977, five-year terms of service for board members were instituted so as to assure rotation and to allow still broader representation of interests among members. An effort is made to have three groups represented on the board at all times: social scientists, the business community, and a group, less easily defined, who are interested in philanthropy and education.

As activities of the Spencer Foundation proliferated, the board established oversight and advisory committees for particular areas of concern. The finance committee reviews and monitors the work of outside investment managers with the intention of maintaining the integrity of the foundation's endowment in the face of inflation. The program committee reviews proposals submitted to it by the president and recommends action by the full board, which meets quarterly for this purpose. There is also a nominating committee charged with the responsibility of recommending candidates for vacancies on the board of directors and for recommending appointment of the corporate officers.

The board of directors is the chief policy-making body of the foundation, and it gives serious and frequent consideration to the intellectual direction the foundation is taking, its chief program areas, and its financial stability. On one occasion, consideration of program was the subject of a "retreat" of several days by the full board.

The staff and board of the Spencer Foundation make no attempt to raise questions for scholarly and scientific study. Rather, they insist that the scholarly community identify the questions and formulate the problems on which they wish to work. Then, if the proposed work is something the foundation can and desires to support, the needed financial assistance is given.

The grant procedure is briefly as follows. A proposal is reviewed first by the foundation staff, frequently with the help of outside consultants, and a report is made to the president, who may send it on to the board of directors' program committee with his recommendation or return it to the staff for further information and investigation. The program committee meets four times a year for consideration of grant proposals, shortly before each quarterly meeting of the full board, which is responsible for final action on all proposals. The entire procedure takes from thirty to ninety days, depending upon the timing of the original request and the amount of staff work required to assess the proposal.

Over the years, the Spencer Foundation has concentrated its interest and support on problems involving intellectual questions and theoretical research, rather than issues of educational policy. It has also tried to stay ahead of—or at least clear of—problems and disciplines receiving government funding, feeling that such a course was necessary if a foundation of this size were to make an impact with its limited resources. More specifically, during the decade following 1971, when the foundation made its first grants, it has tended to concentrate major funding efforts in four areas of study: mother-infant interaction, cognitive development in infancy, the biological mechanisms involved in human development, and the symbol systems by which we come to understand ideas in mathematics, literature, art, and music. Throughout these years, there has been a heavy emphasis on cognition, and the largest percentage of Spencer Foundation granteees have come from various branches of psychology. The foundation has also supported investigations of the educative effects of schooling, hindrances to education, and educational organization and administration.

The staff of the Spencer Foundation has remained remarkably stable. The original corporate secretary, now vice-president and secretary, and the original president both continue to serve the foundation. Program is the responsibility of the president, who is assisted by the vice-president and by research associates who serve one or two years at a time, generally when they are at the dissertation stage of their doctoral work or have just received their degree. Business and administrative matters are the responsibility of the vice-president, who is assisted by a financial and clerical staff.

The severe reduction in federal funding of scholarly and scientific research expected in the 1980s presents the Spencer Foundation, as it does all private foundations, with a challenge to spend its modest grant funds ever more wisely and with an eye on the state of the whole research enterprise. There is every reason to believe, however, that the Spencer Foundation will, for the foreseeable future, continue to serve the area that it knows best and that scholars pursuing research in the behavioral sciences connected with education will continue to encounter an understanding of their problems and help in solving them at the hands of its staff and board.

For further information, see *Annual Reports* of the foundation, published continuously since 1971. See also two informational brochures published by the foundation.

MARION M. FALDET

**STANDARD OIL (INDIANA) FOUNDATION.** See Amoco Foundation, Inc.

**STARK FOUNDATION.** See Nelda C. and H. J. Lutcher Stark Foundation.

**STARR FOUNDATION, THE.** Cornelius Vander Starr set up the Starr Foundation in New York in 1955. Starr, born in California in 1892, was the son of an engineer on a lumber company's railroad. He entered the University of California in 1910 and paid his way by waiting on tables in dining halls. In the course of various jobs following college, he read law at night with a lawyer and passed the California bar examination at the age of twenty-one. Starr then organized an insurance firm, sold it at a profit to enlist in the army in World War I, and, in 1919, arrived in Shanghai, China. There followed a meteoric insurance career, during which he established the Asia Life and American Asiatic Life Insurance Companies. They were active first in China and, by the 1930s, in the entire Far East. Starr also branched out into other fields: he founded the *Shanghai Evening Post and Mercury*, and he invested in real estate and in automobile agencies in the Far East.

An increasingly hostile opposition to Japanese expansion in the Far East led to his return to the United States in 1940. Following the end of World War II, Asia Life, which had changed its name to the American Life Insurance Company, not only returned to the Far East but expanded its operations worldwide. By the time he died in 1968, Starr had built in some 130 countries a group of 100 insurance companies and agencies bearing the title American International Group, Inc.

Up until the time of Starr's death in 1968, the foundation's assets of approximately $2 million, and annual grants of approximately $100,000, were relatively modest. Its activities had been focused on education, particularly the provision of scholarships in the United States and Asia, and local assistance for international studies, community funds, and other civic organizations. This program was continued and expanded through the 1970s, having been made possible by tremendous increases in its assets, which boosted them to over $26 million by 1978 and to over $143 million in 1979. This growth was primarily due to the donation to the foundation of shares of stock in the American International Group, Inc., by that corporation's directors. The foundation's program of activities continued to be about the same as in previous years but on a vastly augmented scale. Thus, grants for 1978 were about $1 million and in 1979 about $3.5 million.

In 1980, assets of the Starr Foundation were valued at about $165 million, and in that year the foundation made grants of about $20 million. That year also marked a significant change in the focus of giving, which switched to a concentration upon hospitals and health groups. As a result of this alteration of focus, 56 percent of the giving in 1980, or over $11 million, went for that purpose. For example, two of the largest grants, $7,634,850 and $3,293,750, went, respectively, to New York Hospital and to the Smith-Kettlewell Eye Research Foundation, of San Francisco. However, the foundation continued its support in its traditional areas of giving. Major representative grants in the fields of education and international relations included the following: New York University—$1,087,750; Columbia University—$1 million; and the Asia Society—$1.58 million. Other grants were made to: American Enterprise Institute for Public Policy Research—$527,500; Hoover Institution on War, Revolution and Peace—$335,000; New York Philharmonic—$92,000; Metropolitan Opera Association of New York—$67,000; and Police Athletic League of New York—$102,000.

The Starr Foundation is governed by a seven-member board of directors, most of whom are officers and directors of the American International Group, Inc., and its member insurance companies. The administration of the foundation is carried on from offices located at 70 Pine Street, New York, New York 10270, under the direction of a president.

Almost the only additional information on this foundation readily available to the public are the annual reports and returns filed by it with the Internal Revenue Service, and the various Foundation Center publications. See, however, Cornelius Vander Starr obituary, *New York Times* (December 21, 1968), p. 37.

**STEELE FOUNDATION.** See Harry G. Steele Foundation.

**STODDARD CHARITABLE TRUST, THE.** Harry G. Stoddard and his wife, Janett W. Stoddard, created the Stoddard Charitable Trust by a declaration of trust dated November 22, 1939.

Harry Stoddard was born in 1873 in Athol, Massachusetts, the son of a Baptist minister. At an early age, his family moved to Worcester, Massachusetts. He chose not to go to college and, after a six-month course at a local business college, entered employment at the Washburn & Moen Manufacturing Company, Worcester, then the largest wire mill in the world. By hard work, aided by a natural persuasiveness and qualities of honesty and integrity, he became, before he was thirty years old, general manager of the company, which by this time had become the American Steel & Wire Co., a division of U.S. Steel Corp. In 1904, he accepted an offer to become president and treasurer of Trenton Iron Works, in Trenton, New Jersey. At the time, he was the youngest president of a company of that size, caliber, and importance in the country. Shortly thereafter, that company, too, was purchased by and became a subsidiary of U.S. Steel Corp.

While in Trenton, Stoddard, who was a fine speaker, quickly became a leader in business, civic, and religious circles. It has been said by people who knew him that had he continued, he would have become head of U.S. Steel Corp. But in 1911, the opportunity to return to his native city presented itself, and this prospect, plus the chance to acquire an ownership position in a smaller company, caused him to return to Worcester as vice-president and general manager of what was to become Wyman-Gordon Company, a firm engaged in the forging business. In due course, Stoddard became president, chairman of the board, and, at his death, was honorary chairman. In 1924, he and a partner purchased the leading local newspapers, of which he became president. He was a leader and participant in civic, political, and charitable causes, as well as in business, giving substantially of his time and substance. In 1920, he headed the first united charities drive, called the "Golden Rule Fund," and later served as president of its successor, the Worcester Community Chest, precursor of the United Way.

In 1939, he established the Stoddard Charitable Trust in order that it might, after his death, continue to support the many charitable causes in which he was interested. During their lifetimes and by their wills, both he and his wife contributed generously to the trust.

The purposes of the Stoddard Trust are to apply its funds for religious, charitable, scientific, literary, or educational purposes, or for the prevention of cruelty to children, within the United States or its possessions.

Grants have been largely to local projects of a capital nature. Major grants have been to the Worcester Polytechnic Institute, Worcester Natural History Society, American Antiquarian Society, and the Worcester Art Museum. In 1980, grants aggregated approximately $1 million. Assets of the trust, a substantial portion of which consists of Wyman-Gordon Company stock, had a 1981 value of approximately $40 million, and since its founding through 1981, it has distributed over nine million dollars in grants. Applications for funding may be made by letter, which should contain relevant information, including proof of tax exempt status, and should be received prior to December 1. No grants are made to individuals.

The foundation is governed by a four member board of trustees which includes Robert W. Stoddard, son of the founder, and his wife, together with Marion S. Fletcher, daughter of the founder, and her husband. Administration of the foundation is carried on from offices located at 370 Main Street, Suite 1250, Worcester, Massachusetts 01608.

The foregoing brief history of the trust was based on a biography of Stoddard by Rae MacCollum Spencer, *The Gift of Imaginative Leadership* (1972); and information supplied by Paris Fletcher, treasurer and secretary of the Stoddard Charitable Trust.

**SURDNA FOUNDATION.** Spelled backwards, the Surdna Foundation bears the surname of its founder, John E. Andrus. Born in a farming district in New

York in 1841, John Andrus worked his way through Wesleyan University, Middletown, Connecticut, then taught school for a brief period and intermittently studied chemistry and medicine. In 1869, he married Julia Dyckman, an orphaned immigrant girl, and it was she who suggested his incursion into the manufacturing of pharmaceutical materials. Prospering, he put his profits into land, mining claims in the West, and other ventures. Shortly, he also invested heavily in many of the companies which became post–Civil War leaders in U.S. industry, such as Standard Oil Company and the Singer Sewing Machine Company. Andrus was taciturn and disliked publicity. He was very frugal and insisted on taking the subway from his home in Yonkers, New York, to the New York City business district long after he could afford travel by other means. Thus, in the 1920s and 1930s he became known as the "Straphanger millionaire." At the time of his death in 1934, at the age of ninety-three, Andrus's fortune was estimated at between $100 million to $800 million.

The Surdna Foundation was established by John Andrus in New York in 1917 on the eighth anniversary of the death of his wife and with an initial gift of $2.5 million. In 1926, Andrus announced that 45 percent of his estate would ultimately go to the foundation and that its principal beneficiary would be the Julia Dyckman Andrus Memorial, Inc., for the operation of the Andrus Children's Home, an orphanage located in Hastings, New York, which he founded in 1927. Thus, after Andrus died in 1934, the foundation began to benefit from his largesse. By 1954, its assets were about $20 million, and it made grants for the year of about $1.3 million.

Thereafter, the Surdna Foundation's corpus and consequent grants grew apace, as the following approximate asset and grants figures for representative years show: 1959—$25 million and $3.5 million; 1969—$103 million and $5 million; 1976—$99 million and $7 million; 1981—$210 million and $9.5 million. In assets, the Surdna Foundation now ranks among the fifty largest in the United States.

The foundation has traditionally supported child welfare programs and those providing forms of aid for the disadvantaged, aged, and the handicapped. Smaller percentages of total annual giving have been allocated for higher education, cultural affairs, and medicine. In 1981, for example, out of grants totalling about $9.5 million, the John E. Andrus Memorial, Inc., a home for the elderly in Yonkers, New York, received $3,618,000; the Andrus Children's Home, Hastings, New York, received $1,694,400. Other large grants for the year included: Industrial Home for the Blind, Brooklyn, New York—$55,000; Pierpont Morgan Library, New York City—$141,000; Museum of Modern Art, New York City—$100,000; and Massachusetts Institute of Technology, Boston—$250,000. The foregoing sample grants illustrate, too, the foundation's general confining of grants to the northeastern United States, with emphasis upon New York.

The Surdna Foundation is governed by a nine-member board of directors, with John E. Andrus III serving as chairman and with other members of the Andrus family on the board. Administration of the foundation is carried on from offices located at 200 Park Avenue, New York, New York 10017, under the direction of a president.

For further information, see *Biennial Reports* of the foundation, published since the 1970s. See also John E. Andrus obituary, *New York Times* (December 27, 1934), p. 21; and articles concerning his estate appearing in the *New York Herald Tribune* (January 5, 1935), p. 1, and *New York Times* (January 8, 1935), p. 23.

**SYSTEM DEVELOPMENT FOUNDATION (SDF).** System Development Foundation has a unique origin. Founded as a nonprofit operating organization to serve the U.S. Air force, it developed assets that now, as a private, non-operating, grant-making foundation, it uses to support basic research in the area in which it made its contribution to air defense.

SDF was established in 1956 by the Rand Corporation. Its major activity through June 30, 1969, was the performance of contracts for the U.S. Air Force designed to meet air defense and other security needs. Its original name was System Development Corporation, and it qualified as a private, nonprofit, operating organization under Section 501(c)(3) of the Internal Revenue Code.

From its inception through June 30, 1969, SDF played a leading role in the growth and development of the information and system sciences and computer technology. It contributed to major advances in the field, such as the development and applications of the first large-scale, real-time, computer-based information processing system. It also undertook significant research and development contributing to higher-order programming languages, time-sharing of computers, user-oriented data management systems, and natural language processing.

During the period 1964 to 1966, the U.S. Air Force changed its relationship to SDF. In June, 1964, it removed SDF from the category of Air Force-sponsored nonprofit corporations, and in July, 1966, it required SDF to compete for Air Force work the same as any other private company. In light of these developments, SDF's board of trustees, in June, 1967, informed the secretary of the Air Force of the board's intention to explore alternatives for the realignment of SDF, with the objective of preserving its ability to operate effectively in a changing and intensely competitive environment. After two years of study, the board reorganized SDF as of July 1, 1969.

The 1969 reorganization of SDF involved the transfer of all contracts, and substantially all assets and personnel, of SDF to a new System Development Corporation (SDC) in exchange for 100 percent of SDC's outstanding stock. The U.S. Air Force concurred in the transfer with respect to all Defense Department contracts, which constituted about $50 million, or some 82 percent of SDF's total sales of about $61 million, in the preceding fiscal year ended June 30, 1969.

In the course of obtaining U.S. Air Force consent to the transfer of the Department of Defense contracts involved in the 1969 reorganization, SDF's board of trustees adopted a program to make voluntary contributions to the U.S.

Treasury in cash equal to one-half of the adjusted book net worth of SDF at the time of the 1969 reorganization. This program of voluntary cash payments to the U.S. Treasury was completed in July, 1977, and October, 1979.

In contemplation of SDF's future role as a non-operating, grant-making foundation, after the completion of the 1969 reorganization, SDF's board of trustees adopted a program to concentrate its grants, over the next five and a half to seven years, among eligible 501(c)(3) organizations doing innovative work in the field of information sciences and man-machine relationships (including applications of this technology to critical governmental problems) where nongovernmental funding offers the prospect of significant beneficial developments. This is the same field of activity in which SDF has been involved since its creation by its parent, the Rand Corporation. The program was implemented initially by grants in 1974, 1975, and 1976 to four qualified grantees doing innovative work in the approved fields: the California Institute of Technology, the University of California at Berkeley, the Rand Corporation, and Stanford University.

In January, 1981, in connection with the purchase of SDC by Burroughs Corporation, SDF completed the sale of its interest in SDC for a cash price of $69 per share of SDC stock or a total of $59.5 million to SDF. Thus it had assets, in 1981, of about $67 million with which to conduct its grant-making programs.

Between June, 1981, and June, 1982, SDF's board of trustees took a number of steps to become better informed about the broad field of the information sciences and how the foundation might contribute most effectively. Board members made visits to eleven important research sites. It commissioned papers summarizing significant developments and problems in several subdivisions of the field. And, it participated in twelve different seminars on a variety of relevant topics conducted by knowledgable experts.

On December 14, 1981, SDF's board of trustees announced its decision as to the fields in which its future grant giving would initially be concentrated. It seeks to advance the information sciences by supporting basic research in these fields:

a. Principles of information science, including information theory, classification, and information structures;

b. Principles of representation in biological and machine information processing, as exemplified by neurobiology, the cognitive sciences, and non-Von Neumann computer architectures, and robotics;

c. Principles underlying the man-machine interface, including engineering and cognitive approaches to human factors in individuals and groups;

d. The interface between the computer and artistic endeavor.

During the fiscal year ended June 30, 1982, SDF's board of trustees approved grants in these areas totalling $25,430,562.

SDF presently expects to continue making grants to qualified institutions doing innovative work in the field of information sciences and man-machine relationships. The board of trustees expects to continue its participation in seminars and other activities designed to help it gain knowledge of the field, thus providing additional background for informed decisions on the allocation of funds. The board also expects to keep closely in touch with the projects supported by SDF.

This is the brief history of a unique foundation. No individual or family furnished its basic assets. No individual or family set forth its purpose or direction. As an operating organization, it developed assets from its pioneering contributions to the growth and development of the information and system sciences and computer technology. It is fitting that these assets should now be used to support basic research in these fields and all be spent during this, the information era.

The foundation is governed by a six-member board of trustees. Administration of the foundation is carried on from offices located at 181 Lytton Avenue, Suite 210, Palo Alto, California 94301, under the direction of the president.

For further information, see "Burroughs Corporation Agrees in Principle to Acquire Company," *New York Times* (August 15, 1980), p. 4.

RALPH W. TYLER

# T

**TEAGLE FOUNDATION, INCORPORATED, THE.** Born May 1, 1878, in Cleveland, Ohio, Walter C. Teagle was the son of John and Amelia Bell Clark Teagle. He received his undergraduate degree at Cornell University in 1900. In 1911, he married Rowena Lee, and they had a son, Walter C. Teagle, Jr., who eventually died in his early adult years. Teagle's lifelong occupation was the oil business, where he came to be known as one of the great "Oil Kings." Starting out with association in the firm of Scofield, Shurmer, and Teagle, of Cleveland, he quickly moved on to the Republic Oil Company and later to Standard Oil of New Jersey, then known as Jersey Standard and the forerunner of the present-day Exxon Corporation. At Jersey Standard, he served in a number of capacities, from director to president to chairman of the board. He also served on the Federal Reserve Board of New York and was a trustee of Cornell University, in addition to being the founder and president of the Teagle Foundation.

Considering it as the "most satisfying experience" of his life, Teagle incorporated the foundation on May 22, 1944, under Connecticut law, and donated successive and substantial amounts of money to it until his death in 1962. Foundation headquarters were set up at 30 Rockefeller Plaza, where it is still located today. The purposes of the foundation were to help the needy and deserving employees of Jersey Standard and its successor, Exxon Corporation, including wives and children; to aid employee children in their college education; and to provide grants to a variety of hospitals, medical research institutes, charitable organizations, and religious organizations, primarily for scholarship purposes unrelated to Exxon personnel. By 1969, Walter and Rowena Teagle had given nearly $20 million to the foundation and had expanded the foundation's grants by appropriating money for nursing scholarships. The foundation continues to fund the activities the Teagles were interested in, as well as others decided upon by the board of directors. It had 1981 assets of about $41 million and makes expenditures of approximately $2.5 million annually. Normally, grants range from $3,000 to $25,000, and nearly four hundred scholarships were supported by the foundation in the program providing aid to families of Exxon employees.

The Teagle Foundation is governed by an eleven-member board of directors. Administration of the foundation is carried on from offices located at 30 Rockefeller Plaza, Room 2835, New York, New York 10112, under the direction of the chairman of the board of directors.

For further information, see *Annual Reports* of the foundation, published since 1979. See also Walter C. Teagle obituary, *New York Times* (January 10, 1962), p. 47; and Bennett Wall and George Gibb, *Teagle of Jersey Standard* (1962).

MICHAEL V. NAMORATO

**TEXACO PHILANTHROPIC FOUNDATION, INC.** In 1979, a $25 million donation from Texaco, Inc., witnessed the founding in Delaware of this company-sponsored foundation. In 1980, the Texaco Philanthropic Foundation received an additional $20 million from the company, and, although no gifts were received in 1981, the foundation's assets in that year were about $39 million.

The stated purpose of the foundation is to enhance the quality of life in the United States by providing support to selected not-for-profit organizations in the following areas: education, hospitals and health, arts and culture, social welfare, environmental protection, and civic, public, and other deserving areas.

In 1981, with grants of about $5.25 million, higher education received about 38 percent of foundation largesse; 27 percent was devoted to cultural programs; health/hospitals and social welfare were also allocated 27 percent; and the remainder of eight percent went for civic, public, environmental, and other purposes. Representative larger grants in 1981 included the following: Lamar University—$500,000; Metropolitan Opera Association of New York—$1.03 million; United Fund/Community Chests and American Red Cross—$546,653; St. Mary's Hospital, Port Arthur, Texas—$100,000; and U.S. Olympic Committee—$50,000.

The Texaco Philanthropic Foundation is governed by an eight-member board of directors, most of whom are affiliated with Texaco, Inc. Administration of the foundation is carried on from offices located at 2000 Westchester Avenue, White Plains, New York 10650, under the direction of a president.

For further information, see *Annual Reports* of the foundation, published since its founding in 1979, and a guidelines brochure issued by the foundation.

**THOMAS AND DOROTHY LEAVEY FOUNDATION.** Thomas E. Leavey and his wife, Dorothy, established this foundation bearing their name in California in 1952 to provide college scholarships. Its assets were relatively small at the time of its founding. In 1957, they amounted to less than $250,000, and grants for the year amounted to only a few thousand dollars. By the end of the 1960s, assets had grown to about $1 million, and the foundation was making annual grants of about $70,000. In 1975, assets were valued at over $12 million, with grants amounting to about $600,000 for the year. Since that time, through successive gifts by the Leaveys, assets have increased to a 1979 value of about $39 million.

The Thomas and Dorothy Leavey Foundation has continued to concentrate on grants for educational purposes. In 1979, for example, about 50 percent of the approximately $1 million granted went to educational institutions and organizations, largely for scholarships. The Freedoms Foundation, which has been a consistent recipient of foundation largesse, received one of the major grants, almost $150,000, in that area. Hospitals and medical research organizations were also major recipients of grants in 1979 and received approximately 35 percent of the total funds awarded for the year. Approximately 10 percent was in the form of denominational giving, primarily to Roman Catholic churches and organizations, with the remaining portion of the foundation giving being directed to various social service organizations.

The Leavey Foundation is governed by a six-member board of trustees composed primarily of members of the Leavey family, including Dorothy Leavey. Up until his death in 1980, Thomas Leavey served as president and a trustee of the foundation. Administration of the foundation is carried on from offices located at 4680 Wilshire Boulevard, Los Angeles, California 90005.

Almost the only additional information on this foundation readily available to the public are the annual reports and returns filed by it with the Internal Revenue Service, and the various Foundation Center publications. See, however, a quarterly *Report From Valley Forge* (Winter, 1982), in which the Freedoms Foundation describes a 1982 grant of $2 million to it from the Leavey Foundation.

**TIMKEN FOUNDATION OF CANTON.** Henry Timken (1831-1909), a German immigrant, was the inventor of the highly successful and world-famous "Timken Spring," used in the nineteenth-century carriage manufacturing business. This invention, and one for a tapered roller bearing, yielded him a handsome fortune. He was the founder of the Timken Roller Bearing Axle Company, which became the present day Timken Company of Canton, Ohio, the active management and eventual ownership of which was left by him to his children.

It was descendants of Henry Timken who founded the Timken Foundation of Canton in 1934. In its first two decades of operation, the foundation restricted its grants for capital purposes and to communities in which the plants of the Timken Company were located. Such grants were largely made to hospitals, secondary schools, and recreation agencies. By the mid-1950s, annual giving of the foundation was about $1 million from assets which by then were about $8 million.

Since the 1950s, the Timken Foundation's pattern of giving has remained substantially the same, although some grants have been made outside of Ohio, and higher education has become a significant recipient of grants. They have usually been for projects in communities in which the Timken Company operates a facility. In 1980, with assets of about $96 million and grants of over $5 million, the largest grant, $3.2 million, was made to the Timken Mercy Medical Center,

Canton, Ohio. Two of the largest grants for that year, ones of $475,000 each, went to Malone College and Walsh College, both located in Canton. Approximately 10 percent of total foundation giving was distributed for civic affairs, arts and culture, and youth projects.

The foundation is governed by a six-member board of trustees, four of whom are members of the Timken family. The four also serve as board members or officers of the Timken Company. The administration of the foundation is carried on from offices located at 236 Third Street, S.W., Canton, Ohio 44702, under the direction of a director-secretary.

Almost the only additional information on this foundation readily available to the public are the annual reports filed by it with the Internal Revenue Service, and the various Foundation Center publications. See, however, "Henry Timken," *Dictionary of American Biography*, vol. 9 (1936), p. 555.

**TINKER FOUNDATION, INCORPORATED, THE.** Edward Larocque Tinker (1881-1968) was born into a New York family which traced its descent from New England seafarers and Huguenots. He received his LL.B. from Columbia in 1905 and a Ph.D. from the University of Paris in 1932. Although educated in the law as well as the humanities, he served only briefly as an attorney. His true avocation soon clearly emerged as a writer. He was the author of *Lafcadio Hearn's American Days, Old New Orleans, Les Écrits de langue française en Louisiane au 19e siecle*, and *The Horsemen of the Americas and the Literature They Inspired*.

An author, scholar, and lecturer, Tinker travelled widely. A visit to Mexico early in his life introduced him to the Hispanic tradition on this continent, which was to become a lifelong devotion. He was a founder of the Spanish Institute, president of the Uruguayan-American Association, and a corresponding member of the Hispanic Society of America, the Instituto Histórico y Geográfico de Uruguay, and the Instituto Gonzalo Fernandez de Oviedo, of Madrid. He was honored in his lifetime by being named a Commendador de la Orden de Isabel la Católica by the Spanish government and was awarded the Order de Mayo al Mérito by the Argentine government.

In 1959, he established the Tinker Foundation in memory of his wife, Frances McKee Tinker; his father, Henry Champlin Tinker; and his grandfather, Edward Greenfield Tinker. His purpose was to promote better understanding among the peoples of the United States and Ibero-America, Spain, and Portugal. Within this geographical area, the foundation has given priority to work in the broad field of the social sciences with particular emphasis on areas such as international relations, urban and regional studies, education, communications, management, and economics, as well as support of projects concerned with natural resource development. Support is also provided for conferences, seminars, and public affairs programs and for limited assistance to programs furthering the education of the Spanish- and Portuguese-speaking peoples of the United States.

In addition to its regular institutional grant-making program, the Tinker Foundation has conducted, since 1975, an annual Postdoctoral Fellowship Competition. This program is designed to assist scholars of exceptional ability and to foster intellectual growth by encouraging field research which will have significant theoretical implications within or between disciplines or for public policy. Each year, a maximum of eight fellowships are awarded, carrying annual stipends of $18,000 with up to $2,000 additional for travel expenses.

In 1979, the Tinker Foundation initiated the Tinker Field Research Grants Program. These awards are open to all recognized centers or institutes of Ibero-American or Latin American studies with graduate doctoral programs at accredited United States universities and are to be used for summer field research only in Ibero-America or Latin America. The purpose of the program is to make it possible for people of ability to work in specific regions of Latin America to acquire as intimate a knowledge as possible of language, terrain, and culture; to gather research data; and to develop contacts with scholars and institutions in their field.

The foundation has also established endowed chairs at five universities throughout the United States: Columbia University; University of Texas, Austin; Stanford University; the University of Wisconsin, Madison; and the University of Chicago. These chairs provide support for distinguished visiting scholars from Ibero-America, Spain, Portugal, or Canada, allowing them to teach and conduct research at the above universities for specified periods of time.

The Tinker Foundation, with 1980 assets of about $34 million, is governed by a seven-member board of directors. Administration of the foundation is carried on from offices located at 645 Madison Avenue, New York, New York 10022. In 1980, a total of about $1.5 million was awarded by the foundation for grants and fellowships.

For further information, see *Annual Reports* of the foundation, published continuously since 1969. See also several pamphlets, published intermittently by the foundation, describing in detail the programs discussed above.

RENATE RENNIE

**TROPICANA FOUNDATION.** See Aurora Foundation, The.

**TURRELL FUND.** The Turrell Fund was established in 1935 by Herbert Turrell and his wife, Margaret. Its original name, the Herbert and Margaret Turrell Foundation, was changed to the Turrell Fund in 1941.

Turrell was born in Newark, New Jersey, on December 3, 1859. When Herbert was about eleven, his father "went West" to seek a fortune and did not return, leaving the mother to provide for Herbert and his half-brother. These early years were hard, and Herbert had to find work to help his mother support the family. He still managed to continue his education, and he graduated with honors from Newark High School in 1878.

Herbert tried several jobs during the next year and ended up with a drug firm in New York, as a salesman. It turned out that he was a born salesman, and in six months, he was the New York and New Jersey sales representative for the company. In 1881, Parke, Davis & Company, a young firm then, bought out the firm for which Herbert was working. Herbert stayed with the company and in two years was head of its traveling service department. He soon presented a plan to Parke, Davis for a private formula department. The company adopted the idea and in 1888 made him manager of the new department.

Turrell was with Parke, Davis until 1907, when he retired after twenty-six years of service although he was not yet fifty years old. He had been investing in the company since he started there. The company prospered, the stock was split many times, and by the time Herbert set up his foundation, his holdings in Parke, Davis were considerable. They became a substantial asset of the Turrell Fund.

Soon after retiring from Parke, Davis, Turrell acquired control of the Oxzyn Company, a New York cosmetic manufacturer, and began to extend its products. There was a quick and booming popular response to the new products, and sales increased many fold.

In 1927, Turrell sold the Oxzyn Company to the American Home Products Corporation, being paid in American Home Products stock. Through the sale, Turrell became one of the largest stockholders of American Home, a position later inherited by the Turrell Fund.

In his mid-twenties, Herbert had married Frances Robinson, and they had three sons. The first two died while still very young, and the third suffered a mental breakdown from which he never recovered. Turrell's first wife, Frances, died in 1921, after a long illness, and the following year he married Margaret Hoberg. There were no children by his second marriage.

Following the sale of the Oxzyn Company, Turrell was increasingly aware that a large fortune, accumulated over the years and steadily growing, was not being used to its full advantage. Even at the age of seventy-six he was full of vitality and enthusiasm, and he approached the problem of what to do with his fortune with his usual energy and careful thought.

He and his wife decided to establish a foundation, and the Turrell Fund's predecesor, the Turrell Foundation, was organized on November 15, 1935. Herbert Turrell died on October 22, 1947. Margaret Turrell died six months later, and she followed her husband's example by bequeathing the remainder of her estate to the foundation.

The certificate of incorporation of the foundation stated rather broad purposes but included among the uses to which its funds were to be put the following provision: "more particularly for the benefit of children... who because of the death, disability or other failure of one or both parents are dependent upon others or are living or being reared in unhealthy, unwholesome or improper environment...." It is probable that the memory of the hardship of his early years and the tragic loss of his own children led him to dedicate his money to providing underprivileged children with the basic elements on which to build a future.

In the early 1940s, the trustees decided to concentrate the contributions of the renamed Turrell Fund on children's causes, and for many years the fund's letterhead carried the legend "Service to Neediest Children." It was also decided to limit grants to the states of New Jersey and Vermont, with special attention to Newark, New Jersey, and its adjacent communities.

Since its early years, the fund has given comparatively small gifts to a sizable list of agencies—which has grown in number as the fund's income increased. These grants have gone to traditional youth organizations—such as Y's, Boys' and Girls' Clubs, community houses, Boy and Girl Scouts, and camps; to special educational efforts on behalf of children and youth; and to other service agencies meeting the needs of children and families. The fund has continued to emphasize help for children, but gradually its approach has broadened into the youth group and, through a special program, even beyond that to young men and young women.

In 1956, the Turrell Fund started the Juvenile Court Fund program to aid in sending court-referred youth to private, nonprofit, residential treatment centers rather than to state correctional institutions. The first year appropriation of $12,000 grew until it was about $200,000 a year for several years. The total for the life of the program came to something over $3 million. With this money, 1,570 boys and girls between the ages of eight and eighteen were placed in over fifty different facilities, almost all of them outside of the state of New Jersey as the available services within the state were not adequate for their care.

In 1978, the state of New Jersey assumed the cost of placement of juveniles in residential treatment centers and adopted a policy against placing New Jersey youth outside the state. This ended the need for Turrell grants, and the state has encouraged the Turrell Fund to use the money that would have gone to the Juvenile Court Fund program for grants to increase the capacity of residential treatment centers in New Jersey. Some grants have been made for this purpose, as noted below.

In addition to this program for teenagers, in 1969 the fund started a College Scholarship Program for young people of high potential but with such disadvantaged backgrounds that without special financial help they would be unable to attend college. Emphasis has been given to those who have been known to the juvenile courts or other law enforcement agencies. Two administrators, one in New Jersey and one in Vermont, are in close touch by correspondence, on the telephone, and in person with all of the Turrell scholars and provide continuing help on the many problems which confront young people today. The progress made by the students is gratifying. Through 1982, 304 scholarships have been awarded; 104 students have graduated from college—24 with honors.

The interest of the fund in the education of underprivileged teenagers has been growing in recent years, as those at Turrell feel that this can be one of the strongest influences for good. The fund has provided, since 1969, 139 annual scholarships for promising inner-city youngsters to attend private secondary schools of high quality in New Jersey and Vermont. In furtherance of this program, the Turrell Fund worked out, during 1977, with St. Benedict's Preparatory School, a program under which St. Benedict's students with academic promise could attend Blair Academy or the Lawrenceville School, residential institutions, for a two-year period to help make the transition from their inner-city home community to the colleges of their choice. St. Benedict's is primarily a day school, and most of the students come from the inner city of Newark, where the school is located. Vermont Academy, at Saxtons River, Vermont, has also participated in the program.

The 1960s and 1970s saw the rise of "alternative schools," with programs especially developed to meet the needs of students who dropped out of public high schools. Grant support has been given in this field in both New Jersey and Vermont.

Some years ago, the Turrell Fund came to the conclusion that there were activities which the states of New Jersey and Vermont should be carrying on for the benefit of children but for which no appropriations could be obtained until their value had been demonstrated. Accordingly, the Department of Institutions and Agencies in New Jersey and various departments in Vermont were asked to propose such projects.

The responses were enthusiastic, and each state suggested several possible projects. Three projects were chosen in each state, and within a year or two after these projects were started, the expenses were taken over by the respective states. Both the states and the Turrell Fund were pleased with the outcome, and it has resulted in continuing cooperation and a number of additional requests from both states. The grants made as a result of this process total $1,018,597 for New Jersey and $585,413 for Vermont. The "seed money" which has been invested in each project has been money well spent. The Juvenile Court Fund program might also be considered as "seed money," even though the amount was large and the period of germination was long. New Jersey has recognized the value of the program and has assumed the cost.

As stated above, many youngsters have been sent out of New Jersey for care due to lack of facilities in the state. In order to help increase the services available within the state, the fund has helped a children's home with a building project, has been working with Bonnie Brae on expansion plans, and, at its December meeting in 1981, voted a gift of $418,000 to the Devereux Foundation to assist in establishing a treatment center in New Jersey.

The Juvenile Court Fund program was only one, though the largest, evidence of the Turrell Fund's interest in residential care for juveniles, and in recent years, numerous grants have been made to private and state agencies for residential programs. Furthermore, much energy and money have been expended on behalf of young people already in trouble. The fund also searches for ways to keep young people from getting into trouble in the first place, seeking additional means to deter the potential wrongdoer. The prevention of the first offense—which may be quite innocent—could be the key to success.

The trustees reached an informal decision a few years ago that the fund's goal should be to divide about equally its income among three grant categories: (1) the rather large list of youth-oriented organizations which the fund has been helping for many years; (2) the Juvenile Court, College Scholarship, and Secondary Schools Scholarship programs; and (3) rather substantial grants for new and possibly innovative activities for the benefit of underprivileged children and youth.

As has been outlined, the first category has been of long standing, and, though the grants are usually not large, the list is long. The trustees have debated whether the number of grants should be reduced so that the fund could make larger contributions with greater impact in the fields selected. However, since the grants are important to the continued services (or even existence) of the organizations receiving them, and the results are good, the trustees feel that this broad-based distribution of grants should be continued.

The Turrell Fund's history has been marked by occasional larger grants. During the last five years, the local YMCA received $450,000 for the construction of a gymnasium in East Orange; the New Jersey Department of Youth and Family Services was granted $176,000 for a Permanency Planning Project; St. Benedict's Preparatory School received $135,000 for construction and renovation; the Salvation Army was awarded $150,000 for the Westside Center (Newark); Smokey House Project and the Greater Burlington YMCA, both in Vermont, received $100,000 each for capital needs.

In earlier years, two Vermont institutions received substantial help from the fund. The Weeks School, a state correctional facility, received funds for two dormitories and other needs, for a total of $334,000 in Turrell grants. New England Kurn Hattin Homes received $128,000 for a children's residence and other capital projects.

The grants made by the fund have grown from the small beginning of less than $20,000 in the first two years to $3,016,552 in 1981. In the latter year, the distribution of grants by board program areas was as follows: youth organizations (Scouts, Y's, Clubs, camps, and so on), $1,113,473; day programs, welfare programs, programs for handicapped, $686,600; residential programs, inner-city programs, state institutions, alcohol and drug abuse, $481,910; schools, special education, $544,825; College Scholarship Program, $189,744.

The following is a summary of grants for forty-seven years: 1935 through 1964 (thirty years), $8,554,129; 1965 through 1969 (five years), $5,059,783; 1970 through 1974 (five years), $8,793,893; 1975 through 1979 (five years), $11,296,807; 1980, $2,775,824; 1981, $3,016,552—totalling $39,496,988. The market value of the fund's assets in 1981 was about $42 million.

The Turrell Fund's staff is small: three people to administer the grant activities and two full time and one part time for the College Scholarship Program, the only program the fund operates. During the lives of Herbert and Margaret Turrell, the fund was managed by a board of seven trustees, which has since been increased to eleven. The fund's assets are managed by the trust department of a major New Jersey bank, under the direction of a trustee finance committee. Fund offices are located at 15 South Munn Street, East Orange, New Jersey 07018.

For further information, see *The Turrell Fund: Report of the First Thirty Years 1935-1964* (1964); *Annual Report* (1970), which includes cumulative totals of all grants, 1935-1970; and *Annual Reports* of the fund, published continuously since 1970. See also *The Juvenile Court Fund Program, A Report to the Turrell Fund* (1975), an unpublished report by Professor Jackson Toby and Associates, Institute of Criminological Research, Rutgers, the State University of NewJersey.

S. WHITNEY LANDON
CARL FJELLMAN

**TWENTIETH CENTURY FUND, INC.** Chartered by the Massachusetts legislature in 1919, the Twentieth Century Fund's founder and president was Boston merchant Edward A. Filene, organizer of the credit union movement in the United States and a planner and co-founder of the United States Chamber of Commerce. Filene intended that the Twentieth Century Fund should study and advance possible social and economic improvements. He favored action-oriented fund support for goals such as municipal reform, minimum wage laws, and labor union recognition by management. In making the series of gifts that came to constitute the fund's endowment, Filene stated that he did not desire to make the organization perpetual, and he provided that the trustees, after 1947, might at their discretion use the principal as well as the income of the endowment.

Although there was some early funding for research studies on subjects such as press freedom, economic boycotts, and anti-Semitism during the first decade of its existence, the Twentieth Century Fund was then mainly a grant-making organization, supporting entities such as credit unions, consumer cooperatives, and the fledgling League of Women Voters. After 1928, this orientation changed, and, although some grants continued to be awarded, the fund became one of the first American foundations to devote itself primarily to research. This shift resulted from the trustees having decided, over Filene's objections, that the fund could achieve more by concentrating upon research than upon grants to activist organizations. In furtherance of its goal to conduct research and disseminate findings, the fund became, in 1931, one of the early foundations to publish an annual report. In 1937, the year of Filene's death, the trustees voted to cease making grants to outside agencies, and from that time on, the fund used its income almost entirely to conduct its own research activities.

During the Great Depression, fund research efforts focused on economic problems, and it sponsored studies of the nation's debt structure, the stock market, health care, and labor unions. It organized small groups of scholars and practitioners to investigate questions of public policy, and the staff was strengthened to assist in this effort. Widening its scope in the 1940s, the fund began to examine international issues as well, and this field received even more attention in the 1950s and 1960s.

The Twentieth Century Fund has thus grown into a highly influential operating foundation, engaged in research and public education on contemporary issues. This has been attained, in large part, through an extensive publishing program, which includes scholarly studies and task force recommendations. In 1981, the broad areas of its research effort included business, economics, and public administration; urban problems and social issues; politics, communications, and the not-for-profit sector; and international affairs.

In supporting inquiry, the fund does not award fellowships or scholarships or support dissertation research. In 1981, the research program comprised one internal research project, three task forces, and forty-three projects directed by individual scholars under contract to the fund. These projects addressed a wide range of issues, including the performance of the public and private economic sectors and their interaction; the effects of uneven economic development on the nation's cities and on social mobility; the responsiveness of electoral institutions to social, economic, and technological change; the role of communications media in public affairs; and the international role of the United States, with particular emphasis on economics and communications.

Since 1929, the overriding purpose of the fund has been the conduct of analytical studies of public policy issues for an audience that includes the informed public, the press, policy makers, and the academic community. It encourages scholars to challenge the prevailing wisdom on significant issues and to evaluate critically the performance of public and private institutions. The trustees and staff seek out individual scholars, regardless of political persuasion or institutional affiliation, who possess not only a fresh perspective on public problems but also the ability to communicate to a broad, lay audience.

Fund-sponsored research has resulted more recently in important publications, such as Jean Gottman, *Megalopolis* (1961); Robert B. McKay, *Reapportionment: The Law and Politics of Equal Representation* (1965); William J. Baumol and William G. Bowen, *Performing Arts: The Economic Dilemma* (1966); Norman H. Nie, Sidney Verba, and John R. Petrocik, *The Changing American Voter* (1976); and Fred Hirsch, *Social Limits to Growth* (1976).

Although, as an operating foundation, the Twentieth Century Fund devotes the bulk of its income to its own public policy research programs, the trustees have over the years made grants to demonstrate the fund's responsibility to the community or in connection with its own research activity. For example, beginning in 1967, it has made an unrestricted voluntary payment annually to the city of New York in recognition of the municipal services (garbage disposal, police and fire protection) that it receives free of charge as a tax-exempt property owner. The first payment in 1967 was $10,000 and the payments have grown through the years to $25,000 in 1981, for a total contribution to the city of $226,500. In 1973, pursuant to a fund task force report, it helped establish the National News Council to investigate complaints against news organizations as well as threats to press freedom. In ensuing years, the Twentieth Century Fund joined with a consortium of other foundations in providing financial support for the council. In fiscal 1979, the fund made a terminal grant of $100,000 to bring its total support to the council to $600,000.

Since the focus of the fund is upon original research, it has sought to encourage innovative investigation of timely issues as they develop. It concentrates upon the conduct of inquiry most likely to produce quality publications for dissemination to the interested public. This inquiry may involve one or both of two long-established fund devices, the book-length project and the task force.

Book-length projects permit individual scholars to take a more reflective view, usually over several years, of particular problems. The fund's usual practice is to contract with a special research director for each new project. Although the scholar works under the general editorial guidance of the fund's central staff, he or she is accorded academic freedom in the preparation of a factual study. The resulting manuscript is offered in fully edited form to those publishers that have expressed an interest in them. (In 1970, because of the rising costs of the expanding publishing program, the fund ceased to publish its own studies.)

Task forces, in contrast to book-length studies, provide a forum for addressing discrete and timely issues and for making specific policy recommendations in a relatively short time. The trustees appoint to these task forces persons from academic, business, and political circles to review a subject from different perspectives. Book-length studies may be used or prepared for a task force, and the combined research and recommendations may be submitted to publishers.

Fund assets had accumulated to about $5 million by 1947. Since that date, there has been a steady rise in their approximate value: 1954—$10 million; 1958—$17.5 million; 1970—$23 million; 1976—$28 million; and 1981—$34 million. In recent years, expenditures of the fund have ranged from $2 million to $3 million.

The Twentieth Century Fund is governed by a twenty-one-member board of trustees. Administration of the fund is carried on under the direction of a director from offices located at 41 East Seventieth Street, New York, New York 10021.

For further information, see *Annual Reports* of the fund, published continually since 1936. See also Adolf A. Berle, *Leaning Against the Dawn* (1969), a good account of the fund to that date.

ROBERT E. McARTHUR

# U

**UNITED STATES STEEL FOUNDATION, INC.** The United States Steel Foundation, a company-sponsored foundation, was established in 1953 in Delaware with an initial gift of $12 million from the United States Steel Corporation. Grants by the foundation have been primarily directed to communities in which the corporation has plants or facilities and to national activities. Organizations located in the Pittsburgh, Pennsylvania, area, where the corporation's headquarters are located, have usually received the larger grants in most categories supported by the foundation.

As with other company-sponsored foundations, the assets and resultant grants of the United States Steel Foundation have been subject to changing economic and industrial conditions. Thus, by 1958, the value of its net assets had increased to $20 million through additional gifts from the corporation, and it made grants of over $4.6 million in that year. By 1969, however, its net assets were down to about $12 million, although it made grants in that year of over $6 million. In 1975, assets were up to about $27 million, again with grants of about $6 million. Since then, assets have grown to approximately $34 million in 1981 with grants rising to about $7 million annually. This ability to give at that rate, despite the fluctuation in value and income from assets, is due to the continued infusion of funds from the corporation. In 1981, for example, the latter provided the foundation with a gift of $15.1 million.

Grants for 1981 are typical of the foundation's pattern of giving. In that year, approximately 37 percent of the total grants went for national and community social services, the largest one in this area being $1 million to the United Way of Southwestern Pennsylvania, which includes Pittsburgh. Higher education received 27 percent of the 1981 grants, with Duquesne University, Pittsburgh, Pennsylvania, receiving the largest grant, one of $500,000. With hospitals, medical, and health organizations receiving 13 percent of the total, the largest grant in this category was one of $400,000 to the Children's Hospital, Pittsburgh, Pennsylvania. Finally, 23 percent of the total was devoted to public, cultural, and scientific affairs. The largest grant in this area, $700,000, went to the Metropolitan Opera Association of New York, New York.

The United States Steel Foundation is governed by a seventeen-member board of trustees, all of whom are officers or directors of the United States Steel Corporation. This composition of the board, as of most other company-sponsored foundations, has been a characteristic of the United States Steel Foundation throughout its history. Administration of the foundation is carried on from offices located at 600 Grant Street, Pittsburgh, Pennsylvania 15230, under the direction of an executive director.

For further information, see *Annual Reports* of the foundation, published each year since 1964.

# V

**VICTORIA FOUNDATION, INC.** The Victoria Foundation was established in 1924 in New Jersey by an initial contribution of $20,000 from Hendon Chubb (1874-1960), and he has been the source of most of its assets. In naming the foundation, he honored his mother, English-born Victoria Eddis Chubb, who died in 1917. Widely recognized as the dean of American insurance men, with more than six decades of experience in the field as chief executive of the insurance firm of Chubb and Son, Hendon Chubb served the foundation as president until his death in 1960.

The grants made by the Victoria Foundation during the first decade of its existence were relatively small and were primarily palliative ones to the local Welfare Foundation and to needy individuals. Sometimes outright grants were made, but often assistance was in the form of loans at no interest, some of which were never repaid while others were repaid years later.

The emergence of governmental welfare programs combined with increasing foundation assets and income resulted in a broader and wider form of preventive philanthropy by the 1940s. One, if not the first, of such new programs was sparked by a siege of rheumatic fever suffered by Hendon Chubb's daughter, Margaret, as a two-year-old. This understandably motivated the father to give support to a hospital in Morris Plains, New Jersey, devoted to serving children with rheumatic heart problems. Thereafter, the foundation entered the allied fields of cardiovascular disease, alcoholism, and so forth. Its giving in these fields continued down to the 1960s.

In the 1950s, the foundation focused its attention on Newark, New Jersey, which was situated close to the homes of most of the trustees of the Victoria Foundation. This declining metropolis suffered from the problems typified by urban centers with their burgeoning nonwhite populations. Three programs, based on support of Newark organizations, received foundation support from the 1950s through the 1970s: planned parenthood, equality of opportunity for minorities, and improved education for the inner-city youth. Representative grants for these programs have included aid for the Newark branch of the Essex County Planned

Parenthood Association, the Newark Urban League, and the Cleveland School in the heart of the most poverty-ridden and poorest ward in Newark. This last program, for which support has continued to the present, came to be known as the Newark or New Victoria Plan. It is one of the few instances in the United States where a foundation and a public school system have cooperated over a long period of time on a major experimental education program. Also, the Victoria Plan preceded the launching of the national Head Start program and probably influenced its initiation and development.

Building from its earlier experiences, the Victoria Foundation has since tripled its annual investment in educational, social, and rehabilitative programs in Newark in the 1970s and 1980s. Support was provided for Newark's Community Information and Referral Services; Spanish-run programs for Hispanic minorities, such as La Casa de Don Pedro; Victory House, a residential center for troubled, crime-prone youths (ages thirteen through eighteen); and more traditional agencies, such as the YMCA and Salvation Army. It was hoped that these philanthropic ventures, plus additional millions of dollars from federal, state, and other agencies, might prevent the total collapse of the city and provide the basis for upturn in the 1980s.

In the early 1970s, without lessening its commitment to Newark, the foundation entered the environmental field. For example, it became and continues to be a major donor to the New Jersey Conservation Foundation's revolving fund for land purchase. This same foundation, with support from the Victoria Foundation, assists the city of Newark in planning for optimum use of its open spaces created as the result of urban decay. The Victoria Foundation has also made grants to the New Jersey Marine Sciences Consortium to serve as a coordinating conservation force within the state. In summary, the Victoria Foundation has made grants primarily for education and welfare programs in Newark and its environs, plus providing aid for environmental projects and occasional and smaller funding for cultural organizations such as museums and libraries.

The foundation, with 1981 assets of about $37 million, is governed by a thirteen-member board of trustees, which includes President Percy Chubb II, son of the founder, and four other members of the Chubb family. Administration of the foundation is carried on from offices located at 40 South Fullerton Avenue, Montclair, New Jersey 07042, under the direction of an executive director.

For further information, see *Annual Reports*, published continuously by the foundation since the 1950s, particularly that for 1974 on its fiftieth anniversary. The foregoing account is primarily based on this report. See also Hendon Chubb obituary, *New York Times* (September 5, 1960), p. 15; and an article by Anthony dePalma, "Foundation Focuses on Newark," *New York Times*, New Jersey Weekly (February 7, 1982), pp. 1, 4-5.

**VINCENT ASTOR FOUNDATION, THE.** In 1784, John Jacob Astor emigrated from Germany, via London, to New York City. The son of a butcher, his only possessions upon arrival in America were his clothes and a small assortment of musical instruments consisting of several violins, clarinets, and flutes. Astor soon became involved in fur trading and subsequently in land speculation, purchasing, at little cost, property in New York City which eventually increased dramatically in value. When John Jacob Astor died in 1848 at the age of eighty-five, he had amassed nearly $20 million, at the time the largest personal fortune in the country.

Vincent Astor, the great grandson of John Jacob, inherited his share of the fortune in 1912 at the age of nineteen, after his father was lost in the Titanic disaster. A man of broad interests, Vincent was successful in many business ventures, including the ownership of the St. Regis Hotel and *Newsweek* magazine. He also had philanthropic interests and in 1948 established the Vincent Astor Foundation. The foundation's stated purpose was "the alleviation of human misery," and it had broad charitable aims; initial grants were distributed to organizations such as New York Hospital, the American Red Cross, the New York Public Library, Astor, Lenox and Tilden Foundations. Vincent Astor founded the Astor Home for Disturbed Children (now known as the Astor Home) and in 1948 turned it over to the Roman Catholic Church; to this day, the foundation supports the home with annual grants.

Vincent Astor died in 1959, and once his estate was settled, the foundation received the bulk of its assets. His widow, Brooke, became the president, and remains actively involved in the operations of the foundation. As the criteria for giving developed, she and the other trustees determined that because the Astor family had been closely identified with New York City for generations, grants should be confined primarily to that metropolitan area. With few exceptions, the foundation supports established institutions and neighborhood programs which broaden the opportunities, enrich the lives, and sustain the vitality of New York City's population. Since its establishment in 1948, the foundation has made grants totalling $116,499,176.

In the early sixties, many of the Astor Foundation's grants reflected the trustees' concern for youth and their desire to make an impact in the field of juvenile delinquency prevention. One of the largest contributions was to the Boys Brotherhood Republic, on the Lower East Side, to build a clubhouse where boys of seven to nineteen years of age could meet for sports, woodworking, and homework assistance. Not incidentally, they are given education in citizenship through actual experience. The Republic is run by the boys, with only a necessary minimum of adult guidance; it serves over seventeen hundred boys each week. Gymnasium, library, and shops have their places in the building, but the courtroom and council chamber symbolize the special qualities of the Republic. In the council chamber, the boys make their own rules; and in the courtroom, infringements of the rules are weighed before the law, with judge, jury, prosecutor, and defense lawyer all peers of the accused. Recently, the Astor Foundation endowed the Boys Brotherhood Republic in the amount of one million dollars.

The foundation is well known for its pioneering work in recreational design.

The Jacob Riis Houses, on New York's Lower East Side, is a notable example. In 1966, the foundation funded an experimental redesign of the three-acre Riis Plaza, which has been called an "outdoor living room" and includes the first "adventure playground" in New York City. An amphitheater was created that seats one thousand and is available to the whole Lower East Side. In Harlem, a three-block courtyard was transformed into a neighborhood center, with an amphitheater in the central portion, a children's play area at one end, and an adult area at the other. In the Bedford-Stuyvesant section of Brooklyn, the foundation funded a prototype superblock that converted two streets into a park, with play areas and paths for strollers. Two years later, in 1969, the board approved a challenge grant of $500,000 toward a capital construction program to provide cultural and recreational facilities for the Bedford-Stuyvesant Shopping and Commercial Center.

Realizing that the quality of life can be improved by even minor changes in the environment, the Astor Foundation, for over a decade, has helped many small community groups create vest-pocket parks and gardens in their neighborhoods. One of the liveliest is the Jefferson Market Garden, in Lower Manhattan—truly an oasis in the midst of a busy section. At the same time, the board continues to support projects in New York City's major parks. They authorized grants in 1978-1979 for the restoration of two fine historic structures—the Belvedere Castle, in Central Park, and the Litchfield Villa, in Prospect Park.

Of the many grants to programs involving children, among the most interesting was a pilot project for gifted children in the New York City school system, inaugurated in 1973. At that time, little attention was given in the public schools to the needs of gifted children. The program started with two pilot classes and soon was replicated in several schools throughout the city.

The Astor Foundation also sponsors a program for gifted teachers from New York City. It consists of a two-month course in the humanities, held at St. John's College, Santa Fe, New Mexico. Upon completion of four consecutive summer sessions, the teachers receive an M.A. degree. The program has been most rewarding, not only for the intellectual stimulation it affords but also for the impact that Santa Fe and the region have on those who have never been West before.

The vitality of a city is, to a large extent, dependent upon the vitality of its institutions—much of New York's greatness lies in its museums, libraries, botanical gardens, and zoos. Major institutions that have received Astor Foundation support include the New York Public Library, Astor, Lenox and Tilden Foundations (founded by John Jacob Astor), the Museum of the City of New York, the Metropolitan Museum of Art, the New York Zoological Society, the Brooklyn Children's Museum, the South Street Seaport Museum, and the American Museum of Natural History. While some grants were for program support, others were designated for capital needs. In recent years, recipients of endowment grants include the Rockefeller University, Columbia University, and the Metropolitan Opera Association of New York.

The foundation's interest in the New York Zoological Society began in 1964, with a grant for the construction of "The World of Darkness" at the Bronx Zoo. Since then, the Astor Foundation has supported several undertakings, the most ambitious of which was the funding of the Wild Asia Exhibit. Since its completion in 1977, over 1.6 million visitors have journeyed through Wild Asia on the Bengali Express monorail and have seen a wildlife collection that is not duplicated anywhere else in the world.

Since 1971, the foundation has contributed over $11 million to the Metropolitan Museum of Art; grants have been made for a broad spectrum of projects. Recently, the foundation funded the construction of a beautiful Chinese garden courtyard at the museum. Initially conceived by Brooke Astor in 1971, the plans were developed with the guidance and knowledge of Wen Fong, special consultant for Far Eastern affairs. It was decided to duplicate from the beautiful southern city of Soochow a Ming dynasty (1368-1644) courtyard and adjoining scholar's room, which still exist in the middle of a garden, now open to the public. The People's Republic of China cooperated with the foundation wholeheartedly, making it the first joint, permanent project between the People's Republic and a western country. In 1979, Brooke Astor went to Soochow to see the original and the prototype; and in December of that year, twenty-seven Chinese workmen came to New York to assemble with their own hands the courtyard they had built in China. By June, 1981, the work was finished, and the garden courtyard was opened to the publc at that time.

A somewhat unusual institution is the South Street Seaport Museum, which is engaged in an imaginative enterprise to preserve part of New York's seafaring heritage. Over the past ten years, the foundation has made several contributions to the museum; a challenge grant of $1 million in 1975 allowed the museum to begin the restoration of its principal commercial block and to enter into negotiations with the Rouse Development Company. Recently, the Seaport Museum and the city of New York have contracted with Rouse for the commercial development of the South Street district.

In contrast to the large, institutional grants is Astor Foundation support for community-based programs. These often involved children or the elderly, and many are sponsored by settlement houses, which serve neighborhoods throughout the city. An example is Project Scope, an experimental program administered by Lenox Hill Neighborhood House, which involves teenagers who "adopt" invalid, homebound elderly. This program started in 1974 and was one of the first of its kind.

In recent years, the foundation has funded a number of community-based organizations working to revitalize neighborhoods and encourage economic development, with particular emphasis on those located in the South Bronx. In 1979, the Astor Foundation and the International Ladies' Garment Workers' Union (ILGWU) funded the plans for a new factory building to be built by the city in the Bathgate section of the Bronx; the building has since been constructed and has two tenants. A year later, the Astor Foundation joined several corporations and foundations in supporting the Bronx division of Local Initiatives Support Corporation (LISC), which will assist local revitalization efforts. It is the foundation's hope that LISC may eventually be involved in attracting large corporations to locate in the Bronx and that they will employ residents of the area.

In the past ten years, several organizations have developed significant expertise in landmark preservation, and the Astor Foundation has suppported their work. The first grant in this field was made in 1974 for the restoration of the Grace Church Houses, in Lower Broadway. The list of buildings with which the foundation has become involved since then is long; it includes the United States Customs House, the Fraunces Tavern Block, the Villard Houses, the Queens County Farm Museum, St. Ann's Church (in Brooklyn), and, most recently, St. Bartholomew's Church. That the foundation continues to be mindful of its origins is evident in a grant toward the renovation of the Astor Place subway station, which is decorated with colorful tiles representing the beaver—the logo of the first John Jacob Astor's fur enterprises.

The Astor Foundation, with 1980 assets of about $56 million, is governed by a nine-member board of trustees, under the leadership of its president, Mrs. Vincent Astor. Its staff consists of four full-time and one part-time employee. The offices located at 405 Park Avenue, New York, New York 10022, are modest; the board prefers to keep the administrative costs low.

For further information, see *Annual Reports* of the foundation, published continuously since 1949. See also the biography by Kenneth W. Porter, *John Jacob Astor* (1931); and "[William] Vincent Astor,"*Dictionary of American Biography*, Supplement Six (1980), pp. 23-24.

MARY EARLE

# W

**WALLACE FUND.** See DeWitt Wallace Fund, Inc.

**W. ALTON JONES FOUNDATION, INC.** W. Alton Jones (1891-1962) was a poor Missouri farm boy who became a pioneer in the development of the natural gas and petroleum industries. He was chairman of the executive committee of the billion-dollar Cities Service Company, as well as chairman of the board of directors of the Richfield Oil Corporation and a director of numerous other major corporations at the time of his death in an airline crash on a trip to join his close friend, former President Dwight D. Eisenhower. By that time, he had become a very wealthy man.

The W. Alton Jones Foundation, which Jones established in New York in 1944, had assets of about $4 million by 1954 and made grants in that year of about $400,000. By 1958, its assets had increased to slightly over $7 million, and its grants amounted to about $800,000 for the year. During this period, the foundation provided financial aid to higher education, hospitals, medical research, religious and missionary organizations, and some assistance to needy individuals.

By 1969, with additional funds from Jones's estate following his death, plus donations from Mrs. Jones, the foundation's assets had grown to about $24 million, and grants for that year amounted to about $1.9 million. In addition to its previously supported areas of activity, the foundation had by that time begun making grants to museums and historic preservation agencies.

In 1980, the Jones Foundation moved its offices from New York City to Charlottesville, Virginia, where a number of its directors and officers were resident. These included Mrs. W. Alton Jones, who has continued to serve as chairman of the board of trustees since her husband's death. In 1981, the value of the foundation's assets jumped from about $67 million the previous year to about $99 million, and it made grants in 1981 totalling about $2.6 million, which reflects the foundation's traditional giving pattern. Thus, about 33 percent went for the support of hospitals and biological/medical research and education; 23

percent for higher education; 24 percent for arts and culture; with the remaining 20 percent going to churches, sports and recreation, and social and child welfare organizations. Representative larger grants in these areas included: $729,000—W. Alton Jones Cell Science Center, in Lake Placid, New York; $583,000—Lake Placid Center for Music, Drama, & Art, Inc., Lake Placid, New York; $300,000—Vanderbilt University, Nashville, Tennessee; $120,000—University of Virginia School of Medicine, Charlottesville, Virginia; $100,000—Episcopal Diocese of Atlanta, Georgia. It should be noted that these traditional program and support patterns began undergoing a reevaluation by its trustees and staff in 1982.

The W. Alton Jones Foundation is governed by an eleven-member board of trustees, which includes Mrs. W. Alton Jones as chairman and five other members of the Jones family. Administration of the foundation is carried on from offices located at 609 East High Street, Charlottesville, Virginia 22901, under the direction of a president.

Almost the only additional information on this foundation readily available to the public are the annual reports and returns filed by it with the Internal Revenue Service, and the various Foundation Center publications. See, however, W. Alton Jones obituary, *New York Times* (March 2, 1962), p. 15, together with other comments on his death: "$55,690 in Cash Carried by Jones,"*New York Times* (March 3, 1962), p. 45; and "Service for Jones Held at St. James'," *New York Times* (March 6, 1962), p. 32. See also the *Annual Report* (1981) published by the foundation.

**WARREN FOUNDATION.** See William K. Warren Foundation, The.

**WEBB FOUNDATION.** See Del E. Webb Foundation.

**WEINGART FOUNDATION.** The B. W. Foundation was established as a nonprofit corporation in 1951 in Los Angeles, California, funded by gifts from Ben and Stella Weingart. In April, 1978, its board of directors voted to change the name to Weingart Foundation in order to identify more explicitly its benefactors.

Ben Weingart was born in Atlanta, Georgia, in 1888. Orphaned at the age of five, he was reared by a foster mother in rural Georgia. After finishing the eighth grade, he headed west and arrived in Los Angeles in a railroad boxcar. He found a job delivering laundry to boarding houses and hotels. From his meager earnings, he saved enough money to lease a boarding house and eventually came to own several rooming establishments and some of the leading hotels in Los Angeles. He built a vast business empire which included not only hotels but apartment buildings and shopping centers. Through his creative ideas and entrepreneurial activity, he helped shape the commercial and residential real estate industry as it is today.

He was best known as the principal developer of the city of Lakewood, the first planned city in southern California. Built in the late 1950s on a thirty-five-hundred-acre tract, Lakewood contained eighteen thousand homes and a shopping center which remained the world's largest for several years. He also initiated housing developments in Seal Beach, the San Gabriel and San Fernando valleys, Las Vegas, and other communities. Although real estate was his main economic interest, he expanded his assets in other enterprises, including the Pacific Employment Insurance Company, which he organized and which is now a part of the INA Corporation.

Ben Weingart was known as an unostentatious man with simple tastes and a spartan life-style. He shunned personal publicity. He was particularly concerned about the needs of the elderly, the disadvantaged, alcoholics, and drug addicts. In establishing the philanthropic foundation which originally bore only the initials of his name, he desired that preference be given charities that addressed these problems in southern California. In 1957, his wife, Stella, died and left her own fortune to be included in the B. W. Foundation to carry on the work envisioned by her husband. Before his own death in 1980, Ben Weingart funded several other foundations, including the Aetna Foundation and the Consolidated Foundations, whose interests were similar to those of the Weingart Foundation.

During its earlier years, the B. W. Foundation made only small grants to local charities. There was no staff, and grants were made by a three-person board of "in-house" directors. Regrettably, records of these grants are not available. Today, a five-member board of directors establishes policies, approves all financial transactions, and reviews and passes on grants.

The principal assets of the Weingart Foundation have consisted traditionally of real estate accumulated by Ben Weingart over several years. Consequently, a large amount of the foundation effort has gone into management of real estate property. Most of the appreciation in the market value of the assets has been due to real estate appreciation, not the securities portfolio. A good part of capital gains has occurred due to real estate sales (primarily apartments) in recent years.

During the fiscal year ending June 30, 1981, foundation investments totalled $143,844,263, of which $48,105,905 were in marketable securities (including U.S. Treasury Notes, Government National Mortgage Association obligations, bonds and common stocks) and $95,738,358 in real estate (including apartments, hotels, commerical properties, and land). The net realized and unrealized gains on investments during the year ending June 30, 1981, were $8,104,000. The foundation, in 1981, had assets valued at about $198 million.

The Weingart Foundation makes selective grants to support well-conceived programs and projects in the following major areas: community programs, social services, health and medicine, higher education, arts and humanities, and governance and public policy. Grants are made for capital purposes, for specific human service programs, and for worthwhile research. There is no fixed minimum or maximum size of grants.

A major foundation objective is to encourage experimental or demonstration projects which promise significant positive results in helping people live healthier, happier, and more productive lives. Such projects must also have the potential to continue beyond the initial funding and be likely to produce a long-term multiplier effect.

Over-reliance upon the Weingart Foundation is discouraged. Applicants are expected to show project support from both internal and external sources. Proposals from organizations outside southern California are not encouraged, nor are requests in the following areas: refugee programs, energy and environment, religion, international concerns, associations of agencies, population studies, consumer interests, federated appeals and quasi-government groups. Grants are not made to carry on propaganda, to influence legislation, to promote voter registration, to finance political candidates or political campaigns. Grants are not made to individuals. The foundation generally does not favor requests for projects that should be financed by governmental agencies, nor does it normally make grants for operating expenses, endowment funds, deficit financing, contingencies, or ongoing, normal institutional operations. As a general rule, it does not make grants for conferences, seminars, workshops, travel, exhibits, or surveys.

Grants made by the Weingart Foundation have increased steadily through the years. In 1974-1975, grants totalled $723,100. During the fiscal year ending June 30, 1982, $13,857,750 in grants was given. During the past eight years, grants amounted to $41,745,750. The largest grant made in the fiscal year ending June 30, 1981, was $2.2 million, given to the Hospital of the Good Samaritan. Other grants in excess of a million dollars were made to the California Institute of Technology, the University of Southern California, Volunteers of America (Los Angeles), and the YMCA of metropolitan Los Angeles. In 1982, the Lakewood Cultural Arts Center was awarded $1,464,000 by the foundation. During the past four years (1978-1982), 49 percent of the grants were made in the area of community services and social welfare; 26 percent in health and medicine; 15 percent in education; and 10 percent in arts and humanities.

When a grant is made by the Weingart Foundation, the directors request an interim evaluation/progress report every six months during the funding period and a final report when the grant funds have been completely expended. The reports must include a summary of the program/project objectives and an assessment of its impact, an accounting of grant funds expenditure, and any other pertinent information about the organization's role in serving the community.

The foundation is governed by a five-member board of directors. Administration of the foundation is carried on from offices located at 1200 Wilshire Boulevard, Suite 305, Los Angeles, California 90017.

For further information, see *Annual Reports* of the foundation, published since the 1970s, together with its *Guidelines and Application Procedure* (n.d.).

RAYMOND L. MUNCY

**WELCH FOUNDATION.** See Robert A. Welch Foundation, The.

**WESTERN ELECTRIC FUND.** This company-sponsored foundation was established in 1953 in New York by the Western Electric Company, Incorporated, a subsidiary of the American Telephone and Telegraph Company. Since its founding, the Western Electric Fund has adopted guidelines which direct its grants to organizations with a national reputation, organizations in regions where the Western Electric Company has major facilities, and organizations which have had an ongoing relationship with the company. Grants are made only to organizations located within the continental United States.

Fund support has been channelled into three broad areas: education, health and welfare, and culture. In the area of education, fund support has been concentrated upon the independent sector, particularly privately endowed four-year undergraduate colleges and universities which confer the bachelor's degree. Such support falls into the following categories: unrestricted grants; capital grants; matching gifts; and small equipment grants. The fund also provides aid to the National Merit Scholarship Program for children of the corporate sponsor's employees and to various educational associations.

In the health and welfare area, the Western Electric Fund has contributed to United Ways, to hospitals, and to youth organizations.

In the cultural area, the fund generally has contributed to the support of the leading three or four cultural organizations in cities where Western Electric has a major facility. Operating grants are restricted to major arts or science museums, arts councils, and performing arts groups. Building grants are restricted to building campaigns for cultural institutions.

The assets of the Western Electric Fund aggregated about $2 million in the 1950s and varied from $5 million to $8 million in the 1960s and early 1970s. By 1979, however, the fund's assets had climbed to around $28 million. Substantial gifts by the company since that time have boosted the fund's assets to approximately $70 million in 1981. In recent years, disbursements by the fund have been ranging from approximately $2 million to $7 million annually.

The governing, nine-member board of trustees is comprised of executives of the Western Electric Company. The administration of the fund is carried on from offices located at 222 Broadway, New York, New York 10038, under the direction of an executive director.

For further information, see *Annual Reports* of the fund, published continuously since 1979. See also *Policies and Procedures*, an informational pamphlet about the fund, published in 1980.

**WHITEHEAD FOUNDATION.** See Joseph B. Whitehead Foundation; Lettie Pate Whitehead Foundation, Inc.

**WILDER FOUNDATION.** See Amherst H. Wilder Foundation.

**WILLIAM AND FLORA HEWLETT FOUNDATION, THE.** Mr. and Mrs. William R. Hewlett and their son, Walter B. Hewlett, established the W. R. Hewlett Foundation in California in 1966. Funded by gifts of stock in the Hewlett-Packard Company, which Hewlett had co-founded, the foundation's assets in

1968 were valued at about $500,000. The emphasis of the foundation's giving at that time was local and grants were relatively small, primarily for the support of medical research, higher education, and a population-control agency, together with limited support for music and the performing arts.

The name of the foundation was changed in 1977 to the William and Flora Hewlett Foundation in order to honor Mrs. Hewlett, who died in that year. Since that time, the market value of the foundation's assets have taken a tremendous surge in value, increasing from about $4 million in 1977 to over $50 million in 1979 and to about $316 million in 1981. Grants for 1979 amounted to about $6 million, and they amounted to about $11 million in 1981. The foundation planned grants of about $15 million in 1982. Although the foundation has continued a regional grants program in the San Francisco area, which takes a percentage of its total annual giving, it has become national in the scope of its operations.

The Hewlett Foundation program now emphasizes support for higher education, population control, environmental projects, the performing arts, and special projects. In recent years, the following major grants in these areas have been made: $300,000—Research Libraries Group, Stanford, California; $402,000—Nature Conservancy, Washington, D.C.; $300,000—Planned Parenthood Association of America, New York; $150,000—the School of American Ballet, New York; and $400,000—Urban Institute, Washington, D.C.

The foundation is governed by an eight-member board of directors, with William R. Hewlett serving as chairman and two other members of the Hewlett family also serving as directors. Administration of the foundation is carried on from offices located at 525 Middlefield Road, Menlo Park, California 94025, under the direction of a president.

For further information, see *Annual Reports* of the foundation, published since 1977. Also available is a ten-year report, which details the grant making of the foundation from its founding in 1966 until the first annual report of 1977. See also a foundation pamphlet (1982) containing general information, policy, and guidelines.

**WILLIAM H. DONNER FOUNDATION, INC., THE.** Established in 1961 to carry on the philanthropic work of its benefactor, the William H. Donner Foundation currently funds projects in the fields of water resources, U.S.-Canadian relations, and nutrition education.

Donner, a turn-of-the-century industrialist whose fortune derived from judicious investments in real estate, natural gas, tin, and steel, originally devoted his philanthropic efforts to cancer research, after the disease caused the death of his son, Joseph, in 1929. The International Cancer Research Foundation, created and endowed in 1932 with $2 million, was the first foundation dedicated solely to the eradication of cancer and related diseases. Its grants enabled the University of Pennsylvania to set up a radiological department in 1937 and an "atom smasher" for cancer treatment in 1940. The foundation also made a significant contribution to cancer research at Memorial Cancer Center, in New

York City, in the late 1930s and furthered the pioneering work of Dr. Ernest O. Lawrence with a gift which created the Donner Radiation Laboratory at the University of California, Berkeley, in 1941. The pioneering work of the Donner Laboratory—applying physics, chemistry, and mathematics to medicine—marked the beginning of atomic medicine.

In 1961, the William H. Donner Foundation was established with funds originally donated by Donner to the International Cancer Research Foundation. E. P. Tatum Smith, Jr., served as president until June, 1967, at the foundation's headquarters in Roanoke, Virginia. In 1967, Smith retired from the presidency, and Dr. Franklyn A. Johnson, former director of the Job Corps, joined the foundation as president and trustee. That same year, the foundation moved its offices to New York City.

At the direction of the trustees, the foundation, in 1967, shifted its efforts away from medical research and instituted two new grants programs: the American Indian and Canadian Studies in the United States. Although first devoted primarily to efforts to increase Indian self-sufficiency through economic development and improved educational opportunities, the former program later expanded to include support for increased Indian law services, the strengthening of tribal administration, and the improvement of health-care services. The Donner Foundation concluded its involvement in Indian affairs in 1980 after more than a decade of involvement, gratified that substantial success had been achieved by native American leaders, tribal governments, and private organizations supported by the foundation, and confident that the emerging Indian leadership was capable of successfully managing Indian affairs in the future.

The Canadian Studies in the United States program was created to increase American awareness of the differences in language, history, and government that exist between the two countries. Foundation interest in Canada reflects its founder's long involvement with Canada, as well as the presence of a "sister" foundation based in Toronto—the Donner Canadian Foundation, one of Canada's largest national foundations. The William H. Donner Foundation's initial grant in this field helped create the first center devoted solely to graduate studies on Canada, at the School of Advanced International Studies of the Johns Hopkins University, in Washington, D.C. Since that important first grant in 1968, the foundation has supported programs in numerous other universities, including Northwestern, Duke, and Columbia universities. In recent years, foundation interest has expanded to include policy studies on issues of current concern to the two countries, such as resolution of the acid rain issue and telecommunications policy.

In the 1970s, under the leadership of Donald S. Rickerd, president, the William H. Donner Foundation undertook two additional grant programs. Aware that the nation's cultural institutions were experiencing serious financial problems as a result of inflation and other pressures, the trustees approved a program, Administration in the Arts, to strengthen the management of cultural institutions in the United States. In 1974, the board instituted the Women in Management grants program to provide support for programs designed to prepare women for successful managerial careers in corporations and academia. Several significant research studies were also funded, and upon conclusion of the program in 1982, the foundation had made a demonstrable contribution to the progress women had made as managers in the corporate, academic, and nonprofit sectors.

The Donner Foundation with 1981 assets of approximately $33 million and with annual grants amounting to about $2 million, continues its involvement in U.S.-Canadian relations through support of select academic institutions and timely policy studies. In 1982, the board of trustees, concerned about threats to U.S. coastal marine resources and inland water supplies, approved a new program area, Ocean and Inland Water Resources, to strengthen the management of these critical natural resources. The foundation will also continue its modest involvement in the field of nutrition education, supporting projects to educate physicians and the public about the role nutrition plays in maintaining health.

The Donner Foundation is governed by a seven-member board of trustees, which includes two members of the Donner family. Administration of the foundation is carried on from offices located at 630 Fifth Avenue, Room 2452, New York, New York 10111, under the direction of the president.

For further information, see *Annual Reports* of the foundation, published since the 1960s.

JANET MAUGHAN

**WILLIAM K. WARREN FOUNDATION, THE.** The William K. Warren Foundation was established in 1945 in Tulsa, Oklahoma, by William K. Warren, the founder of the Warren Petroleum Company, which became a division of the Gulf Oil Corporation. The company is a leading manufacturer and wholesaler of liquified petroleum gas and related products. By 1951, the assets of the foundation amounted to about $3 million and it made grants of about $40,000 for that year, primarily to civic organizations in Tulsa. In 1956, assets were not reported; but income was about $4 million and giving for that year was about $500,000 and consisted almost entirely of a grant for the construction of a Tulsa hospital.

By 1968, the assets of the Warren Foundation had grown tremendously and were almost $90 million. Grants for the year were about $2.25 million and were for a variety of purposes: construction and maintenance of Tulsa-area hospitals, higher and secondary education, church support—particularly Roman Catholic—and cultural projects.

The value of the foundation's assets jumped again, to about $127 million in 1980. Grants for that year totalled over $3 million, with about 65 percent of that amount going for the support of higher education, including a grant of $1,035,000 to the University of Notre Dame and one of $1,002,500 to Vanderbilt University. Grants for medical research and health, with one of $798,880 to the William K. Warren Medical Research Center, Inc., Tulsa, took about 25 percent of the total. The remaining 10 percent was devoted to aid for churches and religious organizations, particularly Roman Catholic, and other purposes. The largest grant in this area of giving was one of $144,000 to the Sisters of Charity of the Incarnate Word, Houston, Texas.

The Warren Foundation is governed by a seven-member board of directors, which includes several members of the Warren family. The mailing address of the foundation is Post Office Box 45372, Tulsa, Oklahoma 74145.

Almost the only additional information on this foundation readily available to the public are the annual reports and returns filed by it with the Internal Revenue Service, and the various Foundation Center publications.

**WILLIAM M. SCHOLL FOUNDATION.** See Dr. Scholl Foundation.

**WILLIAM PENN FOUNDATION, THE.** The principal donors of the William Penn Foundation were Otto Haas and his wife, Phoebe Waterman Haas.

Born in 1872 in Stuttgart, Germany, Otto Haas came to this country in 1902 and was associated for several years with a firm dealing in leather hides. In 1907, he and a friend, Dr. Otto Rohm, established a business in Germany which, prior to World War I, became Rohm and Haas, an American corporation. Utilizing a new tanning process called Oropon, the company prospered; and during the World War I and postwar period, the company expanded its activities to include the development of additional chemicals used in a wide range of industries, including leather, plastics, textiles, and agriculture.

The William Penn Foundation was incorporated in Delaware in 1945 as the Phoebe Waterman Foundation. It changed its name in 1970 to the Haas Community Fund and in 1974 adopted its present name. Otto and Phoebe Haas provided the principal assets of the foundation, which were valued at about $129 million in 1981 and consisted almost entirely of stock in the Rohm and Haas Company. Grants of the foundation from 1945 to 1980 amounted to about $100 million.

Grants have been made primarily to institutions and organizations in the Philadelphia vicinity, including Camden, New Jersey. Health-care and medical research has been a major foundation interest, and over $15 million in grants has been provided to medical schools, hospitals, and so forth, since the establishment of the foundation. Nearly $16 million has been used to provide support for a wide range of creative and performing arts, theatre, and museum activities. Conservation and restoration has been the smallest budgeted category area of foundation interest, with grants amounting to about $3 million. Some have been used, for example, for the restoration of historic buildings in the Philadelphia area.

The two areas which have received the greatest support from the foundation over the years have been education and social welfare. Although they shared about equally for the first thirty-five years of the foundation's existence, approximately $30 million having been appropriated to each area during the period of 1945 to 1980, in the last decade the grants to social welfare have been the greater.

Members of the Haas family have always been involved in the governance of the foundation. The present-day, twelve-member board of directors includes seven Haas family members. John C. Haas and F. Otto Haas, the donors' sons, serve as chairman and vice-chairman respectively. The program of the William Penn Foundation is administered from offices located at 920 Suburban Station Building, 1617 John F. Kennedy Boulevard, Philadelphia, Pennsylvania 19103, under the direction of a president.

For further information, see *Annual Reports* of the foundation, published continuously since 1968, particularly that for the thirty-fifth year (1980). See also Otto Haas obituary, *New York Times* (January 3, 1960), p. 88.

**WILLIAM RANDOLPH HEARST FOUNDATION.** In 1937, William Randolph Hearst faced financial disaster. Control of his newspaper-based empire was stripped from him. Hearst, who never willingly sold a property, watched in furious impotence as a consortium of seventeen banks—Hearst's major creditors—disposed of fourteen newspapers, seven radio stations, the Universal News Service, and other elements of Hearstdom. Hearst was bankrupt and seventy-four years old; if he had written a will at all, it was not consequential. Odds would have to have been heavily against his ever establishing a major philanthropy. As a result, however, of war-induced prosperity and Hearst's longevity, the redoubtable baron was in a position by the late 1940s to establish two foundations which bear his name.

Hearst's assets at the time of his death in 1951 were $200 million to $400 million. The Hearst empire on which the foundations were based encompassed sixteen big city daily newspapers, International News Service, King Features, three radio stations, Metrotone Newsreels, great land holdings, and a group of eight magazines which included *Cosmopolitan* and *Good Housekeeping*.

Hearst was eighty-four years old when his will was written in 1947. Leaving his wife $7 million in liquid assets and his five sons about a half-million each, he put all but one hundred shares of the nonvoting common stock of the Hearst Corporation into two newly formed foundations. The Hearst Foundation, Inc.,* was established in 1945, when work on the will had begun in earnest. The California Charities Foundation followed in 1949, after the will's completion. In two years, Hearst would die at age eighty-eight.

Only nominally are the foundations distinct; their boards and executive structures are interlocking. California Charities, renamed the William Randolph Hearst Foundation in 1952, was established in California and the Hearst Foundation, Inc., in New York, but regional differentiation between the two has faded. They have common headquarters at 888 Seventh Avenue, New York, New York 10106, and make joint use of offices at 609 Market Street, San Francisco, California 94104, and grantees do not exhibit an exclusive pattern of regional identification with one foundation or the other. They share the common purposes of aiding education, health delivery systems and medical research, cultural programs, and poverty-level and minority groups.

Market value of the assets of the William Randolph Hearst Foundation hovers around the 1980 valuation of $131 million. Annual expenditures are approximately $5 million. A large proportion of funding goes to recipients in California and New York. Educational programs receive just over one-third of the money disbursed and health care and research approximately one-fourth. Arts and culture average a little over 10 percent and social welfare a little less than 10 percent. Youth agencies and religious organizations account for about 3 percent each.

Higher education gets the lion's share of educational awards, usually in the $10,000 to $25,000 range for individual institutions. Major grants have been made, however, to institutions such as the University of California and Stanford University, paid in annual installments. The former was recently awarded $1.75 million for rehabilitation of a gymnasium and the latter $700,000 for an endowed chair. The health-field program is characterized by larger grants, such as a $1.25 million grant to the Salk Institute, La Jolla, California, funding the Hearst Research Center, and $500,000 to Harvard Medical School.

Two continuing programs are conducted by the William Randolph Hearst Foundation. One is the United States Senate Youth Program. High school students are awarded $1,500 scholarships enabling them to observe first-hand the working of the Senate and other federal government operations. Randolph A. Hearst, working in concert with former Senator Hubert Humphrey, was instrumental in establishing this program and in gaining the imprimatur of the Senate for it in 1962. Annually, close to $150,000 in scholarships is given, and a like amount is spent in administering the program.

The other is the Journalism Awards Program. It awards scholarships to journalism students and grants of corresponding value to host institutions, whose programs must hold membership in the American Association of Schools and Departments of Journalism. Yearly value of the scholarships approaches $100,000, with operating expenses about half that amount.

The relatively small social welfare program was always much appreciated among recipient agencies, such as the Salvation Army in San Francisco, but it certainly was never heralded among the public at large in a fashion that would identify the foundation with dramatic largesse to the poor. Bizarre events in 1974, however, brought worldwide publicity for a single act in behalf of needy persons. Indeed, all the activities of the foundation since its inception have never received the blaze of attention that was drawn to the 1974 operation dubbed "People in Need."

Patricia Campbell Hearst, granddaughter of William Randolph Hearst and daughter of one of his twin sons, Randolph A. Hearst, was abducted from her Berkeley, California, apartment on February 4, 1974, by a small band of terrorists who styled themselves the "Symbionese Liberation Army." The abductors extorted a food giveaway as a "symbolic gesture of good faith" on which negotiations for her release were conditioned. Her father responded by establishing

"People in Need," using $500,000 in personal funds and $1.5 million granted by the foundation. In a few days, the hastily devised distribution plan was putting free food into the hands of people who would come in and say they need help. Hearst's response to the terrorists' demands did not lead to Patty's release, and she subsequently was recaptured by police action.

As concerns the foundation, "People in Need" was episodic, but Patty Hearst's abduction led, not logically but through a chain of circumstance, to the installation of a new chief executive. Patty, in her converted state as "Tania" while in the hands of the terrorists, had criticized her father for his conduct of the *San Francisco Examiner* as a part of the Hearst "propaganda machine." Randolph Hearst took her comments to heart and began changing the editorial policies of the paper, in something of an atonement, even as she was still with the outlaw band. Being determined to have complete and genuine control of the newspaper, he moved Charles L. Gould out of the position of publisher. Hearst himself assumed this responsibility, adding it to the editorship and presidency he already held. Gould in turn was named executive director of both of the Hearst foundations.

Gould's appointment was in keeping with the tradition of the Hearst foundations. Their officers and directors had long been chosen from among Hearst family members and Hearst Corporation executives. For two decades, their stewardship resulted in levels of funding that were advantageous to the Hearst Corporation and disadvantageous to foundation activities. Then the 1969 Federal Tax Reform Act was passed, containing provisions that led the Hearst Corporation to buy its own stock from the foundations, a $135 million transaction. The foundations, in turn, were able both to build diversified folios and to make more generous disbursements than Hearst family and corporate control had allowed when a dollar spent by the foundations meant one dollar less in the corporate treasury. The corporation's $135 million brought it a bargain, stock which represented about $1 billion in holdings.

The founder's twin sons preside over the twin foundations. David W. Hearst, president of the William Randolph Hearst Foundation, was forced out of his post as publisher of the *Los Angeles Herald-Express* in the 1950s after the paper declined badly under his management. Randolph Hearst, president of the Hearst Foundation, Inc., was more successful in the company than his twin, but the *San Francisco Examiner* was a troubled paper when he left it in 1975.

Save for the presidencies, the two foundations have identical slates of officers and substantially the same directors. The aforementioned Charles Gould, operating in San Francisco, is senior executive in both; and Robert M. Frehse, Jr., in New York, serves both as executive director. Frehse's appointment represents a departure from long practice in that he came to the foundations not from the Hearst Corporation but from a twenty-four-year career with Citicorp.

Many years ago, there was a phrase with which a host of the founder's employees at all levels identified. It might be applied, as well, to the ubiquitous Hearst executives and family members in the two foundations: they are on the "Hearst Service." Symbols of this tradition are found in the "People in

Need"operation and in the foundation's generosity to the University of California, which Randolph Hearst's wife, Catherine, served as a regent.

Beginning in the 1970s, a change began taking place in the Hearst empire. A younger generation of Hearsts were developing influence in corporate affairs, as the founder's sons had never done. Gradually, some of the executives who personified the worst of Hearst were departing as they grew old. A new pride developed in quality operations and the gaining of public respect. These were found to be more profitable, as well. The coming of Frehse to the foundations signals that they, too, are leaving some of the old ways behind. A more open, orthodox foundation operation is emerging. Frehse, a graduate of Northwestern University and the American Graduate School of International Management and a naval officer during World War II, had come on board in 1975 as assistant treasurer and director of administration. In 1979, he succeeded Gould as executive director, and at that time Gould was named senior executive.

The combined assets of the two foundations would place them in the ranks of the fifty largest foundations in the United States. Both are living foundations, spending from income and not dissipating their assets. Barring conversion to an institutional endowment, which is not known to be contemplated, or eventual distribution of assets to beneficiaries under applicable law, this major philanthropy bodes to continue as a source of sustenance for activities within its categories of interest.

While it is common for foundations not to issue publications concerning themselves, it is strange that these do not, considering the basis of their wealth in a business that has published so much. In any case, almost the only additional information readily available to the public on this foundation and the Hearst Foundation, Inc., are annual reports and returns filed by it with the Internal Revenue Service, and the various Foundation Center publications. See, however, Lindsay Chaney and Michael Cieply's book, *The Hearsts: Family and Empire—The Latter Years* (1981); this work contains passages concerning the foundations which, while brief, are extraordinarily informative.

LESLIE CAINE CAMPBELL

**WILLIAM R. KENAN, JR., CHARITABLE TRUST.** The William R. Kenan, Jr., Charitable Trust was established under the laws of the state of New York in 1965, the year of the death of its founder, who was born in Wilmington, North Carolina, on April 30, 1872. He attended the University of North Carolina, with which his family had a traditional interest beginning with his great-great-grandfather's membership on the school's original board of trustees. In 1894, William R. Kenan, Jr., graduated with a B.S. degree and thereafter maintained an active and ongoing interest in the university, not only as an alumnus and as an honorary member of the university's board of trustees but also as a very substantial benefactor.

In 1901, Kenan's eldest sister married Henry M. Flagler, an associate of John D. Rockefeller and a major developer of Florida's east coast. Kenan became closely associated with Flagler in his numerous business enterprises, and upon the death of Flagler and his wife, Kenan and his two sisters inherited a large part of the Flagler fortune. This, combined with Kenan's abilities in the fields of chemistry and engineering and his great business acuity, resulted in the Kenan family amassing a fortune estimated at $300 million at the time of William Kenan's death on July 28, 1965, in Lockport, New York, where he had spent most of his life.

Throughout his business career, William Kenan made substantial gifts to his alma mater, including the construction of the Kenan Memorial Stadium, at Chapel Hill; the establishment of a scholarship fund for athletes; and an endowment of the university's chemistry department.

Upon his death, the major portion of his estate passed to the William R. Kenan, Jr., Charitable Trust. His strong belief in the importance of education was clearly stated in article nine of his will, in the following words:

> I have always believed firmly that a good education is the most cherished gift an individual can receive, and it is my sincere hope that the provisions of this Article will result in a substantial benefit to mankind.

Since its establishment, the trust, with 1981 assets of about $106 million, has used its annual income to fund its programs of educational grants to the extent of about $100 million. Since the trust's primary purpose has been to support education, particularly teaching excellence at private institutions in the United States, one of its major programs has been the establishment of endowed professorships at selected U.S. universities and four-year colleges. Grants for such professorships presently number about ninety. Grants of recognition and support have also been made to a few smaller four-year colleges and college preparatory schools. Also, southern black colleges have been provided continuing support by the trust through projects administered for it by the Southern Regional Education Board, of Atlanta.

A special program for building their endowments has recently been instituted by the Kenan Charitable Trust for a few selected ninth- through twelfth-grade secondary schools under strictly maintained guidelines. Such schools must be of high quality, predominantly boarding, and must have a per student endowment of less than $20,000. During 1980 and 1981, eleven schools along the eastern seaboard of the United States were ultimately selected for participation in this matching grant program, with awards ranging from $200,000 to $2 million. In future years, the trustees anticipate that this program will be expanded to include additional schools in the eastern seaboard area.

The trust's administrative responsibilities are shared by two individual trustees—John L. Gray, a member of the New York City law firm of Dewey, Ballantine, Bushby, Palmer and Wood; and Frank H. Kenan, a member of the Kenan family—and Morgan Guaranty Trust Company of New York, the corporate trustee. Hamilton C. Hoyt is a trust administrator and is located at the Kenan office, 120 Broadway, New York, New York 10271.

Since the Kenan Trust was created for charitable and other purposes, for further information, see the trustee's *Annual Reports*, which provide statements as to historical background, grants, activities, and guideline requirements. The foregoing account is primarily based upon such *Reports*.

**WILLIAM T. GRANT FOUNDATION.** The Grant Foundation, Inc. was incorporated in Delaware in 1936 by William T. Grant (1876-1972), the founder and principal stockholder of the once-successful department store chain, the W. T. Grant Company. In 1977 the foundation's name was changed to its present one. In establishing the foundation, Grant wrote that he wanted "to assist, by some means, in helping people or peoples to live more contentedly and peacefully and well in body and mind through a better knowledge of how to use and enjoy all the good things that the world has to offer them" (The Grant Foundation, *Biennial Report* [1962], p. 5).

Starting with grants totalling $10,000 in 1937, by 1947 grants had increased to approximately $150,000. Its assets were then in the neighborhood of $1.6 million, and it was employing a small staff.

By 1960, the Grant Foundation's assets had swelled to about $14 million, and it was making annual grants of about $1 million. The foundation had refined its program by this time and began to concentrate upon projects designed to contribute to the attainment of positive mental health for children and young people. As will be detailed below, this orientation of the foundation has continued to the present.

The primary source of income up until the 1960s was derived from stock in the W. T. Grant Company. Following Grant's retirement in 1966 at the age of ninety, by which time he no longer played an active role in the company and drew no salary, the foundation began to diversify its portfolio and had reduced its holdings in the company to four hundred thousand shares by 1975. This move was a wise and fortuitous one because the W. T. Grant Company went bankrupt in 1975. With holdings then valued at $50 million in other securities, the foundation has since increased its corpus to about $77 million in 1980 despite grants running about $3 million annually.

The grants made in 1980 by the foundation, while larger and more numerous than in previous decades, are representative of its continuing concentration on research projects dealing with the healthy psychological and social development of children and youth. Approximately 73 percent of the total of about $2.7 million went for support of research programs in colleges, universities, centers, and institutes, both in the United States and abroad. Grants ranged from one of $202,426 to the Albert Einstein College of Medicine, at Yeshiva University, to one for $15,250 to the Medical Foundation, Boston, Massachusetts. Twenty-five percent of the funding was for professional training and youth education programs in the foundation's area of interest, with the remainder being devoted to social policy studies and community service programs.

The Grant Foundation is governed by an eleven-member board of trustees, which includes several M.D.'s. Administration of the foundation is carried on from offices located at 919 Third Avenue, New York, New York 10022, under the direction of a president.

For further information, see *Biennial Reports* (1958-1968), published by the foundation, and *Annual Reports*, published continuously since that time. See also an autobiography, William T. Grant, *The Story of W. T. Grant and the Early Days of the Business He Founded* (1954); and William T. Grant obituary, *New York Times* (August 7, 1972), pp. 1, 18.

**W. K. KELLOGG CHILD WELFARE FOUNDATION.** See W. K. Kellogg Foundation.

**W. K. KELLOGG FOUNDATION.** Will Keith Kellogg, creator of the foundation which bears his name, was in his mid-forties when he launched the cereal industry in Battle Creek, Michigan, that became internationally known and made him a millionaire many times over. He was seventy years old when he created the W. K. Kellogg Foundation. Until his death in 1951 at the age of ninety-one, his concepts and counsel guided both the Kellogg Company and the foundation with energetic drive and innovative spirit.

The story of the W. K. Kellogg Foundation is inextricably tied to its founder. When he provided endowments of nearly $50 million in 1930 to establish what was then known as the W. K. Kellogg Child Welfare Foundation (the name was changed in the same year to the W. K. Kellogg Foundation), the cereal magnate was already engaged in philanthropic interests. Nearly $3 million had gone in previous years to a wide range of worthy purposes, from student scholarships to the providing of clothes for war-orphaned British children. Over half the construction costs of the Ann J. Kellogg School, long a national model in educating handicapped children, came from Will Kellogg's generosity and abiding interest in the welfare of people, especially children.

Believing that a formal structure for stewardship of his wealth was needed, he endowed his foundation primarily with common stock in his cereal company. During its history, the foundation's assets have grown steadily. It now is ranked among the five largest private foundations in the nation and had market value assets in 1982 of over $1 billion. In 1982 over $57 million in grant payments were made—an amount exceeding the organization's entire original endowment.

W. K. Kellogg lacked a formal education beyond the sixth grade. His first job was as a stockboy, followed by the uninspiring life of a traveling broom salesman while in his late teens. He finally went to work as a young man in the Battle Creek Sanitarium—the San—where his older brother, John, was physician-in-chief. W. K. was bookkeeper, manager, and janitor of the world-famous hospital. In fact, virtually any task outside of medicine that needed doing fell to him.

Kellogg's prospects for an illustrious future seemed, in the late 1800s, meager at best. Conditions led him to believe that he would always be a poor man. Adding to the improbability of staking everything on an untried venture was the fact that he had immediate responsibilities: a wife, Ella, and five children, three of whom would die while still young.

Over five thousand patients came each year to the San for treatment of diseases and ailments and in search of a healthier life-style. John Kellogg added his own unique remedies to those of the Sanitarium, including mineral baths and vegetarianism. He also ensured that the patients' menu was well planned, prescribing fare from his own health-food company.

Carrying out his endless duties, W. K. assisted his physician-brother in conducting laboratory research, especially the search for a digestible bread-substitute by the process of boiling wheat. Success eluded them in their basic purpose, but a major dividend was paid from another direction.

On a propitious day in 1894, a pot of boiled wheat was inadvertently left to stand and become tempered. When it was put through the usual rolling process, each grain of wheat emerged as a large, thin flake. W. K. convinced his brother to serve the food in flake form; its appeal was immediate among patients, and it soon was being packaged to meet hundreds of mail-order requests from persons after they left the San. Because John Kellogg had little interest in such business matters, W. K. added another task to his long list of responsibilities: that of managing the burgeoning packaged food enterprise.

When word got out about the wheat flake, a horde of companies raced into operation in Battle Creek. Between 1900 and 1905, no less than forty cereal companies were competing within shouting distance of each other. Competition was savage, and eventually only a half-dozen firms prevailed. Due to W. K.'s shrewd business acumen and tireless vitality, the Kellogg enterprise was among the survivors.

By 1906, the younger Kellogg had thrown off his brother's reins and started his own company, one based on the corn flake, with which he had experimented since stumbling onto the wheat flake process. Using his inborn sense of economics, an uncanny understanding of marketing techniques, and an unflagging dedication to work (he often put in 120 hours a week on the job), W. K. Kellogg constantly increased production, advertising budgets, and sales. He expanded his business to Australia in 1924, guided the cereal company through the Great Depression with hardly a noticeable bump on the road, and brought Kellogg's cereal into England in 1938. As his fortune grew, he also attended to his lack of schooling by becoming a voracious reader and a world traveler.

His premonition that he would always be poor proved unfounded. When told by his treasurer, reasonably early in the company's history, that he was a millionaire, W. K. replied: "I never, at any period of my life, aspired to become wealthy.... It is my hope that the property that kind Providence has brought me may be helpful to many others...'' (Horace B. Powell, *The Original Has This Signature—W. K. Kellogg* [1956], p. 165).

Over the years, his support of charitable causes was enormous and varied. But he became convinced that the most good could be accomplished mainly by helping young people. In that way, help would be extended to the entire world and its future. He wrote:

Relief, raiment and shelter are necessary for destitute children, but the greatest good for the greatest number can come only through the education of the child, the parent, the teacher, the family physician, the dentist, and the community in general. Education offers the greatest opportunity for really improving one generation over another. [Horace B. Powell, *The Original Has This Signature—W. K. Kellogg* (1956), p. 310.]

Hence, the foundation's charter calls for "the promotion of the health, education, and welfare of mankind" emphasizing benefits to children and youth, "directly or indirectly."

Dr. A. C. Selmon, an Adventist medical missionary whom W. K. met on a visit to China, was named as the foundation's first president. But with offices both at the foundation and the cereal company's facilities, W. K. Kellogg was never far from the action.

After examining needs in those formative years, the charter board of trustees concluded that research and relief activities were already being supported by many organizations, including the government. What was missing was the application of existing knowledge to solve problems of health, limitations in community facilities, inadequate schools, and poor-quality hospitals and libraries. The foundation's purpose became one of helping people use available knowledge to help themselves.

At first, efforts were concentrated in the Battle Creek area through a project to establish county health departments in seven contiguous counties. No such departments existed, though they were obviously a sound mechanism for uncovering health problems and organizing to solve them. The Michigan Community Health Project had a profoundly beneficial effect on agencies, professions, and institutions across the region. It conclusively proved the potential of cooperative endeavor for meeting social needs.

The underlying theory of W. K. Kellogg Foundation grant making, established at the outset, holds true today: begin with problems recognized by the people themselves; bring their own leadership to bear on the problems, in addition to the best of current thought; and share the lessons learned with others facing similar difficulties. Though it sounds simplistic, it is inordinately complex. Project successes over the years illustrate that this technique fosters programs that endure and multiply. Publications, workshops, audio-visual materials, seminars, and other outlets are used as mechanisms for disseminating information.

Grant making during the foundation's first decade included support for a world federation of education associations to exchange health materials; a nutritional program for school children; fellowships in various health occupations; and many projects directed at helping the handicapped, such as diagnosing and treating speech defects, preventing blindness and glaucoma, and obviating congenital malformations.

From its inception to the end of World War II, the Kellogg Foundation remained an operating foundation. That is, it managed and directed the projects it funded. By 1942, since the immediate staff numbered less than a dozen professionals who covered over six hundred thousand miles of field trips in one fiscal year alone, the stringency of W. K. Kellogg's work ethos was plainly evidenced.

By the mid-1940s, the foundation had added agriculture to its two other fields of programming interest—education and health—and had moved from an operating to a grant-making organization. The single exception was that it continued to operate its fellowship programs in Latin America, initially established at federal request near the outset of World War II to help foster relationships in the hemisphere. (The Latin America fellowships were discontinued in the late 1960s due to a shift in foundation priorities but were resumed seven years later and continue today.)

In 1955, four years after W. K. Kellogg's death, the foundation convened nearly seventy representatives of state and national agencies and major universities to provide advice on future needs of society. It was a learning technique the foundation still repeats with continued good results.

Flowing out of the advisement, new programs were funded in progressive patient care, emphasizing intensive and coronary care; rural leadership activities; and the nationwide community college movement which brought the "people's college" to the forefront of higher education. Program directors at the foundation, experts in their respective fields, reviewed proposals received, recommended the most promising for board approval, and then were responsible for monitoring grantees' progress. That basic system remains in operation.

Foundation assistance has more recently been extended to efforts such as support of graduate programs in occupational health for primary-care physicians, the associate degree in nursing, and vital hospital administration programs. Centers for continuing education have been established at eleven universities across the country, and the National 4-H Center, in Washington, D.C., was made a reality. In addition, nearly thirty traditionally black colleges were helped to strengthen and expand their curricula in the interest of their students' future opportunities.

The W. K. Kellogg Foundation has been a leader in pioneering the use of computer systems in agriculture, education, and health, with direct involvement reaching back to 1949. At that time, the Southwestern Michigan Hospital Council designed a program to compare medical statistics among its thirteen member-hospitals. In 1976, the funding of the Fast Agricultural Communications Terminal System (FACTS), through Purdue University's Extension Service, brought vital agricultural information to all of the state's ninety-two county extension offices and has led the foundation to aid in development of regional computer institutes across the nation in the 1980s.

The foundation's National Fellowship Program originated in 1980 and represents both an operating aspect of the organization and an abiding interest in the development of interdisciplinary leadership. Annually, as many as fifty professionals from institutional and agency staffs are awarded three-year grants to engage in a set of experiences, largely self-directed, to broaden their social and intellectual awareness. It is believed that the fellows' expanded leadership capabilities return a significant professional contribution to the sponsoring institution and to society in general.

Just over fifty staff members make up the work force of the Kellogg Foundation. All operate from the Battle Creek headquarters except the program director for Latin American projects, who is a native of that region and is stationed there. Considering that the foundation averages six hundred to seven hundred active projects in any year, the number of staff members is lean, representing administrative costs of less than 6.3 percent of the organization's total expenditures in 1982.

Governance is vested in the foundation's nine-member board of trustees. The board also serves as a fiscal review committee. It convenes monthly in Battle Creek. Despite the fact that trustees have come from as far away as New York and Nebraska, in more than a half-century no meeting has been cancelled because of failure to have a quorum. It is an especially impressive record considering the harsh winters often experienced in the Midwest.

Foundation income is derived primarily from investments. A three-member trust administers a major source of the organization's revenues. Foundation Chairman of the Board and Chief Executive Officer Russell G. Mawby serves on the trust as well as on the board of trustees, providing the essential link between the two entities and the institution itself.

Since its beginning, the Kellogg Foundation's total expenditures have exceeded $643 million. In 1982, assets were about $1 billion. During that same year expenditures amounted to about $57 million, approximately a 7.7 percent increase or about $4 million over the previous year. The foundation has traditionally followed the practice of distributing annually at least all of its income.

Grant-making interests are in projects that stress the application of existing knowledge. Seed money is given for pilot projects of potential national or international importance that emphasize the application of new knowledge in addressing significant human problems and which, if successful, can be emulated by other communities, institutions, or organizations with similar problems to solve.

The foundation's activities are linked to the fields of agriculture, education, and health. For many years projects were funded in the United States, Canada, Latin America, Australia, New Zealand, and selected European countries. Revised priorities for the 1980s limit grants outside the United States and Latin America to the Kellogg International Fellowship Program as well as international networks of activities related to the foundation's programming interests. Those interests are: adult continuing education; coordinated, cost-effective health services; betterment of health; a wholesome food supply; broadened leadership capacity; and, in Michigan only, economic development and opportunities for youth.

The Kellogg Foundation does not make loans and does not provide grants for: operational phases of established programs; basic research; capital facilities, equipment, conferences, publications or films, unless they are an integral phase of a project already being funded; endowments or developmental campaigns; religious purposes; or individuals, except for fellowships in specific areas of foundation programming.

To be eligible for support, organizations and institutions must qualify under the regulations of the United States Internal Revenue Service. Grantees must have the financial potential to sustain the project on a continuing basis after foundation funding. To be considered for foundation aid, an institution or organization sends a proposal letter or memorandum which briefly describes the basic problem and the plan for its solution. The plan must include project objectives, operational procedures, time schedule, evaluation process, and personnel and financial resources available and needed. If the proposal is within the foundation's guidelines and interests, and if foundation priorities and resources allow consideration of the requested aid, conferences and staff investigation may follow. The requesting organization may also be asked to develop a more detailed proposal.

Offices of the W. K. Kellogg Foundation are located at 400 North Avenue, Battle Creek, Michigan 49016.

For further information, see *Annual Reports* of the foundation, prepared annually since its founding and published since 1951. See also the biography by Horace B. Powell, *The Original Has This Signature—W. K. Kellogg* (1956); and "Will Keith Kellogg,"*Dictionary of American Biography*, Supplement Five (1977), pp. 378-380. The following histories have been published by the foundation: *W. K. Kellogg Foundation, the First Eleven Years* (1941); *The First Twenty-Five Years* (1955); and *The First Half Century, 1930-1980* (1980).

ROBERT E. HENCEY

**W. M. KECK FOUNDATION.** In 1954, William M. Keck established in Delaware this foundation bearing his name. He also created in his will the W. M. Keck Trust for the sole benefit of the foundation.

Keck was born in Bradford, Pennsylvania, in 1880. Self-educated, he went to California shortly after the turn of the century. Beginning as a roustabout oil worker, he learned all aspects of the oil business, particularly oil drilling. In 1921, Keck founded Superior Oil Company, as an oil and gas exploration and production company. Under his leadership, the company became one of the nation's most successful oil and gas producers. During his lifetime, Keck contributed substantial sums to philanthropy and, upon his death in 1964, fifty thousand shares of Superior Oil Company stock were bequeathed to the W. M. Keck Foundation.

In recent years, the assets and contributions of the foundation have shown a dramatic increase. In 1977, the foundation had assets of about $3 million and made grants for the year amounting to about $125,000. Gifts of cash and stock to the foundation totalled approximately $8 million in 1978; $12.5 million in 1979; and $23 million in both 1980 and 1981. Thus, assets of the foundation increased to about $32 million by 1980. Then, with the final settlement of the estate of William M. Keck in 1981, the foundation's assets in that year grew to about $460 million, making it one of the top twenty foundations in the United States by size of assets.

Before its tremendous growth, the Keck Foundation concentrated primarily on local (California) giving, with an emphasis upon higher and secondary education and hospitals together with some grants to youth agencies, for aid to the handicapped, and community funds. Since 1980, more than three-fourths of foundation funding is still awarded to California-based organizations. The foundation program focuses on grants for the following purposes: to strengthen studies and programs in colleges and universities in the earth sciences areas, devoted to the development of natural resources; engineering; medical research; and, to an extent, other science-related studies and liberal arts. Also, the foundation gives some consideration, largely in the southern California geographical area, to the following institutions: secondary educational; hospitals; arts and cultural; and health-care and civic and community organizations which have been traditionally supported by the foundation.

In carrying out the above program, there follows a sample list of larger grants by the foundations in 1980: Claremont Men's College—$1.3 million; Hospital of the Good Samaritan, Los Angeles—$800,000; Loyola High School, Los Angeles—$100,000; YMCA, Los Angeles—$800,000; Goodwill Industries, Los Angeles—$150,000; and Los Angeles Museum of Modern Art—$100,000.

The W. M. Keck Foundation is governed by a twenty-one-member board of directors, with Howard B. Keck, son of W. M. Keck, serving as chairman, president, and chief executive officer. W. M. Keck II and Howard B. Keck, Jr., are vice-presidents and directors of the foundation; and several other members of the board of directors are members of or related to the Keck family. Administration of the foundation is carried on from offices located at 555 South Flower Street, Suite 4750, Los Angeles, California 90071, under the direction of the chief executive officer.

Almost the only additional information readily available to the public on this foundation are the annual reports and returns filed by it with the Internal Revenue Service, and the various Foundation Center publications. See, however, the foundation's *Annual Report* (1981 and 1982) and the following obituaries: William M. Keck, *New York Times* (August 21, 1964), p. 37; and William M. Keck, Jr., *New York Times* (November 11, 1982), p. 22.

**W. R. HEWLETT FOUNDATION.** See William and Flora Hewlett Foundation, The.

**W. W. SMITH CHARITABLE TRUST.** The W. W. Smith Charitable Trust was established by the will of William Wikoff Smith, who died in 1976. Smith, who headed the Kewanee Oil Company founded by his great-grandfather in 1871, had diversified the company through other business acquisitions and became the principal owner and chairman of the board of trustees of the resulting Kewanee Industries, Incorporated.

The W. W. Smith Charitable Trust was initially funded in 1977 and, from 1977 to 1981, made grants totalling in the neighborhood of $16 million. As directed in Smith's will, the trustees made grants primarily to organizations and institutions in Philadelphia and its surrounding counties. Also as directed, they made allocations in four program areas: 23 percent in financial aid for needy undergraduate students at accredited colleges and universities; 20 percent to hospital programs for the medical care of the poor and needy; 35 percent for specific medical research programs, with particular emphasis on those dealing with cancer and heart disease; and 22 percent for programs of organizations providing shelter, food, and clothing for children and the aged.

The value of Smith Charitable Trust assets in 1981 was about $47 million. Trustees are Mary L. Smith, widow of the donor, and the Philadelphia National Bank. The address of the trust is 100 Chetwynd Drive, Suite 206, Rosemont, Pennsylvania 19010. Its administration is carried on under the direction of a senior trust officer of the Philadelphia National Bank, Post Office Box 7618, Philadelphia, Pennsylvania 19101.

For further information, see *Annual Reports* for the years 1977-1978, 1979-1980, and 1980-1981, published by the trust. See also William Wikoff Smith obituary, *New York Times* (January 13, 1976), p. 36.

## Z

**Z. SMITH REYNOLDS FOUNDATION, INC.** In 1936, the Z. Smith Reynolds Foundation was established as a memorial to Zachary Smith Reynolds, the youngest child of R. J. Reynolds. The father, a native Virginian, came to North Carolina during the late nineteenth century and established a cigarette manufacturing business that grew to be a major corporation. The son was an early adventurer in aviation, receiving his pilot's certificate from Orville Wright while only sixteen years of age. In 1930-1931, he flew an Italian-built amphibian from the south of England to China.

When the younger Reynolds died in 1932, he had not yet come into his inheritance from his father. In the litigation that followed his death, his two sisters and brother petitioned the court to declare them his heirs, with the understanding that they would forfeit any inheritance awarded them and place it in trust for the people of North Carolina. They were declared heirs to a quarter of the estate, and with these funds they established the Z. Smith Reynolds Foundation. Their co-founder was their uncle, William Neal Reynolds; and when he died in 1951, he left his estate in trust to provide income to the foundation.

Since that time, the foundation has made grants to more than one thousand recipient institutions and organizations in almost every county in North Carolina. The total value of grants made exceeds $100 million. In 1980, the value of the assets of the two trusts was about $94 million, and the annual income to the foundation was just over $7 million.

The foundation's one limitation is geographical: its programs and activities are restricted to the state of North Carolina. Within that state, it has supported innovative programs for governmental accountability; improvement of the public school curriculum and the state's judicial system; the development of a state zoo and a school for the performing arts; preservation of natural resources from the coastal Outer Banks to the mountainous west; various programs at a majority of the state's public and private colleges and universities; significant health-care activities; and community projects from small towns to large cities. Since 1946, the Reynolds Foundation has had a contractual relationship that provides for annual support of Wake Forest University, in Winston-Salem. It has made additional and substantial grants to Wake Forest and its Bowman Gray School of Medicine.

In several instances, foundation-supported programs have served as models for permanent state action. The foundation was a major funding source for the North Carolina Fund, an antipoverty program that served as a prototype for national efforts in this field. A grant from the foundation in the mid-1970s helped develop an economic education curriculum for the state's public school system which is now financed to a large extent by tax monies. A current project supported by the foundation will help develop a settlement judge experiment under the North Carolina Court of Appeals, which is expected subsequently to become a part of the state's budget.

While the Reynolds Foundation has avoided developing a specific permanent focus, in recent years it has given special attention to the criminal justice field. Funds from the foundation are supporting the work of a state citizens commission, which is studying alternatives to incarceration. Other funds from the foundation have supported innovative programs of restitution and community service for first offenders.

The foundation board has a majority of nonfamily members representing geographical as well as professional diversity. The board is self-perpetuating and elects five officers—a president, two vice-presidents, a secretary, and a treasurer—for annual terms.

The foundation's staff consists of an executive director, an assistant director, an executive assistant, and a secretary. The board and the staff are assisted in their work by a state advisory panel, consisting of up to nine citizens of North Carolina who perform a number of functions without becoming involved in decision making on grants.

The Z. Smith Reynolds Foundation's offices are located in 101 Reynolda Village, Winston-Salem, North Carolina 27106, a part of the R. J. Reynolds estate. The building which houses the foundation was originally a school in which the Reynolds children were educated.

For further information, see Bryan Haislip, *A History of the Z. Smith Reynolds Foundation* (1967). See also a *Three Year Report, 1967-1969*; a *Two Year Report, 1970-1971*; and *Annual Reports* of the foundation, published continuously since 1972.

THOMAS W. LAMBETH

# appendix 1

# ASSETS

This appendix provides a listing of foundations ranked in order of the size of their assets. The dollar values of assets are based upon a 1980-1981 reporting period in most cases. Figures from a 1979 reporting period are marked with a single asterisk (*), and figures taken from 1982 reports are marked with a double asterisk (**). Sources from which asset values are derived include the Foundation Center and some of the individual foundations themselves.

Some names of foundations in this list are followed by symbols indicating that the foundation falls into one of the following categories: community (cm); company-sponsored (cs); and operating (op). All of the other foundations are in the independent category. It should be noted that 199 of the total of 234 foundations listed in this appendix are in the independent category.

Four foundations, now defunct, are listed in alphabetical order at the conclusion of this appendix.

| | |
|---|---:|
| Ford Foundation, The | 2,565,572,000 |
| Pew Memorial Trust, The | 1,077,735,781 |
| W.K. Kellogg Foundation | **1,046,224,366 |
| Robert Wood Johnson Foundation, The | 1,027,530,645 |
| John D. and Catherine T. MacArthur Foundation | 927,068,344 |
| Rockefeller Foundation, The | 883,200,092 |
| Lilly Endowment, Inc. | 865,568,568 |
| Andrew W. Mellon Foundation, The | 816,855,412 |
| Kresge Foundation, The | 655,408,031 |
| W. M. Keck Foundation | 460,037,974 |
| Charles Stewart Mott Foundation | 428,147,565 |
| Duke Endowment, The | 406,513,218 |
| San Francisco Foundation, The (cm) | 378,975,703 |
| McKnight Foundation, The | 338,143,248 |
| Samuel Roberts Noble Foundation, Inc., The | 336,378,919 |
| Carnegie Corporation of New York | 335,717,107 |
| William and Flora Hewlett Foundation, The | 316,053,089 |
| Richard King Mellon Foundation | 311,455,368 |
| J. E. and L. E. Mabee Foundation, Inc., The | 301,688,871 |
| New York Community Trust, The (cm) | 290,935,166 |
| James Irvine Foundation, The | 272,360,952 |
| Alfred P. Sloan Foundation | 265,649,085 |

| | |
|---|---:|
| Henry J. Kaiser Family Foundation, The | 249,953,751 |
| J. Howard Pew Freedom Trust | 249,010,914 |
| Houston Endowment, Inc. | 242,599,169 |
| Brown Foundation, Inc., The | 239,738,887 |
| Bush Foundation, The | 232,525,444 |
| Cleveland Foundation, The (cm) | 223,713,387 |
| Norton Simon Foundation, The (op) | 218,587,489 |
| Surdna Foundation, Inc. | 210,192,982 |
| Gannett Foundation, Inc. | 207,634,029 |
| Edna McConnell Clark Foundation, The | 200,334,000 |
| Moody Foundation, The | 200,000,000 |
| Weingart Foundation | 197,750,944 |
| Amherst H. Wilder Foundation (op) | 190,662,722 |
| Rockefeller Brothers Fund | 177,087,767 |
| Starr Foundation, The | 164,631,909 |
| Joyce Foundation, The | 164,174,168 |
| Alcoa Foundation (cs) | 151,499,059 |
| De Rance, Inc. | 151,413,317 |
| Norton Simon, Inc. Museum of Art (op) | 147,306,486 |
| Mabel Pew Myrin Trust | 145,419,254 |
| Robert A. Welch Foundation, The (op) | **144,103,315 |
| Commonwealth Fund, The | 138,633,217 |
| Northwest Area Foundation | 131,505,613 |
| William Randolph Hearst Foundation | 131,266,401 |
| Sherman Fairchild Foundation, Inc., The | 130,851,056 |
| John A. Hartford Foundation, Inc., The | 130,536,117 |
| Chicago Community Trust, The (cm) | **130,000,000 |
| William Penn Foundation, The | 129,188,813 |
| William K. Warren Foundation, The | 127,108,204 |
| M. J. Murdock Charitable Trust | 126,798,345 |
| Meadows Foundation, Inc. | 123,509,328 |
| Sarah Scaife Foundation, Inc. | 122,541,347 |
| J. N. Pew, Jr., Charitable Trust | 121,546,176 |
| Hess Foundation, Inc. | 120,406,564 |
| Ahmanson Foundation, The | 119,592,828 |
| Henry Luce Foundation, Inc., The | 118,549,228 |
| Amon G. Carter Foundation | 117,808,825 |
| Olin Foundation, Inc. | 116,324,023 |
| Clark Foundation, The | 113,761,958 |
| Longwood Foundation, Inc. | 112,051,217 |
| William R. Kenan, Jr., Charitable Trust | 105,829,000 |
| James Graham Brown Foundation | 105,541,496 |
| Sid W. Richardson Foundation | 105,016,010 |
| Howard Heinz Endowment | 101,487,076 |
| Smith Richardson Foundation, Inc. | 100,812,536 |
| John Simon Guggenheim Memorial Foundation | 100,014,639 |
| Permanent Charity Fund of Boston, Committee of the (cm) | **100,000,000 |
| W. Alton Jones Foundation, Inc. | 99,241,000 |
| Herbert H. and Grace A. Dow Foundation, The | 98,323,537 |
| Dan Murphy Foundation | 97,432,913 |
| Timken Foundation of Canton | 96,316,324 |
| Z. Smith Reynolds Foundation, Inc. | 93,379,255 |

| | |
|---|---|
| Charles A. Dana Foundation, Incorporated, The | 92,904,175 |
| Claude Worthington Benedum Foundation | 90,498,974 |
| Spencer Foundation, The | **90,347,349 |
| Herrick Foundation | 89,912,788 |
| George Gund Foundation, The | 88,000,000 |
| Danforth Foundation, The | 87,470,731 |
| Champlin Foundations, The | **87,000,000 |
| Ambrose Monell Foundation, The | 83,828,944 |
| Dr. Scholl Foundation | 83,242,000 |
| Aurora Foundation, The | 83,068,761 |
| General Motors Foundation (cs) | 82,084,313 |
| El Pomar Foundation | 81,548,085 |
| Cullen Foundation, The | 81,376,549 |
| Boettcher Foundation | 80,950,239 |
| Callaway Foundation, Inc. | 80,778,525 |
| Geraldine R. Dodge Foundation, Incorporated | 80,507,036 |
| George Foundation, The | 80,455,841 |
| William T. Grant Foundation | 77,330,939 |
| S. H. Cowell Foundation | 76,113,318 |
| Jessie Ball du Pont Religious, Charitable, and Educational Fund | 74,670,333 |
| Ralph M. Parsons Foundation, The | 73,901,167 |
| Charles Hayden Foundation | 73,154,387 |
| Lyndhurst Foundation | 70,494,577 |
| George F. and Sybil H. Fuller Foundation | **70,000,000 |
| Western Electric Fund (cs) | 69,980,538 |
| Mary Flagler Cary Charitable Trust | 69,698,639 |
| Atlantic Foundation,The | 69,268,644 |
| Charles E. Culpeper Foundation, Inc. | 68,602,002 |
| Hallmark Educational Foundations | 67,840,540 |
| McDonnell Foundation, Inc. | 67,636,793 |
| System Development Foundation | 66,757,985 |
| F. M. Kirby Foundation, Inc. | 66,235,952 |
| Maclellan Foundation, Inc., The | 65,926,671 |
| Charles H. Revson Foundation, Inc. | 65,207,257 |
| Communities Foundation of Texas, Inc. (cm) | 60,371,416 |
| Booth Ferris Foundation | 60,328,173 |
| China Medical Board of NewYork, Inc. | 59,876,117 |
| Morris and Gwendolyn Cafritz Foundation, The | 59,726,180 |
| Hearst Foundation, Inc., The | 59,521,553 |
| Conrad N. Hilton Foundation | **59,177,963 |
| Arthur Vining Davis Foundations, The | 58,903,018 |
| Hartford Foundation for Public Giving (cm) | 58,173,945 |
| Saint Paul Foundation, The (cm) | **58,000,000 |
| Edward John Noble Foundation | 57,039,974 |
| Annie E. Casey Foundation, The | 56,298,434 |
| John and Mary R. Markle Foundation, The | 56,221,107 |
| Connelly Foundation | 56,171,801 |
| Liberty Fund, Inc. | 56,096,547 |
| Shell Companies Foundation, Incorporated (cs) | 56,070,096 |
| M. D. Anderson Foundation | *55,699,705 |
| Vincent Astor Foundation, The | 55,658,010 |
| Don and Sybil Harrington Foundation, The | 55,530,780 |

| | |
|---|---:|
| George I. Alden Trust | 54,245,199 |
| Louis Calder Foundation, The | 54,179,516 |
| Adolph Coors Foundation | 54,041,630 |
| Josiah Macy, Jr., Foundation | 53,809,926 |
| Kroc Foundation, The | 53,485,696 |
| Joseph B. Whitehead Foundation | 53,037,241 |
| J. Bulow Campbell Foundation | 52,199,784 |
| Amoco Foundation, Inc. (cs) | 51,916,037 |
| Columbus Foundation, The (cm) | 50,780,782 |
| Kenneth T. and Eileen L. Norris Foundation, The | 50,662,481 |
| John W. Anderson Foundation | 50,527,081 |
| Kerr Foundation, Inc., The | 50,516,537 |
| Kate B. Reynolds Charitable Trust | 50,515,494 |
| Coleman Foundation, Inc., The | **50,000,000 |
| Carrie Estelle Doheny Foundation | 48,663,293 |
| Russell Sage Foundation (op) | 48,604,212 |
| Gates Foundation | 48,415,068 |
| Hoblitzelle Foundation | 48,336,865 |
| R. C. Baker Foundation, The | 48,097,283 |
| Krannert Charitable Trust | 47,802,504 |
| Metropolitan Life Foundation (cs) | 47,401,342 |
| W. W. Smith Charitable Trust | 46,853,566 |
| J. M. Kaplan Fund, Inc., The | 46,572,494 |
| Research Corporation | 46,300,000 |
| DeWitt Wallace Fund, Inc. | 46,094,423 |
| Public Welfare Foundation, Inc. | 45,855,386 |
| Regenstein Foundation, The | 45,683,083 |
| Nelda C. and H. J. Lutcher Stark Foundation | 44,902,899 |
| Helene Fuld Health Trust | 44,755,714 |
| James G. Boswell Foundation, The | 43,698,715 |
| Pittsburgh Foundation, The (cm) | 43,120,759 |
| Retirement Research Foundation, The | 42,893,000 |
| Raskob Foundation for Catholic Activities, Inc. | 42,684,097 |
| McDonnell Douglas Foundation, Inc. (cs) | 42,661,244 |
| Otto Bremer Foundation | **42,409,740 |
| Turrell Fund | 42,266,304 |
| Eastman Kodak Charitable Trust (cs) | 41,242,919 |
| Chatlos Foundations, Inc., The | 41,147,083 |
| Marjorie Merriweather Post Foundation of D.C., The | 40,942,158 |
| Florence and John Schumann Foundation, The | 40,900,000 |
| Teagle Foundation, Incorporated, The | 40,843,911 |
| Del E. Webb Foundation | *40,564,217 |
| Independence Foundation | 40,533,058 |
| Stoddard Charitable Trust, The | 40,158,940 |
| Jones Foundation, The | 40,009,592 |
| New Haven Foundation, The (cm) | 39,616,560 |
| Lettie Pate Whitehead Foundation, Inc. | 39,507,498 |
| Thomas and Dorothy Leavey Foundation | *39,054,644 |
| Texaco Philanthropic Foundation, Inc. (cs) | 38,708,359 |
| Benwood Foundation, Inc. | 38,656,959 |
| McGregor Fund | 37,420,566 |

| | |
|---|---:|
| Eugene McDermott Foundation, The | 37,363,283 |
| Victoria Foundation, Inc. | 36,809,569 |
| L.A.W. Fund, Inc. | 36,686,058 |
| John Motley Morehead Foundation, The | 36,609,391 |
| Exxon Education Foundation (cs) | 36,077,718 |
| Samuel I. Newhouse Foundation, Inc. | *35,983,155 |
| Ford Motor Company Fund (cs) | 35,969,196 |
| Jessie Smith Noyes Foundation, Inc. | 35,271,674 |
| Phillips Foundation, The | **35,000,000 |
| Harry G. Steele Foundation | 34,943,262 |
| Helen K. and Arthur E. Johnson Foundation | 34,751,186 |
| Charles Engelhard Foundation, The | 34,631,695 |
| Henry P. Kendall Foundation, The | 34,482,617 |
| Philadelphia Foundation, The (cm) | 34,470,000 |
| Rowland Foundation, Inc. | 34,069,295 |
| Twentieth Century Fund, Inc. (op) | 33,973,485 |
| Prudential Foundation, The (cs) | 33,934,000 |
| Kalamazoo Foundation (cm) | 33,902,910 |
| Mary Reynolds Babcock Foundation, Incorporated | 33,777,600 |
| United States Steel Foundation, Inc. (cs) | 33,759,854 |
| Tinker Foundation Incorporated, The | 33,620,554 |
| J. M. Foundation, The | 33,543,932 |
| Robert Sterling Clark Foundation, Inc. | **33,280,510 |
| Scherman Foundation, Inc., The | 33,251,100 |
| A. M. McGregor Home, The | 33,240,881 |
| William H. Donner Foundation, Inc., The | 33,239,388 |
| Ira W. DeCamp Foundation, The | 33,198,036 |
| David and Lucile Packard Foundation, The | 32,859,649 |
| Arie and Ida Crown Memorial | 32,605,920 |
| Leland Fikes Foundation, Inc. | 32,558,407 |
| Christian A. Johnson Endeavor Foundation, The | 32,452,712 |
| John McShain Charities, Inc. | 32,432,800 |
| Fannie E. Rippel Foundation | 32,304,395 |
| Beatrice P. Delany Charitable Trust | 32,246,632 |
| Edyth Bush Charitable Foundation, Inc. | 32,047,583 |
| Annenberg Fund, Inc., The | 31,898,249 |
| Charles and Ellora Alliss Educational Foundation | 31,873,111 |
| Robert J., Jr., and Helen C. Kleberg Foundation | 31,363,375 |
| Charles A. Frueauff Foundation, Inc. | 31,189,366 |
| Frank E. Payne and Seba B. Payne Foundation | 31,181,899 |
| BankAmerica Foundation (cs) | 31,053,702 |
| Helena Rubinstein Foundation, Inc. | 30,873,400 |
| Ramapo Trust | 30,729,768 |
| Foundation for Child Development | 30,671,624 |
| Cannon Foundation, Inc., The | *30,366,978 |
| Harold K. L. Castle Foundation | 30,363,795 |
| Hillcrest Foundation | 30,264,638 |
| Godfrey M. Hyams Trust | *30,219,606 |
| Samuel H. Kress Foundation | 30,200,240 |
| Fondren Foundation, The | **30,000,000 |
| Shubert Foundation, Inc., The | 29,601,194 |

Carnegie Foundation for the Advancement of Teaching, The (op)      29,435,220
Jackson Hole Preserve, Incorporated (op)      **29,375,520
General Education Board (defunct)
Julius Rosenwald Fund (defunct)
Laura Spelman Rockefeller Memorial (defunct)
Max C. Fleischmann Foundation (defunct)

# appendix 2

# FAMILY-CONNECTED FOUNDATIONS

This appendix, arranged alphabetically by family name, lists those foundations which have been funded by the same donor or funded by those with connections to the same family. It will be noted that this listing includes those company-sponsored foundations wherein family members hold or have recently held official positions in the foundation.

**BUSH**

Bush Foundation, The
Edyth Bush Charitable Foundation, Inc.

**CARNEGIE**

Carnegie Corporation of New York
Carnegie Foundation for the Advancement of Teaching

**CLARK**

Clark Foundation, The
Robert Sterling Clark Foundation, Inc.

**DONNER**

Independence Foundation
William H. Donner Foundation, Inc., The

**DU PONT**

Jessie Ball du Pont Religious, Charitable, and Educational Fund
Longwood Foundation, Inc.

**FORD**

Ford Foundation, The
Ford Motor Company Fund

**HEARST**

Hearst Foundation, Inc., The
William Randolph Hearst Foundation

**JOHNSON**

Atlantic Foundation, The
Robert Wood Johnson Foundation, The

MacARTHUR

John D. and Catherine T. MacArthur Foundation
Retirement Research Foundation, The

McDONNELL

McDonnell Douglas Foundation, Inc.
McDonnell Foundation, Inc.

MELLON

Andrew W. Mellon Foundation, The
Richard King Mellon Foundation
Sarah Scaife Foundation, Inc.

PEW

J. Howard Pew Freedom Trust
J. N. Pew, Jr., Charitable Trust
Mabel Pew Myrin Trust
Pew Memorial Trust, The

REYNOLDS

Kate B. Reynolds Charitable Trust
Mary Reynolds Babcock Foundation, Incorporated
Z. Smith Reynolds Foundation, Inc.

ROCKEFELLER

China Medical Board of New York, Inc.
General Education Board
Geraldine R. Dodge Foundation, Incorporated
Jackson Hole Preserve, Incorporated
Laura Spelman Rockefeller Memorial
Rockefeller Brothers Fund
Rockefeller Foundation, The

SIMON

Norton Simon Foundation, The
Norton Simon, Inc. Museum of Art

WALLACE

DeWitt Wallace Fund, Inc.
L.A.W. Fund, Inc.

WHITEHEAD

Joseph B. Whitehead Foundation
Lettie Pate Whitehead Foundation, Inc.

# appendix 3

# LOCATIONS

This appendix, arranged alphabetically by states, provides a listing showing the state in which given foundations have located their main offices or headquarters. In the case of four foundations, now defunct, they are so designated, and the state in which they formerly had such offices is provided.

ARIZONA

Del E. Webb Foundation

CALIFORNIA

Ahmanson Foundation, The
BankAmerica Foundation
Carrie Estelle Doheny Foundation
Conrad N. Hilton Foundation
Dan Murphy Foundation
David and Lucile Packard Foundation, The
Harry G. Steele Foundation
Henry J. Kaiser Family Foundation, The
James G. Boswell Foundation, The
James Irvine Foundation, The
Jones Foundation, The
Kenneth T. and Eileen L. Norris Foundation, The
Kroc Foundation, The
Norton Simon Foundation, The
Norton Simon, Inc. Museum of Art
Ralph M. Parsons Foundation, The
R. C. Baker Foundation, The
San Francisco Foundation, The
S. H. Cowell Foundation
System Development Foundation
Thomas and Dorothy Leavey Foundation
Weingart Foundation
William and Flora Hewlett Foundation, The
W. M. Keck Foundation

COLORADO

Adolph Coors Foundation

Boettcher Foundation
El Pomar Foundation
Gates Foundation
Helen K. and Arthur E. Johnson Foundation

CONNECTICUT

Annie E. Casey Foundation, The
Hartford Foundation for Public Giving
New Haven Foundation, The
Sherman Fairchild Foundation, Inc., The

DELAWARE

Longwood Foundation, Inc.
Raskob Foundation for Catholic Activities, Inc.

DISTRICT OF COLUMBIA

Carnegie Foundation for the Advancement of Teaching, The
Marjorie Merriweather Post Foundation of D.C.
Morris and Gwendolyn Cafritz Foundation, The
Public Welfare Foundation, Inc.

FLORIDA

Arthur Vining Davis Foundations, The
Aurora Foundation, The
Edyth Bush Charitable Foundation, Inc.
Jessie Ball du Pont Religious, Charitable, and Educational Fund

GEORGIA

Callaway Foundation, Inc.
J. Bulow Campbell Foundation
Joseph B. Whitehead Foundation
Lettie Pate Whitehead Foundation, Inc.

HAWAII

Harold K. L. Castle Foundation

ILLINOIS

Amoco Foundation, Inc.
Arie and Ida Crown Memorial
Chicago Community Trust, The
Coleman Foundation, Inc., The
Dr. Scholl Foundation
Frank E. Payne and Seba B. Payne Foundation
John D. and Catherine T. MacArthur Foundation
Joyce Foundation, The
Julius Rosenwald Fund (Defunct)
Regenstein Foundation, The
Retirement Research Foundation, The
Spencer Foundation, The

INDIANA

John W. Anderson Foundation

Krannert Charitable Trust
Liberty Fund, Inc.
Lilly Endowment, Inc.

## KENTUCKY

James Graham Brown Foundation

## MASSACHUSETTS

George F. and Sybil H. Fuller Foundation
George I. Alden Trust
Godfrey M. Hyams Trust
Henry P. Kendall Foundation, The
Permanent Charity Fund of Boston, Committee of the
Rowland Foundation, Inc.
Stoddard Charitable Trust, The

## MICHIGAN

Charles Stewart Mott Foundation
Ford Motor Company Fund
General Motors Foundation
Herbert H. and Grace A. Dow Foundation, The
Herrick Foundation
Kalamazoo Foundation
Kresge Foundation, The
McGregor Fund
W. K. Kellogg Foundation

## MINNESOTA

Amherst H. Wilder Foundation
Bush Foundation, The
Charles and Ellora Alliss Educational Foundation
McKnight Foundation, The
Northwest Area Foundation
Otto Bremer Foundation
Phillips Foundation, The
Saint Paul Foundation, The

## MISSOURI

Danforth Foundation, The
Hallmark Educational Foundations
McDonnell Douglas Foundation, Inc.
McDonnell Foundation, Inc.

## NEVADA

Max C. Fleischmann Foundation (Defunct)

## NEW JERSEY

Alfred P. Sloan Foundation
Atlantic Foundation, The
Charles Engelhard Foundation, The
Fannie E. Rippel Foundation
Florence and John Schumann Foundation, The

F. M. Kirby Foundation, Inc.
Geraldine R. Dodge Foundation, Incorporated
Prudential Foundation, The
Robert Wood Johnson Foundation, The
Turrell Fund
Victoria Foundation, Inc.

NEW YORK

Ambrose Monell Foundation, The
Andrew W. Mellon Foundation, The
Beatrice P. Delany Charitable Trust
Booth Ferris Foundation
Carnegie Corporation of New York
Charles A. Dana Foundation, Incorporated, The
Charles A. Frueauff Foundation, Inc.
Charles E. Culpeper Foundation, Inc.
Charles Hayden Foundation
Charles H. Revson Foundation, Inc.
Chatlos Foundation, Inc., The
China Medical Board of New York, Inc.
Christian A. Johnson Endeavor Foundation, The
Clark Foundation, The
Commonwealth Fund, The
DeWitt Wallace Fund, Inc.
Eastman Kodak Charitable Trust
Edna McConnell Clark Foundation, The
Edward John Noble Foundation
Exxon Education Foundation
Ford Foundation, The
Foundation for Child Development
Gannett Foundation, Inc.
General Education Board (Defunct)
Hearst Foundation, Inc., The
Helena Rubinstein Foundation, Inc.
Helene Fuld Health Trust
Henry Luce Foundation, Inc., The
Hess Foundation, Inc.
Ira W. DeCamp Foundation, The
Jackson Hole Preserve, Incorporated
Jessie Smith Noyes Foundation, Inc.
J. M. Foundation, The
J. M. Kaplan Fund, Inc., The
John A. Hartford Foundation, Inc., The
John and Mary R. Markle Foundation, The
John Simon Guggenheim Memorial Foundation
Josiah Macy, Jr., Foundation
Laura Spelman Rockefeller Memorial (Defunct)
L.A.W. Fund, Inc.
Louis Calder Foundation, The
Mary Flagler Cary Charitable Trust
Metropolitan Life Foundation
New York Community Trust, The
Olin Foundation, Inc.

Ramapo Trust
Research Corporation
Robert Sterling Clark Foundation, Inc.
Rockefeller Brothers Fund
Rockefeller Foundation, The
Russell Sage Foundation
Samuel H. Kress Foundation
Samuel I. Newhouse Foundation, Inc.
Scherman Foundation, Inc., The
Shubert Foundation, Inc., The
Starr Foundation, The
Surdna Foundation
Teagle Foundation, Incorporated, The
Texaco Philanthropic Foundation, Inc.
Tinker Foundation Incorporated, The
Twentieth Century Fund, Inc.
Vincent Astor Foundation, The
Western Electric Fund
William H. Donner Foundation, Inc., The
William Randolph Hearst Foundation
William R. Kennan, Jr., Charitable Trust
William T. Grant Foundation

NORTH CAROLINA

Cannon Foundation, Inc., The
Duke Endowment, The
John Motley Morehead Foundation, The
Kate B. Reynolds Charitable Trust
Mary Reynolds Babcock Foundation, Incorporated
Smith Richardson Foundation, Inc.
Z. Smith Reynolds Foundation, Inc.

OHIO

A. M. McGregor Home, The
Cleveland Foundation, The
Columbus Foundation, The
George Gund Foundation, The
Timken Foundation of Canton

OKLAHOMA

J. E. and L. E. Mabee Foundation, Inc., The
Kerr Foundation, Inc., The
Samuel Roberts Noble Foundation, Inc., The
William K. Warren Foundation, The

PENNSYLVANIA

Alcoa Foundation
Annenberg Fund, Inc., The
Claude Worthington Benedum Foundation
Connelly Foundation
Howard Heinz Endowment
Independence Foundation

J. Howard Pew Freedom Trust
John McShain Charities, Inc.
J. N. Pew, Jr., Charitable Trust
Mabel Pew Myrin Trust
Pew Memorial Trust, The
Philadelphia Foundation, The
Pittsburgh Foundation, The
Richard King Mellon Foundation
Sarah Scaife Foundation, Inc.
United States Steel Foundation, Inc.
William Penn Foundation, The
W. W. Smith Charitable Trust

RHODE ISLAND

Champlin Foundations, The

TENNESSEE

Benwood Foundation, Inc.
Lyndhurst Foundation
Maclellan Foundation, Inc., The

TEXAS

Amon G. Carter Foundation
Brown Foundation, Inc., The
Communities Foundation of Texas, Inc.
Cullen Foundation, The
Don and Sybil Harrington Foundation, The
Eugene McDermott Foundation, The
Fondren Foundation, The
George Foundation, The
Hillcrest Foundation
Hoblitzelle Foundation
Houston Endowment, Inc.
Leland Fikes Foundation, Inc.
M. D. Anderson Foundation
Meadows Foundation, Inc.
Moody Foundation, The
Nelda C. and H. J. Lutcher Stark Foundation
Robert A. Welch Foundation, The
Robert J. Kleberg, Jr., and Helen C. Kleberg Foundation
Shell Companies Foundation, Incorporated
Sid W. Richardson Foundation

VIRGINIA

W. Alton Jones Foundation, Inc.

WASHINGTON

M. J. Murdock Charitable Trust

WISCONSIN

De Rance, Inc.

# appendix 4

# CHRONOLOGY

This appendix gives a chronological listing of foundations discussed in this volume. The names provided are those in use at the present time. Some are, of course, different from what they were at the time of establishment of the foundation (see Appendix 5, "Genealogy"). The four foundations now defunct are so listed.

As the reader will note, all of the foundations listed were founded in the twentieth century. Thirty-six were founded prior to 1930; 30 from 1930 to 1939; 66 from 1940 to 1949; 60 from 1950 to 1959; 28 from 1960 to 1969; and 14 from 1970 to 1979.

*1900*  Foundation for Child Development
*1902*  General Education Board (Defunct)
*1904*  A. M. McGregor Home, The
*1905*  Carnegie Foundation for the Advancement of Teaching, The
*1907*  Russell Sage Foundation
*1910*  Amherst H. Wilder Foundation
*1911*  Carnegie Corporation of New York
*1912*  George I. Alden Trust
        Research Corporation
*1913*  Rockefeller Foundation, The
*1914*  Cleveland Foundation, The
*1915*  Chicago Community Trust, The
        Permanent Charity Fund of Boston, Committee of the
*1917*  Julius Rosenwald Fund (Defunct)
        Surdna Foundation
*1918*  Commonwealth Fund, The
        Laura Spelman Rockefeller Memorial (Defunct)
        Philadelphia Foundation, The
*1919*  Twentieth Century Fund, Inc.
*1921*  Godfrey M. Hyams Trust
*1923*  New York Community Trust, The
*1924*  Duke Endowment, The
        J. M. Foundation, The
        Kresge Foundation, The
        Victoria Foundation, Inc.
*1925*  Hartford Foundation for Public Giving
        John Simon Guggenheim Memorial Foundation
        Kalamazoo Foundation
        McGregor Fund

*1926*   Charles Stewart Mott Foundation
*1927*   Danforth Foundation, The
       John and Mary R. Markle Foundation, The
*1928*   China Medical Board of New York, Inc.
       New Haven Foundation, The
*1929*   John A. Hartford Foundation, Inc., The
       Samuel H. Kress Foundation
*1930*   Josiah Macy, Jr., Foundation
       W. K. Kellogg Foundation
*1931*   Clark Foundation, The
       F. M. Kirby Foundation, Inc.
*1932*   Champlin Foundations, The
       Independence Foundation
*1934*   Alfred P. Sloan Foundation
       Northwest Area Foundation
       Timken Foundation of Canton
*1935*   Gannett Foundation, Inc.
       Smith Richardson Foundation, Inc.
       Turrell Fund
*1936*   Ford Foundation, The
       Henry Luce Foundation, Inc., The
       Herbert H. and Grace A. Dow Foundation, The
       M. D. Anderson Foundation
       Robert Wood Johnson Foundation, The
       William T. Grant Foundation
       Z. Smith Reynolds Foundation, Inc.
*1937*   Boettcher Foundation
       Charles Hayden Foundation
       El Pomar Foundation
       Houston Endowment, Inc.
       James Irvine Foundation, The
       Joseph B. Whitehead Foundation
       Lilly Endowment, Inc.
       Longwood Foundation, Inc.
*1938*   Lyndhurst Foundation
       Olin Foundation, Inc.
*1939*   Stoddard Charitable Trust, The
*1940*   Andrew W. Mellon Foundation, The
       Charles E. Culpeper Foundation, Inc.
       Charles Engelhard Foundation, The
       Edward John Noble Foundation
       Jackson Hole Preserve, Incorporated
       J. Bulow Campbell Foundation
       Rockefeller Brothers Fund
       Saint Paul Foundation, The
*1941*   Howard Heinz Endowment
       Sarah Scaife Foundation, Inc.
       Scherman Foundation, Inc., The
*1942*   Hoblitzelle Foundation
       Moody Foundation, The
*1943*   Callaway Foundation, Inc.
       Cannon Foundation, Inc., The

Columbus Foundation, The
Hallmark Educational Foundations
James Graham Brown Foundation
1944 Benwood Foundation, Inc.
Claude Worthington Benedum Foundation
Conrad N. Hilton Foundation
J. M. Kaplan Fund, Inc., The
Otto Bremer Foundation
Phillips Foundation, The
Teagle Foundation, Incorporated, The
W. Alton Jones Foundation, Inc.
1945 Amon G. Carter Foundation
George Foundation, The
Hearst Foundation, Inc., The
John Motley Morehead Foundation, The
Maclellan Foundation, Inc., The
Pittsburgh Foundation, The
Raskob Foundation for Catholic Activities, Inc.
Samuel I. Newhouse Foundation, Inc.
Samuel Roberts Noble Foundation, Inc., The
Shubert Foundation, Inc., The
William K. Warren Foundation, The
William Penn Foundation, The
1946 De Rance, Inc.
Gates Foundation
Kate B. Reynolds Charitable Trust
Lettie Pate Whitehead Foundation, Inc.
1947 Arie and Ida Crown Memorial
Cullen Foundation, The
Dr. Scholl Foundation
James G. Boswell Foundation, The
Jessie Smith Noyes Foundation, Inc.
Public Welfare Foundation, Inc.
Richard King Mellon Foundation
San Francisco Foundation, The
Sid W. Richardson Foundation
1948 Annie E. Casey Foundation, The
Fondren Foundation, The
Helen K. and Arthur E. Johnson Foundation
Henry J. Kaiser Family Foundation, The
J. E. and L. E. Mabee Foundation, Inc., The
Joyce Foundation, The
Meadows Foundation, Inc.
Morris and Gwendolyn Cafritz Foundation, The
Pew Memorial Trust, The
Vincent Astor Foundation, The
1949 Carrie Estelle Doheny Foundation
Ford Motor Company Fund
Herrick Foundation
John McShain Charities, Inc.
William Randolph Hearst Foundation
1950 Charles A. Dana Foundation, Incorporated, The

Charles A. Frueauff Foundation, Inc.
Edna McConnell Clark Foundation, The
McDonnell Foundation, Inc.
Regenstein Foundation, The
Retirement Research Foundation, The
Robert J. Kleberg, Jr., and Helen C. Kleberg Foundation
1951 Annenberg Fund, Inc., The
Brown Foundation, Inc., The
Coleman Foundation, Inc., The
Don and Sybil Harrington Foundation, The
George Gund Foundation, The
Helene Fuld Health Trust
Louis Calder Foundation, The
Weingart Foundation
1952 Ahmanson Foundation
Alcoa Foundation
Ambrose Monell Foundation, The
Amoco Foundation, Inc.
Arthur Vining Davis Foundations, The
Christian A. Johnson Endeavor Foundation, The
Eastman Kodak Charitable Trust
Leland Fikes Foundation, Inc.
Max C. Fleischmann Foundation (Defunct)
Norton Simon Foundation, The
R. C. Baker Foundation, The
Robert Sterling Clark Foundation, Inc.
Thomas and Dorothy Leavey Foundation
1953 Bush Foundation, The
Chatlos Foundation, Inc., The
Communities Foundation of Texas, Inc.
Fannie E. Rippel Foundation
Harry G. Steele Foundation
Helena Rubinstein Foundation, Inc.
McKnight Foundation, The
Mary Reynolds Babcock Foundation, Incorporated
Shell Companies Foundation, Incorporated
United States Steel Foundation, Inc.
Western Electric Fund
1954 Hess Foundation, Inc.
Norton Simon, Inc. Museum of Art
Robert A. Welch Foundation, The
W.M. Keck Foundation
1955 Connelly Foundation
Exxon Education Foundation
George F. and Sybil H. Fuller Foundation
S. H. Cowell Foundation
Sherman Fairchild Foundation, Inc., The
Starr Foundation, The
1956 Charles H. Revson Foundation, Inc.
L.A.W. Fund, Inc.
System Development Foundation
1957 Booth Ferris Foundation

Dan Murphy Foundation
Henry P. Kendall Foundation, The
J. Howard Pew Freedom Trust
Mabel Pew Myrin Trust
1958 Charles and Ellora Alliss Educational Foundation
1959 Hillcrest Foundation
Tinker Foundation Incorporated, The
1960 Del E. Webb Foundation
Krannert Charitable Trust
Liberty Fund, Inc.
Rowland Foundation, Inc.
1961 Florence and John Schumann Foundation, The
Nelda C. and H. J. Lutcher Stark Foundation
Ralph M. Parsons Foundation, The
William H. Donner Foundation, Inc., The
1962 Frank E. Payne and Seba B. Payne Foundation
Harold K. L. Castle Foundation
Spencer Foundation, The
1963 J. N. Pew, Jr., Charitable Trust
Kenneth T. and Eileen L. Norris Foundation, The
Kerr Foundation, Inc., The
McDonnell Douglas Foundation, Inc.
1964 Atlantic Foundation, The
David and Lucile Packard Foundation, The
1965 DeWitt Wallace Fund, Inc.
Kroc Foundation, The
William R. Kenan, Jr., Charitable Trust
1966 Edyth Bush Charitable Foundation, Inc.
William and Flora Hewlett Foundation, The
1967 John W. Anderson Foundation
Marjorie Merriweather Post Foundation of D.C., The
1968 BankAmerica Foundation
Mary Flagler Cary Charitable Trust
1969 Aurora Foundation, The
Jones Foundation, The
1970 John D. and Catherine T. MacArthur Foundation
1972 Eugene McDermott Foundation, The
1973 Ramapo Trust
1974 Geraldine R. Dodge Foundation, Incorporated
1975 Adolph Coors Foundation
Ira W. DeCamp Foundation, The
M. J. Murdock Charitable Trust
1976 General Motors Foundation
Jessie Ball du Pont Religious, Charitable, and Educational Fund
Metropolitan Life Foundation
1977 Beatrice P. Delany Charitable Trust
Prudential Foundation, The
W. W. Smith Charitable Trust
1979 Texaco Philanthropic Foundation, Inc.

# appendix 5

# GENEALOGY

This appendix provides an alphabetical listing of the foundations included in this volume and shows any changes in their titles since their founding.

The foundations in this appendix are titled as major entries by the name they bear at the present time. The year when that usage began follows the name.

In cases where the present-day name is different from that used earlier, the earlier name or names are provided immediately below the present-day name as subentries, and the inclusive dates of the use of the name or names is provided. Subentries preceded by a ")" have merged or affiliated to create the major foundation or foundations listed immediately above.

*Adolph Coors Foundation*, 1975-

*Ahmanson Foundation, The*, 1952-

*Alcoa Foundation*, 1964-
    Alcoa Foundation, The, 1952-1964

*Alfred P. Sloan Foundation*, 1934-

*Ambrose Monell Foundation, The*, 1952-

*Amherst H. Wilder Foundation*, 1953-
    Amherst H. Wilder Charity, 1910-1953

*A. M. McGregor Home, The*, 1904-

*Amoco Foundation, Inc.*, 1973-
    )American Oil Foundation, 1957-1973
    )Pan American Petroleum Foundation, 1953-1973
    )Standard Oil (Indiana) Foundation, 1952-1973

*Amon G. Carter Foundation*, 1945-

*Andrew W. Mellon Foundation*, 1969-
    )Old Dominion Foundation, 1941-1969
    )Avalon Foundation, 1940-1969

*Annenberg Fund, Inc., The*, 1951-

*Annie E. Casey Foundation, The*, 1948-

*Arie and Ida Crown Memorial*, 1960-
    Arie Crown Memorial Fund, 1947-1960

*Arthur Vining Davis Foundations, The*, 1965-
    )Arthur Vining Davis Foundation No. 3, 1965-1965
    )Arthur Vining Davis Foundation No. 2, 1965-1965
    )Arthur Vining Davis Foundation No. 1, 1952-1965

*Atlantic Foundation, The*, 1964-

*Aurora Foundation, The*, 1978-
    Tropicana Foundation, 1969-1978

*BankAmerica Foundation*, 1977-
    Bank of America Foundation, 1968-1977

*Beatrice P. Delany Charitable Trust*, 1977-

*Benwood Foundation, Inc.*, 1944-

*Boettcher Foundation*, 1937-

*Booth Ferris Foundation*, 1964-
    )Willis H. Booth Trust, 1958-1964
    )Chancie Ferris Booth Trust, 1957-1964

*Brown Foundation, Inc., The*, 1951-

*Bush Foundation, The*, 1953-

*Callaway Foundation, Inc.*, 1962-
    Callaway Community Foundation, 1943-1962

*Cannon Foundation, Inc., The*, 1943-

*Carnegie Corporation of New York*, 1911-

*Carnegie Foundation for the Advancement of Teaching, The*, 1906-
    Carnegie Foundation, The, 1905-1906

*Carrie Estelle Doheny Foundation*, 1949-

*Champlin Foundations, The*, 1975-
    )Third Champlin Foundation Trust, The, 1975-1975
    )Second Champlin Foundation Trust, The, 1947-1975
    )First Champlin Foundation Trust, The, 1932-1975

*Charles A. Dana Foundation, Incorporated, The*, 1950-

*Charles A. Frueauff Foundation, Inc.*, 1950-

*Charles and Ellora Alliss Educational Foundation*, 1958-

*Charles E. Culpeper Foundation, Inc.*, 1940-

*Charles Engelhard Foundation, The*, 1940-

*Charles Hayden Foundation*, 1937-

*Charles H. Revson Foundation, Inc.*, 1956-

*Charles Stewart Mott Foundation*, 1926-

*Chatlos Foundation, Inc., The*, 1953-

*Chicago Community Trust, The*, 1915-

*China Medical Board of New York, Inc.*, 1928-

*Christian A. Johnson Endeavor Foundation, The*, 1952-

*Clark Foundation, The*, 1931-
    )Scriven Foundation, The, 1937-1973

*Claude Worthington Benedum Foundation*, 1944-

*Cleveland Foundation, The*, 1914-

*Coleman Foundation, Inc., The*, 1951-

*Columbus Foundation, The*, 1943-

*Commonwealth Fund, The*, 1918-

*Communities Foundation of Texas, Inc.*, 1981-
    Dallas Community Chest Trust Fund, Inc., 1953-1981

*Connelly Foundation*, 1955-

*Conrad N. Hilton Foundation*, 1944-

*Cullen Foundation, The*, 1947-

*Danforth Foundation, The*, 1927-

*Dan Murphy Foundation*, 1957-

*David and Lucile Packard Foundation, The*, 1964-

*Del E. Webb Foundation*, 1960-

*De Rance, Inc.*, 1946-

*DeWitt Wallace Fund, Inc.*, 1965-

*Don and Sybil Harrington Foundation, The*, 1951-

*Dr. Scholl Foundation*, 1973-
        William M. Scholl Foundation, 1947-1973

*Duke Endowment, The*, 1924-

*Eastman Kodak Charitable Trust*, 1952-

*Edna McConnell Clark Foundation, The*, 1950-

*Edward John Noble Foundation*, 1940-

*Edyth Bush Charitable Foundation, Inc.*, 1966-

*El Pomar Foundation*, 1937-

*Eugene McDermott Foundation, The*, 1972-
        )McDermott Foundation, The, 1955-1977

*Exxon Education Foundation*, 1972-
        )Exxon U.S.A. Foundation, 1965-1980
        Esso Education Foundation, 1955-1972

*Fannie E. Rippel Foundation*, 1953-

*Florence and John Schumann Foundation, The*, 1961-

*F. M. Kirby Foundation, Inc.*, 1931-

*Fondren Foundation, The*, 1948-

*Ford Foundation, The*, 1936-

*Ford Motor Company Fund*, 1949-

*Foundation for Child Development*, 1972-
        Association for the Aid of Crippled Children, 1900-1972

*Frank E. Payne and Seba B. Payne Foundation*, 1962-

*Gannett Foundation, Inc.*, 1935-

*Gates Foundation*, 1946-

*General Education Board*, 1902-1964 (defunct)

*General Motors Foundation*, 1976-

*George F. and Sybil H. Fuller Foundation*, 1955-

*George Foundation*, 1945-

*George Gund Foundation, The*, 1951-

*George I. Alden Trust*, 1912-

*Geraldine R. Dodge Foundation, Incorporated*, 1974-

*Godfrey M. Hyams Trust*, 1921-

*Hallmark Educational Foundations*, 1954-
    )Hallmark Educational Foundation of Kansas, 1954-1954
    )Hallmark Educational Foundation, 1943-1954

*Harold K. L. Castle Foundation*, 1962-

*Harry G. Steele Foundation*, 1953-

*Hartford Foundation for Public Giving*, 1925-

*Hearst Foundation, Inc., The*, 1945-

*Helena Rubinstein Foundation, Inc.*, 1953-

*Helene Fuld Health Trust*, 1951-
    Helene Fuld Health Trust, 1951-1969
    Helene Fuld Health Foundation, 1935-1969

*Helen K. and Arthur E. Johnson Foundation*, 1948-

*Henry J. Kaiser Family Foundation, The*, 1948-

*Henry Luce Foundation, Inc., The*, 1936-

*Henry P. Kendall Foundation, The*, 1957-

*Herbert H. and Grace A. Dow Foundation, The*, 1936

*Herrick Foundation*, 1949-

*Hess Foundation, Inc.*, 1954-

*Hillcrest Foundation*, 1959

*Hoblitzelle Foundation*, 1942-

*Houston Endowment, Inc.*, 1937-

*Howard Heinz Endowment*, 1941-

*Independence Foundation*, 1961-
    Donner Foundation, 1945-1961
    International Cancer Research Foundation, 1932-1945

*Ira W. DeCamp Foundation, The*, 1975-

*Jackson Hole Preserve, Incorporated*, 1940-

*James G. Boswell Foundation, The*, 1947-

*James Graham Brown Foundation*, 1943-

*James Irvine Foundation, The*, 1937-

*J. Bulow Campbell Foundation*, 1940-

*J. E. and L. E. Mabee Foundation, Inc., The*, 1948-

*Jessie Ball du Pont Religious, Charitable, and Educational Fund*, 1976-

*Jessie Smith Noyes Foundation, Inc.*, 1947-

*J. Howard Pew Freedom Trust*, 1957-

*J. M. Foundation, The*, 1924-

*J. M. Kaplan Fund, Inc., The*, 1944-
    )Faigel Leah Foundation, Inc., 1948-1975
    )J. M. Kaplan Fund, Inc., The, 1944-1975

*J. N. Pew, Jr., Charitable Trust*, 1963-

*John A. Hartford Foundation, Inc., The*, 1929-

*John and Mary R. Markle Foundation, The*, 1927-

*John D. and Catherine T. MacArthur Foundation*, 1970-

*John McShain Charities, Inc.*, 1949-

*John Motley Morehead Foundation, The*, 1945-

*John Simon Guggenheim Memorial Foundation*, 1925-

*John W. Anderson Foundation*, 1967-

*Jones Foundation, The*, 1969-

*Joseph B. Whitehead Foundation*, 1937-

*Josiah Macy, Jr., Foundation*, 1930-

*Joyce Foundation, The*, 1948-

*Julius Rosenwald Fund*, 1917-1948 (defunct)

*Kalamazoo Foundation*, 1925-

*Kate B. Reynolds Charitable Trust*, 1946-
    )Kate B. Reynolds Health Care Trust, 1946-1946
    )Kate B. Reynolds Poor and Needy Trust, 1946-1946

*Kenneth T. and Eileen L. Norris Foundation, The*, 1963-

*Kerr Foundation, Inc., The*, 1963-

*Krannert Charitable Trust*, 1960

*Kresge Foundation, The*, 1924-

*Kroc Foundation, The*, 1969-
    Ray A. Kroc Foundation, 1965-1969

*Laura Spelman Rockefeller Memorial*, 1918-1929 (defunct)

*L.A.W. Fund, Inc.*, 1969-
    Lila Acheson Wallace Fund, Inc., 1956-1969

*Leland Fikes Foundation, Inc.*, 1952-

*Lettie Pate Whitehead Foundation, Inc.*, 1946-

*Liberty Fund, Inc.*, 1960-

*Lilly Endowment, Inc.*, 1937-

*Longwood Foundation, Inc.*, 1937-

*Louis Calder Foundation, The*, 1951-

*Lyndhurst Foundation*, 1978-
    Memorial Welfare Foundation, 1938-1978

*Mabel Pew Myrin Trust*, 1957-

*McDonnell Douglas Foundation, Inc.*, 1980-
    )McDonnell Aerospace Foundation, Inc., 1977-1980
    )McDonnell Aerospace Foundation, 1963-1977
    )McDonnell Aircraft Corporation Foundation, 1947-1975

*McDonnell Foundation, Inc.*, 1950-

*McGregor Fund*, 1925-

*McKnight Foundation, The* 1953-
        )McKnight Family Charitable Fund, 1964-1972
        )McKnight Family Educational Fund, 1964-1972
        )McKnight Family Endowment, 1964-1972
        )McKnight Family Literary Fund, 1964-1972
        )McKnight Family Scientific Fund, 1964-1972

*Maclellan Foundation, Inc., The*, 1945

*Marjorie Merriweather Post Foundation of D.C., The*, 1967-

*Mary Flagler Cary Charitable Trust*, 1968-

*Mary Reynolds Babcock Foundation, Incorporated*, 1953-

*Max C. Fleischmann Foundation*, 1952-1980 (defunct)

*M. D. Anderson Foundation*, 1936-

*Meadows Foundation, Inc.*, 1948-

*Metropolitan Life Foundation*, 1976-

*M. J. Murdock Charitable Trust*, 1975-

*Moody Foundation, The*, 1942-

*Morris and Gwendolyn Cafritz Foundation, The*, 1948-

*Nelda C. and H. J. Lutcher Stark Foundation*, 1961-

*New Haven Foundation, The*, 1928-

*New York Community Trust, The*, 1923-

*Northwest Area Foundation*, 1975-
      Louis W. and Maud Hill Family Foundation, 1948-1975
      Lexington Foundation, 1934-1948

*Norton Simon Foundation, The*, 1952-

*Norton Simon, Inc. Museum of Art*, 1969-
      Hunt Foods and Industries Foundation, 1958-1969
      Hunt Foods Charitable Foundation, 1954-1957

*Olin Foundation, Inc.*, 1938-

*Otto Bremer Foundation*, 1944-

*Permanent Charity Fund of Boston, Committee of the*, 1915-

*Pew Memorial Trust, The*, 1957-
      Pew Memorial Foundation, The, 1948-1957

*Philadelphia Foundation, The*, 1918-

*Phillips Foundation, The*, 1944-

*Pittsburgh Foundation, The*, 1945-

*Prudential Foundation, The*, 1977-

*Public Welfare Foundation, Inc.*, 1947-

*Ralph M. Parsons Foundation, The*, 1961-

*Ramapo Trust*, 1973-
)Montebello Trust, 1968-1974

*Raskob Foundation for Catholic Activities, Inc.*, 1945-

*R. C. Baker Foundation, The*, 1952-

*Regenstein Foundation, The*, 1982-
Joseph and Helen Regenstein Foundation, 1950-1982

*Research Corporation*, 1912-

*Retirement Research Foundation, The*, 1950-

*Richard King Mellon Foundation*, 1947-

*Robert A. Welch Foundation, The*, 1954-

*Robert J. Kleberg, Jr., and Helen C. Kleberg Foundation*, 1950-

*Robert Sterling Clark Foundation, Inc.*, 1952-

*Robert Wood Johnson Foundation, The*, 1952-
Johnson New Brunswick Foundation, 1936-1952

*Rockefeller Brothers Fund*, 1940-

*Rockefeller Foundation, The*, 1913-
)Laura Spelman Rockefeller Memorial, 1918-1929

*Rowland Foundation, Inc.*, 1972-
Edwin H. Land-Helen M. Land, Inc., 1960-1972

*Russell Sage Foundation*, 1907-

*Saint Paul Foundation, The*, 1940-

*Samuel H. Kress Foundation*, 1929-

*Samuel I. Newhouse Foundation, Inc.*, 1945-

*Samuel Roberts Noble Foundation, Inc., The*, 1945-

*San Francisco Foundation, The*, 1947-

*Sarah Scaife Foundation, Inc.*, 1941-

*Scherman Foundation, Inc., The*, 1941-

*S. H. Cowell Foundation*, 1955-

*Shell Companies Foundation, Incorporated*, 1953-

*Sherman Fairchild Foundation, Inc., The*, 1975-
    Fairchild Foundation, Inc., The, 1955-1975

*Shubert Foundation, Inc., The*, 1971-
    Sam S. Shubert Foundation, 1945-1971

*Sid W. Richardson Foundation*, 1947-

*Smith Richardson Foundation, Inc.*, 1935-

*Spencer Foundation, The*, 1962-

*Starr Foundation, The*, 1955-

*Stoddard Charitable Trust, The*, 1939-

*Surdna Foundation*, 1917-

*System Development Foundation*, 1956-

*Teagle Foundation, Incorporated, The*, 1944-

*Texaco Philanthropic Foundation, Inc.*, 1979-

*Thomas and Dorothy Leavey Foundation*, 1952-

*Timken Foundation of Canton*, 1934-

*Tinker Foundation Incorporated, The*, 1959-

*Turrell Fund, The*, 1941-
    Herbert and Margaret Turrell Foundation, 1935-1941

*Twentieth Century Fund, Inc.*, 1919-

*United States Steel Foundation, Inc.*, 1953-

*Victoria Foundation, Inc.*, 1924-

*Vincent Astor Foundation, The*, 1948-

*W. Alton Jones Foundation, Inc.*, 1944-

*Weingart Foundation*, 1978
    B. W. Foundation, 1951-1978

*Western Electric Fund*, 1953-

*William and Flora Hewlett Foundation*, 1977-
    W. R. Hewlett Foundation, 1966-1977

*William H. Donner Foundation, Inc., The*, 1961-
    Donner Foundation, 1945-1961
    International Cancer Research Foundation, 1932-1945

*William K. Warren Foundation, The*, 1945-

*William Penn Foundation, The*, 1974-
    Haas Community Fund, 1970-1974
    Phoebe Waterman Foundation, 1945-1970

*William Randolph Hearst Foundation*, 1952-
    California Charities Foundation, 1949-1952

*William R. Kenan, Jr., Charitable Trust*, 1965-

*William T. Grant Foundation*, 1977-
    Grant Foundation, Inc., The, 1936-1977

*W. K. Kellogg Foundation*, 1930-
    W. K. Kellogg Child Welfare Foundation, 1930-1930

*W. M. Keck Foundation*, 1954-

*W. W. Smith Charitable Trust*, 1977-

*Z. Smith Reynolds Foundation, Inc.*, 1936-

# INDEX

Page numbers in *italic type* indicate the location of the main entry.

Adair, Kay Kerr, 248
Adams, Thomas, 376
Adolph Coors Foundation, *3*
Adolph Coors, Jr., Trust, 3
Adoue, J. B., 89
Aetna Foundation, 433
Agricultural Education Foundation, 190
Ahmanson, Howard F., 3
Ahmanson, Howard F., Jr., 4
Ahmanson, Robert H., 4
Ahmanson, William H., 4
Ahmanson Foundation, *3-5*
Alabama Space Science Exhibit Commission, 275
Albright, Horace M., 187
Alcoa Foundation, *5*
Alden, George I., 156-58
Alden Memorial Auditorium, 157
Aldrich, Malcolm P., 87
Alexander, Will, 240-41
Alfred L. Willson Charitable Trust, 83
Alfred P. Sloan Foundation, *6-10*
Alger, Horatio, 192
Alliance to Save Energy, 219
Alliss, Charles Clifford, 60; and Alliss, Mrs. Ellora, 60
Ambrose Monell Foundation, *10-11*
American Association of Fund-Raising Counsel, 72
American Council for an Energy Efficient Economy, 219
American Council on Education, 151, 219
*An American Dilemma: The Negro Problem and Modern Democracy*, 49-50
American Graduate School of International Management, 443
American Oil Foundation, 18-19

American Red Cross. *See* Red Cross, American
American Relief Administration, 255
Americans for Effective Law Enforcement, 391
Americans United for Life, 103
American Youth Commission, 151
American Youth Foundation, 95-96
Amherst H. Wilder Charity. *See* Amherst H. Wilder Foundation
Amherst H. Wilder Foundation, *11-18*
A. M. McGregor Home, *18*
Amnesty International, 213
Amoco Foundation, *18-21*
Amoco Production Foundation, 19
Amon G. Carter Foundation, *21-22*
Anderson, John W., 227
Anderson, Joseph A., 73
Anderson, Marian, 240
Anderson, Monroe D., 292
Anderson, Pearl C., 90
Andrews, Edward C., Jr., 59
Andrew W. Mellon Foundation, *22-24*
Andrus, John E., 405-406; and Andrus, Mrs. Julia Dyckman, 406
Andrus, John E. III, 406
Angell, James R., 48
Angier B. Duke Memorial, 110
Anna T. Jeanes Fund, 148
Annenberg, Walter H., 24
Annenberg Fund, *24*
Annie E. Casey Foundation, *24*
*Anopheles gambiae* (mosquito), 366
Appleby, Cornelia Day Wilder, 11-12
Arbury, Dorothy D., 177
Archives: National Jewish Archive of Broadcasting, 67; Rockefeller Archive Center,

153, 259, 364, 372; Sage Foundation Archives, 380; Shubert Archives, 397; Television News Archive, 391
Arie and Ida Crown Memorial, 25
Arie Crown Memorial Fund. *See* Arie and Ida Crown Memorial
Arnett, Trevor, 151
Art collections. *See* Museums and art collections
Arthritis Foundation of Southern California, 4
Arthur Vining Davis Foundations, 25-27
Asia Society, 404
Asibi, 366
Associated Colleges of Indiana, 227
Association for the Aid of Crippled Children. *See* Foundation for Child Development
Association for Voluntary Sterilization, 392
Astman, Fred, 104
Astor, John Jacob, 426-28, 430
Astor, Vincent, 427; and Astor, Mrs. Brooke, 427, 429-30
Atlanta Arts Alliance, 230
Atlanta Medical Heritage, Inc., 230
Atlanta School of Social Work, 257
Atlantic Foundation, 27
Audubon, John James, 306
Aurora Foundation, 27-29
AutoWorld, 72
Avalon Foundation, 22-23
Awards and prizes: Algur H. Meadows Award for Excellence in the Arts, 294; Field, 7; James K. Wilson Silver Cup, 261; James N. Vaughan Award, 396-97; Nobel, 7, 204, 224, 350, 366, 369; Pulitzer, 224, 240; Santa Rita Award, 299; Welch International Achievement Award in Chemistry, 356
A. W. Mellon Educational and Charitable Trust, 22
Ayres, Leonard P., 81

Babcock, Mary Reynolds, 288
Baker, Newton D., 310
Baldwin, Lucian E., 165
Baldwin, Raymond E., 165
Baldwin, William H., Jr., 238
Ballenger, William S., Jr., 73
Ballets. *See* Operas and ballets
BankAmerica Foundation (formerly Bank of America Foundation), *31-32*
Banks and trusts: American National Bank, 324; American National Bank and Trust Company, 33, 382; American Trust and Banking Company, 285; AmeriTrust, 80, 155; BankAmerica Corporation, 31-32; Bank of Delaware, 56; Bank of New England, 329; Boston Safe Deposit and Trust Company, 329; Chase Manhattan Bank, 32, 361; Chemical Bank, 59; Citicorp, 442; Cleveland Trust Company, 80, 155, 164; Connecticut Bank and Trust Company (formerly Hartford-Connecticut Trust Company), 164; Continental Illinois National Bank and Trust Company of Chicago, 140; Fidelity-Philadelphia Trust Company (formerly Fidelity Trust Company), 335-37; First National Bank in Dallas, 179; First Trust Company (St. Paul, Minnesota), 60-61, 382; Glenmede Trust Company, 202-3, 206-7, 273-74, 331-32, 334-35; Harris Trust and Savings Bank, 74-75; Hartford National Bank and Trust Company (formerly United States Security Company), 164; Homes Savings of America, 4; Indiana National Bank, 250; Lincoln First Bank of Rochester, 111; Manufacturers Hanover Trust Company, 271; Marine Midland Bank, 169; Mellon Bank N. A., 26, 182; Morgan Guaranty Trust Company of New York, 36-37, 444; National German American Bank, 324; Northwestern National Bank, 382; Otto Bremer Company, 325; Philadelphia National Bank, 453; Security Pacific National Bank, 98, 190, 348; Shawmut Bank, 329; Simsbury Bank and Trust Company, 164; Southeast First National Bank of Miami, 26; State Street Bank and Trust Company, 329; Trust Company of Georgia, 199; United Bank and Trust Company, 164; United States Mortgage and Trust Company, 310-11; Wachovia Bank and Trust Company, 245; Wells Fargo Bank, 394. *See also* Corporations and businesses
Baumol, William J., 421
Beadle, George W., 368
Beatrice P. Delany Charitable Trust, *32*
Bechtel, Stephen D., 345
Beesley, Eugene N., 266
Belding, Milo M., 137; and Belding, Mrs. Milo M., 137
Benckenstein, Eunice R., 307
Benedum, Michael L., 79; and Benedum, Mrs. Michael L., 79
Bennett, Richard K., 337
Benwood Foundation, *33-35*
Bergman, Ingmar, 294
Berlin, Daniel M., 4

Bertram, James, 47
Better Chance, A (Boston), 271
Better Government Association of Chicago, 220
Bible Alliance Dissemination, 28
Bible Alliance Missions, 28
Bierstadt, Albert, 306
Billings, John, 208
Binger, Mrs. Virginia McKnight, 283-84
Bissell, Cushman B., 235
Board of Regents of the State of New York, 151
Boettcher, Charles, 35-36; and Boettcher, Mrs. Charles, 35-36
Boettcher, Charles II, 35; and Boettcher, Mrs. Charles II, 36
Boettcher, Claude K., 35-36
Boettcher Foundation, *35-36*
Bogert, Mrs. H. Lawrence, 205
Bolling, Landrum R., 267
Bollingen Foundation, 22, 24
Bonel (ryegrass variety), 386
Book of the Month Club, 392
Booth, Willis H., 36; and Booth, Mrs. Chancie Ferris, 36
Booth Ferris Foundation, *36-37*
Borgatta, Edgar S., 379
Borlaug, Norman E., 369
Boswell, James G., 190
Boswell, James G. II, 190
Boswell, Rosalind M., 190
Boswell, Ruth C., 190
Boswell, Walter O., 190
Bowen, William G., 421
Boyer, Ernest L., 54
Boys Club of America, 64, 178, 195, 204, 227, 230, 340, 417, 419
Boy Scouts of America, 20, 46, 99, 163, 194-95, 200, 255, 291, 339, 417, 419
Bradley International Airport, 166
Bremer, Adolf, 324-25
Bremer, Eduard, 324; and Bremer, Mrs. Mathilde Maeder, 324
Bremer, Frieda, 325
Bremer, Otto, 324-26
Bremer, Patsy Raskob, 347
Brewer, Sebert, Jr., 33
Brim, Orville G., Jr., 138, 378-79
Broce, Thomas E., 248-49
Bronfenbrenner, Urie, 379
Brown, Ann Noble, 387
Brown, Esther Lucille, 379
Brown, George R., 37

Brown, Herman, 37
Brown, James IV, 75
Brown, J. Graham, 191-93
Brown, Kenneth J., 96
Brown, Martin, 191
Brown, Patricia, 120
Brown, Rachel, 350
Brown, W. P., 191
Brown Foundation, *37-38*
Bruce, Ailsa Mellon, 22-23
Buck, Mrs. Beryl, 389
Bunche, Ralph, 240
Bundy, McGeorge, 132
Bush, Archibald Granville, 38-40, 116, 282; and Bush, Mrs. Edyth, 38-41, 116
Bush Foundation, *38-41*, 116, 282
Businesses. *See* Corporations and businesses
Butler, Nicholas Murray, 52
Butler, William J., 307
Buttrick, Wallace, 147, 151
B. W. Foundation, 432

Cafritz, Calvin, 303
Cafritz, Morris, 303; and Cafritz, Mrs. Gwendolyn D., 303
Calder, Louis, 270-71
California Charities Foundation, 440
Callaway, Fuller E., Jr., 44
Callaway, Fuller E., Sr., 43-44; and Callaway, Mrs. Ida Cason, 44
Callaway Community Foundation. *See* Callaway Foundation
Callaway Foundation, *43-45*
Campbell, Colin G., 63
Campbell, J. Bulow, 199
Cancer Society, American, 179
Candler, Asa G., 228-29
Cannon, Charles A., 45
Cannon, James W., 45
Cannon Foundation, *45-46*
Career Development Center, 220
Carnegie, Andrew, 46-50, 52-53, 81
Carnegie Commission on Higher Education, 54
Carnegie Corporation of New York, *46-52*, 53-54, 129, 209-10, 212, 239, 290, 378
Carnegie Council on Children, 50
Carnegie Council on Policy Studies in Higher Education, 54
Carnegie Foundation. *See* Carnegie Foundation for the Advancement of Teaching
Carnegie Foundation for the Advancement of Teaching, 47-49, *52-55*, 150
Carnegie Hero Fund Commission, 47

Carnegie Institute, 47
Carrie Estelle Doheny Corporation, 55-56
Carrie Estelle Doheny Foundation, *55-56*
Carrington, Paul, 89
Carter, Amon G., 21
Carter, Edward W., 196
Carter, N. B., 21
Caruth, Mrs. W. W., Sr., 179
Caruth, W. W., Jr., 90
Cary, Mary Harkness Flagler, 286-87
Cary, Melbert B., Jr., 287
Casey, Annie E., 24
Casey, J. E., 24
Castle, Harold K. L., 162; and Castle, Mrs. Alice, 162
Catholic League for Religious and Civil Rights, 103
Catholics United for Life, 103
Center for Advocacy, Research and Planning, 309
Center for Creative Leadership, 399
Center for Non-Profit Management, 295
Center for the American Woman and Politics, 68
Chamberlain, Thomas G., 37
Chamber of Commerce, 84, 220, 308, 310, 338, 420
Champlin, George S., 56
Champlin Foundations, *56*
Channel 11/WTTW (television station), 220
Chapin, E. Y., III, 33
Chapman, Carleton B., 87-88
Chapman, Oscar L., 188
Charity Organization Society, 374
Charles A. Dana Foundation, *56-59*
Charles A. Frueauff Foundation, *59-60*
Charles and Ellora Alliss Educational Foundation, *60-61*
Charles E. Culpeper Foundation, *61-63*
Charles Engelhard Foundation, *63*
Charles Hayden Foundation, *63-64*
Charles H. Revson Foundation, *65-68*
Charles Stewart Mott Foundation, *68-73*
Chatlos, Alice E., 74
Chatlos, William F., 73-74
Chatlos, William J., 74
Chatlos Foundation, *73-74*
Chattanooga Community Foundation, 34
Chicago Community Trust, *74-76*, 308
Chicago Crime Commission, 220
Child Care Association of Dallas, 179
Children's Aid Society, 136
Children's Defense Fund, 66

Children's Home Society, 93, 195
Children's Television Workshop, 67-68, 130
Child Study Association of America, 258
China, People's Republic of, 76-77, 174
China Famine Fund, 255
China Medical Board of New York, *76-77*
Christamore Aid Society, 265
Christian A. Johnson Endeavor Foundation, *77-78*
Christian Business Men's Committee, 34
Christ of the Andes Mission (Ecuador), 103
Christy, Francis T., 315
Chrysler, Walter P., 68
Chubb, Hendon, 425
Chubb, Margaret, 425
Chubb, Percy II, 426
Chubb, Victoria Eddis, 425
Churches and religious institutions: Baptist, 29, 46, 147, 231, 333; Billy Graham Center, 74; Christ Church Cathedral (Indianapolis), 265; Church of God, 46; Congregational, 95; Gammon Theological Seminary, 150; Jewish, 25, 28, 67, 92, 178, 194, 221, 339, 346, 392; Methodist, 28, 46, 108-9; Presbyterian, 28, 46, 199, 340; Protestant Episcopal, 90, 313, 343, 432; Quakers, 231; Roman Catholic, 28, 55-56, 92, 93, 99, 101-5, 107, 194, 221, 339, 346-47, 413, 427, 438-39
Churchill Downs (horse racing track), 192
Cincinnati Reds (baseball team), 291
Civic Action Institute, 220
Claiborne, Herbert A., Jr., 262
Clara C. Hyams Fund, 159
Clark, Edward, 78
Clark, Edward S., 78
Clark, F. Ambrose, 78
Clark, Kenneth, 399
Clark, Ralph, 323
Clark, Robert Sterling, 357; and Clark, Mrs. Francine, 357
Clark, Stephen C., 78
Clark, Stephen C., Jr., 78
Clark, W. Van Alan, 112; and Clark, Mrs. Edna McConnell, 111-12
Clark Foundation, *78-79*
Claude Worthington Benedum Foundation, 79
Cleveland Foundation, 74, *79-83*, 164, 308, 310, 335
Cline, Hugh F., 379
Close, Edward B., 285
Cohn, Edwin J., 86
Colcord, Joanne C., 375

INDEX / 493

Coleman, J. D. Stetson, 83; and Coleman, Mrs. Dorothy W., 83
Coleman Foundation, *83*
Coles, James Stacy, 352
Coles, Rachel L., 336
College Retirement Equities Fund (CREF), 53
Colleges: Adrian College, 177; Agnes Scott College, 262; Assumption College, 154; Barber-Scotia College, 45-46; Bennett College, 72; Berea College, 96, 152; Bethune-Cookman College, 28; Bishop College, 119, 261; Cardinal Newman College, 103; Carleton College, 283; City College of New York, 66, 378; Claremont Men's College, 452; Clark College, 150; College of Saint Catherine, 382; Colorado College, 117; Colorado School of Mines, 38; Constantinople's Women's College, 255; Covenant College, 34; Dallas Community College, 119; Dallas County Junior College System, 120; David Rankin, Jr., Technical Institute, 275; Davidson College, 109, 290; Earlham College, 267; Flint Junior College (formerly Mott Community College), 70; Florida Southern College, 74; Fort Valley State College, 240; George Peabody College for Teachers, 149, 152; Grove City College, 203; Hamilton College, 77; Hampton Institute, 49, 148; Hanover College, 183, 191, 193; Hartwick College, 78; Hebrew Union College, 346; Hillsdale College, 177, 264; Hiram College, 96; Howard Payne College, 261; Illinois Institute of Technology, 32, 83; Jackson State College, 150, 240; Kenyon College, 155; Lafayette College, 125-26, 208; LaGrange College, 44; Lindenwood College, 275; Malone College, 414; Meharry Medical College, 150; Mills College, 163; Moravian College, 140; Morehouse College, 149; Morris Brown College, 150; Mount Senario College, 103; Mount Vernon College, 286; Occidental College, 163; Olivet College, 177; Radcliffe College, 256; Robert College (Constantinople), 255; Rochester Institute of Technology, 111; St. John's College, 428; Salem College, 79; Siena Heights College, 177; Smith College, 380; South Texas College of Law, 94; Spelman College, 149, 363; Springfield College, 46; Stevens Institute of Technology, 118-19; Sweet Briar College, 60, 119; Trinity College (North Carolina), 108; Trinity College (Rhode Island), 164; Tuskegee Institute, 49, 148, 239; Ursinus College, 273; Walsh College, 414; Westminster College, 60; Wheaton College, 74; Whitman College, 324; Williams College, 23; Wingate College, 46; Women's Union Christian Colleges, 255; Worcester Polytechnic Institute, 154-57, 405. *See also* Universities
College Settlements Association, 376
Colonial Williamsburg Foundation, 362
Columbia Foundation, 387
Columbus Foundation, *83-85*
Commendador de la Orden de Isabel la Católica (Spain), 414
Commission on Interracial Cooperation, 240-41, 258
Commission on Public Broadcasting, 50
Committee for Economic Development, 220
Committee on Care of Transient and Homeless, 279, 282
Commonwealth Fund, *85-89*, 171
Communities Foundation of Texas, *89-92*
Community Chest. *See* United Way
Community Service Society, 380
Community Services Planning Council, 338
Conference of Southwest Foundations, 248
Connecticut Women's Education and Legal Fund, 309
Connelly, John F., 92; and Connelly, Mrs. Josephine C., 92
Connelly, William H., 165
Connelly Foundation, *92-93*
Conrad N. Hilton Foundation, *93*
Conservation and environmental organizations, 236, 292, 361-63, 390, 412, 426, 439, 455; Audubon Society, 174, 189; Brandywine Conservancy (Pennsylvania), 270; Chippewa Nature Center (Michigan), 175; Conservation Foundation, 362; Dallas Arboretum, 119; Friends of the Earth, 174; Institute for World Environment and Resources, 216; Midland Beautification Trust (Michigan), 175; Natural Resources Defense Council, 392; Nature Conservancy, 63, 163, 206, 288, 355, 436; New Jersey Conservation Foundation, 426; New Jersey Marine Sciences Consortium, 426; Resources for the Future, 71, 129; Snake River Land Company (Wyoming), 187
Consolidated Foundation, 433
Constance Brown Society for Better Hearing, 243
Continental Classroom (television program), 130

Conway, John H., Jr., 200
Cooperative Assistance Fund, 71
Coors, Adolph, Jr., 3
Coors, Adolph, Sr., 3
Coors, Gertrude Steele, 3
Corbally, John, 214
Corcoran, Walter, 59
Corcoran Community Foundation, 191
Corporate Special Projects Fund, 315
Corporation for Boston, 330
Corporations and businesses: AHW Corporation, 17; Alcan Aluminum, Ltd., 26; Alleghany Corporation, 126; Aluminum Company of America, 5, 108; American Broadcasting Company, 113; American Home Products Corporation (formerly Oxzyn Company), 416; American Motors Company, 68; American Steel and Wire Company (formerly Washburn and Moen Manufacturing Company), 404; American Telephone and Telegraph Company, 435; American Tobacco Company, 108; Anderson, Clayton and Company, 292; Anderson Company, 227; Avon Products, Incorporated, 112; Batten, Barton, Durstine, and Osborn, 313; Beatrice Foods, 28; Bradford Exchange, 213; Bristol Door and Lumber Company, Incorporated, 73; Brown and Root, Inc., 37; Burroughs Corporation, 408; Cadillac Fairview Corporation, Ltd., 197; California Perfume Company, 112; California Portland Cement Company, 98-99; Callaway Mills, 44; Canada Dry Corporation, 319; Cannon Mills Company, 45; Carnegie Steel Company, 47; Carter Foundation Production Company, 21; Charles F. Noyes Company, 201; Coca-Cola Company, 33, 61, 228-30, 262-63; Computer Sciences Corporation, 227; Crane Packing Company, 140; Crescent Diversified Limited, 214; Crown Cork and Seal Company, 92; Dana Corporation, 57; Del E. Webb Corporation, 100; Deloitte, Haskins, and Sells, 195; Douglas Aircraft Company, 276; Dow Chemical Company, 175-76; Du Pont Company, 270, 346; Duveen Brothers, 320; Eastman Kodak Company, 111; Educational Broadcasting Corporation, 63; Eli Lilly and Company, 264-67; Emerson Electric Company, 163; Emery Air Freight Corporation, 59; Engelhard Hanovia, Inc., 63; Equitable Powder Manufacturing Co., 323; Federal Cartridge Corporation, 323; First Wilshire Securities Management, 104; Fleischmann Yeast and Gin Factories, 291; Ford Motor Company, 127, 128, 135, 136; Fruit Industries, Incorporated, 27-28; F. W. Woolworth Company, 125; Gates Corporation, 146; Gates Rubber Company, 145-46; General Electric Company, 349; General Foods Corporation, 285; General Motors Corporation, 6-7, 68, 69, 73, 153, 270, 346; Geophysical Services, Inc., 118; George B. Markle and Company, 208; Great Atlantic and Pacific Tea Company, 207-8; Great Northern Iron Ore Properties Trust, 316; Hayden, Stone, and Company, 63-64; Henry Cowell Lime and Cement Co., 393; Hewlett-Packard Company, 100, 435; H. F. Ahmanson Company, 4-5; H. J. Heinz Company, 181; Hooker Electrochemical Company, 349; Hunt Foods and Industries, Inc., 319; Inland Container Corporation, 249; International Business Machines Corporation, 395, 400; International Flavors and Fragrances Corporation, 10-11; International News Service, 440; International Nickel Company, 10; Investors Diversified Services, Inc., 126; Irvine Company, 194-98; Jacob Schmidt Brewing Company, 324; James G. Boswell Company, 190; Johnson and Johnson Company, 358; Kaiser Aluminum and Chemical Corporation, 172; Kaiser Cement Corporation, 172; Kaiser Industries Corporation, 170; Kaiser Steel Corporation, 172; Kellogg Company, 446-48; Kerr-McGee Corporation, 247; Kevin Roche/Dinkeloo, 127; Kewanee Industries, Incorporated, 453; King Ranch, Inc., 356; Life Saver Company, 113; McDonald's Corporation, 252; McDonnell Corporation (formerly McDonnell Aircraft Corporation), 276; McDonnell Douglas Corporation, 274-77; Maramec Iron Works, 312; Metrotone Newsreels, 440; Miller Brewing Company, 101; Minnesota Mining and Manufacturing Company, 38, 39, 40, 60, 116, 282, 284; Morgan Stanley & Co., 197; Nash Motor Company, 68; National Broadcasting Company, 113; New York and New Jersey Water Company, 57; Norris Industries, Incorporated (formerly Norris Stamping and Manufacturing Company), 246; Norton Emery Wheel Company, 157; Norton Simon, Inc., 58, 319, 321; Olin Industries, 323; Olin Mathieson Chemical Corporation, 323; Paine Webber, 59;

Parke, Davis and Company, 416; Perkins-Goodwin Company, 270-71; Philip Morris, Inc., 101; Polaroid Corporation, 373; Ralph M. Parsons Company, 345; Ralston-Purina Company, 95; Remington Arms Company, 158; Research-Cottrell, Inc., 349; Revlon, Inc., 65; R. J. Reynolds Tobacco Company, 244; Rohm and Haas Company, 439; Rouse Development Company, 429; Schering-Plough Corporation, 107; Scholl Manufacturing Company, 107; Science Research Associates, Inc., 400; Sears, Roebuck and Company, 238-39; S. H. Kress and Company, 382; Singer Sewing Machine Company, 78, 357, 406; Spicer Universal Joint Manufacturing Company, 57; S. S. Kresge Company, 250; Standard Brands, 291; Taubman-Allan-Irvine, Inc., 197; Tecumseh Products Company, 177; Tektronix, Inc., 297; Texas Instruments, Inc., 118-19; Timken Company (formerly Timken Roller Bearing Axle Company), 413-14; Tremont Lumber Company, 235; Trenton Iron Works, 404; Tropicana, 28; Union Carbide Company, 222; United Parcel Service of America, Inc., 24; United States Steel Corporation, 404-5, 423-24; Unity Cotton Mills, 43-44; Universal News Service, 440; Welch Grape Juice Company, 206; Western Cartridge Company, 323; Western Electric Company, Incorporated, 434-35; Western Union, 46; Weston-Mott Company, 69; Whitehead Holding Company and Realty Company, 262; W. L. Moody and Co., 298; W. P. Brown and Sons, 192; W. T. Grant Company, 445; Wyman-Gordon Company, 154, 405. *See also* Banks and trusts; Insurance companies; Petroleum and power companies; Publishers; and Railroads
Cottrell, Frederick Gardner, 349-51
Cottrell, Leonard S., Jr., 379
Council of Southern Universities, 97
Council on Foundations, 116, 165, 267
Council on Library Resources, 129
Council on World Affairs, 90
Cournand, Andre, 86
Cowell, Henry, 393
Cowell, Samuel H., 392-93
Cox, E. Eugene, 223
Cox, John W., 200
Cox Committee (U.S. House of Representatives), 223
Craig, H. Curtis, 193

Creel, Dana S., 362-63
Crippled Children's Relief, 195
Crocker, Ruth C., 190
Crown, Arie, 25
Crown, Ida, 25
Cullen, Hugh Roy, 93-94; and Cullen, Mrs. Hugh Roy, 93-94
Cullen, Roy Gustave, 94
Cullen Foundation, *93-94*
Cullen Trust for Health Care, 94
Cullen Trust for Higher Education, 94
Cullen Trust for the Performing Arts, 94
Culpeper, Charles E., 61
Cummings, Charles B., 73
Cuninggim, Merriman, 97
Cuthbertson, Kenneth M., 199
*cy pres*, legal doctrine of, 336

Dallas Community Chest Trust Fund. *See* Communities Foundation of Texas
Dallas Creative Learning Center, 261
Dallas Day Nurseries, 90
Dallas Heritage Society, 120
Daly, Charles U., 235
Dana, Charles A., Jr., 59
Dana, Charles Anderson, 56-57; and Dana, Mrs. Eleanor, 57, 59
Danforth, William H., 95, 98; and Danforth, Mrs. Adda, 95
Danforth Foundation, *95-98*
Dan Murphy Foundation, *98-100*
Davenport, Erwin, 144
Davenport, Joseph, 33
David and Lucille Packard Foundation, *100*
Davidson, Joan K., 206
Davies, David L., 59
Davies, Joseph E., 285
Davis, Arthur Vining, 25-26
Davis, Jackson, 148
Davis, John M. K., 165-67
Davis, Nathaniel V., 26
Davis, Preston, 84
Day, Osborne, 309
Dayton, Nettie J., 308
"Dead Hand, The," 80
Debevoise, Thomas M., 315
de Forest, Robert W., 374-77
De Kruif, Robert M., 4
Delany, Beatrice P., 32
Delbrück, Max, 350
Del E. Webb Foundation, *100*
Democratic Farmer Labor Party, 325
Democratic Party, 346

Depression, Great (1929), 192, 279, 308, 311, 318, 325, 370, 377, 420, 447
De Rance, *101-5*
de Rance, Abbé Armond-Jeans, 101
Devereux Foundation, 418
Dewey, Francis H. III, 158
DeWitt Wallace Fund, *105*, 314
Dietel, William M., 364
Dimon, Earle, 165
Doan, Herbert D., 177
Dodge, Marcellus Hartley, 158; and Dodge, Geraldine Rockefeller, 158-59
Dodge, M. Hartley, Jr., 158
Doheny, Edward L., 55; and Doheny, Mrs. Carrie Estelle, 55
Dollard, Charles, 48
Don and Sybil Harrington Foundation, *106*
Donner, Joseph, 436
Donner, William H., 183, 436-37
Donner Canadian Foundation, 437
Donner Foundation, 183, 436-38
Donohue, Bernadine Murphy, 98
Donohue, Daniel J., 98
Donohue, Rosemary E., 98
Doolen, Paul D., 213-14
Dorsey, Eugene C., 144
Dow, Alden B., 177
Dow, Herbert H., 175-77; and Dow, Mrs. Grace A., 175
Doyle, Morris M., 198
Drake, Philip M., 63
Drama. *See* Theaters
Dr. Scholl Foundation, *107*
Dryden, John, 341
Duggan, Agnes Brown, 193
Duke, Benjamin, 108
Duke, James B., 107-10
Duke, Washington, 108
Duke Endowment, *107-10*, 245, 289
Duncombe, Harmon, 10-11
du Pont, Alfred I., 200-201; and du Pont, Mrs. Jessie Ball, 200-201
du Pont, Jessie Ball (Mrs Alfred I. du Pont), 200-201
du Pont, Pierre S., 270
du Pont, T. Coleman, 349
Durant, Clark T., 164
Durant, William C., 68
Duryee, Sacket R., 154

East Boston Social Center, Inc., 160
Eastman Kodak Charitable Trust, *111*
Eban, Abba, 67
Edna McConnell Clark Foundation, *111-13*
Educational Broadcasting Corporation, 130
Educational Priorities Panel, 67, 392
Educational Testing Service, 54
Education for Development (formerly University Development). *See* Rockefeller Foundation
Edward John Noble Foundation, *113-16*
Edwin H. Land–Helen M. Land, Inc., 373
Edyth Bush Charitable Foundation, 40, *116-17*
Elbon (ryegrass variety), 386
Eliot, Charles W., 52
Elkus, Marjorie, 387-88
El Pomar Foundation, *117*
Embree, Edwin R., 239, 241
Emergency Unemployment Relief Committee (New York), 311
Emily Griggs Fund, 312
*Encyclopedia of the Social Sciences*, 379
Engelhard, Charles, 63
Environmental organizations. *See* Conservation and environmental organizations
Ernst, Joseph W., 364
Erwin, Sam, 229
Esso Education Foundation, 120
Ethridge, Mark, 241
Eugene McDermott Foundation, *118-20*
Evans, Arthur Kelly, 262; and Evans, Mrs. Lettie Pate Whitehead, 229, 262
Eveleigh, Carl F., 265
Ewald, Russell V., 284
Exxon Education Foundation, *120-21*

Faber, Herbert H., 185
Faigel Leah Foundation, 205
Fairchild, May, 395
Fairchild, Sherman Mills, 395
Fairchild Foundation, 395
Fairlington (housing development), 260
Family Life Association, 103
Family Service Association of Greater Boston, 159
Family Service Center (Houston), 181
Fannie E. Rippel Foundation, *123-24*
Federated Dorchester Neighborhood Houses, 330
Fellowships and scholarships, 5-6, 19-20, 28, 36, 46, 60-62, 65-68, 85, 96-98, 131, 152, 183-84, 190, 200-201, 232-33, 235, 263, 280, 284, 300, 356, 362, 395, 411-13; Bush Leadership Fellowships, 39; Carnegie Fel-

lowships, 54; Charles E. Culpeper Fellowships, 62; Charles H. Revson Fellows on the Future of the City of New York, 65; Commonwealth Fund Fellowships, 88; Congressional Fellowships in Child Development, 139; Cottrell Fellowships, 350; Dana Scholarships, 58; Danforth Associates, 96-97; Danforth College Project Awards, 97; Danforth Graduate Fellowships, 96-97; Danforth Negro College Faculty Fellowships, 96; Danforth School Administrators Fellowships, 98; Danforth Teacher Grants, 96; Dorothy Danforth Compton Fellowships, 97; Ford Minority Postdoctoral Fellowships, 131; Ford National Achievement Scholarships, 131; General Education Board Fellowships, 257-58; Guggenheim Fellowships, 222-26; Harkness Fellowships, 88; Harkness Medical Fellowships, 86; Hearst Journalism Scholarships, 441; Hearst United States Senate Youth Scholarships, 441; Hoover Institution Domestic Fellowships, 204-5; John A. and George L. Hartford Fellowships, 208; Kellogg International Fellowships, 449; Kellogg National Fellowships, 450; Kerr Foundation Fellowships, 248; Lilly Postdoctoral Teaching Awards, 268; MacArthur Prize Fellows, 214-15, 217, 219; Macy Faculty Scholar Awards, 233; Markle Scholarships, 210-11; Marshall Field Fellows, 400; Mellon Graduate Fellowships, 23; Morehead Scholars, 222; National Merit Scholarships, 129, 435; Nieman Fellows, 65; Noble International Fellows, 114; Noble National Leadership Fellowships, 114; Permanent Charity Fund Scholarships for Vocational Education, 330; Rockefeller Foundation Fellowships, 365, 370-71; Rosenwald Fellowships, 240-41; Russell Sage Fellowships, 379-80; Sloan Research Fellowships, 7-8; Tinker Field Research Grants, 415; Tinker Postdoctoral Fellows, 415; Turrell College Scholarships, 417-19; Turrell Secondary School Scholarships, 419; United Negro College Fund Distinguished Scholars, 219; Woodrow Wilson National Fellowships, 129
Ferrell, John A., 210
Fikes, Lee, 260-61
Fikes, Leland, 260; and Fikes, Mrs. Catherine Whitten, 260-61
Filene, Edward A., 420
Fisher, Mrs. Herbert, 165
Fjordbak, Edward M., 90
Flagler, Harry Harkness, 286; and Flagler, Mrs. Anne Lamont, 286
Flagler, Henry M., 443-44
Fleddérus, Mary L., 377
Fleischmann, Max C., 291-92; and Fleischmann, Mrs. Sara, 291-92
Fletcher, Marion S., 405
Fletcher, Paris, 154, 158, 405
Flexner, Abraham, 53, 87, 150, 367
Flexner Report. *See Medical Education in the United States and Canada, Bulletin Number Four* (1910)
Flick, C. Bruce, 36
Florence and John Schumann Foundation, *125*
Flynn, Mrs. Grace B. Kerr, 247-48
F. M. Kirby Foundation, *125-26*
Fondren, Walter W., 126; and Fondren, Mrs. Walter W., 126
Fondren Foundation, *126-27*
Fong, Wen, 429
Ford, Edsel, 127
Ford, Henry, 127, 177
Ford, Henry II, 136, 276
Ford Foundation, *127-35*, 289, 369, 379
Ford Motor Company Fund, *135-36*, 276
Forest Hills Gardens (housing development), 376
"Fortune 500", 92
Foster, Russell T., 165
Foundation Center (formerly Foundation Library Center), 116, 378
Foundation for American Communications, 391
Foundation for Child Development, *136-40*
Foundation for Economic Education, 264
Four (4) H Program, 317, 449
Frank E. Payne and Seba B. Payne Foundation, *140-41*
Frankfurter, Felix, 81
Franks, Robert A., 47
Freedoms Foundation, 413
Frehse, Robert M., Jr., 167, 442-43
French, James H., 59
Friday, William, 399
Friends for Life, 103
Frueauff, Charles A., 59
Fuld, Florentine M., 168-69
Fuld, Leonhard Felix, 168-69
Fuller, Ernest M., 154
Fuller, George F., 153-54; and Fuller, Mrs. Sybil H., 153-54

Fuller, Russell E., 154
Fund for Adult Education, 129
Fund for the Advancement of Education, 128
Fund for the Republic, 129
Furman, James, 215

Gaither, H. Rowan, Jr., 127-28
Gallagher, Donald, 104; and Gallagher, Mrs. Adele, 104
Galpin, Henry L., 308
Gannett, Frank E., 143-45; and Gannett, Mrs. Carolyn Werner, 145
Gannett Foundation, *143-45*
Ganyard, Leslie, 387
Gardens. *See* Parks, gardens, and zoos
Gardner, John W., 48-49
Gardner, O. Max, 241
Garfield, Sidney, 170
Garmany, Howard Hunt, 165
Gates, Charles C., 146
Gates, Charles C., Sr., 145
Gates, Frank, 308
Gates, Frederick T., 147, 364
Gates, Ross Fletcher, 308
Gates Foundation, *145-46*
Gates Fund, 308
General Education Board, *146-53*, 239-40, 256, 367, 370
General Motors Foundation, *153*
George, Albert P., 154; and George, Mrs. Mamie E., 154
George, David Lloyd, 192
George Eastman House, 111
George F. and Sybil H. Fuller Foundation, *153-54*
George Foundation, *154-55*
George Gund Foundation, *155-56*
George I. Alden Trust, *156-58*
Geraldine R. Dodge Foundation, *158-59*
Gerdes, Robert H., 195
Gest, John B., 335
Gest, William Purves, 335
Gilbert, R. R., 89
Gilcrest, Kathleen A., 5
Gilmore, Donald, 244
Girls Club, 345, 417, 419
Girl Scouts of America, 20, 200, 255, 342, 417, 419
Glaser, Robert J., 171
"Glenmede." *See* Pew Memorial Trust
Glenn, John, 374-76, 380
Glenn, Nancy Lee, 331

Glenn, William W. L., 63
Glynn, William E., 166-67
Goddard, Robert H., 350
Godfrey M. Hyams Trust, *159-60*
Goff, Frederick Harris, 74, 79-82, 83, 164, 310, 335
Golden Triangle Project (Pittsburgh), 354
Goode, William J., 379
Goodrich, Enid, 264
Goodrich, John B., 264
Goodrich, Pierre F., 264
Goodwill Industries, 452
Goodwin, Charles A., 164, 166
Gordon, Milton M., 378
Gottman, Jean, 421
Gould, Charles L., 167, 442-43
Gourielli, Helena Rubinstein, 168
*Governing New York City*, 379
Goya, 320
Graduate Record Examination, 53
Graduate Research Center for the Southwest, 119
Grant, John B., 367
Grant, Richard A., Jr., 98
Grant, William T., 445
Grant Foundation, 445
Gray, John L., 444
Gray, Lyons, 262
Great Lakes Exposition (1936), 81
Greene, Jerome D., 149
Green Revolution (agricultural program), 369
Gregg, Alan, 367
Gregg, John P., 235
Gregory, Amos F., 250
Gresham, J. T., 45
Griffin, W. L. Hadley, 172
Griggs, Herbert L., 311-12; and Griggs, Mrs. Herbert L., 311-12
Gross, Spencer, 164
Guggenheim, Benjamin, 226
Guggenheim, Daniel, 225-26
Guggenheim, Isaac, 226
Guggenheim, John Simon, 222
Guggenheim, Meyer, 225-26
Guggenheim, Murry, 225-26
Guggenheim, Robert, 226
Guggenheim, Simon (grandparent), 225-26; and Guggenheim, Mrs. Rachel, 225
Guggenheim, Simon (grandson), 222-26; and Guggenheim, Mrs. Simon, 222, 224, 226
Guggenheim, Solomon, 225-26
Guggenheim, William, 226

INDEX / 499

Gund, George, 155; and Gund, Mrs. Jessica Roessler, 155
G. Unger Vetlesen Foundation, 10-11

Haas, F. Otto, 440
Haas, John C., 440
Haas, Otto, 439; and Haas, Mrs. Phoebe Waterman, 439
Haas Community Fund, 439
Hadden, Briton, 173
Haines, Davis, 343
Hale, George E., 368
Hall, Donald J., 162
Hall, Joyce, 161-62
Hallmark Educational Foundations, *161-62*
Hallock, Robert P., 154
Hamburg, David A., 48
Hamilton, Alexander, 370
Hamilton, Florence C., 56
Hanley, William Lee, Jr., 205
Harbor Branch Foundation, Incorporated, 27
Harbor Branch Institution, Incorporated, 27
Harkness, Charles W., 85
Harkness, Edward S., 85-88
Harkness, Stephen V., 85; and Harkness, Mrs. Anna M., 85
Harold K. L. Castle Foundation, *162-63*
Harper's Magazine Foundation, 216
Harrar, J. George, 368, 371
Harrington, Donald D., 106; and Harrington, Mrs. Sybil, 106
Harris, Albert W., 74
Harrison, Shelby M., 374, 376-77, 380
Harrower, Norman, Jr., 309
Harry G. Steele Foundation, *163-64*
Hartford, George H., 207
Hartford, George L., 207
Hartford, John A., 207
Hartford Foundation for Public Giving, *164-67*, 308
Hartoch, Janice L., 59
Hawkes, Benjamin G., 98
Hayden, Charles, 63-64
Hayes, Ralph, 310-11, 313, 315
Hazen, Elizabeth, 350
Hazen, Maynard T., 164
Hazzard, George W., 158
Heald, Henry T., 128
Health Institutions. *See* Hospitals, medical and health institutions
Health maintenance organizations, 172
Hearst, David W., 442

Hearst, Patricia Campbell, 441-42
Hearst, Randolph A., 167, 441-43; and Hearst, Mrs. Catherine, 443
Hearst, William Randolph, 167, 440-41, 443
Hearst Foundation, *167-68*, 440
Heckman, A. A., 318
Heinz, Henry J., 181
Heinz, Henry J. II, 182
Heinz, Howard, 181-82; and Heinz, Mrs. Howard, 181
Helena Rubinstein Foundation, *168*
Helene Fuld Health Trust, *168-69*
Helen K. and Arthur E. Johnson Foundation, *169-70*
Helming, Carlton T., 323-24
Helsinki Watch, 220
Henry J. Kaiser Family Foundation, *170-73*
Henry Luce Foundation, *173-74*
Henry P. Kendall Foundation, *174-75*
Henslee, Charlyne D., 260
Herbert and Margaret Turrell Foundation, 415
Herbert H. and Grace A. Dow Foundation, *175-77*
Heritage Foundation, 204
Herman Charles and Ellnora Deckert Krannert Foundation, 249
Herrick, Kenneth G., 178
Herrick, Ray W., 177; and Herrick, Mrs. Hazel M., 177
Herrick, Todd W., 178
Herrick Foundation, *177-78*
Hess, Leon, 178
Hess, Robert G., 158
Hess Foundation, *178-79*
Hevesy, George, 368
Hewlett, Walter B., 435
Hewlett, William R., 435-36; and Hewlett, Mrs. William R., 435-36
HFPG, Inc., 166
Higgins, Milton, 156-57
Higher Education Management Institute, 121
Hill, Cortlandt Taylor, 317
Hill, James Jerome, 316; and Hill, Mrs. Mary Theresa Mehegan, 316
Hill, James Jerome II, 317
Hill, Joseph M., 260
Hill, Louis Warren, Jr., 317
Hill, Louis W., Sr., 316-18; and Hill, Mrs. Maud Van Cortlandt Taylor, 317
Hillcrest Foundation, *179*
Hilton, Conrad N., 93
Hirsch, Fred, 421

Hirsch, James G., 235
Hirschberg, William S., 59
Historic preservation projects and organizations, 390, 399, 439; Dallas County Heritage Society (Texas), 261; Danville and Boyle County Foundation for Historic Preservation (Kentucky), 194; Fraunces Tavern Block (New York), 430; Galveston Center for Transportation and Commerce (Texas), 301; Grace Church Houses (New York), 430; Historic Homes Foundation of Louisville (Kentucky), 194; Historic Mobile Preservation Society (Alabama), 194; Missouri Mansion Preservation Association, 275; National Register of Historic Places, 306; Old Salem (North Carolina), 289; Queens County Farm Museum (New York), 430; Reynolda House (North Carolina), 289; St. Ann's Church (New York), 430; St. Bartholomew's Church (New York), 430; Santa Fe Building (New Mexico), 301; Shearn Moody Plaza (Texas), 301; United States Custom House (New York), 430; Villard Houses (New York), 430; W. H. Stark House (Texas), 306-7
Hobhouse, Sir Arthur, 80
Hoblitzelle, Karl St. John, 179-80; and Hoblitzelle, Mrs. Esther Thomas, 179
Hoblitzelle Foundation, *179-80*
Hodges, Luther, 399
Hoffman, Paul G., 128
Hokanson, Patricia J., 59
Holmesburg Prison (Pennsylvania), 337
Homes and houses, 263; A. M. McGregor Home (Ohio), 18; Andrus Children's Home (New York), 406; Astor Home (formerly Astor Home for Disturbed Children) (New York), 427; Bonnie Brae (New Jersey), 418; Boys Brotherhood Republic (New York), 427; Covenant House (New York), 62; Florida United Methodist Children's Home, 74; Granville House (Minnesota), 39; Home of the Innocents (Kentucky), 194; Honey Creek Christian Homes (Michigan), 178; Industrial Home for the Blind (New York), 406; Jacob Riis Houses (New York), 428; John E. Andrus Memorial (New York), 406; La Casa de Don Pedro (New Jersey), 426; Lenox Hill Neighborhood House (New York), 429; McGregor Institute (formerly Helping Hand Mission) (Michigan), 278-79; Misericordia Home (Illinois), 83; New England Kurn Hattin Homes, 419; Smokey House (Vermont), 419; Victory House (New Jersey), 426

Hooker, Elon Huntington, 349
Hoover, Allan, 205
Hopkins, Harry, 279
Horn, Charles L., 323
Horn, William B., 323
Hospitals, medical and health institutions: Allegheny General Hospital (Pennsylvania), 340; American Hospital (Paris), 262; Baptist Hospital (North Carolina), 289; Battle Creek Sanitarium (Michigan), 446-47; Baylor Hospital (Texas), 90; Borgess Hospital (Michigan), 243; Boston Hospital for Women, 174; Bronson Methodist Hospital (Michigan), 243; Cabarrus Memorial Hospital (North Carolina), 45; Chattanooga-Hamilton County Hospital Authority (Tennessee), 34; Chester County Hospital (Pennsylvania), 270; Children's Hospital (Colorado), 169; Children's Hospital (Pennsylvania), 423; Children's Medical Center (Texas), 120; Desert Hospital Mental Health Center, 93; Don and Sybil Harrington Cancer Center (Texas), 106; Edward John Noble Hospitals (New York), 113-14; Evanston Hospital Association (Illinois), 140; Fair Haven Community Health Clinic (Connecticut), 309; Hermann Hospital (Texas), 356; Herrick Memorial Hospital (Michigan), 178; Hoag Memorial Hospital (California), 163; Hospital of the Good Samaritan (California), 434, 452; Huntington Memorial Hospital (California), 246; Hurley Medical Center (Michigan), 69; Illinois Masonic Medical Center, 83; Kaiser Foundation Hospitals (California), 171; Krannert Institute of Cardiology (Indiana), 250; LaGrange City-County Hospital (Georgia), 44; LaGrange Settlement (Georgia), 44; Lincoln Hospital, 258; McLean Hospital, 218; Maine Medical Center, 59; Massachusetts General Hospital, 10, 185; M. D. Anderson Hospital and Tumor Institute (Texas), 293; Memorial Hospital for Cancer and Allied Diseases (New York), 6; Memorial Sloan-Kettering Cancer Center (New York), 7, 77, 204, 363, 396, 436; Methodist Hospital (Texas), 119; Midland-Gladwin Community Mental Health Services (Michigan), 175; Minnesota Society of Crippled Children, 283; Mott's Children's Health Center (Michigan), 69; Mount Sinai Hospital (New York), 346; New England

Medical Center Hospitals, 330; New York Hospital, 404, 427; New York Medical College, 271; Ormond Memorial Hospital (Florida), 167; Peking Union Medical College (China), 76-77, 366-67; Penrose Hospital (Colorado), 117; Polly Ryan Memorial Hospital (Texas), 155; Presbyterian-University of Pennsylvania Medical Center, 273, 337; Regional Cancer Center (Kentucky), 194; Rochester Regional Hospital Council (New York), 86; Roosevelt Hospital (New York), 167; Rush Presbyterian/St. Luke's Medical Center (Illinois), 32, 348; St. Barnabas Hospital (Massachusetts), 185; St. Charles Hospital (New York), 185; St. Joseph (Texas), 21; St. Louis Children's Hospital (Missouri), 277; St. Luke's Hospital (Arizona), 106; St. Luke's Hospital Center (New York), 78; St. Mary's Hospital (Texas), 412; St. Vincent (California), 55; St. Vincent's Hospital (New York), 185; Santa Ana Community Hospital (California), 195; Scott and White Memorial Hospital (Texas), 181; Shadyside Hospital (Pennsylvania), 182; Sloan-Kettering Institute for Cancer Research (New York), 6; Stanly County Hospital (North Carolina), 45; Texas Medical Center, 292-93; Timken Mercy Medical Center (Ohio), 413; Walter O. Boswell Memorial Hospital (Arizona), 190-91; W. Alton Jones Cell Science Center (New York), 432; Western Pennsylvania Hospital, 79, 182; William K. Warren Medical Research Center (Oklahoma), 438. *See also* Research institutions

Hotels: Broadmoor, 117; Brown, 192; Campbell House, 192; Colonnades Beach, 213; Glacier Park, 317; Golden Gate, 74; Kentucky, 192; St. Regis, 427; Suburban Motel, 192

Houses. *See* Homes and houses
Housing Opportunities, Inc., 340
Houston Endowment, *180-81*
Howard Heinz Endowment, *181-82*, 340
Hoyt, Hamilton C., 445
Human Life Center, 103-4
Hunter, George Thomas, 33-34
Hunt Foods Charitable Foundation, 321
Hurricane Allan St. Lucia Rebuilding Fund, 178
Huston, John A., 63
Hutchins, William J., 96
Hutton, E. F., 285

Hyams, Godfrey M., 159
Hyams, Isabel F., 159-60
Hyams, Sarah H., 159

Independence Foundation, *183-84*
Institute for Child Guidance, 85
Institute for Crippled Soldiers and Sailors. *See* International Center for the Disabled
Institute for Educational Affairs, 204-5
Institute for the Crippled and Disabled. *See* International Center for the Disabled
Institute of Medicine. *See* Research institutions: National Academy of Sciences
Institute of Physical Medicine and Rehabilitation, 137
Institute on Man and Science, 71
Institutes. *See* Colleges; Learned and professional societies; Research institutions; Universities
Instituto Gonzalo Fernandez de Oviedo (Spain), 414
Instituto Histórico y Geográfico de Uruguay, 414
Insurance companies: American Asiatic Life Insurance Company, 403; American International Group, Inc., 403-4; American Life Insurance Company (formerly Asia Life Company), 403; American National Insurance Co., 298-99; Bankers Life and Casualty Company, 212-14; Chubb and Son, 425; INA Corporation, 433; Metropolitan Life Insurance Company, 296-97; Pacific Employment Insurance Company, 433; Provident Life and Accident Insurance Company, 285; Prudential Insurance Company of America, 341-43; Prudential Property and Casualty Insurance Company, 342; Volunteer State Life Insurance Company, 33. *See also* Corporations and businesses
Inter-American Center for Community Education, 71
International Cancer Research Foundation, 183, 436
International Center for the Disabled, 203-4
International Committee for the Study of Infantile Paralysis, 204
International Education Board. *See* Rockefeller Foundation
International Institute of the Heart of Jesus. *See* De Rance
International Health Board. *See* Rockefeller Foundation

International Management Development Institute, 220
International Rice Research Institute, 369
International Social Service, 313
Ira W. DeCamp Foundation, *184-85*
Irvine, James, 194-98; and Irvine, Mrs. Katherine, 195-96
Irvine, Myford, 195-96
Irvine Ranch, 194, 196
Isabel H. Hyams Fund, 159-60
Island Center of St. Croix, 178

Jackson, John N., 260
Jackson Hole Preserve, *187-89*, 363
James, H. Thomas, 401
James, Lucy Wortham, 312
James Foundation, 312
James G. Boswell Foundation, *189-91*
James Graham Brown Foundation, *191-94*
James Irvine Foundation, *194-99*
J and R Double Arch Ranch, 252
Janowitz, Morris, 379
Japan Society, 363
Jay, John, 370
J. Bulow Campbell Foundation, *199*
J. E. and L. E. Mabee Foundation, *199-200*
Jessie Ball du Pont Religious, Charitable, and Educational Fund, *200-201*
Jessie Smith Noyes Foundation, *201-2*
Jessup, Walter A., 48
Jewish Community Federation, 82
J. Howard Pew Freedom Trust, *202-3*, 332
J. M. Foundation, *203-5*
J. M. Kaplan Fund, *205-6*
J. N. Pew, Jr., Charitable Trust, *206-7*, 332
John, Harry G., 101-2; and John, Mrs. Erika, 104
John A. Hartford Foundation, *207-8*
John and Mary R. Markle Foundation, *208-12*
John D. and Catherine T. MacArthur Foundation, *212-21*
John F. Slater Fund, 147
John McShain Charities, *221-22*
John M. Olin Foundation, 324
John Motley Morehead Foundation, 222
John Simon Guggenheim Memorial Foundation, *222-26*
Johnson, Arthur E., 169; and Johnson, Mrs. Helen K., 169
Johnson, Barbara P., 27
Johnson, Charles H., 241
Johnson, Christian A., 77
Johnson, Franklyn A., 437

Johnson, Helen D., 63
Johnson, James L., 27
Johnson, J. Seward, 27
Johnson, J. Seward, Jr., 27
Johnson, Robert Wood, 358
Johnson New Brunswick Foundation, 358
Johnson O'Connor Research Foundation, 77
John W. Anderson Foundation, *227*
Jones, Donald F., 350
Jones, Fletcher, 227
Jones, Jesse H., 180; and Jones, Mrs. Jesse H., 180
Jones, J. W., 230
Jones, Mable Irving, 136
Jones, Vincent S., 145
Jones, W. Alton, 431; and Jones, Mrs. W. Alton, 431-32
Jones Foundation, *227-28*
Jonsson, Eric, 119
Joseph and Helen Regenstein Foundation, 348
Joseph B. Whitehead Foundation, *228-31*, 262
Josephs, Devereux C., 48
Josiah Macy, Jr., Foundation, *231-35*
Joyce Foundation, *235-38*
Julia Dyckman Andrus Memorial, 406
Julius Rosenwald Fund, *238-42*
Junior Achievement, 20
Juvenile Court Fund (New Jersey), 417-19

Kaiser, Edgar F., 170, 172
Kaiser, Edgar F., Jr., 172
Kaiser, Henry J., 170-71; and Kaiser, Mrs. Bess, 170-71
Kalamazoo Foundation, *243-44*
Kalleward, Howard, 244
Kane, Paul, 306
Kansas City Association of Trusts and Foundations, 82
Kaplan, Jacob M., 205-6
Karcher, J. Clarence, 118
Kate B. Reynolds Charitable Trust, *244-46*
Kate B. Reynolds Health Care Trust, 244-45
Kate B. Reynolds Poor and Needy Trust, 244-45
Kaufman, Herbert, 379
Kay, Herma Hill, 380
Kean, Beatrice Joyce, 235
Keck, Howard B., 452
Keck, Howard B., Jr., 452
Keck, William M., 451-52
Keck, William M. II, 452
Kellogg, John, 446-47
Kellogg, Paul U., 375, 380

Kellogg, Will Keith, 446-49; and Kellogg, Mrs. Ella, 447
Kenan, Frank H., 444
Kenan, William R., Jr., 443-44
Kendall, Edward C., 350
Kendall, Evelyn L., 174
Kendall, Henry P., 174
Kendall, Henry W., 174
Kendall, John P., 174
Kennedy, Albert J., 375
Kenneth T. and Eileen L. Norris Foundation, 246-47
Kentucky Thoroughbred Breeder's Association, 192
Keppel, Frederick P., 48-49, 209
Kerr, Breene M., 248
Kerr, Clark, 54
Kerr, Joffa, 248
Kerr, Robert Samuel, 247
Kerr, Robert S., Jr., 248
Kerr, William G., 248
Kerr Foundation, 247-49
Kettering, Charles F., 6
Kirby, Allan Price, 125-26
Kirby, Frederick Morgan, 125-26
Kissinger, Henry, 398
Kleberg, Robert J., Jr., 356; and Kleberg, Mrs. Helen C., 356
Kluger, Richard, 67
Knollbrook Trust, 332
Knowles, John, 245
Koshland, Daniel E., 387-88
Krannert, Herman C., 249; and Krannert, Mrs. Ellnora, 249
Krannert Charitable Trust, 249-50
Kreidler, Robert N., 59
Kresge, Bruce A., 250
Kresge, Sebastian Spering, 250
Kresge Foundation, 250-51
Kress, Claude W., 382
Kress, Rush H., 382
Kress, Samuel H., 382
Kroc, Ray A., 251-52; and Kroc, Mrs. Joan B., 252
Kroc, Robert L., 251
Kroc Foundation, 251-53

Ladd, Walter Graeme, 231; and Ladd, Mrs. Kate Macy, 231
Ladies' Garment Workers' Union, International, 429
Lake, Thomas H., 267
Lakewood (housing development), 432-34

Land, Edwin H., 373; and Land, Mrs. Helen M., 373
Lange, Fred M., 89-90
Larson, Roy E., 174
Latimer, J. L., 89
Laura Spelman Rockefeller Memorial, 255-59, 367, 369
Law Firms: Dewey, Ballantine, Bushby, Palmer, and Wood, 444; Fulton, Duncombe, and Rowe, 10-11; Kerr, Irvine, and Rhodes, 248; Mudge, Rose, Guthrie, and Alexander, 185; Musick, Peeler, and Garrett, 98; Whitman and Ransom, 59
L.A.W. Fund, 105, 259, 314
Lawler, Oscar T., 98
Lawrence, Ernest O., 350, 368, 437
Lawrence, William J., Jr., 244
Law Students Civil Rights Research Council, 66
Lawyer's Committee for Civil Rights Under Law, 337
League of California Cities, 213
League of Nations, 255
League of Women Voters, 420
Learned and professional societies: American Academy of Arts and Sciences, 290; American Antiquarian Society, 154, 405; American Association of School Administrators, 97; American Association of Schools and Departments of Journalism, 441; American Association of Social Workers, 378; American Bar Association, 181, 219; American Chemical Society, 349; American Historical Association, 280; American Horticultural Society, 270; American Institute of Graphic Arts, 287; Association for the Study of Negro Life and History, 258; Association of the Bar of the City of New York, 310; Brooklyn Institute of Arts and Sciences, 310; Continental Typefounders Association, 287; Hispanic Society of America, 414; Historical Society of Delaware, 270; Historical Society of Pennsylvania, 221; Indiana Historical Society, 265; Michigan Society for Mental Hygiene, 280; Minnesota Historical Society, 17, 41; Missouri Historical Society, 275; National Association of Secondary School Principals, 97; National Committee for Mental Hygiene, 280; National Education Association, 151; National Society of Automotive Engineers, 275; New Haven County Bar Association, 308; New Jersey Historical Society, 125; New York Academy

of Medicine, 310; New York State Historical Association, 78; New York Zoological Society, 115, 362, 428-29; Panhandle Plains Historical Society, 106; Pennsylvania Prison Society, 337; Phi Beta Kappa, 169, 310; Philadelphia Bar Association, 338; Progressive Education Association, 151; Taos Society of Artists, 306; Worcester Natural History Society, 154, 405. *See also* Research institutions
Learning Exchange, 162
Learning Institute of North Carolina, 289
Leavey, Thomas E., 412-13; and Leavey, Mrs. Dorothy, 412-13
Lebeaux, Elliot, 378
Legal Aid Society, 67, 362, 396
Legal Services Organization of Indiana, 268
Leland Fikes Foundation, *259-62*
Lena Park Community Development Corporation, 159
LeShan, Lawrence L., 277
Lettie Pate Evans Foundation, 228, 262
Lettie Pate Whitehead Foundation, 228, *262-64*
Leukemia Society of America, 4
Levi, Edward H., 213
Lexington Foundation, 318
Liberty Fund, *264*
Liberty League, 346
Libraries: Citizens Task Force for the Library (St. Paul, Minnesota), 382; Dallas Public Library (Texas), 119-20, 179; Folger Shakespeare Library, 120; Huntington Library, Art Gallery, Botanical Gardens, 345; Library of Congress, 265, 303; Moody Medical Library (Texas), 300; New York Public Library, Astor, Lenox and Tilden Foundations, 378, 427-28; Pierpont Morgan Library, 63, 287, 406; Research Libraries Group (California), 436
Lila Acheson Wallace Fund, 259
Lilly, Eli, 265-66, 269
Lilly, Josiah K., Jr., 264-66
Lilly, Josiah K., Sr., 264
Lilly, Josiah K. III, 265
Lilly, Ruth Allison, 265
Lilly Endowment, *264-70*
Lindisfarne Association, 363
Link, Marilyn C., 27
Lipschultz, William H., 325
Lipscomb, James S., 156
Little, Arthur D., 349
Littlefield, Henry W., 59

Little Sisters of the Poor, 93, 194
Lloyd, Glenn A., 213
Local Initiatives Support Corporation, 71, 134, 220, 330, 430
Long, L. D., 245
Long Island Community Foundation, 314-15
Longwood Foundation, *270*
Loomis, Frank D., 74-75
Loper, Ray E., 193
Lorrain, Claude, 320
Louis Calder Foundation, *270-71*
Louisville Development Foundation, 194
Louis W. and Maud Hill Family Foundation, 318
Luce, Henry Robinson, 173; and Luce, Mrs. Claire Boothe Brokaw, 173
Luce, Henry III, 174; and Luce, Mrs. Henry III, 174
Luce, Henry Winters, 173; and Luce, Mrs. Elizabeth Middleton Root, 173
Luce Fund for Asian Studies, 174
Lupton, John T., 229, 272
Lupton, Thomas Cartter, 271
Lyman, Richard W., 372
Lyndhurst Foundation, *271-72*

Mabee, Guy, 200
Mabee, Joe, 200
Mabee, John E., 199-200; and Mabee, Mrs. Lottie E., 199-200
Mabel Pew Myrin Trust, *273-74*, 332
McAdam, Sally G., 145
McAneny, George, 380
MacArthur, John D., 212-14, 352; and MacArthur, Mrs. Catherine T., 212-13
MacArthur, J. Roderick, 213
McCone, John A., 345
McConnell, David H., 111-12
McDermott, Eugene, 118-19; and McDermott, Mrs. Margaret Milam, 118-20
McDermott, Mary, 119-20
McDermott Foundation, 118-19
McDonnell, James S., 277
McDonnell, James S. III, 275, 277
McDonnell, John F., 277
McDonnell, Sanford N., 275
McDonnell Aerospace Foundation, 274
McDonnell Aircraft Corporation Foundation, 274
McDonnell Douglas Foundation, *274-76*, 276-77
McDonnell Foundation, *276-78*
McDonnell Planetarium, 275

McDonnell Scholarship Foundation, 275
McGill, Ralph, 230, 240
McGregor, Tracy W., 278-80; and McGregor, Mrs. Katherine Whitney, 278-79
McGregor Fund, *278-82*
McGregor Health Foundation, 280
McInerny, Elizabeth DeCamp, 184
McInerny, James H., 185
McIntyre, James Francis Cardinal, 98
McKay, Robert B., 421
McKee, Clyde V., Jr., 307
McKenzie, Andrew, 312
McKenzie, Isabel C., 312
McKenzie Fund, 312
McKnight, William L., 38, 282-84; and McKnight, Mrs. Maude L., 282-83
McKnight Family Funds: Charitable, Endowment, Educational, Literary, and Scientific, 283
McKnight Foundation, 38, *282-84*
McLain, B. F., 89
McLaren, N. Loyall, 195
Maclay, Eloise, 315
Maclellan, Robert J., 284
Maclellan Foundation, *284-85*
McNamara, Francis J., Jr., 63
McShain, John, 221
McShain, Mary, 221
McTier, Charles H., 231, 264
Macy, Josiah, 231
Macy, Josiah, Jr., 231
Macy, Thomas, 231; and Macy, Mrs. Sarah, 231
Maes, Robert A., 184
Magazines. *See* Newspapers and magazines
Mahoney, David, 58
Mahoney, Margaret E., 88
Mangelsdorf, Paul C., 350
Manley, Frank J., 69-70, 73
Mao Tse-Sung, 367
March of Dimes Birth Defect Foundation, 62
Marjorie Merriweather Post Foundation of D.C., *285-86*
Markle, John, 208-10; and Markle, Mrs. Mary E. Robinson, 208-9
Marks, Henry J., 165
Marron, Donald B., 59
Marsh, Charles Edward, 343; and Marsh, Mrs. Claudia Haines, 343
Marshall, Gerald R., 248
Mary Anderson Trust, 332
Mary Campbell Center, 270
Mary Ethel Pew Medical Trust, 332

Mary Flagler Cary Charitable Trust, *286-88*
Mary Reynolds Babcock Foundation, *288-91*
Massachusetts Council of Human Service Providers, 159
Mathews, A. Lamar, 29
Matisse, Henri, 320
Mauzé, Abby Rockefeller, 361
Mawby, Russell G., 450
Max C. Fleischmann Foundation, *291-92*
May, Herbert A., 285
May, John R., 388
M. D. Anderson Foundation, *292-93*
Meadows, Algur H., 293-96; and Meadows, Mrs. Algur H., 294-95
Meadows, John M., 293; and Meadows, Mrs. Sally, 293
Meadows Foundation, *293-96*
Mechanics Hall Restoration Fund, 154
*Medical Education in the United States and Canada, Bulletin Number Four* (1910), 53, 87, 150, 367
Medical Foundation, 445
Medical institutions. *See* Hospitals, medical and health institutions
Mellon, Andrew W., 22, 354
Mellon, Mary Conover, 24
Mellon, Paul, 22-24
Mellon, Richard B., 22, 354
Mellon, Richard King, 354-55, 390; and Mellon, Mrs. Constance Prosser, 354
Mellon, Richard P., 354
Mellon, Seward Prosser, 354
Mellon Institute of Industrial Research. *See* Universities: Carnegie-Mellon
Memorial Welfare Foundation, 271-72
Menninger Foundation, 10, 162, 349
Merton, Robert K., 379
Metropolitan Life Foundation, *296-97*
Michael Lynam Fund, 275
Michigan State Board of Education, 151
Milas, Lawrence W., 323-24
Milbank, Jeremiah, 203-4
Milbank, Jeremiah, Jr., 205
Miller, Henry S., Jr., 89
Miller, Paul, 143
Ming (Chinese dynasty), 429
Minneapolis Foundation, 284
Minneapolis–St. Paul Housing Fund, 284
Minnesota State Highway Commission, 317
Mitchell, John C., 36
Mitchell, John E., Jr., 89
M. J. Murdock Charitable Trust, *297-98*
Moe, Henry Allen, 223-24, 226

Monell, Ambrose, 10
Monell, Edmund C., 10-11
Monell, Maude, 10
Montebello Trust, 346
Moody, Libbie, 299
Moody, Robert L., 301
Moody, Shearn, 299
Moody, Shearn, Jr., 301
Moody, William Lewis, Jr., 298-300; and Moody, Mrs. Libbie Shearn, 298-300
Moody, William Lewis, Sr., 298
Moody, William Lewis III, 299
Moody Foundation, *298-302*
Moore, Wilbert E., 379
Morality in Media, 102
Moran, Thomas, 306
Morehead, John Motley, 222
Morgan, J. P., 208
Moritz and Charlotte Warburg Memorial Fund, 311
Morris, Max K., 26
Morris and Gwendolyn Cafritz Foundation, *302-3*
Morrisett, Lloyd N., 212
Morrow, Richard M., 19
Morton, Granville C., 90
Moss, Robert D., 323
Mott, Charles Stewart, 69-71, 73; and Mott, Mrs. Ruth, 73
Mott, C. S. Harding, 73
Mott, C. S. Harding II, 73
Mott, Maryanne, 73
Mount Palomar (observatory), 368
Moyers, Donald P., 200
Murdock, Melvin J., 297
Murphy, Franklin D., 4, 161
Murtagh, Robert J., 37
Museums and art collections: Allentown Art Museum, 140; American Museum of Natural History, 64, 115, 428; Amon Carter Museum of Western Art, 21; Art Institute of Chicago, 83, 220, 348; Arts Council (Connecticut), 309; Brooklyn Children's Museum, 428; Children's Museum (Connecticut), 309; Cleveland Institute of Art, 155; Corcoran Gallery and School of Art, 303; Denver Art Museum, 36; Denver Museum of Natural History, 36, 170; Detroit Museum of Art, 130; Exploratorium Museum (California), 220; Farmers' Museum (New York), 78; Field Museum of Natural History, 220; George Gund Collection of Western Art, 156; High Museum of Art (Georgia), 230; Hillwood Museum (Washington, D.C.), 285-86; Houston Antique Museum, 34; Houston Museum of Natural Science, 94; Hunter Museum of Art (Tennessee), 34; Interlocken Center for the Arts (formerly Interlocken National Music Group), 176; International Museum of Photography (Rochester, New York), 111; Jewish Museum (New York), 67; Kendall Whaling Museum (Massachusetts), 174; Laguna Beach Museum of Art (California), 163; Lamar Dodd Art Center (Georgia), 44; Los Angeles County Museum of Art, 4, 228; Los Angeles Museum of Modern Art, 452; Maramec Museum (Missouri), 312; Meadows Museum of Spanish Art (Texas), 294; Metropolitan Museum of Art, 63, 259, 363, 382, 396, 428-29; Michigan Artrain, 176; Midland Center for the Arts (Michigan), 175-76; Mobile Museum Board (Alabama), 194; Museum of Fine Arts (Dallas), 91, 118-20, 261 (Houston), 38, 181 (Richmond), 262; Museum of Modern Art, 118, 130, 361-63, 406; Museum of Science and Industry (Texas), 21; Museum of the American Indian, 77; Museum of the City of New York, 428; National Gallery of Art, 119, 382; Nature Beach Museum of Art (California), 163; Nelson Gallery of Art (Missouri), 162; Nevada State Museum, 291; Newark Community School of the Arts, 130; North Carolina School for the Arts, 289; Norton Simon Museum of Art (California), 320-21; Pasadena Museum of Modern Art, 320-21; Science Museum of Minnesota, 284; South Street Seaport Museum (New York), 428-29; Stark Museum of Art (Texas), 306-7; Sterling and Francine Clark Art Institute (Massachusetts), 357; Tennessee State Museum, 34; Tennessee Valley Railroad Museum, 34; Toledo Museum of Art, 178; Worcester Art Museum (Massachusetts), 154, 405
Musical organizations and orchestras: Berkshire Musical Festival, 62; Chattanooga Symphony Orchestra, 34; Chicago Symphony Orchestra, 220; Dallas Symphony Orchestra, 91, 119-20, 261; Denver Symphony Orchestra, 36; Detroit Symphony Orchestra, 136, 281; Indianapolis Symphony Orchestra, 265; Indiana State Symphony, 250; Julliard School, 287-88; Lake Placid Center for Music, Drama, and Art, 432; Minnesota Or-

chestra, 41; Moravian Music Foundation, 289; National Orchestral Association, 287; National Symphony Orchestra, 286, 303; Negro Ensemble Company, 130; New York Philharmonic Society (formerly New York Symphony), 62, 286-87, 404; Philadelphia Orchestra, 337; Piedmont Repertory Company, 289; Pittsburgh Symphony Society, 79, 182, 340; St. Louis Symphony, 275; St. Paul Chamber Orchestra, 41, 382; St. Paul Orchestral Association, 317; Winston-Salem Symphony, 289
Myers, Rubie, 265
Myrdal, Gunnar, 49-50
Myrin, Mabel Pew, 331

Nanaline H. Duke Fund for Duke University, 110
Nardi, Nicholas J., 63
Nash, Charles W., 68
National Association for the Advancement of Colored People, 66-67, 219
National Catholic School of Social Work, 257
National Caucus on Black Aged, 337
National Commission on Human Life, Reproduction and Rhythm, 103
National Committee for Responsive Philanthropy, 383-84
National Committee on Aging, 281
National Educational Television and Radio Center, 130
National Family Planning Guild, 103
National Housing Association, 376
National News Council, 211, 220, 421-22
National Organization for Women, 104
National Public Radio, 211
National Research Council. *See* Research institutions: National Academy of Sciences
National Safety Council, 348
National Urban League, 66, 258
National Women's Education Fund, 66
Neaves, Hope C., 56
Neighborhood Housing Services of America, 342
Nelda C. and H. J. Lutcher Stark Foundation, *305-7*
Neuharth, Allen H., 143
New Alchemy Institute, 363
Newark/New Victoria Plan (New Jersey), 426
"New Deal," 346
New Haven Foundation, *307-9*
Newhouse, Donald, 383, 385
Newhouse, Norman, 385

Newhouse, Samuel I., 383-85; and Newhouse, Mrs. Mitzie, 383-85
Newhouse, Samuel, Jr., 383, 385
Newhouse, Theodore, 385
New Jersey Department of Youth and Family Services, 419
Newspapers and magazines: *Atlanta Constitution*, 230, 240; *Bayonne Times* (New Jersey), 384; *CHANNELS of Communication*, 211; *Confluence*, 398; *Cosmopolitan*, 440; *Fortune*, 173, 212; *Fort Worth Star-Telegram*, 21; *Gasden Times* (Alabama), 343; *Glamour*, 383; *Good Housekeeping*, 440; *Harper's*, 216; *Housing*, 376; *Houston Chronicle*, 180; *Life*, 173; *Los Angeles Herald Express*, 442; *Louisville Courier-Journal*, 241; *Mademoiselle*, 383; *Newsweek*, 427; *New York Times*, 173, 241, 250, 310; *Norwich Daily Bulletin*, 201; *Orlando Sentinel* (Florida), 39; *Reader's Digest*, 105, 259, 314; *San Francisco Examiner*, 167, 442; *Shanghai Evening Post and Mercury* (China), 403; *Social Work Year Book*, 378; *Spartanburg Herald and Journal* (South Carolina), 343; *Staten Island Advance* (New York), 384; *Survey, The* (formerly *Charities and the Commons*), 375-76; *Time*, 173; *Tuscaloosa News* (Alabama), 343; *Vogue*, 383; *Washington Post*, 384
Newton, James Quigg, Jr., 35
Newton, J. Quigg, 87
New York Community Trust, 105, 164, 259, 308, *310-15*
New York School of Social Work, 85, 257, 375, 377
New York Yankees (baseball club), 100
Nicosia, Ralph, 28
Nie, Norman H., 421
Noble, Edward, 387
Noble, Edward John, 113-14
Noble, Lloyd, 385-87
Noble, Samuel, 387
Noble, Samuel Roberts, 386
Noguchi, Isamu, 294
Norris, Kenneth T., 246; and Norris, Mrs. Eileen L., 246
North American Congress on Latin America, 66
North Carolina Fund, 289, 456
Northen, Mary Elizabeth Moody, 299, 301
Northwest Area Foundation, *316-19*
Norton, Charles Dyer, 376
Norton Simon Foundation, *319-21*

Norton Simon, Inc. Museum of Art, 319-20, *321*
Noyes, Charles Dennison, 201
Noyes, Charles Floyd, 201-2
Noyes, Jessie Smith, 201

Odum, Howard W., 241
Ogden, Robert C., 147
Old Dominion Foundation, 22-24
Olin, Franklin Walter, 323-24; and Olin, Mrs. Mary, 323
Olin, John M., 324
Olin, Spencer T., 324
Olin Foundation, *323-24*
Olympic Committee (U.S.), 412
"Omnibus" (television program), 129
Operas and ballets: Dallas Civic Ballet, 261; Dallas Civic Opera, 261; Long Beach Civic Light Opera (California), 246; Lyric Opera (Illinois), 220; Metropolitan Opera Association, 62, 106, 259, 288, 392, 404, 412, 424, 428; Opera Company of Boston, 174; Opera Company of Philadelphia, 274; Opera Society of Washington, 303; San Francisco Opera Association, 32; School of American Ballet (New York), 436. *See also* Theaters
Opportunities Industrialization Center of America, 220
Orchestras. *See* Musical organizations and orchestras
Order de Mayo al Mérito (Argentina), 414
Oropon (tanning process), 439
Otto Bremer Foundation, *324-27*
Overstreet, James W., 84

Packard, David, 100; and Packard, Mrs. Lucille, 100
Paley, Martin A., 388
Pan American Petroleum Foundation, 18
Parks, gardens, and zoos: Atlanta Botanical Garden, 230; Bronx Zoo (New York), 429; Cary Arboretum (New York), 287-88; Central Park, 428; Cheyenne Mountain Zoo, 117; Church Memorial Park (Canada), 206; Dow Gardens (Michigan), 175; Glacier National Park, 317; Gramercy Park (New York), 374; Grand Teton National Park, 188-89; Hudson Highlands State Park, 189; Jefferson Market Garden (New York), 428; John D. MacArthur Beach State Park (Florida), 216; Longwood Gardens (Pennsylvania), 270; March Island (Louisiana bird refuge), 378; New York Botanical Gardens, 287; Palisades Interstate Park (New York), 189, 255; Prospect Park (New York), 428; Riiz Plaza (New York), 428; Rock City Gardens (Tennessee), 33; St. James Park (Missouri), 312; Stark Park (Texas), 307; T. W. Davis Memorial Park (Texas), 155; Virgin Islands National Park, 188-89; White River State Park (Indiana), 269; Yellowstone National Park, 187
Parsons, Frank J., 310
Parsons, William, 315
Patten, James A., 75
Patterson, M. K., Jr., 386
Pauling, Linus, 368
Payne, Bruce R., 152
Payne, Seba B., 140
Peabody Fund, 147
Peeler, Joseph D., 98
Pei, I. M., 384
Penrose, Boise, 117
Penrose, Spencer, 117; and Penrose, Mrs. Julie McMillan, 117
Permanent Charity Fund of Boston, Committee of the, 308, *329-30*
Permian Basin (Texas), 397
Perot, H. Ross, 90
Peterson, Jeffrey T., 60-61
Peterson, Kent F., 235
Petrocik, John R., 421
Petroleum and power companies: Amerada Hess Corporation, 178; Amerada Petroleum Corporation, 178; American Oil Company, 19; Amoco Oil Company, 18, 19; Amoco Production Company, 18, 19; Asiatic Petroleum Corporation, 59; Atlantic-Richfield Corporation, 216; Baker International Corporation, 347; Benedum-Trees Oil Company, 79; Cities Service Company, 59, 431; Duke Power Company, 108, 110; Exxon Corporation, 121, 411-12; General American Oil Company, 293-94; General Crude Oil Company, 331; Gulf Oil Corporation, 438; Hess Oil and Chemical Corporation, 178; Humble Oil and Refining Company, 126; Kewanee Oil Company, 453; Mobile Corporation, 197, 277; Mound Company, 355; Noble Drilling Corporation, 386; Pacific Gas and Electric Company, 195; Pennzoil Company, 83; Republic Oil Company, 411; Richfield Oil Corporation, 431; Samedan Oil Corporation, 386; Scofield, Shurmer, and Teagle, 411; Shell Caribbean Petroleum, 59; Shell Oil Company, 106,

393-95; Shell Pipe Line Company, 394-95; Southern Power Company, 108; Standard Oil Company, 106, 231, 286, 406; Standard Oil Company (Indiana), 18-20; Standard Oil Company (New Jersey), 120, 411; Sun Company (formerly Sun Oil Company), 202, 206, 331; Superior Oil Company, 451-52; Texaco, Inc., 412; Warren Petroleum Company, 438. *See also* Corporations and businesses
Pew, J. Howard, 202-3, 331; and Pew, Mrs. Helen Thompson, 202
Pew, Joseph Newton, Sr., 202, 206, 273, 331-32; and Pew, Mrs. Mary Anderson, 202, 206, 273, 331
Pew, Joseph N., Jr., 202, 206, 331; and Pew, Mrs. Alberta Hensel, 206
Pew, Mary Ethel, 331-32
Pew Memorial Foundation, 330-31
Pew Memorial Trust, 202, 206-7, 273-74, *330-35*
Phelps-Stokes Fund, 258
Philadelphia Foundation, *335-38*
Phillips, Elliott H., 281
Phillips, Jay, 338-39
Phillips, S. H., 307
Phillips Foundation, *338-39*
Phoebe Waterman Foundation, 439
Picasso, Pablo, 320
Pifer, Alan, 48-50, 54
Pittsburgh Foundation, 182, *339-40*
Planned Parenthood, 104, 163, 261, 362-63, 425-26, 436
Platten, Donald C., 59
Player, Willa B., 72
Polaroid Land camera, 373
Police Athletic League (New York), 404
Population Council. *See* Research institutions
Porter, John W., 73
Post, C. W., 285
Post, Marjorie Merriweather, 285-86
Pound, Roscoe, 81
Presidents (U.S.): Eisenhower, Dwight D., 188, 431; Hoover, Herbert, 204; Jefferson, Thomas, 278; Lincoln, Abraham, 370; Madison, James, 370; Roosevelt, Franklin D., 144, 180, 325, 346; Taft, William Howard, 349; Truman, Harry S., 221; Washington, George, 262; Wilson, Woodrow, 52, 180, 325, 370
Price, Ed. H., Jr., 28
Pritchett, Henry S., 48, 52-53
Prizes. *See* Awards and prizes

Probasco, Scott L., Jr., 33
Professional societies. *See* Learned and professional societies
Professorships: Dana Professorships, 58; Fletcher Jones Chairs in Computer Science, 228; Fuller E. Callaway Professorial Chairs, 45; Henry R. Luce Professorships, 174; History of Medicine Lectureships, 62; John D. MacArthur Chairs and Professorships, 216; Joseph B. Whitehead Chair of Surgery, 230; Kenan Professorships, 444; Luce Scholars, 174; Welch Chairs in Chemistry, 356
Pro-Life Action League, 103
Prudential Foundation, *341-42*
Public Broadcasting Service, 211
Public Broadcast Laboratory, 130
Public Communication Foundation for North Texas, 179, 261
Public School Bible Study Committee, 34
Public Welfare Foundation, *343*
Publishers: Advance Publications, Inc., 383; American Education Press, 83-84; Gannett Co., Inc., 143-44; Hall Brothers, Inc., 161; Hallmark Cards, Inc., 161-62; Hearst Corporation, 440, 442; King Features, 440; McCall Corporation, 319; Readers Digest Association, Inc., 105, 259. *See also* Corporations and businesses
Puerto Rican Legal Defense and Education Fund, 66

Rabi, Isidor I., 350
Radio and Television Workshop, 129
Railroads: Atchison, Topeka, and Santa Fe Railroad, 301; Chesapeake and Ohio Railroad, 126; Great Northern Railway, 316-18; New York Central Railroad, 126; Pennsylvania Railroad, 46, 57; Union Pacific Corporation, 98; Virginia Railway, 159. *See also* Corporations and businesses
Ralph M. Parsons Foundation, *345*
Ramapo Trust, *346*
Randolph, W. R., Jr., 33
Raphael, 320
Raskob, Anthony W., 347
Raskob, John J., 346-47
Raskob Foundation for Catholic Activities, *346-47*
Ray, Gordon N., 226
Ray A. Kroc Foundation, 251
R. C. Baker Foundation, *347-48*
Reachout, Inc., 34
Reading Is Fundamental, 219

Reardon, Robert J., 325
*Recent Social Trends*, 379
Recording for the Blind, 60
Red, John W., 399
Red Cross, American, 64, 159, 193-94, 203, 206, 255, 331-32, 412, 427
Regenstein, Joseph, 348
Regenstein Foundation, *348*
Regional Plan Association of New York, 376, 380
*Regional Survey and Plan of New York*, 376
Rehabilitation Institute of Chicago, 83
Religious institutions. *See* Churches and religious institutions
Rembrandt, 320
Remington, Frederic, 306
Repplier, Sidney N., 337
Research Corporation, *349-52*
Research institutions: Aberrant Behavior Center, 261; Alden Research Laboratories, 157; Allan Guttmacher Institute, 133; American Enterprise Institute for Public Policy Research, 9, 203-4, 404; Aspen Institute for Humanistic Studies, 219-20; Battelle Memorial Institute, 84; Brookings Institution, 9, 66, 257; Carnegie Endowment for International Peace, 47; Carnegie Institution of Washington, 47, 62; Center for Advanced Study in the Behavioral Sciences, 129, 218; Center for Applied Linguistics, 129; Center for International Legal Studies, 129; ESP Research Associates Foundation, 277; Foreign Policy Research Institute, 398; General Motors Research Institute, 73; Hoover Institution on War, Revolution and Peace, 203-4, 391, 404; Indianapolis Center for Advanced Research, 250; Institute for Contemporary Studies, 391; Institute for Philosophical Research, 219; Institute for Public Policy Research, 290; Institute of Pacific Relations, 257; International Institute for Strategic Studies (London), 129; Leland Fikes Research Institute, 260; Marine Biology Laboratory (Woods Hole), 232; Mind Science Foundation, 277; National Academy of Sciences, 67, 131, 210, 220; National Bureau of Economic Research, 9, 257; National Institute of Agricultural Research (Mexico), 368; Population Council, 87, 129, 133, 362; Psychical Research Foundation, 277; Psychophysical Research Laboratories, 277; Rand Corporation, 219, 407-8; Rehabilitation Institute of Chicago, 218; Research Foundation for Mental Health, 218; Salisbury Laboratories, 157; Salk Institute for Biological Studies, 213, 357, 441; Social Science Research Council, 257, 376-77, 379; Southern Research Institute, 60; Wadley Institute of Molecular Medicine, 260-61; Wadley Research Institute and Blood Bank, 260. *See also* Learned and professional societies; United States Government
Research Triangle Park (North Carolina), 290
Retirement Research Foundation, *352-54*
Revson, Charles H., 65
Revson, Charles H., Jr., 68
Revson, John C., 68
Reynolds, Richard Joshua, 288, 455
Reynolds, William N., 254, 455; and Reynolds, Mrs. Kate Bitting, 244-45
Reynolds, Zachary Smith, 455
Rich, Spencer, 384
Richard King Mellon Foundation, *354-55*
Richards, A. N., 86
Richards, Dickinson W., Jr., 86
Richards, Reuben F., 27
Richardson, H. Smith, 398-99
Richardson, Lunsford, 398
Richardson, R. Randolph, 399
Richardson, Sid W., 397
Richmond, Mary E., 375, 380
Rickerd, Donald S., 437
Riecker, Margaret Ann, 177
Riley, Matilda White, 378
Rippel, Julius S., 123; and Rippel, Mrs. Julius S., 123
Rivers of the Deep South Project, 355
Robert A. Taft Institute of Government, 204
Robert A. Welch Foundation, *355-56*
Robert J. Kleberg, Jr., and Helen C. Kleberg Foundation, *356-57*
Roberts, J. Lynn, 90
Robert Sterling Clark Foundation, *357-58*
Robert Wood Johnson Foundation, 27, *358-61*
Robinson, Marshall A., 379
Rockefeller, David, 187, 361, 363
Rockefeller, John D., Jr., 147, 187-89, 255, 361-62, 364; and Rockefeller, Mrs. Martha Baird, 187, 362
Rockefeller, John D., Sr., 80, 146, 149-50, 152, 158, 231, 255-56, 364, 367, 443; and Rockefeller, Mrs. Laura Spelman, 255, 258
Rockefeller, John D. III, 361
Rockefeller, Laurence S., 187-89
Rockefeller, Nelson A., 361
Rockefeller, William, 158

Rockefeller, Winthrop, 187, 361
Rockefeller Brothers Fund, 188-89, *361-64*
Rockefeller Foundation, 76, 151-52, 239, 245, 256, 258, *364-75*
Rockefeller Sanitary Commission, 365
Rodes, Harold P., 73
Rodin, 320
Rogerson, Charles E., 329
Rogerson, Charles M., 329
Rohm, Otto, 439
Rose, Wickliffe, 151, 365
Rosenberg Foundation, 387
Rosenwald, Julius, 238-39, 241
Rosenwald, Samuel, 238
Rossi, Anthony T., 27-29
Rossi, Florence, 28
Rossi, Sanna, 28
Rowe, George, Jr., 11
Rowland Foundation, *373*
Rubinstein, Helena. *See* Gourielli, Helena Rubinstein
Ruml, Beardsley, 256-57, 369
Rusk Institute, 137
Russell, Charles, 306
Russell, John, 209-11
Russell Sage Foundation, 81, 138, *373-80*
Ruthrauff, John R., 338

Safer Foundation, 219
Sage, Russell, 374; and Sage, Mrs. Margaret Olivia, 373-75, 377
St. Hubert's Giralda, 158
Saint Paul Foundation, 105, *381-82*
St. Paul Winter Carnival, 317
Salk, Jonas, 213
Salvation Army, 90, 162, 200, 206, 251, 345, 419, 426, 441
Sam S. Shubert Foundation, 396
Samuel H. Kress Foundation, *382-83*
Samuel I. Newhouse Foundation, *383-85*
Samuel Roberts Noble Foundation, *385-87*
San Francisco Foundation, 308, *387-90*
San Francisco Study Center, 197
Santa Gertrudis (breed of cattle), 356
Sarah Heinz House Association, 182
Sarah H. Hyams Fund, 159
Sarah Scaife Foundation, *390-92*
Sawyer, John E., 23
Sayre, Harrison M., 83-84
Sayre, Wallace S., 379
Scaife, Alan M., 390; and Scaife, Mrs. Sarah Mellon, 390-91
Scaife, Richard Mellon, 391

Schaefer, John P., 352
Scheie Eye Institute, 221
Scherman, Harry, 392
Scherman Foundation, *392*
Schiff, Jacob H., 311
Schiff, Rosebel G., 311
Scholarships. *See* Fellowships and scholarships
Scholl, William M., 107
Schools, 148, 149, 151, 158, 183-84; Ann J. Kellogg School, 446; Antilles School, 178; Baylor School, 33-34; Blair Academy, 418; Breck School, 283; Cabarrus Academy, Incorporated, 45; Cardigan Mountain School, 77; Cleveland, Ohio, 81; Cutler School, 56; Flint, Michigan, 68-70, 72; Fountain Valley School, 117; Franklin High School, Portland, Oregon, 297; Galveston County High School, Texas, 300; Glenwood School for Boys, 83; Good Hope School, 178; Hawaii Loa School, 163; Hockaday School, 119-20; Houston Independent School District, Texas, 181; Iolani School, 163; Kannapolis, North Carolina, 45; Kimberton Farms School, 273; Lawrenceville School, 126, 418; Louisville School for Autistic Children, 194; Loyola High School, Los Angeles, California; Mary Institute, Country Day School, 277; Merrill-Palmer School, 280-81; Montessori Academy, 261; Newark High School, Newark, New Jersey, 415; New York City, 136, 168, 311; North Carolina Advancement School, 289; Norwich Free Academy, 201; Ohio Military Institute, 291; Phillips Exeter Academy, 316; Punahou School, 163; St. Andrew's Priory School, 163; St. Benedict's Preparatory School, 417-19; St. Mark's School of Texas, 119-20; St. Paul's School, 63, 174; Sewanee Academy, 34; Shadyside Academy, 79; Tower Hill School, 270; Vermont Academy, 418; Weeks School, 419; Worcester Boys Trade School, 157
Schroeter, Donald G., 20
Schumann, John, 125; and Schumann, Mrs. Florence, 125
Schumann, Robert F., 125
Schwartz, Henry L., 346
Schwilch, Gene L., 97
Scientists Institute for Public Information, 220
Scott, Jack, 145
Scriven Foundation, 78
Sears, Richard, 238
Seaton, Fred A., 188
Selmon, A. C., 448

Selznick, Philip, 379
"Sesame Street" (television program), 50, 68, 212, 337
Seven College Conference, 233
Shakespeare, Frank, 205
Shakespeare, William, 145
S. H. Cowell Foundation, *392-94*
Sheinbein, Stanley J., 275, 277
Sheldon, Eleanor B., 379
Shell Companies Foundation, *394-95*
Shepard, Gordon, 325
Sherman Fairchild Foundation, *395-96*
Sherwick Fund, 82
"Shivapuram Nataraja" (Indian art object), 320
Shubert, J. J., 396-97
Shubert, Lee, 396
Shubert, Sam S., 396
Shubert Foundation, *396-98*
Sibley, James M., 230
Sid W. Richardson Foundation, *397-98*
Simmons, Gary D., 386
Simon, Norton, 319-21; and Simon, Mrs. Jennifer Jones, 321
Simon, William E., 213-14
Slater Fund, 148
Sloan, Alfred P., Jr., 6-8
Smith, Athalie Irvine, 197
Smith, Barry C., 85
Smith, David, 320
Smith, E. P. Tatum, Jr., 437
Smith, Homer W., 86
Smith, Lillian, 240
Smith, William Wikoff, 453; and Smith, Mrs. Mary L., 453
Smith-Kettlewell Eye Research Foundation, 404
Smith Richardson Foundation, *398-400*
Solomon M. Hyams Fund, 159
Southern Conference for Human Welfare, 241
Southern Education Board, 147
Southern Regional Council, 241
Southern Regional Education Board, 444
Southwestern Conference of Federations, 290
Southwestern Medical Foundation of Dallas, 119, 180
Southwestern Michigan Hospital Council, 449
Southwest Foundation for Research and Education, 181
Spalding, Hughes, Jr., 263
Spanish Institute, 414
Spelman Fund of New York, 258
Spencer, Lyle M., 400-401

Spencer Foundation, *400-403*
Staats, Elmer B., 248
Standard Oil (Indiana) Foundation, 18-19
Stark, H. J. Lutcher, 305; and Stark, Mrs. Nelda Childers, 305, 307
Stark, Homer B. H., 307
Stark, William Henry, 305-7; and Stark, Mrs. Miriam Lutcher, 305-7
Starr, Cornelius Vander, 403
Starr Foundation, *403-4*
Station Program Cooperative, 130
Steele, Harry G., 163; and Steele, Mrs. Grace C., 163
Steiner, Rudolf, 273
Stevenson, Robert W., 84
Stoddard, Harry G., 404-5; and Stoddard, Mrs. Janett W., 404
Stoddard, Robert W., 405
Stoddard Charitable Trust, *404-5*
Stone, Galen, 63
Suisman, Michael, 165
Sullivan, Dorothy G., 3
Support Center, 342
Surdna Foundation, *405-7*
Swearingen, John E., 19
Symphonies. *See* Musical organizations and orchestras
System Development Corporation, 407-8
System Development Foundation, *407-9*

Taber, George H., 355
Talmadge, Eugene, 239
Tax Reform Acts. *See* United States Government
Taylor, Cortlandt M., 317
Taylor, John D., 318
T. B. Association, 195
Teachers Insurance and Annuity Association, 53
Teagle, John, 411; and Teagle, Mrs. Amelia Bell Clark, 411
Teagle, Walter C., 411; and Teagle, Mrs. Rowena Lee, 411
Teagle, Walter C., Jr., 411
Teagle Foundation, *411-12*
Tenney, Daniel G., 205
Teresa E. Bernholz Fund, 311
Texaco Philanthropic Foundation, *412*
Textile Benefit Association, 44
Theaters: American Shakespeare Festival (Connecticut), 371; Arena Stage (Washington, D.C.), 371; Brown Theater (Kentucky), 193; Dallas Theater Center, 118; Dance

Theatre of Harlem, 130; Frances Ann Lutcher Theater for the Performing Arts (Texas), 307; Goodman Theater (Illinois), 220; Guthrie Theater (Minnesota), 41; John F. Kennedy Center for the Performing Arts, 4, 130, 286, 303; Lincoln Center for the Performing Arts, 130, 167, 363, 371, 384; Majestic Theater (Texas), 120; Margo Jones Theater (Texas), 118; Mitzi E. Newhouse Theatre (New York), 384; New American Drama Project, 130; Puerto Rican Traveling Theater, 130; Shubert, 396-97; Stratford Shakespearean Festival (Canada), 371; William L. McKnight-3M Omnitheater (Minnesota), 284. *See also* Operas and ballets

Theiler, Max, 366
Thomas, Benjamin Franklin, 228-29
Thomas, Franklin A., 132
Thomas and Dorothy Leavey Foundation, *412-13*
Thompson, Elihu, 349
Thomsen, C. J., 119
Timken, Henry, 413
Timken Foundation of Canton, *413-14*
"Timken Spring" (carriage spring), 413
Tinker, Edward Greenfield, 414
Tinker, Edward Larocque, 414; and Tinker, Mrs. Frances McKee, 414
Tinker, Henry Champlin, 414
Tinker Foundation, *414-15*
Townes, Charles H., 350
Travelers Aid, 313
Trebor Foundation, 228, 262
Trefethen, Eugene E., Jr., 170
Trenham, Noble, 104
Treu-Mart Fund, 82
Tripp, Frank, 144
Trowbridge, Hayes Quincy, 308
Truman, David B., 379
Trusts. *See* Banks and trusts
Tsai, Gerald, 104
Turrell, Herbert, 415-16, 419; and (first wife) Turrell, Mrs. Frances Robinson, 416; and (second wife) Turrell, Mrs. Margaret Hoberg, 415-16, 419
Turrell Fund, *415-20*
Tutt, Charles L., 117
Tutt, Charles, L., Jr., 117
Twentieth Century Fund, *420-22*
Twin Cities Public Television, 382

Union of Soviet Socialist Republics (USSR), 286

United Automobile Workers, 68
United Community Charity, Council, Foundation, Fund or Services. *See* United Way
United Hospital Fund, 204
United Nations, 114, 127
United Negro College Fund, 41, 71, 219, 271, 275, 362
United Neighborhood Houses, 271
United States Government: Air Force, 407; Attorney General, 213; Census, 379; Central Intelligence Agency, 180, 206, 345; Circuit Court of Appeals, 310; Civil Aeronautics Authority, 113; Coast Guard, 297; Commissioner of Education, 54; Congress, 147, 150, 364; Department of Agriculture, 148; Department of Defense, 407; Department of Housing and Urban Development, 16; Department of the Interior, 188; Department of the Treasury, 407-8, 433; Federal Emergency Relief Administration, 279; Federal Reserve Board (New York), 411; Federal Reserve District (Ninth), 324; Head Start Program, 426; Home Owners Loan Corporation, 325; House of Representatives, 223; Internal Revenue Service, 180, 272, 279, 332, 351, 398; Job Corps, 437; Library of Congress, 265, 303; National Endowment for the Arts, 166; National Endowment for the Humanities, 290; National Gallery of Art, 22; National Humanities Center, 290; National Institute of Mental Health, 139; National Institutes of Health, 138, 232; National Mortgage Association, 433; National Park Service, 187-88; National Register of Historic Places, 306; National Science Foundation, 223; National War College, 398; Public Broadcasting Act of 1967, 130; Public Health Service, 366; Secretary of the Treasury, 214; Senate, 226, 247; Sherman Anti-Trust Act, 108; Smithsonian Institution, 286, 349, 351-52; Social Security System, 53; Supreme Court, 40, 67, 108; Tax Reform Acts (1969), 39, 51, 84, 112, 195, 197-98, 267, 314, 442, (1981), 98; White House, 221, 353; Windfall Profits Tax, 356
United States Steel Foundation, *423-24*
United Way: 19-20, 31, 46, 84, 89, 153, 164, 178-79, 182, 194, 221, 250, 265, 270, 275, 279, 280-81, 283, 309, 312-14, 318, 329-30, 339, 341, 348, 356, 382, 395, 405, 412, 423, 435

Universities: Adelphi University, 185; American University (Beirut), 255; American University (Washington, D.C.), 260, 275; Atlanta University, 149, 152; Baylor University, 293; California Institute of Technology, 151, 163, 228, 396, 408, 434; Carnegie-Mellon University, 22, 182; Clark University, 154; Columbia University, 52, 56, 65, 67, 114, 118, 150-51, 168, 204, 218, 257-58, 370, 377-78, 380, 396, 404, 414-15, 428, 437; Cornell University, 52, 144, 150-51, 206, 323, 380, 411; Denison University, 96; Deutsche Hochschule für Politik (Berlin), 257; Dillard University, 150; Drexel University, 338; Duke University, 108-10, 152, 289-90, 437; Duluth Business University, 38, 282; Dusquesne University, 423; Eastern Michigan University, 73; Emory University, 152, 230, 262; Fisk University, 150, 258; Furman University, 109; Georgetown University, 275; George Washington University, 66; Georgia Institute of Technology, 44; Hamline University, 39, 283; Harvard University, 35, 52, 62, 65, 68, 81, 117, 121, 129, 151, 155-56, 210, 218, 234, 240, 256-57, 365, 370, 395, 398, 441; Howard University, 150, 258; Indiana University, 227; Johns Hopkins University, 76, 150, 324, 365, 437; Johnson C. Smith University, 109, 289; Lamar University, 412; Lehigh University, 396; London School of Economics, 257; Massachusetts Institute of Technology, 6, 8, 52, 63-64, 119-20, 406; Michigan State University, 135, 177; New York University, 65, 67, 260, 404; North Carolina State University, 46; Northwestern University, 76, 218-19, 275, 437, 443; Ohio State University, 84; Pennsylvania State University, 218; Phillips University, 249; Piedmont University Center, 289; Princeton University, 52, 151, 277, 380; Purdue University, 449; Rochester Institute of Technology, 287; Rockefeller University, 63, 363, 428; Roosevelt University, 401; Rutgers University, 68, 383-85; St. John's University, 339; St. Louis University, 275; Southern Methodist University, 118-20, 261, 294; Southwestern University, 38, 179, 181; Stanford University, 119, 151, 171, 190, 195, 203, 218, 228, 257, 277, 345, 370, 372, 391, 396, 401, 408, 415, 441; State University of Iowa, 258; State University of New York, 54; Syracuse University, 383-85; Temple University, 139, 338; Tennessee Tech University, 34; Texas Christian University, 21; Tulane University, 152, 257; University of Alabama, 44; University of Arizona, 352; University of Bridgeport, 59; University of California, 54, 196, 218, 258, 349, 380, 403, 408, 437, 441, 443; University of Chicago, 39, 66, 75, 150-51, 213, 256-57, 348, 400-401, 415; University of Colorado, 36, 169, 171; University of Dallas, 119-20; University of Denver, 36, 170, 339; University of Detroit, 136; University of Geneva (Switzerland), 370; University of Houston, 93-94; University of Illinois, 83; University of Kansas, 4, 161-62; University of Louisville, 193, 218; University of Michigan, 70, 72, 176, 280, 365; University of Minnesota, 41, 61, 258, 282-83, 339, 380; University of Nevada, 291; University of North Carolina, 46, 222, 241, 256-57, 289-90, 399, 443-44; University of Notre Dame, 438; University of Oklahoma, 386; University of Paris, 370, 414; University of Pennsylvania, 10, 139, 273, 338, 398, 436; University of Pittsburgh, 182, 340, 355; University of Rochester, 111, 399; University of Southern California, 3-4, 197, 228, 246, 434; University of Stockholm (Sweden), 257, 370; University of Tampa, 28; University of Tennessee, 34; University of Texas, 119-20, 257, 260-61, 299-300, 370, 415; University of the South (Sewanee), 201; University of Virginia, 218, 257, 280, 432; University of Washington, 400; University of Wisconsin, 256, 401, 415; Vanderbilt University, 150, 152, 257, 370, 391, 432, 438; Wake Forest University, 46, 289, 456; Washington University (St. Louis), 95, 150, 274-77; Wayne State University, 281-82; Wesleyan University, 406; Western Carolina University, 46; Western Michigan University, 177; Western Reserve University, 87, 310; West Texas State University, 106; William M. Rice University, 37; Wisconsin State University, 401; Yale University, 48, 62, 113, 150, 173, 185, 256-57, 287, 307-8, 316; Yeshiva University, 445. *See also* Colleges

Up with People, 191

Urban Institute, 436

Urban League, 426

Uruguayan-American Association, 414

INDEX / 515

van Amerigen Foundation, 10-11
Van Cliburn International Piano Competition, 221
Van de Graaf, Robert J., 350
van Kleeck, Mary A., 376-77, 380
Veiller, Lawrence, 376, 380
Verba, Sidney, 421
Vetlesen, George Unger, 10
Victoria Foundation, *425-26*
Vincent Astor Foundation, *426-30*
Visiting Nurse Service (New York), 137
Volk, Harold F., 89
Vollum, Howard, 297
Volunteers of America, 434
Voorhies, Paul W., 250

Wadsworth, Homer C., 82
Walcott, Charles D., 349
Wallace, DeWitt, 105, 259, 313-14; and Wallace, Mrs. Lila Acheson, 105, 259, 313-14
Walter, Henry G., 10-11
Walter, W. A., 33
W. Alton Jones Foundation, *431-32*
Wangensteen, Owen, 339
Warburg, Felix M., 311; and Warburg, Mrs. Felix M., 311
Warfield, David, 312
Warren, Roland, 378
Warren, William K., 438
Wars: Civil War (U.S.), 298; World War I, 203, 403, 439; World War II, 192, 207, 243, 297, 361, 377, 390, 403, 443, 449
Washington, Booker T., 49, 238-39
Washington, Lawrence, 262
Washington Center for Learning Alternatives, 219
Washington State Planning Council, 151
Waterman, Robert E., 350
Weaver, Warren, 368
Webb, Del E., 100
Webb, James E., 248
Weingart, Ben, 432-33; and Weingart, Mrs. Stella, 432-33
Weingart Foundation, *432-34*
Welch, Robert A., 355-56
Welfare Foundation, 425
West, Herbert B., 313-14
Westchester Community Foundation, 314-15
Western Electric Fund, *434-35*
West Indies Mission, 28
Wheeler, Kathryn L. (Mrs. Charles), 196
Wheeler, Walton M., Jr., 265
Whitaker, John C., 245

White, Alfred T., 376
White, William S., 72-73
Whitehead, Conkey Pate, 229, 262-63
Whitehead, Joseph B., Jr., 229-30, 262
Whitehead, Joseph Brown, 228-29, 262; and Whitehead, Mrs. Lettie Pate, 229, 262
Whittemore, Clark M., Jr., 59
Whyel, George L., 73
Wildavsky, Aaron, 379
Wilder, Amherst Holcomb, 11-12, 17
Wilder, Fanny Spencer, 11-12
Wilensky, Harold, 378
William and Flora Hewlett Foundation, 41, *435-36*
William H. Donner Foundation, 183, *436-38*
William K. Warren Foundation, *438-39*
William M. Scholl Foundation. See Dr. Scholl Foundation
William Penn Foundation, *439-40*
William Randolph Hearst Foundation, 167-68, *440-43*
William R. Kenan, Jr., Charitable Trust, *443-45*
Williams, Mrs. Bernard T., 165
Williams, Robert R., 350
Williams, Thomas, 311, 315
William T. Grant Foundation, 139, *445-46*
Willkie, Valleau, Jr., 397
Wilson, Robert E., 18
Witunski, Michael, 275
W. K. Kellogg Child Welfare Foundation, 446
W. K. Kellogg Foundation, *446-51*
W. M. Keck Foundation, *451-52*
Women's Action Alliance, 66
Women's Research and Education Institute of the Congresswomen's Caucus, 66
Wood, Charles F., 193
Woodrow Wilson National Fellowship Foundation, 129
Woodruff, Robert W., 230
Woods, Archie, 210
Woods, George D., 171
Woods, Robert A., 375
Woodward, Robert B., 350
Wooley, Walter, Jr., 248
Woolworth, Charles, S., 125
Woolworth, Frank W., 125
World Food Corporation, 220
World Radio Missionary Fellowship, 28
Worldwatch Institute, 363
W. R. Hewlett Foundation, 435
Wright Institute, Oregon Social Learning Center, 218

Wright, John S., 265
Wright, Orville, 455
W. W. Smith Charitable Trust, *453*
Wynn, James O., 323
Wyoming Seminary, 125

Yarrington, Blaine J., 19
Yen, James, 367
Yost, F. Randolph, 19
Young, Donald M., 377-79
Young Men's Christian Association, 20-21, 46, 69, 94, 99, 125, 140, 157, 181, 190, 194-95, 200, 246, 255, 339, 348, 417, 419, 426, 434, 452
Young Women's Christian Association, 194-95, 200, 255, 339, 417, 419

Zen Center, 363
Zoos. *See* Parks, gardens, and zoos
Z. Smith Reynolds Foundation, 245, *455-56*
Zurbarán, Francisco, 320

## ABOUT THE EDITORS

HAROLD M. KEELE is a practicing attorney in Illinois. He served as General Counsel for the Select Committee to Investigate Tax-Exempt Foundations and Comparable Organizations of the House of Representatives (82nd Congress). He subsequently published a number of articles on foundations in various journals.

JOSEPH C. KIGER is Professor of History at the University of Mississippi. He is the author of *Operating Principles of the Larger Foundations* and *American Learned Societies*, and editor of *Research Institutions and Learned Societies*. His articles on foundations and learned societies have appeared widely in periodicals and in standard reference works.